Walking it Through

Stephen P. Smith

An asthmatic's walking diary

First Published 2022
SP Publishing

ISBN: 979-8845944085

Front Cover: Badnambiast (Scotland) © Mike Linnett
Rear Cover: Milford Sound (New Zealand) © Steven Hampton

By Stephen P. Smith

Fiction

The Unsound Convictions of Judge Stephen Mentall
The Veteran and The Boy

Computer Science

Thinking About Computer Programming?
Deriving Prime Numbers by Set Theory

Biography

The Charlie Chaplin Walk

Autobiography

The Munros
Walking it Through

The prequel to this book. ISBN: 979-8-6508560-8-5. Available on Amazon:

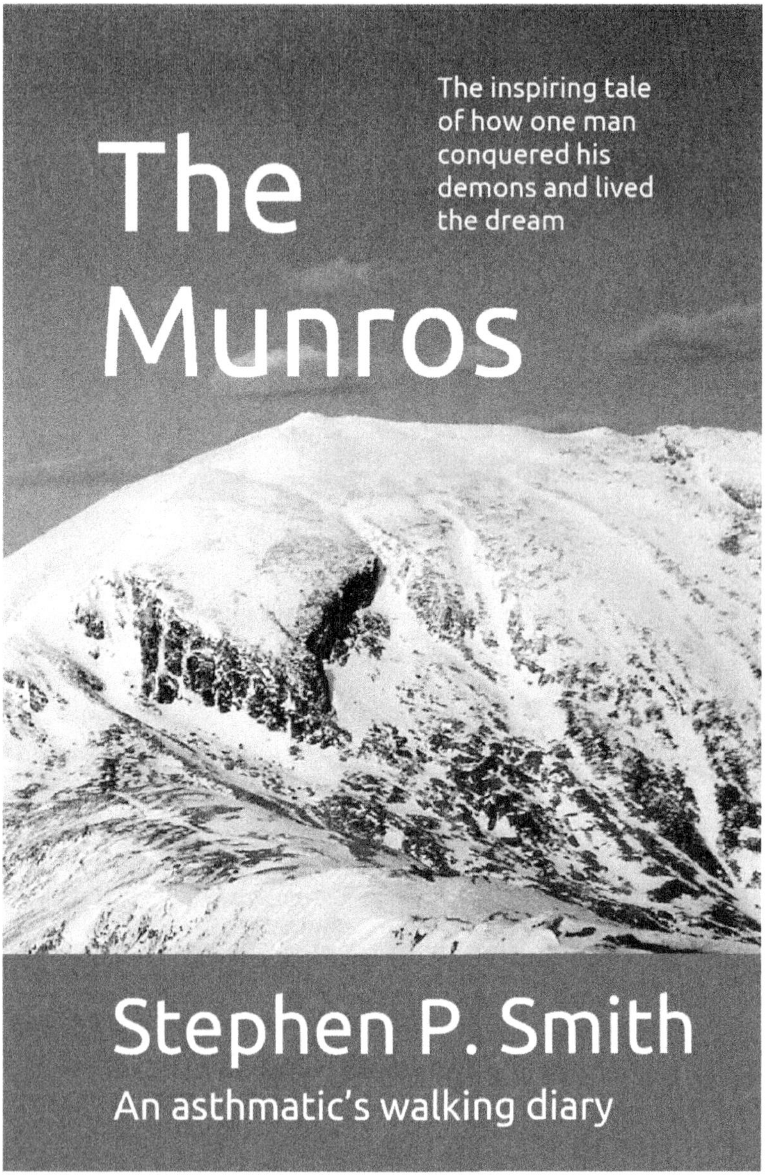

Preface

During childhood my relationship with sporting activities was coloured by severe asthma and the humiliation it brought on the school playing fields. This was back in the 1970s when I was one of a very few diagnosed asthmatics. The condition wasn't properly understood and I was exposed to triggers such as cigarette smoke and dogs. During my worst attacks I was laid up in bed, for days on end, with what felt like a bag of cement on my chest, my mouth and nose taped shut and just a straw to breathe through. The medical profession prescribed tablets to take during an attack, which induced immediate vomiting. At other times I was placed in a steam-filled room to try and drive my asthma out. Both approaches simply caused more breathing problems.

By the late 1980s I had graduated, had a good job and – with my asthma now under better control (but still with the breath intake of a seventy-year-old man) – was looking around for a sport I could do. I found this in the Munros – the 282 Scottish peaks over 3000 feet. Twelve years, 1700 miles of walking, 570,000 feet of ascent later – soaked, blown over, frozen, lost and scared more times than I care to remember – I finished.

And that was supposed to be it. I had promised myself that doing the Munros would conquer my childhood sporting demons. But more was at play for me – I was also an obsessive workaholic who set himself very tough targets. Therefore, I set myself a new challenge – to complete all the 1432 mountains of the British Isles. Twenty-one years later a life-changing event meant I had to retire the idea. But in the meantime, I'd managed to, including the Munros, bag 960 of them. This is my story and I hope it inspires other people with asthma to fulfil their potential.

Author's Note to Guidebooks

If you are inspired to walk any of the mountains of the British Isles please ensure you are equipped for mountain conditions and that you have the correct maps and the recommended guidebooks:

Welsh Nuttalls	Mountains of England and Wales: Vol 1 Wales (Cicerone guides) John and Anne Nuttall ISBN 978-1852845940
English Nuttalls	Mountains of England and Wales: Vol 2 England (Cicerone guides) John and Anne Nuttall ISBN 978-1852845896
Donalds & Grahams	The Grahams & The Donalds (SMC hillwalkers' guide) ISBN 978-1907233197
Corbetts	The Corbetts and Other Scottish Hills (SMC hillwalkers' guide) ISBN 978-0907521716
Munros	The Munros (SMC hillwalkers' guide) ISBN 978-1907233388
Irish Mountains	The Mountains of Ireland: A Guide to Walking the Summits Paddy Dillon ISBN 978-1852841102

Contents

November 2001 – Welsh Nuttalls

I clamber into the rear of Adrian Ogden's car and show him my latest purchase: Harvey's 2000ft Mountain Charts of England, Wales and Scotland.

He shakes his head. "Oh, Steve. You are born to bag."

"Yeah, like Malaria it's in the blood," I reply.

"Steve's got an idea," adds Ali Ashton, settling into her seat. Adrian, and his partner Ali, had accompanied me, in July, on my final Munro (Scottish Peaks above 3000ft). I'm now visiting them for the weekend, and Ali has just witnessed me purchasing the maps.

"Oh," replies Adrian with a curious look upon his face.

"Well," I reply, "I don't think anybody has ever climbed all the two-thousand-foot mountains of the British Isles."

"How many are there?" he asks.

"Nearly fifteen hundred I should imagine," adds Ali.

"Fifteen hundred!"

"Yeah, but I've already done the two hundred and eighty-four Munros, so not that many to do."

"Steve," continues Adrian, "I thought you said you were going to 'accept middle age with grace' now you've done the Munros."

"Well…" I reply.

Back home I lay out the charts on my lounge floor. Do I want to do this? Adrian's words, "I thought you said you were going to 'accept middle age with grace' now you've done the Munros" spin through my mind. The Munros took up every scrap of free time I could spare over twelve years. Do I want to do that again, perhaps taking me way beyond twelve years?

I know deep down I'd like to meet somebody and, with finishing the Munros, I hoped to be a little bit more normal. Between 1990 and 2000 I'd been in two long-term relationships with very strongminded women. It had left me battered. After finishing the Munros an ex-work colleague friend asked me out and we'd gotten together. But then I discovered she'd signed up to a dating agency at the same time as seeing me. I should have walked away then but I kept at it, hoping for things to change, until the inevitable dumping took place.

I then was spending a lot of time with a friend from the village – most Saturday evenings before toddling off home around midnight. The invites stopped abruptly when she got back together with her old boyfriend. When he finished things again the invites for me to visit started up again. I felt second best and withdrew.

I further examine the charts; a steely determination comes over me: getting a relationship is something only partially under my control. Doing these mountains *is* under my control.

Looking further, I discover I've already climbed three of the Welsh Nuttalls (peaks 2000ft or over): Pen y Fan, Cribyn and Moel Siabod plus the Corbett (Scottish peaks between 2000ft and 3000ft) of Beinn Tharsuinn. I'm never one to abandon a project and I've now already started this one! So my next ambitious project begins with the following targets:

Classification	My Total	Total
Welsh Nuttalls	3	188
English Nuttalls	0	251
Corbetts (Scotland)	1	219
Grahams (Scotland)	0	220
Unique Donalds (Scotland)	0	58
Munros (Scotland)	284	284
Ireland	0	212
Totals (18/11/2001):	288	1432

Key:

(i) A Welsh Nuttall is a Welsh mountain 2000ft or over.
(ii) An English Nuttall is a Welsh mountain 2000ft or over.
(iii) A Corbett is a Scottish mountain between 2500ft and 2999ft

with a 500ft drop all round.

(iv) A Graham is a Scottish mountain between 2000ft and 2599ft with a 500ft drop all round.

(v) A Donald is a southern Scottish mountain between 2000ft and 2999ft. Some of these are also Corbetts and Grahams and one is also classified as an English Nuttall (because it is on the border). The term 'Unique Donald' are the Donalds which are not Corbetts, Grahams or a Nuttall.

(vi) A Munro is a Scottish mountain 3000ft or over.

Six days later, Saturday November 24th 2001, my alarm is sounding at 06:00. I'm ready in half an hour for the one-hundred-and-twenty-mile drive to the Brecon Beacons – just to 'have a look'. Fiddling with my radio I pick up my cousin's radio show on BBC Wiltshire Sound. Knowing I must come across as a little unusual I wonder what he'd think of my latest madcap scheme. By Bath, on the M4, I've lost him and retune and get 'Rhyl Radio.' This will put me in the mood I think, something Welsh. Where in the heck is Rhyl? A nagging doubt tells me it's North Wales and I'm currently heading for South Wales. Glancing down at the radio I see the station identifier 'Real Radio'. Either I'm going somewhere where they cannot spell or there is something magical about Welsh radio waves.

Knowing very little about Wales this is a new adventure, the Brecon Beacons and Black Mountains have sat on my doorstep for years and I've hardly ventured to them, instead preferring the 500-mile drive to the Scottish Highlands.

Crossing the new Severn crossing, just after the 'Welcome to Wales' signs, I'm hit by the tollbooth: £4.40 to pay. I'm parked up and walking before 09:00. I'm soon in the mist, but this is easy. The terrain is not as steep as Munro land and the starting point, just north of the Storey Arms, was so high I'm on the main ridge within an hour. But then I'm flummoxed. It is so flat, where is the cairn? I'm poking round a farmer's field in Mid-Glamorgan looking for the summit of a mountain. I stumble on a rise and a small pile of rocks which I settle on being the summit of

Craig Cerrig-gleisiad, at 2064 feet. The Munros, virtually without exception, are graced with cairns, leaving the walker in no doubt of their achievement.

I walk on and bump into the farmer and his dog, tending their sheep and quickly discover these mountains are phonetically harder than the Scottish mountains (judging by the amount of spittle I have to duck). We chat away. With Wales not our common ground, this quickly becomes a talk about Scotland. Welsh through and through he has worked in Scotland for fifteen years so we reminisce about all the places we know.

After parting, I wonder about my new place in the world as a misanthrope. I enjoyed chatting with him, but was eager to press on. I wonder how many other people feel the same? Is there a misanthropy society? Then I realise the irony.

A six-hour round walk takes in Fan Frynych, Fan Llia, a drop down to the dam on the Ystradfellte Reservoir and the haul up to the 2408ft summit of Fan Fawr.

I get a few twinges from my left groin – the results of a hernia operation in August. The operation had left me in agony for weeks. Only now have I been able to get out for a serious walk again.

Seven days later and I'm laid on my couch, the sky is miserable, fifty people from my office have been made redundant in the week and one of my favourite musicians, George Harrison, has just lost his fight against cancer. Flicking through Beatles' tracks I get to 'Here Comes The Sun'. I look out of the window at the precise moment that the sky clears and we get some blue sky with the lyrics 'it'll be alright.' I resolve that if they don't renew my contract I'll go walking.

Next day, Sunday December 2nd 2001, and the six o'clock alarm has me out of bed. And I know I'm hooked. An hour to pack and make sandwiches and I'm leaving my Wiltshire home and heading for the M4. The moon is full in my face and things are going well. One Beatles' CD after another is fed into my car's CD player until I hit junction 19 of the

M4 where a helpful sign says 'Motorway Closed.' There were no advanced warning signs of the road works. Within a couple of roundabouts, the provision of any diversion signs has been abandoned and I'm on my own. A half hour later I'm thumping the steering wheel with frustration as I realise that I have travelled back towards home on minor roads and I'm facing the pointless choice of re-joining the M4 at junction 18, safe in the knowledge that junction 19 would soon kick me off. These people who put diversion signs up need a rocket up the backside. I'd hoped to make it to the Brecon Beacons on the petrol I had but, after losing an hour to the 'diversion' and refuelling, I don't get walking until 10:30. This means that my daylight contingency has gone, and I'm going to have to motor to take in Fan Nedd, Fan Fraith and Fan Gyhirych.

Like a bull at a five-bar gate I'm charging up the hill. Firstly in anger, secondly to try and make up time to do the round in daylight, and thirdly to get away from the quad-bike-driving farmer whose fence I have just scaled.

Fifteen minutes later, with my breathing off tune and blood thumping inside my skull, I slow my pace. Slowing my pace, on ground that I estimate exceeds the grip of a quad bike, I pull myself onto the top of Fan Nedd after just forty minutes.

I walk the ridge from the trig point to the cairn, cracking through ice puddles as I go. Descending west I try and spot the approach to Fan Gyhirych – a cliff edge marked on the map. Nothing there, just a bit of steepness and I wonder at the Ordnance Survey guys who made this map. Desperate for some geographical feature that is up to Scottish standards I could imagine them fighting over who got to draw it on:

"No, bugger off you just do the Churches and Youth Hostels."

"You did the last cliff, it's my turn."

"You got to do the roads, I want this cliff."

I'm convinced this goes on whilst the guys upstairs spend hours agonising over which Scottish features to omit to keep the ink costs down.

I'm soon eating 'umble pie as I'd misread the map and the cliff is there, just not where I had been looking. The two hills yield quite quickly but I'm starving. I dare not stop to eat, or drink, as I'm against the clock. I descend until I reach the slopes back up Fan Nedd where I permit myself to stop and scoff my lunch and slug back water. Back at the car, well before 15:00, with lots of daylight left I curse myself for not have taken it a bit easier.

Classification	My Total	Total
Welsh Nuttalls	10	188
English Nuttalls	0	251
Corbetts (Scotland)	1	219
Grahams (Scotland)	0	220
Unique Donalds (Scotland)	0	58
Munros (Scotland)	284	284
Ireland	0	212
Totals (02/12/2001):	295	1432

January 2002 – Welsh Nuttalls

Early January, sat at my desk at work, my PC pings. There are two new emails, one from my colleague Louise, the other my boss Andrew. 'Boss, colleague' dilemmas swilled my mind, soon settled by 'boss first.'

"Steve, can I take you up on your offer of a warm-up walk in Wales prior to my trekking trip in Nepal. Regards Andrew."

Nothing serious so I open Louise's email.

"Steve, would you be available to go to Scotland next week, Thursday and Friday, to do a 'Due Diligence' assessment on the system the Dumfries and Galloway's Constabulary have developed? Louise."

The obvious strikes me, if I can get Andrew to walk on the weekend after the visit to Scotland, I can save a lot of travelling and somebody else would be paying for the bulk of my petrol.

Pulling up in Llangollen, after a few tiring days away, I find the welcome signs of a hotel with a car park. Early evening, having just driven for four hours, I just want to lie down on a hotel bed.

Wandering into the hotel bar my first sniff of a mistake greets me. A room full of early evening drunks turn and stare at the guy with the £400 suit, £50 shirt and £100 coat. I wish the ground would swallow me up. At first I freeze on the spot before unsticking my feet from the ancient carpet and heading towards the bartender. I wish I was wearing blinkers.

"Got any rooms?" I enquire at the bar.

"Nah," replies the bartender, eyeing me with disdain.

January in the back of beyond and the hotel is full? I try to maintain my pride as I turn my back on the 'Reverse Snob Inn'. Out in the streets I find a B&B, press a bell and await a proprietor.

"Any rooms?" I enquire.

"Yes," a smile and I'm shown to my room. Freezing cold but I take it.

Realising that the warmest place was walking the streets and sitting in my car I walk the streets and sit in my car. The centre was alive, Jack and the Beanstalk is playing at the town hall and the queue was pitiful. That is pitifully long, almost as if the day that 'Jack and the Beanstalk played Llangollen' would be talked about for years to come.

The town, expanded in the Victorian era, is still well kept but has an air of being insular. One building marked 'Expanded 1904' makes me wonder, but not as much as stumbling across 'Uncle Peter's Real Fudge Shop.'

Sat in my car, my stomach full after a lonesome meal, I check the maps for the Saturday's walk in the Berwyn Mountains, prior to rendezvousing with Andrew in The Black Mountains on Sunday. My mistake swiftly hits me in the face; I should be in Llandrillo not Llangollen. They sounded the same and after a long drive my brain substituted 'Llan' for 'well earned rest.' And I've already paid the £20 for the B&B. I check the road atlas, the extra drive in the morning will be okay, but as I do not have an OS map I realise that my daylight hours were now going to be restricted by having to hang around here until the shops open.

I walk around the town again, cupping my eyes against the glass of shop windows to see if I can spy a rack of maps. Pedestrians view me with suspicion: "Was that not the guy in the posh suit at the 'Reverse Snob Inn'," I could hear them say. Okay, I made that bit up but I felt people were eyeing me with suspicion.

Selecting a hit list of shops I settle into the freezing bed for a nights sleep with lucid moments grappling for every inch of covering that could be mustered.

At breakfast on Saturday January 12th I realise that the landlady is so sweet that I can't bring myself to mention that perhaps the room I had would be better suited as a fridge. The first shop has maps and I purchase OS Sheet 125, ideal for the Berwyn Mountains. But I start to feel hesitant. I don't want to push myself too hard and I've booked a plush hotel for the evening in Hay-On-Wye. I had to go up market as it was the only place that served breakfast at 08:00 on a Sunday and I was due to meet Andrew at 09:00 in Capel-y-ffin.

Instead, I scale back my plans and decide to walk Post Gwyn, a single mountain requiring just 1200ft of ascent. Finding the start of the walk proves difficult with the normal procedure of relying on signposts to only then be duly dumped.

Starting in a glorious crisp morning I walk beside the Afon Disgynfa stream and ascend the mountain where I promptly freeze until I don extra clothing. I enjoy the views then descend via the recommended route in *Nuttall's guide to the 2000ft Mountains of Wales.* Then I remember the pitfalls of following a guidebook rather than the map. The author of a guidebook can only ever assume that you have managed to follow their route: off course and you are on your own. I'm trying to find the paths surrounding the old mine workings that the book eagerly instruct me are the best route back to the start. But I must have missed it and I'm now facing a very steep escarpment with the advice of 'cunningly finding an easy but exposed way down the cliff' ringing around my head like the advice somebody gives you after you have made a blindingly obvious mistake. Now with the guidebook abandoned and my eye off the map, I have to use visual terrain to pick up a known point to make my successful drop back to the car for the drive down to Hay-On-Wye.

Playing with the remote control at the Swan Hay Hotel I realise that Wales only has three channels decipherable to the ear of an Englishman. Here Channel Four is in Welsh after a referendum, that voted to keep it in English, was ignored.

At 08:10, sat waiting to be served the 08:00 breakfast, I take my problem up with somebody that vaguely looks in charge. They don't respond helpfully, actually she barely responds at all, and if she could get away with shrugging her shoulders I'm left in no doubt she would. "Look," I protest, "I stayed in this hotel because when I booked you said I could have breakfast at 8 a.m. and I paid my bill at quarter to eight so I could get going." Something dawns when I add about it being an expensive hotel, that has made me late and I'm disappointed. Breakfast comes, but I feel stressed and hurried to get going.

Walking with one's boss is an interesting experience. At work Andrew always looks for me to take the technical lead and, of course, today was to be no different. Instead that this time I also had to take full responsibility for any decision made, at work the buck stops with him. I've memorised the route by heart and we set off into mist, cloud and light rain.

"What's it like in Wales?" I ask.

"Fine," replies Andrew, "why do you ask?"

"Well I'm in England!"

"Oh we are on the border then?"

"Yes, this is Offa's Dyke."

Unable to see anything, due to the mist, we make the round of Black Mountain South Top, Black Mountain, Hay Bluff and Twmpa in about six hours. But Twmpa has another name, anglicised it has been converted to 'Lord Hereford's Knob.' Now I don't know who Lord Hereford was but he must have been one hell of a lucky guy.

Descending back to Capel-y-ffin Andrew is hesitant about the final descent. To me it is a fine slope but to Andrew all he can see is a steep drop and I realise how dependent he is on me for his safe trip. It is humbling and reminds me of when I started the Munros and how scared I could be on terrain that now I'd hardly take a second glance at.

January 27th and the 05:30 alarm goes off, I have had hardly any sleep having been out until gone midnight. A three-hour trip to Capel-y-ffin awaits and, having just purchased a three-year-old Golf, this is to be the last major trip in my 194,000-mile Toyota.

Floods plague my journey and it is with welcome relief that I reach The Black Mountains, meet with Andrew again and set off.

We are hesitant walking through the grounds of 'The Grange'; eventually stumbling upon the path beside relics of cars, crumbling back into the ground, nature reclaiming them. It strengthened my resolve to properly lay up the Toyota and not let a most trusted thing rot.

Andrew keeps a good pace and we reach the cairn below Chwarel y Fan with little difficulty before bagging the mountain in the beginnings of a gale. Backtracking we take the long route out to Rhos Dirion where I sense Andrew is struggling: the hard wind and rain sapping his strength. "What now boss?" he asks.

From Rhos Dirion we try for the path directly back to Capel-y-ffin but I am unhappy with the route as it will take us onto high ground again. So we take in a re-ascent of Lord Hereford's Knob. I make good ground, looking back after a few minutes there is no Andrew. I wait and see his head bob in the distance. Realising the boot was now on the other foot, asthma made my trailing people up the Munros miserable, I allow him to catch up, wait until he is ready to set off and keep to his pace.

At the summit, in miserable conditions, I say, "Andrew, now you can say Lord Hereford's Knob has blown you off."

"Had to be said Steve, had to be said."

We descend to the Hay-On-Wye to Capel-y-ffin road where Andrew is in a happier mood. "Looks as if the sun is about to shine," he says.

"We might make Hay while the sun shines then," I reply.

"Had to be said Steve, had to be said."

February 9th and another 05:15 alarm clock for another walk with Andrew. I'm in my new car and New Radnor is where I'm heading. Andrew parks his Volvo behind me, a little out from the kerb.

"It'll be fine," I say as he inspects it.

"I think I should tuck it in a bit more."

"Nah, it'll be okay."

"Steve, would this be anything to do with the fact that it is protecting your rather expensive shiny new purchase?"

"Andrew, you've known me long enough. It's got everything to do with that fact that your seventeen-year-old Volvo is protecting my rather expensive shiny new purchase."

"Okay, pack, map and guidebook," I say as I check I've got everything.

"Do you always follow the guidebook?"

"Well no, it's just a guide you see. And I'm rather put off by the first sentence describing this walk. 'Leave the ancient town of New Radnor by Mutton Dingle'. It's not so much the 'Mutton Dingle' that's the worry but the oxymoron in the first part of the sentence: I'd hate to see the state of Old Radnor."

The path has us climbing almost immediately, passing through a wood then onto clear ground where tracks and paths take us to the summit of Bache Hill. An easy stroll follows to Black Mixen where its huge transmitter dominates the surroundings. Andrew pulls his phone from his pocket. "No mobile phone signal," he announces with a dash of wry humour.

The weather is clear and blustery, but the best we've had so far walking together. We walk north-west to avoid a sharp drop into the valley, then south-west over Great Rhos before south then steeply south-east, passing the firing testing ranges for Ely bullets. This takes me back to my days of firing handguns with my dad. It was for years his main hobby, having been raised on a farm guns were the norm for him and he'd taken that into adult life as a police marksman. One day he took me along to a gun club. I remember the Ely bullets in their pale blue boxes, the smell of the discharged bullets and the kick of the gun as he let me have a go.

We make it to the bridge over the stream, which runs down the valley, surrounded by the hills of the day. We pause awhile and Andrew removes his hat.

"Does my hair look okay?" he asks.

"Yes, does mine?" I reply.

"Yes fine, you've got less to stick up than me. Well what I mean is..."

"Do you want to stop there?" I ask.

"Okay."

At the cars we decide to find a pub, the five-hour round has left Andrew with time before he needs to get back. We sit and discuss work opportunities. I'm freelance with the company whereas Andrew, who I report to, is a manager of a number of projects. There's just a matter of weeks left on my contract and I sense after five years I've had enough of the place and, coincidentally, so many permanent people are being made redundant, there's not much prospect of an extension.

"What are the prospects of winning new business?" I ask.

"Poor, Steve. Poor."

We drink up and get set to depart.

"Would you do a weekday for the next walk?" he asks, knowing how somebody on contract rates hates taking a day off. "Do you have any free dates?"

"March looks good," I quip, "I think I might just have a diary full of free dates."

March 2002 – English Nuttalls

Saturday March 2nd and Kate Wilson, Ali Ashton and I are looking back to where Adrian Ogden had stood a few moments before. "It's the faff factor again," explains Ali.

Kate and I wait for Adrian to reappear, scooped up by Ali. Reunited we continue the walk out of Ambleside and then the start of the climb up Heron Pike. We soon meet surface snow, the remains of weather forecasts that threatened to reduce our weekend away to board games and tearooms. But the weather is being kind and we make good progress, even though I sense I'm making a slower pace. Over Heron Pike North Top and Great Rig and it's clear I'm struggling. Ali and Adrian have the illusion I'm a fast walker – a hangover from when I met them on the Cuillin Ridge where adrenalin, and the fear of being left behind, had me raising my game. But now they're seeing the true me – lagging, heavy legs and struggling with my asthma in the cold conditions.

Just before Great Rigg we rest for lunch, where Ali produces a fantastic bivi tent. A device where a group sit in a circle, place the large sheet over their heads and tuck the edges under bottoms.

Adrian elects to sit outside, gentlemanly still sitting on the edge of the sheet, while Kate, Ali and I enjoy the warmth of the interior

I'm wearing my rarely-used Gore-Tex boots (the soles on my leather ones having become a little thin) and I have developed blisters on both heels. As I remove the first boot there are cries of 'pooh' – my reassurances of not having smelly feet were countenanced by overwhelming evidence to the contrary.

I manage to get away with taking the second one off when Kate through the smog says, "They are nice little ankle gaiters you've got."

"They were Barbara's, a relic of a failed relationship."

"She's still snapping at your ankles," replies Ali. I cannot stop laughing and we have to relay the humour to Adrian, still sat outside enjoying the views. I reflect that it's good to be able to laugh – Barbara had an anger towards men, simmering to the point of hatred, which she'd taken out on me on a daily basis. Humour is a relaxant.

Continuing on we begin to lose Adrian as he insists on 'Crinkle Bagging' – a term for exploring every bump, hump and outcrop. For a man of about fifty his energy knows no bounds.

On the approach to Fairfield we begin to meet other walkers doing the horseshoe in the opposite direction. The cold requires hoods to be drawn and scarves to cover mouths. But each walker we pass smiles with their eyes, and we smile back.

The wind picks up to mop us with the icy spindrift and, combined with my slow pace, the others offer a quick descent from Fairfield. However, I'm keen to continue so we start the return of the loop taking in Hart Crag, where we have to wait for Adrian, still intent on further exploration, and Dove Crag

While waiting for Adrian, Ali and Kate decide to build a snowman that is soon transformed into a snow penguin. Feeling the cold, I just look for his beak and eyes amongst the rocks and hand over suitably-shaped rocks for the inclusion in the rapidly-forming Antarctic beast.

Ali and I stand admiring the work as Kate, bent over, puts the finishing touches on the snow creature, now looking ever so sweet. A group of young chaps arrive and one stands admiring the work. Kate has not registered this and after some loving final touches she looks up and with a shocked bemused voice says, "Oh hello."

"We are a bit mad," I say.

"Don't worry, we are students."

Adrian joins us to admire the fine fellow and it was decided that Penguin needs an igloo to live in. Adrian and Kate set about the task, a few false starts and rethinks but an igloo begins to form. Unfortunately, on near completion, Adrian's fist goes through the rear wall causing the majority of the structure to collapse.

"Oh no, poor Penguin comes from a broken home," I say.

Kate pelts me with snowballs.

After a further few minutes Penguin is equipped with a 'cool pad' and he stands proudly by the entrance. He is a little oversized for his new abode but this is soon explained by it being Tardis like. One of the students comes over and says, "The guy that lives in that igloo is going to have one hell of a shock when he comes out to find a giant penguin sitting outside."

Continuing on we descend, making full use of the snow to have some wonderful bottom sliding, over Little Hart Crag and, missing Red Screes, descend back to Ambleside to a relaxing evening in Kate's parents' cottage. A game of limericks ensues with Ali coming up with:

> There was a young penguin from Ambleside
> Who's partner refused to lie by his side
> He stomped up a mountain
> And cried like a fountain
> 'til he caught influenza and died

I reflect how much I enjoyed the walk, a nine-hour roundtrip that I was more than happy to allow the others to lead and navigate. I really enjoyed that, not having the added pressure of being responsible if we got lost. Ali, Adrian and Kate's company was so good I wonder, after having known them only nine months, how that has come about. But then being strapped to Ali and Adrian for a week on the Cuillin Ridge did accelerate the friendship by a good few months. Friendships are much stronger by having lived through something together.

May 2002 – Scottish 2000ft Mountains

I'm in Scotland meeting and re-supplying Ali Ashton, Adrian Ogden and Kate Wilson, at Ruigh-aiteachain Bothy, on their TGO Challenge (The Great Outdoors Challenge) cross-Scotland walk. I walk with them for half a day, taking in Mullach Clach a' Bhlair, my first Munro since completing, before a return to the bothy, a walk out and a drive south to climb a Corbett – a sub-3000 foot Scottish mountain.

Sat in a B&B on Sunday May 19th the landlady, serving me, looks out the window and exclaims, "Oh my god." I look in the direction of her gaze, towards the opposite hotel, to witness the tail end of six naked male motorcyclists whizzing through. The landlady is out like a shot to get a better view; I continue my breakfast whilst checking the menu for streaky bacon.

I meet Willy Newlands at 09:00 to walk the Cobbler – one of the most famous Corbetts. Remembering guide book descriptions of a perilous ascent I ask, "We can get to the top?"

"Aye, Steve."

"Just that I heard it was a bit tricky."

"Nah, it's a flat summit."

Through the mist we plod, with me back to my normal slow self. But it is good to walk with Willy again and his edgy humour.

The route to the Cobbler takes a sweeping arc as you encroach the summit through one of its weak defences. A ridge connects its twin summits and we head for the most southerly, the highest. Stood on the plateau I look to the east and ask, "Willy, this is the top?"

"Aye, Steve."

"Just that bit is higher," I add, pointing.

"That's the eye of the needle, you won't catch my going through that. It's too exposed."

"But this is not the top."

"Well some might say that, Steve."

"Well that bit is higher, so it must be the top."

"Nah, this is the top, Steve."

"But that is higher."

"You want to try it?"

"No," I reply.

"Then this is the top."

I leave the Cobbler, for another day and perhaps a paid guide.

August 2002 – English Nuttalls

With a recession in IT procurement hitting the computer industry hard, leaving me struggling to find work, I spend some of my free time taking extra professional exams. Come August my mind drifts back towards hill walking. So, on August 2nd I'm off to Dartmoor to climb its pair of two-thousand-foot peaks. Yes Tor and High Willhays.

I get lost trying to find the route to the car park at Meldon Reservoir. The local planners and sign writers conspiring on decades of games of 'guess where it is' delays my start by some hour. Once I get going I enjoy a heavenly five-hour round trip of Yes Tor, High Willhays, Dinger Tor, Lints Tor, Steng-a-Tor then Shelstone Tour. On the approach to Yes Tor I'm humming the Beatles' 'Yesterday' for 'Yes Tor Day'.

September 2002 – Welsh Nuttalls

I continue to struggle for contract work over the summer, eventually picking up a commission to produce a report, for Unisys, on business opportunities that might come out of the forthcoming freedom of information act.

September 11th is a glorious day, clear skies and warmth in the air. However, I'm stuck in an office in Colwyn Bay discussing workflow and document management with North Wales Police.

Having set off at 04:00, I am relieved when the meeting ends and I can set off for Llanberis Youth Hostel to take up my bed. When I'd phoned through the booking the warden had sounded reluctant to make a note of it. On arrival I understand why – I am the only guest. My heart sinks – living and working alone, I hadn't fancied the impersonal hotel offered on business expenses. Instead I'd opted for the Youth Hostel in the hope of some company from likeminded hillwalkers.

"Do you want an evening meal?" the warden asks as I sign the register.

"I think I won't," I reply and he looks a little disappointed – I guess he needs the business.

"I'd feel a bit strange eating on my own," I add.

I skulk around the hostel. In the common room I read a plaque on the wall, commemorating its opening in 1968. I recall my last visit here, chatting to two nurses, of a similar age, I'd remarked that I was three when it'd opened. "Are you still free?" asked one. Too shy to take the bait I'd always wondered, "What if".

When my stomach starts to indicate it's supper time, I walk back into Llanberis. I enjoy hearing Welsh being openly spoken on the streets. I find an impersonal hotel and eat on my own.

Waking early I set off in the dark for the short drive to Pen-y-Pass, the starting point for walking Snowdon. I pull up in the car park. It was once free, now the charge is £4. I dig around in my car for enough coins to feed the meter and set off, at just after 06:00, in the half-light of the breaking dawn.

The initial pull is gentle and guides me, in the brightening light, to rough terrain. As I approach some disused mine buildings, my eyes are drawn to around thirty orange sacks, laid out side by side. On closer inspection I note each contains a human being – a party camped out, on the lower slopes just before the path becomes vague, scree ridden and hard on the legs.

A notice saying 'Footpath erosion control, please keep to the paths' causes me some amusement – there is no obvious path through the scree.

The walk is now in thick mist, in contrast to the glorious day of sun cooped up in an office yesterday. I plod my way up and, on meeting the main ridge, check my watch – I'm three hours from the start. The Snowdon Mountain Railway drifts off down to Llanberis. I follow the tracks for a few yards before the climb to Crib y Ddysgl and a backtrack to reach the summit of Snowdon – my fourth visit since the age of eleven. Unlike the previous times I do not descend to the start but instead take the oft-narrow ridge around to Y Lliwedd, Y Lliwedd East Peak (one assumes that an Anglican tacked the last bit of the name on) and Lliw-edd Bach. Now on slightly lower ground the weather is a bit clearer and I walk out and back on the ridge spur to Gallt y Wenallt before dropping back to the track to Pen-y-Pass.

Classification	My Total	Total
Welsh Nuttalls	25	188
English Nuttalls	10	251
Corbetts (Scotland)	1	219
Grahams (Scotland)	0	220
Unique Donalds (Scotland)	0	58
Munros (Scotland)	284	284
Ireland	0	212
Totals (12/09/2002):	320	1432

March 2003 – Welsh Nuttalls

The winter passes and I start to play five-aside football again, in my beloved position as a goalkeeper. I enjoy being back on the pitch but various knocks, and a foot-on-foot collision with an opposing attacker, has me delaying a planned trip, to finish off The Black Mountains, by a day.

Thursday 13th March starts with a 05:00 alarm which, after two beeps, promptly gives up with a failed battery. However, it's just enough to rouse me to breakfast, make sandwiches and set off on the three-hour drive to South Wales and The Black Mountains.

The swelling and bruising on my right foot makes squeezing it into the boot a bit tricky. But once in it protects the joint and I only get minor niggles from it.

I set off at just before 09:00, in thermals, shirt and fleece. This proves okay until I meet the first main ridge where it becomes very cold with the ground frozen under foot. I don my Gore-Tex jacket and three layers of gloves. Things start to feel warmer.

I take a few tumbles; the soles of my boots are worn. I rest at the first summit, Pen Cerrig-calch: my only companion the orange peel of previous walkers. In the distance I can see what I think is the furthest mountain of the day, but after closer inspection I realise it is only halfway – Pen Twyn Glas. I look at my watch, consider dusk and calculate I have to reach the furthest point, Waun Fach, by 13:30.

I stride on, bagging Pen Allt-mawr, Pen Twyn Glas, Mynydd Llysiau and Waun Fach (bang on 13:30). It's then Pen y Gadair Fawr and Pen Twyn Mawr, making seven 2000ft tops in this seven-and-a-half-hours' elongated horseshoe.

High cloud made navigation easy and I distributed my sandwiches amongst the peaks. The eastern side was warmer, the ground squelched underfoot, not frozen like its westerly counterpart. In the afternoon the sun started to break through and I could see my morning's work now offset by its rays, dusting the folds of the hills with shade. Towards the end, the skies cleared further but I had dropped most of my height to appreciate the full effects of the light bouncing off the hills.

Back on a minor road a car pulls up, two old ladies offer me a lift. I decline graciously yet appreciatively. From trips and tumbles I am filthy, their car is immaculate and somehow I figure we'd both end up looking dishevelled.

September 2003 – Welsh Nuttalls

After so long away from the hills it feels the time is right to venture back to the Brecon Beacons. A summer of failing to secure proper work is playing on my mind as wasted time. I could have been in the hills after all. Instead, the only walking I did was to plod the streets of my village, delivering leaflets asking people to register interest in broadband. We got the requisite number signing up, hopefully BT will now install it.

On September 24th, with my alarm clock set for 05:00, I wake at 03:48 to a distant alarm alerting me that my water softener needs more salt – a First World irritant. Laid in bed I contemplate for a few moments before leaping into action. Perhaps I could get even more walking done.

Loading the car I notice how the clear sky has caused frost to settle. It takes a while to locate the windscreen scraper, but I am on the road by 05:00, paying the Severn Bridge toll after 06:00 and walking in the Brecon Beacons at 07:30.

The air is chill, the sky blue – perfect for me. As I ascend I drink in the purity of the day, the smell of the hills. Reminding me of my true love, hill walking.

The ridge around to Bwlch y Ddwyallt gives me views towards the highest points of the Brecon Beacons. Sheep graze, birds soar and streams gently trickle. The sun rising over the ridges warms me and I shed clothing and make an even better pace. I am motoring: Bwlch y Ddwyallt falls before 09:00 then Waun Rydd followed by the soft descent and ascent to Allt Lwyd.

Without another soul in sight I have the hills to myself. I get back to the car well before lunch, pleased with my progress. A summer with no hills has made me suspect my fitness but my body is still there and I contemplate an early journey home. But the day is too good to miss so I drive down the road a bit and take in Cefn yr Ystrad.

I ascend towards this featureless plateau, ideal for a day of great visibility with a gentle stroll to the summit. A few cairns on the way fool me, in mist it would have been a difficult walk. Yet at each cairn I can see a higher one ahead, to tempt me on; beckoning in the Brecon Beacons. I reach the top in just over an hour and a half, sit awhile and enjoy. A bird of prey is circling, gracefully swooping, to catch and to kill? Or just having fun like me?

I choose a different descent and soon come across an ugliness of disturbed nature: disused quarry workings, unattended, abandoned in mid-slice. An ugly scar – why can't the granters of the license insist on an environmentally-pleasing end result? Instead millions of years of weathering will be required to give this a natural look. Some old cars, now burnt out, have been driven up on the old quarry roads: joy riders, who rob others of their joy. Some workers are towing the cars away, removing the eyesore from the eyesore.

Past this my spirits lift and I return to my car for the drive home.

Classification	My Total	Total
Welsh Nuttalls	36	188
English Nuttalls	10	251
Corbetts (Scotland)	1	219
Grahams (Scotland)	0	220
Unique Donalds (Scotland)	0	58
Munros (Scotland)	284	284
Ireland	0	212
Totals (24/09/2003):	331	1433

March 2004 – Welsh Nuttalls

It's March and my sleep has become sporadic but on the evening of the 26th, with a walk planned for tomorrow with Ali Ashton, I force myself to stay awake while watching the classic film, *Random Harvest.* Afterwards, and feeling half asleep, I drag myself to the kitchen and painfully bash my knee before making cheese and pickle sandwiches and packing an apple along with my day's walking kit.

I drag myself to bed, the alarm sounds at 04:00 and I'm on the road an hour later. I avoid the toll bridge on the M4, into Wales, and take a cross-country route to meet Ali at the Talybont Reservoir. Her partner, Adrian couldn't make it due to work pressures.

I arrive early and wait an hour for Ali. We drive down to a small parking area in the Taf Fechan Forest (which requires caution when pronounced) and get walking at 09:30, ascending to the Graig Fan Ddu ridge where the mist descends. We speak with a bald-headed, out-of-shape walker on his route to Pen Y Fan. Being the pompous experienced walkers that we are we advise him to put his hat on.

We then go along to the crossroads in paths, past the obelisk in memory to wee Tommy Jones who in 1900, at the age of five, perished on this spot after becoming separated from his father. Then it's onto Y Gyrn and, at five hours into the walk, we backtrack across Corn Du and drop some height. Here we meet a man and his incredible three-year-old son doing the hills. We now ascend Pen Y Fan, Cribyn and Fan Y Big. I'd previously walked Pen Y Fan and Cribyn in March 1990 but was happy to repeat them.

From some of the summits we had views, though misty. Some of the ascents were hard going; Ali and I are both out of shape. Some of the edges were sheer drops: I kept away which was fortunate as I did take one very heavy tumble on wet ground. At the final summit the mist came down again and, having previously seen car lights in the valley below, I asked Ali if we could descend quickly. She was fine about it, a very compatible walker is Ali. We were soon safely on the final track, navigable in the fading light. We got to the cars at the last light of 19:00

April 2004 – English Nuttalls

On April 11th I arrive at Ali and Adrian's house in Rotherham at one minute to nine. Ali opens the door with a bemused look. My ability to turn up spot on time is gaining humour with Ali, we'd said 09:00 and I've done the three-hour drive with a minute to spare. Adrian chooses to look after their baby, Ellen, for the day, allowing Ali and I to drive down into the Peak District to walk Bleaklow Head and Higher Shelf Stones – a walk of about six hours, nine miles and 1500 feet of ascent. High cloud gives us views, not superb, yet views worthy of the walk. Starting at just before 11:00 from Old Glossop, we make our way by joining the Pennine Way (the long distance path to Scotland). In areas the peat is thick and boggy and make it tough going. Many people are out on this Easter Sunday with some very young children wondering why their parents have brought them to this wild spot.

Having brought a full pack, in practice for the upcoming cross-Scotland walk (The Great Outdoors Challenge), I require more rests than normal. On the descent we sit, allowing a party to pass us, and I say 'hi' to one guy, over sixty and overweight. He turns to return the 'hello' and promptly falls over. Fortunately Dr Ali is here to offer advice, but I do feel a bit guilty.

May 2004 – The Great Outdoors Challenge

"Lindisfarne Castle," says Ali Ashton.

I glance out the train window to where she's pointing. The sixteenth century castle is dappled in sunlight and, on its raised mound, stands out from the stunning East Coast of England.

"We've not even started the walk," I reply, "and we're already getting glorious views."

We pass through Edinburgh, on our way to Oban to start of The Great Outdoors Challenge (TGO Challenge): an annual two-week self-supported Scottish Coast-to-Coast backpacking adventure which, now I have completed the 284 Scottish Munros, Ali has convinced me to have a go at.

We have a two-hour wait in Glasgow where, in the early summer sun, I act as a tour guide showing Ali my old haunts from my time working here.

The train trip from Glasgow, through the Southern Highlands, branching west through Tyndrum to Oban, offers stunning scenery of mountains towering over moorland and light glistening on lochs. I get a mix of excitement and apprehension about the trek we are about to embark upon.

We arrive at Oban Youth Hostel (one of the permitted Challenge starting points) in the afternoon. It's a picture postcard port with stately Victorian buildings and a folly looking down over the town. A ferry goes out to the islands, fishing still appears to be an occupation. An imposing cathedral hangs heavy at one end. In the distance is the Isle of Mull with its mighty Ben More.

Friday May14th we breakfast, sign the register to mark our start then, at 09:15, set off walking. However, we are soon halted by my desire to purchase new insoles for my boots. I sense Ali is itching to get going but my right heel is heavy, hot and complaining it needs something more comfortable to spend the next 200 odd miles on.

With a shop located, and new insoles purchased, I find they lift my sole pushing the top of my feet against previously unreachable leather. I'm now in danger of blistering. But, having taken up Ali's time, I keep quiet and rejoice that at least my soles are now comfortable. I follow as Ali begins to guide us along the twelve miles of roads to Taynuilt.

Now Ali goes quiet. I sense what's coming. "How's your love life?"

"Quiet," I reply, "still waiting on Mary to make a decision."

"The Canadian lady?" asks Ali.

"Yup."

"Nobody else a possibility?" she asks encouragingly.

"To be honest, after the daily dressing downs I went through with my last two partners, I'm glad of the break. It's left a few bruises."

"Isn't Mary older?"

"Yes, six years older than me."

"That'd rule children out, Steve."

"I've never thought of myself as a dad," I reply, surprised by her question.

"You seemed pretty broody when you played with my three the other day."

"Really?" I ask, again surprised by this revelation.

"Oh yes," she replies with certainty in her voice.

With this new angle on my character to ponder we pick up other TGO Challenge people. I joke with Geoff Yarnell, who resembles Michael Palin, he should be walking the other way (i.e., around the world) to get to Montrose and the end of the walk. The joke falls flat, I must make a note not to be so obscure in my humour. Or at least attempt to be funny.

Geoff is an interesting and engaging chap and soon is very much part of our day. Like me he is new to the TGO Challenge and we are given the title of 'first-time challengers'.

We bump into John Jordan, a companion at our Youth Hostel breakfast, who, despite having seven tumours and no bladder, is making great progress. This well and truly out trumps my dodgy knees and asthma. But, given I slept in the bunk below him last night, I may have had a narrow escape from this bladderless man.

Our tents in Glennoe

We criss-cross with Penny and Bernie Roberts throughout our day and another walking couple, Stuart and Maria Scott. Stuart and Maria met on the Challenge two years ago and were married within months. They are still smitten with each other. I struggle with conversation, I'm always a bit shy and awkward with new people. It takes me a day or so to bond, this will be another challenge.

At the pub in Taynuilt we have a welcome meal, a welcome rest and more bonding with fellow TGO Challenge participants. We then take the forestry track to Glennoe where we pitch our tents for the night. I wander back and wait, just north of a group of farm buildings, for Kate Wilson and Amanda Cowking, joining us for the weekend. A dog with more bark than bite warns me of their arrival.

I lead them back to our campsite where we all huddle into one tent for food, completing the day of low cloud and a bit of rain.

It's Saturday May 15th and, due to low cloud Ali, Kate and Amanda give up on their high route. Instead they accompany me from Glennoe around to where the Allt Hallater stream meets the River Kinglass. I find it tough going and, with the weight of my pack, I am painfully slow.

The weather is okay and, with Geoff having left us, we pitch the three tents facing each other.

I grab an hour of sleep before the evening brings a joyous game of guess the area covered by an OS map from the map number. We then become a bit risqué and confess the OS map number on which we each lost our virginity. Ali can't decide which of two neighbouring maps it is which prompts me to ask if she were travelling in a car at the time. It's one of those moments where you know you've pushed your luck and await the response with icy tendrils dancing in one's stomach. Fortunately, after the split second for the joke to sink in, it is received with good cheer.

We take a short evening walk to a bridge across a stream, disturbing deer who greet us with their graceful bounding off.

It's Sunday May 16th and nearly noon as I sit on a rock, overlooking Loch Dochard. The cloud is high and broken. The hills are alive with patches of sun, shadow, snow, heather and rock. An underground stream is echoing its way down towards the loch. I'm surrounded by mountains – some are Munros, conquered with a lighter pack. I've been struggling today. It was to be a day of going into the hills, leaving my tent for a whole day. But I need to get a day ahead to claw back the time I've lost by being so slow. Therefore I have separated from Ali, Kate and Amanda.

I plod on and meet challenger 326, Brian Hill. I take his number and promise to phone in for him at Bridge of Orchy. He plans to walk on beyond Bridge of Orchy, perhaps as far as the bothy at Gorton.

The tar-sealed road from Victoria Bridge to Bridge of Orchy, is hard and painful. It's taking me a while to settle into the Challenge. For 'Challenge' is what it is generally termed. "Are you doing the Challenge?" you enquire of fellow walkers. No need to mention TGO Challenge, just 'Challenge' is the currency of comradeship.

I arrive at the Bridge Of Orchy Hotel at 17:00. Adrian Ogden, Ali's partner, is due later, with baby Ellen and a resupply for me. I phone into 'Challenge Control' and speak with Roger Smith. He congratulates me on getting so quickly involved as I mention the legends of Brian Hill and John Jordan. I really have Ali to thank, she warned me what to expect so I was able to speak with Roger in a knowledgeable way.

I eat then check into the hotel bunkhouse and rejoice in the luxury of a twin room, all to myself for the mere sum of £10.

Adrian arrives at 21:00 with my spare clothes so I can now shower and change. We then have a couple of hours in the non-smoking end of the bar. Baby Ellen, eleven months, is into everything, including a passion for Adrian's pint of beer. It starts with a curiosity Adrian attempts to satisfy by allowing the beer to touch her lips. Like a Microsoft product there is a delay as we wait for a response. The response is a wide grin and two outstretched arms to begin her drinking career. I'll remind her of this when she is older. It's a good couple of hours chat with Adrian. I admire how Ali and he have got a good balance where she can do the Challenge with his support. I couldn't imagine any of my past girlfriends prepared to do that for me. As Adrian is a doctor I show him the pack rash on my shoulders. He winces. It must look bad.

On Monday May 17th I set off at 07:00 for Gorton Bothy. The first section, along the A82 road, is unnervingly hazardous and I'm glad to turn and head across the glen towards Gorton. The weather turns to rain and I feel miserable as my jacket lets water. I sing and whistle and dream of soup at the bothy. Fortunately nobody else is around – it sounds awful. I pass a tent, probably Brian Hill's. I consider etching 326 and an arrow into the dirt track but think better of it.

They say the early bird catches the worm, but I've long held the view life is down to timing and indeed an early bird can be thwarted if the worm chose to have a lie in – my being an early bird today got me very wet.

The weather perks up and, at 11:00, I'm relieved to be inside Gorton Bothy, sipping soup. It's a classic bothy, two rooms and that's it. I read in the log book, like many bothies, it was once a shepherd's cottage.

This morning I passed the ruin of Barravourich, unroofed and falling down. Due to the rating system owners of unused cottages remove the roofs to avoid paying tax. The Mountain Bothies Association (MBA) agrees with the owners to re-roof the odd ones as mountain shelters. Due to a quirk in the law they remain free of the rates tax because the owner doesn't own the roof. Long may this quirk last.

Brian Hill joins me, I should have carved his number into the ground: he said he'd have enjoyed the joke. Brian is seventy-five, like most challengers he looks ten years younger than his true age.

I leave Gorton and soon realise I've lost the clip for my drinks tube. I backtrack to the bothy but cannot find it. Brian makes me one from a piece of string and a slipknot. I enjoy accepting his help and I think he enjoys helping me.

The afternoon's walk is over wet ground, tough going with no track. I camp at 1500ft above Rannoch Forest. The tent takes a bashing in the wind and its outer skin thumps against the inner, doing nothing for my nerves. It could be a rough night. I hope all will be well. On a positive note, I'm snug in my sleeping bag and have managed to find my drinks tube clip in my pack.

It's Tuesday May 18th and it's been a rough night. I wake many times with the tent being pounded, like I'm bedded down with an excited Labrador. Fortunately only a bit of rain falls. At 07:00 I stick my head out and the sky is every conceivable shade of colour. Light, dark, angry, enticing! A call of nature requires me to get up. With every limb aching it takes all my composure to haul myself out of the tent.

It's a painful task to break camp. My biggest fear is getting the tent down without it taking off in the wind. In a rare calm moment, I pull out the pegs, slide out the hoops and pack it away, swing my pack onto my back and set off.

I follow the tall deer fence (though I see no tall deer), which I'd followed for an hour yesterday evening, to the south of Rannoch Forest, looking for the route through to Bridge of Gaur. I have no luck and follow the deer tracks running parallel to the fence. At one point I pause to take in the stunning view up the distant Glen Coe.

My confusion with the map is explained when I realise the fence is new and the forest has changed its geography. I survey my options then pluck up courage and cut through the forest on a stream and pick my way down.

I follow a faint deer track (ironic as the deer fence is supposed to keep them out). It's hard going, with ups and downs and continual re-crossings of the stream to get myself onto lower ground. Then where? The tracks on the map have disappeared. I get a feeling of despair that, by cutting through the forest, I've compounded the problem of finding the route. I opt for a new track which by luck leads me out of the forest. After an uncertain two hours I heave a sigh of relief and allow my nerves to calm down.

At Bridge of Gaur I cross to civilisation and hope for a tearoom or pub. I have no luck so take the long haul to the bothy of Ben Alder Cottage which, by all accounts, is haunted. It rains and is tough going. My energy is poor and with 1km to go I slump down and have to will myself to get moving again. I keep chanting, "Come on, Steve, just 1km more".

On arrival, after ten hours, I make soup and am grateful for the dry pair of socks in my pack. I read it was last occupied, as a home, by Mrs McCook. I feel the pit of loneliness, this could be the low point of the crossing – it's now twenty-nine hours since I last spoke to anybody.

With a fire lit I find some cheer, hang my sodden socks up and watch them steam.

It's Wednesday May 19th and I wake at 04:30. There's been no disturbances from the ghost, but two mice did disturb me with their rustling.

Last night's rain caused me to postpone a call of nature, this morning there's an urgent need requiring the use of the bothy spade. A sign gives guidance as to where one might crap (their words not mine). It pleads using the outhouse, open ground, the bothy wall or porch, covering over with a mole hill or building a nice little rockery over ones steaming achievements is not on. I have to grab walking boots and spade and make my way to the recommended turd graveyard some two hundred metres from the bothy.

I set off at 07:00 and find it very tough going with a complaining body. In places the path meets the shore of Loch Ericht and I have to scramble around rocks to avoid an icy plunge.

The weather varies, and I can't get comfortable with my kit. Passing the shore in one place an oystercatcher decides I'm too near its nest. I have to pull my hood up and attach the mouth protector as it continually dive bombs me.

It takes me six hours to get to Ben Alder Lodge and I'm disappointed the estate has, with consent, rerouted the path around the lodge. This makes a full pass up the side of the loch impossible and adds considerable height to the walk. Somehow the planners who agreed to this, along with permitting a series of buildings with every conceivable piece of Scottish architecture crammed into a building too small to accept it, missed the point somewhere. They look like castles from a Scooby-Do story and are a 'face lift too far' for the Scottish hills.

It's now a three-and-a-half-hour further trudge to the hotel at Dalwhinnie to collect a resupply parcel. When I'd phoned, to check if I could use them as a postal address, I asked if they had a room for this night. Alas they were full so, plodding wearily on, I consider my options for a bed for the night.

A mountain biker passes me, being my first human contact in two days I all but pull him off his bike to engage him in conversation. I'm low, down and convinced everybody else is ahead of me on the Challenge.

I glance back down the loch as the sun hits it. Trees, mountains, water and the shades of light conspire to lift my spirits and remind me of why I do this.

I continue to the calls of a cuckoo. A solitary bird I am convinced is also doing the TGO Challenge. I keep myself going by allowing daft things to enter my head, like is this 'The TGO Challenge' or just 'TGO Challenge' – TGO Challenge stands for The Great Outdoors, thus 'The TGO Challenge' would imply a stutter as it expands to The, The Great Outdoors. Or should it be 'TGOC', standing for The Great Outdoors Challenge?

The event used to be called The Ultimate Challenge, which never, to my knowledge, got the acronym of TUC. You could imagine it in its early days:

"Now brothers we are on TUC. We've made it half way and now we propose to strike out—"

"Right, strike. Everybody out."

I'll spare you the rest, it's all tripe coming into my mind to keep me company. You poor reader, are lucky as you only have a snippet of the constant rubbish that churns inside my head.

On the approach to Dalwhinnie it begins to rain. Desperate for a bed and a bath, I try the railway station to see if I can get a train to the next town, Newtonmore. If successful I'd then get the first train back in the morning to pick up where I left off.

As I'm reading the timetable a train comes in, stops for a moment and then sets off again. It's then I realise there are no more trains for over six hours. With my plan thwarted, and my head hung low, I trudge to the hotel, to collect my package and, convinced I'm going to have to camp in the rain, half-heartedly enquire of a room, keeping the hope in my heart in check. The manager peruses his books and says, "We've one left." I ask him the price. I'd have taken it at any price, but £25.50 is a bargain.

He leads me to the room, opens the door and shows me around. I spout the most painful series of words of praise, gratitude and gratefulness ever to have passed my lips (well apart from to the girl on OS sheet 198 some twenty years previous). I run a bath and lower my aching limbs bit by bit into the pool of warm water. It's the most pleasurable bath of my life.

When I eventually extract myself from the bath (believe me this is a long time later) I make my way to the restaurant and settle into a seat.

"TGO Challenge?"

I look up to an enquiring face. "How did you know?" I ask as it dawns on me there might be other TGO Challenge participants taking refuge in the hotel tonight.

"Tanned, tired, unshaven and no shoes!"

Yup, that about sums me up and I shake hands with John Hooper as I contemplate how dumb my question must have sounded. John goes to fetch another challenger and I'm introduced to the infamous Di Gerrard. Soon we are joined by John Jocys. From forty-nine hours alone, which surprises them, I'm now buzzing, alive and feeling part of something. All the pain now feels worthwhile as we share stories of our adventures.

It's Thursday May 20th and I wake feeling a bit peaky, my stomach has been churned up. A voice comes into my head telling me what is wrong. Vitamin C! Okay scurvy hasn't yet kicked in but, whenever the waiting staff are distracted, I take another glass of breakfast orange juice. Eight in all with the last one being sank with my rucksack on my back ready for the off.

As I make to leave I spy a familiar figure alighting from a car. At first glance it looks like Geoff Yarnell. At a second glance I notice the odd handles on his trekking poles and realise it is indeed Geoff. I shoot out to humiliate him, whatever the excuse, over the use of a vehicle. Of course it is innocent, a train trip to Newtonmore the night before and a lift back to restart his walk. We are both pleased to see each other, it has been five days.

I'm able to introduce him to John and they set off together. I walk with Di after briefly meeting Val Hadden and Mary Brook. Walking with Di is fun, and we make good progress alongside the aqueduct with various connections with Val and Mary.

Near Coire Chuaich there's a parting of the ways and I'm left alone to walk down the Allt na Fearna before the cut across the lower reaches of Maol an t-Seilich and a cut down to the bridge at the dam on the loch north of Gaick Lodge.

As I approach the dam two figures pause and wait for me. It's Geoff and John, having taken the longer route via Gaick Lodge. We make good progress and, with their encouragement, I revise my plan to camp and instead make Ruigh-aiteachain Bothy my target.

With my breathing on the ascents making every few metres feel like I've just done a 100m dash, I lose John and Geoff on the lower slopes of Can Dearg. I can't find a maintainable pace and have to rest every thirty seconds.

Some of the views today are stunning and I recall why Scotland is so beautiful. The Alps, for sure, are beautiful yet it's the ideal image of mountain scenery. Scotland has the moods of the weather and unlike an artist's canvas you can be amongst it, part of it, embracing it and not just looking on.

Cutting through the forest above Allt na Cuilce, picking between the fallen trees on a track, I meet with John Jocys again. We keep each other going and share the pain of the track down into Glen Feshie. My quick-fire appalling jokes keeps John's mind from the pain of the walk.

I carefully pick my way across the River Feshie, stepping from stone to stone, watching out for currents when splashing across wider sections.

It starts to rain and I can't really make out the bothy in the poor light. I plod on for a bit then my nose picks up the scent of a fire. It feels warm, welcoming.

Bursting through the door, after over ten hours' walking, I'm met by a huge array of people, a hearty log fire and John Hooper and Geoff ready to spring up and shake my hand. A chair opens up for me. The comradeship strikes me. We are all individually trying to get across Scotland, but to each one of us the success of each other's crossing is just as important as the success of one's own. The Munros are about the mountains you climb, the TGO Challenge about the people you meet. Yet in both cases the soul is worked upon. Both offer long, tough, gruelling days yet when rest comes a satisfaction descends that warms away your worries.

Also in the bothy is Maggie Hems, a retired teacher, who'd I'd met in this bothy two years previously; Alan Hardy, a well-known walker who had vetted my route and Bob Lees who falls prey to my bad jokes: he has bought some Super Glue to mend his boots and the chap in the shop reluctantly sold it to him, saying he doubted it would solve the problem. I suggest he go back and say it had fixed the problem, but now how does he get the boot off?

The evening passes by with good stories of the hills, simmering hot drinks and simmering socks.

It's the morning of Friday May 21st and I'm making a cracking pace by tailgating Alan Hardy. He's interesting to talk to, very knowledgeable about the hills. I also like the way he engages in conversation and is interested in my tales too: I have met other well-known walkers in the past and have been disappointed by their self-interest.

After an hour or so I lose Alan, he's just too quick though I'm grateful for him having got me through what is normally the slowest part of my day.

I pick up with John Jocys and Mike Fallon. We get a thing going about craving for fried eggs, beans and chips. Every excuse we can we get it into the conversation. Continually adding to our fantasy meal. We fantasise that a distant communications mast is perched on the roof of a café, selling fried eggs, beans and chips.

We lose John and then I lose Mike so I walk alone towards the

Linn of Dee. Mike is heading for Braemar with John planning to camp at White Bridge. Other people pass and through them I hear stories of a couple, MA and Mike. As they never catch me up they must be evenly paced to me, but through the various stories I hear, I build up a mental image of them.

I camp, on a bend in the river, just short of the Linn of Dee, avoiding hitting the road into Braemar. I sit with the tent open enjoying the views of where I walked from. Within a few feet the wide river floats gently past and snow-capped mountains frame the horizon. Heathers, trees and grass pick out contours and gullies. Rocks mark the crags.

I lay in the tent and draw a compass on to my TGO Challenge cap with the peak facing east.

After eating I spy a fellow challenger descending the path. I wander up to meet and greet him. He's a wee fellow called John Dodd from Liverpool – full of personality, bubble and enthusiasm. It's great to meet him.

Saturday May 22nd dawns bright and it takes three hours to walk to Braemar, arriving at 10:00 in the beautiful morning sunshine. The Fife Arms Hotel has a single room for me which I can have at 15:00. So I stroll contented around Braemar, eating in cafés (enjoying fried egg, beans and chips) and chill with fellow TGO Challenge participants. I soak up the atmosphere.

Bernie and Penny Roberts approach me. "We are having a small gas problem," she says.

I'm about to reply "Oh please" when I realise she isn't referring to dehydrated meals but a lack of camping gas on which to cook them. I'm able to donate a half-used cartridge and promise more when Adrian arrives with my resupply. Scotland never ceases to amaze me when such basic supplies as gas cartridges aren't available in the shops.

A good evening is had in The Fife Arms. Plenty of atmosphere with a jamming session involving Steve Wagstaff and John Jocys on squeeze boxes and a superb itinerant fiddle player playing the most amazing music. His pace and Steve's alcohol consumption make an amusing contrast with Steve often left with swinging arms trying to regain a hold on the proceedings.

Adrian arrives, baby Ellen recognises me which is very sweet. They both enjoy the music too.

I meet MA and Mike. MA's mouth drops with slack-jawed amazement as I recount her life history I've heard from people feeding the information down the TGO Challenge line.

On Sunday May 23rd Adrian (carrying baby Ellen) and I walk, in wonderful sunshine, to the view point overlooking Braemar to meet Ali. As we approach I can see her on her mobile.

I turn to Adrian. "She's on the phone."

"To me," replies Adrian as he lifts his mobile to ear. Ali's request for our progress is met with a more primitive form of communication in the form of hand waving.

It is good to catch up after a week. I thank her for the dehydrated food she'd made me and the maps she'd laminated for me. She tells me I'm animated and enthusiastic, a far cry from how I appeared when she last saw me.

We lunch and I then set off and walk into the mountains, towards the bothy at Lochcallater Lodge. I soon bump into Val and Mary and am embarrassed as I cannot recall when I saw them last. They soon fill me in and we are able to fill each other in on our progress so far.

I follow the twisting well-made track up the side of the Callater Burn in the beautiful sunshine. Water glistens in the sun as it scampers over rocks and tumbles on minor falls.

Next to the bothy is Lochcallater Lodge itself. The custodians, Stan and Bill, are inviting TGO Challenge participants in and I have tea. Sat on one of an array of odd matching chairs I survey the kitchen. Wood clad walls, papered with photographs and newspaper cuttings. A fire does its bit, drawing a focus, warming the room and heating two blackened kettles with water for tea.

The lodge is owned by the Invercauld Estate and Stan and Bill get the use of it in return for maintaining and keeping it available for the odd needs of the estate, including royal visits and stalking.

I had been warned of their hearty greetings and that a bed for the night would be offered. I'm one of the lucky ones, having a room on the first floor, high in the mountains, with gaslights (no electricity here) and an original iron-framed Victorian bed which has been in situ for over one hundred years. Stan and Bill are kindly chaps, in their 60s who welcome TGO Challenge people in this remote mountain location.

As I settle down for the night there are a number of people downstairs enjoying drams, including the larger-than-life Dennis Pidgeon who let me know my night will be disturbed by an internationally recognised award he has for snoring. I stuff ear plugs in.

It's Monday May 24th and I wake early, 05:00, and sneak downstairs, passing Alan Fox in an adjoining room, to make my breakfast. Dennis stirs and comes into the kitchen, I think he'd passed out in the lounge, on route to going out for pee on the grass. He says something about it being the middle of the night and wishes me luck for my day ahead.

I'm off at 05:45, my earliest start of the Challenge. Yesterday and the day before were the best two days, weather-wise, of the Challenge and were, unfortunately, my two half days. My route today is high (1100m across Lochnagar) and I'm hoping it will be wonderful views. Unfortunately it's nothing like it, instead it rains and I have to use map and compass all the way but still manage to get myself lost twice.

At one point a piece of metal catches my eye and I descended to it. It's part of a Wellington Bomber that crashed on Carn an t-Sagairt Mor during the war. One of the engines is on display in Braemar, it held my fascination while I was there: a memorial to the British, Commonwealth and USA mixed crew. The damage to the lower cylinders, the elongated hole where the propeller shaft was mounted gave forensic clues the plane crashed into the mountains nose first, with the engines running.

After passing over Lochnagar I look back to see it now bristling out of the cloud – so much for the early bird.

At 15:00, after nearly nine and a half hours of walking and barely a rest, I make it through to the bothy at Shielin of Mark. Two other TGO Challenge participants, Myra Watson and Terri Lane, head off as I arrive. Val and Mary pass through but head off to camp a bit further on.

The bothy is a dingy small place, I miss the bed of Lochcallater Lodge. In all seven tents appear, its small confines encourage most to camp and I get the bothy to myself.

I recall my younger working days, the stresses of life and my then aim to 'buy a bothy' and hide myself away. Friends sometimes remind me of this, so I must have mentioned it a lot. I think the life that was paved out for me (degree, professional job etc.) was, at one level, rewarding but inwardly I've always struggled dealing with people. However, the people I meet in the hills give me hope that there is a life beyond the cut and thrust.

Alan Fox emerges from his tent and lights the fire in the evening, I drift off to sleep with it blazing. I don't remember him leaving, just remember being cosy in my sleeping bag.

I start at 06:55, on Tuesday May 25th, and walk over Muckle Cairn and then drop down into Tarfside, taking about six hours in all. The top is heathery and I have to pick my way down to avoid turning an ankle on the uneven ground. My right leg slips into a hole and I buckle over, disturb a grouse which launches into the air with its familiar squawk. Or was it laughing?

On the shores of Loch Lee I bump into Val Hadden and Mary Brook for the fourth time of the walk. An ancient tractor rattles past and Mary remarks on its age.

"Nineteen eighty-one," I say.

They both give me a curious glance.

"X registration," I explain.

Val and I then have a flowing conversation reminiscing the various years and the registration letters for them. How 1967 was cut short as they only ran an 'E' plate for seven months. Mary listens with a bemused interest of witnessing two people with such a weird interest connecting in such scenery. I recount one my first holidays to Scotland in 1978 when 'T' registration had just come out. Being in the licensing region of 'SH', and to my parent's dismay, I spent the week looking for the car number plate 'OSH1T' ignoring all pleas of my parents to enjoy the fantastic scenery they'd brought me to see.

It's great to walk with Val and Mary. I really enjoy their company. Although Mary now lives in Scotland we discover she grew up near to where I live. We dream of the hostel in Tarfside. With countless people heading that way we pick up the pace to ensure we beat off the opposition for beds. We strike a deal if there are two beds Val and Mary will get them, just one and it will be mine.

On arriving at the hostel we all get single rooms - though my socks, having been on my feet for the last twelve days, could have done with a single room of their own. An Austrian chap is also staying, enjoying the TGO Challenge. He looks at me somewhat puzzled when I ask if Austria has a coast-to-coast walk. Some jokes just fail.

The hostel is clean and comfortable with neat bedrooms and a well-laid out common room. It's cheap at just £8 for my own room. Belonging to the church it is opened to the TGO Challenge and staffed by kind and welcoming lady volunteers. It is another one of the treasures of the TGO Challenge. The Challenge does get me talking to people, this is good.

Ali arrives and we will now head to the coast together.

The hostel has showers and in it I notice my right hand is browner than my left. This is an incredible effect of walking west to east. If I get lost I could check which side of me the moss has grown on and navigate from that. I imagine a Sherlock Holmes story called 'The Brown Sided Man':

"By Jove Holmes," said Watson, "not another corpse."

"I'm afraid so, but this man was not killed in London, Watson."

"What makes you say such a thing?"

"Elementary, my dear Watson. You'll observe the poor wretch's right hand is browner than his left. Clearly he was walking west to east on the TGO Challenge when he met his fateful end."

"Great Scott, Holmes!"

"He could be but it has been noted many of the TGO Challenge participants are from England."

"What about those tartan underpants then Holmes?"

"That could be the clue we've been looking for."

It's Wednesday May 26th and, sat in a café in Edzell with Ali, Adrian and baby Ellen, I reflect on the four-hour walk so far. Walking with Ali along, what is now, flatter terrain I realise the walk is starting to come to an end. With the mountains behind us, the east coast will be reached tomorrow. I'm feeling fit, my pace is good and I reckon I could do it all over again.

"How are the Nuttalls going?" Ali asks.

The Nuttalls are the 2000 foot mountains of England and Wales – making up part of a life's aims to walk all the mountains of the British Isles.

"Thirty-seven, so far," I reply.

"And how many are there?"

"446."

"You set yourself some tough targets," Adrian replies, shaking his head and smiling. "As a chronic asthmatic wasn't finishing the Munros enough?"

He's probably right, but I feel the need to defend myself. "Well," I flounder, "I've always set myself tough targets." I'm not kidding. Both with education and work I set my goals high, needing to attain the best results. In short I'm a workaholic. Even my first house was a project, buying a wreck and over four painstaking years renovating it.

"When do you think you'll finish them?" he asks.

"It'll be a good ten years," I explain.

Two further hours of walking take Ali, myself and Ros Stokes to the

North Water Bridge campsite. Along the way we pass the disused air base that has recently been rejected as a centre for asylum seekers – hopefully the tap-tap of passing *trekking poles* doesn't alarm the locals!

Passing a beautiful house with perfectly-kept lawns, I pose the idea of knocking on their door and asking, "We are doing the TGO Challenge and you either allow us to use your loo or we cut little holes in your lawn. And by the way where can we camp?"

In a warm summer's evening, with blue sky and a gentle breeze, twenty tents fill part of the official campsite. A party atmosphere ensues with people strolling and chatting. I meet Sue Oxley, her and Ali had connected earlier in the walk.

Ali gets a leg massage from Keith Leonard. I ask if he is a professional masseuse.

"No, I'm a chippy by trade," he responds.

"You should have a word with that Paul McCartney," I suggest.

"Why?" asks Ali cautiously.

"Well you can do both Heather's legs."

They look at me blankly.

It's Thursday May 27th and a beautiful clear sunny day as Ali, Sue and I walk from North Water Bridge towards the beach at St. Cyrus. There's a sense of closeness in sharing the experience of the last leg together. Our conversation is free and open as we enjoy the views of the countryside. The wheat shimmers in the gentle wind like the waves on a sea.

On the beach I strip to my undies and charge straight in, leaving me gasping as the freezing cold water grasps my chest. Both Ali and Sue say they are impressed. Ah, at the age of thirty-eight I finally manage to impress some girls on a beach.

Adrian joins us and we chill on the fine pale sand with the sun warming our bodies. We share handshakes and applause with other finishers. We all agree this is one of the most relaxed and chilled moments of our lives. Neither Sue, Ali nor I want to leave. We go for some fine dining on a beach restaurant where Adrian buys us champagne.

We report into the Park Hotel and go to 'Challenge Control' to sign in, receive certificate, badge and handshakes. The obligatory T-shirt is handed to each person perhaps, to the delight of the waiting staff, as an attempt to ensure each participant has a fresh top to wear for the evening meal.

I'm sad now the walk is over. I slip off to my room to shower and return to 'Challenge Control' to be warmly shaken by the hand by Dennis Pidgeon. It is now I realise the question of was I smelly when I arrived is given an overwhelming affirmation. Now being washed and fresh my body's own odour is unable to mask that of the others. As Dennis continues to pump me warmly by the hand, I'm gripped in an embrace that even at an arm's length has me saying, "Aye, Dennis, aye so nice to finish. Must dash, catch you later."

The evening of festivities includes the meal with speeches etc. It's a grand occasion with over 200 people present. Also some famous British hillwalkers are here, names I'd just read about now all in one place. It is good to sit with John, Ali, Adrian, Sue and John Jordan. Good to chat with Val, Mary, Geoff, the Johns, Brian Hill, Di Gerrard and everybody else I'd connected with on route.

It tugs on my heartstrings to leave on the Friday morning, it's sad to say goodbye to so many people who have become friends. Friendships are made through time or by sharing adversity. Going into a café for lunch on the way home I glance around to see if there are any fellow challengers. Of course there are none, but I had got used to being on the look out for fellow challengers. My car keys in my pocket remind me of home, work and responsibilities. Only fifty weeks to go before the Challenge starts again.

June 2004 – Welsh Nuttalls

On June 28th, I stir at a little after 05:00 and, with my stomach still full from yesterday's birthday meal, I skip breakfast, pack my rucksack with a big bag of leftover food courtesy of my mum, back my car off the drive at 06:00, and am walking by 09:00.

My first intention is to follow the Nuttall guide book and start from Glyntawe, but I soon spy a minor road that gains me about five hundred feet. I set off at a cracking pace for Fan Hir, the left hand of two peaks on the horizon. After doing the TGO Challenge cross-Scotland walk in May my body is on fine form and I reach the Bwlch Giedd in an hour and am soon standing on Fan Hir. I can't believe how light my daypack feels after the thirty-three pounds on the TGO Challenge. I cut round via Fan Brycheiniog, Picws Du and Waun Lefrith, admiring (and avoiding) the sharp cliff down to the waters of Llyn y Fan Fach. A whisper of wind is in the air, cool yet warming but I keep my fleece on. I then strike out for the fifth 2000ft top of Garreg Las which I reach in just over three hours into the day. Now clad in my Gore-Tex jacket, I admire the twin tops of two fine ancient cairns.

I now have a dilemma. By adding the best part of three hours to this walk I can take in Garreg Lwyd and complete all of the 2000ft mountains in the Brecon Beacons. However, I have it in mind to get back to Bristol before 20:00 to buy a garden shredder – another First World dilemma. It's one or the other until I realise the alternative option of using my car to get closer to Garreg Lwyd. So I backtrack (avoiding a man lying on the ground in a most disturbing pose, only to be waved at by his female companion in an attempt to say this is normal) and get back to my car at a little after 15:00.

I drive around to the summit of the A4069 where I reckon it's an easy walk up. I break all the rules and take no map, no pack and no waterproofs. Instead, I just set a compass bearing and go. I'm soon standing on the summit, just an amazing twenty minutes from the car and only 400ft of climbing. Pleased with myself, I promptly set off down the wrong side and have to backtrack and then head back the way I came. It takes me fifty minutes from the car and back before setting off for Bristol – where a navigational error gets me horribly lost.

September 2004 – Welsh Nuttalls

I set off from home at 06:20 on September 11th and make excellent progress. I get walking on the hills at 11:00. Starting from Cwm Penmachno I ascend past the woods and break onto the ridge where I am met by strong gusts of wind. I make a blustery crossing to Moel Penamnen, jutting up above the surroundings.

On the way back, the wind and the rain conspire and look for a victim. Finding me, I'm placed in a wind tunnel with a hosepipe. Rueing my luck I return to the ridge – the last two weeks have been busy at work and spent in glorious sunshine. There are quarry workings to pass and I'm a bit too close to a steep drop. In one place there is a deep shaft right on the edge of the path. This is no place for a slip. Fortunately I pass safely but wonder at the lack of warning signs. Quarry and mine workings take you by surprise; they belie the lie of the land and you are upon them before you realise.

I set off for the blustery ascent of Manod Mawr. My body aches, the cloud is down and I only make the Manod Mawr North Top. It's sensible to turn back, though not without incident. I put a foot in a boggy area and my leg disappears to the knee, quickly followed by the other. It takes two seconds for the icy cold water to penetrate my boots. I haul myself out, wet, exhausted and wondering how much I am destined to enjoy this.

I arrive at my rented cottage, Squirrel Cottage, Penmachno. The cottage is one up, one down and nicely done out. I spend a little while making it my temporary home for two weeks.

On Sunday the 12th I set out for the hills again. The weather looks grim but my determination lasts only to the first peak, Allt-fawr. Looking towards Moel Druman, standing at about 2000 feet, I reflect on my ageing. When I was doing the Munros today's weather would not have deterred me. Yet the wind and the hail are lashing in to me and, knowing there will be little view to be had, I turn back with just one mountain climbed of the five planned summits. Two days of uncompleted walks is the equivalent of not setting out at all. It's just too wild and wet to go on. I don't need these mountains like I needed the Munros. I only want them, not need them. That difference aids caution, reminds one of waiting for another day. Reminds one that the risk is just not worth it. I return to the car, as many ancient trucks pass on what appears to be a rally.

The book *The Mountains of England and Wales – Volume 1 Wales* is split into sections. The mountains attempted so far are The Moelwyns, which are in turn split into four walks. Fortunately I climbed Moel Siabod in 1999 which means, despite two incomplete walks, I have still made some headway into this area.

Moel Siabod is probably well remembered by the party I was in at the time. I was in a group of chaps and when you get a group of chaps together on a hillside it's only a matter of time before the sheep jokes start coming out. In fact I'd be decidedly worried if a group of chaps failed to discuss such matters; it's a rite of passage, a badge of honour. During a rest stop, the subject matter duly turned to the topic of sheep buggery. My friend Greg put in an initial bid, "Why do you do it with a sheep on the edge of a cliff?" His joy of explaining that it was because they push back harder was not denied by anybody claiming that the lack of response was because we had heard it before: most likely on the last walk with Greg. Anyhow in true style the stakes were upped (including the use of Velcro and oversized wellington boots) until I announced, "Oh yeah, you need a bull dog clip on a piece of string tied around your neck."

"Why?" somebody enquired, his voice full of caution.

"To hold their tales up."

The previous few minutes of joyous hilarity were curtailed. The silence was awful.

Greg, with comic timing, asked, "You've done this haven't you Steve?"

I was just about to chip in with, "Surely we all have, lads?" when I realised that immediate denial was the better option.

It's Monday 13th and I'm in Blaenau Ffestiniog looking for the path to Saturday's abandonment, Manod Mawr. It proves elusive: car and foot are used to inspect a multitude of possibilities. At 08:20 I'm walking having found the route, tucked up a side street. I soon get a soaking yet make good pace, doing the round trip in just two hours. Saturday's route would have taken me through a steep quarry so I'm now grateful that the weather steered me back.

Many hours later I'm sat at the foot of the Snowdon area having just failed in my three-hour attempt of Crib Goch. Arriving at the pay car park at 11:20, and realising it is £4 before noon or £2 after, I make the excuse that I'm waiting to see if the weather will hold and go in search of food in Llanberis.

At 12:20 I'm back, paying the £2 parking charge and setting off in the dry. The weather soon turns to passing rain. The summit of Crib Goch stands at 923m and it looks, from a distance, very steep. This is often the way and I have an imaginary conversation with a friend – she was walking this with me and questioning how steep it looks and I give reassurance that it looks worse from a distance than it actually is. Well today is an exception: up close it is just as bad. I try many different angles, go on many fruitless scrambles, following paths that peter out. My boots, veterans of many a Munro and over 2000 miles of walking, do not have enough grip. I turn back, the shakes have kicked in and when confidence goes it's time to give up.

So I'm back in my car further realising these hills don't need to be conquered like the Munros. I'm ambitious but self-preservation is now in charge.

The 14th is a complete wash out but the 15th brings a better day. With a good forecast I set off early, walking by 07:40. The ascent to Pen yr Ole Wen is soon into mist and I rue my trust in the forecast. I have to pick my way up the east face, bits of scrambling then many places with no obvious path. But I make it to the top and then set forth, still in the mist, to Carnedd Dafydd, which I reach with ease.

The thorny issue of Foel Meirch now arises. In 1997 Myrddyn

Phillips pored over maps and determined that an 800ft descent, followed by a very short rise constituted another 2000ft mountain. As I start to descend to it I fail to share the excitement he may well have had. I soon abandon – no way would I find the small rise in this mist. So I set off back up and walk around to Carnedd Llewelyn where I meet a nice chap, Roger. We end up spending the rest of the walk together. As the mist lifts, to reveal wonderful views, we take in Yr Elen and Pen yr Helgi Du: the latter having a narrow ascent to it. In all I am out for just over nine hours. It feels good to have got a dry high walk in, with some views.

It's Thursday morning, the 16th, and I check the TV forecast: wind and cloud this morning, rain this afternoon. I set off to attempt the four that I abandoned on Sunday. Starting at a little before 08:00 it's a long, three-hour pull around Moel Dyrnogydd and up onto the high ground. The wind is now giving me quite a hammering while I survey the long ridge walk before me. The first top, Ysgafell Wen Far North Top, is soon captured, as is its near neighbour, Ysgafell Wen North Top. But by now the mist is thick and the wind very blustery. It is further to Ysgafell Wen itself, following a fence I keep on the safe side such that the wind pushes me against the fence. I'm pleased for its company and protection.

To reach the summit means climbing over the fence and crawling across rocks to touch the cairn followed by a quick descent to line up Moel Druman. It is now a shade after midday and the rain begins. Moel Druman is in thick mist and I try and get a compass bearing onto it. Occasionally it emerges for a second or so, teasing me yet not enough time to line the compass up. I give up and set the bearing by the map and lay one of my trekking poles on the bearing and, like a drunk waiting for the room to stop spinning, I wait for it to emerge for confirmation. It does, I'm right and I set off but get drenched and blown all over the place. I make the summit then descend quickly to the north side for some protection. There is little. A fence is still with me and I cling to its loose top wire. When it becomes detached from the posts I cling to the next one down. On a steep downwards section I cling to the wire and use it like an abseil by running as fast as I can go.

Skirting Allt-fawr (bagged on Sunday) I make the ridge again to its east. As I approach I can see the wind thrust up from both sides and battle it out at the top. On the final descent the wind subsides and I meet a group having a break: it looks like a leader and paying novices. I wander across and mention how windy it is. I get the cold shoulder from the guide.

Friday the 17th and I discover, on my trip over to Croesor, that Wales still has gated roads. It reminds me of our 1982 family holiday. Dad would hop out and open the gates and I, as a learner driver, would lurch the family car forward whilst he shut them. It felt daring, a learner always needs a tutor by his side: fortunately my mother and sister, in the back seats, were not slow in offering me the benefit of their expertise.

I set off at 07:30 and it is a long pull up Cnicht then Cnicht North Top. Navigation becomes tricky over to Moel-yr-hydd. On route I bump into the party I had spoken to yesterday.

"Was it windy?" I ask.

"Just a little breeze," replies their guide.

There are some pulled faces and harrumphs from his group.

The route I am now on is a little tricky and I triangulate off two tops to confirm my position. This is something I rarely do but a useful technique to have in one’s toolbox.

The route up is via old quarry workings, disused buildings and mounds of spoil. I make the top then set my compass bearing for what I think to be Moelwyn Mawr North Ridge Top. But it does not line up, instead it lines up with some insignificant bump. I dig around for my guidebook and am alarmed to find that Myrddyn Phillips has been up to his tricks again: a Welsh 2000ft mountain is defined as having to have at least 50ft rise all round, and I imagine Mr Phillips poring over maps looking for new humps which serve only to add to the challenge of walkers like myself. When he's laid to rest I'm convinced it'll be in some hitherto undiscovered part of his local graveyard (on a gentle rise).

After this I ascend Moelwyn Mawr proper then take the wrong direction but am rewarded by a Broken-spectre and its glory. This is where I look down my own shadow and see my silhouette surrounded by a rainbow. After correcting myself I take in Craigysgafn and Moelwyn Bach. I return to the car in a round that has taken eight hours and seven mountaintops.

Moelwyn Bach and Moelwyn Mawr

On Saturday the 18th, wishing to right the missed summit on Wednesday, Foel Meirch, I drive to Bethesda and, having waited for the rain to pass, start walking at 11:20. It's an easy walk yet, due to previous walks and a restless night from eating cheese, I feel oh so tired.

It takes me two hours to the summit and about an hour and twenty back down. I remind myself of a childhood story. When visiting Wales at young age I rather fancied buying a small witch that I had seen in a shop window. Being a shy type I mustered the courage and went in and asked for, "A witch".

The shop assistant glared at me, middle age and fearsome. "That, my boy, is not a witch. It's a Welsh lady dressed in our national costume."

I wonder if over the years she has seen it as funny as I have. Needless to say her words failed to secure a purchase and, with her eyes penetrating into me, I rapidly left the shop. I probably begged my parents to drive me out of town.

Starting at 08:30 on Tuesday 21st I'm pleased to be walking again. The weather has been so bad that it was impossible to walk over the last two days. Last night I tried to offset the boredom by venturing out for a beer only to find the sole pub in the village closed on a Monday.

I make good progress and, after climbing a ladder stile and finding a handy spare compass, am soon atop of Tal Y Fan. I then descend and have a 1000ft pull up Carnedd Y Ddelw. Here the wind is cold and fierce. Not as bad as last week but it is draughty and a couple of times I feel insecure for my safety. I then walk over to Drum: these middle two mountains have ancient cairns on them which have been broken down to form welcome shelters. I then continue to Pen Y Castell and along the ridge before descending to the road and then a long, hard-on-the-feet, walk on tarmac. A few minutes from the car I rue my luck as it starts to rain leaving me damp for the return drive.

Wednesday brings rain and I contemplate a walk but plump to keep my kit dry for the better forecast for Thursday. So at 09:00, on Thursday 23rd, I'm sitting up the end of a single-track road, three miles south-west of Tal-y-bont, waiting for the rain to ease. It pours and pours then at 10:30 things ease and I set off. I decide to split the one long walk into two: with five peaks in all I reckon that, even with the late start, I could pick one peak off then return to car and reposition for the last four.

All is going to plan, Craig Eigiau climbed, until I take a wrong turn in the car and get lost. By the time I spot the error my entire contingency has gone and it is pointless setting off. The forecast for tomorrow is better and I'm hoping for some good weather to leave Wales on a high note with. Though I have suspicions that next week is going to be nice and I'll be back at work.

Friday 24th indeed brings much better weather and promises to be the best day so far. I start from Abergwyngregyn at 08:40 at a good pace. As I pass over some waterfalls I slow down, picking my way across the sharp scree. The pull up onto Llwytmor is tough going but once made I find the rest of the walking okay. It's usual for me to find morning ascents tough, it always takes me a while to become broken in. It could be that my asthma is worse in the mornings.

I then cross to Foel-fras where I spy a man with a tripod. I wonder if it is Myrddyn Phillips and his trusty theodolite looking for extra summits. Here follows Garnedd Uchaf and a pull up the distant Foel Grach. Some of these hills I'd observed from other walks and it is good to connect them together. Then across Yr Aryg to the rocky summit of Bera Mawr where the last few steps involve climbing. Good views are had, inland to mountains and out over the sea. From here I do Bera Bach, Drosgl and Gyrn Wigau. I take an odd route back, extending the walk for safety sake, as I do not fancy the waterfalls again. However I find the walk along the side of Moel Wnion steep, freaky and requiring care.

It's so good to finish the holiday on a high after an eight-and-a-half-hour round.

November 2004 – English Nuttalls. Over The Hill Club

Driving up to Derwentwater Youth Hostel on Friday November 19th I stop at the Cotswold Outdoor shop to buy new walking boots. Both the assistant and myself admire my old pair; worn through in places it's sad to finally retire them after they contributed to over 200 of my Munros, one TGO Challenge and numerous other walks.

Joining a walking club was something that I'd never considered, especially one by the name of The Over The Hill Club. However, the enjoyment of the TGO Challenge and Sue Oxley's good sales pitch has had me filling in forms and attending the club AGM.

Saturday 20th brings my first walk with the club. A fine winter's day dawns over Derwentwater Youth Hostel. Usually one to walk solo, and nervous about my pace, I pump myself full of my Salbutamol inhaler, grab a lift with Maggie Hems and am off walking with the group at around 09:45.

For once I am flying and by Cat Bells I'm heading the procession. Not even being reduced to one trekking pole (the other having become unthreaded) deters me. My usual place at the back, puffing and panting, has been promoted by medication and the hangovers of many. That beer barrel in the Youth Hostels Members Kitchen is clearly not for show.

I take a minor tumble on ice, causing my hand and knee to smart. Picking myself up I'm pleased to be momentarily out of sight. But my position, of being out in front, is a false one; I really had gone to town with the medicine. On from Cat Bells is the broad top of Maiden Moor. As my height rises the views became more stunning. There are mountains all around with a view out towards Scotland. With the tops of High Spy bagged, I wait for the others as I survey the snow-dusted peaks and the winter's light spreading its shadows out across the tops, cliffs and crevasses. The sun hovers low in the sky, gently warming and lighting, gently shadowing and freezing. No wind, blue sky and a light crispness of snow under foot tells me that this is my best day in the hills for many years.

I set off again, dropping steeply past the water of Dalehead Tarn before the pull up Dale Head. I am slow, others quickly catching me, overtaking me. This was no race, I was not intending it to be. I was just enjoying so much the pace that I've found. Rare, to be savoured. I use my inhaler, take on food and am soon flying again. The proposed walk takes in Hindscarth, but not Robinson. I fancy both; it would help my 2000ft tally. At the summit of Dale Head a number of us congregate. Mountain stories are abound, including the strange tale of an Irish visit where a walker was discovered hauling a porcelain toilet with him. "Was there something wrong with the man?" asks somebody.

"Potty, I guess," I add.

Dale Head (looking west)

There are a few groans but then Gordon Coventry stands up for me, "No, that was very good." A nodding agreement seals my joke.

So I now have a friend and he fancies Robinson too, so off we set. We take Hindscarth in half an hour, slipping our way in the sole-deep snow. On the approach a man and woman are descending. I recognise them and assume they are other club members. He stops and points at me in some form of recognition, clearly not members. We both agree we know each other but cannot think from where. Somewhere out in the hills, no doubt – Wales or Scotland.

Backtracking from Hindscarth we fly round to Robinson. The snow is starting to harden underfoot. Ice patches form and young children, being introduced to the hills, slide across and shriek with joy. From Robinson we descend back towards the cars. The light is starting to fade as the sun heads for its set. A few icy rock descents have to be negotiated before a steep grassy slope towards Scope Beck. The remaining trekking pole buckles and collapses and dumps me on my backside. I start to slide on the icy grass (I could have made this rhyme) but keeping my right foot flat I come to a halt. That would be the end of the story if only my backside stopped too. Alas not and, like a slow motion car crash, I sense what was going to happen as my body slides into the back of my boot.

Robinson and its north-facing descent

After sliding the remainder of the slope I catch Gordon up and, a few octaves higher, amusingly explained the story of my collapsing trekking pole. We wonder if the figures coming off Hindscarth are members of our party or some of the many other people out on the hills today. Back at the car all is revealed. Gordon's pace, from Hindscarth quicker than mine, has got us back ahead of the others. We sit in his car and watch the others emerge from the shadows, some half an hour later.

Classification	My Total	Total
Welsh Nuttalls	79	188
English Nuttalls	16	252
Corbetts (Scotland)	1	219

Grahams (Scotland)	0	220
Unique Donalds (Scotland)	0	58
Munros (Scotland)	284	284
Ireland	0	212
Totals (20/11/2004):	380	1433

May 2005 – The Great Outdoors Challenge

It's a wet day in May as I descend the steps of the Airbus at Inverness Airport and exclaim, "Bloody Scotland!"

Other passengers, equally blasted by the wind and rain, shoot me bemused glances. I sense they know I have a greater tale to tale.

The hood of my jacket is in my pack, in the hold of the aircraft – I didn't want to risk it becoming un-popped and lost in the inevitable crush with the business suits who, at this moment, are fighting past me.

So far my trip has consisted of train, bus and plane. There is another bus to come, another train ride followed by a car ride to my hotel to start the 2005 TGO Challenge cross-Scotland walk.

At the airport bus stop I meet David Lee, an American. This is his first visit to Scotland, and he's planning to get the bus down to Cannich and walk towards Glen Affric Youth Hostel. I tell him some things he may encounter. He's interesting, interested and asks many questions. He's nice and polite – a good American. There are many, but in the shadow of Bush it's easy to imagine a different country. We say our goodbyes as we reach Inverness and, given he'll be heading west on bits I'll be heading east on, joke we may see each other on the 'trail'. I think we like that connection.

I've a number of hours to kill in Inverness. First things first, I buy a gas canister – they weren't allowed on the plane. This will be additional weight to the 28lbs my pack weighed when checking in at Heathrow. There will be water to carry too

I post a few things home, my passport and the handy plastic

wrapper British Midland protected my pack with. Passport? After 911 we all need photo id to fly.

I buy a copy of Orwell's *Animal Farm* (lightweight and easy reading) then sit in a café and start to read it.

I take a walk, a drunken woman approaches me and asks, "How are the love bites on your bum?"

Perhaps it was Gaelic and I misheard? No, I'd heard all right. You'd never get that in my village. I laugh, kill more time, feast and walk to the station.

There's a group with backpacks. They look like TGO Challenge. I catch their eye, they catch mine and I'm welcomed across. I've made the mistake of thinking I'll be alone on the train. Far from it. We pack it out and tell tales of the previous TGO Challenge. We travel through fantastic scenery, a prequel of our two weeks to come. There's snow on the high ground, or is it Orwell's sheep huddled together to fool us? I'm inspired by the company, the light shines between the hills forming searchlights on the ground below. Rick Smith, partnered by Sue Graeme, mentions Alan Sloman's pictures in the TGO Challenge magazine. How they were credited to another fellow. I admit I was this 'other fellow' and am determined to track Alan down on this walk and explain the mistake wasn't mine.

From Strathcarron Station I phone the Lochcarron hotel, asking for the lift they had promised me when I booked. It isn't on offer now, instead they give me the number of a taxi firm. I phone and arrange the ride. A taxi feels decadent but there's something psychological about walking coast-to-coast, the walk is so important to me I didn't want to risk any additional footsteps.

The train gets in on time, Dennis Pidgeon disembarks from the next carriage and we shake hands on the platform. The taxi is waiting but, after the ride, I find nobody is at the hotel to serve me. After what feels like a long wait, somebody appears and I'm led to a room in poor repair. I sleep on and off with the TV broadcasting the election night news.

It's Friday May 6th and I wake to my own labours, breakfast and a taxi back to Strathcarron. I sign the TGO Challenge register, one of the twelve dotted along the west coast, then set off.

I walk along the road, then dive off to the beach, wetting my boots in the sea water of the loch – a TGO Challenge tradition along with gathering a pebble to deposit on the east coast.

A washed-up football, amongst the rocks, catches my attention and I kick it along for a few hundred yards. I contemplate being the first man to kick a football across Scotland. Soon bored I give it one last kick into the distance.

Lochcarron, on the opposite shore, is lit by the sunlight, a morning glow picking out the white buildings of a village sprawling the coast of the loch.

At Craigton I take a path across the hills. Battling with heather and my pack I make steady progress, using map and compassing through the hills in poor visibility.

At one point I slip, steadying myself I take an immediate sip from my water pipe. Something primeval, perhaps? When I disturb a lamb it will run to its mother and suckle. I get a deep sense of self exploration, closer to my primeval brain. Closer than our 'perfected' world would normally allow? Perhaps the TGO Challenge gives two weeks a year to satisfy a deep sense of what our society has lost, yet not enough to turn our backs on everything it gives us? I ponder some more, as I'm prone to do amongst the Scottish mountains. It isn't just about the beauty of the outward view of my eyes, something clicks, those eyes turn inwards for resolution and understanding.

Passing through Killilan I discover the hotel room key in my pocket – I have a stamp with me so post it back. I'm now on a good track, a sheep follows me, bleating. I wonder if it is saying "Four legs good, two legs bad." I start using my trekking poles and I'm sure it bleats trekking poles don't count.

I intend to stop at Faddoch but instead decide to keep on the track and camp by a bridge which will make a good starting place for tomorrow, Saturday. I miss the bridge and, imagining guiding a companion, apologise profusely until I find the next bridge along.

By now the rain is heavy (I could do with that hotel room key) and I quickly erect the tent. As I sit inside, slowly drying under my own heat, I realise this is no fun.

I have a disturbed night, lashings of rain wake me, then later the cold. I shine my head torch on the label of my new sleeping bag, it says good down to three degrees. The catalogue had advertised it to zero degrees. I invent the argument in my head with the shop as The Three Degrees' songs, 'When Will I see You Again' and 'Woman In Love' echo around my head.

At 02:00 a call of nature beckons. I take my socks off and stand on a plastic bag just outside the tent. The stars light the heavens, one just poised above a mountain top.

I get back into my sleeping back and, to try and keep warm, slip into my plastic bivi. I wake an hour later with the sleeping bag drenched in condensation.

Saturday May 7th dawns in drizzle. I procrastinate; hoping for a break in the weather to be able to get the tent down. Only when I begin to feel stuffy, and accept the weather isn't going to improve, do I brave it and get the tent down, packing it away in the wet.

As I swing my pack onto my back I view the scene, snow on the hills, fallen in the night. Other hills scooped out like ice cream. Things could be worse, things could be better. Things could be dryer, not wetter!

Braving the steep path it takes me a few hours to reach the Falls of Glomach. Once they come into view I settle on a rock, wishing to take it all in – savouring and remembering it for days in the office. The falls are amazing: a torrent of water with mist lifting from the spray. A buttress of rock, never to give in to erosion, protects a flank.

I make the tiresome walk along the streams and lochs, boggy in places. I come across a tent and call fruitlessly to anybody inside. Out, asleep or abandoned: I'm unsure. I continue on and see distant figures walking up Gleann Gniomhaidh. I join the path but alone, sometimes the way I prefer it.

It's a seven-hour trudge through peat hags and rough tracks, requiring frequent rests. By the time I approach Alltbeithe (Glen Affric Youth Hostel) I'm wet and muddy. With a hundred or so metres to go, I duck down out of sight to relieve a call of nature. I've never had a tick bite before. Apparently they can cause serious illness as these little biters anaesthetise the area then sink their teeth in and suck your blood. I reel back in horror: one is burrowing into the end of Mr Naughty.

I hurriedly finish the call of nature then spend some fifteen minutes, with my manhood laid on my left hand, trying to extract this beast – both with our teeth firmly fixed. After a few minutes I realise what a sight I must be. Hunched over, 'examining myself'. One could imagine mothers hurrying their children past.

I get a grip on it (the tick that is) and remember the advice of turning them anticlockwise. But I'm sure this bastard is reverse threaded, it won't give. Half of it breaks off, but its front end is still buried. Not wishing to feed this thing, I resolve to think of nothing other than mathematical puzzles.

I get to the hostel. I love this place. No roads, a wind generator and a bed spare! I am relieved.

The warden, Ellen, is bubbly and friendly and explains how she recently went to a meeting of hostel wardens in Inverness. She turned up, covered in mud announcing she is from Alltbeithe. "We'd gathered that," was the response.

The remoteness appeals. I ask around about ticks, though not advertising where I'd been bitten. I get some advice, "They breathe through their arses."

"They breathe through their arses," I repeat while pondering the full ramifications of this. "Well I've broken the back end of it off," I add.

"You've killed it then."

I was pleased to hear this. Just the little devil to get out. I have an attempt in the shower. Still no joy.

The evening passes, talking to other challengers, guests and Ellen. John Hall and Richard Smith are good to chat to. The last arrival is at 21:30, in the dark and pouring rain. He takes the last bed, relief written all over his face.

A small gathering remains in the lounge until late. Ellen tells of how she is escaping life to be warden of this place, and we get round to talking about our home areas. One chap is from Huntingdon.

"I once had a curry there," says Ellen.

"So did John Major," I reply.

I end up having to explain the joke.

Sunday May 8th and I wake early and sort my wet kit out in the lounge. I take my time getting ready and ask around for a loan of a pair of tweezers. The guy who turned up late last night has a pair. I borrow them, it works and I sterilize them. As I hand them back, and fail to mention what I used them for, I realise he has very poor eyesight. I've no idea how he made it to the hostel in the dim wet light.

Today is pleasant and it takes me two hours, on good track, to reach Loch Affric. A dusting of snow holds the contour on each mountain – nature's spirit level. From here I ascend the muddy path and head east along to the forest around Cougie. Passing a sizeable loch which appears tiny on the map, I'm relieved to bump into Richard and John again to confirm the map is wrong.

Not having the map to cover the ground to Cougie my plan is to skirt up the edge of the Cougie forest. The intended path is barren, wet and boggy. I'm deterred. I keep the company and arrive in Cougie, planning to trace their map for my different route out.

Craig, a nineteen-year-old who has abandoned the walk with a groin injury, is billeted in the same cabin as me. To my relief he has a copy of the map I need and kindly lets me have it. He also donates a Gore-Tex patch for a tear in my jacket and keeps his fellow cabin mates, myself, Richard and John entertained with his tales.

I go up to the house and accept the tea and scone on offer. I chat for hours with Val (the owner) and Craig. David Lee, the American I last saw at Inverness Airport, appears. We did bump into each other after all.

I ask after people who I met living in this vicinity when I visited in 1989. Did the Lawaetz still have the cottages up Mullardoch? What became of the Birmingham couple who took the Loch Affric hotel? Val is able to fill me in.

She married fifty-three years ago aged seventeen and has lived here for forty years. Seven children arrived in the first eight years. I guess she eventually realised what was causing it! She's entertaining and later tells how she incubated a ducks egg in her bra and describes its untimely hatching during a Friends of the Earth meeting.

David, trekking the opposite route (or rowt as he says), asks about paths and tracks. Craig mentions about tick bites. David takes an interest, wishing to avoid them.

"I guess you call them check bites in the States," I suggest.

"Check bites?" he asks.

"Don't you call ticks checks in the US?" I'm beginning to rue this joke, the moment you have to start to explain...

"Oh you are thinking of when you get your work checked."

"Yes." And I give up there.

It's Monday May 9th and I wake cold and shivering in my sleeping bag. I peer out the cabin window, snow is falling. It takes me a while to get up.

I make good use of Craig's map and, to start with, the route from Cougie goes well. Richard and John keep to the tracks, but I decide to cut a corner, effectively doing one side of a triangle.

To start with I follow a stream through ascending woods before an open hill climb and a marshy descent to Glen Moriston. I bypass a Graham (mountain between 2000 and 2500ft), instead electing to keep a pace.

Dropping down into the glen I take a last look back at the snow-covered mountains I'm leaving. Passing a number of ancient abandoned cars (anybody wanting bits for an ancient Vauxhall Wyvern would do well to visit here). I cross the river at Torgyle Bridge and start the tortuous ascent via the electric pylons. It takes hours, soft ground and uphill.

On reaching the top I spot Richard and John on the track across the glen. I pick up pace and, in the warmth, navigate sweet-smelling wooded tracks down to Fort Augustus – almost back at sea level.

I walk through Fort Augustus, exhausted after an eight-hour walk but glad of only the odd rain shower. A fatal combination of my credit card and a hotel with a vacancies sign is too much temptation for me. The hotel owner assesses my unshaven, tanned and sticky appearance. I can see a pattern formulating in her brain. "Are you on this TGO Challenge thing?" she asks while possibly weighing up the price of carpet shampoo in comparison with the £40 for a night's stay.

I'm grateful to have a nice room and my own space to dry, sort my things and wash clothes. The shower rail, which takes the weight of my damp tent, is an added bonus.

I pop out to the village shop. It's easy to have one's view of Highland communities tainted. I imagine gossip in the shop, between the assistant and well-known customers, to be along the lines of, "Did you hear about Mrs MacPherson? Well would you know she unpicked her husband's best jumper to make herself a new hat." Or "Hello, Mrs Macleod, I hear you won first prize in the church raffle." No, when I'm queuing to pay I'm confronted with the conversation between two women as another young woman explains to the assistant, "'e took 'er up the bee-hind and he didnae use a condom."

It's Tuesday May 10th and I'm eating the hotel breakfast at the earliest possible time of 08:30. At 09:15 I set off along a road before a long pull up General Wade's Military Road (built in 1731 as a pass through the mountains for troop movements). I stop for lunch at Blackburn Bothy – a neat stone-built cottage with a new bonnet-style tin roof. I find Stuart and Catherine Brown and their friend, James Spittal, inside. They share their soup and company with me.

I continue up the Corrieyairack Pass – a popular funnel for the TGO Challenge. I see and chat to a good many people over its long slog of a rough track and ancient bridges.

To the right is the distant Ben Nevis towering above its surroundings. During the final pull over the summit I take a last look back at the snow-capped peaks of the mountains I'd spent the previous days coming through. I pick out most of the previous day's route. I enthuse to Stuart, Catherine and James how much I love Scotland, how beautiful a place it is. Being Scots I can sense their pride.

I plod on, feeling the strain of the walk, and pause, in the late afternoon, at Melgarve Bothy. I consider sleeping here but sense I have another hour left in me. My feet have hot spots so, fearing blisters, I plaster up. My body packs up at 18:20 and I camp in glorious sun on a small island, which I paddle out to, near the edge of the River Spey.

The late sun is just above the trees. Heather, peat and shadows adorn the hills. The trees on the edge of the forest have their bark stripped, probably by deer. I saw many today, high up on a mountain breaking the skyline with their ears pricked and alert. Streams tumbled down that mountain, flowing into the river which now gently gurgles past me.

I eat noodles. Tasty outside though the couscous I've mixed in make it a chore to get through. I also eat lots of peanuts for protein and take a daily vitamin C tablet, having suffered from a lack of it last year.

I wake on Wednesday May 11th, it's been a cold night. This darned sleeping bag is going to be the centre of discussion with the shop that sold it. I put on two tops, two pairs of trousers, gloves and socks and still feel cold. Around 06:00 I struggle out, eat a cold breakfast, collapse the ice-covered tent, and pack it away wet.

I'm wrapped up and walking at 07:00 sensing a glorious day of weather lies ahead. After half an hour I pass Garva Bridge where a battalion of ice-encrusted tents are pitched. A few folk are emerging including a downcast Richard and John. I say hello and plod on.

As the sun gets higher I shed garments, down to my shirt. And even that has to have its sleeves rolled up. I make good progress on the track, crossing a mix of old and new bridges. Some are the originals from 1731, one now in the middle of a field as the track had been diverted.

I pass a lodge house where an elderly lady resident is stood outside. I stop for a chat. Her dad had taken the place, as an estate tenant worker in 1948. She's been able to stay on. She tells me how a barn, now fallen in, was disused in the 1940s when the dam came. How the road had been diverted. How the estate won't repair her beautiful decaying house. We speak for ages.

With barely a cloud in the sky the mountains are cast in a mixture of sunlight, snow and shadow.

I plod on to Laggan and get a phone signal and call in to 'Challenge Control', reporting my progress. A check of emails, on my palmtop computer, reveals my Canadian friend, Mary, has just lost her father. I'm sad, I knew and liked him. I send my condolences and don't feel like the hill walk. Instead I walk up the road to Newtonmore. It's very hot. I've no water and I start to dehydrate. I stop at a fallen tree, its trunk snapped at the base yet enough still connected for shoots to ascend upwards like the teeth of a comb. Its fight for life remind me of the descriptions of how Mary's father had been the last months. A newborn lamb, umbilical cord still dangling and mother licking its coat, nibbles the grass as it balances on its wobbly legs and takes in its first view of the world. I pass a duck with its chicks following on behind. So wee and tiny. Renewal.

I'm now very dehydrated and have a headache. On reaching Newtonmore, I bundle into the first hotel and am offered a room with ensuite if I'm prepared to wait for forty minutes. Instead I take the room without ensuite. My head is thumping. I need water. The lady of the hotel asks me to fill in the form, then looks at me. "No, you get yourself sorted then come and register." I'm grateful, kind of her to realise my plight. I drink lots of water, the headache becomes distant. I go for a walk and bump into the lady from the lodge I'd spoken to during the day. It's a small world.

Richard and John arrive, I sit with them in the bar. I also chat to Bryan who I discover was walking with Craig and his father, Peter. Peter has now dropped out too and Bryan, at the age of sixty-six, is the last remaining member of their team. Peter had been passing blood in his urine and had been evacuated from Melgarve the night before. Bryan tells me he comforted him by saying, "I expect that's your aorta leaking."

Cameron McNeish, the editor of TGO Challenge magazine, arrives and a former Doctor Who, Tom Baker ('The Doctor'), stands at the bar opposite. Sat in the middle I sense an anti-vortex of anonymity. At one stage I catch Tom Baker looking at the time. *You're the time lord!*

Thursday May 12th and I wake early and go for a walk up the main street of Newtonmore, buying a few supplies. I keep an eye out for a blue police box, but alas there is none. The doctor must have made an early start.

It takes just over an hour to walk from Newtonmore to Kingussie. Bryan is behind me, the last of Craig's party. I purchase a few more provisions then spend a minute or so sitting in the Memorial Park before setting off. Passing the ruined eighteenth century Ruthven Barracks I take the tracks to the forest and, on breaking tree cover, head for a bridge. Here I sit in the glorious sun. I'm joined by Doug Cockburn, Tom Ietswaart and Nik Lawcock. Their company is great and aids the trip down to Ruigh-aiteachain Bothy. I'm glad we stick together.

When we get to the bothy we find Bryan has already arrived, getting ahead of me at Kingussie. We pitch our five tents; a couple of teachers (leading a Duke of Edinburgh award party) use the bothy. Bryan has us in stitches with tales of his own disasters, jokes and mannerisms. He lights a fire in the bothy and a number of us pile in. Bryan mentions how lucky in love he is despite his first wife leaving him and his second dying. It was also a delight to meet Heike Lies and her walking partner, Karl. Bernie Marshall, on his nineteenth crossing, joins us around the fire.

Around 01:00 I stir in my tent to the arrival of a group of noisy people. With the F and C words being used as aggressive punctuation, I snap out of my doze. I listen intently for any hassle, worry about the two female teachers in the bothy, Nik alone in her tent but I don't hear the door open or any disturbance. I get back to sleep and then awake and wait for the sun to dry my tent.

Friday May 13th and it is a late start. The revellers who arrived in the night, all men in their thirties and forties, are rough. Although now sober their talk has an edge about it. I'm nervous. Nik privately speaks to me, saying how anxious she is. So I hang on for her to be ready. I didn't want them to observe a lone female setting off down the glen.

At 10:00 we set off. Nik and I soon talk deeply about life. I'm sad over Mary's dad so I'm grateful for her company, explaining to her my mixed emotions because this, to some extent, now makes Mary a free agent. As we pass the glen which I entered Glen Feshie from last year, I remark to Nik how I kept John Jocys' company last year, in the pouring rain, with the most awful puns and jokes.

We catch up with Bryan, Bernie and his wife, Pauline. They say they are pleased to see us, having been worried about the aggressive guys at the bothy. I expect the guys were okay but with alcohol it sounded very, very different. Then, seemingly out of nowhere John Jocys appears. I explain to Nik this is the John I was mentioning earlier.

John says, "No jokes, Steve. No jokes."

Nik gives me an odd look of, 'What jokes?' The three of us set off and I'm glad Nik gets along with John okay. With the drunken guys I feel responsible for her. John and I descend into silly jokes, and Nik mentions how a man she considered to be a deep thinker is now revealing a rather different side. I blame John: a man has as many personalities as his friends.

We pass the obvious watershed coming off the hills, leaving another walker preparing to take a very early night under nothing other than a tarpaulin.

The glorious day continues and we walk the nine and a half

hours to White Bridge, finishing a bit weary at 19:30, and camp. One usually looks forward to snuggling into a sleeping bag. Not this one. I sit outside and, as the sun goes down, I dread another freezing night.

In the early hours of Saturday May 14th I wake to find my drinks bottle, housed between the tent inner and outer, frozen. I get up to relieve myself and prod John's socks he's left to dry on his trekking poles – they are now frozen solid.

The three of us walk towards Braemar, via the Linn of Dee. My mum and dad, up on a week's holiday, are waiting where it joins the public road. It's nice to see them and I introduce them to my friends.

We walk on, Nik's feet are playing her up and she doesn't have a room booked. Mum and Dad go down to Braemar and book her in then return. Nik is delighted. John aiming for Lochcallater Lodge, goes ahead and Nik and I walk on to Braemar.

A challenger stops to talk with us, a second or so passes before I exclaim, "Bernie!"

Bernie Roberts is on his twelfth crossing – solo crossing this time as his wife, Penny, is taking a break this year. They are the couple who announced a "gas problem" in Braemar last year. As Bernie sets off Nik and I sit on a seat while an entire herd of deer paddle in the River Dee below us.

In Braemar I eat with Mum and Dad. I feel drained. It has been a long hot walk in from White Bridge. I apologise profusely for my tiredness, they understand. Back in my hotel room I glance in the mirror and take a moment to recognise the somewhat bearded figure peering back at me.

I pop to the local outdoor shop and buy a sleeping bag liner. I rue the £40. It is also bulky and heavy but the thought of another freezing night isn't appealing.

The evening is a combination of eating and chatting to other challengers. I briefly speak with MA Harper. I catch up with Alan Sloman and explain the crediting of his photographs, in the TGO magazine, to me wasn't of my doing.

After breakfast, on Sunday May 15th, I talk with MA and Mike Akin-Smith. A kind, well-spoken pair who give me their time and make me feel very welcome.

At 11:00 I set off and meet Mum and Dad at Auchallater on the A93. We then set off to Lochcallater Lodge. I assume the role of a tourist guide and, after about two hours, am thrilled with their reaction to the lodge. Bill and Stan welcome them in and I can see their enthusiasm for this remote escape. Bill and Stan maintain the place for the right to use it. Gaslights and a roaring fire are its modern conveniences.

As I erect my tent I take in the views. Mountains surround the lodge, and a loch lays before it. To the left is a bothy. The lodge is L shaped with green windows and a slate roof. It's been a gentle afternoon with numerous challengers congregating for a chat. Basking in the sun. It's been good.

The evening brings one of Bill and Stan's legendary parties. Not one for drinking and singing, I find myself as an observer. So imagine your name is Sheila Matheson and you live in a remote spot on the west coast. You plan a high-level crossing and you've been out for over five days without passing through any town or village. You've heard of Lochcallater Lodge but are unsure what it's about. Very late in the evening, you stumble upon this wild and remote place without a neighbour for miles. You make your entrance to a wild whisky-fuelled party taking place. Packed full of people, singing, dancing and drinking. Your eyes shoot around, bemused and unsure. She was quite a picture but soon became part of the atmosphere. I get to my tent at 23:30.

During the night it gets very windy and when, on what is now Monday May 16th, I stick my head out of the tent I find it is snowing. I grab a brief weather break, take the tent down and bundle into the lodge. I have a quick breakfast and learn the revelling went on until 03:00.

At 08:50 I set off, the rough terrain sapping my strength. I had the impression Jock's Road might just be that – a road. In places it is nothing, not even a path. A remote rights of way sign stands at the head of the glen, oddly pronouncing a route that would require many other such signs if it were to be of any guide. I can only assume it serves some legal requirement to keep the access open.

This is a hauntingly lonely place. Just before the TGO Challenge I flew to Switzerland, to see my friend Steve Hampton, and we bagged Chli Aubrig as a warm-up for my TGO Challenge. Higher than any Scottish mountain it was easy in comparison, no wind and even the knee-deep snow was easily manageable. Scotland's mountains aren't high but they are steep, rugged and harbour atrocious weather.

I struggle with the final ascent at the head of Glen Callater. There's a walker ahead of me and two in red behind me. I get myself onto the high ground, weary, demoralised and forsaken. I consider changing my route and heading for the Shielin of Mark bothy. The two red jackets join me: MA and Mike. I'm elated to have their company – it lifts me and I walk with them a few miles.

We come across Alan Keegan, making very slow progress. At seventy-seven the oldest challenger. I'd seen him walking into Braemar and was concerned at how tired he looked. We walk on together but soon find I'm on my own as MA and Mike drop back to support Alan.

I descend towards Clova stopping only to investigate a mountain shelter. An iron door opens into a flat tin-roofed low housing – damp and uninviting to all but those in need of refuge.

The Clova Hotel Bunkhouse is a welcome sight after seven hours of walking. I'm given a room in a dorm of ten. I hope there isn't too much snoring.

Tuesday May 17th and I start at 06:10, hoping to get over to the hostel at Tarfside while beds remain. I start with a long pull up Green Hill (870m) then make my way to the Corbett (peak between 2500 and 3000ft), Ben Tirran. It's 09:14, and Munros start from 914m. I can also see the sea! Yipee!

I check my phone; I have a signal and text a friend saying I'm atop my first Corbett. She replies "What's a Corbett? A sexy woman called Elizabeth!"

I also pick up a text from my dad. "Have seen Nik's kit in foyer she is in bar knocking it back with a girl missed as a newt!" I'll have to have a chat with Dad about predictive texting.

It's now a long route over with changing weather – all sorts blow through. Approaching Burnt Hill I glance to the glen below where a snow storm is blotting my view like an air brush in Paint Shop Pro. It soon nabs me. I drop down to the road and, with my body now in fine form, walk along to Tarfside: arriving at 13:10, too late for a bed.

The cheese on toast at the hostel, made by the ladies who staff it for the TGO Challenge, is very welcome. I put the tent up in a snow storm, shame about the bed. Again I'm warm with the sleeping bag liner. I observe one other walker sleeping below a raised sheet – rather him than me.

Wednesday May 18th and I follow the river and road to Edzell, taking five hours in all. It's the same route I took last year and I'm amazed by how well I remember it.

There's blood on my nose, no idea how I did it. Each time I wipe it away it seeps back. I bump into MA and Mike and we have lunch together, lingering for ages in the Tuck Inn café. I scratch my calf muscle, and I am alarmed by its size.

After some hour and a half I start to walk on to North Water Bridge. Just beyond Edzell I notice a penned-in bull with unfeasibly large testicles. Last year Ali Ashton and I talked about posing with it for a captioned photo, 'A couple of nuts on the TGO Challenge.'

MA and Mike catch me up as I'm sending a text to Ali. One might imagine I was sending a message enthusing over the scenery but instead I'm describing how the bull with the unfeasibly large testicles is still here. Funnily enough Ali doesn't reply.

MA, Mike and I walk on and pick up Russ Manion. The night

before I'd got talking to Boyd Potts. What great names some people have – I'm left with a pure simple 'Steve Smith'. Russ, early sixties, has long white hair which a wide-brimmed hat perches on. We make our way through the farm tracks, avoiding the road and get to the campsite at North Water Bridge.

It's been sunny all day but as I erect my tent it starts to rain, cocooning me for the evening. Having mentioned my tasteless couscous to MA and Mike I'm thrilled when MA's hand appears under my flysheet and passes me a couple of sauce mix packets. Later in the evening I take my newspaper to them, passing it through a small gap I'm immediately returned with strawberries and cream. A true delight.

I'm lifted by the day.

Thursday May 19th and I wake at 04:30, sensing something isn't quite right. A quick check around reveals that I'm soaked from the waist down. I've rolled onto my drinks bottle, now in the tent to prevent it from freezing. I get up and shower and use the hair dryer in the Gents to dry my wallet out.

The rain is pouring as I set off, reaching St Cyrus just before 11:00. Mum and Dad are waiting for me and accompany me down to a rain-soaked beach. I paddle my feet and throw my pebble into the North Sea. That's it. The TGO Challenge complete.

Room is made for me in Mum's car to give me a lift to the hotel. I can see Mum eye my sodden gear up and down. "I'll walk, Mum, honest it's okay." Her car is her pride and joy.

The hotel room doesn't have ensuite – after two weeks of roughing it I feel disappointed. As if a comfy bed wasn't enough for me? Mum and Dad stayed the previous night and, not for the first time, had got talking to challengers in the bar. I begin to wonder if they'd talked to more challengers than me as they relayed tales, names and faces.

The evening celebrations in Montrose go well. I catch up with Di Gerrard and hear how a torn calf muscle had her crawling to Barrisdale followed by an evacuation by boat. The story of Dennis

Pidgeon's trekking pole collapsing on the first day, relegating him to retirement, is passed around.

I'm lucky with my table, sharing it with MA, Mike, Richard and John. I catch up with Nik and exchange tales of our final days. Later catching up with John Jordan and Bernie and Pauline Marshall. Seeking out Roger Smith, thanking him for organising the event.

I also catch up with John Dodd. A man who has every piece of equipment clipped about his person. He describes each of the items, many I've never heard of, in his cheeky-chappie kind of way. I assume when he visits a shop the assistants clip items onto him and debit his credit card on the way out.

The TGO Challenge has gathered a life of its own. An eclectic mix of people, ages and professions. Could the originators have perceived how the human spirit would drive it to what it now is? Any competition has gone out of it – it's all about the wonderful people you meet and helping one another across Scotland. Nobody can invent a legend or a tradition. They just happen, guided by the human spirit. A few years ago somebody invented 'The Metros' – a list of peaks above 1000m. It's never caught on – formulated at a desk humans have rejected it. There has to be a special something people find.

The term 'Challenge' is a catch-all for the multitude of challenges that go to make up one person's Challenge. Whether that be an injury, a missing piece of equipment, being downcast, exhausted, lost or just soaked through. The Great Outdoors Challenge is just a title that encompasses so much.

June 2005 – Welsh Nuttalls

It's June 10th, just before noon and a glorious day. I've driven up to mid-Wales on the spur of the moment, and I am now sat on Gorllwyn, an ancient trig point supporting my back. It's been an easy pull up. Tracks, streams and tadpoles have graced my way. The weather is gorgeous. A light breeze is teasing my neck. A bird is accompanying the weather in a delightful tune. Gentle hills are all around me, I can see for miles. Distant farms and tree plantations lead the eye to the Brecon Beacons standing proud on the horizon.

Later and I'm sat atop Drygarn Fawr. It's been a good walk across, boggy in places. The gentle breeze is still with me and I think about looking for a B&B and do another walk tomorrow. A group of Gurkha soldiers have arrived, the view is amazing in any language. It feels like the world is laid out, horizons enlarged from day-to-day living. The Gurkha soldiers come to say hello, so polite, so sweet and so young. I wish I were twenty years younger, and possibly female.

The walk back from Drygarn Fawr is a little complex, navigating a number of deeply-cut streambeds. I come across a disused mine and am grateful for its track; still good enough to follow leading me most the way back to the car. At the car I feel very dehydrated and, to make things worse, I find I've not packed enough water. I think through my options. In this area are three walks containing 2000ft peaks. It would be nice to get them all in this weekend. I plot my route via Rhayader, reckoning on getting a drink there then driving onto Devil's Bridge. Very soon after setting off I come across a sign "Mountain Road" to Aberystwyth. A quick look at the map and I am sold. The rehydration will have to wait. It is glorious, sun and mountains and I play a Woodstock CD – it fees oh so good.

Arriving at Devil's Bridge I rouse the hotel owner with the help of an elderly couple who are also seeking accommodation. I let them check in first and then do the same. Though when I ask for a single room she asks, "Just for yourself?" Was she trying to out fox me or had she heard about Greg's theory of me and the sheep? We all ask about food, the elderly couple are directed to the dining room but when it comes to my turn the bar menu is mentioned. Target market or just a lucky guess? I ask for an early meal and they oblige. I wonder if I can get one of the walks in this evening – it looks short; three hours. But tiredness descends and I plan to walk tomorrow morning.

The hotel is glorious: Victorian opulence of an imposing

building. With high ceilings the view from my window is straight up a wooded gorge with twists and turns hundreds of feet high. It's amazing.

June 11th and, having woken at 04:30 with a dehydration-related headache, I sit it out and set off at 09:25. I make good going and in just over an hour I'm sat on top Y Garn. It's cooler today and the exercise is doing me good. Below me are a dam and a reservoir. In the distance is mist; a cool breeze forces me to put my fleece on. On the ascent I passed foxgloves – I always loved them as a child, collecting their seeds for the next year and littering our garden flower borders with them.

Crossing east then north I find the pull up Pumlumon Fawr a gentle affair. I meet an older lady and we share company to the cairn and trig point covered summit. A shelter is to my right, not required today. Some mist has just blown through. It's all very peaceful and gentle up here. The Welsh hills are easier on my lungs than the Scottish.

It's now 12:50 and I'm sat on Pen Pumlumon Arwystli having taken in Pumlumon Fach then passed over Pen Pumlumon Llygad-bychan. A light breeze accompanies my thoughts that I'm glad I brought more water today: two and a half litres versus the one litre yesterday. I'm used to being spoilt in Scotland where there is lots of water in the hills. My night-time-dehydration-fuelled headache has now gone.

An hour and a half later I'm sat in the warm grass having passed over the final bumps of the walk.

I make a positional move by car, gain a puncture and change a wheel in blazing heat on a steep mountain road. I start walking again at 17:00 to claim Pen y Garn, electing to do it this evening instead of first thing tomorrow. The weather is so glorious I want to make the most of it.

The walk up is through very hot forest tracks and I make the summit horseshoe shelter at 18:15, a break from the sun. A wind farm is behind me. There is much protest against them on hill-top sites. I can hear a constant drum of noise. In one way they are graceful. I'm unsure what I feel but would not want to see many more. They do spoil the tops.

July 2005 – Welsh Nuttalls

On July 25th I set off into the hills – now a forty-year-old with my head full of thoughts. For the last year I've returned to playing five-aside football, as a goalkeeper, in a last bid to assuage that childhood dream of being a great keeper. The opportunity came with new employment, providing systems support for Wiltshire Constabulary, and after work five-aside games. Playing every week my skill levels soon came up until I was again rueing not having had an opportunity as a youngster. In some games my form dipped, but by and large I played well with whatever team I played for, winning more often than not.

On one occasion I made a string of saves from an aggressive attack, with me flying around, scooping the ball away with each shot. Finally a blast came, a hammer of a shot and I upturned myself and, from near ground level, cupped my fingers, flicking the ball over the bar. There was a pause, "Gordon Banks" was mentioned and one of my teammates dropped to his knees and worshiped before me. My ego loved it.

Another game stays with me as a favourite. The opposition had two sharp shooters who, at one stage, were two to one onto me. The first one struck, I saved it but into the path of the other and promptly saved his strike. Later in the same game the younger of the two launched a rocket from outside the penalty area. I flew backwards and tipped it over the bar. The strike was with such force I had no idea how I travelled backwards faster than the ball. Nor did my teammates or the striker, who congratulated me at the end of the match. I dwelt on it for days then the reason came to me. When the ball was struck I could see I'd not be able to get to it as it passed me, but my brain worked out, before the ball was even struck, that if I immediately dived backwards my hand would be ready for it, on its flightpath, a couple of yards behind me. And there at the age of thirty-nine I discovered the art of goalkeeping. No instruction manual teaches this: the art of goalkeeping is that you start the save before the ball is struck. And if you watch the old footage of Gordon Banks' save against Pele, in the 1970 World Cup, this is exactly what he did. Of course, if I were up against Pele I'd have no chance.

The crunch came in March, again we were under pressure, and the ball was flying in as quickly as I could push it away until a power shot smashed into my nose and eye socket. I don't remember the ball being struck, I don't remember it striking me but I do remember coming to, on the ground, with one of my team mates standing over me and the sweet taste of trickling blood from my nose. Reassuring everybody I was okay, I staggered to my feet, feeling anything but. I played on but was wobbly, groggy and glad when the match finished.

The next morning I woke stiff necked and achy. I had displaced two neck vertebrae, which had to be reset along with the bones forming my nose and eye socket. So I was more Bert Trautmann than Gordon Banks!

It took me a few weeks to play again, my confidence had dropped and it became very easy to pull muscles in my neck; there was likely long-term tissue damage. This made stretch saves very difficult and I was beginning to make judgements based on the risk of injury rather than as the true role of a goalie. From then on I could play about one game in three, a painful neck ruling me out for the other two. I played my last game three days after my 40th birthday. I just wanted to have played one competitive game in my forties. There was no hero ending, we lost. But one of the opposition team, in the changing rooms, asked if I'd be interested in training with his eleven aside team with a view to playing in goal. I was flattered but explained that, despite not quite looking it, I was forty. I did not explain to him, or anybody, that this had been my last ever game. Instead, I did that by an email, to the organiser, a few days later.

The reason for this, less than humble, tale, amongst my diary of mountain ascents, is tucked away in the first pages of my Munro diaries: having failed miserably as a sportsman at school, I found hill walking as a sport I could do while secretly knowing I had a talent for goalkeeping. It goes a way to make up for what I lacked at school and later missed out on.

The ending of goalkeeping coincided with leaving my career in police IT. I'd taken the job with Wiltshire Constabulary after struggling for work following six years developing a Home Office system used for major crime investigations (HOLMES). During that time web technologies had come to the fore and, with HOLMES based on older technologies, it had been career suicide.

Though I'd enjoyed working for an end user, the politics were rife and I concluded Wiltshire Constabulary was structured to build careers rather than provide a public service. Also I was not developing software, my true love and for which the pay is better. Leaving police IT became a necessary decision. When I started in it, after graduating in 1987, I was delighted to be able to use my skills for what I thought was the public good. But all along I'd struggled with career builders either dumping on me or plagiarising me. And Wiltshire Constabulary brought that to a head and I decided 'Enough is enough'.

I'd been interested in police IT because my father had been a police officer and, knowing a bit about the business, it felt like a good way to deploy my skills. Back in 1987 the main other options for my skills were military or finance. Neither appealed to me but, wise to now having to look after myself, I found a new job, as a software developer, in finance. Between leaving one job and starting another I had a break, still carrying the football injury, in Wales.

I'd set off from home at a little after 06:00 and get walking around 10:30. Starting from the west side of the lake Llyn Ogwen, in North Wales, I thwarted the £2 parking charge by parking in a layby. Soon ascending I follow the path then a faint one beyond Llyn Idwal (Llyn means water) up the steep ascent around Devil's Kitchen. I notice a number of places in the hills called the Devil's something or other. His elbow, punchbowl, staircase and penis are scattered throughout the land. It must make his daily routine a logistical nightmare.

The ascent requires a bit of scrambling and the use of polished handholds. Then I reach a plateau before a final ascent where the handholds are jagged and come away. Fortunately it is just steep; there is no risk of falling. I pull myself onto the ridge at about 14:00 and strike west for Glyder Fawr. After following cairns and a well-trodden path I soon find the twin-peaked summit. Many people are around and echoes and clanks come from the mist until it clears enough to enjoy a view. I then head east for Glyder Fach, climbing amongst the boulders to reach its summit. I visit the famous cantilever stone before the steep descent via Llyn Bochlwyd where my companion is drizzle.

July 26th dawns a glorious day, views all the way but I am slow. I drive up to Nant Peris (just a mile or so) then set off for the hard slog up Elidir Fawr; first passing some cottages then onto the open hillside. Initially I strike to the east of the stream but change my mind and, having passed a bridge, descend the gully before picking my way across. Then it is the long slog, over three hours, as I haul my way up this steep gradient. My trekking poles, left behind yesterday to ease a painful shoulder, assist the 3000ft to the summit.

From the top I have views of Snowdon and its mountain railway, emitting clouds of smoke as the engine ascends. I peer over to the modern and functional reservoir before descending and ascending Mynydd Perfedd.

I then walk out to Carnedd Y Filiast and back before the pull up Foel Goch. Here I can see down the other valley, where I ascended from yesterday. The final peak, Y Garn, the highest of the day, is the next. At its summit I can see all of my walking of the past two days. I descend to Llyn y Cwn and take a poorly-defined path back to the road and a mile walk back to my car, arriving at 16:50.

I'm staying in the Heights Hotel, Llanberis – staffed by very sweet, polite, smiley and helpful eastern European girls. This is the sign of the times with the expansion of Europe. I eat then go for a stroll and pass a group of Welsh youngsters. I was heartened to hear them speaking their mother tongue but gather there is no Welsh equivalent for that well-known Anglo Saxon phrase F*** O**!! It was the only part of the conversation that my passing ear could understand.

July 27th, I start walking at 07:50. Following the Llanberis path I make a good pace. Passing the railway line, seeing the diesel locos then later a steam one. Pausing at the Halfway House café it is time to branch off, leaving the path I walked when I was eleven years old. I soon reach the rocky outcrop of Llechog. Fitting the criteria of a 2000ft mountain (requiring a 50ft drop on all sides) it looks humble within the shadow of the towering Snowdon. Behind is my walk of the previous day, easy to make out. I chat to an older guy and we agree that the rules defining the mountains are, at times, elevating minor bumps above their status.

I descend to the lake of Llyn Du'r Arddu, in a basin with towering cliffs above me. The train hugs the ridge, almost balanced, precariously. I slip twice amongst the boulders yet am glad to catch my balance and move on. I break into my second water bottle of the day – yesterday I took just one bottle and it was not enough. Today I remembered the lack of water available in the Welsh hills.

I then take the undulating walk across Moel Cynghorion, Foel Gron and Moel Eilio making it back to the hotel at 15:30. There were descents then long hauls back up, my legs feel heavy the boots like weights hanging off each. I wonder if trail shoes would be better. On these final three peaks I have good views west and back east across the ground I covered today. The older chap catches me up and we rue the guidebook appearing to have measured map distance, not catering for extra distance caused by ascent and descent.

As I descend the final mountain I see two people arriving at the top – no gear and just jeans and trainers. Further down I chat to a lovely Welsh girl, ascending the mountain. It was nice for a couple of minutes. Her Welsh accent music to my ears.

August 2005 – Welsh Nuttalls

Setting off from home at 07:30 on August 27th it takes me three hours to get to Oswestry. There is one signpost for the B4580 road but there are three roads it could refer to. Three tours of the town, and a few wild guesses later, I'm out on narrow Welsh single-track roads. With signposts to places not on any map, I frequently pull up to try and make out where I am. I miss the relative ease of Scotland that has long glen roads with no web of alternative routes. I spread the map out, on the passenger seat, and use my compass to navigate.

Feeling rather agitated, I'm walking at 12:30 but ruefully back along the road I'd just driven along. I bump into a young man and woman; people are a rare sight today. I ascend up a track and then follow the gentle pull up to Godor. Then onto Godor North Top followed by Moel yr Ewig: a minor bump above the 2000ft line where a drop of 50ft all round gives it an undeserved status.

I then make a sharp pull onto a glorious ridge – North Wales is saying hello beyond with summits and valleys beckoning. I turn left and take in Moel Sych before a reverse turn has me passing the ridge entry point. Here there is a cross, carved in marble, to Fiona McWilliam. "Remember me." says the inscription. I do not know of her but pause and take in here years: 1965 to 1999. The same year I was born. I wonder why she was robbed of her life. What was her history? It would be unfair to pick mountain flowers so I pick some grass and make the small gesture of laying it on her memorial. I then bump into the same couple I'd met earlier, they've done a different walk, covered more ground with their lighter sacks. Though I am doing well, breathing good, coping with the 13Kg sack, including 3.5Kg of water and camping gear. There is no water on the walk, so all has to be carried.

I continue and take in Cadair Berwyn North Top and Cadair Berwyn for real. Ploughing on, soaking the views and gentle breeze I bag Cadair Bronwen and Cadair Bronwen North-east top before a descent and re-ascent to meet Pen Bwlch Llandrillo Top (also known as Moel yr Henfaes). With the time at 17:30 I view the next part of the walk, a six-mile round trip to Moel Fferna. It feels too late, I'm tiring and wish to look out at the sunset. I pitch my tent below the summit cairn and eat my cold food. No stove packed, zero luxuries on this walk. I had a large veggie breakfast at the M54 services: my hot meal of the day.

I call Ali Ashton on my phone, just to say hi – she loves the hills.

Then I text my friend, Andrew Rodda for the football results. He obliges. I eventually zip myself into the tent and am asleep before sundown,.

My "room" for the night

Waking to a howling wind I remain snug until I get the urge to move on and get the tent down. I set off at 08:10: it's a ninety-minute trip out to Moel Fferna and the smashed remains of its summit cairn forming two horseshoe-shaped summit shelters. It takes eighty minutes back. I pass back near my campsite and then the difficult re-ascent, with accompanying strong wind, of Cadair Bronwen NE. I'm now tired, aching and very slow. People I first spy as being miles behind me catch up and overtake. I use extra medicine but am still plodding. I settle in for a slog and eventually hit Cadair Bronwen and cut across to Tomle, using a short cut across the escarpment. At the top the wind is howling and I have to put everything under stones as I take my pack off to sup water. It's then Foel Wen and Foel Wen South Top; the wind is so strong I am blown against a wire fence. There is long grass and the wind rushes at it sending it brushing like the waves crashing on a shore. I plod my way up

Mynydd Tarw, noting how the fence divides grazing styles, giving one side grass and the other heather. I then start my drop to the car, getting there at 15:30 and the three-hour drive home.

November 2005 – Walking Home

It's 04:45 on Saturday November 12th 2005 and I'm letting myself out my front door, to make the twenty-four-mile walk home – many years have passed since I referred to my parents' house as home.

There's a chill, starlight accompanies me and my torch is silent. I pass through the graveyard, making my way to the canal towpath. I stop by a war grave of a WW2 flying officer. Each year I leave my poppy on his grave, I apologise for disturbing him so early and promise to visit again next year.

Crossing the railway tracks then the 18th century canal bridge, I start my first leg proper, leaving the confines of my village and heading for my parent's village, Bromham.

My torch is needed for narrow stretches where the water's edge and the towpath are ill defined. For wider bits I walk unaided. A torch narrows one's vision to its immediate beam, in darkness the eyes look further, and the shades of grey make sense.

I press the button on my new toy, my altimeter watch, bought from Lidl's, a bargain at £25. The price made me doubt its accuracy but it tells me the canal is level.

It takes about two hours to reach Wootton Rivers, my path being called by pheasants, owls and other birds setting the trees alive. Here I leave the canal, dawn breaks and I take the roads to the car park below Martinsell Hill, my altimeter climbing all the way, accurate to within one metre.

I rest, remove my fleece but keep my Gore-Tex jacket as an outer. I plaster my painful right hip with Deep Heat. An elderly gent pulls up in his car, to walk his dogs. They bark at the stranger, he asks if I'm hitching. I explain myself and press on, using compass to navigate across the grass downs and round clumps of trees.

A handy post points me to Oare Hill. Crossing the Marlborough to Pewsey road I take in Huish Hill. Now high up, on one of Wiltshire's backbones, the views become outstanding with rich blue skies and distant hills rising from the flat lands. This walk is part of wishing to understand the county of my birth a bit better, wishing to interconnect hills and tracks.

Past Gopher Woods I get a twinge from my right knee. A bit unusual with the heavy strapping I wear. All my Scottish and Welsh mountain walks have taken their toll. I continue on the beautiful ridge to Knap Hill, looking back to see the progress of paragliders, then cross up to the Wansdyke – a large dark-aged ditch and bank which once stretched from Bristol to the edge of Savernake Forest, guarding against threats from the north.

The Wansdyke

Checking altimeter and watch I predict I'll be at Shepherd's

Shore for noon. The Wansdyke proves long and tiring and my right knee, which a tribe of pin jabbing patella fetish pygmies has settled behind, starts to complain bitterly. Lateral movement becomes impossible and I lead with my left leg and merely trail my right for balance.

To my right is Silbury Hill, nestled low on the floor in contrast to its towering appearance as one drives past. I'd wondered if I'd see deer on this walk. Here I'm treated, three breaking cover from the defences of the Wansdyke. White bottoms springing across the field in their wake.

Feeling the strain, I trudge on and rest at Shepherd's Shore. I consider abandoning, phoning Dad for a lift. Pressing on I search for the reserves of a steely determination that has seen me through many tough times.

I start to meet a few more people: dog walkers, normal walkers and joggers. Limping on, I notice my progress is adequate. Ibuprofen relieves the pain. Passing through Hill Cott I anticipate the treat of Roundway Downs. The corrugated steep slopes, carved by the ice age like the knuckles of a giant hand.

I find the old London Road. Long abandoned, a mere cart track – for that is all it ever was. I squelch and slip my way down. I have feet of clay. Big clods of the stuff, my right knee smarts as sucking sounds accompany the lifting of a foot. I try for solid ground where I can until I reach Netherstreet. Then it's the simple plod into Bromham.

I'm stopped by an older couple who tell me I look as if I've walked far. I explain I have, a few words pass and they know my parents. They'd just seen them at the Methodist Church Bazaar. I join them, completing a ten and three quarter hour walk. I'm introduced to other people, "This is Steve, our son, who set out before 05:00 to walk here." I feel like a celebrity.

Dad fetches me tea and cake, other eyes glance at the mess that's just walked in. I wander around. Passing one stall a chap asks me "Test your sense of smell for thirty pence?" I reply. "If I sat down I'd be testing your sense of smell!"

November 2005 – English Nuttalls. Over The Hill Club

Meeting TGO Challenge, Over The Hill Club (OTHC) friends and trying new technology are the thoughts when I lay keyboard to rest, pack the car and set forth for an M6 Travelodge, halfway between Wiltshire and the Lakes. Will the £25 altimeter watch bought from Lidl's be any good? Will the impressive Travel Lodge voice-recognition booking system see me with a bed for the night or a sleepless night in a chilly car?

"No Mr S Smith on our booking list," says the Travelodge receptionist. My heart sinks before he adds, "There's a Mr F Smyth, but no Mr S Smith." After my reasoning of "In the balance of all probabilities, with all things taken into consideration and given the similar sounding names and the slim likelihood of a Mr F Smyth showing up later," I'm handed my room key.

Passing the time with a M6 service station meal, a quick wander around, sleep and chipping the car free from its ice tomb I set off around 05:30 on Friday 18th November. I make good progress, consume a large breakfast at a different service station (I was desperate for a change of scene), take it easy on the ice-covered A592 and set foot on the hills at 08:30. My first target is Red Screes, left wanting after a long walk back in March 2002. Risking an ungloved hand I set the altimeter and make good progress across frozen marshy ground that on another day would have had my feet plunging into peat-ridden mire. Today I'm spared the familiar walkers treat of a sunken foot, a random Microsoft-style pause while one waits for the wet to soak to the skin.

As I climb the altimeter does too. It kindly points out to me that I've screwed up and have ended up on Middle Dodd instead of Red Screes. The lack of trig point, much higher ground to my left were clues too but I'm pleased to see that it had hung in there. Not given into arguments, stuck to its guns and resolutely informed me that I'm not where I think I was. It would have a comrade in a GPS – perhaps even a voice-recognition booking system would back it up too. Oh, that reminds me, the other great thing about the voice-recognition booking system was that when I made my little jokes it replied "I did not understand that. Can you repeat that again please?" The more traditional, anthropological-induced method always met my jokes with silence.

From Middle Dodd I start the easy ascent to Red Screes. To my left the hills fall away into the Kirkstone Pass, only to rise again leaving the road snaking towards Ullswater on the valley floor. At the summit the mountains open out, an optimum viewpoint for a theodolite that would have once been mounted on the trig point of local stone. A crisp blue sky with low-hung winter sun dances the light and shadows like an artist with a rarely-used palette.

Views from the top

I make a quick descent back to the car, and look back to take in the mountain, living up to its Red Screes name. If only I understood Gaelic then the Scottish peaks would have been more navigable. Carn Mor Dearg – big red hill, so simple if you know.

The previous weekend I walked twenty-four miles across the Wiltshire downs from my home to my parents and, for my troubles, a long-term knee complaint remerged. Having hobbled for most of the week I'm pleased that it has held up on Red Screes, and I decide to attempt another this afternoon. I set off for Grange, the small village at the south end of Derwentwater. After the OTHC Newlands round of last year, I convinced myself that I'd missed out High Spy North Top. I wish to ascend again to be sure I've taken this in. Taking the minor road, from Keswick, to the west of the lake, I twist and turn to avoid oncoming vehicles and patches of ice. Having already seen one car slid into a wall I'm cautious.

The combination of an adverse camber, a shaded spot, a bend and a hill conspire to form sheet ice and for me an impressive zero point turn pointing me perfectly back to Keswick. I take the hint, pass through Keswick again and tackle Grange from the better road the other side of the lake.

I'm slow up the sharp incline to Narrow Moor. During the week I've spent time with a neighbour's dogs and its probably playing my asthma up. I puff, pant and beg the altimeter for each increment that it slowly meters out. My confidence in the wrist technology increases and both my new toy and the sun touching the ridge, count me down for the unending views out towards Hindscarth and Robinson. The many shades of blue sky contrast with the shades of green, brown and grey of the mountains. I'm grateful for the ridge, views and nearby summit of High Spy North Top with its adorning cairn. Looking back towards Grange, Derwentwater sits in her full glory above the hamlet. Its islands and glistening water punctuate the mountains rolling down.

On the descent, my knee starts to groan, not quite up to the levels of the tribe of pin jabbing patella fetish pygmies that had settled in during the previous weekend, but nonetheless I become aware of it.

I finally reach my car and set off for an evening at the Youth Hostel. Like my breathing shyness holds me back. I always feel bad, fearing I come across as aloof and rude when people welcome me into their conversations. Being a reformed drinker the two OTHC barrels of beer, which do look tempting, cannot be used for rescue. But slowly I relax, take in the surroundings, the people. Skulking put to one side, I join in.

I sleep well. Steve Wagstaff's attendance at the international snore-athon finals (this year being held in the remote reaches of the Amazon) aids my comfort. I join Big John's Scafell Pike walk along with Sue Oxley, Jacqui Hutchinson, Gordon and Gavin Coventry, Dave Skipp, George McKendry, Dave Wilkinson and Andy Sayer. I chat to Sue, we finished the 2004 TGO Challenge together on a warmer, yet equally blue sky, day. In front of us George slips on ice, Sue goes over on the same piece. We turn to see if Big John will fall foul of the same ice-covered rock. Nobody considers shouting a warning. We just wait and watch. It's Gordon that takes the slip, a great cheer goes up and he manages a bow as part of the steadying process.

We pass up the Corridor Route, the mountains tower above us. Where the sun's fingers have touched the ground it is safe, other places are covered in ice. Sometimes it's layered like uninviting steps. It takes us three hours, with me firmly at the back, for the final ascent to the summit. A large summit cairn come shelter marks my arrival. I try and recall the 1958 picture I have of my father on the same spot. Even in black and white the grey, misty day is obvious, in contrast to the glorious winter day we are blessed with.

I've been struggling, my breathing down. Grateful for the rest, I dose up with food and my asthma inhaler. I check with John about the route off. He makes a casual comment about people could do Great End. I eye it up, along with Broad Crag and Ill Crag. I fancy them all and ask about the route off Great End. We set off and I'm flying. Something's kicked in, an extra cylinder is firing. I go over Broad Crag then take a look at Ill Crag. I try and make a quick ascent yet it's frozen in its own shadow. Feet slide around like a newborn horse. Reaching the summit I set off again, keeping my eye on the rest of the group, I pass them as they just start the descent to Esk Hause. I belt up Great End with the view to descend and meet the party on the path to Sprinkling Tarn. I intersect them easily. Too easily. There's been a misunderstanding about my intentions. They've waited for me and John is still waiting for me on higher ground. We'd talked about Great End but the communication had broken down somewhere. I now make a big mistake. I leave my kit with the others so I can nip back up and tell John I'm okay. It is longer and harder to re-ascend than I'd imagined. I'd estimated my energy reserves and now they are burnt up. I end up crawling the last hundred yards to the point where the others left John waiting. No John. I can see figures in the fading light, high on the ridge. My stupidity hits me. I've fallen into a trap. I've left my kit assuming I'll soon be collecting somebody with a map and compass. Now I feel alone and wonder where John is. I cannot risk going any further, looking for him. The temperature is dropping and my rucksack, packed with survival gear, is safely making its own way off the hills. I descend, past the spot where I'd met the others and come across a junction in the paths. Bugger. Straight on or go right? I have no fix, no map, no compass. The light is fading and I'm feeling colder. In the distance I see two figures, I make my way to them and ask to take a look at their map. I think they want me to be more lost than I truly am – alarmed that I cannot remember the name of the start point it takes me a few goes to claim some level of competence by remembering the grid reference of 235123. This is as good as remembering the name of Seathwaite. Once I get a look at their map I set off and catch the others up. Sue reassures me that John is very experienced, he'll turn up. Jacqui, his wife, looks unconcerned.

We reach the cars in the last of the light. Gordon and Gavin and the two Daves are waiting for us. We discuss the situation, wondering on the best plan. Admitting we've "lost John." Gordon finds it funny; Dave and Dave express their concern with a proposed visit to an off licence. Gordon, Sue and I start back up the hills, hoping for some sign of John. Latecomers are stepping off the hills. Torches can be seen on high ground but always in groups. Not the single torch we are hoping for.

It is Sue that spots John. Friends for many years she picks out his shape in the darkness.

The hills normally let one get away with it. Today was such a day. Nobody was hurt on the ice. Nobody was lost. A misunderstanding introduced some risk but we all survived. Yet things can always turn out differently. I couldn't believe that I left my kit. Something in all my years in the hills I vowed never to do. A lesson learned.

Classification	My Total	Total
Welsh Nuttalls	112	188
English Nuttalls	21	252
Corbetts (Scotland)	2	219
Grahams (Scotland)	0	220
Unique Donalds (Scotland)	0	58
Munros (Scotland)	284	284
Ireland	0	212
Totals (19/11/2005):	419	1433

February 2006 – Wilsons Prom: The Southerly tip of Australia

Where does one begin to describe a hike like none ever taken before? Where kookaburras, wallabies, lorikeets, lizards and paper bark trees adorn one's path. Where the magpies have evolved into what their European cousins would run and hide from. Where previously unseen species of trees and plants appear so abundantly one feels like a modest collector stumbling over the lifetime's work of an expert. For this is a small description of the wonder of Wilsons Promontory National Park. The most southerly tip of mainland Australia.

After driving along the 30km park road Steve Hampton and I set up our tent at the Tidal River campsite.

As an excursion to pass the afternoon we head off on the trail, cut through the dense undergrowth, to Squeaky Beach. Unlike the national parks of the UK, which are there to preserve what has already been changed, this is untouched, never cultivated or abused. Our aboriginal predecessors were good custodians of Australia and this one area shows what we could have done if only we'd followed the wise ways of the ancient people.

We climb steadily and easily, signposts guiding us and the

vegetation shading us from the brutal Australian sun. A wallaby munches on a tree and allows us to video him, unfazed by our presence. A kangaroo in miniature he reaches for the tasty high pickings, intent on filling his belly before loping off onto higher ground.

Navigating through a headland we, from our high vantage point, take in the splendid views of the vegetation-covered land spilling into the sea.

On Squeaky Beach we discover its apt name. Grains of granite make up a nearly white beach, every footstep makes a satisfying squeak as we made our way across.

Back at Tidal River we make supper and camp among the new smells and noises. The kookaburras laugh at our every move. The vicious bull ants swagger their way around seeking out campers to sink their hot ember of a bite into. And all the time the irritating march flies leave their calling cards of red blotches.

We join in the laughs of the kookaburras as one swoops down and thieves the burger filling from the bun held by an American. Cries of "Gee, did you see that?" were soon added to with, "It's done it again", as another American falls victim.

We sleep well in the tent then, after driving to Telegraph Saddle, set off on our three-day trek.

I'm struck by the size of the grasses shading the path. I've only seen such things in garden centres before – what might be rare to one is common to another. Black bulbous stems with a shock of grass protruding as a head battle for space with tee trees and eucalyptus. And there are hairy trees too – Australia is so butch even the trees are hairy!

We pass through areas blackened by bush fires, part of the cycle here with some species only germinating after a fire.

Many of the plant species we see are only found in Australia and Tasmania. Once connected to a greater continent this is a time trap of a world forgotten elsewhere. The land bridge to Tasmania, broken some 15,000 years ago, allow trees, animals and people to be shared. The aboriginal people are a further testament to this once isolated continent: a people for whom buildings, money and ownership don't mean a lot. Broken away tens of thousands of years ago they, like the flora and fauna, are a living testament to the world as it once was.

Sealers Cove

It takes us three hours to reach Sealers Cove, named after earlier seal hunting settlers attracted by its fresh water supply. As we break off the path onto the white sands of the beach I'm unprepared for its breathtaking beauty: a perfect horseshoe cove with tree covered hills folding down towards it. Clear blue sea laps against the shore. Rocks the size of buses litter the edge of the beach. Truly one of the most beautiful places on the earth. For me it outdoes Scotland and that takes a lot of beating.

We pause a few hours, swimming in the sea before setting off for Refuge Cove. On the trail we come across an echidna, a spiky ant-eating egg-laying mammal. Proof of the reptilian past of mammals and like so many Australian species the females nurture their young by way of a pouch.

We set up camp at Refuge Cove and are soon surrounded by the tents of others doing the trail. One couple, camped opposite, catch our attention. She is slim and good looking, probably in her late twenties. He is a few years her senior, fat, moonfaced and bald.

By basic observation of body language we ascertain they aren't an item. However, he is making the most pathetic attempts to win her heart but, by the flirtatious glances she gives my handsome friend Steve, she isn't in the least bit interested. I point her glances out to Steve.

"You embarrass me," he replies.

"Well she isn't looking at me," I reply.

"What's the situation with your Canadian friend, Mary?" he asks, half changing the subject.

"Well her father died last year, she was caring for him. So she's planning to come to England."

"Good luck," says Steve.

"Thanks," I reply.

I pick up our water bottles and ask our hopeful neighbour, "Do you know where the water taps are?"

"They're screwed into the water tank," he replies, looking pleased with himself.

I give him a sick smile and set off to find this water tank. It's just a short walk and I'm entertained by the only piece of graffiti on the entire prom: 'Yeah but, No but' added to a sign advising all to carry their rubbish out. In a country inhabited by the British even the sayings of Little Britain made it this far.

When I get back Steve whispers to me that Baldy has just had a severe bollocking from his female companion for being so rude to me. I whisper back it serves him right for trying to play the tough guy and impress her.

She goes for a solo walk, leaving Baldy looking lonely and forlorn. On her return she gives Steve another longing look.

I snuggle down in my sleeping bag and drift off to sleep to the most pathetic attempts I've ever heard of a no-hoper trying to win the heart of a woman. Everything she says he laughs and agrees to. Every opportunity for a cheesy compliment is taken.

We wake to a chorus of bird cries, squawks and calls I've never heard before. Steve fills me in on what I missed after I went to sleep. He's managed to ascertain they are work colleagues and we surmise he must have leapt at the chance of doing some trekking with her. He managed to get her to read to him and, in Steve words, the thanks he gave her for his bedtime story were, "Stomach-churningly nauseating."

The day is dull making the walk to Little Waterloo Bay easier yet still testing with all the ups and downs as the narrow path finds the line of least resistance.

At one point we break out of the bush cover and find an open bit of sand. I pick up a stick and scratch out, "Baldy is Gay".

Steve snorts with laughter and then says, "And you turned forty last year."

"And you are laughing," I reply, "and are turning forty in a few days' time."

We then look at my words. "Do you know what?" I ask, breaking the silence.

"What?" replies Steve.

"I'm feeling a bit sorry for him."

"I was just thinking that too," says Steve. "I suppose we've all been there, making a total arse of ourselves trying to impress a girl."

"It reminds me," I said, rubbing out my words with the stick, "when I was twenty-four and went on a walking holiday with a girl."

"You made an arse of yourself?" asks Steve.

"Not quite, but I felt a bit of an arse, that's for sure. She knew I was interested in her and she suggested we walk the Cotswold Way together. It takes a week and we planned to stay in B&B rooms each night. So you might say I was a bit hopeful."

"And?" asks Steve quizzically.

"On the first day, while taking a rest and enjoying the views, she announced she'd met a chap called Graham and he was the love of her life."

"And you still had another six days to walk with her?"

"Yup!" I reply.

"Great!" replied Steve sympathetically. "How did you cope with it?"

"Well, I just kept it all in until the Tuesday when I noticed she was using a contraceptive pill packet to work out which day of the week it was."

"What, openly?"

"Yup. She held it up and counted off the days."

"You're kidding!"

"Nope."

"That's rubbing it in."

"I know. I think she was showing off. The final straw was when she was going on about him playing American football, and how bruised he got. All over his back, thighs and legs – as if I needed to hear that. I topped it off by saying, 'He must be *very* brave'."

"What did she say?" asks Steve.

"Told me off for being sarcastic."

"If you don't mind me saying," adds Steve, "you've got a knack of choosing women who don't give a stuff about your feelings."

"I know," I reply, shaking my head.

"What was that one about the work colleague and the internet TV?"

"Yeah, right," I reply, raising my eyebrows. "We went out together, it lasted about six weeks then she finished things. A couple of weeks later she phoned me, saying she wanted to get on the internet and could I help her choose an internet TV. Anyhow, ever hopeful of being reinstated, I picked her up and drove her to a branch of Currys. There were a few TVs with web browsers but the functionality was limited. I was knelt down, with my back to her, reading the blurb on one of them when I asked her what she wanted to use it for. 'Internet dating,' she replied."

Steve lets out a snort of sympathetic laughter. "And you think Mary will be different?"

"Oh yes," I reply full of optimism.

"Well, go careful," replies Steve.

We take a brief stroll out to Kersop Peak to a high view of the route to come and the numerous little islands guarding the coast.

I wake early on our final day, long before dawn – the quarter moon picking our tent out from amongst the tress. I stroll onto the beach at Little Waterloo Bay then walk up and down soaking in the mood and the stars. It's so hot I take off my shirt and let the breeze air my body.

I gaze up, the Milky Way glows centre stage. The four stars making up the Southern Cross shine; marking out their distinct pattern – unique to south of the equator as The Plough is distinct to our northern hemisphere.

With the sun beginning to rise I get back to the tent – first a red glow then the sun's orb breaks the horizon.

We pack up the tent and set off for the inland trek back to the car at Telegraph Saddle.

My body, more akin to the northern climate, doesn't take well to the thirty plus degree temperatures. What should take four hours (the park route guide is that informative) takes us six with heat exhaustion grabbing me for the last two hours.

I'm desperate for shade and copious water but both are in short supply as we survey the damage of an accidental bush fire which, in 2005, wiped out our shade and many square miles of bush.

We admire the vegetation regenerating, the bullish determination of nature. We press on but have to rest often, the heat is too much and I'm relieved when we reach the car.

To the final laugh of a Kookaburra I'm bitten by a bull ant and am left poleaxed and writhing on the ground as the hot ember of the bite sinks into me.

May 2006 – The Great Outdoors Challenge

It's Thursday May 11th and a sunny day in Glasgow. Via a text rendezvous I meet up with Ali Ashton, a fellow participant on this year's TGO Challenge.

After greeting with a hug I point towards the device next to her trowel tucked into the side meshing of her rucksack and ask, with a puzzled look, "What's that?"

"My trowel," she replies.

"No," I reply, wagging my finger at the plastic scoop-like thing next to it. "I *know* what trowels on hikes are for."

"Oh that," she exclaims. "It's a Shewee."

I furrow my brow.

"It acts as a penis for women," she adds.

"Where do the batteries go then?"

"It's for peeing through, Steve," she replies forcefully.

"Oh." I'm trying to absorb this.

"You don't know how hard it is to squat."

"No," I concede. "Have you tried it out?"

"Yes, at home."

"What you mean you *stood* at your loo at home?"

"Yes."

"What did the children say?"

"They were *out*." This was said with some emphasis.

"They didn't comment on Mummy leaving the loo seat up now? And which way round does it go, this scoop affair?" I ask, ignoring Ali's right to remain silent. "Does that go at the front or to the rear?"

I must have gone on about it a bit because Ali eventually adds, "I wish I hadn't told you now."

I was of much the same opinion.

We meet up with Sue Oxley and join other TGO Challenge participants gathering and greeting on Glasgow's Queen Street station. Ali is catching a bus whereas Sue and I are taking the Mallaig train with me set to alight at Lochailort.

The journey goes well, through the suburbs of Glasgow then into the Southern Islands. As we cross the glorious Rannoch Moor, with the hills out basking in the sunlight, we spot the point, near Loch Ossian, at which we've arranged to rendezvous on Wednesday.

It's the morning of Friday May 12th and I paddle my feet in the sea loch of Loch Ailort. I sign the register and set off walking on the short road leg before turning into the hills.

My first uphill slog takes me to the long hassock, tussock and hillock boggy walk across to the Graham (mountain between 2000 and 2500ft) of Glas-charn, at 633m. The weather though a bit wet, doesn't hamper me and I'm pleased my new altimeter ascends at the same rate as myself. I'd never appreciated how useful it could be, not only is it a countdown to the summit but it reduces the need to pace (or estimate the distance travelled) when wishing to change course on a slope.

The descent takes me to a small stream before the ascent of the Sgurr an Utha. At 15:00, realising my knees have had enough, I perch my tent at 430m on its westerly slope. The weather has cleared for a nice evening and my open tent flap reveals a view down a glen. A rocky mountain ahead, a loch to its right and folds of hills guarding the head of the loch. The heathers and grass are a deep mustard colour, flattened by the recent snowmelt.

It's Saturday May 13th and I start the day by resetting my altimeter to the reading when I finished walking yesterday. It's then a two-hour pull, in good weather, up to the Corbett summit of Sgurr an Utha – heavy going with ascents, bogs and bumps to navigate.

Sat at the summit I take in the views out to the sea, and beyond to the Cuillin Hills on the Isle of Skye – towering majestically, their menace hidden from all but those who dare to cross them.

The view from Sgurr an Utha

I then make the steep drop down to Allt a Chaol-ghlinne where I meet fellow challenger, David Boyd. He's had a tough day crossing the absent path alongside Loch Beoraid.

We descend to the bothy at Glenfinnan where I leave David resting as I set off north-east to the bealach. My aim is to then ascend Streap and take in the mountains east to Spean Bridge.

At the bealach, after a long old pull, my plans change. Streap appears to be impregnable from this angle and my own fitness is sending me a warning signal to stay low.

My low level alternative involves backtracking and heading out via Glen Finnan. I'm demoralised my lofty expectations have been halted. The idea of throwing open bothy doors late in the evening with tales of grand adventure, has been set to one side.

Wondering what to do, my eye casts to the top right of my map. The slither of yellow road and the tiny hamlet, Strathan. I know my way from there to Spean Bridge. In better spirits I descend a bit and camp. It's a low level route for a few days yet better than backtracking.

Sunday May 14th and I'm descending through Gleann Cuirnean, following its burn. I glance back, Streap looks more menacing than ever. There doesn't appear to be an angle on view through which it could be breached. The decision to change route is the right one although the long road walk down Loch Arkaig will be a tiresome alternative.

I reach the little hamlet of Strathan and play a game of dodge the bog as I fight my way to the road. I pass what was once the school house for the glen, now nothing more than a shut-up tin shed. Here I meet fellow challengers Stuart Brown and James Spittal who I shared lunch with at Blackburn Bothy a year ago.

I start the long road walk, the weather is good, the loch is fine yet I'm disappointed by the amount of rubbish strewn along the loch side. Beer cans the modern graffiti, saying 'I was here. I got drunk here and am so stupid I left these tins behind.'

A car draws up, offering me a lift. I explain the Challenge and get a good luck wish. I catch up with the LaBorwits. Gretchen, their granddaughter, is this year's enlistment. Her Achilles tendon is sore, I hope she makes it.

I bump into David Boyd again. It's a long walk and we chat away, covering numerous topics.

"What I need, Steve is a wife waiting at the end of each day. With a camper van."

"What about lunches?" I ask.

"Yes, that too. Lunch. She could pull up and have my lunch ready too."

"And supper?" I ask.

"Yes, supper too. Just when it's time to end the day."

"If only Carlsberg made wives?" I suggest.

After seven hours of plodding I camp at 16:00. The spot isn't so great, on the side of a hill in unfenced farming land. I spend a dull, long evening worrying about getting run over by some farm vehicle. Sleep comes slowly.

I wake in the early hours of Monday May 15th with rain pelting against the tent and only the BBC World Service to keep me company. I don't sleep again and come 07:00 pack my rucksack and brave the rain to dismantle the tent.

With it hastily shoved into the pack I'm off walking, hood up and pulled tight. I pass the end of the loch and its sign saying not to dump rubbish. There is so much in the glen a couple of carrier bags, full of empty beer cans, leant against this sign would have set the scene off a treat.

I soon realise my over trousers are on back to front, and the pack is so badly arranged I have the choice of it pressing into various parts of my back or hanging off one shoulder.

Not until I reach Achnacarry can I find enough shelter to sort myself out. Hurrah for an 1930's K6 telephone box but. But with the proliferation of mobile phones the phone is now disconnected and the directory mouldy and decayed. A lack of cleaning gives that oh so familiar K6 whiff, so familiar of a Saturday morning. I rue its demise.

I set off again and I'm passed by two logging lorries, neither acknowledge my hasty retreat into the verge. An elderly man on a mission in his VW Polo looks nothing but ahead as I dive out his way. Only an old lady in a red hatchback manages to raise a hand of acknowledgement. There again it could have just been an age-related twitch, I shouldn't get my hopes up.

I plod on, struggling with the pack, hunger, the weather and my morale. I need to stop to eat but the Little Chef in Spean Bridge beckons and sets my focus. After three hours of clouded hill tops, tar-sealed roads I reach the Commando Memorial. I'm dripping wet and know the sign announcing, 'Spean Bridge' is a bit optimistic: there's still a good trudge to go. The fantasy of eating in the Little Chef keeps me going.

On the last bend into town a sign saying 'All Day Food' grabs my attention. This will do. As I approach, dreaming of fried eggs on toast, the small print comes into focus – '12 noon to 9 p.m.' Now call me Mr Picky but 'All Day Food' really does mean twenty-four hours, possibly a 07:00 start at a push. But 'all day' is not a noon start.

I'm weary, hungry and grumbling. I pass my hotel, The Spean Bridge Hotel, and set forth to the last building, The Little Chef. A waitress points me to a table and I slump exhausted into a chair.

I take out a menu card from the rack on the table. I can barely focus. The print is swimming in front of me in a dyslexic haze, everything looks odd, double. I begin to see strange things on the menu. The waitress approaches and by dead reckoning I fancy she wishes to take my order. I mutter about being vegetarian and, "Could she point out what dishes I can have."

"The vegie dishes are the ones with the wee green men next to them."

Thank Christ. I really was beginning to worry I was hallucinating.

I eat well, set off back to my hotel and announce to the receptionist, "I've a booking in the name of Steve Smith."

She scours the booking list, taking just the right amount of time to cause my heart to sink.

"Nobody of that name. When did you book?"

"A few weeks back and I arranged to send a parcel," I reply.

She looks at her feet, "Sorry we've only got a parcel for a Mr Smith."

"That's me then."

"But you are Mr Stephenson."

"No, Steve Smith."

"But you said in the name of *Stephenson.*"

It takes a couple more seconds to convince her and she produces a key.

"You're in the annex."

My heart does sink. An annex is all too often an euphemism for a long walk. She attempts to show me on a diagram how many corridors, stairs and the amount of open ground I need to cover. She realises the game is up and leads me through the maze of different eras and styles of additions until we break cover to the car park.

"It's over there, in the corner and up the stairs," she adds (I've just knocked a painting off the wall with my pack).

"Behind the hut?" I enquire.

"Hut! It's a chalet," she replies, offended.

"Call me Mr Picky," I add, "but that *is* a hut."

I decide it's time to solo this out, time to not try my luck or her patience any further. I find the door, ascend the stairs (18ft by the altimeter) and open the door. The bed is unmade, the bathroom a mess, bin full and half a cup of tea in the cup. I drop my pack and wander back. She's settled back in reception.

"The room hasn't been serviced," I announce.

"Thought it might not be," she replies, "it's a bit early for you to check in."

It's 11:30 and I bite my lip as I'm about to say, "Call me Mr Picky but aren't I already checked in?" Instead I ask when it will be done.

"Hard to say," she replies, "they are doing the rounds. Could be hours yet."

"Do you have any other rooms?"

"No."

We then enter into a staring competition. It's a battle of wits as to who will break first. On one hand I could offer to wait, on the other hand she could offer to find the cleaning staff and ask for a change in the order of room cleaning. We look at one another, both holding out. She breaks first, I thank her and head back.

Slumped in the armchair the cleaner arrives in minutes. Diligently and efficiently he cleans the room, changes the bed and scrubs the bath. He then empties the bin and deals with the dirty tea cup. It's left spotless. We exchange regal nods of approval. Twenty minutes later I've trashed the place.

The bath is excellent, welcome. The shower rail perfect to hang the tent over. Following my escapades last year I check the 'Hewee' for ticks. Fortunately I am spared. I resolve to ask Ali if the 'Shewee' has been spared too.

I check my upper half, my shoulders have erupted in septic spots from the pack straps. A problem I'm prone to. These are beauties. The type that, as a teenager and if on one's face, one would spend a happy hour in front of the bathroom mirror with.

I head down to breakfast on Tuesday May 16th and make use of the self-service-style buffet, piling my plate high with a monster-sized portion.

At 09:00, feeling somewhat full, I set off, sluggishly making my way along a small public road. Trees shroud my path, full of the falling rain. I branch into the glen towards the Lairig Leacach and make a slow pull up a track.

I struggle with the weight of the food supplies to last me to Braemar. To help myself along I empty my water container and take extra medication for my asthma.

I bump into Colin Tock, a route vetter who does about thirty reviews a year. He asks me my views on organising the Challenge. I enjoy the chat.

A Land Rover stops, an elderly gent gets out and, without us needing to ask, describes his life on the hills, berating those who move the stones or leave the bothy messy. He goes on a bit, retired from hill farming but now in charge of checking the water supply fed from the hills to the houses, below.

"Is all the local water passed by you?" I enquire.

"Aye, aye."

Jeff Rowe joins us as he continues on about the beer cans left in the bothies.

"I told them if they felled all the trees," (it's the forestry's turn for admonishment), "the water would be undrinkable for days. They said it'd be fine. Well bugger me it was undrinkable for days."

None of us takes him up on this offer. I once did get a kiss from a girlfriend on top of Driesh but nothing like this. His admonishment then turns to young men who venture out not wearing ties. Apparently he never leaves the house without one.

"I guess it's a generation thing. Not meaning you are old like," adds Jeff. This breaks the flow and I accompany Jeff, a fit sixty-three-year-old himself. Yet not sixty-three in mind or body.

We walk on up the glen, the mountains coming in and out of cloud. As we pass the Corbett of Cruach Innse it clears. Temptation gets the better of us and I pump myself full of drugs to help my breathing. We set off on the long slow pull to the summit. There are fine views from the top with snow still in the Grey Corries across the glen. The track is now far below. These wild places capture your heart. Where life is lived in the moment.

We give the next mountain, Sgurr Innse – a menacing-looking affair like a spot risen from a face – a miss and descend to the bothy. Graffiti on the door dates back to 1937, its age giving it permission to be there. The later stuff has me feeling scorn.

Jeff brews tea, drinks it then moves on. His company was good. I'm now alone, writing by torchlight as it is dark inside. I wonder if I want company tonight. As time ticks by I begin to feel I own the place, resenting the thought of anybody else arriving. With the fading light I set a candle in the window to welcome any walker. I'm pleased when the bothy door swings open in the late evening and Graham Brookes enters. It's good to have somebody to chat to.

On Wednesday May 17th I set off down the glen, planning to camp and meet Sue Oxley where the track, after passing Loch Treig, passes under the Corrour to Tulloch stretch of the railway. It's tough going and I mean that in many senses of the word. Diarrhoea has set in, my pace is poor as is my navigation which has me peering, with frayed nerves, into a 100-foot drop to the Allt na Lairige. The diarrhoea beats the fear to it.

It takes me five hours to do what should have been done in three and I'm almost in tears when I turn a corner and see how far my destination still is.

Sue and I plan to do an evening hike up Beinn na Lap. She arrives one hour after me (having walked twice as far, starting around the same time). I set off with her but feel weak, and uneasy.

One normally needs to find a secluded spot every other day in the wilds, today so far it's been seven times. I make my excuses and return to the tent. Unable to eat an evening meal I try some cereal.

Sue returns later all smiles having done her Munro and got a phone signal which she used to explain to her husband he should open the laundry package she'd posted home at his peril. Now I always thought it was the norm only to send such things to an ex.

She says a storm is blowing in. Within an hour we are hunkered in our respective tents, being buffeted and blasted by wind and rain. It's a real gale. I'm desperate to relieve myself but hold on and on. I hear an engine and peer out. Two guys on a caterpillar vehicle are heading up the hill. It looks like madness in these high winds and rain.

At 01:00, having not slept, desperation gets the better of me. I don waterproofs and head out. I'm violently ill, both diarrhoea and vomit. High on the hill a powerful light is moving around. Who would be out on a night like this? Then I remember the two guys. I retreat to the tent in agony. Constant stomach cramps have me groaning.

A couple of hours later I venture out the tent again to be ill. This is about as welcome as Albert Pierrepoint a pair of scales and a tape measure. The light is still moving around on the hill, mixing with the wild and lonely shadows, lashing rain and howling gale.

I root through my first aid kit to see if there is anything to make me feel better. The kit has been added to over the years but never turned out. I find no sign of anything for stomach bugs, instead there's a mixture of plasters, safety pins, creams, blister second skin, more creams and a condom. Oh how I rue the irony of the last thing I need right now. I rue further as I discover its use by date has long expired.

In all I have ten bowel movements during the night, eight of which I manage to get out of the sleeping bag for.

At 06:00 on Thursday May 18th I get up and discover Sue and I are now on an island, our tents due to be flooded within minutes. We have to rush to get our tents down, doing one at a time as it's just too windy to be able to do alone. I explain how ill I've been and I need a hotel room with ensuite. Sue said she heard everything above the howling wind, including my groans of agony. She was relieved when she heard me vomiting, knowing I was still alive.

Our next challenge is to get off the island. This proves difficult: what were trickling streams when we set up the tents are now raging torrents. Our only hope are the three iron bars of a derelict bridge. With each three inches wide I balance my way across, knowing one slip would land me in this raging torrent. Sue, with shorts and sandals, prefers to wade and hang onto one of the iron bars. It looks perilous.

"I'll be glad to be out this swirling brown stuff," she shouts.

"Hmmm, I know the feeling," I shout back ruefully.

When she is halfway across the current starts to take her. Her body rises as she clings to the rail. I lean forward to reach out, shoving my lower right leg deep into the water. But she manages okay, regaining her own balance and arrives at my side giggling at our bizarre encounter.

"This isn't going to be a night I'll forget," she says.

"Never had a woman say that to me before," I add.

With that the mood is set and we make for Corrour Station making the most bizarre puns. The ground is so wet the only way out is to walk up the railway track. There are moments where there is no escape if a train were to come – we hurry past these.

Sue sorts her things in the station shelter and sets off towards Loch Ossian. I'm relieved to be getting out. I'm joined, on the platform, by two teachers and a group of adolescent school children from Edinburgh. They are polite and we chat, waiting for the train. For some of the time they're in part as they act out the scenes, shot at this station, from the film *Trainspotting*.

We flag down the sleeper up from London and I travel, in a luxurious seat, to Fort William – the nearest place with medical help. The school kids alight at Tulloch and wish me well.

I find a hotel. The receptionist takes one look at me and asks if I need a doctor.

"Just a room, for two nights? I need to lay down."

She books me in and I struggle to my room. The walls are bright yellow, the sheets are pink. The counterpane and curtains a matching tartan. Nausea returns.

I rest up for a number of hours, thankful for the ensuite. Imodium improves things and I'm able to hold down some soup. I stroll around Fort William, checking out the map section in WH Smith reference library for alternate routes out.

I get commiserations from 'Challenge Control' and a call from Ali. "Steve, if you get going on Saturday you can still do your original route."

"Do you reckon?"

"It'll be long days. Corrour to Dalwhinnie, Dalwhinnie to Ruigh-aiteachain. Ruigh-aiteachain to Braemar then Braemar to Clova. But it might be possible."

"I was thinking of perhaps walking out via Kinloch Rannoch."

I later get a text, relayed via Ali, from Lorraine McCall (the first woman to complete a continuous round of the Munros), saying the Kinloch Rannoch route is the quickest, yet hard on the feet.

On Friday May 19th I manage to eat more. Gradually rehydrating and rebuilding my strength. Unsure of my route I purchase a road atlas and tear out the pages for the road walk out from Kinloch Rannoch.

I wake on Saturday the 20th battling with the decision whether to cross from Corrour to Dalwhinnie, staying as low as possible, or to walk to the road leading to Kinloch Rannoch. The latter entailing a road walk out for six days.

I get the train from Fort William and alight at Corrour Station and, in true purist style, make sure I stand where I boarded the train on Thursday morning. This way I can say I've walked every step of the way across Scotland.

I start walking at 08:25, I still haven't made my mind up which route to take. Over the last twenty-four hours I've swayed between one and the other. It isn't until I pass the quaint Loch Ossian Youth Hostel I make a decision: Dalwhinnie and my original route. My aim is therefore to meet Ali and Sue in Clova on Tuesday night, requiring eighty-six miles of walking and 11,000 feet of ascent in four days. This is a challenge within the Challenge.

I make good pace along the side of Loch Ossian, passing the fabulous rhododendron bushes I get to the end of the loch in an hour and a half. I look for the path and start to panic I might be inadvertently walking up Strath Ossian. With careful map checking and sifting through the myriad of paths and tracks, I gain confidence I'm bound for Dalwhinnie.

The Uisge Labhair is fast flowing and its numerous feeders are difficult to cross. Twice I have to ascend high to find crossing points. The bealach forever feels like it's in the distance, yet I set a good pace and, unlike the remains of the crashed WW2 plane that lies up there, I make my way over it, four and a half hours from setting off.

Down the other side the path is good, much work has been done on it. I get to Culra Bothy at 14:15 and pop in, hoping to also get a signal to call the hotel at Dalwhinnie to book a room. No luck on the signal but the maintenance officer is staying and a log-burning stove explains the pleasant smells I'd been getting wafts of. It's snug and warm, gorgeous in fact. He's pleased I'm a member of the Mountain Bothies Association and makes me a welcome cup of tea.

I depart at 14:40 and decide to follow the tracks around Loch Pattack. A longer route but better looking than the path. This, like a wrong turn at chess, is a bad move. After forty-five minutes of walking I discover the track is flooded, impassable. The alternative, via peat hags, has me swearing, cursing and blaming everybody but myself. It's an endless maze of swamp, tufts and filthy slopes of peat. After half an hour I realise the game is up and backtrack to the bothy to take the path.

I'm annoyed, angry and emotional. I say 'fuck' about twenty times a minute, all the time gained by my earlier pace lost by a single wrong turn. My lower legs are filthy from constant sinking in the peat, it's been two hours of walking in treacle.

This two hours has cost me. It takes, in all, eleven and a half hours to get to the hotel. I know nine is my usual limit. To add to the pitiful day the last two, the lost two hours, are in a downpour and I discover lightweight kit comes at the price of not being so waterproof.

I cannot get a signal on route so I arrive at the hotel very wet with no room booked. My heart sinks when they tell me they are full but, after seeing the despair on my face, they open up another room. I'm grateful yet I ache and my heart is racing.

I wake on Sunday May 21st and get ready to set off.

The hotel is under new management and they have been so good to me I am sorry to be leaving. I could quite easily sit out the rest of the TGO Challenge here: my feet are blistering after the hard walk up Loch Ericht.

I plaster up and set off at 09:30 via the leat, and its path, towards Loch Cuaich. Looking back, a wonderful rainbow hangs across The Fara, setting off the snow that has fallen in the night.

From Loch Cuaich I close navigate around every piece of high ground – making the journey longer but less of a climb. I'm not as quick as yesterday, instead this is more of a plod. I follow the loch's feeder burn with my compass angling towards the right of Clach-mheall Dubh. This is a delightful passage which includes the picturesque estate bridge, over the Allt Bhran, at Bhran Cottage.

I then make the hard slog above the Allt Bhran. With long drops, heather and an intermittent path I take frequent rests. At one point I nearly sit on an adder before it slithers away. It's then an uphill pull to meet the track to take me into Glen Feshie. I urge myself on, needing the bothy, unable to face the tent. My feet are painful, my right heel especially.

I fancy the River Feshie will be too deep to cross, unlike two years ago when I crossed with John Jocys. This time I have no company, just pressing on alone.

As I turn into the glen I'm met by the most delightful scene imaginable: smoke from the bothy chimney. There will be warmth to dry my wet things. I try to imagine who is there. A party of walkers? Surely I must be the most westerly TGO Challenge participant remaining?

I have to go past the bothy to cross the river by the dilapidated bridge 1km upstream.

Arriving at 18:45, I meet Colin Pritchard who, having set out on the Monday, is pleased to meet his first challenger.

I thank him for the fire, I'm so grateful. I'm amazed at his high-level route and how far he has travelled in one week. Able to run up and down Ben Nevis in under two hours he's a league ahead of me. I congratulate him on his route so far.

"You haven't seen my feet yet," he replies. At about this time I'm removing my right sock. We both look astonished at the red slug attached to my right heel.

"Forget *my* feet," he continues, pointing towards mine. "My goodness."

It is mightily impressive. I puncture it to release the blood and lymph, nothing happens so I apply gentle pressure with my fingers. It then turns into a garden sprinkler system, dousing everything in reach.

We talk about our lonely walking; I mention the loneliness of the long distance walker. Colin gets my reference straight away and we discuss the films of Tom Courtenay.

We drag camp beds down from the upstairs and arrange them to sleep by the remains of the fire. As we are about to doze off Colin says, "I think it's you who's the most westerly challenger."

"Why?"

"You're on the west side of the bothy!"

I wake about 03:00 on Monday May 22nd. The fire is out and it's very cold. I go upstairs to get some blankets, climbing the ladder through the hatch in the floor. I miss my footing and have to throw myself against the lip of the floor to rescue myself. So nearly a 6ft drop, so nearly out the Challenge again.

I get back to sleep, then wake then pop and dress my blisters with Colin's help.

I get going just after 08:00. My feet are sore, yet workable. It's day three of my catch-up, the longest at twenty-five miles. I make good progress, picking off the bridge near the watershed, Geldie Lodge then the Linn of Dee. My right foot is sore and after about eight hours I slip my boot off and inspect it. The dressings and padding are dripping with an unpleasant red and yellow mix of body fluids.

All day I walk alone, just the footprints of the wave of challengers ahead of me remind me I'm still part of the greater thing. I was heartened to see all the names in the bothy book, especially the LaBorwits. Gretchen, their granddaughter, was still making progress, her Achilles tendon at least getting her this far.

The final road walk to Braemar is hellish. I go via Mar Lodge but it doesn't detract from how depressing and draining the walk is. I keep counting grid squares, timing myself and predicting my arrival time – continuously adjusting it.

The weather varies, the hills on view are fine. My feet ache and every time I press down on my right foot it feels like I'm stepping on a bed of pins. The River Dee is in fine form flowing its way towards the sea – encouraging me with it.

I get to Braemar at 18:45 and arrive exhausted at The Fife Arms and present myself at reception. "Do you have a room for tonight?"

"No," replies the receptionist.

My heart sinks, I can't imagine stepping out of the hotel and wandering around looking for a room. I'm too exhausted. I don't know if it's the dour side of the Scottish humour but seconds later she's found me one. She apologises for there being no bath, I'm happy to just have a room. I ask about dinner in the restaurant she gives me one of those 'you're asking the impossible' kind of looks.

"It's too late for that."

It isn't even 19:00.

The apology for the lack of bath turns out to be a moot point, there's no hot water. Though believe me, I am so grateful for this room.

I wake at around 05:00 on the Tuesday May 23rd aware I've been muttering in my sleep, like my mind is competing with hallucinating drugs, I keep coming in and out the land of lucidity. It's sheer exhaustion, my body aching alongside my mind. This four-day catch-up is a gruelling test. I visit the ensuite and realise I can put no pressure on my right foot. The second toe is swollen and the heel is equally complaining. I wonder if I'm out of the Challenge.

I manage to sleep for another two hours and feel good enough to get going. While patching up my feet I lose count of the blisters, though more than a British Leyland paint job. I gingerly take my first steps: it's like walking on a bed of pins, but I can just about do it. I make it down to breakfast, busy with an elderly coach party staying in the hotel. To a person they look in better shape than me.

I set off at 09:15, hobbling towards the Lochcallater track, aiming to make it across to Clova. Stan, the joint custodian of Lochcallater Lodge, is driving down the track, looking about as bad as I feel yet for different reasons.

I stop at the bothy, 11:50. My right foot hurts with each step but I press on and make my way through to where the Jock's Road path runs out during the last sharp ascent.

I've had word from Roger Smith, at 'Challenge Control', Ali and Sue will be waiting for me at the Clova Hotel. This is the tonic to keep me going, a precious incentive to keep me focussed. I know if I can just get to Clova I'll then have moral support for my last two days.

The weather varies from sun, to rain, to hale to sleet, to snow. I get impressive views back towards the hills above Braemar. I make it to Crow Craigies, over 3000ft high. The weather clears and I peer down

Glen Doll and just above I catch sight of the sea, forty-five miles in the distance. I'm overcome, overwhelmed. My body aches, this catching up is so painful. I can't believe I can see the sea. My eyes well up, seeing the sea just means so much. Never ever, ever give up. Ships are safest at harbour but they are designed for the high seas. No person can realise their dreams, find their potential or fully know themselves by staying in harbour. I repeat to myself, over and over, "There's the sea. The sea." I can't believe it. A man must break his back to earn his day of leisure. This was reward in itself. This moment made the days of pain more than worthwhile. Nobody would have blamed me if I'd pulled out when I was ill. Yet I'd have always had a nagging doubt I should have given it another go.

From here the descent to Clova is long and tortuous. Jock's Road into Glen Doll has my feet yelping at each press on the ground. The forest walk dank, long and tedious, the final four-mile road walk painful on the feet. I'm utterly drained. It's nine hours into the day already. I swagger in the pouring rain, the hard road sending shockwaves through my feet. I fall asleep while walking, with my eyes shut I stagger into the centre of the quiet, single-track road, coming to with a dazed jolt.

Counting off landmarks, I reward myself with sips of water. If I can just get to that clump of trees, then that building. I break it down into chunks.

It takes me until 19:10 to get to the hotel. I'm hoping Sue and Ali have got my text asking for them to get me a room. Staggering into reception, with restaurant guests staring at this sodden mass, I start to ask if I have a booking. I hear footsteps running. It's Ali. She doesn't care how wet I am, her arms go round me and I get a huge hug. Then Sue hugs me too. They give me permission to be very proud of myself! Eighty-six miles in four days is a long walk.

"Let's get you to your room," Sue says.

I turn to the receptionist, "What do I have to do to check in?"

She takes the form back, "I think just the key will do."

Sue and Ali help me to my room. I shower and meet them and

order supper. The stories of our last days pouring from us. I have to swallow hard. I appreciate them waiting so very much, having got a day ahead of themselves..

On this, their day off they climbed Driesh and Mayar and kept looking west towards Jock's Road observing the weather I was walking through. They'd been in touch with 'Challenge Control', this rendezvous was made by message passing through Control as phone signals became poor. Knowing they'd be there was the biggest thing that kept me going. They tell me my story has got around, the guy catching up after two days off sick. I'm deeply moved by all the messages I've received. Texts, relayed phone messages. Roger, Pauline, Robin and Alan in 'Challenge Control' keeping me going. Fellow challenger John Jocys coming on the line to give me encouragement. Texts from my mum and dad. So many people urged me on.

Wednesday May 24th starts with a knock at my door. It's Doctor Ali with her medical bag. My feet are dressed with the correct dressings for open and closed sores. I stand up, it feels good. I can exert pressure on my right foot.

There's a different air at breakfast. Sue and Ali truly mothered me last night (and I truly revelled in it) but I'm quietly aware we have about thirty-five miles to make it to the coast. They tell me of the route, straight up 2000 feet of ascent. It's the quickest route.

"Are you okay with that?" they ask.

"Yes, I'm in your care now. I'll do whatever you tell me to."

"Now if you'd only said that yesterday," jokes Sue.

It took everything I had to get here. From now on all I want to do is to follow in their footsteps.

We set off at 09:00, Sue is a strong walker and I find myself ascending at 400m per hour up Green Hill. From here it's misty, requiring close navigation which I take no part in. We drop down and then take the long descent to the road to Bridge End. I find the road tiring, exhausting and tough on my feet. It's a three-hour power walk. Sue and Ali fancy Brechin, I can only promise to get to the next milestone.

"Every mile we walk today is one less tomorrow," says Ali. Sue repeats this later, so does Ali. Elementary mathematics hasn't escaped me, yet I sense an underlying plot to keep me going. They deal with me in a business-like way. We've still a long walk. I sense they are in cahoots, if they allow me to dwell, offer too much sympathy about my aching body I might give up. Yet it's a long way for all of us. We keep one another's spirits up by a long discussion of Enid Blyton books.

"The Infamous Three," Sue calls us.

I point out the unfortunate acronym.

"We are the TITs," yells Sue.

About an hour from Bridge End I pull up. I've been getting stitch in my side, my feet ache but now my calf muscle, where it attaches to the Achilles tendon, pulls tight. It's a hobble from there on to Bridge End. I lean to my left to reduce pressure. Ali and Sue get ahead and, to add to my misery, water is now wetting my chest, soaking me: the bite valve has come off my water pipe. I follow the trail of water back to pick it up.

Now out of water I press on and meet Ali and Sue at Bridge End. Ali straps my calf muscle, I can proceed at a measured pace. If I quicken I yelp, slower and I'm okay. We're now in remote farm land, no place to camp, no B&B. It's nearing 18:00.

I fantasise about each dwelling offering B&B. Only to be thwarted as we reach a sign-less dwelling. I start to lag behind. Most the day I was determined to keep pace but now I'm sluggish. I start to get chest pains.

"Ali, I'm getting chest pains," I call out. I've no wish to take chances.

"Whereabouts?" she calls back.

"High up, above the breast line."

"Does it hurt more when you twist?"

I do a test, and call back it does.

"It's just muscular then," she reassures me.

Not a stride was lost in this conversation.

We make it over the twin hill forts at Caterthun and then in the distance is the sea. We shout with joy and look back to the hills basking in the evening sun. The earlier mist, snow and rain now behind us. We are walking into the nicer weather of the coast. Now ten hours into our day.

A cyclist pulls up, out training. "Where are you heading?" he asks.

"Brechin we hope," adds Ali, "but Steve here's pulled his calf muscle."

He gives us his address. "I can put you up. I've lots of room."

As he pedals off we confirm with one another if what we heard was true. Ali goes ahead, saying she needs to walk at her natural pace, oh and to buy some wine. Sue helps me through the next two hours. Again I fall asleep while walking, stumbling into tree branches on the edge of the road.

We arrive around nine, after a twenty-five-mile day, at the address offered. A beautiful Victorian Manse with matching grounds. Simon and his wife, Jill make us supper, add in pudding, wine and damson gin. Then we are each shown to our beds. And there was us thinking we'd be having rehydrated food, in a tent with mere water to wash it down.

On Thursday May 25th we are given porridge and toast for breakfast. As we make our way down the long drive we look at one another.

"Did that really just happen?" asks Ali.

"I think so," I reply. "But to be honest I'm so tired I'm struggling with reality."

"Doesn't feel quite real, does it?" adds Sue.

Carlsberg do make people you meet on the road.

It takes us four hours, in a gentle sunny breeze, to get to the edge of the beach at Montrose. Ali and Sue get chatting to an old chap with a dog. As they are all dog lovers I drop my pack to the ground and wait it out.

"Nice talking to you," says Sue after a few minutes, bringing the conversation to an end.

"Can you hear water running?" asks the old chap.

"No, that's just the sound of your dog relieving itself on my pack," I reply sardonically.

Hugs and photos follow on the beach. Ali and Sue apologise for slave driving me the last two days. It needed to be done, all my emotional energy went into getting to Clova. I'd not be here without them.

Checking in at 'Challenge Control' news of my plight has got around. People approaching me to say well done.

This has been very tough for me, my toughest Challenge yet. However, I appreciated the small things. A loo is a luxury, a bath and a good meal an unimaginable dream. All the things that just happen in our daily lives have to be planned and fought for on the Challenge. But it's the word 'challenge' that sticks with me. Not just because it is a challenge to get across Scotland but there are so many challenges met along the way. It's having the resources, the determination and the help to get through them.

November 2006 – English Nuttalls. Over The Hill Club

November 18th and we pile out of David Handley's Land Rover into drizzle. Most of the peaks are hiding in cloud, those on show are covered by snow. A far cry from the last two OTHC AGM club meets where blue skies and crisp weather made for fine winter walking days.

John Hutchinson produces a dog lead and clips me on. On the walk last year I parted company with the group to bag a few extra peaks. "I'm not taking any chances this year," he says.

"I promise not to hump any legs, sniff any butts, however I can't promise to spare any handy lampposts we might find." At the sound of leg humping John unclips me. I don't think he heard the word 'not', or if he did he was not taking any risks.

Seven of us set off towards Base Brown. I feel tired. Sleep has come poor. The OTHC snoring gene has evolved in the last year and now easily penetrates wax earplugs and radio headphones. As far back as the nineteen eighties, when canoeing and rock climbing were more my thing, I remember, at Derwentwater Youth Hostel, the words "You're in Room One" with dread – the scrap yard for men who are single because their snoring is beyond what any wife could take. The reputation of Room One is now becoming part of the OTHC folklore.

I'm also stiff from the drive up yesterday. I'd fancied doing a walk in the Dales but when out on the high roads I'd pulled up, wound down the window whereupon somebody sprayed my face with a power shower. It was not just the force and quantity of the water it was also the freezing cold temperature which had me heading for an early arrival at Derwentwater Youth Hostel.

We climb west from Seathwaite, following the path, taking care of the wet and slippery conditions. Sue Oxley is nursing a knee injury and elects to keep on the main path around Base Brown while I accompany Dave Skipp and Gavin Coventry on the rocky scramble to its summit.

It's wet and slippery in places, we stick together yet give one another space on the scrambles in case of a slip. As we approach the exposed summit hail strikes us, sandblasting our faces. We are pleased for the brief shelter of its summit. Sue and John join us, having ascended from the rear. David Handley and Dave Gothard are already heading for Green Gable. We press on, Dave Skipp hangs back for me. I'm a little slow with my breathing today and I find the trudge through fresh snow an added burden.

We all congregate at the summit of Green Gable, taking refuge in its horseshoe cairn. Wind, rain and hail join us. John and Sue decide to head down via Brandreth and Honister. I ask after her knee and the response leaves me in no doubt that it is rather painful.

I'm now the guy with the map and Gavin the guy with the compass. The string has come off mine and my hands are too cold to fix it. Gavin lends me his, making no fuss in having to take his pack off to retrieve it. I can loop my frozen hand through its string and check the navigation to get us to the fine summit of Great Gable. My first ascent of this classic hill, we can see nothing but each other.

As we descend towards Sty Head so does our conversation. Five men out together is the cue to practise the art of political incorrectness. The weather picks up, the wind drops (apart from that caused by the two barrels of beer drunk the night before) and we can see peaks in the distance, now sat below the cloud. Snow and the sun conspire to draw our focus. We each take it in turns to halt the party to admire the view.

Having the breath sucked out of you, your face pummelled by wind and hail, tired and achy joints can so quickly be rewarded by a fine view. Then there's the healthy glow and the hill camaraderie of the OTHC.

Classification	My Total	Total
Welsh Nuttalls	112	188
English Nuttalls	24	253 (i)
Corbetts (Scotland)	4	219
Grahams (Scotland)	1	220
Unique Donalds (Scotland)	0	58
Munros (Scotland)	284	284
Ireland	0	212
Totals (18/11/2006):	425	1434

(i) Birks Crag was promoted on 04/10/2006

May 2007 – The Great Outdoors Challenge

It's a week before the TGO Challenge, and I'm sat at my kitchen table in a state of realisation. You see I don't cook. Never have. I just heat things up. Cooking to me is heating a jacket potato and pouring a can of beans over it. A balanced diet comes with pouring yogurt over chopped banana.

When I left home in 1983 I was packed off with a cookery book. Many years, and many moves, later it ended up unopened in a charity shop. Years after this a great aunt asked me, "Do you have a cookery book, Steve?"

Assuming I was about to receive an unwanted family heirloom I replied, "It always says what to do on the packet." This left Auntie Joan in stitches: somehow this was the funniest things she'd heard in eighty years.

So here I am, a week before the TGO Challenge and I'm reading the instruction booklet of the dehydrator my generous parents bought me for Christmas. I'd asked for it but now I'm seeing the flaw. You can't stick a jacket potato and baked beans in, nor yogurt and banana. No, you actually have to cook things then dehydrate them. There's recipes for all sorts. I'm cornered. Mum is bound to ask how I got on with it. I look for inspiration. On my kitchen table I spy a flyer for a home delivery Indian takeaway, my mobile phone and my wallet. I don't even have to get out of the chair. The Indian voice answers and I put in a large order of main dishes.

"Rice?" he asks.

"No," I reply.

"Nan?"

"No," I reply.

"Pepsi?"

I hear suspicion in his voice. "No," I reply.

"You have credit card."

I'm really sensing some suspicion.

It's Wednesday May 9th and I'm waiting at Heathrow for Mary to arrive from Canada. We first met in Braemar Youth Hostel in 1998 and have met three times since, spending eight weeks together in total. Now we are starting our life together by doing the TGO Challenge.

The friend I have with me, to take her life's possessions back to my house, politely hangs back while we embrace. I then eye Mary's boots (a bit feeble) and her rucksack (a bit small).

Undeterred we board the short flight to Glasgow with my rucksack bulging with dehydrated Indian curry.

We eat out at an Indian restaurant in Glasgow, spend the night in a hotel then take the train to Fort William. I'm excited to be showing her the views from the train window across Rannoch Mor: one of the finest rail journeys in the world.

"I think this is the same route I did in 1998," she says, "when I took the train from Glasgow to Mallaig! It was lovely."

I'm deflated. I'm wishing to show Scotland off to her. Instead, I hunt around my pack and pull out my reading material for the trip.

"What's the book?" Mary asks.

"It's on calculus," I reply.

I get a bemused look.

"Both integral and differential," I offer as if I need to explain its merits.

"You told me to pack light," she says.

"Well it isn't that heavy. I've wanted a chance to read it for some time. It's an old text, written by Sylvanus P. Thompson, published in nineteen-ten. I managed to hunt a copy down on eBay."

There's silence, a hole. I can see she's pondering this.

"It was only ninety-nine pence," I add.

"You mean there were no other bidders."

"Yes, that's right."

I get a bemused look.

We talk more about the TGO Challenge. Mary hasn't got herself fit and I'm a bit alarmed she doesn't understand the extent of what she's letting herself in for.

"It sounds rough going, and the boggy ground must be tough," she replies, summarising our discussion.

"Sorry, you'll get wet, muddy and suffer pain," I say.

"You almost say it with glee, a badge of honour. A badge of war."

"Well you will. I never said it was going to be easy. Scotland and walking are synonymous with rain and pain. If you go to Cyprus you wouldn't mention you were going for the sun: it'd be obvious. So with Scotland it's rather assumed it'll rain and you'll encounter bogs and pain on the TGO Challenge. Sorry if I forgot to mention it."

I return to my book.

In Fort William we have a six-hour wait for the coach to Shiel Bridge. To allow time for delays I hadn't booked on the earlier coach. But Mary's flight and everything since has been bang on time. We resign ourselves to sit it out, buying food, gas and having lunch.

Fort William claims to be the outdoor capital of the UK. I find the place a bit boring and I look forward to spending six hours wandering around as much as Mary would relish reading a book on integral calculus. A TGO Challenge tip is when walking in a pair bring reading material both can share.

We meet Ken and Nina Stimson who tell us they are on the earlier coach. We decide to ask if we can bring our tickets forward.

With a few minutes to spare Mary goes off to check the internet and I dash into Tesco to buy the lunches for the next three days.

With Mary's parting words of, "No chocolate, Steve," echoing in my head I grab flapjack, fruit bars and some chocolate.

Back with Mary I'm trying to convince her. "Chocolate is great energy food. High calories for the weight. Very efficient."

"It just sends you on a high, crashes you to a low then gives you spots and fillings," she retorts.

At the bus station I volunteer Mary to sweet talk the driver into allowing us to use our tickets earlier. He directs us to the inspector and we throw ourselves at her mercy. She tells us we'll have to wait for the departure time and if there is space we can switch.

We watch with anticipation as other people board, hoping for two spare seats. The time approaches and the bus is being readied for departure. We await our fate: Fort William for another four hours or an early ride to our hotel.

"Okay, there's room for you," the lady inspector says as the bus driver takes our packs to load.

"Can I say something," I say.

"Yes," she replies.

"We love you."

She smiles and the driver asks if we feel the same towards him. Mary confirms yes, I remain silent. There's a coach ride ahead, I don't want any misunderstandings.

It's Friday May 11th and we sit in the bay window of our bedroom taking in the glorious views down the loch and checking through our kit.

I show Mary the international distress signal to a helicopter, letting them know it isn't just a friendly wave. I tell her the correct procedure for attracting attention with a whistle and ask her to tie hers to the outside of her pack. It's an impressive school teacher's whistle.

We make a leisurely start after breakfast. An initial stroll to the beach of the sea loch where we each gather a pebble and paddle our feet in the usual TGO Challenge traditions.

Mary has brought a pebble from the shores of Halifax, Nova Scotia (New Scotland). She throws it into the sea here to mark the start of her crossing and we set off up the main road before branching onto the minor road past Morvich and the slow climb towards Bealach an Sgairne.

We pause for numerous rests, we both struggle a bit but I'm impressed by her speed. We take in the mountainous views, the forest opposite in deep commercial green with just the odd birch intruder in a lighter shade.

There's high cloud and a bit of rain. We pause by Joan and Bryan Crick, resting with Peter Lumley. I like Bryan's tales and take on life, Joan jovially trying to silence him. We chat for a moment before crossing the river and taking the climb through the bealach where we soon pick up the path I joined in 2005 after coming up via the Falls of Glomach. From here on we are in path, bog and path.

Mary's fabric boots soon leak and she feels uncomfortable. I worry if this will get her down on the Challenge. I offer chocolate, predicting her response. She settles for flapjack. We make it to the hostel at Alltbeithe in seven hours where a good evening follows chatting to Jenny Wheeler, Barbara Peers, Margaret, Chris and Peter Lumley.

Barbara is proud to carry a hairdryer and no tent.

"If you carried a tent you'd keep your hair dry," I offer. The point is lost. She asks us our route and I mention it including the Lairig Ghru.

"You're not taking Mary down the Lairig Ghru are you?"

"What's the Lairig Ghru?" asks Mary.

"Oh, nothing really," I add.

We retire early to our bunks in the annex. I feel strained from its confines, losing pieces of equipment only to rediscover them tucked down inside other things.

We wake early on Saturday May 12th and move into the main hostel lounge to gather our gear and repack.

We breakfast then set off. Barbara soon passes us on her seventy-year-old legs. We, in our forties, are mere youngsters on the Challenge.

"You've got a good pace!" says Mary.

"Oh it's just having long legs. I merely sit on top of them," she replies.

We start well on the tracks, enjoying the moody clouds hanging around the peaks, the beauty of Loch Affric and the peace of the wilderness. Mary does well but is concerned about the distance. I reassure her this is a 20km day, just 2km further than yesterday. She takes it in, mentally preparing.

We meet with Bryan, Joan and Peter and join in with their banter. I tease Bryan about his 2005 crossing where on this day, the second day, he lost one of his trio and later lost Peter and finished alone.

"You do realise you are jinxed walking with Bryan," I say.

"Thank you very much," replies Bryan.

I struggle uphill via the Allt Garbh. The weight of my pack pulls me backwards.

We meander on the easier sections before a left turn and pull up then down towards the loch which is shown as much smaller on the map. Mary has to watch her footing on burn crossings, trying to avoid soaked feet where I can just splash through in my Scarpa boots.

From a distance I hear the generator running at Cougie. "Nearly there," I say reassuringly. "Let's hope they have beds for us."

"You didn't book?" she asks.

"Ah no," I reply apologetically. I sense Mary is at the end of her energies: 20km a day is the most she can manage.

Val, who runs Cougie, doesn't have a room, our hearts sink but she sends us up to her son's place – a wooden house which started as a caravan, has been extended and extended until the caravan was eventually cut free. We have a room under the eaves, welcome amongst tools, sawdust and the lifestyle of a bachelor.

We return in pouring rain, fortunately missed on the trail, to Val's kitchen for tea, cakes and sharing our day with other challengers. Cougie is one of the Challenge institutions: homely and warm. It's still the family home where Val and John's children and twenty-six grandchildren visit.

"Some people are so fast," says Barbara, who has made it in long before us, "I lead for the ramblers and there's me with my asthma."

I shake my head in despair.

Bryan starts telling one of his long stories, Joan signals him to zip his mouth. There's real banter between this couple but obvious genuine love. We catch up with Peter and Jenny too.

After a fine supper, cooked and served by Val, Mary and I retire to her son, Paul's house.

Before bed we sit and listen to music as the resident bat does a circuit of the lounge. We both sigh with relief when the monotonous rhythm of the generator falls silent at 11 p.m. We can now almost hear the silence. I sleep fitfully, waking after just a few hours. Then a rooster starts in the early hours. It kills any hope of further sleep, I slip out to use the loo.

"Where have you been?" Mary asks when I return.

"I went to strangle that bloody rooster," I reply. At that moment it starts up again. "Trouble was there was four of them and I only got three," I add.

Mary make an ironic laugh and then dumps me. As a sweetener she explains she'll try and finish the Challenge with me. *For Christ's sake,* I think. People meet on the Challenge, have got married on the Challenge and there's me setting a new record of having been dumped on the Challenge.

At breakfast Barbara cheerfully asks, "How did you sleep?"

"Good," replies Mary.

"Awful," I reply.

Mary shoots me a glance.

I'm in no mood for keeping up appearances.

With my poor sleep and Mary's apparent 20km limit we manage to phone a B&B at Torgyle Bridge, cutting our day back from a 30km day into Fort Augustus.

We follow the easy track to Hilton Lodge then the uphill and cross-country tracks, following the power lines, to Torgyle Bridge. I feel every step is laden with bog and despair

We look back towards our trodden route, the mountains in cloud yet sparing us of rain. I point out the pass we came through to reach the hostel on the first night then Cougie on the second – following a fold between the hills which towered above us.

We meet with Bryan and Joan. Peter has taken off on a different route wanting to try a shortcut. Bryan has a mix of concern and annoyance for his missing companion. We continue, enjoying the fabulous mountain views to our right. Peaks, snow and sunlight dancing through.

We arrive at Torgyle Bridge where we find Peter, forever a striver, having beaten us all. We are desperate for the B&B and excuse ourselves.

I'm always cautious with B&Bs. With hostels and hotels there's an acceptance for drying boots and making a mess. With B&Bs you are entering another's home. We make do, rinsing out shirts and draping them over radiators, hanging rinsed-out undies from a conveniently-shaped lampshade.

A peacock struts in the grounds, its call competing with the rooster of the night before to deprive me of sleep.

I wake early on the Monday May 14th and use the bathroom. I spy a bottle of 'Skin So Soft'. This is the best midge repellent known. Discovered by chance, by foresters finding its properties repel midges. I have my own product in mind called 'Midge so Dead'. I'll breed midges in my own midge farm then immerse them in water and fill atomizer bottles. When the purchaser sprays some on they'll be amazed at the instant success as dead midges will immediately be found on the skin.

Back in the room I explain to Mary we need to head for Blackburn Bothy on the Corrieyairack Pass. It'll be a night in either the bothy or the tent.

"Is Fort Augustus too near to stop?" she asks.

"We need to do 20k a day, at least. We can stop there to eat. Then it's the curry for supper tonight."

"Will there be crockery at Blackburn?"

"Erm no," I reply, feeling a heavy burden of responsibility to solve every problem.

"What do we use?"

"We eat out the cooking pots." I wait, worried I haven't really explained things so well. But it's fine, she just needed to know.

We have breakfast with Jenny Wheeler, a solo first-time challenger. She's lucky to be on the Challenge having seriously put her back out when lifting her cat. These things can happen so easily. We chat about our days.

"We'll need to buy some more lunches at Fort Augustus," I say, directing my voice to Mary.

"Not chocolate," Mary adds.

"It'll help you," I reply. "A good boost if you are struggling."

Personally I feel like shutting myself away in a hotel room, watching TV and eating chocolate.

Jenny, who works in the medical field, now gives a thorough explanation of the fallacies of using chocolate on the trail. She explains slow-release food is much better. I sense the expertise I had professed to Mary is now in doubt.

We get going and make our way up through the pylons above Torgyle Bridge. It's a tortuous route, boggy and uneven. Mary's boots leak and it gets her down. We press on and, after what feels like an age, cut through Jenkins Park where we are greeted by the tarmac of Fort Augustus. It feels an affront, roads and massive tar-sealed car parks. We've gotten used to the open country, paths, tracks, trees and rivers. It just feels so wrong.

It takes us another three hours to get to Blackburn. A long pull up the track, Mary does well. Although she is struggling, sometimes feeling unwell she does okay on the uphill sections. We arrive and I'm surprised nobody else is here. I was half expecting Bryan, Joan and Peter. We manage to get the tent up before a fine drizzle sets in. We cook and sort things in the bothy then munch through our home delivery curry – amazing the distances they will deliver!

Retiring early to the tent we ponder what to do. It's a bit early for sleep but good to be warm and cosy – even if in separate sleeping bags.

"How about doing some five-minute writing I suggest?" We both like writing, Mary makes copious notes of her journey.

"How does it work?" she asks.

"We pick a topic and both write nonstop for five minutes. We then read to one another. It's good for developing writing skills."

"Okay. What topic? How about if we jot down all kinds of ideas on bits of paper and then draw for a topic?" she replies.

"It needs to be a more instant topic we can both leap into. Anyhow my hat is tucked into my pack for putting the bits of paper into."

"Fine, fine, fine!" she says laughing, "Have it *your* way!"

She's sounding more cheerful and I wonder if I'm 'still dumped'.

"Not like you're 'put out' or anything?" I drawl. "I know, that'll do the topic can be 'Being Put Out'"

So we embark for five minutes on this exercise, both silently and intently scribbling away. Time's up. I go first, reading out my ponderings on all forms of being put out, including putting the cat out but excluding being dumped.

It's Mary's turn. I hear repressed glee as she starts. "Being Put Out. It's NOT that I'm 'put out!!' The Shit!! How come he gets to choose the topic? ALL I said was, 'How about if we jot down all kinds of ideas on bits of paper and then draw for a topic?' Well, that was quickly dismissed! We didn't have a hat at hand.... Like who needs a hat?! 'Fine, fine, fine!' I said, 'Have it Your way!' 'Not like you're 'put out' or anything?' he glared. 'Okay,' he went on, 'The topic is 'Being Put Out' .. ..' and he went on outlining the rules, timing, and blah, blah, blah. But you know what?! He was just going on, making noise in the background as my mind raced off. 'Being put out????,' I thought, 'It's NOT that I'm 'put out'!!... the Shit!!'."

Fair enough.

"I need to go and pee," says Mary.

I lay flat to let her climb over me.

"Is it okay if I go in the porch?" she asks.

"No, it bloody well isn't."

"But it's cold out there."

"Same for me."

"But you don't have to squat."

"We need a chat about tent etiquette," I reply. "Peeing in the porch is *not* allowed."

"How about peeing in the tent?" Mary asks mischievously.

"Nor the tent. Nor is rolling over in the night allowed. Excessive use of the torch or snoring." I pause, "But farting is."

"Oh I might have guessed farting would be allowed. Along with telling silly jokes I suppose."

"Yup farting and telling jokes are allowed. And they're not silly jokes. And farting is funny."

"Steve..." it's said in a way I sense the need to turn to face her. She looks earnestly at me, "I teach eight-year-old boys."

I look a bit hurt.

Mary adds, "You look just like an eight-year-old boy now, just like at breakfast when Jenny told you chocolate isn't a good trail food."

We wake early on the Tuesday the 15th, both shivering with the cold. Mary more than me, she's had poor sleep. She peers out the tent. "There's been a frost."

We emerge into the sharp air, yet enjoy the blue skies. The gas stove, heating water, gives us a bit of warmth in the bothy while we eat our breakfast and sip tea.

We set out for another long incline on the excellent track, enjoying the mountains in the beautiful light of the morning sun. The odd snow slither setting off the high corries of the mountains.

Looking back we make out our passage of the last few days. A lone deer stands on the high pass, its ears and head silhouetted against the blue sky. We soon pass Joan, Bryan and Peter packing up their tents. Peter is in a bad way with his feet, Bryan is tending them. Joan is bantering with Bryan over his stories. We chat and Bryan asks us our route.

"Glen Banchor, Newtonmore, Feshiebridge, Lairig Ghru."

"You're not taking Mary down the Lairig Ghru are you?" asks Bryan.

"Well, it's the bit I've never done, I've only ever peered down into it from the surrounding Munros."

"You do like this girl don't you?" asks Bryan.

"Yes."

"She might not like you after the Lairig Ghru," adds Peter.

I'm beginning to sense she's gone off me anyhow. "Well we'll judge it when we get near," I reply. "Glen Feshie is always an alternative."

We press on, passing large puddles full of tadpoles. I spy a sleeping lizard, submerged and point it out to Mary.

"The tadpoles are like sunflower seeds with tails," she says.

"I was thinking they look more like sperm," I add.

"What was I saying about the mentality of an eight-year-old boy," she adds with a heavy sigh.

We meet Bryan and Joan again near the summit of the pass and sit with them. Bryan is worried about Peter but is a bit frustrated at the differing pace being kept. We sit and enjoy the views and food.

As we descend the Corrieyairack Pass, we find great chunks have been washed away leaving it in a sorry state. River and path often becoming one.

We make it to Melgarve Bothy, our planned stopping place for the night before. We sit outside on worn-out chairs, looking at the hills opposite, ever changing in the sunlight. A glorious place to rest up and, though we are the first walkers to arrive having had our head start from Blackburn, the stream of challengers soon start coming through.

Birds join us, knowing the titbits of food surround walkers.

We get talking to Jenny and many others. I'm asked about our route again and mention the Lairig Ghru. There's some silence.

"You're not seriously taking Mary down the Lairig Ghru are you? There's boulders the size of small cars."

For God's sake, I think.

A few others join in and I concede perhaps we'll go via Glen Feshie. I'd chosen this route to give Mary the best TGO Challenge experience. The Lairig Ghru was the one day for me.

Mary quietly says to me, "When you realised the Lairig Ghru was no longer an option your bottom lip quivered."

"Oh," I reply.

"Just like an eight-year-old boy refused an ice cream," she adds.

I close my eyes in despair. I know this trip isn't going well, but I could do without the reminders.

"You always have that face when you're disappointed," she informs me.

I take a deep breath. "Well you are giving it quite a few chances to make an appearance."

She goes quiet.

I think the point hit home.

Bryan and Joan arrive, no sign of Peter and his bad feet.

"He's determined! He'll crawl in on bleeding stumps," says Mary.

I'm reminded of Monty Python's 'It's just a flesh wound'.

We press on and camp on a small piece of high ground above the road after Garva Bridge.

"What's for supper?" asks Mary.

"Curry," I reply, "it's the main meal of our camping nights."

"Every night!"

"Just the camping ones," I add.

On the Wednesday May 16th we make an early start, 06:20 and get to Laggan in two hours, passing Bryan, Joan and Peter on route. We rest, enjoy the views back towards the way we've come, make use of the public loo and village store. It's a nice gathering of many challengers.

I always wonder how much I pong while walking. And how shopkeepers and accommodation providers manage to cope with smelly walkers. As Mary walks back from the loo I can clearly smell the soap on her, but nothing else. I now realise you only notice the smells that aren't on yourself.

We set off up Glen Banchor. It proves boggy and our energy is sapped in the depressing drizzling rain. We stop at the bothy for rest, damp and smelly – just like us.

There's a rough old table with some packaged food and magazines that past visitors have left behind. Some soup sachets look tempting. Mary reads the details on one. "They're out of date."

I take a look. "No, we print the month and the day the other way around to Canada."

"So much to learn," she replies.

There's a pile of 'Lads Magazines' she sifts through. "Pornography," she announces scathingly.

I'm about to say, "That's not porn", but just stop myself in time. Such a declaration would leave me open to having to explain certain material which circulated when I was at school.

Mary really struggles from here on, she starts to fade and feels ill. She hasn't slept well. The path is sporadic, her boots are leaking and the terrain is boggy and rough. Light rain doesn't lift her spirits. We make it to Newtonmore and grab the first hotel room we can find.

It's Thursday May 17th and Mary is feeling poorly. She's struggling. We walk into Kingussie with Rob, an American doctor. He offers some reassurance but we book Mary into the doctors. My heart sinks at a 16:30 appointment. This wouldn't make for a good day.

We bump into Nik Lawcock and Andy Desmond. Nik and Mary discuss the merits of walking with "schoolboys".

Mary braves a return to the doctors, asking for an earlier cancellation. A nurse takes her blood pressure but isn't qualified to listen to her chest to see what's causing the tightness. However, the nurse does say she thinks it's probably exhaustion.

We go for lunch with Rob and I leave it to Mary to make the decision. Do we head for Ruigh-aiteachain Bothy now or wait for the doctor's appointment? After lunch and a rest she picks up and decides we can set off.

We transfer Mary's sleeping bag, sleeping mat and share of the food to my pack. She is just left we the bare essentials: water and her clothes. I'm weighed down, my GoLite pack isn't designed for this weight.

Peter and George (from Holland) offer us extra food as their resupply parcel, they have just collected, now represents oversupply. I make an exception to my pack weight and take a couple of handfuls of the bars of chocolate being offered by George: otherwise destined for the bin they're keen to get rid of it.

We start walking, Mary picks up and we do well. As we pass Tromie Bridge we meet another group of TGO Challenge participants. Having done this route before I offer to lead. Dutch George asks if I'm sure of the way through a myriad of tracks. Privately I am. "I am sure, George," I reply, looking him earnestly in the eye, "but if I'm wrong I'll give you a bar of chocolate."

He grabs my face with both hands, shakes his head and grins at me.

In the woods we reach a junction that isn't marked on my map. I'm a bit unsure so make use of my new GPS to confirm where we are. We press on, losing the group of people we have spent the last hour or so with.

When we meet the tar-sealed track down the edge of the Feshie I reassure Mary we are doing well. She is doing a bit better, the weight off her.

In the distance I catch sight of what looks like MA Harper and Mike Akin-Smith. It is and it's great to see them both. I like their company and so does Mary.

We cross the new Land Rover bridge and walk the east side of the Feshie. This is better than risking the dilapidated bridge near the bothy. As we approach Ruigh-aiteachain the hills above are lit by the sun, the pine trees and the Feshie guide us in.

The bothy is surrounded by a shanty of tents. Mary and I claim upstairs places as it is threatening to be a wet night. In the cosy downstairs room Dave Skipp is getting a good fire going. Nik, Andy, Mick Hopkins, Peter Sheppard, Bryan, Joan, Peter, Fran and Allen Mellors enjoy the fire. It's a nice evening and I'm glad Mary can see a true bothy night and it cheers her up.

On Friday May 18th we set off into the rain. Mary, reluctant to risk further damp and cold on top of how unwell she's been feeling, asks if it is possible to get a bed for the night. The only place possible is the Youth Hostel at Inverey. I warn her it's a risk, a long day and perhaps no bed. She wants to press on. I'm being drilled into the ground with all the weight. Mary takes just the two lightweight pots and the stove. We walk on and she goes quiet.

"You okay?" I ask.

"I'm feeling ill again."

I try something. I readjust her pack so all the weight is on her hips, none on her shoulders. We walk on.

"How are you now?" I ask.

"Better, I don't feel unwell anymore."

"I'm wondering, Mary. There's something called extraneous cervical ribs."

"What are they?"

I'm sensing my pronunciation might have sounded a bit gynaecological.

"They're small extra ribs, high up. The weight of a pack can press them down and cut off vital blood supply and make you feel ill. I'm just wondering. It'd explain you feeling unwell and why you picked up when I shifted the weight off your shoulders."

We pass through the often trackless terrain, picking it up again before the welcome junction with the Geldie where a Land Rover track will see us through to White Bridge and onto the Linn of Dee.

We sing, in the rain and the wind, to keep our spirits up on this lonely route. When we arrive at White Bridge we rest.

"There's nothing here," says Mary.

"What did you expect?"

"Well. I'm not sure. So many people mentioned it."

"It's just a landmark. Like Geldie Lodge on the map. That's just a ruin."

Mary is now understanding the remoteness of the Highlands. She is an outdoors type but has never been through this kind of terrain before.

Looking up at the bridge there's a box with wires protruding from it. "Looks like a scene from *The Bridge on the River Kwai*," I say.

"I never watch war films," replies Mary.

I sigh. "Well, I seldom do too. I tend to restrict myself to ones with good stories like *The Bridge on the River Kwai*. Or just ones where our brave boys blast the Hun out of the sky."

Fortunately Mary sees my irony. It's something I find myself explaining often to foreign nationals who believe we really mean what we say.

We reach the hostel at Inverey and are told there are two spare bunks but it's in a room of four and we have to wait the arrival of the other occupants to see how they feel about sharing. Then we're told it is fully booked anyhow. We resign ourselves to camping.

I'm worried about Mary. She'd said she needed a warm bed. We'd pressed on to near 30km, way beyond what she was used to. She feels the walk into Braemar tonight would be possible. I doubt it. I'm concerned. A young Australian couple arrive, pre-booked for two of the bunks in the room of four. They are clearly city dwellers and the look on her face is one of 'I'm not staying here'. I think the outside loo and cold tap have put her off a bit.

The Australian chap is asking the warden about a refund of his £30 if he moves on. The warden gets flustered and confused and retires to his upstairs office to check other people in.

By now a large group of us are sat in the lounge sipping tea. I make the Australian an offer which I consider fair. "If he won't refund you I'll take the beds and give you twenty pounds."

The room looks aghast at me. I'm surprised. It was a fair offer I felt. After all I'd be paying for the beds too, and an extra £20 on top.

I repeat the offer, trying to look earnest. Again the room looks aghast. I'm shocked at the shocked faces. Am I being too generous? Somebody pipes up I'm being mean.

"Mean! He wants to move on and is worried he might not get a refund. So I'm offering to help him. What's the problem?"

"You could offer him the full amount."

"The full amount. But then I'd be paying twice over. Once to him and once to the Youth Hostel association."

There's a look of realisation about the room. But nobody apologises. They'd all thought I was trying to buy the beds on the cheap when I was offering to pay more. I'm very put out. Mary teases me if everybody had mistaken me then perhaps it was the way I said it.

"Well I am put out," I continue. "I'd never have ripped him off – that's your sad interpretation of my honest motives."

I go and see the warden with the Australian chap and it proves too complicated to do a refund. But the warden says if I pay the chap £24.80 it'll be okay if we stay under their names.

"Would I only get a £24.80 refund then," he asks. "What about the credit card fee and the booking fee?"

I feel sorry for him. His partner is giving him a hard time over this booking. At this precise point I know what getting a hard time from a partner feels like.

"Don't worry, I'll give you thirty," I say.

So we leave the warden but I'm struck by a minor concern. Paying out cash on a verbal agreement with the warden, who often looks a bit confused, would leave me vulnerable.

"Where is your partner now?" I ask. Wondering if she might be resting on one of the bunks I was about to unofficially purchase.

He looks me in the eye and firmly says, "She's sat in the car."

I'm unsure if this was offered as a reflection on their relationship or to reassure me. She'd obviously point blank refused to stay here and he'd been sent back into get the money back.

I feel sorry for him, give him £30 and wish him all the best.

Later Phil Lambert arrives complete with Dan Pawlak, a Polish guy, who has collected an antler and skull set. He has it strapped to his outer pack. It's quite a sight and Phil is using it to dry things out on.

I wake early, after poor sleep, on Saturday May 19th. We breakfast in hushed whispers then sort our kit while others stir. Soon the kitchen is busy as we make to leave. I peer out the window and see it's raining.

"Mary, shall we hang on until the rain's passed?"

"Steve, you're not really the outdoorsy type are you," says Phil.

We start the wet walk to Braemar at 06:30. It takes just two hours. The highlight is when we look back to see around a hundred deer, just off the road stood in line watching us. As is typical of deer they stared for a few seconds before their leader, a proud stag, leads them off.

We find a café open and have a welcome hot breakfast, catching up with a few other challengers. I'm worried about Mary, she is very tired. I've already said we'd walk out via Ballater, an easier route then going over Jock's Road or Lochnagar. "There's a few nice art shops in town," I venture, trying to cheer her up. "It's where I bought one of my pictures of the Inaccessible Pinnacle."

"Where's that?" she asks.

"It's on Skye. One of the Munros."

"So you haven't done it then."

"Yes, I have."

"So why is it called the Inaccessible Pinnacle then?"

"Well…" I begin but I'm floundering with the teasing. Or is it? I'm beginning to wonder if it's petulance.

We wander around, check into our pre-booked hotel. Mary rests and I go out in search of maps to get us to the coast and to book a hotel for the next night. I realise Mary needs some comfort to see her through.

In the map shop I rue, to the shopkeeper, this purchase as I have the very maps at home.

"No use to you there," he commiserates in practised dour tones.

At another store I witness Rob, the American, asking a shopkeeper if he can draw cash out anywhere.

"The machine's no working."

"Can I draw cash here?" he asks.

"You should have asked me before you bought your things then I could have given you cash back."

"I didn't realise," he said.

"You should have asked first," retorted the dour shopkeeper.

"How was I supposed to know?"

I suggest to Rob he buy something else small to get cash back.

Standing in the Tourist Information shop I find myself in a

dilemma over the opportunity of a hotel in Inver, 10km away, for Sunday night. Not cheap at eighty-five pounds but we have the choice of that or a 30km-walk to Ballater. There is no alternative accommodation on route. I book the Inver hotel and with relish return to the hotel and explain to Mary she'll only have to do 10km tomorrow.

She announces the 30km walk will be better and informs me it was a mistake to book such an expensive room. Furthermore, I should go back and unbook it.

Given the accommodation is on me, I take a sharp breath and overrule her. Plans, like accommodation and my goodwill, are in short supply and at least this is one.

We eat, at a fine food bistro, with Phil Lambert and Di Gerrard. Di is about to emigrate to Kazakhstan to marry her man from Kenya. She wonders how he'll fare on the Challenge next year.

"We could get married on the Challenge," she muses.

"That's getting a bit old hat," says Phil.

I fail to mention I've been dumped on the Challenge.

"What about giving birth on the Challenge," I offer.

"That'd confuse Roger," says Di.

"Three hundred start and three hundred and one finish," I add.

"It could be just like a nativity scene at Callater Stable," says Phil.

"Would we find three wise men on the Challenge?"

"You can imagine the scene," says Phil, "the first thing the baby sees is Mick Hopkins peering down with his headlamp."

After the meal we pop into The Fife Arms to catch up with people. Many are milling around: Sue Oxley, MA, Dave Albon, Humphrey Weightman to name but a few.

On Sunday May 20th we see Bryan setting off alone. We'd heard Joan had twisted her ankle. My prophecy of him losing his entire party again appears to have come true.

We kill the morning, walking around then pop into a café where we catch up with Dennis Pidgeon, Bernie Roberts and Russ Manion. I ask

Dennis his route.

"To The Fife Arms," he replies.

We set off on the short walk to Inver and its hotel, chatting with Margaret and David Brocklehurst on route. At Invercauld Bridge we branch off, taking the forest track, enjoying more mountain scenery. We try some more singing, I'm pretty tone deaf.

"We'll need to train your ear," says Mary.

"I've already trained the left one to fetch me a beer each evening," I add.

Mary likes the hotel, it's a nice room. "Does it go up to five stars?" she asks after observing the three-star rating sign.

"It does, I don't," I reply sardonically.

There's a luxurious bar of soap, impeccably wrapped that Mary bags. I have to use the cheap one I'm carrying.

I wake on the Monday May 21st, achy and stiff.

Mary takes one look at me. "Do you feel like you've just been hit by a truck?"

I give her a sick smile and she then realises what she has said: in February I had the misfortune to be driving on the M25 when Mr Radisa Radovanovic, having just driven his truck up from Serbia, mistook me for a piece of tarmac. Being sent into the crash barriers at 70 mph hadn't done any favours to my back or left knee. Or my car for that matter.

Indeed, given the constant pain, I'd wondered whether I'd have to withdraw from the Challenge. Other things have had to go by the wayside. I was voluntarily doing up a Victorian pump house, on a hill beyond the village, but, given the ladder work, I have had to put that on hold. Fortunately on the TGO Challenge the pack has acted as a splint. I'm minded of Jenny Wheeler who did far worse to her back by lifting her cat. It's a strange world when fate takes a hand.

We set off in glorious weather to walk along Royal Deeside. Just a few wisps of cloud hang in a royal blue sky. It's a very pretty walk, though hot on the minor roads.

Just before the final stretch into Ballater we meet with Andy and Nik on an otherwise challenger-free day. We stand at the shrine at the Bridge of Muick built to the honour of Queen Victoria who once inspected a line of soldiers here. This was prior to them going off to be slaughtered in Africa. Well it actually said they laid down their lives for Queen and Country but I prefer to say it as it is.

Nik and Andy are in good form. Mary reconfirms with Nik that they are both walking with men whose humour hangs around the eight-year-old mark.

We set off and I say, "There might be a shrine to my jokes one day."

"There's another one that died," quips Mary.

At Ballater we follow the course of the disused railway towards Dinnet. We hope this will be easier but it's a bit tedious. Mary takes some of the weight back and soon feels ill again. I offer to take the weight back, she assures me she can manage.

We stay in another three-star hotel in Dinnet, changing rooms to get away from a noisy kitchen fan that's stopping Mary from resting.

Having a scalp riddled with eczema I step from the shower and announce, "I've just done something I haven't done since Christmas day."

"What's that?" asks Mary, her voice sounding concerned.

"Washed my hair with shampoo. I normally just rinse my hair with water."

On Tuesday May 22nd I wake and look at Mary's sunken eyes.

"How did you sleep?" I ask.

"Not at all."

We talk it through, we are just thirty-five miles from the coast. She is exhausted. I offer her a day off, offer her a 17km-walk to the next hotel. It's no good. I can see she is finished. I've done all I can with varying the route and taking more weight, I've no more options left to ease it for her and, to be frank, I'm starting to feel a level of criticism which is somewhat unfair. Having done my best, any further persuasion would be bordering on bullying.

I book her on a National Express coach from Aberdeen to London, give her the key to my house and my spare cash to cross London and buy a rail ticket. I then put her on the local bus to Aberdeen.

Setting off alone, I just want to finish now. I stop for lunch at the Potarch Hotel and from there I feel very alone, missing Mary.

I camp in a glorious wooded glade near Moss-side. Just wishing the time away now. I want to finish, am excited about completing my fourth Challenge but it feels different now. I used to walk the hills alone, now I seek more company. However, I manage to enjoy the meadow grass and Scots Pines. During the night I hear animals moving around, the morning brings close calls of deer and pheasant.

On Wednesday May 23rd I make an early start through Fetteresso Forest, close navigating and frustrated that my brand-new map is already out of date with forest operations. I also feel annoyed with an estate sign claiming they'll be shooting from May through to February. It's a ploy to distract walkers.

I make it through and at Mergie I pass the house of a former challenger, Lorraine. She invites me in for tea where I join Suus and Bert from Holland. It's welcome company and the three of us walk into Stonehaven with Bert suffering from a sore ankle he picked up on the second day. We make for the beach. I throw in my pebble, call Mary on my mobile and throw her pebble as we speak. She sounds tired and drained and bemoans the long coach trip.

On Thursday May 24th I spend a leisurely day before the end of Challenge meal. I find out Joan did make it. This is good news. I catch up with many other challengers milling about.

As I set off from my hotel to the meal I spy Polish Dan walking in. This time minus his stag's antlers and skull. I catch him up and find he has posted them home. He says he has run out of food for the last three days and was relieved to find spare food at a bothy. I make conversation and ask him what he does for work.

"I work in a factory making sure everything is in the right place for production control. Sort of stock control if you like."

"And you ran out of food?" I ask.

"Ironic isn't it," he adds.

On Friday I get the train home, Mary greets me at my house with a big smile, and she appears excited to see me.

On the Saturday we go shopping in Marlborough, she tries to tempt me into buying lots of expensive wooden garden furniture. Something holds me back.

On Sunday Mary wakes and announces she has the unused half of a return plane trip to Canada she can use today. She's hatched a plan to fly back, with empty suitcases, and collect more of her things, then get a cheap flight back.

Knowing how she is prone to changing her mind I warily drop her at Heathrow, she's full of smiles and reassurances as she kisses me goodbye.

I never see her again. I later read an online account of her walk across Scotland staying in tent and hostels. No mention of me, no mention of the three-star hotels and no mention she didn't actually make it across. I think I'm destined to be a solo walker.

I spend the next few months wondering what life's all about. To take my mind off things, I finish restoring the Victorian pump house I mentioned earlier then embark on a new project of writing a book called, *The Charlie Chaplin Walk.* On Saturday mornings I'd take the train into Lambeth and Kennington and walk the streets which Chaplin did as a waif in the 1890s. His father, having abandoned the family, and his mother mentally ill and absent, he often fended for himself. I researched the places of his childhood and how they influenced his films and adult life. I find a publisher and become a 'biographer of Chaplin's'. It was fun walking in his footsteps, piecing his childhood together. Another case of 'walking it through'.

July 2007 – Welsh Nuttalls

July 14th and I'm trying to find Bristol Airport. For an international airport it's proving remarkably shy. Many about turns and a process of elimination home me in. I arrive a few minutes before the arrival of Steve Hampton's flight from Rome. It's good to see him but I notice that like me he's recently lost a lot of hair. Alas mine to ageing, his to a barber. After negotiating the way out, signs pointing to dead ends, we set off for the Gower to camp.

Both starving we try various service stations. The first one is closed, the second has run out of everything vegetarian, and the third is a rare combination of being open and serving vegetarian. However, it's a slow service Burger King. It'll do yet there is some confusion between Steve's antipodean accent and Welsh.

"Do you have water?" asks Steve (a rare request in a Burger King).

"You want a whooper," she replies.

It takes some explaining.

We find a campsite and enter the office and explain we wish to camp for one night. The proprietor, a middle-aged man, looks us up and down.

"That'll be," there's a pause while he thinks about what he can get away with, "sixteen pounds for the night and a ten pound deposit for the car." Neither Steve nor I are awake enough to enquire why property belonging to ourselves merits a deposit.

"You've got your own toilet paper?" he asks. Steve and I give one another an incredulous look: this guy's taking the mick but making it sound as if he's doing us a favour.

"And it's twenty pence for the shower. You get ten minutes."

Next morning, after a rain-soaked night, I discover that indeed you do get ten minutes, four of which are waiting for the warm water to come through. What with the recent rains and flooding making the UK a less desirable holiday destination, we could only wish this chap a rapid business failure.

We go in search of breakfast, first trying an open café in Port Eynon. We pop our heads around the door.

"We're not open to eight thirty," says a woman dismissively. It's 08:20 and this woman is trying her charm. "And the oven's still heating up," she adds. "Might not be ready until nine." She's busies herself with tasks, not aided by an apparent hatred of customers. No offer to take a seat and wait. Why oh why do the UK tourist boards wonder why they suffer so?

In the end we find a post office store's open and eat hot pasties in my car whilst watching the rain stream down the windows. Welcome to Wales. We avoid paying £3.30 for the privilege of parking the car on some wasteland, then do a short walk.

After a late afternoon drive, following the west coast, we camp at a site just above the beautiful Beddgelert. The campsite office is closed so we find a pitch. In the morning we discover it does not open until 09:00. We decide to leave the tent and pay later; I'm itching to bag Yr Aran. At the car park I discover I've left my jacket in the tent so we return to collect it and pay the £14.70 per night. At least there are free showers and toilet paper.

We get walking at just before 11:00, following the easy mine paths, watching out for the literal pitfalls. The water glimmers and the mountains look down.

I'm having a bad day with my breathing and Steve has to frequently wait for me to catch up. Some mist and cloud greets us on the high ground but the final pull brings in some glorious views, arriving around 14:00.

After another night of heavy rain we pack the car up, park in Beddgelert, lunch and get ready for a night out in the hills. I'm wishing to string two walks together by climbing Moel Hebog today, wild camping then taking in the Nantlle Ridge tomorrow.

After the rain subsides we set off for Moel Hebog, a fine hill that overlooks Beddgelert. Though getting out of the village proves one of the hardest parts of the day. The map and the ground barely tie together and we find ourselves crossing the new Welsh Highland Railway and struggling through dense woodland. Ferns, brambles, ruts and trees all have to be negotiated. Our frustrations mount when we are blocked by a stone wall, crowned by a length of barbed wire. I attempt it first and, by managing to sit myself just the other side of the wire, I throw my titanium trekking poles to the ground and jump the five feet to the forest floor below. My over trousers catch and rip on the wall. I land on one of my trekking poles and exclaim 'Oh God'. It snaps in two bringing the total cost of negotiating the wall to £140.

"Are you okay?" I hear Steve asking.

"Broke my pole and ripped my trousers," I reply.

"Oh, thank God. All I heard was a nasty crack and you saying 'Oh God'. I thought you'd broken your leg."

"It's worse than that," I reply, "I've just trashed £140 of kit. If I'd broken my leg the NHS would have fixed it for free."

We pass some empty cottages, apprentice ruins, before making for the open hillside. I find the walk tough going yet Steve is happy to rest often. He magnanimously says that my frequent needs for rest allow him to take in the views in a way that he would not have done if he were alone.

It's a long pull to the summit to Moel hedgehog (as we've christened it), arriving around three hours after leaving the woods. Steve, in true fellow Kiwi Edmund Hillary style, says, "We knocked the bastard off."

From here we ascend Moel Yr Ogof and Moel Lefn. Really bumps in the ridge before the descent to find a pitch. This proves difficult as there is real steepness and we have to take it step by step with our heavy packs.

We camp around 19:30 on a shelf in the hills with running water. The weather has joined the idyllic scenery to set a peaceful evening of relaxing after a days walk. Only when we finish eating do the rains come in – ideal timing.

In the morning, breakfasted and tent taken down, Steve asks me to point out the route up the Nantlle Ridge. I detect some hesitation. As we get to the point where we could ascend it or cut back to the car, via Beddgelert Forest, Steve admits he'd like to give it a miss. With a long day ahead I'm glad he spoke up. Instead we walk out, navigating forestry tracks not always matching the map, and drive up to Caernarfon to look around.

We get a free night's camping at the Beddgelert site by unintentionally arriving after the site office shut and leaving before it opened in the morning.

The following day, July 19th, Steve surprises me by saying that he fancies the Nantlle Ridge: I'm in no mood to disagree – a fine day of weather, despite the week of rain, is forecast.

On the Nantlle Ridge

It's a steady pull up Y Garn where the beauty of the ridge, and its six 2000ft peaks, lay before us. Twists and turns, boulders and grass, slopes and sheer drops snake into the distance with views into the valleys below. There are views over to Yr Aran and the Moel Hebog ridge of the days before. Days like this are to be savoured.

The walk up Mynydd Drws-y-coed involves a rocky ascent, with some entertaining drops if one chose to wander off course. I find the rocky ascents helpful with my breathing as they force a pace better suited to my windpipe. Trum y Ddysgl is the next peak with a splendid walk between the two, sheer drops to one side, a col and steep pull to its summit. From here we take the twisting ridge, with one small scramble and sharp drop to negotiate before reaching the wall leading to the summit of Mynydd Tal-y-mignedd where the obelisk, in celebration of the diamond jubilee of Queen Victoria, towers over the valleys, making it an easily identifiable landmark.

It's a good descent and steep, boulder ridden, climb up Craig Cwm Silyn. Some mist blows in but, on the easy walk on to Garnedd-goch, it nicely picks out some of the hills for us. We are spared rain and get good views over to Caernarfon, its castle, the Menai Straights and Porthmadog.

Now at the furthest point, we descend into the south-east valley, steeply with much backtracking to find a route down. Eventually bum sliding to save a fall, the closeness to the ground causes my hay fever to come on. An overgrown gate means we have to negotiate a fence to reach the road. Steve get harangued by a farmer on a quad bike for not using the gate. He points out that the gate was covered in stinging nettles – which has the effect of ending the discussion.

From here I have to apologise to Steve for having promised him no further ascents. For we have to pick our way through a series of abandoned mine workings. It looks a grim place to have worked, far from home with poor conditions. Steve and I agree this would be the place to bring the one or two angry feminists we have encountered in our lifetimes.

Some map or navigational error means we lose ourselves near the Beddgelert Forest. The GPS confirms where I think we are but we've lost the path. We force our way through the commercial forest on a bearing, pick up the track again and walk out. My estimate of finishing around 17:00 is woefully inadequate as we finish at 20:20, having started at 08:40.

We quench our thirst in the pub at Rhyd Ddu. The landlord, having got wind of our long walk back, takes glee in pointing out a leaflet advertising a bus service back from the end of the ridge. We try, on a few occasions, to point out we've not heard of it, we've just completed the walk, but he's having none of it. The pleasure in pointing it out is all his. Even our comment that, if back earlier, we'd not have used his campsite cuts no mustard with him. After leaving him to his pleasure we put up our tent and are treated to an incredible sky at sundown.

Sundown from our campsite

Friday dawns wet, no chance for the hills. I've arranged to meet with my friend Sandra Davies in Llandudno and mention to Steve we have five hours to kill. Steve picks up on the emphasis – he sees it as an opportunity to explore the historic Conwy. I sit in the library reading a book on electronics.

August 2007 – Welsh Nuttalls

It's 05:50 on August 11th and I'm setting off. I make the M54 in two hours then reach Wales where the A roads are B roads and the B roads are C roads, yet get parked and walking at 09:50. In the twenty minutes of readying myself not one car passes, this is peak season in Wales.

It's a high start, around 500m; the weather is blue sky and cloud. The air is clear, the views are good. Behind me are the three tops for later in the day, or tomorrow – a ridge guarded at either end by Foel y Geifr and Foel Goch. But for now my ambitions are set on Pen y Boncyn Trefeilw, just off the Land Rover track of ascent. This Nuttall could almost be done in a car.

I make the summit in half an hour, crossing a fence from heather to grass field. The summit is one of a number of minor rises in the high ground, so I stand on them all to be sure I've bagged it. A panoramic vista greets me, Cadair Idris guarding the view of the coast with the hills unfolding into more mountainous terrain. For today I'd describe what's beneath my feet as hill not mountain. The slopes are gentle and suit me well. I set off and battle the heather, a trade for a steep slope. Heather, grass and commercial forest break the view of the terrain; cloud builds from the horizon greeting blue sky.

I make Stac Rhos in around half an hour and again have a game of guess the summit. Minor rises and bumps deter an outright contender so again I visit each to convince myself of my achievement.

I turn east, following a fence and pass a rare hillside feature: a ploughed field. It's then tough going through heather before I find a path slowly opens up to the summit of Cefn Gwyntog: my 125th Welsh 2000ft mountain.

It takes an hour and a quarter to the next, Cyrniau Nod, the highest of the day at 2188ft – bagged by returning to the Land Rover track, heading north-east then heading into the heather land once more where fence posts guide me to the summit.

The odd conifer tree sprouts up, an offspring of the nearby

plantation; a phenomenon not known to Scotland where the deer stunt any growth. And the only deer I've seen today is a young one that ran in front of my car just outside of Swindon. A fellow car driver, the deer and myself all swerved and managed to avoid one another.

The guidebook describes this area as looking and feeling a long way from anywhere. The hills are mere minor bumps in an expanse of moorland. I miss the 'mountains' yet am glad for an easy day on my breathing.

I head back to the track then carry straight on where it turns sharply left. Alone on the hill I quickly make Y Groes Fagl, a tall post marks its summit. In front of me is Foel Cwm-Sian LLwyd, an hour and a quarter walk – the longest stretch of the day. I decide to battle its heathery slopes and include it today. These mountains are nothing more than bumps in the ground on a high moor. I ponder whether they are rightly individuals or whether just part of a massif. Yet this classification of mountains draw me to Wales and I tick them off, greeting them as individuals.

A classic trig point, built from stone, adorns the final summit of the day. As I approach I spy a shape and wonder if there is company but, on further examination, I conclude it's a raven sat against the cairn. It flies off. There is no company today. The hills stretch out in all directions and I'm at my furthest point after six hours.

I start to make my way through the heather-clad slopes, back towards the Land Rover track, but am soon stopped by the curious spectacle of an infiltrator in the heather. It's a balloon with a card attached. As a boy I always hoped to be the finder of one of those balloons that are set off at fetes. At the age of forty-two my wish is granted. I read the card and determine it was launched a few days earlier (on the 8th) from Aberystwyth. It's a chance find and I use my GPS to record its location to within a few metres. I hope it's the winner.

After just over an hour, from the furthest summit, I'm back on the Land Rover track. I'm out of water and thirsty. A Land Rover passes, the only people I see on the hills today. I trudge back, rueing each incline but satisfying myself that they are not too steep.

I make it back to the car at 18:35, and set my stove to boil water for a pot noodle. Lack of gas pressure and gusty wind conspire to make it a slow boil. A man is hunting for a mobile signal to call the AA to rescue his broken-down car. I wonder about driving him to the phone box in the valley below. Yet I need to eat and direct him up the track to get a signal, promising myself that I'll be more altruistic if he should return with no signal. Alas he gets one, my water boils and I eat pot noodle.

I plan to camp but wish to not show my car as having been left too long. Therefore I turn it around then quickly realise I've parked it facing the same way again. I turn it properly again. I gather things for the night and set off into the moorland to camp. My dry feet sink into a bog, coming up smelling and dirty. I pitch and get into the tent moments before the rains set in. Visible from the road I feel a little nervous. I wake often in the night, uncomfortable on the uneven ground.

I wake properly at just after 06:00, eat peanut butter and jam sandwiches for breakfast, get the tent down and head back to my car. A change of pack contents has me setting forth for the trig point of Foel y Geifr. I'm soon in cloud and mist – I had vowed not to go up in such weather. The Munros required ascents in all weather, less ambition and an ageing body have conspired to cause me to take it easy. Yet I'm already cold and wet and not getting out of a nice warm car makes for an easier transition. In two hours I make the round trip of Foel y Geifr, Trum y Gwragedd and Foel Goch. My only companions being two birds perched on the fence that follows the ridge. They look at me, and I at them. We conclude I am the maddest.

Late August, and feeling cheated by a summer of constant rain, I check the forecast. It looks good for the bank holiday weekend and I plan a trip to Wales.

I set off on August 25th at 05:45 and make good time until I get to navigate the shores of Lake Vyrnwy. In perfect sunshine I turn up what I think to be the minor road to Bwlch y Groes. As I ascend the grass in the middle of the road spreads and the tarmac narrows until I'm driving on lawn. Finding a place to turn proves fun and by the time I hit the right road I'm driving through cloud. Parking up I start walking at around 10:45. I can see the Aran Ridge, for today or tomorrow but first I have a single mountain to be bagged with a day pack.

I have brassy ideas of doing the fourteen peaks of the Aran Mountains in two days with perhaps making a start on the Arenig mountains on Monday. A fence shows the way, from a very high starting point, for the half-hour brisk walk, in the warm sun, to Moel y Cerrig Duon. I survey the fine view down to the shimmering Lake Vyrnwy. On my way down I'm a little unsure about a junction in the fence that I cannot remember from my ascent. Fortunately a boot print, which lines up with the pattern of my own, puts me back on track.

Back at the car, after an hour round trip, I switch day pack for camping pack, have a brief chat with some holiday makers then make a noon departure for Llechwedd Du. I keep peaking at the folded map to judge my progress against my plans. Although my pace is good I soon realise that this will take two nights of camping, not one and I'm glad I've packed two days of food.

I make my way across the modest peat hags – terrain where one can easily get bogged down. Fortunately my footing remains firm and my pace good. I have the presence of mind to rest awhile, from the weight of the pack, and survey the glory. I make Llechwedd Du at 13:00.

Skipping the proliferation of peat hags, I follow the fence north, cross it and briefly, meet a fading streambed before the pull onto the slopes of Foel Rhudd (Red Bare Hill). I make the modest summit on a compass bearing yet the rising ground was the greater clue. From here I can see the Bala Valley and the Arenig hills.

A helpful fence takes me west then south to the unmarked peak of Esgeiriau Gwynion, or 'White Ridges' to the anglicised. Views are again superb, even my car glistens two miles away.

A steep descent and re-ascent catches my breathing out. A heavy pack, with 3Kg of water to be sparingly used, sun and asthma has me at a snail's pace on the 400ft of ascent from Bwlch Sirddyn. I make the summit of Foel Hafod-fynydd at 15:55, and look back to see the west face of Esgeiriau Gwynion sporting its white quartz from which it gets its name. Foel Hafod-fynydd has a couple of peaks to its summit, reminding me of the Python sketch with the double-sighted expedition leader wishing to build a bridge between the two summits. The valley to left has farm, spots of commercial forest and cultivated fields.

I drop to the lake, Creiglyn Dyfi where the rising wind makes waves and keeps the most tenacious midge grounded. Feeling dehydrated, having rationed and not peed all day, I finish the water I'm carrying, refill from the lake, use purification tablets to be safe and hesitate putting the tent up. I'm tired, it feels like a boring job and I procrastinate until I pitch alone, not having seen another soul since I left the car. Good rocks form a shelter for my stove; an east face guarantees the morning sun.

I wake around 05:00 but cannot get enthusiastic about leaving the warmth of my sleeping bag. It's over an hour before I poke my head out and see blue sky with mist wisping around the peaks. Some red sky reminds me of the old saying, "red sky in the morning shepherds warning". I slowly get prepared, heating breakfast in the shelter of the rocks, placed for this very purpose by another long-gone camper.

I set off at 07:10 taking the sharp incline towards Erw y Ddafad-ddu. It's a little easier than it appears and soon opens up as a broad ridge spur. Mist wisps over the col, exposing and covering the lake. Aran Fawddwy stands guard with its sheer, beautiful south face towering above.

I reach Erw y Ddafad-ddu in around an hour then twenty-five minutes later I'm at the far end of the Aran Ridge on Aran Benllyn. I take in the views of Lake Bala, Lake Vyrnwy and even my distant car.

Backtracking over Erw Ddafad-ddu I then take in the rocky ascent to the highest point, at 09:45 and a shade under 3000ft, of Aran Fawddwy. Here I see the first person since I started – a fell runner with his two Jack Russell dogs. With the sea to the west, and a stone-built trig point marking the summit, the scene is a real treat.

Mist over the col

I drop away and make a rough crossing to Gwaun y Llwyni, at 2250ft with its good views to the east. I then follow the fence to the 2038ft lump of Waun Camddwr, so much of the surroundings feel higher yet this point has a 50ft rise in all directions and consequently gets a name, and a place in the tables, of its own.

Now I'm struggling and my brassy expectations of finishing the fourteen today feel curtailed. I reckon on twelve instead, a high camp and the last two tomorrow.

It's a hard pull up the 2557ft high Glasgwm. An unusual cone-shaped cairn greets me just after 13:00. From here I survey the route out to Pen y Bryn-fforchog, following the fence then the forest edge. I haven't quite appreciated the amount of drop and re-ascent between the two. I reach it at 14:10 and, being the furthest point from the car today, I feel out of my comfort zone. Beyond is the sea and the mountains of Cadair Idris and the Rhinogs. I make it back towards Glasgwm. As I rest for chocolate a dog appears, followed by its owners. I descend steeply passing Waun Camddwr and, wondering if the true summit is the peak I stood on earlier, stand on its twin.

Aran Fawddwy

After a ten-hour day I camp by a water source, 350ft below the peak of Drysgol. Pen yr Allt Uchaf and Gwaun Lydan will have to wait for tomorrow. I face the tent entrance to the setting sun: with flap open I snooze in the cool breeze, stir and watch the sun sink ever further.

I wake around 05:00 having managed over eight hours sleep, stirring from time to time as my hips felt sore from the pressure on the ground. The thought of bank holiday traffic, and the M6 to be tackled later in the day, is enough to get me motivated. I winch myself out of my sleeping bag and get going at 06:45.

My pack is lighter today because I've used most of the water, just enough left for the day ahead. I ascend a lovely shoulder leading first to Drws Bach, and then the pull up Drysgol is manageable. A few sharp drops into the gulley of Hengwm have to be avoided. I look across to the connecting ridge to Pen yr Allt Uchaf and am reminded of the Fannichs in Scotland– a group of mountains carved with interconnecting ridges giving choice of route.

At Drws Bach I stop by the memorial to Mike Robert Aspin who was killed by lightning near this spot. I'm reminded of the walking press recently deriding mountain memorials. My conclusion is simple: memorials are appropriate near the spot of a mountain tragedy. If you die elsewhere your memorial belongs elsewhere.

This peak looks, to the eye, to be an individual mountain. Yet it does not have a 50ft rise in all directions whereas the 2038ft bump of yesterday, simply a rise in moorland, does. Sometimes I think you can't define a mountain on paper, it's how the eye perceives it and the vista from the summit that makes a mountain. To the north-west I see the lake where I camped the night before last; slowly I'm coming full circle.

From the summit of Drysgol I descend the faint path before the pull up Pen yr Allt Uchaf, crossing a fence to meet its summit. I then cut the best line to Gwaun Lydan, catching the ridge to its west then ascending. An indistinct summit yet offering a good panoramic view of much of what I have walked.

From here I walk east hoping to drop height at the end of the ridge. I soon spy a route off to the north, although steep I take it to stop having to chance an even steeper path off. I sit awhile and admire the chasm cut by the stream in Ceunant y Bridell. Steep sides constantly being eroded have opened a deep wide course.

Crossing the Llaethnant stream I pick up the path. I'd panned to ascend back over the second peak of yesterday, Llechwedd Du. It looks steep so instead I follow the path, losing height all of the time. I look to my right – the way off the end of the ridge would have been very steep: waterfalls on the map are a hint to keep away. At the road I realise my error. I've descended so far, to avoid the re-ascent of Llechwedd Du that I now have 1000ft of steep, hot road walking back to my car. It is long and tough, taking about an hour and a quarter. I arrive back at the car around noon. A five-hour day, completing the fourteen peaks of my three-day walk into the wilds.

November 2007 – English Nuttalls. Over The Hill Club

It's the night of Halloween and my email has gone ping. Big John's on the cyber line asking if I can lead this year's main AGM walk up Skiddaw, in the Lake District. I'm flattered to feel trusted so I say yes straightaway, then it hits me: I've never led a walk before. I've wandered into the hills around three hundred times yet never once been asked to lead.

Getting out my 1:50,000 map, I survey Big John's proposal: a non-tourist route taking in Ullock Pike, Long Side, its brother Carl Side then the scree slopes to Skiddaw, the most northerly of the English three-thousand-foot mountains. It then follows the fence down to Whitewater Dash (a waterfall), but my maps don't have a fence marked. Apparently the 1:25,000 series does. My eyes drift north and spy a peak called Cockup. It's all too probable so I email John to ask for some grid references of the fence from his 1:25,000. He replies that his map is 1:63,000. I thought they were older than the hills!

Not wishing to end up causing a mountain rescue, I drive to the Lake District a day early to practise the walk ahead of the Saturday. Arriving early evening in Keswick I seek out a modest hotel. The landlady shows me around and informs me breakfast is at eight thirty. As I fancy extending my Friday practice walk to take in Skiddaw Little Man, Lonscale Fell and Sale, I ask if an eight o'clock breakfast would be possible. Well I might have well accused her of being a lady of ill repute. I hold my ground, needing the early start and get my way while being left in no doubt why the British tourist industry is struggling.

At 09:00 on November 16th I set off negotiating the hardest navigational part of any walk – the bit between the car and open ground. It's where I normally get lost and lose the most time. At least, having found the route, I'll be able to instil an early confidence into my troupe for tomorrow.

I take in the staircase of climbs and straights on the way to Long

Side, making it in two hours. I enjoy the sun glinting on the many inlets of Bassenthwaite Lake, but perhaps not so the distant wind farm. Now I'm in the mist for the deviation to Carl Side then the long pull up Skiddaw and the walk along to its trig point. Here I get chatting with two older gents. One hands me a GPS, a gift from his son, "How do I use it?"

It's the request you dread. I know with my model it takes about seven button presses to see the OS grid reference. The designers, having never set foot in the hills, do not know that all you want is the grid reference. Track logs, waypoints, memories all have to be scrolled through until you find the nugget that everybody is looking for. His model is not my model and the qualification of being younger does not help me discover how to use it. I think we both end up feeling embarrassed.

I backtrack and head south, picking up a fence that neatly guides me to the summit of Little Man. On route I pass four women, none of which smile back or says hello. Even their Jack Russell growls at me. The wind is now quite strong, and I'm in danger of losing the map clenched in my fist; I wish I'd brought a map case.

Descending I pick up another fence line which acts as a handrail to the summit of Lonscale Fell. The mist briefly clears to offer a view for my efforts.

I descend to Jackson's Fold and break out into the late afternoon sun. The views to the north-east make the day worthwhile and I hope the later afternoon sun is not too late as I've quite a walk out. I make it to Sale How then descend to the remote Skiddaw House, the long Land Rover track out to the road and the walk in the dark back to my car.

Only Big John, David Handley and Dave Goddard accompany me on Saturday the 17th. I'm not sure if it's the poor weather or my quiet nature that turns people off.

Being blown along by the wind, and having to up my pace to stay in the lead, we reach the first summit twenty-five minutes earlier than yesterday. Other than taking in less hills, and it raining on the descent, it's very déjà vu.

Mountains looming in the darkness

Classification	My Total	Total
Welsh Nuttalls	144	189 (i)
English Nuttalls	30	253
Corbetts (Scotland)	4	219
Grahams (Scotland)	1	220
Unique Donalds (Scotland)	0	58
Munros (Scotland)	284	284
Ireland	0	212
Totals (16/11/2007):	463	1435

(i) Carnedd y Filiast North Top and Castell y Gwynt promoted and Cadair Bronwen NE Top was demoted

March 2008 – Welsh Nuttalls

It's Good Friday and I'm boarding the 06:31 train from my village with gusty ambitions to add the nine Rhinog mountains to my list of bagged peaks. The worst Easter weather forecast I've ever seen is of small concern; surviving the British railway system is my first challenge. My route involves changing trains at Reading and Birmingham then, via the Cambrian coast line, I'm due to alight at Tygwyn. I then plan, over the weekend, to walk across the mountains and, on Easter Monday at Talybont, submit myself again to the mercy of the railway system.

True to form the train is sixteen minutes late into Birmingham for a fifteen-minute connection. It's times like this that the hope gets you. The despair is easier – a two-hour wait for the next train and the short evening mean I'll not be able to walk as far as I want today. That I can deal with. Yet it's the small hope that the Pwllheli train is also delayed that has me, politely as possible in the circumstances, hurrying my way to the main station concourse to find the departure board.

My heart sinks when I find it has left so I make my way to the information counter and join the queue of other would-be travellers that have equally just had their journey ruined. A young lady pushes to the front of the queue, suddenly all around me are comrades in arms as we look at one another and frown. Mr Indignant kicks in and I go forward and explain, "There's a queue you know." Fortunately the counter lady has seen it all before and sends the girl packing to the back of the queue.

When it's my turn at the desk I announce, "My train was late for the 10:33, can you endorse my tickets for the 12:34?"

"No, it'll be okay."

"Can I have a seat reservation?"

"You're too late for a seat reservation."

I can feel Mr Indignant, who has already been aroused, starting to elbow out Mr Nice and Pleasant.

"I'm not late! It's the train that was late."

"I'm sorry, a reservation is not possible. There's bound to be seats available."

"Are you sure my tickets don't need endorsing?"

"Yes."

The strain is showing on both of us.

"There are lots of other people in the same situation as yourself going for that train. The guard will know."

"So if there's lots of other people in my situation how come there will be seats available?"

I get an ill-tempered look and depart to pace around the concourse, probably covering the same amount of ground as I'd have covered in the lost two hours on the hills. I'd planned to bag Moel Ysgyfarnogod and Foel Penolau then camp high. Now I'll only get as far as a thousand feet before the light defeats me. Not even a free cup of coffee is offered for my pains.

I find a corner to sit and read. At the last minute I'd packed a slim volume, Agatha Christie's *Dead Man's Folly*. I realise my mistake, it's dated and reminds me of the last time I'd read it in the mid-nineteen eighties. As an engineering student I had to do a year out in industry and, leaving behind the lights of Brighton, wound up in north London digs. My landlady, a Mrs Joy Rose, had clearly spent a lifetime bringing very little joy to anybody. Indeed Mr Rose had bailed out to the cemetery some seventeen years previously leaving Mrs Rose as a merciless, and embittered, landlady. I'd discovered the best defence was tucking myself away. Agatha Christie and Dick Francis became easy reading.

Rueing my choice I take consolation as the pages feel absorbing and may come in useful later on the trail. I had considered bringing Jon Krakauer's *Into the Wild* for its slim, lightweight qualities. Yet, with snow forecast, reading a book about a guy freezing to death does not feel the best of choices. I pace around some more and visit WH Smiths. No book takes my eye, not even the well-thumbed copy of the *Aston Villa 1980/81 Season*. Trust me, I'm not joking.

The time comes and I board the train, duly find a seat and, given that Tygwyn was not listed on the board, check with the guard that I am on the right train.

"This is the Cambrian coast train? I'm aiming for Tygwyn."

"I've never heard of Tygwyn," he says, "there's a stop called

Tywyn, they've probably printed a G by mistake."

"This is the Pwllheli train?" I ask in case mention of the Cambrian coast has flummoxed him.

"Yes, but it divides in two."

"Okay am I in the right section of the train for Pwllheli?" You really have to spell it out to these guys and I'm wondering if he is pre-Cambrian himself.

"Yes." With that I take comfort and after the train divides, and the guard is replaced I ask again.

"Yes, Tygwyn, that's right. Glad you told me as that's a request stop. I'll tell the driver."

I wish I were dead.

It's around 16:30 when we get to Tygwyn. I'm pleased to at last be walking and my annoyances and aggravations are left at the station. Alan Sloman, who I met for a day when he was doing his Lands End to John O'Groats walk, described me as the kind of person that lightens up any meeting. His words shocked me at the time; although welcome I felt them a little on the generous side. Then I realised Alan only ever meets me in the hills, the place where I can truly relax. He never meets me trying to get there on the British railway system!

To my right I see Harlech Castle basking in the low sun, to my left mountains gleam with snow. When the light starts to fade, and the wind picks up I camp by the small lake of Llyn Eiddew-mawr. I have to stand on bits of my tent as I erect it – until the pegs are in I can't risk it to the wind.

I sleep on and off, grabbing a couple of hours to be woken by the wind again. Waking fully around 06:30, I feel the cold. I unzip the inner tent to find the wind has unzipped the outer. It must have been flapping for hours.

I set off at 07:25, needing three pairs of gloves to keep warm. The ground is slippery, icicles claim every place they can, a dusting of snow marks my track. I reach Moel Ysgyfarnogod at 08:50 and then battle my way across to the well-fortified Foel Penolau. Rock battlements defend its twin summits. I have to scramble to ascend both, taking care on the ice-coated rocks. Two mountains quickly bagged which I literally started from sea level, a rare thing amongst the peaks. My celebrations are brief as the wind picks up and carries me towards a four-foot drop. I'm just deft enough to sidestep it into being a mere two-foot drop.

I descend via gorse, rock and heather-clad slopes towards the edge of the forest, east of Rhinog Fawr and Rhinog Fach. It's a long pull over and many a time I question my location. Eventually, on the horizon, I see a couple of self-seeded trees: a sign of an impending forest. I make its boundaries and struggle with the rough ground, dry stone walls, undulations, pitfalls and scrambling. I'd planned to climb Rhinog Fawr by its north face but the approach looked impenetrable. Rueing my lack of planning, I contemplate the long walk, via Llyn Du, to attempt its west flank. Two people pass me, having exited the forest, causing me to glance further at my map. I spy a network of forest tracks and paths that could bring me out between the two Rhinog mountains with a route up from Bwlch Drws Ardudwy. It requires close forest navigation and I begin the ascent of Rhinog Fawr. After no more than seventy metres up, my self-preservation alerts me to the risks. The wind is likely strong on higher ground, I am very tired and it is getting late in the day. Needing a water supply, I descend west looking for the stream marked on my map. Water gurgling under the ground teases me and I have to keep descending until it breaks through and I can fill my bottle and camp.

It's another rough night in the tent, listening to the radio and eating my daily luxury of a Cadbury Cream Egg followed by the frustrations of continually losing things. By now I've planned to skip Rhinog Fawr and Y Garn and instead walk out via the five remaining peaks. I get a text from Ali Ashton warning me of snow during the night.

When I wake it is raining but a calling card of snow has blown under the flysheet. The end of the tent is damp where snow has laid heavy and melted into a pool formed in the outer. I peer out and see the tops in swirling cloud with snow well below. I realise that the game is up. My Easter weekend relegated from nine summits to just two. Fitness, weather and lack of planning have conspired against me.

I set off for the hamlet of Llanbedr, spying a Youth Hostel marked on the map. The weather cheers up. The peaks are now possible. Yet the early decision to bail out can't be revoked and I make the long road walk out.

I pass a field with tents in it. I wonder about pitching up alongside then seeking out the farmer. It reminds me of the Famous Five with Julian and Dick always going off to find the farmer who was always only too grateful to allow some terribly nice middleclass children make use of his land.

The Youth Hostel is boarded up, a sad state of affairs. They are closing at an alarming rate.

I visit the station and, finding that there are no trains today, walk back to the village and find a room in The Victoria Inn. It's luxurious yet noisy, next to the boiler room and above the bar. I sleep on and off.

On Easter Monday I arrive at the deserted station, an hour early for my train. I get talking to two women, around my age up for the walking. They're heading north for a day's circuit, myself south and home.

On the train trip I forget the challenges of the weekend and realise that I should have been more ambitious. In my twenties I'd have thought nothing of ascending higher in those conditions. What happened to that young lad? Somewhere along the line I've lost some confidence. Or is it the enthusiasm of youth? I remember my mum coming home from work and finding me dismantling large parts of my Morris Mini.

"What are you doing?" she asked with alarm.

"The clutch suddenly failed."

"Have you changed one before?" she asked.

"No," and lifting the Haynes manual I added, "but it describes all about in here."

May 2008 – Welsh Nuttalls

For the first time in five years I'd failed to get on the annual cross-Scotland walk (the TGO Challenge). Having booked the time off work, in the hope that my name would advance up the waiting list, I sat resolutely in a position requiring an almighty set of coincidences, and possibly a murder enquiry, for sufficient numbers to vacate their places. It felt time to be proactive and time for a crack at finishing the Welsh 2000ft peaks: therefore I withdrew from the TGO Challenge reserve list and started to make plans for Wales.

With forty-two mountains remaining (two of which have just been added after some resurveying) I reckon I can do them in sixteen walks. I book a holiday cottage for two weeks, with a few days either side, to give me a good chance.

The advantage of Wales is that, with careful planning, the travelling day can also be a walking day. The nearest remaining mountain to my house, Foel Goch, has a start point that I reach in less than five hours, courtesy of my new in car toy, a 'Sat Nag'. Gone are the days where one is obliged to follow the main roads around. The minor roads are now championed as it threads me through the most direct route. In the village of Knockin I look out for a shop. No such luck, 'The Knockin Shop' would have made a good photo.

It does not take me long to get my kit on, the beating sun only requiring a T-shirt and cap above the waistline. Newborn lambs skip in the fields: like me they are enjoying their first day of summer.

Less endearing animals await my arrival at the Pendre Farm. Five collies and a drop kick sized terrier circle and yap at my feet. Like all farms the dogs bark but nobody appears but the sense of eyes upon you is unnerving. I climb two gates and make for the hills as the barking fades into the distance. I follow a hollow grassy lane, then a stream until I turn left and ascend the easterly flanks of Foel Goch. A cuckoo calls my progress. Some faint paths indicate not too many people have beaten me to it on this route. A warm wind, cairn, trig point, ancient marker stone and distant wind farm, await me at the summit. I get clear views out to the mountains of the north and north-west. A single cloud in the sky emphasises my luck with the weather. With a clear forecast for the weekend I'm determined to make use of every clear day. I'll rest when it rains.

Returning to my car I set off for Bala and the search for fuel and two nights' accommodation. A filling station catches my eye. But a newspaper board, on the forecourt, proclaiming Bala has the most expensive diesel in the country, flattens my enthusiasm.

I park then wander up and down in search of a place to stay. Pricey-looking places without a price list. Rundown places with detracting signs saying live music and drinking until 02:00. I eventually select The Ship with its Bed & Breakfast sign. I enter.

"How much for one night bed and breakfast?"

"We don't do bed and breakfast," replies the bar lady. I'm in no mood to take this further and exit. I find the Plas Coch Hotel has room and not too much of a surcharge for being single. The owners and staff are Welsh and I love hearing the language. Even the sink taps are in Welsh – perhaps in England we should have them in Polish to help the workers.

May 9th and I wake early and pass the time until breakfast. Always the downside for me is the wait for the hotel breakfast: it's why I've booked a holiday cottage for the next two weeks.

I have a big breakfast and plan a day to match in the hills: twelve miles, six peaks and 3300 feet of ascent to include the king of the area, Arenig Fawr.

I find my way round to the minor road from Bala, passing the Llyn Celyn, park under the buzzing electric pylons and set off shortly before 09:00. The cloud is low yet I sense it will clear later. I pass an old railway line, a quarry then pick up the run of an old fence onto the high ground. I'm very slow on the steep sections, of which this mountain has many.

It's misty so only when the wind picks up do I know I'm

approaching the exposed summit ridge. The final pull to the windless summit is a gentler incline, where, after just under two and a half hours, I reach a trig point and memorial stone to the eight American crew members of a Flying Fortress that crashed on the mountain in 1943.

I take a short descent and re-ascent to take in Arenig Fawr South Top, my 150th Welsh two-thousand-foot mountain. It's then a longer descent and short re-ascent to take in the cloud-free Arenig Fawr South Ridge Top. I then lose around 700ft of height as I drop down and prepare for the ascent of Moel Llyfnant. The summit is a series of rocky knolls and I rest at the highest and take in the views with Arenig Fawr still shy behind the clouds.

It's a drop of 1000ft to the low point before the final ascent of the day to Foel Boeth and Gallt Y Daren. These prove to be a hard-going, tussock-ridden climb. I continually have to circumnavigate knolls and debate whether to follow the stream or head straight towards the summit. In the end my poor navigation has me hitting Gallt Y Daren first which should have been on my return leg. I waste no time in striking out for Foel Boeth.

It's a long walk back to the car, taking two hours of steady descent. My right knee causes me to yelp and I stop to readjust my knee strapping. The outer one is a Velcro sports support, the inner a surgical knee sock. Peeling this back I'm surprised to find a mass of congealed blood. The desk in my hotel room had a sharp edge and I'd earlier knocked my leg against it. I'd forgotten the incident until now. I make repairs and enjoy the evening sun, following fence, stream then disused boggy railway line back to my car.

May 10th and as ever I wake early and await the hotel breakfast before my departure. Breakfast eaten, bill paid and I'm off to do Y Garn before taking possession of my holiday cottage for two weeks.

Walking at 09:25, I follow the track through the woods as described in the Nuttalls guide book, adjusting for changes in the years since it was written. Once on open ground I elect my own route.

I pass former gold mine workings with their eerie drops into the abyss, fortunately these are fenced. I sit and rest and experience one of the few perils a water bottle can throw at you – filled some 1000ft lower, where the air pressure is higher, when I undo it water explodes out all over me.

As I ascend, cloud hangs in the valley to my left. It's rough terrain, navigating walls, bogs and tussocks. On the pull to the summit of Y Garn I have to cross a final wall topped with a fence. I put my weight on the top it, it crumbles and I'm left using the fence to stop myself going with it. I hum the song "Like a dry stone cowboy" as I try and make some repairs. At the summit quite a crowd of people have formed. From eavesdropping it looks like some kind of singles event. A hopeful woman has come minus bra and her hot sweaty top does not leave too much to the imagination.

I descend with more walls to cross and bog to contend with. Finally I'm on a staircase arrangement of massive rocks as I pick my way down to the forest track. My right leg slips between a rock and the ground, dangling in air; no harm is done. Once in the forest I make good progress. Crossing a stile I put my left leg onto the leaves carpeting the floor. Unfortunately there's nothing below them other than a boggy sinkhole. My leg descends into a wet mass and jars against firm ground as it takes the full weight of my body. I wait for the crack and searing pain. But I'm lucky, just mild aching as my lower leg slurps its way to the surface. I get back to the car at 14:15, rather relieved.

I wake on May 11th to birds serenading the sunlight pouring through the bedroom window of my holiday cottage in Llan Ffestiniog. I decide to make today the biggest walk I have left – the six remaining Rhinog mountains. It's a surprisingly long drive around to the start and, from the luxury of my car, I recognise the road walking that I did at Easter.

At 07:25 I'm parked at the very end of the minor road leading from Llanbedr to Nantcol. A cloudless sky and warm sun welcome my first steps, heading for the skyline then the right turn onto the flanks of Rhinog Fawr. I ascend in the beautiful sun, disturbing mountain goats sleeping on the path. Climbing a wall to find the best attack point for the summit I play mathematical games over how long this walk will take. The final leg, of the two-and-a-half-hour climb, requires the ascent of a scree chute, then the flatter rocky summit with welcome trig point marker. The views are outstanding, just a distant haze hiding some of the mountains of Snowdonia.

I set off south for the steep descent into the pass between Rhinog Fawr and Rhinog Fach. It's tough going across scree, heather and rocky terrain. From my high vantage I can see where I camped at Easter and wonder if the sweltering sun of today will curtail my efforts as the snow and wind did then. My left knee is very sore after the jarring I gave it yesterday and I gingerly finish my descent.

The guidebook describes a very steep ascent of Rhinog Fach. I elect for a longer route, ascending to its west and taking a final sweep to its summit. I have a love-hate relationship with guidebooks – I wouldn't be here without them but on the other hand I grumble when they only give one option.

As I cross the ladder stile (this is an area of many walls) I spy another party heading towards the steeper route but, undeterred, I press on with my plan and find this steep enough. It feels like I walk for thirty seconds then rest for a minute. Continually I park myself down, timid to refresh myself with water as I've only brought two litres for the entire day. More would have been extra weight. Like at Easter I'm teased by the sounds of water passing underground, too shy to emerge and be drunk.

The wind picks up and I reach a level plateau that was likely once a tarn. Its northerly bank long breached, draining it forever. Looking back to Rhinog Fawr I see the long layers of rock at forty-five degrees, ancient activity having pushed up this mountain from the horizontal.

I push on up the final steep section before the easier walk to the summit. My right knee starts to jab and I remove all strapping, apply Deep Heat, swallow ibuprofen and re-strap my knees. At the summit I meet with the guys that I saw taking the steeper route. They beat me by just ten minutes. The wind is now stronger, the air cooler. At first I welcome this until I hear the sinister sound of thunder rumbling around.

I consider leaving the last four but elect to press on: if I did pull out it would cost a day to return and a lot more ascent to regain the ridge.

Making it to Y Llethr at 14:45, I move my waterproofs to the top of my pack for the imminent need. Welsh farmers are obsessed with building walls and I hug the ones following the ridge as the thunder and lightning crack overhead. The going is now much easier and I can retain a pace. I take in Crib-Y-Rhiw then Diffwys. Translated this means precipice and very aptly it is named too. Its eastern flank just falls away, fantastic views all round and a lovely stone-built trig point. About eight guys join me and proceed to add to the wind with their own variety, each attempting to out trump the other. One takes off his pack and places it on the ground, it starts to slip towards the precipice. He catches it in time.

I climb back over the wall and make for the final summit, Diffwys West Top. A late afternoon breeze keeps me company. From a distance it looks lower than some neighbours but the optical trick is soon revealed. Descending to the water of Llyn Bodlyn I then follow the track awhile before cutting up over the bealach and down to the road. It's then a mile walk back to my car, completing a twelve-hour day.

I'm glad I still have my tenacity. I could easily have pulled out earlier in the day; I feel that I was a bit of a wimp at Easter.

May 12th and, after my twelve-hour epic of yesterday, I decide to take the day off. Wishing to support a local business, I visit the Llan Ffestiniog store. Picking up a strategically-placed basket I enter and realise that locals do not to use baskets: the shop is narrow and short, the shelves sparse. It takes me fifteen minutes to find things to save the embarrassment of having walked around with a basket – two cans of soup and a Mars bar.

Having eaten lunch I decide to see if I can find the cottage we had for our last two family holidays. This was in 1981 then 1982, the cottage inherited by a work colleague of my mother's. I'd asked my parents of the location before setting out on this trip. They were a little unsure.

"Was it near Llandrillo?" I asked.

"Yes, I think you are right," replied Mum, "it did start with a double ell."

Dad and I gave one another a look that only a father and son could.

We plumped on Pennant on a minor road out of Llandrillo and this is where I aim for. Turning on to the minor road potholes, ruts and loose stone hinder my progress. It's not been resurfaced since I was last here. Half way down and I find that the local authority is of the same opinion as the road is closed. A sign says work started last week. How unlucky am I? My first visit back for twenty-six years and this is the time they've chosen to resurface it. The road reminds me of the holidays. The place was an eccentric time warp, two wooden army huts joined to form a T-shaped single-storey house. It had been furnished in the 1940s and had remained untouched. We found a tin of plum pudding in a cupboard dated 1948. But what has remained with me was a sadness: my mother's colleague's brother had been killed in 1940, at the age of sixteen, in the merchant navy – his ship sunk by the German Navy. His aura still touched the place – photos, possessions and citations. As I was sixteen, at an age when death felt more terrifying than taxes, I dwelt on it a lot.

On the good side the place had an old record player and a pile of 1960's singles. I even stripped the player down and cleaned every component to get a better sound. My family must have got fed up with my repeated playing of the 1962 hit, "Let's Dance" by Chris Montez and the Dusty Springfield hit "You don't have to say you love me…". The love of the music of this era has remained with me to this day and it always makes me think of that cottage.

On turning around, from my thwarted visit, I set north for an evening in Llandudno with Sandra, Alan and daughter Megan. Megan, just five years old, promptly draws my portrait. Every limb is out of proportion with head too big for the body. Yet the receding hairline she draws to perfection. Sandra and Alan produce maps and guidebooks which we spread out on the lounge floor. Sandra and I discuss routes. As I've been looking for help to do Tryfan and Crib Goch, Alan searches the internet for guides.

May 13th dawns with another beautiful day and with it comes an urge to get up on the mountains. It had been a tough call to take yesterday off but, even though the weather was beautiful, my body demanded rest.

I elect to do Tyrrau Mawr and Craig-y-llyn, in the Cadair Idris range. A track rises from 30m to 500m giving me an ascent rate of 250m an hour. I barely stop for rests, a warm wind keeps me cool and the gradient is fine for my breathing. The Rhinogs had not been helped by my inhaler running out. Armed with a new one, today's ascent is easier.

At the top of the track I virtually sidestep onto the ridge for the final 160m to the summit. Fantastic views of Cadair Idris, the town of Barmouth and my next peak, Craig-y-llyn await me. The sky is a rich blue, the wind is moderate and warm.

The drop down and re-ascent feels easy compared with the Rhinogs of Sunday. I walk to the end of the main ridge then drop to a track which, heading north-east, takes me to the track I ascended on. My left knee starts to give trouble so I add Deep Heat and tighten the bindings. Arriving back, in just over five hours, I am pleased with the quick round.

May 14th dawns and, having booked a guide for tomorrow, I decide to hang back on the temptation to do the big round of Cadair Idris and its neighbours. Instead I cast my gaze further south and plump on the Tarren hills.

At 07:50, and worried about my left knee, I gingerly take my first steps on a sharp road incline. It feels okay, I think just descending is the issue. When I had it un-strapped in the cottage it gave me pain but now it feels good enough.

I turn off the road and enter a forest, walking on paths and tracks. The sky is a perfect shade of blue, streams gurgle, light dances through the trees, birds chirp and the gentle smell of pine reminds me of my Canadian summers. I ascend and zig-zag, passing an old slate railway, until I reach a felled section of forest. I make a beeline for the ridge, it proves tough going with, what to the eye looked like a good route, soon turning into a stumbling ground of stumps and unwanted branches. At the ridge the wind is stronger and I pull on my fleece to make a more comfortable ascent of Tarrenhendre. I cross steep grassland then follow a fence to reach the stunning views. Mountains all around, the sea to the west, a faultless sky and a good view of the walk I did yesterday. A grand reward for all the effort.

View to Cadair Idris

I follow the fence and the line of the forest to head for Tarren Y Gesail. It's a fair old descent and I feel it in my left knee. I need to cross the forest to get to the open hill of the second peak. Following a path, marked on the OS map, I become concerned as the path dwindles while the density of commercial trees increases. It gets to the point of no return, no path and no sight of where I am. I plough through the trees, their sharp needles and branches attacking my face and neck. The only way of protecting my face is to put my back to it and reverse downhill out of a densely-planted forest. After ten minutes I emerge, like a cork out of a bottle, into the daylight feeling very angry. I'm scratched and uncomfortable and annoyed with the forestry people for planting over a marked path. If I had a box of swan vestas with me I'd have risked the ensuing enquiry. I strip to my waist and spend time picking pine needles from my clothing.

It's then a looped ascent, first following the line of the forest then an old fence for the long old slog to the summit. Many of the posts are rotten so my virtual handrail is intermittent. As I approach the summit a jet fighter passes, so close I can see the cockpit. I turn left onto the final ridge and across to the trig point. At 666m it's not the actual summit but I'm amused by the number of the beast. I make a short detour to pick up the true summit then return to the trig point for a rest. Here I drink in the fine views and survey the route I've taken.

Both Crib Goch and Tryfan fill me with fear. Guidebooks warn of exposure and scary sections and, having previously turned back from Crib Goch, I conclude that this is the time to pay for a guide. Finding a guide is a challenge. After a few emails, texts and leaving answer phone messages, Libby of Llanberis Guides calls me. She takes my needs in hand and arranges that I'll do Crib Goch with her, then the following day a colleague will guide me up Tryfan and the other three peaks that I need to get done.

It's May 15th and we meet at just after 09:00 in the layby on the Pass of Llanberis. A very fit woman, not an ounce of fat. I hope she'll slow to my pace. We are soon off and walking, taking the seldom-used route to Llyn Glas.

"Few walkers come this way as there are no paths marked, but as you can see it's easy going to start with," she says. I gaze up to the jagged ridge of Crib Goch, silhouetting the skyline. Her mention of, "It's easy going to start with" concerns me somewhat.

Libby and I chat away, finding the common ground. Spending around eight hours in somebody's company, where one is entrusting his life in the other, makes for an interesting dynamic. My mobile phone beeps, an incoming text.

"Was that you?" asks Libby.

"No it was my mobile," I reply.

She gets the humour and laughs. I turn my mobile off, I don't want it bleeping when I'm about to make a move with a vertical drop.

"You have got the rope in that pack haven't you?" I ask.

"Yes, Steve I have."

I feel bad for asking but it feels sort of important to me.

We reach Llyn Glas. A beautiful tarn, with an island, covered in vegetation that the sheep can't reach. The mountains tower on three sides and Libby points out the proposed route up the right flank to join the ridge at Bwlch Coch. This is a beautiful place with mountains hogging the pure blue skyline. We ascend well, Libby's pace just perfect for me to follow.

At Bwlch Coch it's a left turn onto the ridge and the reason I'm paying becomes obvious: not just to be shown the way but to also be talked through the handholds. Polished rocks show the good places to put hands and feet as we twist and turn across the rock. It's no place to have a slip; long drop offs and deep gullies.

People head towards us – the classic way of tackling the ridge, but Libby has listened to my need to only bag Crib Goch itself and feels this is the easiest way to the summit. It will then be my decision as to whether we complete the ridge or turn back.

A couple with a free roaming dog pass us. The dog 'Sam' needs a lot of encouragement to make progress. I do well, just nervous at one point where a large step is required with a simultaneous twist of the body to take in the handholds. Libby has to talk me through it, my nerves taking a beating as I make the move. I'm over but have caught my right hand on the sharp rock. A minor thing but like a paper cut it bleeds well.

Being no place to worry about first aid kits, I just rub the blood into my hand and allow a few drips to worry other walkers.

On the Crib Goch Ridge

We pass the 914m lower peak, then easily assail Crib Goch itself.

"You did well," says Libby, "you undersold yourself. You moved well on the rocks."

"Thanks," I reply, handing her my camera, "I really just brought you along to take some photos." She smiles and I add, "I couldn't have done it without you. I needed to be shown the route to the top. It'd have been too easy for me to have taken a wrong turn and this is no place for a wrong turn. And I needed to be talked through the moves."

She asks if I am up for the rest of the ridge. I am and we make good progress, I deal well with the exposure and we make the 921m endpoint in good time. I peer down and look at the way I attempted the ascent years ago. It's not surprising I turned back, too many options with only one good way, the preserve of those in the know.

I peer into the valley below, "I can see the cars," I say.

"If you look to the left you can see our route up and Llyn Glas."

"Oh yeah," I reply.

Crib Goch

We take the north ridge off and Libby points out a face about a kilometre ahead, the opposite side of the road.

"See those climbers?"

I peer at the face and make out three people ascending the vertical pitches.

"Yes," I reply.

"I was working on that yesterday. See the climber on the right, he's doing a route called Cemetery Gates and the guy, or girl, on the left is on a pitch called Cenotaph Corner."

I raise my eyebrows just as my left knee starts to play up. Something is moving around in it. I stop to adjust the strapping and we both bask in the sun and soak up the surroundings.

"How many days like this do you get a year?"

"Few. Very few. It's often cloudy and raining."

We hit the road. I'm able to repay Libby's tolerance and good company by inflating her flat rear tyre on her van and buying her a coffee in Llanberis.

Having read scare stories about Tryfan, and wishing to take no risks, Libby arranges a guide for me today. I meet Garry, a tall Geordie chap with a gentle manner, at Capel Curig. Garry, like Libby, has never previously met somebody doing the Welsh 2000ft mountains.

We head down the pass, in both vehicles, dropping mine off and continuing in his for the short drive to the start of the walk, taking Tryfan from a northerly approach. Like Libby we get on well, joking and ruing our political system. We then survey the sky, a blanket of grey cloud is making for a cool day.

Adam and Eve

We climb beyond Tryfan so we can approach the final stretch from its upper southerly flank. Although exposed, you'd have to be rather foolish to fall off, just one small section to navigate with a nasty drop.

Then the summit plateau with strewn boulders and the famous 'Adam and Eve': two vertical rocks, each about six feet high that form the summit. I watch a chap climb on to the highest one. I walk over to take a peek and see the drop off behind them. When he's off Garry gives me a leg up and I'm sat on the rocks I'd read about and feared.

Garry tells me of the record for running from the top of Tryfan to the tarmac of the road below. It's an unimaginable nine minutes and six seconds. One would simply be flying over the rough ground.

We eat, drink and descend. Garry, doing his paid guiding job, stays on the danger side of the one exposed section. I then proceed to take a tumble on an innocuous section and rather embarrassingly slide on scree tripping over my trekking pole and bending it into the bargain.

We ascend the steep scree slopes of Glyder Fach. A repeat mountain for me but I need to reach the newly-promoted top of Castell y Gwynt – Castle of the Wind. It is a rocky outcrop that requires a scramble to ascend. I sit atop and munch some more lunch while an ever hopeful seagull joins us. Giving up, it swoops off in hope of sustenance elsewhere. Garry points out the interesting lichens, some bright as a yellow highlighter. By the road they've all but died out – a victim of car fumes.

We press on for Y Foel Goch, the wind now giving icy blasts in complete contrast to the week just gone. We chat away and I ask him about his guiding. He gets all sorts of requests, always turning down ones involving children because of the overbearing child protection laws. We are of the same age; both did degrees at the same time. He tells me of a city university where he has to take 'freshmen' out into the hills – a social engineering attempt to get the youngsters to bond and bridge the gap between home and university.

"So many of them feign injury at the first sign of tough ground," says Garry.

"What's the most stupid?" I ask.

"One guy collapsed ahead of me in absolute agony, holding his groin," replies Garry. "I got to him and asked what had happened and he replied that he'd just touched his knob against an electric fence. I asked him why he'd done it and he replied because the guy next to him had told him to."

We both rue the quality of university intake and then I collapse laughing. Through my near tears I manage to say, "It's not his stupidity in doing it that's funny it's the fact he told you."

We talk further and discover we have walked together before. Though it's not surprising we could not remember one another as it was the two million strong anti-war march before the invasion of Iraq.

We pass over Gallt yr Ogof and the easy northerly drop, observing the goats grazing on the high ground. We continue to my car, which we then use to return to Garry's van.

May 17th, being the day of the FA Cup Final, I elect to do the straightforward round of Dduallt and Rhobell Fawr. I set out early and wind my car, through single-track roads, towards a suitable starting place. The cloud is low, the windscreen wipers on, I'm pleased for the early start. In the middle of nowhere I happen upon a traffic jam; a series of low-loader trucks containing rally cars – some event in the hills. There are marshals way ahead checking people, taking ages over each entrant as some paperwork is obviously being done. Tens of minutes drag by and I reach the head of the queue, window down I ask, "Is the road blocked, I'm going hill walking."

"Oh sugar," replies the female half of the pair of marshals.

"If the road is closed it'd have been decent to have signposted it from the main road," I say.

"The road isn't closed," replies the male half.

I compose myself, "Well it does look fairly closed to me."

"Where are you going?" she asks as the man wanders off. I point to the map and she tells me I can get through.

Driving on, I park at the end of the road below Cwm-hasgen. I don full waterproof kit, the fun of the last few days is over even though the forecast said it'd be clear today. My short-sleeve shirt now sits below fleece and Gore-Tex jacket. My cap, which protected me from the sun, replaced by one that protects me from the rain.

I set off, initially up a track, passing old farmhouses that are being allowed to fall down, just some minor repairs to the roofs would save them but they are destined to be ruins. Not wishing to expose my guidebook to the elements, I closely follow my annotated map. I keep to the track by crossing a bridge over the Afon Mawddach then re-cross it via stepping stones, to break for the slopes of Dduallt. It's then a long pull towards the top, through heather and wet ground with an old fence acting as a guide.

It's a miserable sightless summit where I eat and drink water. Then on a compass bearing I head for the forest, skirt round until I find an entrance. A row of trees has gone over simultaneously in the wind, the roots and the earth all still connecting the toppled row. I pick my way through, going off track into the forest's clutches to avoid fallen trees. When I emerge it's on to a track which I follow until a decaying wall leads the way to the summit of Rhobell Fawr. It's a higher mountain and I struggle to find a consistent pace across the rough terrain, sometimes having to scramble through rocky sections.

Four hours into the walk I tag the summit trig point and feel miserable in the rain as the icy wind clips the back of my neck. A wall runs near to the summit and the group of sheep, huddled in its shelter, stare across to me. I descend quickly to the track on the south side of the Afon Mawddach and to the car.

May 18th and I wake early, before 05:00. I feel so tired. I manage to snooze until my desire to do these mountains, coupled with good weather forecast, gets me out of bed, fed, packed and driving to the start of the Cadair Idris circuit of five 2000ft mountains.

Pulling up in the car park I read signs saying no camping and no starting fires, symbolised by the activity with a red line through it. Strangely, the symbol indicating smashing a car window and nipping off with the contents does not have a red line through it. Presumably a local by-law allows such activity.

At 07:50, with compass aligned, I swing round in the car park and point it directly at the sign for Cadair Idris. Perhaps I'm being too fastidious for this popular tourist route. I set off, climbing the well-made steps yet I feel tired. Dog tired. I ache through and through and rue not taking yesterday, which was wet, as a rest day. I rest often, press on often, sit down often, sip water often. Unable to shake it off I'm grateful for the advantage of a marked path. That is until I reach a fork, Cwm Cau to the left and Mynydd Moel to the right. It's just like driving through a British town. You are following the signs for a place then it dumps you at a junction with different signs you've no clue of. I revert to compass and follow the cwm signs and rest before the path branches to the high ground around to Craig Cym Amarch.

Cwm is Welsh for a valley and when Everest was being mapped they borrowed this Gaelic word, hence the Western Cwm on Everest.

Here, on more mediocre terrain, I get chatting to an older chap, who's doing the Cambrian Way which stretches from Cardiff in the south to Conwy in the north. It's good to connect with a likeminded sort and I hope when I'm his age I'm still able to venture into the hills. I press on up the long pull and experience the beauty of the Llyn Cau. Nestled in the horseshoe of the Cadair Idris Mountains it sparkles blue in the sun. I stand and admire, with the mountains like a group of men admiring a debutant.

My knees ache. I stop and rub in Deep Heat, tighten the strapping and take Ibuprofen. I reach Craig Cwm Amarch, rest and catch up with the Cambrian Way man. Then a drop down and ascent up much of Cadair Idris before branching north-west and out to do Cyfrwy. The views are stunning, out to sea in the west, Llyn y Cadair in a drop to the north and Cadair Idris itself to the north-east. To my south are Tyrrau and Craig-y-llyn that I climbed just five days ago.

I make Cyfrwy at around 11:20, good going given I feel so tired. Many people are now around, a change from the lonely hills I've been experiencing. The nice weather lifts me and I start to feel stronger. I find the pull up Cadair Idris easier. I meet the Cambrian Way man for the third time before resting at the white trig point of the summit. A shelter is perched a few feet below. I peer in, a large group of people, having taken residence, peer back.

Cadair Idris and Llyn Cau

An icy wind chills my neck as I make good pace, keeping to the right of the sheer cliff, towards Mynydd Moel. The route pans out ahead and I take the summit in, followed by the lesser peak of Gau Graig which I reach at 13:30. I keep looking back to the sweep and splendour of the mountains just completed then it's down to the road – a long way down. I pick a careful route which eventually has me out on the A road. Keeping to the right edge, most cars give me a wide berth. Raising a hand in acknowledgement to any car that breaks the centre line for me, I then flick a V sign at a car that comes way too close. Here I am, pushing forty-three and still flicking the V sign, I regret my behaviour. I'm glad when I reach the branch off onto the old road, if the driver comes back he will not be able to find me. I make the car at 15:35.

May 19th and, despite waking early, I find it hard to get out of bed. A deep fatigue keeps me under the quilt until it's countered by the urge to complete the Welsh two-thousand-foot mountains. By now I sense they are within reach to complete.

I drive south and play the game of 'hunt the start point' from the village of Aberllefenni. Things don't tie with the guidebook. I start by following the track, next to a field studies centre. This soon fades to the edge of a wood with no obvious path on. I cut down to a track to find it's the road I've parked on. I drive on a little further and pick a track marked on the OS map and make good progress, climbing steadily into the warming morning sun until a doubt causes me to check GPS. It places me on a trackless hillside to the east of where I want to be, yet I'm stood firmly on the track. With the guidebook, map and GPS disagreeing I'm left with the casting vote. I trust the GPS and take a bearing and head uphill through a field of bemused sheep. Making the skyline I stare ahead into the doom of an impassable forest and to my left a steep drop to the track where I should be. Losing hard-won height is a bitter pill to swallow, but I have no choice. I head down the steep slope, protecting my knees as I go, to the corner of the forest where it meets the track. I then follow the track via old slate workings, admiring the decaying buildings made of right-angled slate blocks. From here I could return to the suggestions of the guidebook, but this takes in forestry tracks that could have changed.

Climbing steeply along a south-west spur, I zig-zag to ease the gradient. Taking a few deep breaths, to alleviate my mind's worry over the drop, I look to the forest across the valley to my left. Above it are the final two peaks of the day and I keep an eye on the tracks through the trees, working backwards plotting my route out as it unfolds parallel to my current ascent.

It takes an age to make the ridge but when I do the gradient eases and I follow a fence across a couple of minor tops until I reach Craig Portas – a steep drop off. A little nerve is required to follow the narrow access way to the flanks of Maesglase and its fairly featureless top. I return to Craig Portas and follow the north-west connecting ground for the long pull up to Cribin Fawr. Free of the steeper drops, my heart rate settles and I arrive at its tussock riddled summit with no obvious conclusion as to which is the true high point. I circle, visiting each bump until I'm certain the mountain has been claimed. I feel a spot of rain in the air as I survey my route up.

It's a quick descent then a sharp incline, following a fence, to make the attractive trig point of Waun-oer – six hours into my day. I can see my route of yesterday with the final ridge drop off and return to the road. I sit awhile and look around. A chill has me reaching for my fleece as sadness descends. I realise that in any gain there comes a loss. I doubt I'll ever sit here again, doubt I'll ever experience this mountain or precise view again. In doing these mountains one gains so much, yet part of life passes by in the conquering of each. This sadness stays with me as I drop back to the low point, between Cribin Fawr and Waun-oer, and descend a slate streambed, picking up the forestry track for the two-hour walk out. New trees give a wide view then mature pine hides all but the blue sky and the sadness stays with me, I sense a goodbye happening. I've enjoyed Wales but my two-thousand-foot mountains are fast running out, as is my reason for coming. It feels like the departure at the end of a wedding reception where people who seldom see one another, or have just become acquainted, make never to be upheld promises to call by "if they are ever passing." Everyone knows the words are hollow yet necessary to soften the sadness of the goodbye.

May 20th and, having cricked my neck while rolling over in bed, I plan this as a semi-rest day with just the interruption of the newly-promoted peak of Carnedd y Filiast North Top. Having previously done the circuit including Carnedd y Filiast itself I spy a route from a high parking place on the minor roads to the north of Llanberis. It's so easy, following a long track and a path with a kind gradient, that I'm up and down in two hours. It feels a little like taking the low hurdle yet this newly-promoted peak, after a resurveying of its ascent and re-ascent, could have been taken in on a previous walk if its status had been known about.

I'm due to meet with Sandra again in Llandudno. I'm early off the hills so retire to Llanberis to buy a postcard and a coffee. Queuing behind an old lady, of at least eighty, she turns to me and starts to speak. After a second or so she says, "Oh, I'm sorry I thought you were my husband."

I cannot resist, "Madam," I reply, "either you have a very young husband or you have just insulted me."

I drive over to Sandra's and we go out for lunch. I'm introduced to a new concept of collecting a child from school. For Megan, Sandra and Alan's five-year-old daughter, Mummy's friend coming along to collect her is an adventure. For me I'm trying to blend in and not cause any 'questions to be asked'. "Don't worry, Steve," says Sandra, "I feel odd too, I'm older than some of these children's grandmothers."

We have a nice evening, the company is good. Living on my own, working on my own, holidaying on my own and walking in the mountains on my own has its freedoms but also its costs. I leave wondering about my future, whether I'm missing out on not having a family life of my own. But a series of bad choices have left me more settled in a life of solitude.

May 21st and I wake very early, make sandwiches and head north beyond Betws-y-Coed to take the minor road to the Llyn Cowlyd reservoir. This is a steep minor road, where my fuel gauge alarmingly drops back as the diesel tilts in the tank, the road disappears as the angle of my bonnet hides the immediate tarmac and the pong of the clutch has me wondering what permanent damage is being done. The narrow road twists and turns, sharp bends on unbelievable cambers and gradients rarely gets me out of first gear.

I park at the very end of the road; I can see the dam of the reservoir to my left with a distinctly unattractive riveted steel pipe heading from it to feed unknown taps in faraway anonymous households.

I'm walking at 07:25, my earliest start of this trip. A short track takes me to the dam and then a long pull up Creigiau Gleision North Top. I hope to meet the fence that plots the way to the summit but, after squelching through marshy ground, do not pick it up until I'm only 100m from the summit.

The backs of my leg have pulled tight between the ankle and the calf muscles. I use Deep Heat to free them. I make the first summit at 08:50 and admire the spreading surroundings. The horseshoe walk around the reservoir is before me, further Tryfan, with its rigid back, introduces The Glyders with Snowdon behind. I press on over the broad heather ridge to Creigiau Gleision and, with some minor scrambling, Craiglwyn beyond. It's then a sharp drop to the west end of the reservoir before the slog up Pen Llithrig-y-wrach. My altimeter, counting me down to an 11:30 arrival, keeps me company before a cold wind greets me at the top.

I take the long, parallel to the reservoir, north-east ridge until I spy the road I drove in on. Turning right, and crossing rough ground, I hit the track back to the car where, after my five and a half hours in the hills, the smell of the brakes replaces the smell of the clutch.

I wake on the 22nd, the forecast of rain has not yet hit but I don't sense the need to get going for my penultimate day in the hills. Even with a late start, I'm walking at 08:15. An initial short stretch on the road then a pull up through trees and I follow a useful track to reach the flanks of Carnedd y Filiast. This is to be the second of the day – it's easier to initially bypass, walk out to Waun Garnedd-y-Filiast then follow the fence line to the first summit.

As I pass the flanks I see a rare thing – another walker. Initially I think there are two but then realise his companion is no more than a slab of slate marking the summit. He is descending my way so I wait for a chat. Not only is he another walker in the hills, all but extinct save for the popular routes, he's also here finishing off his Welsh 2000ft peaks. Just fifteen for him to do he's bagging Waun Garnedd-y-Filiast, which he'd previously missed, having been promoted between the first and second editions of the Nuttall's guidebook. The third edition is not yet out but will surely include the two extra that I've had to do. It's a great chat, Kevin Guest is an interesting chap and very pleased to know I'm on my penultimate day.

Setting off alone, unlikely to see another soul all day, I take in Waun Garnedd-y-Filiast, Carnedd y Filiast then Carnedd Llechwedd-llyfn. Here, I branch out a little as another peak looks higher. By my altimeter it's two metres lower but to the eye appears higher. I head back towards the fence then survey Arenig Fach in the distance. It looks a long way off and massive. At only a few metres higher than where I'm standing it's hard to accept that some visual deception is taking place.

I drop down, following the fence, crossing the stream then taking the hard heather-clad slog of the flanks of this mountain. I curse the route. It's not the best, the heather is draining on my energy and I don't know where I'm placing each foot as it drops out of sight. A rock is an island to aim for, a place of sanctuary for a moment's rest. As the gradient increases my annoyance and discomfort grow. I find a fence – a much-needed handrail. It soon gives up and I'm again alone working my way to the summit where I'm rewarded by a cairn, a shelter and the rain.

It's taken over three hours from the last peak, a long slog but I'm blessed that it was not through wet heather. I descend more heather-clad slopes to the road and a long walk to the car to complete the seven-and-a-half-hour round. I think the guidebook authors were keen to make this a circular route – Arenig Fach needed to be approached by any angle but this.

I wake early on May 23rd and it feels like I'm going on a date. My last Welsh 2000ft mountain deserves this treatment. I shower, shave, don my best and clean walking kit and, after the drive over, I'm walking at 07:15. Few dates start this early. Good ones end this early!

Climbing the forestry track, from Rhyd-Ddu, it fades to a path, then a sharp incline to a ladder stile. Open ground includes a sharp incline up the nose to the east of Craig y Bera. Steep enough for the path to be a series of earth-carved steps as hillwalker after hillwalker has placed boot on the very same spots. Though this is my first foray into the hills without boots – I'm trying out some new Meindl hill shoes. They are like trainers but with a stiff sole and waterproof upper. Not wishing to risk tried and tested technology until my last hill, I'm wondering whether I'm going to fully get to grips with the lightweight revolution.

I continue on the steep ground until the large rising curve, swinging out to the left, draws my eye to the summit: Mynydd Mawr. The wind rises too and it's a chill walk around to the top. A hundred feet short of the summit I stop and look around. Snowdon stands proudly, shafts of sun rays pouring through the cloud lighting up the undulations of the distant ridges. The Nantlle Ridge, bagged last year, to the south. I get my camera out, capture the scene then switch to video. Speaking into it I record my last few steps. I'm alone, I decided it to be this way. I'd thought about a summit party, as I did for the Munros, but recently a friend pointed out to me that I tend to focus too much on outcomes and that I don't enjoy the passage – one of those passing comments that got me thinking of my own life path and passage. If I'd organised a party I'd have been focussing too much on the outcome and, likely, trying the impossible of keeping everybody happy. Alone feels best or perhaps to celebrate with a sheep! I remember all those day trips to South Wales and weekend trips to North Wales. Lonely times on the motorway, nights in tents. It's been worth it.

This is a double celebration: not only is this my 190th and final Welsh 2000ft mountain, I reckon it's also my 500th British mountain. I chatter this into the microphone as I reach the summit and celebrate at just after 09:00.

I sit awhile, admire the surrounds then send a text to family and friends: "Hi All, I'm sat on top of Mynydd Mawr my 190th and final 2000ft Welsh mountain. It is also, by chance, my 500th British mountain. It is a bit cold and windy but a good view of everything and even Snowdon has its head out of the clouds. Cheers, Steve."

Jerry Webb calls and we have a good chat as he congratulates me.
Jane Brown: Well done. Enjoy the moment. Have a glass of sparkling mineral water on us! Jane X and Yv.

Liz Barker: Must b magical! What a gr8 feeling it must b.
MA Harper. Well done!
Mum. Well done glad ok and on top of world.
Amanda Seymour. Very jealous – well done!
Sue Oxley: Well done Steve! What next?
Ali Ogden: Well done. u r barking mad of course! It would b terribly boring to be sane though
Andy Glover: Steve, Congratulations on your achievement! Cheers Andy
Alan Sloman: Well done sir!
Kate Wilson: Congrats. What will you do next?
Kate Mackenzie: Well done you! I'm full of admiration.
Nick Green: Wo that's where you have been then!
Garry (the Tryfan guide): Nice one Steve.
Rona Waldon: Steve, that's fantastic. Love Rona.
Glynn Seymour: Yeah, well I got donuts, :-P

November 2008 – Welsh & English Nuttalls. Over The Hill Club

On September 19th I was sat at home watching Hitchcock's *The Wrong Man.* A text from Ali Ogden arrived: "Oh no another Welsh 2000fter". I press pause and amble to my computer. She is right, Mynydd Graig Goch, previously 1988ft after more than 7,000 readings, has been resurveyed at 2,000ft and six inches. If only they could have done it when the tide was in! I read the news report online:

At 1,988ft, Mynydd Graig Goch in Snowdonia was always classed as a hill because it fell just two feet short of the requisite height for a mountain.

Three Welsh volunteers decided to challenge the status quo and, using state-of-the-art satellite equipment to carry out more than 7,000 readings, concluded that its actual height was 2,000ft and six inches.

And of course my old adversary Myrddyn Phillips was part of

the resurveying party.

Classification	My Total	Total
Welsh Nuttalls	189	190
English Nuttalls	30	253
Corbetts (Scotland)	4	219
Grahams (Scotland)	1	220
Unique Donalds (Scotland)	0	58
Munros (Scotland)	284	284
Ireland	0	212
Totals (19/09/2008):	508	1436

Then an email from Big John had me scrabbling for books and maps – The Over The Hill Club AGM weekend big walk is 'Glaramara'. I wonder if this is some foreign adventure, I'm used to the comfort of anglicised Lakeland names. But no, there it is amongst the pronounceable in my Nuttall's guide to the English 2000ft mountains. A route taking in eleven mountain summits with Glaramara sat between Looking Steads (Lookout Place) and Combe Head (Valley Summit). Glaramara translates to 'Hill with the Mountain Hut by a Chasm'. Well pardon me for not guessing that one; I can only assume that this contraction came at a time when the use of spoken words had some form of taxation levy. And believe me, any computer programmer worth their salt would be proud of writing a compression algorithm that got 'Hill with the Mountain Hut by a Chasm' down to 'Glaramara'.

So I plan to combine bagging Mynydd Graig Goch in Snowdonia on the same weekend as the Glaramara round in the Lake District.

It's Thursday November 13th, the day before The Over The Hill Club AGM in Derwentwater and I'm headed to Caernarfon. I find a B&B and negotiate a 07:30 breakfast. I then visit Sandra, Alan and Megan for an evening meal.

The following day, I set off from the hotel, park near a transmitter and am walking at a shade before 08:50. I need this fairly early start as North Wales to Derwentwater is still a fair drive.

I buy more time by wearing my lightweight walking shoes instead of traditional heavy boots. The hype in TGO magazine has at least got me to give it a go, I intend to wear them for all the walking of the weekend to see if they'd be up to next May's TGO Challenge.

I plod on, feeling the effects of a bad sleep – a chap in an adjoining room, separated by a paper-thin wall, had his TV on loud and made mobile calls until the early hours.

My car soon becomes a distant object and I am pleased the walk is straightforward with the only obstacle being a wall to climb over on the final summit approach to Mynydd Graig Goch. I celebrate at the summit with an apple – after all I have just finished the Welsh 2000ft summits for the second time.

I'm in cloud so I have no view to enjoy; the weather is warm, balmy for this time of year. I check the GPS. It confirms a shade over 2000ft.

My outer garment, a black fleece, has turned grey under a fine layer of mist. I wipe my sleeve and grey turns to black like the scene in *The Good The Bad And The Ugly* where a line of dust covered Union soldiers are mistaken for Confederates.

I send just a couple of texts, to family and friends, to share the formality of finishing the Nuttalls again. Descending I reach my car at 11:00 for the trip to the Lake District.

My arrival at Derwentwater is rewarded by the warm welcome of other members and the YHA staff. Sheet sleeping bags have now become fitted sheets and duvet covers. At last they realise the regulation way of fitting a sheet sleeping bag is never adopted and body against duvet has been a tradition since they replaced blankets.

Another change is the introduction of personal alcohol restrictions, which appears to have reduced the numbers of club members making this weekend meet. Although I don't drink (for a medical reason) I do miss Waggy's well-organised barrels of beer. Club members now complain of the hostel prices starting from £2.75 for a bottle of beer. As ever, the OTHC members are up to the challenge and like a sixth form field trip beer, wine and whisky is smuggled in, hidden in packs, under jackets or secreted in large pockets. YHA soon becomes an acronym for Your Hidden Alcohol.

It's 09:00 on Saturday November 15th and the intrepid high-level walkers are gathered outside the hostel, admiring the lake and high cloud; a good sign for the day ahead. In any organisation there's an unwritten rule that the chairman should have the most expensive car. The OTHC is no exception as our eyes are cast to Graham Gledhill's five series BMW, unoccupied with the engine left running to warm it up for the short journey to Seathwaite. When Graham appears there is no mercy from his flock of members.

David and Ross offer me a lift, seconds later Big John chips in an offer and I explain I am already sorted. Fortunately I'm used to John's humour as an uninitiated man, straying within a hundred yards, could be killed by the scowl.

At Seathwaite we pile out of assorted cars. Graham arrives, the only occupant of the BMW. He tries to plead that nobody took up his offer of a lift, but we are not having it. We take the unwritten rule that, in the absence of any legal representation, we'll believe what we want to believe and the kangaroo court found him unanimously guilty of the root cause of the planet's greenhouse gas problems.

We set off and, with my lightweight walking shoes, I manage to keep near the front of a sizeable group of OTHC members tackling this round. I've already explained to John that I wish to deviate from his route to take in Seathwaite Fell and Seathwaite Fell South Top. However, I'm in two minds as it looks quite away over these two summits and I wonder if I'd be able to meet the rest of the group at Sprinkling Tarn after they'd followed the path around Styhead Tarn. John and I peer up towards

Aaron Crags and spot a number of routes. I like the look of the third and John tells me to go for it. I climb quickly and steeply, it's true that normal walking boots do weigh you down. Though the gradient gets steeper and I soon have to rest. It takes around half an hour to reach the 601m Wainwright summit, short of the elusive 2000ft marker that claims my interest. But I can see Wainwright's point of view; from here is beautiful. The cloud shadowing the reds, greys and green of the hills before me with the sun spotlighting areas as the clouds swish with the winds. There's a simple purity about the Lake District.

I carry on and bag every high point, using my GPS to confirm which are Seathwaite Fell and Seathwaite Fell South Top. I realise that there is only a very short drop to Sprinkling Tarn, which means the rest of the party would have to ascend, over a longer distance, the same height as I'd just done. Wondering if I am ahead or behind the group, I decide to press on to find a good viewpoint where I can check the path both forward and astern. As I take the path through the shallows of the tarn, fish break the water and dart away from my approach. In 2006 some 130,000 Vendace eggs were taken from Derwentwater to Sprinkling Tarn to establish a new habitat for this endangered breed of fish that date back to the ice age.

I press on and the good path soon takes me to the crossroads where a north-east branch leads to Allen Crags. I planned to wait here but it's so cold and I'm not yet convinced that I'm ahead of the rest of the group. Instead, I press on and make the summit where I can see the path to Glaramara, absent of a large party of walkers. I duck down to gain shelter from a biting cold wind. I don jacket, scarf and gloves and comfortably settle in the lee of the summit for the rest of the party.

Half asleep I'm brought back to reality by Big John peering around my hood to check it is me: I'd gotten twenty-five minutes ahead. He pretends he doesn't care about my whereabouts, nor that of the rest of the group but I often observe him keeping an eye out for his charges.

We all settle for lunch, having already eaten much of mine I just enjoy the views. I remark on the cute-looking black-faced, brown-coated sheep. I get some strange looks and sense some rapid shifting of immediate neighbours.

In all groups there comes a mutual sense of when it's time to press on. One or two packs are being fastened which spreads amongst the group until, without a word being uttered, we are all standing and ready to take the challenges of the cold wind.

For the rest of the group the next summit is Glaramara, but for me there are the summits of High House Tarn Top, Red Beck Top and Looking Steads to collect en route. I gain some humour from the others as I dart off again.

These mountains are mere bumps, off the main track but for anybody hooked on doing the English 2000ft Mountains they are important deviations. In my view these should be referred to as the 2000ft mountain summits, not each a mountain in its own right.

One has a bit of scrambling to reach the top. On the descent I slip and ungraciously land heavily on my bottom, sliding a few feet. Fortunately the group are a distance away and my embarrassment is spared.

At Glaramara there is an amicable split in the group with half wishing for a quick return to Seathwaite and the rest, including Big John, wanting to make use of the good weather to take in Rosthwaite Fell. I'm delighted as Rosthwaite Fell will be another bag with three additional summits in between I can take in.

So off I set again, darting off up Combe Head, then following the crags to the leftmost of the two rocky and grassy knolls: Combe Door Top. I catch the group before bagging Dovenest Top and catch them again at the pass to the right of Rosthwaite Fell. I branch up it and am initially presented with what appears to be an unscalable group of rocks that form the summit. Traversing around, I find a point where I can, with a few easy rock-climbing moves, scramble to its summit.

I must have lost time here as I'm now a long way behind the group. I make a pace and slowly reel them in on the lower slopes. It's dusk as we return to the cars and a welcome return to the hostel where a shower and the annual dinner are very welcome.

So how did the lightweight walking shoes serve me? On the descent from my walk in Wales yesterday, I caught my left ankle on a rock and cut it. This would not have happened with full height boots; otherwise I did not miss the ankle support. I noticed my toes moved around more, which meant by the end of Saturday I was developing hot spots that would have eventually blistered. Though I am susceptible to blisters and covering the hot spots with plasters would have stopped them getting worse. On the plus side I was much quicker and the ascents much easier. In traditional boots I'd not have been able to do all the peaks in the Glaramara round and kept up with the group.

December 2008 – The Footsteps of a Forefather

It's just before 07:00 on Boxing Day 2008 and I'm parked on the edge of The Green in Urchfont (a village on the north of Salisbury Plain), waiting for a lift. Dad pulls up and I switch cars.

"Which house was it?" I ask, peering out of the passenger window. Though I once knew the cottages well they were sold from the family in the early nineteen eighties. I'm struggling to remember which pair my great grandfather bought in the early nineteen twenties and then which house he occupied with his family. Dad points it out and I make the mental note for this to be the exact finishing place of my walk.

Dad's car eats up the miles as we travel the forty-five minutes to the village of Whiteparish, between Salisbury and Southampton. Darkness slides into the pale light of dawn, and a cloudless sky becomes full of promise for the day ahead. However, I get a sense of foreboding for the challenge ahead: every mile Dad drives is a mile I'll have to walk back.

I direct Dad to pull up outside the shop and post office in Whiteparish. We step out into the cold. I don't know how Dad feels but it feels a bit weird for me. This is the spot that for years has been in the folklore of our family.

"Fancy walking the first bit with me?" I ask.

"Yes, alright."

Both wrapped up against the chill of the dawn air, we set off at 07:45, from the very same spot Peter Andrew Smith, my grandfather and Dad's father, did on Boxing Day, 1938 – seventy years ago to the day. Having not got leave from the navy until the morning he'd set out, in his Standard Nine car, from Gosport and at Warren Farm, some three miles to our east, he'd come off the road as he met a formidable snow storm that had swept down from the north overnight. He called at the farm but even with the help of the farmer the car remained steadfast in the ditch. He recovered a pair of navy-issue boots and a small attaché case then the farmer and his wife gave him a lift to Whiteparish in their gig. From here nothing was moving and, with the attaché case tied about his neck, he set off on a thirty-three-mile epic walk to get to the church on time: at 11:00 the following morning he was due to marry my grandmother.

I'm unable to precisely follow the route, though I have it pencilled on my map in Gramp's own hand. He had followed snow-covered roads whereas for reasons of safety, comfort and enjoyment I intend to deviate up paths and bridleways. The first being north-west from Whiteparish up a rising track, carved out from years of use. At the highpoint Dad and I say goodbye, with a polite handshake and then a more demonstrative hug. I relieve him of his scarf as there is a bitter chill in the air and my neck tube doesn't cover my face. The walk had been touch and go and only yesterday, after recovering from a cold, I finally made up my mind.

Soon the muddy incline becomes a gentle grassy track through moor-like grassland, then drops down towards the minor road leading to West Grimstead. To my right, the east, the deep glow of the sunrise reminds me of the early hour.

At the road I have to re-strap my left knee, after adding Deep Heat and taking an Ibuprofen. I don a fluorescent bib and head towards West Grimstead, crossing the near silent A36 before regaining Gramp's route through Whaddon and Alderbury. By now the spectacular blue sky is in full winter glow. The occasional garage door opens, a front door squeaks on its hinges and a car starts as the country yawns and stretches its way into Boxing Day.

I meet the A36 just south-east of Salisbury and follow the pavement, past Petersfinger, into the city. Now about 11:00, the traffic is in full flow heading to the outlets of Argos, Land of Leather, Currys and Next adorning the edge of the road. When Gramp passed this way it'd have been a deserted snow-covered road with these shops likely still farmland. I once asked him what he'd noticed as the biggest change in his lifetime. I expected him to say traffic, or attitudes to marriage or one of a whole host of changes. But he simply replied "The availability of finance" – likely a common denominator to most changes we see today.

Ahead the spire of Salisbury Cathedral stands proud above the trees and commercialism – perhaps a beacon for Gramp all those years ago. He didn't know what was ahead, both with the looming war and the more immediate issue of whether a bus could be caught from the centre of Salisbury.

At the bus depot he was told, "Nothing's moving, you know – no chance at all. You'll have to walk". As I approach the city centre I'm a bit lost, the layout being difficult to follow from the internet street map I downloaded. I navigate my way through using my compass. Passing the soon-to-be-closed Woolworths, I wonder if it was in the same place seventy years ago.

I pause at a public loo to dress my blistering feet with plasters. I use the river as a guide until I meet the A345 before taking a left, deviating from Gramp's route up the then quiet A360, to Stratford Sub-Castle.

Unlike Gramp I know I'm aiming to do the walk – he was ever hopeful for a lift. I get texts of well wishes from family and friends – he'd have been out of contact. His family, and my grandmother, not knowing where he might be. I pass a Braemar Lodge nursing home and hope I haven't headed too far north!

The winter sun strikes the minor roads, the odd car and group of Boxing Day walkers pass. I sit for a while on the wall of the house where my sister was born, munching a peanut and jam sandwich – a large van in the once front garden protects me from any glances of the occupants.

I continue on one of the more tedious parts of the walk – a lengthy stretch of road. High to my right is the ancient hill fort of Old Sarum – one of many scattering the Wiltshire hills. I press on, mindful I need to hit the carless tracks across Salisbury Plain by dusk: walking along darkened road has no appeal.

My route is set to take me through the Woodfords, a mile or so to the right of Gramp's route. First it's Lower Woodford and, before heading for Upper Woodford, I pass the war memorial at Middle Woodford. A group are packing away wine – it looks like the end of a Boxing Day celebration.

"Walking far?" asks a middle-aged grey-haired man.

"I started at dawn from Whiteparish and am aiming for Urchfont, the other side of the plain."

"I know where Urchfont is," he says with surprise. His curious look has me telling the story. He calls the others over and tells them, "This man is re-creating a walk his grandfather did seventy-five years ago today."

"Seventy years," I correct then explain the story again and add we only lost Gramp in August and Gran is still alive. There's looks of admiration to bask in and I'm wished well and given the location of several pubs I might wish to call at.

I walk on, my feet and knees hurt and my pace drops. I think of Gramp often now. His last three weeks in particular. He was an active man, still giving and preparing lectures on his wartime service in the submarines, right up until the evening of his stroke.

Tenacious and always adept, his wartime stories are of the *Boy's Own* variety. During the evacuation of Crete HMS Thrasher, his submarine, surfaced and Gramp, an accomplished swimmer, swam ashore with a line to rescue eighty trapped allied personnel.

Another time his keen hearing got them out of a minefield as he guided the captain to steer the vessel between the mines. Though my favourite is when they were submerged and trapped in a harbour by enemy ships. He identified a particularly noisy fishing vessel putting out to sea and was able to guide the captain to steer the submarine to sit just under it. As the enemy allowed the fishing boat to pass through their blockade the HMS Thrasher was submerged just a few feet beneath it. Once in open sea they legged it.

For these and his other antics he was awarded the Distinguished Service Medal (DSM).

The Germans, Japanese, Italians and later throat cancer in his fifties never got him. Being one of only two submarine ASDEC operators who started the war to survive, he even escaped a 'friendly' bombing from the RAF. In later life a triple heart bypass and a failing heart were not to take him. Even a week after his stroke we thought he was going to make it. His speech had lost its slur, his eyes were alive to the nurses and he was sitting up and engaging. But his ninety-two-year-old body couldn't bare the strain, another minor stroke and heart attack laid him gravely ill. A few days before the end my cousin, Matthew, and I were visiting. One open eye flitted between the two of us and he whispered, "I'm worn out."

On August 4th, a month before his ninety-third birthday, he passed away with my uncle and myself at his side. Stroking his head as he took his final breath, keeping count while the seconds ticked by and the realisation he'd gone.

Some say at death the life is gone, the animated spark has died the person no more and just a shell remains. For me it was nothing like this, he was still there, I could still speak with him. As Colin, my uncle, left to tell the family I had some time alone with him. I stroked the remains of his hair and chatted away to him. He was still there as he's still with me on this walk. Maybe a few miles to the left, or looking down or wherever but he was such a strong character he'll always be around me. In me I inherited his tenacity as for whatever I do in life I too never bloody well give up.

A mile past Upper Woodford I'm glad to take the path and

bridleway towards Normanton Down. I rest for a welcome coffee break and a piece of my friend Rona's birthday cake she'd packed me off with yesterday.

Peter Andrew Smith – DSM

The walk here is beautiful, the pure blue sky and track winding its way across the field are stunning in the cool winter air. If Gramp had arranged this he did me proud and if looking down it wasn't from a cloud.

On the approach to Normanton Down the path splits and I ask a family, likely walking off the turkey, for confirmation of the route to Stonehenge. The lady confirms and says, "It's a long way." I smile, thank her and add no more. For a family it might be a long way but it's under two miles.

On Normanton Down I admire the succession of Bronze Aged burial chambers. In the distance is the magnificent Stonehenge. Now fenced in as a visitor attraction I recall the times when we'd just pull up in the family car and run into the farmer's field and play amongst the stones. This was in my lifetime – adding to the pace of change of the last seventy years.

I drop down to the A303, streaming with traffic I pick a moment to cross and follow the bridleway to the edge of Stonehenge. I chance the café for food and drink but the lengthy queue turns me back onto my walk. It's about 15:45 and I head north to Larkhill – a stark military town with streets of bland austere order.

Absent of graffiti and litter it's difficult to find a comfortable fit with previous experience so I press on, turning left on to the minor road then north and west on to bridleways.

Normanton Down Bronze Age Burial Chambers

I reach the outer edges of Salisbury Plain, the sun and temperature are starting to drop. To my left are neat ordered fields of green, to my right the scrub of the military land where the ban on chemicals has kept the plants the same as seventy years ago.

I pass a long line of trees and, in the setting glow of the sun, a murmuration of starlings swish and swoop in a perfect synchronised display.

I make it to The Bustard Inn at 16:45, alas it is closed. A warm drink would have been good. Gramp stopped here on his walk. He fancied the track across the plain but, with the snow swept up to above head height, a group of imbibing soldiers said, "Don't you dare do it." Glad of the company he teamed up with two of the soldiers, trying to get through to Lavington, and skirted the edge of the plain. For me the dark tracks Gramp took are now dark and menacing roads and I elect to take the direct route across the plain.

As I follow the track for the final nine miles the night sky starts to open up with stars. The clear sky gave me extra useable daylight and now Venus glows bright with the fainter Jupiter in the background. With each step a new star appears, which one is Gramp's I wonder. It was a clear night for him too and I am warmed as I realise some of the light I see now was already on its journey seventy years ago.

Rabbits dart across when I pass through trees. I jump as my phone goes. It's Rona, my friend of nearly thirty years. She and her sister are willing me on. The few minutes of company are good and as we say goodbyes I mention I can see a light on the path ahead. It's a long plod to meet it, the grass becoming crunchy with ice and the puddles forming their frozen skin. But just south of Devizes Cross the light becomes a figure: Peter Smith. Not a ghostly apparition but Gramp's namesake (and my last two names) in the shape of my dad, having walked in from the north. I'm glad of his company and a flask of hot coffee.

The final walk takes three hours accompanied by a cold, biting wind blowing from the north. We are treated to a wonderful view of the heavens. The Milky Way is a streak across the sky with the Plough and Orion standing out. From this high ground of Wiltshire we can make out various settlements as clumps of street and house lights interspersed with the darkness of the rural roads. We talk of Gramp, the last seventy years, the year just gone.

We pass a fingerboard, in the middle of nowhere, pointing out tracks to Salisbury, Devizes and Lavington. A relic of when this was a route for those travelling by horse or foot. Military signs warn us not to stray off the track: there is much unexploded ordnance scattered across the plain.

"I remember coming up here as a kid," I say, "and seeing abandoned tanks used for target practice.

"There's still a few around," replies Dad, "and when I was a kid there were many abandoned spitfires used for target practice up here."

At Redhorn Hill we pass Dad's, now very icy, car then take the track to the left, hoping to pick up the same track down into Urchfont Gramp had taken. He'd hoped to walk the road between Market Lavington and Urchfont but it was impassable. Instead, he had to climb up onto the plain and descended White Road into the village.

Dad and I can't find the right track so we descend pass Dogtail Plantation and head towards The Green in Urchfont.

We are both worn out and try to assemble one good set of body parts between the two of us. We fail. To our right is the shimmer from the village pond and beyond is the ghostly silhouette of the church where seventy years ago tomorrow, Gran and Gramp married. For years Gramp was the Church Warden and just nine days previously we buried Gramp's ashes in its graveyard.

At The Green the products of the union walk to the very gate Gramp passed through at around 22:30 to be greeted by his sister with an, "Oh – you got here then."

A light is on, the occupants having no knowledge of the little family ceremony taking place at their gate.

For me it's 20:45 and I'm finished. Truly finished, my right hip, both knees and both feet ache. It's been thirteen hours and thirty-two miles, just one fewer than Gramp and, given the poor weather conditions he endured, surprisingly an almost identical time. Perhaps being twenty years my junior and a bride to claim helped him on his way.

I was at my limit at the Bustard some nine miles back but I'm glad to have done it and perhaps, in the history of the human race, just become only the second person to walk from Whiteparish to Urchfont in one day.

Classification	My Total	Total
Welsh Nuttalls	190	190
English Nuttalls	41	253
Corbetts (Scotland)	4	219
Grahams (Scotland)	1	220
Unique Donalds (Scotland)	0	58
Munros (Scotland)	284	284
Ireland	0	212
Totals (15/11/2008):	520	1436

February 2009 – Glenmore Lodge

Before May 2008 I hadn't paid much attention to Glenmore Lodge. I was only vaguely aware of its existence from the TGO Challenge magazine and seeing their emblazoned minibuses travelling the roads of the Aviemore region. But on May 16th last year, while completing all the mountains in Wales above 2000ft, I hired a guide, Garry Smith, to get me safely up Tryfan. A former guide at the centre himself he spoke of its virtues and I duly booked an introduction to winter skills course. This is my story, from February 1st to the 6th, told through snow-goggled eyes.

Having travelled up, with an overnight stay in Edinburgh, I'm waiting in the cool of a winter's Sunday evening at Aviemore station. Anything looking like a minibus raises my hope for the pre-arranged pick up to Glenmore Lodge. From along the main street a suitably sized red vehicle approaches, but my heart sags as I realise it is a van and not a minibus. Then the coincidence hits me for along the side of the van is a simple logo advertising 'Get High'. It's Garry's van – the Wales based guide who put me on to this place.

Coincidences set to one side I'm grateful when the Glenmore Lodge minibus arrives and whisks a few of us up into hills. The centre is clean and neat. The first evening is spent with a bar meal and, with questions like the following, it reminds me of my first night in halls of residence when I was eighteen:

"What course are you on?"

"Where do you come from?"

The only difference being is the years have killed the need for discussions about driving tests and girls.

My room is excellent, hotel like, ensuite without the telly. The centre has grown from its simple beginnings to offer incredible value for money. I get the sense this is a significant step up from the YHA centre-based courses I've been on before.

At breakfast I still haven't met anybody from my course and sit with a police officer, Andy, on the further winter skills course.

Mark, who I met the night before, joins us and I get to introduce him to the police officer who is on the same course as him.

The food is fantastic, a clear difference from halls of residence. We discuss our winter experiences, mine pretty low with some bad mistakes I've made while soloing in snow. Andy describes his life as a police dog handler. I chip in with, "I guess you're looking forward to the ice axe arrest training."

"Aye, we did that on the introductory course, Steve," he replies with no hint of having got my joke.

With my humour pride dented I collect a packed lunch and fill my flask with coffee. All provided inclusive of the price, unlike my YHA experiences where the misunderstandings between the warden and the suppliers of the course are legendary including what nights' accommodation is included, what meals, packed lunches, coffee and use of drying facilities are permitted. And here there is a distinct lack of notices instructing you to take your boots off, it's left to the individual to determine when boots may or may not be worn.

I make my way to the handsome lecture theatre for the introductory talk by Nigel Williams, head of training. His professionalism and confidence exude and I like his straightforward approach, even his words "I can't guarantee your safety" have an air of reassurance about them.

Then it's time to meet our instructors: an Englishman, an Irishman, and a Spaniard. For the want of this being the opening line to an old joke their names are Rupert, Clive and Rafael, but I'll leave you to wonder whether I have listed them respectively.

We gather by the stores, a cavernous garage-like area with a climbing wall in one corner. Large double doors protect us from the elements and the line of minibuses waiting to take us further into the mountains.

We queue and the store man lists the kit we need, surveys what we've got then fills in the gaps. With bits of kit dangling from every place possible we are instructed to head for the bar. This is fast becoming like the first day in halls of residence but, alas the bar is shut and we use the space to adjust crampons, try on goggles and helmets.

The instructors circulate, testing the fastness of our equipment. I'm keen on the loaned plastic boots, they are solid, fit well and I feel my feet will just be along for the ride.

It's then off to the minibus and the trip up to the ski centre car park. We disembark and start to make our way into Coire Cas – first following the funicular railway, a raised concrete structure snaking its way up the hills like the route illustrations in one of Poucher's guides. Its conception, construction and concrete are still heaped in controversy.

The instructors circulate amongst us, getting to know us. Rupert asks me, "Have you done any hill walking in snow before?"

I recall my first Munro and a companion's helicopter rescue when his bum sliding in snow got out of hand. Then the time I was ascending Stob Coire Raineach, in Glen Coe, and climbed into such a steep snow face I had to rely on a couple of other walkers to bail me out. And the time I was following a ridge in the mountains in the Ben Alder area, using what I thought was a line of boot prints to lead me to the summit until it dawned on me I was walking on the gash in a cornice about to break away.

"No," I reply.

I find the walk tough going, the boots give excellent protection but I'm aware of their weight. We are soon taught how to navigate an icy slope by using the side edge of the boot to kick and form steps. How to turn safely and how to descend through snow by kicking one's heel in.

At Coire Cas we drop our packs by a collapsed igloo and Clive instructs us to don helmets. "Treat your helmet like a tortoise," he says.

"What leave it in the shed for the winter," I reply. The wind wisps my words away and I'm spared a glare from Clive. I then discover his advice is useful as it refers to placing the helmet on the ground open side down so it doesn't take off on the ice.

I note we each listen by way of our own personality. Some offering quips, shared ideas or past experiences. People like John listen quietly and thoughtfully. A character can be judged simply by the way he or she listens.

We are then instructed in a selection of ascent and descent techniques using the ice axe. Sticking the shaft in, cutting steps, digging a ledge to sit or stand on. The biggest thing I learn is the importance of making flat ground to move or rest on.

The cutting of steps nags at my back, each swing just touches the snow to create a ledge but it's a long way down for me. Rafael, Rupert and Clive circulate, correcting our mistakes, watching until we get it right then moving on to the next.

Rafael speaks perfect English, narrated through a distinctive Spanish accent. From the Basque region he's settled in Scotland, distinctive in looks, as well as accent, with the blackest hair I've ever seen, nose stud and earring sleepers.

The sinking of the ice axe shaft requires aggression. Clive tells me to pretend it's somebody I don't like. I adopt a "Yer bastard" each time I thrust it into the snow. This catches on with Clive, and he explains my technique to the rest of the group.

A Motley Crew

The exercises require frequent regroupings at the rucksacks. Each time we are reminded of the conditions as our packs are covered in new snow. Things could easily disappear.

Snow Buntings hang out and move in for crumbs each time we graze on our lunches. It's good to see the wildlife, earlier a mountain hare darted across the slopes above us.

I'm glad when Clive calls an end to the day. I'm tiring and we've been at it a good few hours. We don crampons, aiding a comfortable descent. As we meet the ski runs snow boarders zip past at great speed, their equipment built to not stick to the mountains whereas ours is built to do the very opposite.

The evening passes with a three-course meal and instructional talks in the lecture theatre.

Tuesday dawns with the news of snow in the south of England –

according to the reports, the biggest for years. I'm reminded of my 1999 Christmas in Canada, hoping for my first white Christmas. For the first time in living memory Southern Ontario was devoid of snow while family and friends back home experienced the first southern England white Christmas in my lifetime.

I purchase a pair of inner gloves from the store. Goggles and gloves are a few of the items not provided free of charge. I'd found it very cold having to remove gloves to eat yesterday so I welcome the chance of a handy base layer.

Again it's a drive up to the ski centre and this time a walk into Coire na Ciste in search of a suitable slope to practise ice axe arrest. Again I find it tough, I ask Stefan how he is finding it and am reassured I'm not alone in finding the walks in hard. I'm glad when the instructors find some sloping ground, test the gradient and snow quality and declare it suitable.

Glenmore Lodge

We kit out in wet gear consisting of a pullover top and over trousers. This is to protect us from the worst of the wet and damage to more expensive clothing beneath. With my goggles and balaclava Jon says we look like we're equipped for biological warfare.

"After that breakfast I think we all need it," I reply.

Both my hands ache from the "Yer bastards!" of yesterday so I'm glad when the first lessons are axe free involving (i) throwing yourself downhill head first, (ii) throwing yourself downhill feet first on your stomach and (ii) throwing yourself downhill on your back. These are then repeated many times with the axe as we learn the art of correcting your position and braking.

I envy our youngest member Ben, not much older than a student with a laid back attitude to match, making the moves without fear of his limbs aching later.

We stop for lunch, and I take a look at the relics of an ancient chair lift we are working beneath. The timbers of the seats are rotten through as they gently swing in the breeze. We sit beneath the dilapidated wheel house and munch our food and sip our warming coffee.

When the day's work is done we return to the centre and practise and count our pacing on a 100-metre stretch of woodland path. We need to know this for navigating in poor conditions. Mine is around sixty paces for 100m on the flat and, once we migrated on to the uphill paths, rose to seventy-two paces and ninety paces on descent. There was a considerable variance across the group so it's important to know your own.

There then follows a series of navigation exercises amongst the trees. Each designed to take you back to the start via squares, rectangles and triangular courses of varying lengths.

The evening lecture is on avalanche awareness. We learn for the things to look out for in the weather forecasts and how to review the information supplied at the Scottish Avalanche Information Service website. Avalanches occur because of snow build up on the lee side of windblown hills – you need to keep an eye on the weather from the previous few days.

Like cavers who review the rainfall of the last few days, winter mountaineers need to review the snow fall and wind patterns of the last few days. Each day the warnings are about 80% chance of avalanching in the Aviemore area. I'm glad of the instructors' careful checks.

Wednesday I wake to a corking bruise on my stomach – with the countless times I'd thrown myself down that slope yesterday I can't recall which slide was the culprit.

I pull back the curtains and find a large snow dump has fallen during the night. This turns out to be more snow than any self-respecting mini bus will tackle so the trip up the road to the ski centre is postponed. A change in plan, which we are told is key to mountain safety, has us walking on the track towards Ryvoan Bothy then the Corbett overlooking it.

Clive says, "You can leave your extra wet-weather gear behind, we shan't be practising ice axe arrests today."

I'm relieved to shed some weight then catch Clive eyeing my pack, focussing on an extra outer piece of material. "Can you take the snow shovel there Steve?"

"Is that what that loop is for?" I ask.

"Yes."

"I rather wished I'd known before."

"Why?"

"I'd have taken it off."

We pace off landmarks (with accuracy ranging from good to appalling) to reach the bothy. I'm looking forward to our group being able to congregate within its confines, eat and drink our coffee. Alas the romantic ideal is scuppered by a large group of well-behaved youngsters who have filled the single-roomed shelter.

We manage to eat and survey the Corbett of Meall a' Bhuachaille. We make out two paths, branching a few hundred feet above where we stand. Although the left one appears more tempting we opt for the straight up option, following the path marked on our maps. Clive says we don't need to pace out sections as the way looks fairly clear – welcome words to me. He also talks about Naismith's rule which is to allow a minute per contour. Worried about my pace, and preferring Steve Smith's rule of two minutes per contour, I set my altimeter and tuck in behind Jane and Roger, clearly fit for the hills.

We spy reindeer on high ground and pass over areas of soft powdery snow, pure ice and ice covered in snow. I notice the tread on Jane's boots is caked with snow and, assuming mine must be the same, kick off the snow. I now have much better grip and tell Jane to do the same. She thanks me, unaware it's her boots that helped me.

We traverse west over steep ground and see how avalanches happen by no more than a desktop-sized piece of snow breaking away from frozen older snow below.

We make the summit in eighty-five minutes, just twelve minutes longer than Clive's rule of thumb calculations. Like us it's all very iced up. The Velcro on my sleeves is covered in thick ice, my jacket is stiff and I'm covered in what one would describe as a sharp frost.

It's piercingly cold and Clive urges us to get moving. We are set the task of heading west into the col. We have to each calculate, agree and set bearings before setting off and pacing the downward slope to meet the col.

After a few minutes, Clive calls a halt to the shambles. We've headed south-west instead of west. He does a half-hearted job at disguising his frustration. Checking my altimeter I'm not sure if we are as far off as he says. Fortunately we aren't made to re-ascend and we are instead given instructions to follow a sweep search downhill to meet the path leading through the forest and then to the lodge.

The visibility is good and our sweep search fails to hold a line. With each of us falling into holes and struggling across the deep snow it's welcome when the gradient slackens off and we meet the outer edges of the forest. Alas, with the snow, there is no path to be seen so I surreptitiously take a peek at my GPS. It has us not far from where we need to be but I know I need to keep quiet about my sudden 'expertise'. We head to the right, still searching out the path into the forest.

Jane quietly says to me, "It could be by that signpost saying footpath."

"Looks about right," I say as I share the irony of the situation with her and reveal my GPS. I then quickly put it away and in doing so drop my compass. This gives Clive delight in telling us how important it is not to drop your kit. In all my years of walking this is only the second time I've dropped a compass and it had to be in front of an instructor.

It's a long final slog through the woods and back up the track. We do a final pacing on the 100m course we used yesterday when it was free of snow – today it's covered.

Back in the lodge we sit around a circular table in the dining room and, while being debriefed, munch our way through the free tea and cake. Outside the window the principal is taking photos of a hastily-built snowman.

"I never thought I'd see something so bizarre," says Clive.

"Not as bizarre as if it were the snowman taking a picture of the principal," I suggest.

In the evening I take a walk around the centre. Photographs from the 1950s, showing young people having fun in the early basic accommodation, fill the walls of the stairs. It gives me a level of sadness, moments in time snapped for history. The subjects will be bordering on old age now. Photographs and artefacts from renowned lost climbers, lives cut short in the pursuit of dreams.

I'm cheered by an enthralling evening talk by Kirk Watson. As a climber he's spent a number of winters and summers at the British Antarctic Survey base. His film clips, stills and stories are entertaining and have us dreaming of spending some time there. In particular Alan Maw, a welder from the north-east of England, learns his type of skill is in high demand. Alas I couldn't see a role for me – a software engineer doesn't fit into the category of climber, scientists or skilled manual labour.

Thursday I wake to see the snowman up to his neck in snow. Rafael is unable to make it in and we are allocated Kirk to take his place. The snow is too deep to even get out of the centre so we start with building snow holes, something Kirk had covered with some instructional video clips the night before.

We split in to two groups and the party I'm in pile their rucksacks in a heap. Mine is still in my room, which gives me mixed feelings of guilt and relief as we pile on snow.

We continually pack it down before adding layer after layer. A couple pass and the woman of the party asks what we are doing. Clive replies, "Making a snowman."

"Why not a snow woman?" she asks.

"Ours is going to have snow balls," I offer.

"That's the tone just lowered," says Clive.

"If a guy can't just have a joke," I mutter. "Only trying to cheer people up, I thought it was quick, witty and relevant."

"Steve, shut up and keep digging."

Jane is sent in to dig the entrance. She reaches the packs which are then pulled out. We then take it in turns to slide in on our stomachs and hollow out a cavity. It's unlikely this form of shelter would be used in emergency as it's a lengthy process. The other group start to dig a snow grave. However, it becomes more of a snow wall and is used to shelter a group bivi.

During all of this a RAF search and rescue helicopter lands three times. Once to pick up search and rescue dogs. Two people have been out all night in the hills. Texts had been received the night before and they were told to, "Dig in." This morning the ominous lack of contact has rescue workers concerned.

The dogs are eager to board and be taken high up into the mountains. The snow, and wind kicked up by the helicopter gives us an idea of what whiteout conditions are like. Our beautiful blue sky day, with mountains edged with snow as an artist would pick out shadow on a picture, is turned in to howling snow swirling conditions. We have to turn our backs in to it and brace ourselves. On the third landing the snow cave is sufficient for Jon and me to dive in and take refuge.

Birger, our dry-witted Danish representative, has some fun with me. I'd earlier explained the helicopter rescue I was involved in on my first Munro. As it lands this time he says, "They're here for you again, Steve."

A BBC camera crew turn up and we learn the two climbers have been found alive and well.

The blue skies continue into the afternoon and the instructors find snowshoes to kit us all out. These are solid plastic flipper affairs, which you fasten into with a hinge at the toe end, and make for easier travelling across the deep powder snow.

We set off on a circular route, following forestry tracks, with the aim of touching the shores of Loch Morlich before the return to the lodge.

We are all taken with the pure beauty. Each lump and bump on the ground is picked out by rises in the whitewashed blanket that's folded into every contour. Blue sky sits above the higher branches, rays of light draw our eyes as it splashes its way from canopy to carpet. Trees hold snow on every skyward face, rocks in streams like sleeping polar bears, bridge rails with perfect vertical white extensions.

We meet cross-country skiers and they share our enthusiasm for the nearest to perfection that Scotland can produce. As a group we fall into a line, grouping into a circle when it's time to rest and talk. A skier who Kirk knows passes us. He's young, designer stubble and shades, flowing dark hair. "Russ!" calls out Kirk.

"Hey, Kirk," comes the reply from the biggest smile I'd seen in a long time, "Perfect day, man."

If he'd been smoking a spliff the scene would have been complete.

We reach Loch Morlich and all fall silent. Beyond are perfect snow-covered hills, the sun lowering yet still above them casting its light over the secrets of their folds and bringing a shimmer across the loch.

Ducks float in ice free flowing water. It's a long time before anybody speaks. We walk along the snow crusted beach with our heads turned left, savouring every moment.

Sat with coffee and cake in the lodge we reflect on the day. It's been the biggest snow fall for ten years. Clive tells us it's been years since he's been out on snow shoes. They've done us proud, what earlier looked to be a day of hasty improvisation became an unplanned experience nobody expected.

Clive asks each of us for our personal highpoint of the day. I reply seeing a party disembark from a luxury coach with 'McPhallus' emblazoned down the sides.

Clive pauses, raises his eyes and says, "McPhails Steve, McPhails."

I explain my dyslexia. Stefan asks, "Do you know what DNA stands for?"

I shake my head figuring somehow deoxyribonucleic acid isn't the answer.

"National Dyslexic Association," he replies, smiling broadly.

I've struggled all my life with asthma and dyslexia, two things that don't get a great deal of sympathy when compared with more visible ailments. I never had any help with it when I was at school or later when I was a student. It was never picked up, so I never got help or additional time in exams. This is something which grates with me.

Though I have to admit Stefan's remark is very funny.

Friday and the road to the ski centre is open and becomes our first day out by minibus since Tuesday. The car park feels alpine, skis being unloaded from roof racks, folk kitting themselves to the gentle anticipation of the hum of ski lifts.

We opt to walk and trail up into Coire Cas. It's tough going, the blue skies of yesterday now hidden by low cloud and occasional wind whipping up snow. Clive keeps an eye on Stefan's broad frame. He's trailing at the back and I can sense a mental calculation is being made whether he's fit for the summit of Cairn Gorm. We hear the instructors talking, via radio, to the three other courses, all more advanced than us and one by one we hear thc news they've turned back. It just leaves us, the least experienced, having picked the route where conditions are most favourable.

Clive and Rafael huddle in conference. I pick up that Clive wants to walk Stefan off and there is debate too whether the summit is really suitable today for any of us. Stefan is then spoken to but says he feels up to it. Clive isn't convinced but we settle on splitting into two groups. On we march until time for a coffee and a snack is called. Clive starts to dig a snow grave.

"It doesn't look good for you, Stefan," I quip.

We are instructed to each dig our own hole for shelter and a comfortable place to eat. A few minutes of flurry ensues as we each open out our homesteads.

We carry on, Rafael selects Jon to lead via bearing and pacing. Deep snow is negotiated until we reach the ice-encrusted building and weather station marking the summit. It's no place for a lengthy rest and we are soon instructed to move on. I'm far from ready and feel frustrated when the group moves off while I'm still adjusting my kit. My frustration grows during the descent as my goggles freeze over to the point I'm seeing the white ground, white sky and blowing snow through a couple of square centimetres.

I desperately try to find the footsteps in front of me, tripping often. We don't get many rests but when we do I'm grateful for Ian's realisation I'm struggling. I'm also grateful when he improves my vision by chipping the ice from my goggles.

Rafael's paces us on a bearing to the Ptarmigan Restaurant which adorns the top of the ski lift. I'm relieved when we halt and our destination is declared – though we cannot see the building as the visibility is so poor. An exploratory party sets forth and then calls the rest forward.

We are now amongst skiers, stepping off the ski lift, with their bright clothing and cool ski wear without a drop of snow or ice on them. We are ice and snow encrusted like an Edwardian photograph of an Antarctic expedition. It is surreal, we must look surreal. We get some strange glances, but with them I sense a mark of respect.

Amongst curious gazes we follow the edge of the ski slope back to the car park and to the end of our week.

Saturday morning I wake in Euston Station, having come down by the sleeper. The bulk of London's snow has melted but as I get the train to my village the snow scenes of Scotland return. At 08:30 I step into our village bakery, hearing how our village, three miles from the nearest main road, remains cut off to all but those with a 4x4. I'm glad for the train, and my newfound skills, as I make the final short walk home.

May 2009 – The Great Outdoors Challenge

It's the Friday evening of the week before the TGO Challenge and I'm sat in my favourite Marlborough coffee shop. A text comes through from my sister and we arrange weekend visits for our ninety-two-year-old grandmother.

"Just out having a curry this evening," she adds.

To outdo her I reply, "I've just ordered eight curry dishes to take on the TGO Challenge and I'm having a coffee waiting for them to be cooked."

"What at an Indian take away? Do you then dehydrate them?"

"Yes and yes."

"You are joking aren't you? Tell me you are?"

"No and no."

"Have you ordered rice?"

"No, I managed to do that bit myself."

"Nan?"

"I thought we'd already sorted the visits."

Like all things culinary I've left it until the last minute, leaving no time to cook anything. Therefore I dragged myself, without much protest, to the Raj in Marlborough. Through language difficulties and our opposite meaning of shaking and nodding our heads, I made the order. They apologise for keeping me waiting and give me a couple of bottled beers. I take them – trying to explain I don't drink might have sounded rude.

It's the evening of Wednesday May 6th, the food is dehydrated and my bag is packed. I'm online double checking tomorrow's train journey from my village to Strathcarron. As it requires the first train out and the last train in, with five accompanying changes, I'm in the middle of debating whether I should print off a compensation claim form to take with me when the doorbell rings. It's a neighbour and, in my role of running the local rail passenger group, she asks, "Do you know what's happened to the trains?"

"No," I reply.

"Well, the line is blocked: a woman and her dog have been killed on the crossing."

I text my friend Susannah, who lives by the crossing, concerned it might be her. I'm thankful for the text back but she says it's pretty awful.

Later I check the trains, they report the line blockage, due to a fatality has been resolved but there are now scheduled engineering works for the rest of the night. I've had experience of this before. Although reported to clear at 03:00 there's often an overrun which causes the first train to be cancelled. With nervous anticipation I don't sleep well and find myself at 04:30 checking online. There's no useful information so I ring the helpline number. It's voice activated and we struggle to get my start station into the system, then it's the destination of the first leg, Paddington.

It starts off with, "Did you mean Cuddington?"

We then go through a series of options which, after I'm not sure what got said, culminates in, "Did you mean Pluckley?"

I give this up and wander down to the station and press the helpline button. They know no more than I do. By the time I leave the house for the second time, I can hear the 06:07 pulling into the station. If I'd left it all to chance I'd have had the same result.

The journey goes well with changes in London and Glasgow. I meet with Ali Ogden (formerly Ashton as Adrian, her partner has now made an honest woman of her) and Sue Oxley at Perth and we journey on together to Strathcarron.

Ali is lucky to be on the Challenge: a torn cruciate knee ligament and a cartilage operation two months ago, have curtailed her preparations.

The weather, viewed from the train window, varies from sun to cloud then descends to lashing wind and rain. We step out of the warm railway carriage at Strathcarron Station into the foul weather.

"Come on," says Ali, heading towards the overbridge.

I follow on, impressed by how her knee holds out as we start to run.

A wet and sorry mob land in the hotel, some checking in, some just buying a drink, or two, before pitching their tent. Routes and plans are exchanged, my eyes light up when, amongst the tales of dire weather forecasts, I hear of a previously unknown bothy that might suit my Friday night.

On Friday May 8th we set off in the dry towards the bothy at Bendronaig Lodge. I am sluggish, the weight of the pack, which hasn't been on my back for two years, pulls heavy on my left shoulder, and the poorly-distributed weight doesn't need much excuse to dig into my lower back.

I rest to repack and lose Ali and Sue as they walk on. With large items now stowed transversely it's easier but the rough incline has me wondering about my 'get fit on the Challenge' philosophy to preparation.

It starts to rain and I catch Ali and Sue at a beautifully-refurbished bridge crossing the River Ling. I enthuse and point out the craftsmanship of the restoration.

"How do you know it's restored?" asks Ali. "It could be new."

"Not with rivets that size," I reply.

"I guess you have to be male to know about rivets," she adds.

I'm unsure whether this is praise or mockery but am happy to plod on in company. There's then a few moments when it's just Ali and me walking side by side. I wait for the question.

"Any luck on the girlfriend front?"

"Oh, one of my old commuter friends tried to set me up with one of her friends. So we all met up in London."

"Any joy?" asks Ali.

"Well no. She was ten years older than advertised—"

"That'd rule children out," interrupted Ali.

"Well," I said, getting myself back on track, "they also told me she was an actress. But I was a bit taken aback when I asked her what roles she'd been in."

"Oh, what were they?"

"*Adventures of a Plumber's Mate* and one episode of *On The Buses*."

"What kind of actress was she?" asks Ali, chuckling. "I suppose you've still got your hill walking. How are the Nuttalls going?" she asks.

"I finished the Welsh ones last year and to date I've done forty-one of the English ones."

"How many does that leave you?"

"Well over 200."

It's a wet group that arrives at the bothy after some three and a half hours of walking. My jacket is leaking and I'm grateful to be able to sit down and rest my legs.

People pour in and, having just experienced more rain on this Challenge than in the entire previous one, are grateful for a roofed structure. Our oldest comrade arrives – Jack Addison, aged seventy-three, who soon announces his intent to press on.

Only myself plus Ann and Alvar Thorn declare our hand and

decide to cut the day short with a night in the bothy. The ensuite loo, complete with paper, bucket to flush and toilet duck is too tempting.

Ali and Sue feel the bothy is too far to the west (there's no pleasing some people) and elect to make this merely a rest stop before pressing on to Loch Calavie in the hope of positioning themselves for some Munros tomorrow. I have my eye on an afternoon walk up the Corbett of Beinn Dronaig but not before lunch and rest.

"I'm cold," complains Sue, sat huddled in her coat.

"You could chop up the firewood for us later," I suggest.

I get a scowl and then Sue tries to cheer up engaging in conversation with each person who arrives which unfortunately becomes a series of gaffs.

"Bad hair day," she says to the arriving Gordon Green, noted for his full head of long white hair.

He looks mildly affronted.

"Men can have bad hair days too," she adds. "Let me guess your age, most people on the Challenge are about ten years older than they look."

It was just one of those days where the foot was firmly stuck in it.

I strip my pack to the bits required to do a day walk up the Corbett and set off. But I can't get comfortable. First my insulated, waterproof hat is loose on my head: my recent number two head shave, a brave and long-thought-out decision to outwit baldness, doesn't offer much purchase. And second I've forgotten my trekking poles – I return to the bothy and, amongst curious glances, reclaim them. I then head up the rough craggy slopes of Beinn Dronaig.

I find it easier going without the full pack weight, though I take frequent rests to peer back towards the bothy and admire the snow-capped peaks with angry cloud above them.

My ascent is entertained by periods of rain blowing in followed by snaps of blue sky and chill wind to blow the water off me. I reach the bealach of the undulating, rocky summit plateau with the wind picking up. I get to see out towards the Mullardoch hills whose peaks are picked off by a strip of snow.

As I approach the summit a hailstorm strikes in a void between clouds above and below me. I'm grateful for the guidance of light snow on the ground which marks out the shallow indentations of otherwise indistinguishable paths. At the top I get some welcome shelter.

The first part of the return is a hundred metre drop back into the hailstones, pelting and sandblasting my face as I hurry to escape their domain.

Back at the bothy I'm pleased with my efforts. To have sat out the day in the bothy would have left me feeling stuffy and unfulfilled with this remote Corbett left unconquered.

Alvar had tried to get a fire going, but the stove just smoked the room so we are warmed only by a succession of gas stoves heating the evening meals – curry for me.

Five challengers sleep the night and the morning begins with the rustling of plastic bags and the flaring of stoves. I take my time gathering my things, not looking forward to the day ahead which appears to be one of grotty weather.

Setting off towards Loch Calavie on a good track, I'm soon hampered by a deteriorating path which becomes a bog hop on the approach to Pait Lodge. I am slow, it takes five and a half hours to get to this lodge: an oasis of construction and garden in the boggy wild shores of Loch Monar.

I decide, through a conspiracy of fitness and weather, not to ascend An Cruachan and instead cut up Allt Riabhachain to a bridge Ann recommended. The advice is good and I reward myself with munching lunch in the heather.

I'm passed by Phil Turner, setting an impressive pace as I ponder the rough walk through the bealach to collect the path towards the hydro works below Beinn Dubh an Iaruinn.

The going is tough, each step, each ascent is a strain while I stagger under the weight of eight days supply of food. I use each stream to try and wash my boots and gaiters from all the peat gathered in the bog hoping and sinking.

Descending the glen I feel miserable as the rain pelts down. I approach my camping spot: I must look a sorrowful figure. Only the arch of a rainbow cheers me and there's just enough let up in the weather to erect the tent. I'm glad to be inside, snug as the rain pelts the outer skin. I wonder where Ali and Sue got to and am a bit surprised to be camping away from any other challengers.

It's Sunday May 10th and I wake and survey my sore feet. I patch up as best I can and pull on my wet socks.

Last night it was too wet to get out of my tent to clean my teeth and I'm glad to clean up this morning and rid myself of the taste of curry. Tonight I'm heading for the Struy Inn so the evening meal will be a change.

The day is nice, but I make slow progress in the sun. Ann and Alvar set off from their camp and I pass Terry Leyland as he packs up. I look back to the route I covered yesterday, snow-capped peaks and high cloud tease me with the missed mountain of yesterday, An Cruachan. You have to catch them on the right day.

My feet get wet as they squelch into Glen Strathfarrar. The bridge at Inchvuilt requires a climbing move to overcome the locked gate at its entrance and, by the time I hit the road, blisters are coming on. I stop to add surgical padding and find they are bleeding. After doing my best to patch myself up, it's still painful to walk.

I catch up with Ann and Alvar but, with them having stopped for an hour for lunch, I realise my pace is poor. It becomes a route march down the glen and my heart sinks when I pass my 2001 parking place, to capture a couple of Munros, and recall the time it took to drive up the glen – ground I now have to travel on foot.

A single pine tree, alone on an impressive mound, becomes my focus as the road twists and turns towards it. I'm glad the glen isn't straight. The walks in Glen Clova and along the side of Loch Ericht, are straight, boring, long and in the latter case a dam teases you by forever being on the horizon. Here there is a pretty twisting glen to enjoy.

I arrive at Struy Bridge after an eight-and-a-half-hour trudge. My heart sinks when I find it locked up and note saying it doesn't open until 17:30. I flop onto a bench, glad of a rest and am grateful when I'm rescued by the hotelier.

"I'll get the wee lassie to open up," he says.

The 'wee lassie' turns out to be a very tall Polish girl with the most amazing black hair. She shows me to my room where I settle down to check my blisters. I find a scene of gore on my right foot. A red grape appears to have taken root between my big and second toe. Like an ageing car, where surface rust implies worse to come, there is a horror story on the underside. A large blister has popped leaving a raw area, on the ball of the foot, about the size of a fifty pence coin.

I limp my way to the shower to get it as clean as possible and soon find a new danger: the ancient shower appears to have two settings: freezing or third degree burns. A further hidden danger is that it doesn't appear to have been cleaned since the first challengers passed this way in 1980.

Discovering the trick is to control it by the stopcocks on the inlet pipes, I find a balance, clean up then patch up and limp my way down to the bar. I order food and am soon joined by Alistair and Lynsey Pooler, at twenty-eight and twenty-seven they look so young. They do well to reduce the average Challenge age. Ali and Sue join us, tired but elated to have achieved the four Munros to the north of Glen Strathfarrar.

The conversation flows and for Ali and Sue so does the wine. The purchase of an extra bottle, to decant into a plastic platypus, sees them off to bed with the rest of us following and limping.

I get a text from my mum saying they've been to look at a new cat. They lost 'George' recently and, as tradition has it, the vet then phoned them about six weeks later saying 'They've had a stray just handed in.' I don't know if the vet is influenced by my parents' gullibility or whether their income stream is dependent on the bills my parents willingly pay in order to keep old cats on the road. Anyhow, this cat is called Bobby and was found wandering in a local park. The vet had him in, whipped off his testicles and are now offering him to my mum and dad. Mum sounds uncertain, saying he looked a bit aloof. I reply, 'I'm not surprised he's a bit aloof, he was probably just out for a walk. If I'd been strolling through a park and somebody whipped my testicles off I think I'd be a bit aloof!'

Breakfast on Monday May 11th is a fine affair. The hotelier, realising we are all on the Challenge, sits us together and it's a feast of fine food and conversation. We depart to pack, and I bargain with every item to see if I can throw it away to reduce weight

I meet Ali and Sue outside. "I need to walk with you today."

"Why particularly?" asks Sue.

"Well the forest tracks of my planned route look pretty boggy. Your road walk is my foul weather alternative but I forgot to print the maps."

She raises her eyebrows.

We need to be at Drumnadrochit for 17:00 to catch a pre-booked ferry across Loch Ness. I sense a quietness about Ali and Sue, I'm not noted for my speed walking so know I have to raise my game.

The roads are steep, hot and unforgiving to both my blistered foot and Ali's knees. We pass through hamlets – Kiltarlity we rename as 'Kill a Tity' (I tried for 'Lik a Tity' but got outvoted). We rest by a chapel and the entertainment begins with an inspection of my foot followed by Sue's wet pack.

"Looks like your platypus is leaking," says Ali.

We find a leak near the neck.

"This isn't good," says Sue. She isn't kidding, without a watertight container the Challenge is nearly impossible. "This could be me out of the Challenge."

"I've got a spare," I say and am immediately declared a hero. Once the spare is in place, and as much water transferred as possible by the careful hand of Doctor Ali (a self-claimed expert in decanting urine samples), we are set to go.

I don't mind the small risk the platypus I'm using will spring a leak and curtail my Challenge. The TGO Challenge is all about helping one another out by selfless acts.

"Thanks for that, Steve," says Sue, "my spare is full of wine, I didn't want to waste it."

Setting off, feeling I've been somewhat duped, I keep my cool by dipping my cap in clear puddles. The water drains down, running between my shirt and skin, cooling me on the uphill sections.

We pass lamas, alpacas and the cutest ponies. I feed them longer grass and they look sorrowful as we depart.

"You'd make a great dad," quips Ali.

We turn onto the Great Glen Way for the final leg to Urquhart Bay, which protrudes from Loch Ness to the shores of Drumnadrochit. We stop at a picnic area for lunch. It's nice to sit at a table and enjoy the sun. I'm low on water so refill from the tap in the loos and emerge into the sun with a plastic bag with contents resembling something you'd find hanging on the side of a hospital bed.

The walk between the trees is gorgeous, light shining through, dappling the path in sun and shadow. Trees bend against the blue sky and a chorus of birds share our delight in the day. Sue keeps us paced but I bargain for a two minute break, which turns out to be a longer one as we sit on a viewpoint overlooking Loch Ness.

By now the muscle, which connects my right leg to my bottom has strained. It's painful, especially on uphill bits.

"I could massage it for you?" says Sue.

I await the punch line.

"With my boots," she adds.

"And what state of dress would I be in?"

"Naked," says Sue.

"It's rumoured one normally has to pay good money for that," I add.

We make the ferry at five past five. We realise we are on the second boatload so rest, bask in the sun and chat to other challengers. I'm grateful to Ali and Sue, for Ali's navigation and Sue's pace got us here in time.

There's no time to walk into the centre Drumnadrochit. My last visit was in 1995 when there were two museums, one proclaiming it to be 'The Official Loch Ness Monster Museum' and the other 'The Original Loch Ness Monster Museum'. I did wonder if there was a bit of competition going on.

Ten of us crowd into the open topped ferry for the crossing. The engine putters off and the subtle glow of the evening sun lights the water and surrounding hills.

As the western shore shrinks, the eastern shore grows and what were faint outlines become clear to the eye and what was clear to the eye dwindles into pinpricks of memory.

We alight at the hamlet of Inverfarigaig onto the derelict jetty and plod our way to the Sutherland's hill billy ranch at Ault-na-goire. Others find pitches or head to B&Bs.

We approach the ranch apprehensively and enquire if the rumour of free pitches is true. We are welcomed in, fed tea and biscuits then directed to camp in the field.

In glorious evening sun we chat with Shirley Worrall, Peter Shepard and many others. A sink and a welcome loo make it all mod cons amongst eccentric sculptures involving ancient bicycles and Dyson vacuum cleaners.

I don't get much sleep. The welcome cups of tea went down a bit too well and caffeine now pumps through my system. Sleep becomes snatched moments between periods of trying to get my aching body comfortable on my Thermarest.

An early hour's call of nature has me admiring the heavens, millions of stars lighting those who choose to sleep away from the lights of the cities. I sense a frost in the air and crawl back to the welcome warmth of my sleeping bag. Life is simpler in a tent, just the bare necessities of survival with the attendant list of jobs to sustain a twenty-first century lifestyle left far behind with their significance. The TGO Challenge is a leaderless travelling community, full of comradeship with just a few basic rules in which to flourish. I've always been unsure of what love means but somehow the TGO Challenge fosters that spirit – at the very least it's one definition.

The Sutherland's hill billy ranch at Ault-na-goire

On Tuesday May 12th the calls of animals and the roar of neighbouring gas stoves serve as an alarm clock. A frost has settled on the tents and we wait for the sun to clear the high trees and dry the worst off the tents. In the meantime we all sing 'Happy Birthday' down Ali's mobile to her fifteen-year-old daughter, Madeleine. Ali is younger than me and has a fifteen-year-old daughter, the years creep by and one barely notices until a little reminder, and an aching body, awakens us to a world getting younger.

We get going at 07:45 in a long procession of people, funnelling from where they rested towards Errogie and the splendour of the Monadhliath Mountains beyond.

With the lack of a hearty breakfast I make a weary start and soon need to rest. I ask Ali to check my foot. Sue turns away as she sees the gore, fortunately this is all in a day's work for Dr Ogden and she patches me up with an appropriate dressing, supplies me with a spare and off we set again.

I'm slow and don't mind Ali and Sue getting ahead. I sense I'm becoming a burden and feel their concern each time I catch them at a rest stop. Finding myself in a second party, I chat to new people as we find ourselves unintentionally trespassing through a well-manicured garden with the destined hills beyond. A woman emerges from a grand house and, before she can say anything, I'm apologising on behalf of us all. If there was wind in her sails it is taken away as we explain our mistake and she gives helpful route advice. Catching the front runners we choose to ignore said advice and find ourselves in an even more beautifully-manicured garden. This time there's only a gardener and from him we receive a cheery wave.

At a junction in the path I lean on my trekking poles, beat with tiredness. I've already decided to tell Ali and Sue we should separate as I'm holding them up. I'm just about to make my magnanimous gesture when Ali, who's obviously been in conversation with Sue, says "Is it okay if we go on, Steve?"

"Yes, no worries," I say. So I bid them and Phil Turner farewell and settle for a rest. My right foot has been painful with each step so I take Ibuprofen, drink lots of water and graze on nuts and raisins.

Due to Jenny Wheeler's dietary advice in 2007, and recent follow-up emails and texts on the same subject, I haven't dared pack any chocolate.

I'd kill for a Mars bar right now.

But the healthy Steve, who at this point can barely move, sets off again and forces his legs along the track.

I'm soon passed by Peter Shepard and companion as I follow the steady pull towards the Corbett of Carn na Saobhaidhe. Passing the additional tracks to the wind generator – a solitary structure requiring access roads and power lines – I lose myself in a work problem. It switches my mind away from my fitness struggles as my mind plays through ideas, possibilities and scenarios. Like life, the purity of walking, the purity of the mountains, makes everything simpler. The solution comes to me and even the lack of timesheet to record the event isn't a bother.

As the map indicates the track's imminent demise, I catch sight of a group of three huddled over a map. Realising it's Ali, Sue and Phil I catch them and ask, "What happened?"

"We stopped for lunch and dried the tents."

"I'll accompany you to the top," I reply, "then let you off the leash again."

Accompanying to the top becomes a tortuous bog hop over the final slopes to the bealach between Beinn Bhuraich and Carn na Saobhaidhe. Super fit Sue and youthful Phil leave Ali and I standing. We are left to work our way with tender knees, and tender feet, to the higher ground.

I rest often, allowing Ali to catch up, though I sense she's happy to make her own pace. It's tough going and I'm glad when the south-westerly climb becomes an easier south-easterly final ascent to the Corbett's summit. I expect to spot Peter but he's long gone (though oddly he didn't pass Sue and Phil) so instead I rest at the high, breezy plateau of the summit cairn.

The deal to separate isn't required as we all descend at equal pace to the Allt Odhar and its short, yet impressive, waterfalls.

"You're a new man," says Sue.

"Something clicks in with me," I reply. "Sometimes I'm on a roll other times I'm just so slow."

We follow the river downstream to Dalbeg, where I rest by the closed-up bothy. Peter is camping and comes over to say hello.

"We were shouting to you from the track to the wind turbine, didn't you hear?"

"No," I reply.

"That was the way to the Corbett."

For the life of me I couldn't see how, and a later inspection of the map makes me none the wiser.

I press on for the bridge south-west of Coignafearn Lodge where an evening appointment with MA Harper awaits me. Having said goodbye to Ali, Sue and Phil I lose myself in my thoughts as I follow the comfortable track along the banks of the river. I'm glad of the gentle descent but wary this will require more ascent tomorrow.

As the bridge comes into view, and the new Victorian-styled lodge building fills the glen beyond, I spy my three comrades of the day sat resting by the bridge.

"We can't lose one another," I say, slumping myself down having completed my day of ten hours' walking.

"We miss your sparkling company," says Ali.

I sit next to her and trim my nails.

"You are showering me with bits of nail," says Ali.

I pitch my tent, alone and admire the evening light as the sun drops below the hills to a deepening blue sky. With no sign of MA, I slip into my sleeping bag and have a restless night: each time I turn, my body reminds me of my aching hips.

I snatch just enough sleep and wake to Wednesday May 13th dawning another glorious day. I heat my breakfast in the unwashed pot in which I cooked curry last night. The smell of gas reminds me of the static caravan holidays of my childhood. Rain-soaked south coast sites, making model Airfix kits to try and take the mind off the tedium.

Muesli and dehydrated skimmed milk isn't the most appetising and I won't claim the twang of curry sets it off any better. After I scrape the last of it into my mouth I set to patching up my feet then packing up the tent. It's the bit of camping I like the least, the bit of camping that will always make my preference a bothy.

I head south on the track as it rises away from the river. Looking back I spot a fellow challenger following the river. I wait for a while in case it's MA but as the figure draws closer and the distant movement grows legs and arms, I work out it's a man. I press on, making reasonable time and making use of the tracks. Oystercatchers and cuckoos keep me company; the sky is a promising shade of blue and the burns emit a cacophony that can be listened to intently or phased out at will.

As I rise I find the wind cooling. I rest for a while and the male challenger catches me up. His map shows more tracks than mine and I memorise them for my walk to the Corbett of Carn an Fhreiceadain. I skip a tempting bridge, continuing on the track until I have to boulder hop the Elrick Burn. Then it's a rough, ascending walk following an ever-diminishing stream until all that remains is the sound of water pouring through underground sumps. Then it's a drop to a shelter. I peer into the structure, a table crowds the room and I only guess at its purpose.

A rest then a track has me ascending to a window to the right of the Corbett. I go well past it before the track turns back and leads me to its summit. I rest, phone in to 'Challenge Control' and, at just after one in the afternoon, I'm pondering my descent to the Insh House at Kincraig. My options are to either follow the ridge then drop almost on to Kincraig, drop in to Kingussie for a meal or aim for Balavil then take the old A9 route to Kincraig. This latter option becomes my plan and downfall timewise.

At first I take the wrong track and have to traverse east across heather and peat to pick up the right track. I stick to the track to Balavil. I'm slow, it's tough going and I don't make the road until 17:30. It's then a gruelling road walk, my feet reminding me of their blisters and the unforgiving tarmac doing nothing to help.

I count the kilometres off against my watch, every few minutes re-estimating my time of arrival in Kincraig. Cars are forgiving – mostly I'm given a wide berth, a few people smile and wave.

It's 19:00 when I reach the village – one of the first buildings is a hotel serving bar meals. I've been going twelve hours, unsure just where the time has gone. Hot, weary and dehydrated, I fall inside, prop myself at the bar and order two pints of orange juice and lemonade. The barman becomes distracted, a food order to take to a table, a phone call to answer, a local to pass time with. Doesn't he realise the gravity of the situation! My head is tipped forward, or to be precise, slumped. He then pours me my two pints and like John Mills in *Ice Cold in Alex* I savour them then slug one back then take my time over the second. A third follows before I recover enough to order food.

I take a seat and heave a sigh of relief. I'm sore and tired and feel I couldn't have walked another yard. As I wait for the food I begin to feel ill. It must be dehydration, I'm getting a 'three in the morning' alcohol-fuelled sensation that the room is swimming.

The three courses of food are welcome. I check the map over two coffees and realise I've another mile and a half to walk. This is painfully cruel, the bar is no longer the welcome end to my day and is relegated to a mere rest stop.

I wearily shoulder my pack and wonder if this is the end of my Challenge. My right foot is really bad, it's been painful with each footstep today and another hour on it isn't going to help. Cars pass me, headlights on. The cool of the evening descends and I keep checking my watch, counting off any kind of marker I can see. The walk is in two stretches, I'm grateful for the first turn then the walk down the side of Inshriach Forest and the final welcome view of the B&B.

Sue and Ali should be there I think. Actually I'm not thinking at all for when I walk up the long drive, ring the doorbell I'm met by three concerned faces. The owners, Nick and Patsy Thompson, and Ali are all by the door. In an instant I realise my lack of thought.

"We've been worried about you. And I've just reported you as overdue to 'Challenge Control'," says Ali.

It rapidly sinks in. I should have phoned from Kincraig and reported my recovery at the local hostelry. It's 21:35.

"If I had my time again I'd have phoned," I offer.

I just about get away with it.

Ali phones 'Challenge Control' and reports my safe arrival. Patsy offers me the floor to collapse on to remove my boots, a room with a bath is supplied and I crawl off to refresh and recover.

With rinsed-out clothes draped on radiators; I pull myself between the sheets. I ache from head to toe. Pains shoot from my hips to meet those on their way up from my feet. I feel I'm out. Too tired, too blistered.

On Thursday May 14th I wake in a positive mood. The will to keep going and a few hours of sleep tip the balance back in my favour. It's a short day today, no rush. Ali comes in and dresses my right foot and gives me a prescription for antibiotics: in case it gets infected.

It's my last day with Ali and Sue as our routes diverge. I make use of their redundant resupply box and post back everything I can. Spare hat, gloves, used-up maps, book, radio, spare top, undies, hankies and just about everything else I can think of.

After a cooked breakfast, and a £20 note to Mr Thompson to cover the postage of our three parcels south, we are out the door. That's the easy bit because between the door and the road is a long drive with one or two rather inviting picnic tables. The three of us slump at the first and wave the Thompsons goodbye as they depart for their day.

Once every excuse to rest has been exhausted, we set off. It's still painful to walk, the first few paces making me wonder 'how on earth?'. But after a few minutes I find my stride and the pain becomes a less tiresome companion.

I notice a horn tucked into Sue's pack. "What's that doing?" I ask, "I thought you were telling me I was carrying excess weight."

"Phil Turner gave it to me."

"Phil gave you the horn then?" I chip in.

There's silence. The world stands still while I prepare for a reaction and prepare my response for every reaction. Fortunately there's a laugh and I'm off the hook.

We take the pretty forest track to Feshiebridge. I still feel drained but, with Ali and Sue both being dog lovers, my humorous negotiating for a rest is circumvented by a team of resting husky dogs, chained to individual stakes. Their owners, a middle-aged couple, are sorting their mobile support unit, in the guise of a long wheel-based van. The wheeled cart, the huskies pull, is parked to one side.

The dogs bark our entrance and are calmed, one by one, by their owners and our stretched out hands. Ali and Sue embark in long conversations on dog ownership while I take the chance of a rest. My contribution to the intellectual conversation is restricted to the following:

"Do you compete with them?" asks Ali.

"Yes," replies the man.

"You must do well to keep up," I chip in.

Ali raises her eyebrows; it's lost on the chap.

We set off and enjoy the forestry tracks, a freshness in the air and a rich blue sky. Ali and Sue become deep in conversation about buying their own B&B. Even the respective labour divisions of their husbands are discussed. My only contribution is to request disposable razors in each room.

We bump into another dog owner, I realise how useful they are as I take another rest. It's hard to get going again: after each stop, my right foot is very painful to get moving. I'm also troubled by a multitude of smaller blisters, but the TGO Challenge is about tenacity and the human spirit. The Montrose check in, at the end of the Challenge, is made up of the walking wounded.

At Drake's Bothy we pause to rest, chatting to some cyclists. The familiar voice of fellow challenger, the Reverend David Albon comes from the entrance to the bothy. Ali and Sue abandon our conversation and leap towards him, greeting him with hugs and kisses. I take my time and offer a polite handshake.

We lunch then set off for a camping pitch that David knows. This consists of careful navigation around forestry tracks, the crossing of the Cairngorm Club Footbridge then about a one mile walk to meadow grass on the bend in a river by a clutch of Scots Pine trees.

It's a beautiful setting, the hills behind us glow in the light, the water of the river glistens, high trees gently bow and swish in the light breeze. We pitch our tents in a circle and sort out our kit.

The weather forecast is poor for the next few days. I use a welcome phone signal to try and book in for Saturday night at The Fife Arms in Braemar. They can't confirm the booking until the next day so I leave them my parent's number, assuming I'll be out of signal range before office hours.

MA, who has had car troubles, bikes in to meet us, stays and chats for a while. We then prepare our meals in the warm evening sun. David, like all blokes, thinks dehydrated takeaway is an excellent idea.

"The trouble is you've got curry every night," says Ali.

"And your point is?"

Ali then points out I don't attach the security tabs on the central hoop of my tent.

"What happens if I don't?"

"The guy lines don't work unless you attach all the hoops."

"That's something I now have to worry about. Ignorance was bliss."

The conversation goes on in to the evening, Ali and Sue crowd into David's tent, I elect to sit in the doorway of my own.

When I turn in I recall my walk of yesterday and my state of tiredness when I arrived at the B&B. What a difference a day makes.

Friday May 15th dawns overcast with drizzle, the forecast likely accurate. I say goodbye to my departing camp mates and make a slow start on the fifteen kilometres to Corrour Bothy, over the infamous Lairig Ghru.

Tumbling streams and Scots Pines accompany the gentle forestry ascent, my body copes better and the softer ground is kind to my feet. The skies grey and the clouds hang low on the mountains ahead. A light rain starts. As I rise, the temperature drops, the wind picks up, the clouds descend and the rain meets me with gusting lashes.

I meet others passing the other way, brief words are exchanged about the conditions offering not much hope of improvement. My jacket starts to leak. I rue not having donned my fleece, now too windy to contemplate opening the pack for. The wind cuts into my chest and I have the persistent feeling of having just jumped into a swimming pool.

The conditions aren't the worst I've experienced, in my younger days I was the archetypal southerner who'd drive to Scotland and head into the mountains whatever the conditions. At times I haven't been able to stand on summits, a crawl being all the elements would allow. Today is poor though and I have to stand and brace the wind and rain with all my efforts going into staying put rather than moving forth. Lulls allow progress into the headwind. What a difference a day makes…

I dread hypothermia, the wind and rain are ripping the warmth from my body. I've experienced it once before, sat soaked and sorry at a Munro summit cairn. Again with no fleece the wind and rain had sucked the heat out of me. My co-ordination had gone, my reactions sluggish and a little voice, deep from inside, prodded me awake and got me off the mountain.

I grip the map in my soaked glove and, with the aid of my altimeter, which serves to keep me mentally alert, reach the high point of 2750 feet and a hailstorm to keep me company. Over the summit and after a bit of descent, I get some shelter. The wind is still in my face, but it's now bearable as the worst of the weather is funnelling over the high pass between the steep Munro slopes guarding the Lairig. I'd planned this TGO Challenge to take in areas I hadn't previously done. This includes Glen Strathfarrar, the ferry across Loch Ness, the Monadhliath and the Lairig Ghru. These conditions are awful, I'm having no fun and make a mental note to make a diary entry for October marked 'Don't apply for the TGO Challenge'.

My hands go numb under my soggy gloves, making a call of nature impossible to attend to. The descent is long, over five kilometres until the roof of Corrour Bothy comes into view. It's welcome. Up until now every rock face that came into view I'd imagined as its gable end. I cross the bridge leading to it, admire the attached toilet block, enter into the porch then the main building.

"Hello," I say.

"Hello," reply two Belfast accents.

"Are you on the TGO Challenge?" I ask

"No, what's that?"

I explain and they mention the larger than usual number of people they've seen. They are two brothers, Stuart and Andy, snatching a week in the Highlands before Andy's return to Afghanistan. They are kitted out in army gear.

Rainwater is draining out of my pack so I attempt to lift one of their packs to save it from the puddle. I can only just manage it, the weight is unimaginable. We pass the time discussing the futility and hopelessness of the wars in Iraq and Afghanistan. I hear first-hand accounts of what the politicians would rather not hear, or perhaps rather not tell you.

My day has taken six hours and it's now 15:00. I'm aware the bothy may get busy so I choose to cook early. The parcel I sent home included as much food as I could do without, so this is my last food of the day.

I use the nails, driven into the walls, to hang my wet gear on. Stuart and Andy mention they plan to camp so I bag the one raised sleeping platform. I explain the bothy will get busy. Andy promptly goes out and sets up his tent.

"That's the last we'll see of him," says Stuart.

Over the course of the next five hours twelve more challengers arrive into the tiny confines of the bothy.

"Trust you to take the best bed," announces Maggie Hems, greeting me for the first time in two years – her charm hasn't deserted her.

"I simply got here first," I explain.

Frank Row with Lesley and Lawrence Dark arrive. Frank elects to camp but after an hour reappears asking for rescue. The central pole of his tent had bent down in the wind. His companions dart out and his tent is rescued. This halts all plans Stuart had of camping, and he decides to stay in the bothy.

Fiona Bennett, Marion Mitchell, Fran Mellors and Marie Donohoe arrive. Glad to be out of the growing storm yet in good spirits. Stories of the pass through the Lairig Ghru are exchanged.

I venture out to the loo. A wooden structure attached to the southerly gable. By now the roof of the main building is rattling ominously. A couple of times we'd all just stopped and looked at one another as a ferocious gust had blown through and tested the workmanship of the Mountain Bothies Association.

I fight the loo door open and pull it closed behind me and drop the simple latch built into the handle. I take my seat which is a hole on a raised platform. The door blows open and smacks my bare right leg. I now begin a wrestling match to close it and am reminded of the 'who owns the sock' game one plays with a determined Labrador. The wind is so strong all I can manage to do is hold it back from bashing my leg. Its power is equal to my power to push against it, like stalemate in an arm wrestle. It's the first time I've ever sat on a loo fighting off the wind!

The wind relents for a few seconds and I manage to close the door and hold it fast with my right foot. This doesn't make the job in hand any easier yet my modesty and fear of being beaten to death by a wooden door, are protected.

Back in the bothy Fiona offers chocolate. I'm grateful for the fine Green and Blacks as by now I'm hungry and have no food spare. Vicky Allen her aunt, Barbara Johnson and cousin Kathy Powell arrive. Barbara is eighty, on her tenth crossing and appears in the doorway in a very sorry state. Soaked through and exhausted she's been caught out by a day that started mildly then turned into a storm which increased by the hour until the safest course of action was to keep going to the bothy.

Fiona, Marion and Fran go to her aid. Barbara has reached an age where her reserves are low, we can all dig deep and find the energy to keep going – all Barbara's have been spent getting here.

Her clothes are changed and I exchange worried glances with

the others. Never having used my foil blanket I'd posted it back from Kincraig. I ask if anybody has one, Leslie has a fine one and that is then draped over the barely lucid Barbara as she is offered a hot drink. She vomits and I wonder if I need to walk on for help. Fiona, Marion and Fran do an excellent job.

By now I've pushed my gear to one side of the sleeping platform so I can share it. The place is booked for Barbara and she is lifted up. I take her right hand, Fran her left as we try and get warmth into her. A spare tin of Heinz tomato soup was in the bothy when I arrived. I'd nabbed it but now offer it back and, while it is being heated up, I'm given the job of talking to Barbara to keep her awake.

"Where did you start?" "How many crossings have you done?" "Where will you finish?" are all met with a whisper of an answer. The soup is ready, Barbara takes sips then vomits again. Though by now her voice is stronger and her temperature is getting back to normal. We think it'll be okay.

Koos Schellevis is the last to arrive, making fourteen in all in the small room. He's dripping wet and is shown the toilet to change in. Looking nonplussed, he leaves his things in the porch and takes the last place by the door. Leslie gives Koos some food, and, full of embarrassment for my own short rations, ask if she has any spare. A bread roll and a piece of cake are very welcome.

We settle for sleep, many sit up as there isn't enough floor space for laying out. I manage to sleep well, the platform being shorter than me means I have to bend my knees. Each time I move I disturb Barbara and am relieved to feel her move.

The long wild night is replaced by the dim glow of dawn through the tiny bothy window. People start to move and everybody is polite and considerate when moving round one another. Kit had been disbursed to the four corners of the bothy and it's a major operation to reunite people with their belongings. Stuart, the youngest person in the bothy and the only one not on the Challenge, is a true gent. He'd slept sat up (a generous gesture and one I hadn't made) and uses a powerful torch to guide anybody searching for a lost item. Koos, with his dry Dutch manner, says "Careful" after every trip or slip.

Barbara sits up and speaks. "Thank you everybody for saving my life. This is my tenth and last crossing."

"This is my first and last," adds her daughter, Kathy.

I get going at 08:00, out into the rain again, unsure if I have a room in Braemar or whether it'll be the campsite. A room would be welcome to sort my gear, feet and get dry. I soon catch up with Barbara and Kathy, then Vicky just ahead. She asks me my name, in the melee of the wild night we hadn't been introduced. As soon as I mention it she reels off my adventures, written up online. I'm touched yet embarrassed: I don't tend to remember other people's accounts.

Ahead on my own it's a squelch to the Luibeg Bridge. I recall my Munro exploits to this area – a fifteen-hour walk that had me making a late evening bid to return to Braemar Youth Hostel before closing time. Today I'm not against the clock, just against myself. I count the distance off, passing small patches of trees before the track through the forest and the drop to Mar Lodge. I cross the well-kept grounds and emerge on the road to Braemar, sparing myself the tiresome and feet wearing tarmac between the Linn of Dee and Victoria Bridge.

A check of my texts reveals I have a room in Braemar. This lifts my spirits and I make good progress and bump into Jenny Wheeler as she makes her way east to Mar Lodge after a shopping trip to Braemar. It's good to see her, it's been two years. We chat for a while, exchange stories and I hear of how her new boots hospitalised her in Fort William with badly-blistered toes. She praises Mar Lodge and I wish I'd called in for at least a cup of tea. I confess to having had chocolate the night before, she forgives me the one slip.

"Time to move on from the rabbit," I say as our conversation comes to an end.

She catches my gaze, looking down at the decaying corpse we've been stood alongside.

"Thanks for pointing that out, Steve!" she retorts.

Braemar takes its usual form, checking into the hotel, showering, hanging the tent over the shower rail, milling around, chatting to people, sharing stories. My foot inspection shows swelling and tenderness and has me visiting the chemists and making use of Dr Ali's prescription for antibiotics.

I phone into 'Challenge Control' and speak with Alan Hardy. He's done a quick crossing and is manning the desk. He is such a quick walker I wonder if he's ever phoned in and answered it himself. I ponder what it must be like on 'Challenge Control'. There are over three hundred people heading your way, trying to keep tabs on them all, concern at those overdue. I wonder if it's like wartime Bomber Command, counting the planes home with worry about those not answering.

I get a text from my mum saying they've taken Bobby, the cat their vet was offering them, on. However, he appears to have overcome his aloofness by being rather over friendly in the hormone department. He's trying to create kittens from anybody's leg that appears within grabbing distance.

I have supper in the hotel with Russ Manion. He's on his tenth crossing, celebrating by wearing a kilt which, with his long white locks, sets him distinctively apart. We are the only two TGO Challenge guests in the hotel, long gone is this the throbbing hub of the Challenge. It's now owned by a tour company which has this hotel catering for those seeing Scotland from a coach.

We get on to the topic of our routes to the coast.

"I don't fancy putting up my tent again," I say.

"You were one of the first with a Laser Lite tent," says Russ in his smooth fireside voice.

Again I'm flattered by the memory of another.

"What's your route to the coast?" he asks.

"I don't feel up to the high ground or the road walk."

"Have you thought of Gelder Shiel?"

I admit to my lack of knowledge so he promises to bring maps to breakfast. I spend part of the evening in the bar, catch up with sleep then rise before six to sort my kit.

Russ is true to his word and, over breakfast, shows me the route to Gelder Shiel bothy. It looks like a fine route out, and perhaps within my capacity of being tired to the bone and sporting feet which bleed at the slightest knock. My maps don't show the entire route so I sketch in the missing portions.

The last few days have reminded me of the non-competitive nature of the Challenge: people are there for you and you for them. It's an often said thing when you have a problem it's the Challenge folk who are the first to be in touch.

The TGO Challenge represents what we yearn for: a community offering freedom and support. It brings out the best in a world which otherwise encourages prosperity by the worst of behaviours.

I'm in no hurry to set off and instead relax in the hotel lobby. The standard residents, grey, pale and overweight, wobble their way down the stairs. They are no older than many of the challengers but their life path so different. Ali, on her first Challenge, realised the TGO Challenge folk are the people she doesn't see in her doctor's surgery.

I wander around, Jenny sees me and I shyly show her my purchase of chocolate. I have lunch, visit an outdoor shop to buy the one extra evening meal needed to get me to the coast. The first one I find is dehydrated vegetarian curry, I elect to try something different so choose pasta in tomato sauce.

It takes an hour and forty minutes to walk to Invercauld Bridge where I take a welcome turn off the traffic-ridden A93. I navigate the forest in rising temperature. I sit, contemplate, free from all worry other than what's in my pack and the few days ahead. The skies are good again, fluffy white clouds intermingle the blue sky. Scots pines are either side of the track but with room for heather, luscious grass and light to pour through.

Out of the trees, on high ground I walk below the towering cliffs of Cnapan Nathraichean. I look back and bid the Cairngorms farewell, gracious in the gentle calm – innocent to the storm of forty eight hours before.

I make good progress on the track. Ahead is Lochnagar, a long mountain towering from the plains. I arrive at Gelder Shiel bothy, a simple building on the opposite side of a track to an attractive lodge.

Vicky, Kathy and Russ greet me at the door. Barbara is asleep inside. I choose a cot-like bunk, making keeping one's possessions together an ease. Shawn Grund, an American and the youngest challenger, joins us. Barbara at eighty the equal oldest means we have an age range of fifty-nine years below our roof. We are also joined by the spirited Anna Tertel from Poland. Both she and Shawn are making solo crossings having planned it all from foreign lands.

Compared with Corrour Bothy the space is luxurious. Many camp and use the bothy to cook and chat. It's a peaceful atmosphere in a beautiful setting with the sun sinking to a low glow over mountains and burns. Behind the bothy is the loo, a back window allows us a view of those opening its door. To a person there's the same reaction: an eager face (pleased not to have to poo and bury it in the wilds) opens the door, pauses, draws in eyebrows, drops chin and reels back. I choose to hold on and not pay a visit.

I get a good night's sleep – the bothy's layout offers comfort and reassurance as companions lie a few feet away. The stir starts a bit before 06:00, people dress, stoves go on and I stay put. It's a short day today, over to the next bothy, the Shielin of Mark.

Vicky comes in from her tent to ensure Barbara and Kathy are making progress for the day ahead. I stay in my bed as others, who have camped outside, make use of the bothy's tables and chairs for breakfast and repacking.

I'm last to rise. I pull my things together, breakfast on Jacob's Cream Crackers then set forth. Suckered by a useful-looking bridge, I find myself on a rising mountain track. I return and pick up the right path, following the stream then branching across a boggy mush to reach the Land Rover track heading south then east to the head of Loch Muick.

Lochnagar has her head in the clouds, and I recall a long day up there doing a succession of Munros. It starts to rain as I bump into Russ and others. They rest and I set off, Anna a bit behind me. We play rest and catch up for a while before we walk together. I struggle a bit with her accent, as I'm sure she does with mine. She's good fun, strong minded and, judging by the size of her pack physically very strong too.

The rain is tiresome, damp penetrates my arms and chest as we drop down the track, through a brief pine forest before reaching the visitor centre at the Spittal of Glenmuick. It is unstaffed so we make use of its dry confines and the drinks machine does a roaring trade with sixty pence after sixty pence exchanged for hot chocolate and soup. I'm glad to be out of the rain and stay as long as I can, making use of the clean loo before setting off up the steep south-easterly path that follows an impressive river in a deep gorge.

It rains, it drizzles and I keep my spirits up by thinking how lucky I am to still be in the Challenge. I thought I was out at Kincraig but now it all appears to be coming together, even if a bit damply. I catch Barbara, Kathy and Vicky. They urge me to go on but I want to stay with them. They're good company which I enjoy but also the terrain is rough, the day is short and there is security in numbers.

As we emerge from the gorge and break out on to open land, we estimate it's just a mile to the bothy. Yet this is no ordinary mile, a mile can be short and a mile can be long because when said quickly no account is taken of the terrain. And this is tough ground, few routes are fitful through the peat hags and bogs. Then there's the matter of the bothy being out of sight. Situated in a dip you almost stumble onto its roof before you see it.

Barbara is slow, her age having caught up with her over the last year so we stay on a compass bearing to ensure we hit the bothy and don't waste unnecessary steps. Keeping on a bearing is impossible so Vicky and I 'box'. This involves agreeing on the bearing, one person staying rooted while the other walks forward, avoiding bogs and hags then drifting back onto the bearing. The rooted person then waves them left or right to get them aligned, then goes forward, passing the other, who is now rooted, and getting ahead is then waved onto the bearing. We do this half a dozen times until I spot the bothy, just a dozen or so metres off bearing.

The bothy is welcome, yet dingy and damp in comparison to the fine one of the previous night. There are two raised platforms. Anna joins us and ponders whether to go on. The river, usually an easy crossing, is high, swollen as it gutters the water off the high ground. Vicky is concerned and surveys the bank.

"There's a possible crossing upstream," she says.

I ponder this as I try to dry Barbara's, Kathy's and my jackets in the breeze between showers. I leave the jackets to hang on a line and wander up with her.

"You see that island, I think you can easily wade to it. It's then a short knee-deep crossing. Though I'm worried about Barbara being able to withstand the current."

I peer at the proposed route, it isn't enticing, nor is a long walk north to avoid the crossing and risk finding an even worse swollen river. I decide to take the head in the sand 'worry about it in the morning view' and return to gather the jackets as the rain blows in again.

Anna is still debating whether to stay or go. I make her a platform out of an old door and two benches. This does it for her and she decides to set off with Russ, Mick and a few others. Vicky and I go to watch. Mick crosses, throws his poles back which I gather for Anna. She makes it but looks somewhat wet. The rain blows in again and without my jacket, I return to the bothy. Vicky returns and reports them all safely across.

The evening starts to slip by with supper and new arrivals falling between those staying and those attempting the river crossing tonight. Jenny arrives and camps, so does Bernie Roberts and a few others. Maria and Stuart Scott arrive late, eat then decide to make use of the last of the light and cross.

Shawn, having climbed Lochnagar and arrived after us, makes use of the final sleeping platform.

Last night, at Gelder Shiel bothy, somebody read from the bothy book, "Walked in with twenty kilograms of coal to find no fireplace." That has to be the hamlet cigar moment of all bothy nights. Tonight is more typical: a fireplace but no fuel. We make attempts with some pre-cut peat but all that burns is the methylated spirits we try to light it with. It gives a few moments of hope, then, like the preverbal Christmas pudding flickers and dies.

"Lovely fire," we all say with irony as we edge forward for warmth from the imaginary flame.

Kathy and Barbara share a platform, both for warmth and consideration to not use up two. Barbara, who has been alternating between resting and chatting, sits up in her sleeping bag wearing her hat. She touches Kathy's arm through gloved hand and in a soft mesmerising voice begins to recite the 'The Cremation of Sam McGee' by Robert W. Service. We all fall silent as the rain drums on the bothy roof, the wind gentle wisps and howls and the bothy feels oh so cold. Barbara lifts and lowers her voice to the rhyming flows, lifts and lowers her hand to Kathy's arm as the poem flicks between speech and narration.

There's silent reflection when she finishes. I'm amazed anybody can commit such a long poem to memory. The best I ever did was a playground limerick about a young lady from Leeds who swallowed a packet of Suttons finest.

Tuesday May 19th dawns after a night of rough sleep. It's starting to feel like the Challenge is coming to an end – today will be the last of the mountains as we cross to Tarfside via Muckle Cairn and Glen Lee.

We rise and breakfast. Barbara offers me a triangle of Dairylea – welcome with my dry Jacobs crackers. I shall never forget this piece of Dairylea, it's up there with the excitement of going to the theatre or seeing a great film for the first time. Everything is relative and in a society where food is taken for granted what gives us a thrill is getting bigger by the decade. Rollback to the basics and the small things become big things, they shine through with the people who come with them.

I finish packing, including the daily routine of setting my curry and rice to rehydrate. This involves emptying the dried flakes into my cooking pot, filling it with water, covering with thin plastic, pushing the lid on, taping over the steam hole then securing in a plastic bag.

With postulations long aside there's a river to cross and seven of us to do it. I go first and, on Vicky's advice, unclip my pack so if the worst happens, and I go under, I can free myself from it. The first part is easy, made with ankles above water. I pause on the island, spot a submerged rock, park one foot on it then scramble up the bank. To my relief my gaiters have held tight.

As the others begin to cross I realise I have to be the anchor man. I slip back down the bank, perching myself on a peat hag that's determined to wobble with my every movement.

One by one people cross. I guide them with instructions, which rock to aim for when to jump and when to make a grab for my hand. I have to tailor advice based on age, weight and leg length. Barbara is escorted and we manage to lift her out onto the bank.

A rest involving draining out boots and changing socks follows before the damp trudge up Muckle Cairn in the company of Barbara, Vicky and Jenny. Barbara tells me of her exploits, trekking the world in her senior years. She then recites a poem her son, Frank Johnson, wrote from his home in Australia on the day of President Barack Obama's inauguration:

I sat and watched his speech today
This man who will lead the USA
and though I was a world away
I had to brush a tear away.

He's given all of us some hope
Not just the usual old soft soap.
The world is on a slippery slope.
Is this young man our safety rope?

He called to us, the teeming throng
to listen to his stirring song.
Now come my people let's be strong.
The course we take is steep and long.

Six billion people heard that man
The sceptics wondered if he can
affect the change in uncle Sam.
The crowd roared YES, OH YES WE CAN!

"Your memory is amazing," I say.

"There are lots more where that came from," adds Kathy.

I love the company and we join with Ian Shiel who, in his true gentlemanly style, trades his better trekking poles with Barbara's for the descent into Glen Lee.

A river crossing has Ian as the anchor man, helping us cross through the funnelled rush of the waters draining from the mountains. Ian, the son of a sure-footed shepherd, has us all over in no time.

As it's raining Barbara and family urge Jenny and I to walk on ahead. I'm a bit unsure but the track is now good so it'll just be a slow plod into Tarfside for them. Jenny and I know, given the hour, there's no chance of getting a bed at the hostel but elect to go ahead to spend more time enjoying the social scene. As beds can't normally be booked ahead Russ has been tasked with asking if one can be reserved for Barbara.

"I do hope mum has a bed," says Kathy.

"With Russ's charm I've no doubt they'll hold one for her," I add.

It's good to walk with Jenny, great company and I lose myself in conversation with her and forget about my foot pain. When it's time for a lunch stop we sit, out of the rain, in the porch of a derelict house. Glass and dead mice have to be evicted before bottoms can be parked.

"Is that your lunch?" asks Jenny as I unwrap a single piece of flapjack.

"I've reduced my rations to keep the weight down."

Jenny takes pity on me and I'm offered pita bread and peanut butter which is delicious.

We reach Tarfside and pitch our tents on the village green. Retiring to St Drostan's Hostel we drink the tea and eat the cake supplied by Ann, Janet and Carole. As ever the ladies do a sterling effort amidst the chaos of people arriving and what must be a pungent whiff of unwashed walkers.

Given the number of tents we reckon about a third of the Challenge are here this evening. You spot a face, think hard and recall you spent a few hours' walking with them just a week ago. Others call hello and you stop to remember when you last met them. Val Hadden and Mary Brook are all smiles and it takes me a second to remember I walked with them into Tarfside on this day of the Challenge five years ago. Old acquaintances become renewed acquaintances and I feel guilty I'm abandoning the people I've walked with over the last day or so. Alas I worry needlessly for everybody is deep in conversation with others. Tales abound of wild nights, wild drinking and the bizarre and peculiar people one meets along the way.

News of our wild night in Corrour Bothy has travelled far and, with most of us from that night now in Tarfside, we become legends. We are referred to as 'The Corrour Fourteen'. We discuss T-shirts and reunion events.

It feels good, a buzz, and we all eat at the hostel before drifting back to our tents. For Barbara and Kathy there's a welcome room in the hostel. Jenny and I have pitched next to one another. A sorry-looking Sue and Ali are a few yards away, Ali's knee is playing up and Sue's dog, sick back at home, is causing her concern. I try for conversation but realise the timing isn't right and slink back to my tent.

Tent sorting and chatting follows, Jenny goes off to the loo and a few minutes later she is being helped back to her tent.

"Steve, guess what I've done," she says. Her face looks pained and distressed.

"What?" I ask, concerned.

"The wooden ramp out of the ladies loo was very slippery. I went flying and landed heavily on my back."

Tarfside Tents

This could be serious for Jenny. She has osteoporosis, three slipped discs and, due to associated nerve damage, can't lift her right foot. She drives a modified car, is amazing to be on the Challenge and doesn't allow adversity to get in the way of the life she wants to lead. But if a slippery ramp out of ladies loo has ruined her crossing this would be unjust in the extreme.

Myself and John, who helped her, are very concerned. She also has a badly-bruised and cut arm. We help her to her tent where she begins to sort herself out. I spy in the distance a council grit bin, borrow Jenny's bright orange trowel and set forth to help prevent another accident.

I'm waiting for the calls of, "You don't need a trowel for these loos, Steve" but I'm spared it. About a dozen trips between the grit bin and the ramp (there is no suitable bucket to hand) has it more or less safe.

I return and see Jenny is very uncomfortable but she says she's taken strong pain killers and is waiting for them to take effect. I ask if she needs to visit hospital but she assures me rest is better. Having been hospitalised once already on this Challenge I'm sure she's reluctant to add to her visits. I promise not to wear ear plugs and she promises to shout and wake me if she needs help in the night. She gives me an energy bar which I enjoy in my sleeping bag.

I lay awake, a distant car sound system is blaring away as local youths share their pleasure with all who'd rather sleep. Though I count my blessings, it isn't raining.

I wake a bit before 06:00 on Wednesday May 20th. The tent is damp and I struggle to get myself moving. I survey the unappealing cream crackers for breakfast then my cooking pot. Having eaten at the hostel the curry and rice, I set to rehydrate twenty-four hours ago, is still there. It'd be a waste – wouldn't it? I put on the stove and perhaps become the first man to purchase a curry in Marlborough and have it for breakfast in Scotland.

Jenny and I set off just before 07:30, deep in conversation we miss each bridge that crosses to the pretty tracks on the south side of the River North Esk. Instead we remain on the road realising, each time too late, we've overshot a crossing point. Cars, buses and lorries give us space until a large Vauxhall comes round a bend towards us. Tilted at speed he honks and shakes a wild fist gesticulating us to walk single file. We return to our peace and let him speed on to wherever his life is taking him.

Jenny shows me how she manages her right foot. Unable to lift it she lifts her leg, to clear the foot of the ground, and manages to drop it down with an almost imperceptible limp.

"How is the back?" I ask.

"I used a hand mirror this morning to check the bruise on my coccyx."

"That'll be a rear view mirror," I quip. Realising I'd just been a tad flippant I ask, "What was it like?"

"Quite large."

Dead rabbits litter the road. It's as if they've been dropping out of the trees. Not one or two but an exceptional crop interspersed with the occasional bird (which could be excused for dropping out of its tree). They are in varying states of decay and we ponder the quantity.

We pass Millden Lodge and, with the realisation we've overshot another bridge, we turn back.

"Don't let me hold you up, Steve. You can go on and I'll meet you at Edzell."

"No, it's okay," I reply.

"I worry I am too slow for you."

You're going at a perfect pace, keep it up, I think. We venture back and walk into the grounds of Millden Lodge, cross the bridge only to find it gated and locked on the south shore. Covering the same ground again we try for the bridge just north of Haughend.

"I think we've missed it again," I say.

"Let's try this track," replies Jenny, pointing.

It leads towards the river then loops back. Jenny gives me a GPS reading and we've overshot. We climb down to the banks of the river and make a determined northward charge along the riverbank. After ducking overhanging growth, circumventing undergrowth, twists and turns we find the bridge, dilapidated yet serviceable enough for our purposes. We emerge amongst a strange array of wooden barrack like buildings. Now on the beaten track we celebrate with a rest and a pre-Edzell lunch break which involves me eating more of Jenny's pita and peanut butter.

We take more care over navigation and manage the tracks cutting the corner off the road into Edzell. Proud of ourselves we indulge in a game of inventing acronyms for the three letters of each car number plate that passes us. We award bonus points if they are relevant to the TGO Challenge.

"TSW."

"Tired Scottish Walkers."

"BSF"

"Blistered Sore Feet."

"JSB."

"Jenny's Sore Back."

In Edzell we stop at a familiar café where I lose all interest in healthy eating and order deep-fried mushrooms followed by a kaleidoscope of ice cream. Sat opposite Jenny, a vegan, I worry about what the deep-fried mushrooms will do to me. As for the ice cream – the blue sauce was delicious.

Once lunched, we shop for evening food, make use of the post office where upon a lapse of concentration has me leaving my bank card in the machine. Fortunately the next customer spots it and, with Jenny still in the shop, it is returned to me.

Outside an elderly gent, accompanied by his wife, arrives on his bright red three-wheeled tricycle.

"That's a fine machine," I say.

"I'm unstable on two wheels now, so I bought this," he replies.

"Great basket too," says Jenny admiring the white-framed basket which I secretly wonder if his wife rides in.

We mill about for a bit, chat with Kathy, Barbara, Vicky, Bernie and many more. We then set off down the track between the post office and the garage.

Part way down the dropping track we come across 'Mrs Trike' trying to push the bike downhill. It's tilted towards her, riding on just the front and one of the back wheels. She's having trouble controlling it.

"Do you want a hand?" I ask.

"Oh would you, I'm having some trouble with it."

Jenny takes her in conversation as I take over steering the fine, bright red machine. At the bottom is a T junction in the path.

"Where do you live?" asks Jenny.

The lady points to the other side of the river and for the first time I observe her closely and realise she is very elderly, likely in her nineties.

"Did your husband come across the footbridge?" asks Jenny.

"No, we came round on the road."

We wheel the trike to the left then onto the footbridge. It barely fits, just a half inch either side. By now Jenny and I are pondering the wisdom of this.

"I think we should turn back," says the lady.

We do so and back on the path a long line of challengers pass us and I'm mercilessly ribbed for my new mode of transport.

"There's an old chap in the high street looking for his trike," says one.

Once the crowd has passed the lady says, "I think I should wait for my husband here."

"Do you normally bring the trike this way?" asks Jenny.

"No, we don't."

"Let's go back to the high street and find your husband," I suggest.

"Yes, yes I think we should do that now."

We set off, at a snail's pace with Jenny holding the old lady in conversation. At the foot of the slope, leading back to the main street, the elderly gent appears. I don't know if he's more pleased to see his wife or his trike.

"Thank you," he says, "I'll push it on from here."

I look at him, look at the trike, look at Jenny. She kits him out with two walking poles as I begin to push the trike. I stay just ahead of them so they can keep me in sight in case they are concerned I'm making off with it.

We make it back to the high street amidst a conversation of her explaining her reasons and him, unable to fully appreciate his wife's confusion, saying what trouble she's put this nice young man to. At the top I swap the trike for Jenny's poles and he takes my hand to shake.

"God bless you, you've booked your place in heaven."

I look into his elderly eyes, observe his height and build and see my grandfather who we lost last year, just a month before his ninety third birthday. He even takes my hand as Grampy did, shaking my right, covering it with his left.

I return to Jenny and we bask in the glory of our good deed of the day.

"He must have cycled that in on the main road," says Jenny.

I ponder this, "Yes, he must have."

"I'm full of admiration for him to want to keep going but it must be dangerous," she replies.

"You sense they shouldn't be out on their own, especially in charge of a tricycle."

We make it back onto our route and I explain we are about to pass the bull with the unfeasibly large testicles. "Believe it or not these are the biggest pair of nuts you'll see on the TGO Challenge," I explain.

Alas he isn't there, his field empty and my chance of further schoolboy humour in tatters.

We pass through farmland tracks, avoiding the straight road to our left with its speeding traffic. Beyond is a disused airfield with associated hangars. Then there's the bull, quietly munching in the field. I point him out with glee. Actually I point out nothing more than his pendulous assets but Jenny gets the idea.

We decide the farm tracks are getting too complicated, the ground too boggy and head towards the road. Bert Hendrikse is on hand to drive away nosey bullocks and help open heavy gates. On the road we are joined by Shawn and we wonder on his take of our number plate game.

"HTS."

"Helping The Seniors."

"NAC."

"Nearly across."

Shawn is softly spoken, and there are gaps in conversation as we play our game interspersed by chat about his university life and plans. Then quietly he joins with our game, coming up with acronyms to wile away the monotony of the road.

At the North Water Bridge campsite the volume of tents grows in the evening sun. I count over fifty, Shawn had counted sixty-seven at

Tarfside. There's the chance to wander around and I'm called to two groups to explain the story of the red tricycle. Back at the tents Kathy joins us for a chat, then Ali and Sue. Ali, forever the one to champion my love life, takes me to one side and, nodding towards Jenny, asks, "Who is she then?"

I phone my mum to report that I've nearly finished the walk and ask how Bobby, the hormonal leg baby-making cat, is doing.

"Hmm," she replies. "It's a bit of a concern, he's hanging on to your dad's leg right now and 'rubbing himself'."

I then hear the phone being rested down. "Bobby, bobby, get off him. Get off." She then comes back on the line. "The little bugger," she adds.

It sounds worse then she'd described.

It's sunny when I wake and I can't quite believe this is the last day of the Challenge. Tonight it'll be the celebratory meal and a hotel room. Tomorrow will be the train ride home and home is where somehow survival feels a bit harder. More chores to distract, phones to shrill, emails to answer, bills to pay and more than one pot to wash each night.

I hear Jenny moving then call out to me to see if I'm awake. We then have a conversation through the tent material. I head for the washroom and make use of the hot water.

Dave Skipp is using the sink next to me. "Steve, mate I'll tell you. People actually use this campsite for their holiday, right next to the A90. I don't know what lives they live but if this is a holiday they must live by the M8 in Glasgow."

Packed up, we set off for St Cyrus following the familiar road walk to the foot of Hill of Morphie (or Hill of Morphine as I indulge a fantasy) where we rest.

Jenny hands me chocolate and a banana. "Thank you for seeing me to the end."

The mutual appreciation society lingers in the air. Ignoring her previous dietary advice she's bought me a bar of chocolate.

I spot a discarded Kit Kat mug behind a post. I pick it up and clean it off. It's a fine red one.

"We've had a break and a Kit Kat mug! I've got lots of chocolate mugs," I say, "but not this one."

I wrap it well in my pack and we set off for the final three miles.

"How are the back and foot?" I ask.

"Fine and you?"

"My foot is still killing me but otherwise okay." I think of another *Ice Cold in Alex* analogy where the truck breaks a spring on the final ride in.

We get to the top of the cliffs and survey the pure sand stretching between the land and the blue, blue sea. We can see south towards the lighthouse and on to Montrose. It feels a long way since I started at Strathcarron.

We make our way to the beach. Shawn is with us now and Jenny paddles her feet. I survey my options and decide to do it. I strip to my undies, run into the sea, hesitate, hesitate again then duck under for a second or so. A couple of strokes to say, 'I swam in the sea' and I'm running back up the beach.

We shake hands with Shawn and both congratulate him wholeheartedly on his achievement. "Shawn, you chanced by the TGO Challenge on the internet, applied, planned your own route, kit and transport. Arranged for time off university and came and did it unsupported. And you are only twenty-one. That's incredible."

He smiles, shyly then says, "I'll regret it if I don't." Strips to his underwear and runs into the sea.

We walk back up the long cliff path, a car passes.

"SBY, Shawn, Shawn..." I say reading off the letters of a car that passes us.

"Shawn's Bloody Young," says Jenny and we get a broad smile from our North American colleague.

We eat at a café then head for the bus. We just miss one then realise it's an hour wait to the next. This turns out to be fortunate as

Shawn realises he has left his wallet and passport in the café. I order a taxi. A big red one arrives with room enough in the boot for a big red tricycle, if such a thing were being carried (the rumour going round is I have it stashed in my pack and am cycling to the coast).

It drops us at The Park hotel, Montrose. We prepare for the ribbing of arriving by taxi but we are spared. We make our way to the Kinnaird Room to sign out and receive handshakes from Roger Smith and Alan Hardy. Our badges, certificates and a bright red celebratory T-shirt follow. Oh and a small bottle of malt whisky which lasts as long it takes to bump into Mick Hopkins.

So I'm happy and far from seeing red, despite the T-shirt, taxi, tricycle and Kit Kat mug. But just a bit sorry this is the end. Jenny is booked on tomorrow's meal so we say our goodbyes for now. She's been great company and we swap contact details and promise to 'Meet soon'.

I wash and clean up in my hotel room then mingle around Montrose and its proliferation of charity shops. Back at The Park Hotel I start to feel guilty with dividing my time, not wishing to appear rude when needing to flit from one person to another. There are many familiar faces to catch up with, but even more I never met on the trail.

The time for the dinner comes and I sit with Shawn, Barbara, Vicky, Kathy and Maggie. I gaze around the room. There is so much noise, so much contrast and a sea of red shirts with the occasional sunburned face to match. People lean forth, turn to their left and their right for conversation. Some wander between tables, catching up and taking photos with people who mean so much. Shawn with his backward baseball cap and black body warmer makes the TGO Challenge commemorative shirt look cool. I feel this is my most memorable crossing, the one I'll miss the most, the extremes of weather offered a variety and despite my own hardships I've enjoyed this crossing the most. As this is my fifth crossing I must have past the one thousand mile point somewhere on the trail.

I await my vegetarian option and, in true Park Hotel tradition, I'm left waiting and waiting. A bowl of pasta arrives, just a bowl – no salad or extras. It looks like five-minute pasta with a cheap sauce. Before I can say, "You're having a laugh" the waiter disappears knowing he's having a laugh. I tuck in to what I could throw together in five minutes.

"I feel I've been done," I announce to the table, "this must account for about ten pounds of the cost of the meal."

Everybody nods in agreement. As I finish it pudding arrives. Sat at the end of the table I slip the bowl of profiteroles onto my lap and cover it with my napkin. As a waitress does the other side I catch her eye and say, "I didn't get one."

"Did you not?" she asks, sounding surprised.

I shake my head and she pops a bowl in front of me. I eat it then, with deft hand, switch the second bowl up.

"Steve," says Vicky, "you've just shot up in my estimation."

Sat next to the eighty-year-old Barbara I ask, "Is this still your last?"

"Yes," she replies with a definite voice, "I'm too slow to do it again."

"Will you do it again?" she asks me.

I nod and make a mental note not to make a mental note to make a diary entry for October marked 'Don't apply for the TGO Challenge'. The TGO Challenge community is too good to miss.

I look over to Kathy and ask, "Your first and last still?"

"At Corrour I said so, but I think Vicky would like me to do it with her now Mum is retiring."

I smile. "And there's this fantastic comradeship," she adds. And we look around the room.

Back home Jenny and I keep in contact and we make plans to meet up in August. She later cancels, explaining she's now seeing a chap from her walking club. I *am* destined to be a solo walker!

July 2009 – Scottish 2000ft Mountains

After completing the May TGO Challenge, and having feet full of blisters to prove it, I decide to press all the easy buttons for a July trip to Scotland. A rather nice cottage, in Blairgowrie, takes my eye and I book it for two weeks. The sleeper up on the night of Friday 3rd of July is added to the shopping list of ease coupled with a hire car, to be collected in Perth.

At 19:00 on the Friday evening of my departure I'm sat at my home computer checking that the 19:17 from Westbury will leave on time. It duly does and I gather heavy rucksack and holdall for the stagger to the station. I feel a sense of pride as the HST pulls in: we'd campaigned for connections to and from the west and, although going east, I am pleased to board the service from Westbury.

It's a hot, sticky evening and, with restricted luggage space, I just wear a T-shirt and jeans, taking the risk that my one packed fleece will see me through two weeks.

Paddington brings a transfer on to the Hammersmith and City line where a series of delays has me arriving at Euston with only two hours to spare; such is my caution at not wasting expensive onward tickets. I kill the time with some not so healthy food before a very tired, hot and weary person drags himself the full length of the sleeper service to find his bunk. Whereupon he promptly wakes up and spends the seven-hour journey snatching no more than an odd hour of sleep.

The romantic idea of breakfast in the early morning of Glasgow is soon relegated to a marmite panini in a Costa Coffee shop. This is all that is hot and vegetarian, and you either love it or hate it. I've always been on the hate side of the marmite fence. But needs must.

The onward trip to Perth goes smoothly with a collection by Enterprise Rent-A-Car at the station. After being whisked to their offices things begin to not go so smoothly.

"So that's £231 plus £150 deposit, Mr Smith, which gives you the two weeks and basic insurance."

I checked my booking form then asked, "But it says here it

includes collision damage waiver."

"Yes, that's right a basic insurance."

"I'm a bit worried by what you mean by basic."

"Well there is the £500 excess."

"It doesn't say anything about that here."

"If you'd read the small print online you'd have seen it."

"I did read the small print," I add (I am that sad).

"Here it is under the optional extra link," he adds.

"But I just read that it included CDW. I did not think to look under any optional extras."

"Well," he drew that word out, "if you had you'd have seen that there was an excess for £500 which you could bring down to zero by paying an additional £10 per day or £100 for a week."

He's truly having a laugh, I think. What's the difference between a collision damage waiver and an excess? Clearly £10 a day. My mind then heaves with the obvious thoughts that it should tell you under the primary text that there is an excess, not under optional extras. And then there's this matter of £10 a day for a week (i.e. £70) can be reduced by paying £100 instead. But before I could respond he adds, "But for a two-week hire we keep it at £100."

"But it does not state there is an excess here."

"Where?" he asked.

"Here on the contract."

"That's not the contract, that's just the booking confirmation. This is the contract," he said tearing off a form he'd just printed which would require a magnifying glass to go through the detail. "I'll tell you this, sir," he adds, "nobody has ever raised this before."

There was no point arguing, he was not going to budge and I was not going to insure £500 for a £100 premium. A 20% of value insurance for a two-week period is a lousy rate in anybody's money. We then go and inspect the car where he marks up any pre-existing damage on a sheet. There were just a couple of scuffs to mark down before I inspect the front valence.

"Are all these marks damage?" I ask.

"No, they are all just dead insects."

I stopped myself from adding, "I see you've washed it then." I can't be bothered, even with cleverly put sarcasm.

"This is how you start it," he says, showing me.

"Oh, I put the key in that little slot."

"That's right," he adds.

Two miles down the road I suspect that showing me how to adjust the door mirrors would have been more useful. I eventually spy the button and make it to Blairgowrie. Two hours early I take the chance to wander round and have an early lunch. It takes me a while to sort out the geography, find a supermarket and a café for lunch.

Again being a vegetarian in Scotland does not work so well. "I'll have the vegetable lasagne," I say, selecting the only choice that is free of meat. She gives a grunt and I add, spying the option of French fries or baked potato, "with baked potato."

I also order a decaffeinated coffee, which comes quickly enough to leave me to believe it is instant. It takes a few minutes before another girl brings a plate with a microwaved jacket potato and a few bits of relish. All it is missing is a baked potato and the vegetable lasagne.

"Is that right?" she asks, having caught my stare of disbelief. It takes me a few seconds to think straight, "Well I ordered vegetable lasagne with baked potato."

She calls over the girl that took my order.

"The customer says he ordered vegetable lasagne but you only put baked potato on the order."

"Oh, did you want vegetable lasagne then?" she asks.

"Yes."

"We've no got any," adds the serving girl.

"So where is this on the menu?" I ask as I gesticulate towards the plate and the menu.

"It's that there," a deftly finger directs me.

"It says it comes with filling," I add.

"You did not say you wanted a filling when you ordered," says the girl who took my order. I'm about at the 'God give me strength' stage but simply add, "but that was a baked potato with a lasagne where one would not expect a filling."

"Which filling would you like," adds the serving girl seeing a way through this.

"I'll have cheese."

It is whisked off and comes back with cheese. I do not follow the path of a baked potato is not actually a microwaved potato (it's a jacket potato) nor do I rise to the temptation that this particular tuber would fit in any oven ever created – and that includes those in a dolls house. There is a phrase called 'choose your battles'.

Lunch taken, shopping done, wandering around complete I pull into the drive of the holiday cottage proprietors; their house and cottage sharing the same grounds. I'm hoping all will be okay: two weeks ago I received a letter from the agents explaining there would be a £20 deposit for 'good housekeeping'. I phoned and explained, having dealt with many a dodgy landlord in my time, I was concerned what I'd have to do to see the money back. They contacted the landlord who agreed to waive it.

So I arrive hoping I'd not got off on the wrong foot. I need not have worried, the major is a charming chap and spends time showing me round the magnificent coach house, explaining where everything is and how they'd restored it.

In the utility room he stops by the fire extinguisher and fire blanket and shows me in detail.

"Sorry, I have to do this. Health and safety you know."

"That's okay," I say and add, "I've managed to get myself out of four burning buildings I've been in." There's a pause as I suspect he wonders whether the £20 deposit would have been a bit on the low side anyhow.

I unpack, shower and have another walk around. I love the wooden floors, the open plan and the minimalist effect. After my escapades with cars and cafés I feel relaxed, too tired to hit the hills but just right to relax and enjoy. I settle down to write this account and become engrossed.

I'm shaken back to the present with a small bird traversing my eyes and coming to rest against the window to my right. It's flown in through the upper half of the stable door and is now convinced that a solid, un-openable piece of glass is the best way out. It goes through periods of calm, its tiny breath steaming the window then turns, looks at me and flutters its wings in desperation.

I'd often wondered if birds pee. One of those little queries on existence that one is either too embarrassed, or not interested enough, to ask. The bird shows me that they do, and also a good display of what they are more noted for.

Each time I make a move he flutters wildly then stops and turns his head towards me. "This isn't easy for either of us," I say.

I get a pair of thermal inner gloves and just manage to catch him. But I'm not firm enough and he escapes half way between window and door. Of course he flies back to the window, the open door possessing no interest whatsoever. It lands on the little opening section at the top, which duly does not open because it is locked and no sign of keys. I move everything out of the way, make another grab which only results in him dropping to the original resting place. With confidence rising, I make a firmer grab, surround his body with gloved hands, walk him to the door and launch him into the air. He takes to it and, with a little chirrup, flies high and away.

I then wander up to the Co-op, a fair hike but the only supermarket around. Blairgowrie is a plethora of small shops serving every need. I'm glad that there is no Tesco to rip the heart out of this micro-economy.

I wake after 08:00 on Sunday July 5th, pleased to have got some rest. A leisurely breakfast and kit preparation precedes the drive to the road east of Cray and the start of the ascent of the Graham, Mount Blair. This is a mountain of many shoulders and I've chosen the gentlest. As ever my navigation fails me on the drive to the start of the walk. I overshoot the starting place, turn around, drive back and pull off the single-track road just on the Angus side of the Perthshire border.

I step out of the car and take a few moments to enjoy the sun shining from a sky of mixed blue and cloud. My enjoyment is blighted when, in the bright light, I notice a series of dents in the roof of the hire car. Up to this point I'd found the Toyota Auris, at just a few months old, an enjoyable little machine. Now my heart sinks. I did not spot these dents when I picked it up and, having only done thirty miles so far all thoughts of 'conspiracy' fly through my head as my mind races to the worst possible scenario and the loss of the £500 excess.

So, it's a disillusioned walker who takes to the hills. Choosing a hire car for ease is now causing me stress. I make good progress on a grass track, through the knee-high grass, with high voltage markers at varying points. The sky is now a mottled picture of the whites and greys of high cloud. Duchray Hill, to the north, looks tempting for the afternoon but I continue to the top, resting every few minutes on its manageable slopes. The summit, which takes less than an hour and a half, is made up of a series of transmitters (which explains the high voltage cables), a trig point and a well-constructed circular windbreak which serves additionally as a memorial. A semi-decayed panoramic board points out the more significant peaks in the area.

I return to the car and decide to give Duchray Hill a miss. It'd take me about three hours to bag and the recent voices of my friends Rona and Kerry play on my mind. "Go careful, Steve, you've been overdoing it." It rains on the drive back to Blairgowrie, making the decision feel even more right.

The evening is warmer and I stroll into the centre of Blairgowrie and sit in the central park area. I read, enjoy the sun and listen to a distant pub band. On rising, I turn to head back to the cottage, that's when I see it. Blazoned in bright letters, standing proud of the buildings before it is Tesco. I vow not to go there and to continue to use the Co-op instead.

Mount Blair (from Duchray Hill)

Monday July 6th begins with hints of both sun and rain. I check the forecast and it's expected that the day will be a mixture of thunder, rain and sunny spells. I set out on the same road as yesterday, passing my starting place before taking the dead-end road to Auchavan with the view to climbing the Corbett of Monamenach and the Graham of Duchray Hill.

With just a thin T-shirt, to protect my upper body, I set off after 10:00 on the easy westerly track which gently lifts me, via the course of a stream that drains a high plateau, to the south-westerly slopes of Monamenach. Resting, and taking a compass bearing, I realise that the lack of response from my Silva compass is due to all the fluid having disappeared from the bezel housing. This is the second compass, of the same make, that this has happened to inside a year. I could just be unlucky but I make a mental note to see if any friends have had the same problem.

Fortunately I have an old Eurohike spare in my pack. It's not that great, very sensitive which is proving the complete antitheses of its travelling companion. With a bearing set, and the hills alive with birdsong, I climb the north-east slopes, pausing only to don waterproof top, as the edge of a storm, from clouds lowering themselves on to the southerly hills, clips me in its wake.

The rounded, smooth summit is shy to the storm's presence, only the wind picking up over the top, and my altimeter, tell me I am almost there. With the summit bagged I sit and admire the rough, rocky and sunny slopes of Creag Leacach to the north-west. To the south is Mount Blair, looking menacing with a storm over its head and lightning flashing down. I time the flashes to the rumbles and confirm the distance with my map.

I inspect the map closer – to include Duchray Hill requires a three-kilometre south-westerly descent then a sharp pull up the final kilometre to its summit. Setting off, I'm in two minds as the clouds look menacing. I alert a mountain hare that bounces off in to the distance. A herd of red deer are gathered in the basin shelter of the hills: it's around this time that they give birth.

As I descend the clouds blacken, the light drops and the time between lightning and thunder claps reduce. Kerry and Rona's words revisit me; sometimes you need your friends to be wise for you. The exposure of Duchray Hill is not worth the risk so I head east to pick up the ascent track. With the rain closing in and ensnaring me as its victim, it proves to be the right decision. By the time I reach the car it's a heavy downpour. The radio weather forecast and persistent crackle of each lightning strike reaffirms the correct decision was made.

Tuesday 7th is a non-hill day and instead I meet with Val Hadden, a TGO Challenge friend, and her partner, Merv Savage. They are lovely people to spend the day with, and we do a circuit from east of Dunkeld to Loch Ordie and back. Her daughter's dog, Ollie, a friendly bull terrier, accompanies us and is great fun – even if a little dim at times.

Merv quickly gets used to my little quips while Val plays catch up as he raises eyebrows. And the kid in me is never too far from the surface. At Loch Ordie Val clips Ollie on to his lead and holds on to him.

I pick up a stick, get Ollie's attention and throw it into the loch. He pulls while Val hangs on.

It's a good walk round in a day of high cloud. Val and Merv, both retired, are about to set off on a bicycle ride to Australia. I think today in no way counted as a warm-up.

We part in Dunkeld and, after a visit to a coffee shop, I head back to Blairgowrie. I aim to pull up outside the Co-op but the few bays are taken and the rest is double yellow lines. I try Tesco, the parking is free and plentiful. They get you!

Wednesday July 8th and it's time to finally bag the Graham of Duchray Hill (also known as Mealna Letter). It feels like a daily commute via the A93 and B951, though today, with not walking until 10:30, I'm a late starter.

I walk through a boggy field of buttercups, flowering thistles, moss-covered squelchy ground and tall grasses – all thriving in the wet conditions. I pick my route carefully, keeping in line with the wall and fence that edges the forest plantation.

The climb proper takes a varied route, avoiding the undulations of the nose of the hill. I meet the corner of the forest and, after donning my waterproof top, I can follow the wall, and its offset fence, to the summit of Duchray Hill. The top appears to be right on the line of the fence, though I spy a cairn the other side. This requires a quick step from Angus to Perthshire to ensure that the mountain is claimed.

I stand and survey my walks of Sunday and Monday before heading downhill, crossing the bog and the return to the car at 12:20.

Thursday July 9th and I'm taking it easy again. A leisurely start and breakfast rules out an attempt on the Corbett of Ben Vrackie and instead Blath Bhalg, a Graham a little to its south-west, catches my eye. Travelling the almost single-track A924, and using a telephone box as a navigation aid, I park at Dalnacarn and am walking at 09:50.

I follow a good grassy track and, avoiding the temptation to follow spur paths, which, through experience tend to soon peter out, reach a small wooden hut with a tin roof, red with rust. It's in dilapidated condition, windows almost out of their frames, cladding either having fallen off or tempting me to give it a prod. I try the door, it opens and the inside is good in comparison. A long bench, with accompanying seats, fills the length. Candles on the table and in the windows hint at some purpose.

I shut it up and take a bearing to the summit of Blath Bhalg. The route is through heather, which I find hard going. It's slog, rest, slog with tempting grass sections being too boggy to bother with. I make the summit line and, crossing a fence, pick off a minor bump before the summit proper. The views are extensive, Schiehallion to the west, Mount Blair and its transmitter to the north-east. To the north the mountains are in rain, heavy in comparison to the very light precipitation of my ascent. Hints of rainbows hang in the glen below.

View from Blath Bhalg

The roof of the hut makes for a handy reference point as I descend through the heather. From its waypoint I pick up the track and arrive back at the car within three hours of my start.

Friday July 10th dawns bright and sunny which has me soon out of bed, packed and driving to Kirriemuir, then minor roads to Glen Prosen, north-west of the town. I have my eye on the Grahams of Cat Law and Corwharn. Soon lost, I stop the car to check the map and work out where I have gone wrong: I now have to go to a spot called Spott and backtrack the car down the other side of the glen. Another glance at the map shows how close I am to Glen Clova. Glen Clova has featured in two of my TGO Challenge crossings of Scotland and it is typical of me that I did not link its proximity to today's walk.

I drive to Easter Lednathie and wonder how this place is connected with a Christian festival. Then I notice Wester Lednathie, where I drive to and park. I suppose these are geographical and not religious names.

I'm walking at 09:00, initially through a farmyard where, as always, dogs bark my entrance but not a soul is in sight yet I feel eyes are upon me.

Following the track I then cut up through open fields to meet the track that rises to Monthrey. It is hot and I wear a thin top and a baseball cap to keep cool. I slowly reach a digger working on the high ground: cutting a track to the summit of Cat Law. Unsure why, and fearing I might be enjoying this mountain pre-wind farm, I bypass it and follow a faint track to a gate where a conveniently-placed stone allows an easy passage into an enclosure containing trig point and summit.

It's taken an hour and twenty minutes and the views are well worth the climb. I can see right up into the Highlands in one direction and out to sea in the other. I sit with my back to the trig point with the sun gently warming me. A bee buzzes around, birds scoot past and the wind picks up the grass in waves. It starts from a distance and the rush, the swish and the moving grass pass me in a stroke. I wait in anticipation and it happens again, nature finding some cyclic formula.

I return to Monthrey and follow the track to the wide mouth of Glen Quharity. A small burn trickles through what was once a mighty river of the ice flows. It takes me a moment to spot the track north.

It's easy to follow the tracks, preferable to the heather slopes, and I make good time to the foot of Corwharn. A flowing stream allows me to drink and take on a spare supply. I survey the slope west, not too steep but it's enough to have me frequently resting. As it levels out I swing right for the final pull to the top of Corwharn. An impressive pillar cairn sits to its east where I rest my back and survey Cat Law and my route over.

I then head south-west, cutting across heather, to pick up the ascent track to bag Cat Law. It's then an easy route off and I'm soon on the main track, swinging into the steep and very narrow Glen Uig. The slopes tower above me until I reach another dried-up riverbed with a burn running through its middle.

I drop back to Wester Lednathie, completing a five-and-a-half-hour round. Feeling hungry I stop in Kirriemuir for a late lunch and ice cream. It's a typical rural Scottish town with some shops empty, some boarded up, some not having changed in fifty years and others giving the appearance of being modern and thriving. I don't know if I'm tired but I have trouble picking up the local dialect and wonder if this is an enclave of Gaelic, or just the modern influx of Polish people.

July 11th dawns bright and sunny, appropriate for a highlight of my two weeks in Scotland. Big John Hutchison, who I know from The Over The Hill Club, is finishing his Munros today on Schiehallion. It's effectively a club meet with many members converging on the Braes of Foss car park. People of different ages and states of health set off at different times with the aim of a summit rendezvous.

I make a start at 10:00 and rise quickly on the well-engineered path, taking in the stunning views that open up as this whale-backed mountain is conquered. I find a steady pace, unusual for me who tends to walk, rest, walk, pausing only once to take on water.

At the summit, a shade before noon, I join the gathering crowd. My ascent was quicker than the three hours it took in 1997: I put this down to better medication and lightweight footwear.

Half an hour later John, in his distinctive red T-shirt, and his companions, come into view. They step onto the final, rocky rising plateau to the summit cameras. Whisky, champagne, applause and Steve Wagstaff on his accordion are at the ready for those final few steps into the hall of fame as a Munroist.

He stands, looks around, says a few words, the applause begins and the corks pop. Celebratory cake is handed around; views and memories are shared. Ben Nevis is clear to the north-west, mountains surround us doing justice to Schiehallion's status as the most recognisable mountain in Scotland.

It takes me an hour and a half to descend, spent mainly with Sue Oxley and her dog, Susie. From there I travel on to Val and Merv's leaving party for their cycle ride to Australia.

Big John's summit party on Schiehallion

Monday July 13th brings a second day of rest from walking but not a day without feeling part of the walking community: I'm visiting MA Harper, a TGO Challenge friend, and also plan to catch up with her neighbours Val and Dave Machin plus Doreen Stewart who I also know via the TGO Challenge.

The drive to MA's house takes me along the B9512 that was a tiresome, lonesome and painful walk back in May. Today the road feels long, even by car.

After meeting up we decamp to The Insh Water sports centre for lunch. I passed the place in May with wistful eyes – behind schedule and unable to rest. It proves to be a let-down as MA and others are forced to return their poorly-prepared food.

Redemption comes in the afternoon when taking a Canadian canoe out. We circle the loch and pause to observe an osprey nest on a RSPB island. Built high in the tree we watch wings flap and await the return of a parent that had circled us earlier. The rain comes on so we paddle to the shore.

Tuesday July 14th and I'm back on the hills again for an attempt on Ben Vuirich – a remote Corbett with a lengthy walk in from the west. I spy a shorter route, from the south, breaking off the A924 at Tarvie. My parking is disturbed by a local resident who asks me to park further on as he is expecting a delivery of gravel. He's very helpful, apologetic but I'm only too pleased to move the car away from anything that might dent the £500 excess.

At 09:20 I'm striding up the tarmac path which, after passing an impressive Victorian mansion, buried in the trees, dwindles to a gravel then grass track. Rain sweeps in and I pause to don waterproofs before pressing on to a small hut. It's likely a hunting bothy – the key is in the door so I take a look around. Wooden tables, chairs, benches and brushes fill the one room wooden structure.

Leaving the hut I disturb a young deer that sets off into the distance with a repeating bark. It stops, looks back towards me, barks and sets off again.

It is wet underfoot and I feel water seep through my trail shoes. However, it does not hamper my ascent rate and I pass over Druim Moor before the pull up Carn Dubh – I could avoid this but I fancy taking it in on the way around. A slight drop takes me into cloud, rising up onto the col, before the final ascent of Ben Vuirich. I find the trig point, at spot on noon, ducked down behind a protective horseshoe-shaped summit wall. Ptarmigan call and take off, distant rain clouds hint at what's in store for my return journey. At some 30ft below Munro height I enjoy the views until a cooling wind has me setting off south, crossing boggy ground, picking up the hut, track and then the car at 14:10.

July 15th brings a day of forecast poor weather. I downgrade my ambitions of the Ben Vrackie Corbett to the Graham of Badandun Hill and a familiar drive, on the B951, past Mount Blair. I pull up near the hamlet of Fergus and take the track through a collection of buildings undergoing renovation. A short pull through a forest takes me onto a track that, although shown on the map as petering out after a mile, now winds its way to the summit of Craig Lair.

Badandun Hill

I break off the track and head south-east up the steep slopes of Badandun Hill. I climb slowly against my altimeter through short heather. Flies swarm around me: flicking them away has them returning within seconds. I rest on the occasional rock sat amongst the greenery, batting the flies away.

I spot a track snaking down from Craig Lair that likely goes to the top of Badandun Hill. Breaking my steep ascent, I head on a gentle diagonal to pick it up. A thunder clap greets me.

It's now an easier ascent to the summit where I'm met by a trig point and a cairn. There's not enough wind to see off the flies. I rest briefly, take in the views across to Monamenach, Duchray Hill and the infamous Mount Blair. Lightning flashes from the easterly mountains urge me to get a move on. I descend quickly on the track to rapidly lose height.

Nearing its low point I break left, onto the rough ground, and cut across to the track from Fergus. An easy walk takes me back to the car: seconds later the storm breaks overhead.

The evening brings a ride out to Letham to visit Graeme and Marion Dunsire, son and daughter-in-law of Val Hadden. I drive down to Perth, out towards Cupar and thread my way down to the small hamlet and call Graeme.

"Hi Steve, where are you?"

"In Letham."

"Ah good. Where about?"

"By the bus stop, near the phone box."

"Okay, I'm just trying to picture that. Can you see the hotel and the pub in the square?"

Having just driven around Letham the idea of a square and a hotel feels a bit of a farfetched luxury.

"You do live in Letham, Fife?" I ask while things start to dawn on me.

"No, Letham, Angus."

"Ah!"

"I did not think to tell you that."

I'm thinking the evening is in ruins when Graeme adds, "It's only a forty-five-minute drive."

He plies me with directions and I set off and forty-five minutes later I phone again. "Hi Graeme, it's Steve I'm in Letham, Angus in a square with a hotel and pub."

I get directions, easy and quick and I'm pulling up the lane where they live. And my chin is dropping as I look at their house. Well, house is not quite the word. Let's start with the clock tower and the adjoining hall. It would be more than worthy of a slot in Channel Four's *Grand Designs* programme.

I'm shown in, welcomed and we sit and eat in the vast kitchen. We discuss walking, they are soon off to do the Aonach Eagach (which I privately know as 'The A-n-E') in Glen Coe.

"Is it bad?" asks Marion.

"Yes, many places it's one slip and you are dead."

She looks a little concerned while Graeme adds, "It's no that bad. I don't remember anything like that."

"We are talking the same Aonach Eagach aren't we?" I ask in case the theme of the evening is repeating.

We agree we are and that likely I was misguided over it. It's then time for the tour. And it is a tour. The kitchen, diner, and lounge leads onto a sitting area with office, loo and other rooms off it. A mezzanine floats above which we reach via a most beautiful wooden spiral staircase. From here we survey the ground floor. Three bedrooms and a family bathroom lead off. Up another flight and the floor is completely open with internal windows looking down on to the mezzanine and the ground floor. Internal solid oak roof trusses set it off. I think we are nearly done.

"There's more," says Graeme. That's when I remember the tower. It's three or four more flights of stairs, each with a floor of its own, one housing the clock. We break onto the roof with stone battlements and a view across the village and the surrounding hills.

It was originally built as a church, never used and mothballed for a hundred years. Then it became a joiner's workshop for sixty years before falling into disuse. It's been an amazing project. I dare not ask how much was spent but what they've produced is both beautiful and likely highly desirable.

We chat some more and it comes time to depart. Passing through the utility room I notice what can only be described as a plant room. They've rigged up a ground thermal system to heat the water and the house. It consists of large cylinders, and an array of pumps, pipes and valves. We slip into deep conversation on its merits, until it's time to go again.

"Head for Coupar Angus," says Graeme. He must catch my look, "Not the Coupar in Fife, that is."

"Thanks," I reply.

"Do you know the way, from there?" he adds.

"Yes. I'll be fine, I checked the map and there's only one Blairgowrie."

Sleep comes poorly – having had three cups of coffee, to make my late-night drive safe, I toss and turn and snatch two lots of two hours, finally waking with memories of disturbed sleep in Youth Hostel dormitories.

The day has dawned clear with very high cloud, the forecast rain free and I fancy a go at Ben Vrackie. It's a fifty-minute drive to Moulin, passing its geographic and lexical neighbour Ben Vuirich, and a further few minutes to navigate track-like roads to find the car park in a wooded enclave.

This is an unusual mountain as its route is signposted through the woods and out onto the open hill. I climb steadily, passing lochs and burns, only resting occasionally for a sip of water or a top-up of food. The path is well made, no bog or heather to negotiate. It drops slightly to the small Loch a Choire before the final steep pull to a noon rendezvous, after an hour and three quarters, with the summit of a fine trig point and memorial cairn. There's a fine circular, bronze direction finder pointing out Ben Nevis and many other hills. The views and the way the land drops off, leaving a rocky island of a summit, leaves me feeling this is a rather special place.

A few other walkers join me, various nationalities. A trio of Scots with a dog, Clover start to chat. They ask me what I'm up to. I explain I'm staying in Blairgowrie, walking Corbetts and Grahams. They are impressed I've made the effort from the south of England.

"Ever tried a Munro?" Clover's owner asks.

"Actually, I've done them all," I reply while munching my way through a peanut and jam sandwich. They are impressed and Clover moves closer and eyes my sandwich.

"What about Wales, it's closer to you."

It's a gift. "I've done the Welsh two-thousand-foot mountains too." Clover moves even closer. She stares me out and gets the last bit of sandwich before begging an apple core off a group of French people.

Clover's owner demonstrates his new GPS to the other two. He reads off the location and height. "See this, it's a breadcrumb trail of our route up."

At the mention of breadcrumbs, Clover pricks up her ears.

A few words are exchanged with others but largely it's just the view we are all here for. To the north are the fine and mighty Munros of Carn Liath, Braigh Coire Chruinn-bhalgain and Carn nan Gabhar, to the south the more gentle Perthshire hills. I stay half an hour, until I feel cold and make it back to the car in just over an hour.

Friday July 17th brings my last chance to walk. I've loved having the cottage, a relaxing place to spend the late afternoons and evenings. My eyes flit over OS Sheet 43 for an easy Corbett to finish the fortnight on. I've had good use of this map – there's a series of Munros where I'd written 03/05/1994 against.

Initially I have it in mind to head up to Braemar and take in Morrone – an easy Corbett which always eludes me on the TGO Challenge. However, just north-west of Spittal of Glenshee, I notice the nearer Ben Gulabin.

The trip up is familiar, passing the roads that have been my stomping ground of late. I park up, kit myself out and start the pull up the track in the chill air. The weather for the afternoon has been forecast as poor so I'm pleased for my 09:50 start.

It's easy going on the track. At the remains of an old building it divides in two, one track leading around to Creagan Bheithe and the other, to the left, heading to the col between the two summits of Ben Gulabin.

The wind assists me up the steep northerly slope, meeting a path at the top. By now the wind is blustery, the straps on my pack feel abandoned to the wind. The sleeve of my jacket finds a harmony of vibration. I turn right and, having set my altimeter wrong, claim the summit earlier than anticipated in just an hour and ten minutes from the start.

I settle for a while but feel chilled through my thin top and walking shirt. Looking around, from what is likely my last Scottish summit of the year, I spy the distant Mount Blair – I don't appear to be able to shake him off! I head down, the wind now acting as a useful brake while I descend the steep slope. I meet a couple on the first part of the track. They confirm the poor forecast, ending my lofty ideas of taking in Morrone too. We discuss the Corbetts, I know I've been doing the easier ones. They confirm how remote and hard many are.

Back at the cottage it's a leisurely afternoon of writing and gathering kit together for the trip home. I reflect on the two weeks, four Corbetts, six Grahams and of course a repeat Munro.

Saturday morning and I arrive at the Enterprise Rent-A-Car depot before it opens. Fortunately it's raining, making the dents in the roof harder to spot. I park it up a slope, away from the door. The same wee guy that served me before arrives. This is good, part of my plan.

"Any problems?"

"None at all," I reply.

"I'll just go and take a wee look around the car and I'll be back with you."

I watch him walk to the car, as before he bends down and looks around the bodywork. His stature does not draw him to the roof. And the uphill walk to it kept the dents over the horizon – which are now puddles in the rain. He comes back. "That's all perfect," he says.

July 2009 – Scottish 2000ft Mountains

On 15th July 2009, Sgurr nan Ceannaichean (NH087480) south of Glen Carron was resurveyed by the Munro Society at 913.43m. I climbed it as a Munro and, given it's re-classified a Corbett, I've added one to my Corbett count and deducted one from my Munro count.

Classification	My Total	Total
Welsh Nuttalls	190	190
English Nuttalls	41	253
Corbetts (Scotland)	11	220
Grahams (Scotland)	6	220
Unique Donalds (Scotland)	0	58
Munros (Scotland)	283	283
Ireland	0	212
Totals (15/07/2009):	531	1436

May 2010 – The Great Outdoors Challenge

The TGO Challenge is oversubscribed this year and I only get a place via the standby list. Too late to dehydrate my own food I order freeze-dried pouch food off the internet and visit the Cotswold Outdoor shop at South Cerney.

I cast my eye over gear and start with the practicality of a long-handled, aircraft aluminium, spoon to scoop out food from the deep pouches. As spoons go this is the most expensive I've ever purchased but, having become a lightweight freak, the new type of food means I don't need a knife or fork, just a long-handled spoon. An added bonus is, with the pouches just requiring boiling water, I no longer need any pot-washing utensils.

I've also decided to take the plunge and switch from walking boots to trail shoes. There's mixed opinions about their merits. One frequent complaint is they don't offer any ankle support. However, with my strong ankles I figure I'll be okay – my knees are my Achilles' heel. Instead my concerns lay in how my feet will fair getting wetter than usual. I wander to the sock display and select a waterproof pair and hope for the best.

Next lightweight over trousers, a new trekking pole, lightweight fleece, map case and energy bars drop into my basket.

Now for the tricky bit, I need a lightweight trowel. I ask a female assistant. She looks at me at me in a 'This isn't a garden centre, sir' kind of way.

"I mean for camping," I add in a hopeful manner.

She still appears confused. By now I'm a bit hot under my collar and wishing this conversation hadn't begun. I try humour and chip in a, "We're not talking geocaching," smile and nod hoping this will get through. No such luck and we part company before she starts to list various ironmongery shops I might care to visit. I escape the shop with just under £300 spent, return home and book my tickets for the sleeper train to Scotland.

As my new work's mobile phone contains a camera I pack this, and its lightweight charger, instead of my usual digital camera.

The final task is to find the smallest tube of toothpaste to see me through two weeks. This proves harder than one might imagine. I try the local shop, I try Tesco, I try the Co-op then Waitrose. None has a small tube of toothpaste instead they appear to be targeting the family market or those with a rather excessive number of teeth. In desperation I look to the children's end of the market. 'Age 3 to 6' has me doubting whether it'd be right for me but then on a perfectly-sized tube I spy 'For Ages 6+'. Well, correct me if I'm wrong, that does, at the age of forty-four, include me. Okay the DreamWorks picture of Shrek and his lady friend might not have me falling into the target market but there's nothing else to indicate it isn't for me.

Friday May 14th and I step out of Glasgow Central Station into the cool air of a grey morning. I am pleased to have had the sleeping cabin to myself, glad to have managed to get some sleep despite an annoying buzz from the cabin's electrics. My radio picked up nothing but white noise but this was preferable to the buzz and I dozed off to what, I recently was amazed to learn, is the noise of background radiation leftover from the Big Bang.

Judging by the niggling of the couple in the cabin next to mine I'm grateful, for a moment, to be a bachelor. When I boarded the woman was saying, "I don't want you in here" as she evicted the man so she could attend to their child. He protested from the corridor about how hard he works and he'd, "Bloody paid for the tickets." Later, when he'd been allowed back in, he began negotiating for leave to go to the buffet car. "It's only a nightcap," he repeated and protested. I never found out whether he got permission but the only other sound from their cabin was some serious snoring.

I've become savvy to the limited choice of vegetarian breakfast available in Scotland and have brought two boiled eggs and some slices of bread – gone are the days of the sleeper ticket including breakfast. With these munched I walk to Queen Street Station with my 10kg pack swaying on my back in retaliation to my failure to fasten the waist and chest straps.

People mill around, day trippers, cycle touring parties, pie-eyed revellers and the odd hopeful hobo. I'm glad when the train to Mallaig is called, glad when I find my seat, force my pack into the overhead rack and sink into my reserved seat. If nothing else I've made it this far and now just have to sit for five hours.

It's a journey of small station stops, trains dividing, meeting and crews chatting. A journey of bridges, viaducts, curved tracks, snow tunnels and the rhythmic clacking over the old-style short rail lengths.

We cross Rannoch Moor with its mountainous views being snapped by those doing the journey for the first time – others gaze out the window onto old friends.

As we approach Mallaig I get chatting with an Australian and an American girl, both touring Scotland. The Australian is on a tight schedule, the ferry leaves Mallaig ten minutes after the train gets in and the ticket advises to be there ten minutes early – such is the British joined-up transport system. A man joins our conversation, he's trying to get the ferry too, a hired sailboat his destination.

He directs a question at me. "What are you up here for?"

"I'm walking across Scotland."

This gets some appreciative comments from all around.

"Have you got your Skin So Soft?" he asks.

"What for the midges?" I ask.

"Yes."

"It's a bit early for them. And as long as I don't camp in still air near water I should be okay."

"They never fly across salt water," he adds.

"Superstitious are they?" I ask and he looks at me as if I'm some form of cretin.

Mallaig brings lunch, the purchase of food for the evening and a quick hunt for the West Highland Hotel to sign the form saying I've started the TGO Challenge.

"I'm on the TGO Challenge, do you have the signing out sheets?" I ask at reception.

"You're the last to sign out," replies the man.

I'm surprised, it's only 14:35.

And so I set off down the road, make good time and take a track east to a small loch. From here I trail south-east, picking up the road and track along the north shore of Loch Morar.

I've yet to set up my drinking water bag and pipe, so repeatedly fill a small plastic bottle from the frequent streams. A man with a camper van offers me a cup of tea, I decline but we chat. He advises against collecting water and cites the preverbal tale of a dead sheep being just upstream. Actually in my twenty years of walking the Highlands I've never come across a dead sheep in a stream, yet, according to folklore, there are literally thousands bunging up the water supplies.

He does convince me a camper van is the ideal walking accessory. It's something I've pondered many a time. I take the dream along the track with layouts and body styles pouring through my mind along with unrealistic assumptions of cost and whether it would make a practical daily vehicle too.

My mind then wanders to natural navigation, how, in reality, so much is done subconsciously. For example one would never pass through mass forestation, or ascend a crag where indigenous trees, escaping the mouths of even the most agile deer, grow. And when you climb in mist and the wind picks up, indicating a sudden change of terrain. And a flowing stream, or the position of the sun give a rough idea of direction. My mind goes through many.

These thoughts fade as I admire the light on the distant hills, the cloud, the blue sky and a rainbow. The breeze catches my neck and I realise how drained I am. It's now 19:45 and I haven't yet reached my planned stop at Tarbet. A small piece of flat ground, just beyond a remote house, tucked out the way with a stream running past has me putting up the tent.

With erecting and packing away a tent the least favourite part of wilderness travel I procrastinate over sorting inner from outer, peg from pole and front from back. I realise I'd forgotten to make all the repairs to the tent I'd promised myself I'd do over the winter. A midge attack speeds me up and I realise I've camped in still air near water.

I eat, the pouch food is tasty and filling and I'm so grateful I'm not rehydrating this year and bulking out the meals with couscous. I've eaten so much couscous on TGO Challenges I doubt I could ever stomach it again.

My grandmother who died, aged ninety-three, last September, comes to mind. She outlived my grandfather by thirteen months. Like most from that generation the war was a pivotal point in her life. Her life had three epochs: 'Before the war', 'During the war' and 'After the war'. My grandfather was on the submarines and whenever he was in a British port she'd gather up my father (then a babe in arms) and travel to whatever port he was in. Given they got caught up in a few 'lively' air raids it made my father a reverse evacuee.

When she died she'd lived in her house for eighty-three years. When I say house it was a rundown three-storey former Victorian wool mill with an attached warehouse. Five bedrooms in all with room for a further seven on two unconverted floors. Her parents then, along with my grandfather, dutifully filled the place to the rafters with redundant items from a bygone age. It required a lot of sorting and, with my dad and uncle suffering with their health, I'd done the bulk of the physical work. Now with the place sorted, and a few repairs to try and make it more saleable, I'm in my tent reflecting. I miss my grandparents and their home. Years of family history have been decommissioned. An abrupt halt to my family story. But the idea is the generations continue and I'm certainly not doing my bit! I'm forty-four and Miss Right still eludes me.

It starts to rain. I hold off a call of nature and slip into sleep only to wake in the early hours with a pressing need. I slip out and add to the sounds of flowing water. Pulling myself back into the sleeping I grope around for my watch, find it and press the button. It briefly lights the tent and tells me it's 02:45. I shut my eyes and have a strange glowing image of Shrek printed on my retinas. I press the watch light again and see my toothpaste tube.

Saturday May 15th and, having struggled to find the energy to get going, I set off at 09:40 and make my way round to Tarbet Bay. I pass through the buildings of a tiny community and, with the sea of Loch Nevis lapping the shore to my left, don't see a soul.

A polluting generator rattles from within a building, a hostel, with beds laddering its walls, teases one to believe others do venture this far. Moored boats bob against gentle waves and I follow the path on, seeking out the steep route to take me onto a 15km ridge and the Corbett of Bidein a' Chabair.

The cliffs steepen to my left and, with no visible path, I set my compass for the ridge.

I get into an inefficient stride where my pack weighs heavy on my back and my upper legs ache as I put foot in front of foot. Each step is deliberate and I sense the mountain wishes to pull me back down into the sea each time I lift a leg.

I make it to a highpoint and, realising I've ascended a minor hillock, rue my lack of close navigation – only a descent will get me onto a course for the main ridge.

I make it to the ridge at just after 13:00. Mentally pacing my route, I realise, with many separate mountains to be gone over, there's at least another 3000ft of ascent. I eat as much as I dare from my rations and follow the ridge at a painfully slow pace while my mind jiggles the days ahead against this benchmark of my fitness.

It's a sorry walker who, at 18:15, after numerous undulations and circumnavigations, pulls himself onto Bidein a' Chabair and promptly gets swept over by a snowstorm.

I settle down and send a text or two describing the view then look up to find the view has disappeared in the mist.

I get going and drop height. The mist lifts and my aim of A' Chuil Bothy looks, and feels, an unbelievable distance. My legs begin to wobble so I hunt for a place to pitch my tent. The ground falls away for nearly 3000ft and is a myriad of rock, heather, moss, lochains and forest. A small lochain and a square of flat ground above its north-east bank catch my eye. With each pace towards it my mind reassesses my entire life, wishing to be safe and secure it jettisons all plans and has me virtually nailed into my home toasting my feet by a log fire.

I quickly put my tent up, fighting the threatening clouds and my shaking, tired hands. I collect water, dive inside and cook my meal, thankful to make my world as small as possible. When I start to warm up, my strength returns and my mind expands with lofty plans and ambitions.

It's Sunday May 16th and I wake knowing my ambitions of the three

Corbetts, at the head of Glen Dessarry, will have to be abandoned and the best I can hope for is to get myself back on schedule by making my way direct to Kinbreack Bothy. An alternative of taking in the single Corbett of Carn Mor also feels too ambitious.

My mind swings to the more pressing need of getting myself off the mountain I've camped on. This isn't aided by taking two and a half hours to get ready.

With tent packed and rucksack on my back I gaze along my chosen route – the ridge continues to undulate and doesn't bode well for an easy start to the day. If I'd pressed on last night I'd have been passing through forest in the fading light.

I peer south-east, surveying the route down to the river that gathers the mountain burns into Loch Morar. It looks passable through a deep slit of a glen.

My pace gathers as I drop to a deer fence guarding a forest. I curse the thing, climbing high and swaying on its wire. With my right foot slung into one of its wire squares I swing my left leg over and pray not to rip my jacket or Gore-Tex over trousers, donned against the rain. Taking a leap of faith I stagger up on the other side.

I can't find the marked path so follow the fence to where a burn passes below it. I then find the path, complete with a proper passage for walkers through the fence. It's hard on my feet, the thinner soles of the trail shoes means the roughness of the track digs into me.

I emerge from the forest and, after missing the required track, begin to coax myself to the one above A' Chuil Bothy. It's off my map but I reckon I can navigate it from memory. However, as I ascend I glance back and spot the track I missed. I cut across bog and peat to reach it. With the rare sight of two other walkers I carry on and meet the good track passing the houses of Upper Glen Dessarry and Glen Dessarry.

I keep an eye out for the north-east track around to Kinbreack Bothy and am relieved to see three ladies heading down it, showing me where it branches from my track. On exchanging pleasantries they warn me the ground floor of Kinbreack is uninhabitable and advise I use the upper floor.

As I ascend to the 350m bealach between two of my missed Corbetts I glance back and spy a party of men trying a number of false paths until they branch onto mine. I'll have some company tonight. I expect them to catch me but as I swing into Glen Kingie, and look for the bothy, they are still a way behind.

There's a light breeze and the afternoon sun cheers me but it feels slow, I am slow, this distance today should be easy but instead I'm hours late. I can't find a pace.

It's 18:30, and eight and a half hours of walking, before I approach the bothy on the edge of the wide basin floor of the glen. An identical shaped ruin lies to its left and a tiny ruin lies beside the burn rolling past it. At the very moment I wonder if the ground will be wet and soft, my right foot sinks deep into a soft wet bog. It makes a satisfying pop as I extract it but I fear losing a shoe in such circumstances and make a mental note to splay my toes and take great care when it happens again.

I make my way up to the bothy loft. My pack catches against the hatch, and I lean in and negotiate my way on to the floor. Two sleeping mats are already laid out. I grab a pitch and sort my kit as the chaps behind me arrive. None of them is on the TGO Challenge – I'm twenty-four hours in and feel twenty-four hours behind.

They are kindly, retired men. I'm surprised when I get speaking to Joe to find he's seventy-one. He knows a town near me, Devizes (where many of my ancestors came from) having done his national service there. He could pass for fifty.

I make my meal – these pouches are great, everything you need already mixed in. And, of course, there's no couscous.

I wake on Monday May 17th after sleeping fitfully with Radio 4 and then the World Service, drowning out the inevitable snoring. As I take my headphones off I'm treated to a dawn chorus of farting, burping and the hissing of gas stoves. I conclude the ear is the best behaved orifice.

I set off and find I'm now able to move well. After an hour I rest on a high vehicular track looking east along the wide Glen Kingie. Passive high cloud casts its shadow over the glen. The river and the track I'm on, meander towards a forest. My plans have changed: the Tomdoun Hotel, just east of my planned camping spot, has proved too tempting. My struggles with fitness, my tiredness and achy feet of the last few days deserve a hotel.

I press on, wishing to make the most of the good weather. I put my trust in the track through the forest as it bends and dips and climbs around the forested slopes. I tick off the odd bridge, the odd junction against the map and am glad to emerge on the minor road just over a mile short of Tomdoun. A walker passes me at speed – he looks like he's on the TGO Challenge. I find him in the hotel bar, pausing for three pints of Guinness on route to Invergarry. But before I ask if he's on the TGO Challenge I pose a question to the Australian bartender. "Do you have a room for tonight?"

"Don't know, mate, I'm not in charge," he replies.

"Who can I ask?"

"The fellow who does the bookings is out."

"When will he be back?"

"Within the hour I guess. But it's a bit pricey, might not be right for you."

It'd have to be quite pricey to see me walking on. I order sandwiches and soft drinks.

"What's your name?" I ask the fellow challenger, the first I've met.

"Anthony Driscoll. And you?"

"Steve Smith."

He pauses, looks at me and asks, "Do you write a blog?"

"Yes."

"I've read it. It's good."

"Thanks, I enjoy doing it," I reply and feel famous in my own lunchtime.

In the event the owner is back within fifteen minutes and Room

3 is available for £40. I take it and he points me up the stairs. A few seconds later he's sprinting after me, pointing me the right way down a corridor. I'd turned the wrong way, west, at the top of the stairs.

"East, the Challenge is east. I must remember to always turn east," I reply.

I spread myself out in the room, wash out my clothes then notice two toenails have turned black and my heels and big toes have an irritating sore itch about them. The bath is welcome, sinking an aching, sighing body below a warm water line.

In the bar I find the menu isn't vegetarian friendly, there's not one option I can have. The owner is now smartly dressed in chef's attire.

"Can you do me something vegetarian?" I ask.

"I'll just go and check."

I wait expectantly, thinking I'll even take the Scottish standard response to vegetarianism of macaroni cheese and chips. As long as it doesn't contain couscous I'll eat anything vegetarian.

He returns, "I can do a lovely range of lightly roasted vegetables on couscous base," he says.

My face quivers with disappointment.

Back on the landing, just before I turn east, I try and work a piece of couscous from between my teeth as I survey the bookcase for reading material. The complete works of HG Wells (never knew he was so prolific), some Penguin classics, two copies of a Leeds & Bradford street map and the Brownie Annual, 1939 get flicked through. That's the thing with pub and hotel bookcases, they're never put together by the same collector. I choose a Sherlock Holmes and read two short stories.

Tuesday May 18th dawns another bright day. The breakfast is welcome (vegetarians well catered for) and I set off at 09:40 on the road walk – destination Invergarry, destination hotel.

I keep a leisurely pace, it's just a twelve-mile walk, and am caught up by Nicky Crawford, a sprightly sixty-nine-year-old who, as it turns out, lives not far from me.

We walk until the road meets Loch Garry and turn off south to Greenfield where I bid my fellow challenger, only the second I've met so far, adieu and promptly sit down for a jolly good rest. The jolly good rest becomes tempered by a desperate need for water so I set off and follow the wide forest tracks, and its logging lorries shuttling back and forth, until I find a good stream where I can gulp back the water.

I press on with Pete and Dud sketches spinning about my mind. It's only when I reach Mandally I realise why - I'd been on the road to it and, it being one of their sketches, I must have subconsciously picked this up from the map. Another mile takes me to the hotel and, after just over four and half hours from Tomdoun, I'm sat on another barstool.

I explain I've booked a room and am directed to reception where I'm handed my pre-posted resupply package and shown to my top-floor room - negotiating the two flights of narrow stairs with the pack, becomes the hardest part of my day.

I shower, change, wash out my clothes and return to the bar, order lunch and a drink. Supping outside, I watch the world go by, chat to two guys cycling from Land's End to John O'Groats and gaze across to an impressive road bridge over a deep river.

I inspect the bookcase. All the books are long novels, you'd have to be staying awhile to start one. I spy a Conan Doyle, but it isn't a Sherlock Holmes. But it does reinforce my suspicion Scottish hotel bookcases are littered with the works of Conan Doyle. Southern hotels tend to have a proliferation of Dick Francis books. Realising these thoughts indicate the onset of boredom I walk to the local garage and buy a paper.

I read in the garden, read in the lounge. A food safety test is going on where the examiner appears to be telling the delegate the answers which he dutifully writes down. I go for a wander, pass an alcove where a large table is surrounded by suits on some management meeting. "I see this as a learning centre conduit," announces one. I make a hasty retreat.

Finally 19:30 comes and it's time for dinner. I have the choice of a single table by the bar or by the kitchen door. I elect for the latter and get an insight into how a hotel kitchen is run.

"Fucking hell, don't tell me we are out of cod," yells the duty manageress. She then emerges, crosses the bar to the offending table and says, ever so sweetly, "I'm really sorry I'm out of cod would you care to order something else?"

As I get through my soup, which I daren't complain is a bit cold, the kitchen door swings violently amongst the crashing and gasps of exasperation from the kitchen staff.

A young waiter brings me my main course, a piping hot vegetarian lasagne. "Can I get you anything else?"

"No," and I flick my eyes to the kitchen door, "I wouldn't put you through it."

"Yes!" he says, "Result!" and salutes the air.

Given I missed the three Corbetts on Sunday, today (Wednesday May 19th) is to be my biggest day so far. From Invergarry I try and spot the tracks through the forest but end up on the A82 for well over an hour. I walk in the right-hand verge and wave to the car drivers who indicate and move out to give me room, to those who just move slightly I raise the fingers of my left hand from its trekking pole. To the bastard who crossed onto my side of the road, while overtaking a car approaching from behind, and misses me by no more than an inch, I give an angry V sign. I'd have made it two handed if I didn't have to hold my trekking poles.

On reaching Aberchalder I enjoy the sight of the swing bridge being opened, to make way for boats to pass into Loch Oich. I then tentatively make my way through a farm searching out the track up onto the hills. By a process of elimination, and sniffing out the general direction, I climb a steep track before cutting into forest which leads to Glenbuck Bothy. I rest awhile, enjoying its comfy chairs and plan how I might come back and spend more time here. After eating lunch, I press on to the 815m summit of Carn Dearg.

I stand in the bealach before Carn Dearg with warm wisps of

wind tickling my face. High cloud is scattered across a blue canvas. A stag stands in the coire, staring down at me. He bounds off, stops, turns and looks at me some more. At last he bounds off again and the last glimpse of him is high on the skyline, silhouetted by the sun, his short antlers bold above his head.

I take in the 815m Corbett of Carn Dearg at Grid Reference 349967, missing its namesake Corbett at 357948. It's then slow progress towards Luib-chonnal Bothy. I arrive at 17:30 to the shadows of the evening light. Deer graze on the flat grounds. A sense of loneliness envelopes me. The bothy book entry describes how Alan Sloman, Phil Lambert and Alistair Pooler spent a good evening here the night before. I'd have welcomed their company.

All there is to keep me company is a copy of *Zoo* magazine. Not my choice of reading material and something that always winds me up in WHSmiths as such magazines are listed under, 'Men's Lifestyle'. I always think, *Not my bloody lifestyle*. Anyhow, with nobody around I figure it's safe to have a flick through, indeed it would feel rude not to. It's all headlines with no substance, somewhere between the *Daily Sport* and *Daily Star*. The centre spread is a young lady by the name of Alice. She reveals, shall we say, her upper half with an invitation to text a code to a particular number (where one is presumably charged a sum similar to the length of the code) with the promise to be sent (presumably to one's mobile) pictures of various other parts of her anatomy. It actually doesn't say which parts but I'm guessing it isn't her left knee or ankle.

With bothies always colder than a tent I'm thankful it's a warm night.

It's Thursday May 20th and I make an early start on the route through Melgarve, Garva Bridge to the Laggan Gaskmore Hotel where hopefully a resupply package awaits me. It's to be my longest day, by distance, so far but the ascent is minor, the tracks are good and I'm confident of making the hotel in good time to clean up and relax.

To the calls of the cuckoo, the diving of the oystercatchers I make my way along the River Spey. I'm fooled by a building at Shesgnan – from a distance it looks like Melgarve Bothy, the approach is similar. When I reach it I find it's boarded up and realise my mistake. I now follow the forest edge and wind round to Melgarve and Wade's road.

The walk now becomes boring, not only is it a repeat of ground travelled before but the ground is straight, monotonous and distant landmarks take their time to be passed. In the backdrop are glimpses of the Cairngorm Mountains, their tops encrusted by snow. It reminds me of the road between Linn of Dee to Braemar, a pitiful route of tar-sealed road and distant landmarks refusing to become part of the foreground.

I reach Laggan around 15:00, ready to make use of the excellent public loo (I'm sure many a challenger has fond memories of its spacious confines) and stores. I buy what I need for lunches and see one pastry-shaped item in the 'hot counter'.

"What's in that thing?" I ask. Somehow, perhaps because I haven't spoken to anybody for forty-eight hours, my words sounded scornful for the assistant falls about laughing.

"That thing, as you put," she says, "is a vegetable pasty."

"Okay, I'll take it then," I reply.

I sit on the bench outside, chewing my way through the thing (which judging by its brown outer, dryness and high temperature has been being heated all day) and hear the two assistants having a chuckle at the way I said it. One comes out and is surprised to see me there, "Oh, you're still here," she says, embarrassed.

I smile back.

I walk the mile to the hotel, it's a bit run down and I have to circle the building to find a door not surrounded by weeds.

"I've a booking, Stephen Smith," I say

"Ah yes, and a package."

This is good.

"What time is breakfast?" I ask.

"It's between eight and eight forty-five. But tomorrow it's at seven."

My room is on the ground floor, functional and designed for those on coach parties. I make use of the bath, wash out my clothes and end up watching *Deal or no Deal* on the TV. The fact that the contestants think which box they chose is significant, amazes me. It's merely a game of chance and the skill is knowing when to quit and not play it to the last box. I recall a conversation with a fellow challenger, the late and dear Bob Lees. He'd recently bought a lottery ticket and chosen the numbers one to six. A friend of his had said, "I thought Bob was brighter than that. Doesn't he know he'd have more chance if he spread them out?" We'd then had an in depth conversation about maths and how frustrating it is to hear non-mathematical people (friends, colleagues, media and politicians) making sweeping statements when the maths doesn't back them up.

I make my way to the conservatory and find the preverbal Sherlock Holmes anthology and start to read *The Sign of Four*. I shouldn't have switched the TV on, it always annoys me. Reading calms me down.

The coach party arrives, a large group of older Australians making jokes about Haggis Farms and recounting endless visits to the distilleries.

The evening arrives and I order a meal and am told I can eat it in the conservatory, away from the coach party. A piper appears and pipes in the meal for the Australians. I'm near the bar, the bar tender a jolly stoutly-built Scot, chats to the piper as he returns, covered in sweat, and gasping for a drink.

"Do you want a Sheepshaggers?" asks the barman.

I assume he means the beer and not one of the Australians.

Friday May 21st comes and with it 07:00 and no sign of breakfast being ready. Come 07:30 the Aussies are fed up and break their way into the breakfast room. I follow, food is being readied and I select a feast to help me through the day.

Classic mellow music of the sixties plays. It leaves me doleful, emphasising for many this coach trip is a swansong.

Next follows the tricky bit of trying to pay. I wait at the reception desk, there's no sign of anybody. I notice a buzzer, press it and Glenn Miller plays in the distant bar. At first I think it's coincidence. I wait and press it again and find the buzzer does fire Glenn Miller into life.

A member of staff passes and I grab him and force him to take my money.

I have to head the mile back into Laggan before taking the road east towards the A9. Passing another hotel I realise better planning would have saved me this backtrack.

The road is hard on my feet, the thinner soles of the trekking shoes offer less support than a boot and I wriggle my feet to free the pain. It takes me around three hours to hit the A9 where road works, and associated traffic lights, make it easy to cross to the wide east verge. I walk north, looking for the track up to Phones, a hunting lodge. Peering amongst the trees to my right, I hope to see a shortcut up but the track comes before I'm brave enough to chance it through the trees. I negotiate my way through workmen and heavy machinery and set off on the switchback track. It's a good one and has me elevating the contours. Phones is a clutter of buildings freshly painted in cream, tying the 19th century and 1930's architecture together. The odd building might stem from the Second World War.

I rest by the stream running past it, eat my lunch, rationing myself a packet of peanuts for later, slug back water, swing my pack onto my back, fasten the waist strap, tuck the map into it then secure the chest strap. I then set off up the incline onto open moorland.

With so many mountain tops to choose from my mind plays a game, guessing the correct route over to the Corbett of Meallach Mhor. Minor adjustments in compass bearings have me pointing at wildly different hills. I take a GPS co-ordinate, set my compass and take off over the moor hoping covering some ground will narrow the options and show me what I'm aiming for. The ground rises gently and I negotiate around bog and peat hags. I begin to notice squares of cut peat, stacked as little turrets on the tops of rises in the ground. On each are scattered grey pellets. I wonder what they are for and am alarmed they might be the estate attempting to poison birds of prey. I check my phone for a signal, it's strong and I phone into 'Challenge Control' and speak to Alvar Thorn. He speaks to Ann and they reckon it's to feed the grouse. I feel they are right as the sheer number of them would leave the estate vulnerable to being caught out.

Feeling better I press on and drop down to Bhran Cottage, cross the bridge onto the tar-sealed road. It's a remote spot for such a fine road. A car passes me full of children just collected from school. The time is drifting and I review the map. My aim of Meallach Mhor and Carn Dearg Mor now looks ambitious and I temper my plans to just the first Corbett. The bargain gives me new zest until part way up the tiring slopes of Meallach Mhor I tire to the point of having to rest after every other pace. I reach the summit at 17:45, around nine and a half hours into my day.

Making out the distant village of Laggan, I plot my route. I shovel peanuts into my mouth as distant rain greys out distant glens. Then I'm pelted from behind by rain at a forty-five degree angle. It isn't just heavy, it's a jet wash. There's no chance to get my over trousers on. Fortunately I'd put my Gore-Tex jacket on to keep warm so I'm able to zip it up and then press on. The rain pings musically off my trekking poles as my legs get soaked and my trousers cling to my skin. It takes over twenty minutes to pass. My plans to camp are put on hold as I walk until I'm dry.

Before the slopes of Carn Dearg Mor my watch clicks over to 19:00. Alarmed by the late hour I find a small water source and force myself to muster up the energy to put the tent up. I place it just off a track, always fearful of late-night poachers' quad bikes, and just manage to bundle myself in before the next shower hits. So ferocious is the storm I'm able to channel rain water, from the outer of the tent, into my cooking pot to boil.

I wake on the Saturday May 22nd and force myself to get a move on. To get myself back on target I need to bag the missed Corbett of yesterday, Carn Dearg Mor, and also complete the two Corbetts already planned for today.

I struggle to pull on my soggy knee supports, I hadn't appreciated how wet they'd got below my trousers. Plastering my knees with Deep Heat I hope it will keep the joints warm while the supports dry under my own body heat.

I'm off at 08:00, dropping down to the good track heading north-east to below the bealach that approaches Carn Dearg Mor. From here I head north over sharp, steep ground until I hit the gentle pull to the summit. As I do the beautiful clear sunny weather slips into minor puffs of cloud. I admire the views from the top and am chuffed I have managed to get myself back on target for one and a half hours' effort.

I gaze across to the route ahead. On the horizon, and on the track to be followed, is the Corbett summit of Leathad an Taobhain – just shy of 3000ft. It looks a distant dream yet it's only a small part of the day.

I drop back to the track and start following its passage east. I peer down the long glen into Glen Feshie and consider cutting down to Ruigh-aiteachain Bothy then follow the route around to Linn of Dee and Inverey. It'd be an easy option but the road walk into Braemar is pitifully long, boring and far worse for tedium than the one from Melgarve to Laggan. I also recall putting on my route sheet, as reason for not submitting a foul weather alternative, 'If I make it this far wild horses won't make me walk that bloody road from Inverey to Braemar'.

I press on, rest then stagger in the heat while trying to plan water stops, against streams on the map, so I can keep the weight I'm carrying to a minimum. At the final bealach, before the pull to the summit of Leathad an Taobhain I rest by the remains of a shelter.

I'm struggling for energy: my light lunches aren't proving enough. Having the unscheduled night at the Tomdoun Hotel I have an evening meal spare. I set up my stove, boil enough water to hydrate the meal and make a cup of tea. It's enough to replenish me and I follow the track that dwindles out at the summit and arrive before 14:00.

I now drop down and follow a high-level plain across to the foot of Beinn Bhreac. I feel solitary, it feels remote. For once the lack of companions haunts me and I rely on my GPS for reassurance. I feel each step is taking me further from safety, like a conversation you wished you'd never started – such as buying a trowel from the South Cerney Cotswold Outdoor shop.

In the distance deer graze, they clock me, stand and stare before lolloping off. A single one, an outsider (perhaps a young male being cast from the herd) stands in my path until he decides it's his turn to move off. A walker is passing far to my left across the high flat ground. I steer towards him, crossing bog, hags and areas of quartz grit. I'm desperate for company. As I approach he waves but his pace is too good and he gains on me until I give up the chase.

I keep north of Beinn Bhreac before tackling its north-easterly flank. I wobble and pant my way to the top. In all it takes three hours to regain the identical height of Leathad an Taobhain.

The bothy is five miles away, I'm keen for it but bargain with myself if I don't reach it in three hours (twelve hours since the start of my day) I'll camp.

With this deal in mind I drop to the head waters of the Tarf Water. It's easy to cross here and I follow the southerly bank through broad flood pains and narrow paths on steep banks where I cling onto heather to avoid a slip. The water flows east, meaning I'm following a welcome downhill route. I cut corners where I can but am always glad to return to its safe confines. It's wide, rocks peek through the flowing water and the evening sun glints from the surface like a million dazzling diamonds.

I reel in the bothy, from a distance it looks like a large structure but as I near its two chimneys give a sense of proportion. I arrive five minutes within my self-imposed twelve-hour day. Two people sit outside, a man and a woman. They aren't on the TGO Challenge. I sift through its rooms and plump on an uninhabited, concrete-floored one with its own entrance. Even with the company of people I still need the privacy of my own area.

I make my dinner and sit outside and chat.

"Where are you from?" asks the woman.

"Marlborough, Wiltshire. And you?" I reply.

"We've lived in Aberdeen for the past twenty years but I went to school in Chippenham."

"So did I. Which school?" I ask.

"Sheldon."

This was getting spooky.

"Me too, which year?"

It turns out she was two years behind me and we discuss the teachers we shared, for good or for bad.

The three of us talk until the sun disappears and the long evening light turns into a cool chill. I make my way into the bothy, close the door and check my route for tomorrow. "What the hell was I thinking of!" I exclaim. I'd worked out an eighteen-mile route with 1123m of ascent and all to claim one more Corbett on the way into Braemar!

My lofty ambitions mean I've planned no alternative and I only have the maps for this mad route. On the bothy wall is pinned an OS Sheet, the very one I'd need to make my way to Braemar via the Linn of Dee. I eat my route sheet words, 'If I make it this far wild horses won't make me walk that bloody road from Inverey to Braemar'.

I have the subversive thought of stealing the map but, with captain conscience getting the better of me, instead sketch out the missing section to White Bridge, from where I know I can get myself to Braemar from memory.

Waking on Sunday May 23rd at 04:00 I recall that the other bothy inhabitant, a middle-aged man who had briefly joined the evening conversation, had cast doom on my choice of room. "The sun will rise through the window and you'll be awake by four."

It takes me two hours to get myself going, but I'm grateful for the early start. To my bothy colleague being woken at 04:00 would be a nuisance. One man's meat is another man's poison as the saying goes. Well actually I am a vegetarian so I set off pondering that one.

My aim is Mar Lodge, on the road into Braemar: they offer accommodation and a warm welcome to those on the TGO Challenge.

I follow the Tarf Water on its south bank, east towards the Falls of Tarf, looking for a suitable crossing place. I have a number of abortive attempts seeing me perched on rocks, midway across, before backtracking. When I finally accept it isn't going to be possible to cross and keep my feet dry, I find a wide patch, change into my canoe shoes and step out as far as I can on the rocks. I then wade the rest, using my trekking poles to keep balance in the flow yet moving swiftly to save my nerves from falling victim to the current.

Back into my trekking shoes, I reach the Falls of Tarf in thick cloud, a beautiful area where four deep gorges meet. I take the northerly route along a narrow path. It's a wild deep place, the mountains tower opposite and four decomposing deer are testimony to this being a place to avoid when the snows come.

From the ruin of Bynack Lodge the going becomes frustrated by a multitude of shallow rivers and streams which I have to cross back and forth to reach the track to White Bridge.

By the decaying parapets of an old bridge I make my final crossing. On the other side I lean against a concrete stump, which once formed part of the bridge, and eat my lunch.

As I'm set to leave I'm attracted by moss which covers it and, by chance, appears to be spelling words. I peer closer and see the moss has formed in sunken lettering – I just manage to make out the bridge was built in 1966.

I pass a few folk walking into the mountains, we bid our hellos and I reach the Linn of Dee eight hours into my day. A forty-five-minute road walk takes me to Mar Lodge, it feels further than on previous years.

In the grounds of the lodge I follow the helpful TGO Challenge signs and arrive at reception. "Do you have room? I'm on the TGO Challenge," I say as if mentioning I'm a smelly damp walker will help my cause.

"If you don't mind sharing," says Jane the helpful manageress. I'm shown the kitchen, and am told I can pretty much help myself to whatever food I want for an additional £5. I can't pay the total of £20 quickly enough, nor can I get into the bath at the same speedy pace.

The lodge has been rebuilt after a fire, though my room is furnished with old beds, wardrobe and chest of drawers. It feels like I'm staying at the house of an aged relative.

I make my way to the high-vaulted kitchen, make a cup of tea and sit at the long table. Another challenger arrives, sixty-nine-year-old Alan Kay sporting a pack twice the weight of mine. Jane introduces us as roommates and Alan's first words to me are, "You don't snore do you."

"No, do you?" I ask.

"No."

"That's good," I reply, "we'll get along well."

Another challenger arrives (making him the fourth I've seen since the west coast) and the evening drifts into eating and chatting. They are good guys to talk with. Both are carrying huge packs and we compare notes and weights.

I take a wander around the ground floor of the lodge. The corridors are a mix of straights and bends with the heads of deer, shot in the nineteenth century, peering down at me from the high-hooped ceilings.

Alan asks Jane to show me the ballroom. Over one hundred years old it sits in a separate building. I sense from the mood I'm about to be shown something spectacular. We walk across the well-manicured lawn and Jane unlocks the door. If I'd only looked down I wouldn't have seen this as anything more than a large village hall with furnishings to match. But I don't, I look up. One could not fail to look up. The walls and ceilings are lined with no fewer than 2435 sets of deer antlers and skulls

"This place is macabre," I exclaim. Jane and Alan smile at my reaction.

The evening continues with food and chatting before we retire to bed whereupon Alan starts a chorus of snoring. I reach for my radio, plug in the earphones and tune into the only available radio station.

I stir throughout the night and finally come to, on Monday May 24th, with Neil Diamond's 'Beautiful Noise' playing into my ears with the backing track of Alan's snoring.

Over breakfast Alan asks how I slept.

"Well you snore," I say.

"I was going to say you snored," he replies and it appears we had had a shift system going of keeping one another awake.

We share the concerns of the package waiting for Mark Storey. He's two days' late and no sign of him. 'Challenge Control' had phoned the night before trying to locate him. I reach Braemar, along the boring wet road, and phone in. He still hasn't been located and they are now out looking for him.

Braemar is cleared out of food. Challengers have been through the stores like a plague of locusts. Missing the wild open spaces, I feel constrained by the narrow shop doorways and people milling around.

I manage to pick together a few things then go to the outdoor shop and buy additional breakfasts and evening meals. I lunch in a café then set off for Gelder Shiel Bothy, road walking south, taking the tracks past the Lion's Face, enjoying the viewpoints and road walking to Invercauld Bridge. From here I feel very achy but am glad to be away from the traffic on the open tracks that curve their way on the flatlands to the bothy.

In all it takes me five hours and I'm surprised, yet pleased, to find TGO Challenge company in the form of Paul Farrar. He's a police inspector and, having previously had a career in Police IT myself, we find lots to talk about. He's practical and down to earth in his views of policing which is always refreshing to hear.

Tuesday May 25th dawns cool with high cloud. I make it a lazy start, chatting to Paul and aiming for just the eight miles to the Shielin of Mark

Bothy, via the Corbett of Conachcraig. Paul's aiming for Lochnagar but it's likely we'll meet at the bothy later.

Conachcraig stands proud (occupying the inside of a bend in the track) with its three summits forming a shallow coire. I start my climb towards the middle summit, taking it slowly through the cold air and gentle wisps of wind. I keep catching sight of a fringe and fool myself I have a full head. When I realise it's no more than my eyebrows growing bushy with age, I sink into disappointment.

I reach the middle summit in over two hours then bend south-west to the true 865m top. From here a good path leads west. Although it is in the wrong direction I follow it, meeting the track in the glen below which I follow round to the Spittal of Glenmuick.

I recall my last visit here, in pouring rain, taking shelter and making good use of the hot soup from the dispensing machine. This time I'm able to sit outside and enjoy the weather and sip my soup.

I press on up the steep gorge and take Ian Shiel's, my route vetter, recommended route around to the bothy. It avoids the bog hop of previous years, following a stream upwards until it dwindles to sump holes and water gurgling underground.

I drop down the easily crossable burn (a marked contrast to the raging torrent of last year) and as I approach the simple structure of the bothy I stop to speak to a man. He's older, late sixties, wild in features with a full head of grey wiry hair. He wears tweed trousers down to the shin, below are wrapped homemade cloth gaiters, tied with string, sitting above stout boots. His jacket is white, cloth and multi-pocketed. In his hand is a substantial pair of garden secateurs.

"What are you looking for?" I ask.

"Heather for me bed."

He follows me into the bothy, his manner kind, his voice a thick Scottish brogue. I look around, his kit is substantial and old. It could have been the 1940s: he's spread tins and things tied up in string over the bench. It took both my grandfathers a lifetime to litter a bench with so many eclectic items, it appears he's done it from the contents of his pack in one afternoon. The five bottles of whisky make me cautious and I plan to camp.

Bernhard Koeglmeier arrives, a challenger from Germany, having just walked in from Braemar. We exchange glances as the man lights his ancient stoves. He chats away, saying he has two bottles one of petrol and one of paraffin. The flames shoot high, three to four feet. The fire then spreads to the floor and he does a dance to put it out. "Don't ya worry, it'll ney explode," he says.

He heats his food then transfers it to a smaller stove to simmer (such is his method of controlling a flame). Paul arrives and sits with us – our eyes can't avoid the eccentric activities of the man.

There's just one bed space spare. "Bernhard and I are camping," I say, "as you've only a tarp you can have the bothy."

Paul nods gently, "That's very kind."

I feel a bit stuck. I hadn't really been honest. Cautious about all the whisky (not to mention the petrol and the paraffin), I didn't really fancy the bothy.

I put my tent up then return to the bothy to eat. The man says he'll get a fire going. He does, a roaring success and we toast ourselves as he stirs the fire with his bare hands. There is wood to be chopped up, this is when I notice the axe and the bow saw (tied up with string).

"Did you bring those?" I ask.

"Aye."

"How heavy is your pack?"

"About seventy pounds there."

And I struggle with mine at twenty-two pounds.

He puts on large spectacles and lights his pipe. I wonder if he is a lover of combustion as I find a pipe smoker spends more time reigniting the thing than ever drawing breath through it.

I pick a piece of wood to cut for the fire. "You'll be better with this," he says, drawing a handsaw from his trouser pocket.

"Will you take a dram?" he asks Paul and me. I decline, am glad he doesn't push it. His manner is so gentle and kind. He pours a generous measure for himself and Paul. As I start to nod with sleep I make my way to my tent and sleep well.

Wednesday May 26th and I enter the bothy to make my breakfast. The fire is still going and the man offers me the nearest seat. I make my food and notice that half of the five bottles of whisky have been drunk. I wonder if Paul has further imbibed but he looks fit and ready to go and assures me he has slept well. We bid farewells to the man, cross the burn and head for the summit of Muckle Cairn to pick up the track to Loch Lee.

"That wasn't exactly true about a good night's sleep," says Paul.

I'm not altogether surprised to hear this but ask why.

"I think I had the measure of the man but he stayed up very late drinking. When he finally laid down he snored, was restless, talked and muttered endlessly in his sleep and frequently sat up and yelled, 'For Jesus Christ's sake' in a Father Jack kind of fashion".

"While admiring his axe?" I ask.

"I didn't look," replied Paul.

We peep into a bothy at the head of Glen Lee. It's strewn with straw. A large open fireplace, with spit hook for meat, is the centre piece of the gable wall.

"Is this the bothy that chap said he'd be moving on to," I ponder.

"I think so," replies Paul.

"I don't like the look of that hook in the fire. It looks just right for roasting a challenger's head," I reply.

"With an apple in its mouth," adds Paul.

From here our conversation continues until we have convicted the poor fellow of a multitude of crimes. Some of which are quite heinous indeed. We chat further and discover we both know Garry Smith, a mountain guide from North Wales. Like the lady, who grew up in the same home town as me, staying at the Tarf Hotel Bothy it feels a small world at times.

The conversation then extends to the mating habits of deer and how the male rolls itself in his own urine to make himself attractive to the female.

"Not something that'd work for us humans," says Paul.

"He could say 'sorry love I've been out on the piss, it was a stag night you know'," I add.

"Very good. Did you just make that up?" he asks.

"I have to confess, no. Although it's my own joke I made it up years ago and have been waiting for an opportunity to use it. Today was the day."

I recall last year's route march with a procession of soggy walkers heading for Tarfside. Being a day late this year it's just the two of us until we break onto the track to Westbank. Here we are caught up by Roger Wiltshire.

I eye him up and down and can't help but notice he's wearing odd boots. His two companions have dropped out at Braemar, leaving some of his essential kit in the wrong rucksack – including matching boots, his cigarettes and the money with which to purchase them. Paul lets him have one and Roger draws on it with relief.

We walk into Tarfside, we are the first to arrive, just missing the rain, and lap up the kindness of Ann, Janet and Marion. There are rooms galore and we each have one to ourselves. The evening passes with the meal, endless pieces of cake, conversation and tea.

It's the morning of Thursday May 25th and I take my time getting going. I'm a bit daunted by the long walk to North Water Bridge but the thought of lunch and a rest in the café in Edzell cheers me up.

Setting off again, I amble down the road in the wake of Roger and Paul. I look for the bridge to cross the River North Esk to the good path of its south bank and like last year, miss it. I pick a later bridge which, now in a ferocious hailstorm, I only find by ploughing through marshy ground then following tracks back to the bridge.

On the far side I find a new pace and make good progress via Dalbog then the footpath cutting the corner off the road into Edzell. I pass the corner of a wood and jump out of my skin at a large explosion. It's right by my left ear and, as my heart rate rescinds, I discover it's a gas-powered crow scarer located right by a public footpath.

This is my second experience of these. Many years ago, while walking with Andy Glover, we settled down for lunch without knowing one was right next to me. Just like this time when it went off my whole world stood still for a moment.

The pine trees of the wood sway and bow in the breeze and the wind rushes through the tops like the sea running up a sandy shore. To my right the short wheat shimmers in the wind, and gleams in the sun, as it rushes up the hillside. So perfect and green that if two Teletubbies came bounding over the horizon I'd not have been surprised.

I rest and eat in Edzell and visit the Mace Shop. It's closed, early closing Thursday. I go to the post office for cash, this is closed too. I reflect if the shop had been open, and not the post office, I'd have spent my money and now be short of the fee for the campsite at North Water Bridge.

Taking the familiar route across the River North Esk, I pass the bull with the unfeasibly large testicles (he's a landmark and a legend in my book) and make my way through the farm roads to Chapelton before breaking off towards the public road leading to the campsite.

This involves crossing one more field and, with my mind away with my thoughts, I then become aware of a herd of young bulls prancing towards me. In a group of males there always has to be a cocky one: this is no exception as one stands forth, leaps and bounds and kicks its back legs like an Irish Setter. It takes me a second to realise it's attracted to my red jacket.

"Oh bullocks," I exclaim as the bastards move in. I'm walking next to a fence so I press my left hand down on the top wire and go to vault it. The next moment I'm yelling, "For Jesus Christ's sake." The fence is electrified and my hand has just been flung off and is now stinging like crazy. Perhaps the man in the bothy was dreaming of a thousand bullocks chasing him towards an electric fence?

In the ensuing excitement one of the bullocks tries to hump another, his prey isn't having any of it and darts forward which sets the others prancing closer to me.

Nosey Cows

I raise my trekking poles. "Goo onnn, get out of 'ere," I yell while discovering why farming communities often have deep West Country sounding voices. I'm surprised but this does work and they back off, though I do have to practise my newfound skill twice more before I make it to the field gate.

On the roadside they gang up against the fence and stare at me. It takes a while to switch on my mobile to take a picture. However, my red jacket taunts them, keeping their minds focussed on the impending photo opportunity.

At the campsite I spend my last £7.31 on the camp fee, an ice cream and a bar of chocolate.

Roger Wiltshire is already here and watches intently as I make a mess of putting up my tent.

A bearded, long-haired chap arrives. I ask his name, it's Mark Storey who we were concerned about at Mar Lodge. I ask of his adventures, how come he was missing for two days. It appears he'd changed his route and his message didn't reach 'Challenge Control'. We are joined by a couple from Surrey and Sheila Farley from Coulsdon. Just five tents – the night before there'd have been seventy or eighty.

When I wake on Friday May 28th I breakfast then peer out. Roger has made one of his early starts and kindly left me an egg by my tent flap. While wondering what to do with it Mark stirs and claims it for his breakfast.

I change my destination to Montrose Bay, the plan of St Cyrus has been shelved because of the lack of money for bus fare to then get me to Montrose.

I pass more bullocks that, safely behind a fence, skip and charge towards my red jacket. As I rise over a hill I get the first view of the sea. A welcome sight on what's been my quietest crossing. It's the first where I haven't planned to meet anybody else on route and I wonder at myself for working alone, living alone and holidaying alone.

I pass through the sand dunes, paddle in the sea and throw the small pebble I've carried from Mallaig on the west coast. As I walk along the beach towards Montrose the sea runs up the sandy shore like the breeze rushing through the tops of the pine trees.

November 2010 – English Nuttalls. Over The Hill Club

It's Friday November 19th and I'm battling my way through London to catch the 09:30 Euston to Penrith. The automatic announcements are cajoling us to "Move right down the car", the doors are shutting and I'm regretting wearing my thermal top, fleece and Gore-Tex jacket. Oxford Circus is a good few stops so I venture beyond the vestibule and grip one of the balls that hang from the roof by a spring.

With my arm raised I recall deodorant adverts and am now pleased to be wearing my jacket. Coupled with walking trousers, trail shoes and pack I'm conspicuous amongst the suits.

The man stood next to me, smart raincoat, neatly done hair, speaks, "Your spikes are flying all over the place." I look behind me and figure this is not the time to point out that what is strapped to my pack are actually trekking poles. And if I'm not mistaken I'm detecting some irritation in his voice.

I swing my pack off and offer my apologies all round. The tube train then jolts and I fly forward and smack him full in the chest.

"Sorry about that," I say, "rather looks as if I'm flying all over the place too." The quip doesn't work, or if it did he has some issue with his facial muscles. I add, "I had to let go of the strap to take the pack off." This time I see that he is in full control of his facial muscles. I catch the eye of a seated female passenger, she smiles and I reckon she knows what trekking poles are for.

The train lurches from station to station, people join, people leave and I'm feeling more and more trapped in the middle of the car. At Baker Street I start to wonder if I should make my way to the vestibule. By Regent's Park it's beginning to feel like a necessity and, as the train begins to slow, I survey whether the quickest exit will be to my left or to my right. It's clearly to my right and I've clearly got to ask the man I've stabbed with my poles and smacked in the chest, to allow me to pass.

"Excuse me, sorry," I start, "I've got to..." But he's an expert, parts the waves and I'm then edging myself closer to the doors. Like Crocodile Dundee in New York I ascertain who is getting off, who is staying on as I sidestep my way.

On the platform a waft of cool air clears my head and soothes my body. I find my way to the Victoria Line, board the waiting train and wait. And wait. An announcement explains there is a broken-down train ahead. I check my watch. The minutes tick by. I'm sweating, plotting and finally running for the Central Line to Tottenham Court Road then the Northern Line to Euston whereupon one of my trekking poles decides to descend, catches the door lip and I fall into the carriage, just righting myself before I clatter into somebody else.

I catch my train at Euston and emerge some three hours later in Penrith basking in blue skies. The ruins of the sandstone castle perch over a neatly-mown moat – the pride of any Tory MP's expense claim. But it's the McDonalds restaurant that catches my eye, not because it spares me crossing the road, not because there's a crisp chill in the air but because I'm bloody starving: needs must and all that.

I enter and, being a vegetarian, I scan the menu of delicacies that do not involve the remains of bovine, ovine, porcine or piscine.

Although, to my untrained eye, some of it distinctly looks canine. Failing dismally, and finding myself at the head of the queue, I ask the assistant (who on first impressions would appear to have sampled the entire menu, daily), "What can you do for a vegetarian?" Realising that my question has left me somewhat open I'm pleased when she points out a 'Vegetable Deluxe Burger'. I order that, chips and we then go through the charade of ordering me a drink. This is where it gets more complicated for I'm waiting, like a hand paused on a fruit machine, for her to mention something that does not contain caffeine or lots of sugar.

"You can have Fanta, Sprite, Coke, 7UP, milk shakes, a fruit shot, coffee or tea." At this point I'm looking her straight in the eye and she's fazed by my impassive face. I can see she's struggling, she's running out of options, I doubt she's ever had to get this far through the list before. I glance at the cabinet to my left and she follows my gaze. "Oh we have pure orange juice," she says.

"That'll be great," I reply and she looks more relieved than me. The meal comes and I have to admit it's rather tasty.

I take my time over the final morsels, allowing each chew to be a countdown to the bus departure time.

I wander to the bus stop, enjoying the coolness of the air and the blueness of the sky. I check then double check and accept the safety in numbers of the correct stand.

The bus rattles to a standstill and my compatriots murmur and stir. A loose order of boarding is formed between perceived early birds, the elderly and mothers with young children. I pay my dues, perch my pack on my lap and take in the views while the bus wanders north and south of its A66 route, collecting and depositing people as it goes.

Nearing Keswick the mountains rise from the earth until they tower above the road. Russet brown of their lower slopes propping darkened upper reaches. I don't know their names and I pledge to walk them, to know them, to spend more time in the Lake District. I spy paths, routes and scrambles amongst their folds. It's a day for surveying, a day for planning and if one is lucky a day to be basking on the ridges in this cool, clear winter day.

The bus reaches the outskirts of Keswick and I ask an aged, capped headed man, in the seat in front of me, if he could let me know where the centre is. He turns, gives me a rundown of all possible stops, their merits for different purchases, attractions and drinking hostelries. I notice his hands; aged tattoos of LOVE and HATE are engraved above his knuckles. I wonder if he ever glances at them, ponders at them and remembers the man he once was. But I accept the kindly old man, the man pleased to be offering advice, the man pleased to be asked.

I pick the best recommendation from many, accept his directions, thank the driver and step from the bus into the bustling hub of Keswick. I wander awhile, survey the market stalls, and make a donation to a man rattling a tin for mountain rescue. He'd spotted my poles, my pack and my jacket. "You look like a man that doesn't need rescuing," he said. The compliment worked and a sticker was added to my lapel to prove it.

It takes a while to meander my way to the B5289, the route to Derwent Water Youth Hostel, the route to The 'Over The Hill Club AGM' weekend. There's a nice path that sits on the lake side of the road. It wanders eagerly from shore to road, through dips and rises. Down the lake the view unfolds into a plethora of mountains, light heather, trees and snow are set back in ever increasing layers of beauty.

I sit awhile, time is on my side. Mesmerising waves pound the shore until they settle into gentle laps. A brown spaniel races ahead of its owner, its nose close to the ground sniffing past then climbing the rise behind me. Its owner follows on as the dog stands proud from its eyrie plotting her progress.

I take my cue to follow and stroll leisurely into the Youth Hostel. As ever I'm assigned a bunk in Room 1, the resting place of all males single. Graham Gledhill announces an ability to snore so I move further into the room's reaches where the two Daves (Skipp and Wilkinson) are making up their beds.

"What are the numbers like this weekend?" I ask.

"Not good," says the Wilkinson half of the pairing, "we tried a membership drive but have attracted no young blood."

"The clue could be in the club title," I add. I quickly rue my quip as evidently this has been discussed at length on Facebook.

I slope off to enjoy the evening, the meal and to catch up with old friends.

Wiping away the condensation on the tall windows of Room 1, I dry my hand against my fleece and peer towards the mountains. They stood glorious in yesterday's sun, now they are hidden by the low cloud of the dawning Saturday morning.

The veggie cooked breakfast cheers me and the packed lunch, a first ever purchase for me, looks substantial. I wander to the car park, I need to bag a lift and Graham Gledhill comes up trumps with his shiny new VW Touran. Peter Goodwin joins us. Sue Oxley appears, joining a variety of vehicles carrying Dave Handley, Big John, Jacquie Hutchison, Ann and Alvar Thorn.

We rendezvous at a car park below the Grisedale Pike Horseshoe. There's some confusion over the grid reference matching the visual description of the car park. Nobody dares to question Big John as he arrives and, after packs are sorted, boots donned and waterproofs pulled on we set off. I make a good pace, keeping up – I need to keep near the front for a planned deviation to Hobcarton End. Sue and I take the lead up the cloud-clad spine of Grisedale Pike. As I touch the summit we confirm mobile phone numbers and I head north for Hobcarton End. It's a steep descent in scree and I fail to find a path on what should be a popular route. I stop and survey the surroundings. Unclaimed voices of distant walkers funnel eerily onto the slopes. To my left I reckon the land falls away, to my right, in the swirling mist, I fancy I can make out a ridge spur. I clamber to it and find a path which, over undulations and detours takes me to Hobcarton End. I motor back, reclaim Grisedale Pike and follow the south-westerly path, with its steep drop into the valley below, around to Hobcarton Crag. Studying the map, I can't understand why Hopegill Head does not count as a 2000ft mountain. I survey further and conclude its listed in another walk and, my tunnel vision of marking up a map, has let me down.

I descend to Coledale Hause and study map, compass and GPS to pick up the right path around to Crag Hill. The distant sound of Sue's voice rolls off the mountain with the mist. I wait, allowing my ears to pick up closing voices and figure the rest have taken in Hopegill Head. By chance I'm now ahead of them. They are a little surprised to see me standing in the mist on a junction of paths at 2000ft.

The wind has picked up and we head south until a culvert, with babbling stream, shelters us for lunch. Alvar's ankle is playing him up and a debate about route ensues. He and Ann are adamant that we should not change our plans for them and point out the many ways off they could take. I pitch in for the route over Causey Pike as it'll give me the seven peaks described in this round in the Nuttall's guide to 'The Mountains of England'.

I finish the Youth Hostel packed lunch, substantial and tasty. We pull packs on, stretch legs and chat freely while we ascend Crag Hill. Ann and Alvar drop down into the valley as we take in Sail. An ever-decreasing number of routes off, clearing cloud and the desire to stay high take us over the decaying waveforms of Scar Crags and Causey Pike. A minor piece of scrambling, requiring hand and footholds, has us bunching up, offering advice and taking it easy as we complete our round.

We all look back, whence we came and admire the terrific views. The sunlight that escapes through the cloud forms layers of tone on the side of the hill, mixed with the ever-changing colours of the heather and peat it forms a colour wash that only an artist can understand yet the eyes of all admirers can appreciate.

We pick up the minor roads then paths that skirt us around Braithwaite and, in the fading light, find the cars and make our way back to the hostel for the AGM meal, merriment and, thankfully, for this evening no talk of changing the name of the club. Over the hill we have been. Over the hill we will become.

Classification	My Total	Total
Welsh Nuttalls	190	190
English Nuttalls	48	253
Corbetts (Scotland)	20	220
Grahams (Scotland)	6	220
Unique Donalds (Scotland)	0	58
Munros (Scotland)	283	283
Ireland	0	212
Totals (20/11/2010):	547	1436

March 2011 – The end of the line

I'm on my way to give a product demonstration for Solchar, the company I work for. I get a text from my dad telling me my grandfather (Mum's father), who has been ill in hospital, has just died. That's my last grandparent gone. With them dying when I was aged twenty-seven, forty-three, forty-four and forty-five I knew them all very well. It's also another home to break up. He'd lived there for sixty years and, like my other grandparents, it's a large rambling rundown place full of redundant items that were never thrown away. Full of memories too. Time passes on.

I get through the day, thinking of him and worrying how his two older brothers are coping with the news: Uncle Laurie at 103 and Uncle John at ninety-eight. Our family tends to hang around a bit.

Like the men of that generation he rarely talked about the war but he did tell me he landed on D-Day plus three at Arromanches, on the Normandy beaches, and on the advance through France the chap next to him got his head 'blown clean off'. Ending up in Vienna, as part of the British occupying forces, he got home in 1946.

He was famed for his bizarre remarks. When his friend Barbara died, while sitting on the toilet, he was convinced it was from hypothermia. It was August and in the bathroom of her upstairs flat. On showing the plaster wobbling behind wood chip wallpaper in my house I described how I intended to get it re-plastered. "I wouldn't bother with that," he said, "it's only lost its suction." On entering my parents partly-replaced kitchen he began to admire the side not yet replaced and, on running his hand along the chipped Formica top, announced, "They are making a lovely job of it." On listening to my description of a walk I'd just made he suggested, "You should get a dog." On pointing out to him that I had a life-long allergy to dogs, brought on by his Jack Russell when I was just two years of age, he replied, "That needn't matter." When he asked me what a word processor was I gave a rather full explanation, including the ability to easily correct errors before printing. He told me, "That's daft, you can do all that with a bottle of Tippex." On discussing his care he sung the praises of his polish carer before adding, "She's got a twin sister. She's polish too." On my mother visiting him in hospital he announced, "I saw a proper doctor today." To which my mother replied, "You mean a man don't you?" On my mother asking if he'd been wetting the bed he replied, "No more than anybody else."

And there was the time he phoned me up one evening and asked if I'd lend him £100,000 because he'd seen a flat he'd like to buy. He had many other strange ideas and, when questioned, he'd back then up with an angry look. But he loved being outside. He also loved being a great grandfather, courtesy of my sister last August.

He loved an argument, loved winding people up. But he gave me a love of the outdoors. When I was growing up we'd see him and my grandmother about once a month. We'd always go for a walk, along a nearby disused railway line or the then redundant Kennet and Avon Canal. These walks with him sparked an interest. As did my bedroom window when I was a boy. I had the back bedroom which looked out across six miles of open countryside to the hills beyond. I'd spend many an hour alone, sometimes with my eye to an antique brass Victorian telescope, surveying the fields and Wiltshire hills. They looked faraway, only when I was a bit older did I explore them on my bicycle or walk out towards them with friends.

April 2011 – English Nuttalls

Friday 15th April sees me visiting a customer on the outskirts of Liverpool followed by a holiday in the Lake District, bagging peaks. The close proximity of four bank holidays (Easter, The Royal Wedding and the May bank holiday) means I have three weeks away for just eleven annual leave days.

With my company kindly paying my mileage to Liverpool and back, I emerge on Saturday the 16th from a Travelodge, feeling that so far this has been very efficient. The dawn skies look promising and a gentle cooling breeze wafts across the M6 service station. I make my way to the service area with the hopes of a hearty breakfast.

My diet has become tiresome: no wheat (due to a digestive issue), no meat, no sugar or alcohol (both of which dump me in a low mood). Not that an alcoholic beverage is on my agenda but I soon realise that an M6 service station is not prepared for no wheat, no meat and nothing sweet. I plump for two fried eggs, beans and tomatoes. Back in my room I devour a couple of rice cakes for my carbohydrate.

I then set off on the drive over to bag a couple of mountains above Grasmere and to the west of Thirlmere. It takes just over an hour, punctuated by a number of stops to convince myself that I'd not left anything behind in the hotel. Arriving at the car park I find there's a charge for it, but I'm without any change. So up and down the road I drive, kerbed by the waters of Thirlmere and a rock face. Each time I spy a pull-in I also spy a no parking sign until one pull-in, with abandoned track beyond, fails to have a note of deterrent.

I begin walking through a gently-rising track; grateful for its even ground and easy navigation. Trees fall away to my left and climb to my right. A stream gently gurgles below me as the sun dodges in and out of cloud, cooling and warming me. I navigate the track, drop down to a stream and pick up a path which, via a double-gated break in a forest border fence, has me out onto the hillside.

The well-marked path, on the map, is difficult to find and, by use of GPS and compass, I set a direct course for Low Saddle. The direct route becomes one of deviation as I navigate round knolls, streams and boggy ground. I rest often – having injured my neck in January I've been unable to exercise. After two and a quarter hours I clamber the final few paces to the summit.

I munch on some food, eat a rice cake, sup water then make the half-hour crossing to Ullscarf. This is a simple cairn, marking the highest point of its upland plateau. I return on the same route, saying hello to the same breed of sheep I saw on the way up (grey or brown bodies with white faces), before dropping sharply east across Standing Crag. The going becomes hard when I have to lower myself down a steep grassy wet slope. Safely on gentler ground I slip, go flying and bum slide a few yards with wet penetrating my backside and legs.

I return through the forest, following the same track as on my ascent, and return to the car in a total of four hours.

I wake in the Ambleside holiday cottage that I have taken for three weeks. It's bijou, well thought out and rather lovely. I take my time getting up, there's a Formula 1 race to watch before I head to the hills. A relaxing breakfast takes me through the build up and an exciting hour and a half sees me through the race. Then it's a packed lunch to make, maps to check and the trip round to the start of Harter Fell.

I soon discover the delights of the Wrynose Pass. Being one of the steepest roads in England, linking to the more famous Hardknott Pass, it is narrow, tortuous and not averse to having your left wheels running along a very sharp drop.

There's lots of starting and stopping and braking to do, not aided by getting entangled in a cycling event with a stream of cars and motorcycles. Having just had all four discs and pads replaced the rather substantial bill came with an advisory note of "Avoid heavy braking for 500 miles." I don't know if lots of braking constitutes heavy braking, but my foot is more often than not wedded to the pedal.

Fortunately everybody is being sane, allowing room for the mass of cyclists to make their way through and even the motor bikes wait patiently for their turn.

The start of the walk, requiring a short deviation down the Seathwaite road, is from a National Trust car park. I set off walking at 11:35 and, rarely for me, have the guidebook in my hand as I make my way across a tracked bridge and turn left onto a riverside path. There are a series of paths branching off, not mentioned in the guidebook. I view each in turn, wondering if I should be taking it. I press on, hoping I'm following the footsteps of the authors.

Relieved to pass a farm house mentioned in the guidebook, I dutifully turn right onto the track beyond then seek out the path to the left. It's now a climb through the remnants of a felled conifer plantation. After a kilometre I glance down at my compass and realise that I am heading due north. This is not good; in fact any navigational direction without the word 'west' in it is not a good idea at this precise moment. As the plantation has been felled I strike west over rough, steep ground.

I find this slow going and rest every few paces. I'd planned yesterday and today as easier walks, wanting to build up some fitness. It's been a tough few years with my dad's parents dying in 2008 and 2009, then my last remaining grandparent just a month ago followed by his

103-year-old brother last Sunday. These things fatigue you more than you realise and I certainly feel fatigued treading my way in the ripening sun.

I pass through rocky crags, using them as place markers or things to aim for. Then the summit appears on my horizon: a castellated array of rocky crags. Sheep stand and stare while I ascend the grassy slopes and tread onto the first of the rocks. I master the slabs, say hello to a group of feasting people, and climb, with a few easy moves, what looks like the summit at 13:55. The views all around are magnificent. I track my route up then gaze out across to the Wrynose Pass and to the sea beyond.

I drop down and rest by the trig point before climbing one of the lesser peaks of its battlements, just for the hell of it. A fellow walker asks for the trig point, I direct him but also tell him which the true summit is.

I wander between the jagged outcrops of rocks like a laird prowling his estate. I take out map and guidebook and rule out the recommended way down: too much tree planting has taken place since the route was worked out.

Picking a south-easterly path, I navigate carefully down, hoping for an easy route off with no wrong turns and extended timings. I run out of water and do the only thing I can do to help my thirst – donning a cap to break the heat from the sun. Opposite is Seathwaite Tarn, its distant waters teasing my thirst.

There is loose small scree and I stumble twice, slipping a few yards and jarring my body at the same time. I pick my way very carefully, feeling tired, a little wobbly and determined not to slip again.

I drop onto the track with a metaphoric thump, turn left and keep on it until I reach the car after another four-hour walk.

On Monday April 18th my ambitions have become loftier and, with the Langdale Pikes in mind, I pack my rucksack with food and water then make the short trip to Great Langdale. Fortunately this time I have change as the parking is £6.50 for the day and few other alternatives appear to exist.

I make a slow plod up the well-made path, some people overtake, others roughly keep the same pace as me but I don't get ahead of anybody. Feeling tired, I rest often, either perched on a slab on the path or laid out on the grass. I slug back a litre of water then refill my bottle from a fast-flowing stream. A path repair team are attempting to reposition a large boulder in the stream; a ratchet lift, metal poles and some brute force do little more than rock it on its foundations.

I'm grateful to the path builders for this stepped path. It gives me an even pace that the steep grassy slopes, where I frequently slump to the ground for a rest, fail to.

Harrison Stickle from Stickle Tarn

I arrive at Stickle Tarn at 11:00, an hour and a half into the walk. It's a lovely tarn, some 400m long and in the shadow of Pavey Ark and Harrison Stickle. A walled dam restricts its draining back toward Great Langdale, its northern shore laps against the gentle slopes of my route to Codale Head. Its western shore sits below the menacing peaks of

Harrison Stickle and Pavey Ark.

I stagger my way north-east then north-west, following the dwindling path to the rocky peak of Sergeant Mann; not being a 2000ft summit in its own right I head east to Codale Head. In the distance is High Raise but it's an illusion of the terrain – it takes me just twenty minutes to pace my way there. I'm pleased to be on the high ground, the steep climb is done and it looks now to be a pleasant walk around the seven summits. Despite the brilliant blue skyline the wind chills me and I don my jacket as I make my way south to Thunacar Knott.

A dip and a rise and a minor scramble have me on Pavey Ark. I sit awhile, allowing the throngs of people to pass. I watch crows hover and call. Seagulls call too. Paragliders turn and swoop from Harrison Stickle. Looking back, from whence I came, I pick out Sergeant Mann, Codale Head and High Raise. Below me is a sharp drop back to Stickle Tarn, glistening blue in the afternoon light.

I try a direct route to Harrison Stickle but it has me negotiating rocky outcrops. Instead, I drop and pick up the path that leads me to the summit. This is tough going, taking me forty minutes in all.

A welcome cooling breeze fans me as I survey Stickle Tarn from yet another angle. I head west towards Pike of Stickle. The route gets a little confusing with the best I can find to be via a sharp descent of a rocky wall. I gingerly take steps before leaping the last few feet and steadying myself as I land. It's then a good drop before the ascent of Pike of Stickle starts. At the low point a grey sheep, with a white face, blocks the path. "Hello you," I say and then realising my pun reiterate the joke. The sheep is not having it, not one twitch of a laugh or acknowledgement. It just stands there staring at me. I walk around and begin the rocky climb which takes me to the summit.

I rest awhile at the top, surveying the views, the late afternoon light playing off the mountains, the deep blues of the sky and the cool breeze remind me that it's only April.

On my way back, I drop down the rock face until I meet the path and, with my lack of fitness showing, take my time to Loft Crag. From here I navigate carefully, the 2000ft view down into Great Langdale looks a long way and I'm mindful of getting my bearings wrong and joining the road miles from my car. So I check compass and GPS at every twist and turn as the path takes me back to Great Langdale. After just over eight hours in the hills, I arrive at 17:40. I don't fancy cooking so pop into the Stickle Barn pub. I'm served by a monotone Scandinavian gentleman, likely Finnish by the sounds of him. As I dump my pack and trekking poles down I order jacket potato with cheese and a side order of chips.

"Will you be eating inside or outside?" he asks

"Inside," I reply, "I'm not really the outdoorsy type."

My humour is lost.

After a rest day, using up another day of glorious sun, I feel fit enough to tackle the Bowfell group of mountains – a big day in the hills. I plan a route in the reverse order of the guide book so, if I feel fit, I can also take in the ten summits to the south. But first I have to contend with the car parking in Great Langdale. Misreading the starting point I pull up in the very same car park I'd used on Monday, pay my £6.50 and set off up the track. I then discover that I'm in the wrong place as the terrain does not match my map. Back at the car I drive further up Great Langdale and, unable to spot the car park at the head, I turn back and park at a midway car park. My heart sinks when I see that this one is operated by the National Trust and my ticket is for a car park belonging to the Parks Authority. I put a note in my window pretending to be ignorant saying, "Sorry I bought this ticket at your other car park, hope that's okay."

I take the track to Middle Fell Farm, a gentle stroll through fields, where I find the car park that I should have been in. I consider going back but think better of it and, at 09:00, take the well-made and gently-rising track of the Cumbria Way.

It's tough going, the sun is blazing down but as I rise I'm treated to great views of the Langdale Pikes that I climbed on Monday. Unbelievably some of the high folds of the mountains ahead have snow still in them.

I rest at the junction of tracks, to my right are Black Crags and to my left my intended route to Rossett Pike. I drink a litre of water and refill from the flowing stream.

The walk becomes a tortuous staircase of laid stone. Bags of rock, brought in by helicopter, line the edges. I look up, it's a perfect sky, the ridge lines are rock sitting below the rich blues of the sky. My cap protects me from the blazing sun; my legs feel tired and heavy. I rest often and sup water. People pass then I pass them as we migrate our way up.

Below Angle Tarn I branch off right and ascend Rossett Pike, reaching the summit just before noon. I stand and admire the panoramic views with peaks dipping and undulating, great ridges connecting them. Some tops are great battlements with unclimbable faces spewing scree to the valley floor below.

I press on, pass the dark Angle Tarn and follow the track around to Esk Hause. Here I rest amongst couples sitting and chatting, families sharing a picnic and a man fussing over his two dogs. It could be a city centre park on a mid-summer's day, apart from the 2500ft views and the cool breeze of the mountain air now gently cooling me.

Pressing on I stagger my way up Esk Pike, negotiating my way through its boulder field until I pull myself onto the summit. A bit of cloud has formed in the sky, high, white and no danger. A distant paraglider catches my eye before two single engine propeller driven RAF trainer aircraft blast down the valley. Decorated in shiny black with yellow markings they make a beautiful sight and a lovely sound as their piston engines drone into the distance. Like steam trains have the romantic advantage over diesel, propeller planes do so over jet.

Following another boulder field, I inadvertently come up between the two Bowfell mountains. I turn back to take in Bowfell North Top, the final leg being on crunchy dry grass, before the leg-draining clamber to Bowfell, at 902m the highest point of the day. From a higher vantage point, I survey my Monday's walk before dropping south-east to pick up the track back to Great Langdale. I help out a woman with a searing headache by giving her a couple of Ibuprofen. The descent is steep, tough on the legs and I take a good three hours over it. The last 2000ft is over the sharp nose of 'The Band' where the ground falls away so steeply, to the valley floor below, I'm glad of the path.

At the foot I get chatting to a couple of women, one of their husbands has gone for their car and they offer me a lift to my car park. I gratefully accept, the sun is so hot and the heat is wafting from the tarmac. They drop me off, I'm grateful for not having received a parking fine. I then set off and realise I'm only a hundred or so yards from the first car park of the day. I could have just gone back there and saved the worry.

Due to my tiredness the 21st becomes another rest day where I amble in Ambleside, buy some DVDs, food and generally relax.

The 22nd becomes my third trip down Great Langdale since Monday. This time I have the parking sussed and am walking at around 09:15 for a day doing the ten tops of the Crinkle Crags round. The first peak entails a road walk before I branch off at a stream then follow a well-trodden path. The weather is clear and the sun steadily warms me. I carry 2kg of water but at every opportunity stop, drink a litre and refill from the flowing stream. I'm wondering if my struggles this week have partly been due to dehydration.

The first top is Pike of Blisco, which I reach in two hours. Many people are gathered here for its fine views. I then head for Great Knott but it's not at great knots I'm travelling. The summit is a rise to the north of the path; here I'm alone as, unless you are setting out to bag every 2000ft top, the temptation is to head straight for Crinkle Crags. However, my path now deviates via Cold Pike, Cold Pike West Top and Cold Pike Far West Top. Again the views are fantastic: Monday's walk is fully on view again and part of Wednesday's appears on the skyline. The extremity of the day is Little Stand where I use my GPS to confirm I have gone far enough.

It's now a yomp across open ground, followed by a sharp rise, to Crinkle Crags South Top. The wind is still until I reach the ridge and its many cairned summits. I climb them all and use GPS to confirm when I'm sat on Crinkle Crags, Shelter Crags then Shelter Crags North Top; each time sitting on my map case to save it from the strong warm breeze. I'm tired and rest often, my legs a little shaky and my heart pounding in protest. Dropping rapidly to the track I took on Wednesday I make good going, reaching my car at 17:40.

Views of Crinkle Crags from Cold Pike

I visit the same pub I visited on Monday and Wednesday, ordering the same food – jacket potato, cheese and chips with two pints of orange juice and lemonade. The same, head shaven, Czech Republic girl is serving as on Wednesday. Her colleague, the humourless Finn, takes my order – I don't risk any jokes this time.

Saturday 23rd I wake early, feeling fit enough for another day in the hills. A visit to the bathroom proves otherwise – my feet ache where the ball of the foot meets the arch. I return to bed, doze, wake, breakfast and inspect my trail shoes. They've both cracked across my pain line so I wander into Ambleside to look for new ones.

I'm never a good shopper, need to feel good about a shop even before going in. Then when I'm in the simplest of things can put me off, have me heading for the door. I look in a few windows, wander in a few shops, wander out. Then I find Millets, the vibe is good, I wander in. Footwear upstairs. The assistant is helping another chap. I feel all the shoes for weight, turning the lightest towards me as placeholders. She finishes with him, smiles cheerily and asks how she can help.

"Well size ten or eleven in any of these," I say, pointing to those I'd picked out in a price range of £28.99, £64.99 and £104.99.

Only the £64.99 and £104.99 are in stock and then only at size eleven. I try them both and, would you believe it, only the £104.99 ones fit properly.

In the evening I go to the cinema and see the very funny film, *Submarine*. Though I'm equally amused by the screen advertising. The first advert is for the Advertising Standards Authority – saying if you see an advert that is not accurate you should complain. A later advert is for 'Visit Scotland' which says 'You will get a warm welcome, a very warm welcome.' In my humble experience, not if you are a single English bloke you won't – frequently downright hostile I'd say.

Sunday 24th (Easter Sunday) dawns as beautiful as any day this week. I manage to get myself out of bed early. I fancy the Coniston Fells. At eleven and a half miles coupled with 4400 feet of ascent, I'm set for a big day.

Arriving in Coniston around 07:30 I consult the guidebook. Apparently I need to find the old station car park. I find Station Road but there's no sign of an old station let alone an accompanying car park.

Setting off at 07:50, after finding parking on the road to the Copper Mines and Youth Hostel, I find my new walking shoes are a nice fit. I feel fit and make good progress towards Wetherlam. The disused mines and the Youth Hostel come into view but I branch north-west, taking the path through the curves and undulations. I hear voices below and my gaze spots a group of wild campers; their voices carrying high up the mountain. A sheep with its new born black lamb blocks my path. It's the first lamb I've seen this year. I pause until it moves, the wobbly-legged youngster keeping close to its mum. A fell runner passes me before I make Wetherlam at 10:15. Coniston Water glitters in the morning sun and I recall its dark history, Donald Campbell and his Bluebird boat. Opposite is The Old Man of Coniston – a peak for later in the day. There's a little haze through which I can make out much of my walk, around the twisting ridges and their peaks.

I make the easy half-hour walk to Black Sails, arriving at 10:45, then, via a rocky scramble, the summit of Swirl How some fifty minutes later. Here I chat to a woman, only the fifth person I've met so far, who started from Keswick a few days ago with backpack, tent and faithful collie called Pluto.

The walk round to Great Carrs is simple but tinged with sadness as I come across a cairn built around the remains of the undercarriage of a Halifax Bomber. It marks the site of the crash on October 22nd 1944. I survey the area and see that there are the remains of molten metal where it caught fire. The aircraft would have only needed to be a few metres higher to have made it over the ridge.

It reminds me of an old chap, Jack Taylor, I met in Canada who'd lost his brother, Robert William Taylor, in a Halifax Bomber during the war. He mentioned he'd wished he'd visited his grave in England, but now felt too old. Back home I contacted The Commonwealth War Graves Commission and they were able to tell me where he was buried. I went and took some photos and researched the circumstances of the crash. Next time I was in Canada I caught up with Jack and gave him the photographs and details of the crash.

I take in Great Carrs. The drop off is steep into the valley below and I'm cooled by a breeze as I take in the surrounding mountain vista.

I take the drop and ascent to Grey Friar where I stop for lunch, relaxing with my back to a rock and surveying the sweeping mountainside, the sharp fall away, round to Coniston Old Man.

I retrace my steps then take the contour-like path around to Brim Fell (with its ancient cairn) before the long pull up The Old Man.

Here I'm on the beaten track and there is quite a crowd at the summit. The views over Coniston and its water are just so beautiful, sail boats are out as birds gently swoop for tourist titbits. Many fellow walkers head straight back down but for me I have the walk around to Dow Crag, Walna Scar and White Maiden.

The remains of Halifax LL505 and its fallen heroes

Dow Crag has an unnerving exposed scramble to its summit. I pause only briefly, patting the summit, then return to safety.

The pull over to Walna Scar and White Maiden feels like a remote corner of this walk. I'm glad for the stunning weather – in wind, rain or mist, I could imagine being uncertain about taking such a spur from the well-beaten track. Even with the good visibility I make a navigational error and find myself having overshot onto the lesser summit of White Pike. Either side there are views into the valleys below.

The view from The Old Man

My legs feel very tired and I feel drained as I retrace my steps to meet the path between Walna Scar and Dow Crag. Here I turn right and drop quickly on the good path. As I get closer to Coniston, four mountain bikes shriek by and I notice how many cars have driven up the track for their occupants to free camp.

A woman opens a gate to allow her partners BMW 3 series cabriolet through.

"Thanks for opening the gate for me," I quip.

"Would you like a ride into Coniston?"

I grab the opportunity, a ride in an open-top car on a lovely day and the saving of about a mile road walking.

The 25th brings a cooler, cloudier start to the day but I feel fit enough for another walk. I start to look slightly further afield and fancy Great Dodd and its surrounding hills.

After finding the minor road to cut me across to the A592 I park at High Row and am off walking at 08:15. Firstly it's a walk down a metalled road to the farm at Dowthwaitehead and a chat with a farmer about the pleasures of the day. Then it's an embarrassing root around his farmyard while I look for the path onto the hills. Path found, and my eyes averted from any checking by the farmer, I make my way across the heavy, boggy grass slopes.

I miss the paths of the last few days as my legs feel heavy and tired. I make a navigational error and have to correct myself to find the stone wall that climbs near to the top of Birkett Fell. This is not a true 2000ft summit but it's a nice perch, although blustery, from which to rest. I check for phone signal, put on my fleece, and call my parents, it rings awhile but I assume 10:00 is not too early. Mum answers.

"Hello."

"Hi, Mum, it's me."

"Who?"

"Steve."

"Where are you?"

"Birkett Fell."

"Birkett Bell?" she replies (Mum is known for her mishearing).

"No, Firket Bell," I correct her (I'm known for mixing the first letters of successive words), then correct myself with, "No, I mean Birkett Fell," while thanking my lucky stars it's not called 'Hirkett Fell'.

I cross to the true peak of Hart Side then drop to the col and climb the beckoning Green Side before the short sharp ascent of

Stybarrow Dodd. I note fell runners around, I get chatting to one (while I shyly inspect the footings of an ancient derelict wall). They are on an Easter egg trail, running from peak to peak seeking out clues.

I have a good wander around, taking in all the cairns before the grand sweep and rise round to Great Dodd. At Watson's Dodd I rest. It's 11:50 and I take an early lunch to have some energy before the end of the day.

I arrive on Great Dodd at 12:30, it feels like a real mountain, there are drop offs all round with accompanying views. There's also an ancient shelter.

I drop, on the ridge, to Calfhow Pike before the quick pull up to Clough Head and its trig point made of local stone. There are great views of the higher mountains to the north-west and the long and winding 'Old Coach Road' (my return route to High Row) snakes through the valley floor below.

I drop rapidly, making my own zig-zag path, before climbing over an ancient wire fence and picking up the coach road. A mountain bike approaches; it, and its rider, are both heavily laden. I comment on this, the reply is a pure Glaswegian accent so consequently I don't understand a word of it.

It's now a route march back to the car with an undulating track, and tired legs, to keep me company.

As I drive over 'The Struggle' from Ambleside to Glenridding I notice a drop in temperature and low hanging cloud. I'm second to arrive at the car park and part with £7 to park for the day. I collect my ticket and the credit card receipt for the previous payee and tuck it under their wiper.

At just after 08:00 I'm off walking and struggle as I look for the guidebook's recommendation of a ladder stile with a sign for 'Helvellyn via Greenside Mine and Red Tarn'. By poring over the map and checking GPS, I pick my way through a series of other 'Helvellyn via' signs to find the 'Helvellyn via Greenside Mine and Red Tarn' sign. I make a mental note, if I ever write a guidebook I need to mention all the signposts you are likely to come across and tell you which way to go at each; otherwise it's just educated guessing.

The steadily climbing track towards Red Tarn is good. In low mist I turn up the dinosaur-like, spine ridge to Catstye Cam. I don fleece, bandana around my ears and gloves to take away the sting of the cold.

As I approach the top I keep away from the sharp drop off to the right. I make the summit at 10:30, feeling very healthy. Through the swirling mist I can make out Red Tarn and the path to Helvellyn Lower Man. I drop down to the col before climbing the path through the rocks which appear to hang like a rickety cartoon staircase. I climb cautiously, the drop to the left being a steep fall off. Placing foot and hands carefully, I reach a steep grassy slope which has a series of useful footholds which lead me to the summit plateau. Before me is a trig point and I realise that I've inadvertently strayed onto the summit of Helvellyn (which was due to be part of another round connecting the mountains to the south). I tag the trig point and stroll the short distance to the summit cairn. The cloud has lifted and the views are a stunning array of encircling peaks with criss-cross paths stretching between each.

I walk around to Helvellyn Lower Man and appreciate what a fine, conical, mountain Catstye Cam is. From the Lower Man I drop towards the col. I briefly chat with a chap before the most piercing freezing wind hits from the east. Despite my fleece it rips the heat out of me so I'm grateful to make the col where the wind is gentle. I ascend White Side where I fancy breaking for lunch. However, the summit is adorned with some human waste so I press on to Raise and its impressive cairn. It's now 12:10 and, very pleased with my progress, I duck below the cairn, out of the wind, and eat my lunch.

I line up Sheffield Pike by compass bearing. It involves a drop to Sticks Pass then an easterly turn. Here I note the optimistic ski lift on the north side of Raise. I wonder how many people make the walk out to it as this would be a remote spot on a winter's day.

Sheffield Pike requires a detour from the main path and a sharp pull across an energy-sapping grassed slope. After briefly speaking with a family tackling the Wainwrights I make the summit at 13:40.

From the top it's a steep easterly descent. I backtrack a few times as I pick my way down, keeping my nerve against the sharp drops before returning to the car.

April the 27th dawns without a cloud in the sky. A good day to try and complete the Scafell group of mountains. It's a bit of a hike over, requiring travel across the Wrynose and Hardknott passes. I take much of it in first gear while the bonnet rises above my nose or sinks beneath my knees. As my Sat Nav constantly revises my arrival time the car's temperature gauge remains rock solid. I'm thankful for modern cars and imagine the scene in the 1960s with overheating cars parked up on each bend.

At a shade before 09:00 I'm parked at the top of Wast Water, grateful for one of the last remaining free parking spaces. The day starts with the regular chore of getting into the mind-set of the writers of the guidebook: working out which unmentioned bits on the ground to ignore. After one backtrack I'm on course and climbing the steep slopes towards Lingmell.

From high up Wast Water glistens behind me, I hear the cattle grid rattle with each new vehicle coming up the valley and watch as the final free parking place is swallowed up.

In the hot weather I find it very tough going, taking me an hour and a half to conquer the steepest part of the path before two distinct raises become part of the trail. Sat, studying the view in surreal still and quietness, I ponder my pace; yesterday I was so fast in cool weather on rock and slab paths. But on grass or scree, combined with the sun, I slow right down.

I long for some wind, sometimes it's your friend, sometimes your enemy, right now I want a gentle breeze to cool me. My prayer is answered on the higher slopes where, on slipping off my pack and map case, the soft wind cools my dripping wet torso.

I make Lingmell's summit at a little after 11:15. A few people are already here, enjoying the views. Others join me. Great End and Great Gable stand proud either side of a valley. Birds dive from their tops and hang still in the air as they study the ground below. I study the map, and set the compass for the next top. However, I can't see the one beyond so drop to the col where I see what I thought to be the next is actually the one after.

Wast Water (and the sea beyond) from the slopes of Lingmell

Middleboot Knotts and Round How are really knolls nestled, with the prerequisite height and drops, amongst the grander mountains adorning the main ridge. I pass over the sharp-falling stream of Piers Gill before dropping and ascending the two. On Round How, which was a heavy legged, energy-sapping sharp pull to attain, I stop and eat lunch and survey the view in the peace of my own company.

I drop to the Corridor Route and join the masses heading to Scafell Pike; too many people for pleasantries as everybody passes with barely an acknowledgement. The route feels familiar – I'm pretty sure I climbed it from this route in 1990 when I found it equally tough going. I rest often, sitting on the polished rocks, as people pass. A multitude of cairns claim the way before the boulder-strewn summit appears and, after careful steps, I make the summit for the third time.

Next are Symonds Knott and Scafell. A daunting rock face appears to block the path. I check the guidebook and it advises almost getting to the face then a three hundred feet descent before a rock-strewn gully climb through the stream of Foxes Gill. As I approach the rock face it all feels very serious. Climbers work their way up. Others discuss the best routes. For me I'm following the guidebook, actually it's now my best friend as I descend through the steep scree to the route up. Eerie echoes and clatters fill the scree-ridden cauldron. I chat with a few people, everybody is taking it steady.

The pull up the gully is thick with fallen boulders, trickling water and ringing wet moss. I take a few steps at a time, careful not to dislodge anything to the path below and listen carefully should anybody be dislodging anything on to me.

I rest, studying the guidebook: Symonds Knott and Scafell are both above 3000ft and are my last two English 3000ft mountains. It takes me just a second to realise that I'm about to complete all the 3000ft mountains of Great Britain (308 in all). This gives me a new spring as I squeeze past, clamber over or avoid large boulders.

At Foxes Tarn, no more than a puddle, I turn right to the pull to the ridge. I take in Symonds Knot. A few people are already there, peacefully surveying the view. It feels so different to Scafell Pike where the tourists sat, chattered and made endless mobile phone calls. Here it feels more serious.

The views are outstanding, back across to the Pike, the valleys and mountains behind and the sea out to the west. I cross to Scafell and have a private celebration of my sudden 3000ft achievement. I explain to a couple and ask them to take my photo.

The day becomes longer than I ever anticipated. The walk back to the car is on gruesome scree and steep slopes. It takes me until 17:45 and I mess up my navigation on the drive back, not arriving back in

Ambleside until way after 20:00.

Scafell, having completed the 308 3000ft mountains of Great Britain

April 28th brings another day of continuous sunshine and it begins to dawn on me how lucky I am seeing the mountains of the lakes, and their waters, in the bright sunshine of an English spring. With thoughts like these, I take my mind off navigating my car across to Swindale, to take in the not oft visited Sleddale Fells, and get lost.

Back on track I approach the recommended parking area at around 09:00, only to be thwarted by a sign saying, 'No parking beyond this point'. So I start further back with the sun catching the back of my neck as I walk the undulating tar-sealed road to Swindale Head.

At Swindale Head I branch right up the gruesomely-steep twisting path. On a frequent rest I conclude that air temperature, gradient and terrain can conspire to all but bring me to a halt and this, without exception, is such an occasion – studying the map I see it's called 'The Old Corpse Road' so I quip to myself that it could soon become 'The New Corpse Road.' The sun is brutal, right on me as I try to swing my way around to Selside Pike.

I make the top, sink into its summit shelter, slip off what feels like a heavy pack and raise my tired legs onto a rock. I rest awhile before the brief descent and ascent of Branstree North-east Top before a drop down to a rather spectacular pillar – which, according to the guide book, was used for surveying.

Branstree is gained by following a fence, with its predecessor at its feet lying dead in the grass. Where the fence meets a fine wall I cross and make my way to a small cairn (the least impressive summit cairn I've ever seen) and a more interesting ground-level circular structure that has the hallmarks of Ordnance Survey about it. Shortly to the north-east are two more impressive cairns but, below the summit line, I wonder what the motives were for building them.

It's just before noon and, after taking in the fine views down to Haweswater, I park myself on the south side of the wall and eat my now familiar lunch of cold jacket potato and cheese. An older chap, who followed the fence up from the south-east, wants to chat; I'm a man that clearly does not want to chat. I answer his questions, am friendly but ask him none in return. He moves on and I'm grateful for the peace.

The surveying pillar between the Branstree summits

At 14:10 I make the fourth summit of the day, Tarn Crag, which is adorned by another of the interesting pillars, standing proud over the valley below. Next to it is a peaty bog where sawn timber, likely from the structure, is being preserved as bog wood.

I make my way over to Grey Crag and turn north-east to Harrop Pike. This is a remote corner and I touch the summit, cross the fence and admire the cairn: a stack sitting on a level rock.

I drop back and cross a ridge and descend to the bothy of Mosedale Cottage, taking in the views of my walk from earlier in the day. I find it a depressing place and all my thoughts of having, perhaps, found a bothy I'd like to revisit for a few days are ended.

At Swindale Head I get lost amongst the farm buildings. As I navigate myself amongst farm vehicles and gates my stress levels are heightened by a dog calling my presence. When I get to the road I'm grateful for the straightforward plod back to the car. Arriving at 16:40, I set off and get very lost on the myriad of lanes which lead to the main road.

Getting lost is the theme of my Saturday April 30th trip round to Kentmere to meet with Sue Oxley. We plan to do the Kentmere Fells, starting at 08:00. I make the drive over, which should have taken half an hour, in just under an hour.

It's a warm day but a stiff breeze in the air has me setting off wearing my fleece and bandana wrapped about my neck. Sue and her dog, Molly, are in fine walking form and I'm glad for the pace as we shoot up Yoke. I think to myself 'This is great, we'll have these seven hills ticked off in no time.'

Towards the top of Yoke the blustery wind, under a perfect blue sky, turns to a persistent attack. We fight to stay on the path, Sue fights to keep one trekking pole on the ground as she clutches Molly's lead in the other hand. I brace myself with two trekking poles.

A man wheeling a mountain bike passes us and, after we pass over Ill Bell and Froswick, he struggles his way up Thornthwaite Crag. At one point his mountain bike takes off and we watch him struggle to hold it parallel to the ground.

Sue gets ahead and I catch up with her in the col before the ascent. We can barely stand up in the 75mph winds. Sue had previously mentioned a drop into the valley to the west. As I catch her I ask if she wants to take it.

"It's not going to get any better," I say.

"Are you sure that's okay?" she asks.

"Yes, this is supposed to be a holiday."

It's a long drop before the wind abates. We meet two older chaps, one with a blister. We sort him out with some Compeed I'm carrying. They plan to press on for an ambitious day as Sue and I drop to the more settled confines of the valley floor.

We rest behind a wall to eat before the tough re-ascent, keeping well away from Yoke, to return to Kentmere.

May Day brings a rest day and a catch up with Kate Wilson, her family and friends. It's almost ten years (July 2001) since I met Kate when she joined mutual friends on my last Munro.

May 2nd and I'm back to the hills with the plan to do the Hartsop (or heart stop as I call it) horseshoe and two of the hills that were abandoned on Saturday.

The drive over 'The Struggle' from Ambleside to Hartsop village is stunning in the early morning light. The radio is playing out the news of the deaths of Henry Cooper and Osama Bin Laden. Again there's not a cloud in sight and when I've parked I'm glad for the cooling breeze. However, I am concerned what it'll be like on the summits.

I make an early navigational error and find myself too far up Pasture Beck. I cut steeply, across rough ground, north-west to regain the steep path up Hartsop Dodd. Wind catches me and I worry it's going to be like Saturday but on reaching the path it abates.

I find it a hard pull, resting often but I'm glad for the cooler conditions as, although I'm slow, I make progress. The sun is directly in my eyes which gives a morale boost by stopping me from directly viewing the ascent. To the north I'm able to view the Kirkstone Pass and Ullswater in the distance – a rich blue that snuggles into the lower contours of the hills.

At the summit I chat to a husband and wife pair who clearly are avid hill goers – as fellow Munroists we chat about mountains climbed and those to be climbed.

I let them set off first then follow on to Stony Cove Pike then north-east, on steep path and scree, to the impressive summit beacon of Thornthwaite Crag. Here I am on the same ridge that Sue and I turned back from on Saturday. Again the wind hits hard and I duck below a wall to rest.

Haweswater Reservoir

I break from the guidebook to take in the previously-abandoned High Street. High Street is both the name of the summit and the Roman road that graces this ridge. It's an easy walk and the wind, although very blustery, is manageable. Like many other people out today I use the confines of the wall, leading to the summit, to eat my lunch. From here I branch to the furthest point in the day by dropping around 240 metres before the simple rise to Rough Crag. The drop is through a twisting entertaining ridge path with rock, grass, steps and fantastic views. To my right is the tarn of Blea Water, rippling in the wind. Ahead of me the waters of Haweswater Reservoir have dropped, leaving a white ring that defines the shore like a contour on a map.

I'm pleased to find the re-ascent to High Street easier than expected – the twisting ridge allowing natural points at which to catch my breath. I head back to Thornthwaite Crag before taking the long north ridge spur to Gray Crag. The wind is now bashing me hard but, as I drop below the High Street ridge line, I find some protection.

It feels a long way out to the summit. I stand and survey the views, my walk up and the steep descent ahead of me. I make my way down, trying to be gentle on my painful knees before arriving back at the car eight hours since I started.

Tuesday May 3rd and I wake early but very tired. I lie in for an hour then drag myself up, breakfast, pack lunch, pack gear and a drive round to Patterdale to take in Place Fell, High Rise and five other surrounding peaks. The guidebook recommends starting from Martindale Church, instead I elect to start it from Rooking.

I set off at 08:25 following first a delightful walled track with sun glimmering through the trees then a river bank with birds chirping in the fine weather.

The ascent is long and tough as I begin the lower flanks of Place Fell. I have my usual thoughts of 'why am I doing this?' and 'why not turn back if it hurts this much?'. It's really tempting and I'm sure one day I will and that'll be it. But, for now, as ever I push on, stumble and rest, press on until I make the summit in just under two hours, a typical timing for my Lakeland ascents.

I survey the walk ahead, it looks massive. The walk over to Rest Dodd looks far enough but the swing round to Loadpot Hill looks a very long way.

It's a sharp drop then another climb until, at 11:50, I get to the very pretty Angle Tarn. It has peninsulas, coves and small islands where trees grow, free from nibbling sheep.

The ascent of Rest Dodd is steep. I feel tired, slow and annoyed. I place one foot in front of the other, keeping my head down. On a break I look back and see the snaking path that drops from Place Fell. I pick out my route past Angle Tarn until my eyes run up to where I stand.

It takes an hour to the summit where I eat my lunch before tackling a cruel drop and a 600ft ascent to Rampsgill Head. This takes a further hour and as I survey the six-mile round trip to Loadpot Hill I realise that it and Wether Hill will have to be for another day. I find relief with a decision made, and it makes the closer summits of Kidsty Pike and High Raise more achievable. Pressing on would take me into a late evening to finish and spoil any enjoyment – ten years ago I'd have done it.

At High Raise I hear the distant voices of other hill-going folk carried on the wind. I make out the odd word, the odd phrase but seldom does a conversation hold across the open ground.

It's a route march back, mainly descent but the odd rise in the path has my legs complaining. I pass Angle Tarn at 15:10, Canada Geese protest my intrusion and swim across the tarn. From here I take the direct paths to Patterdale with my chatterbox mind annoying me about every topic it can think of. It's about 17:30 when I wearily reach the car, dump my pack and head to the local inn for food and orange juice.

I wake early on May 4th feeling very tired, and it's 10:00 before I'm navigating the car through the muddle of single-track roads and farm tracks to Hallow Bank, north-east of Kentmere. My plan is to finish the two mountains of the horseshoe Sue Oxley and I tackled on Saturday. I hope the high winds will have abated.

I make steady progress until, just after 11:00, I sink into the grass and survey the view. The flatlands of the valley floors, either side of the ridge, are a rich green of walled fields; a wall runs the line of the ridge before me like a sharp trouser crease. The mountains rise either side of the fields, the lush green merging into army camouflage before rocky outcrops steer the eye to their ridges and summits. In the distance is the sea, glimmering through the light haze of a lovely spring day.

I pass the summit cairn and trig point of Kentmere Pike before the easy ridge walk out to Harter Fell, arriving at 12:15. Sat with my back to the iron fencepost spiked summit cairn I survey the vista before me: the familiar Haweswater Reservoir glimmering and High Street (with the dots of moving walkers) to my left. I rest until my back feels uncomfortable against the rocks, I say hello to a few passing walkers then set off back to my car.

The weather forecast proves correct and the unprecedented sunny, dry weather is at an end. However, I fancy taking in the Helvellyn circuit which includes the notorious Striding Edge.

I set off, from Patterdale, at 08:20 with an overcast sky, a few dots of rain in the air, and the welcome result of only having to carry one litre of water instead of the two required for hot weather.

I follow a track for the first summit of the day, Birkhouse Moor. After missing a turning around the 300m contour, I stop to inspect the map. Instead of backtracking, I figure I can continue and break off at the 490m contour to get onto the track for the summit. At 510m I stop and look back. I've overshot. After a quick descent I pick up the right path, cross a wall which I follow to near the summit. I branch off to visit a cairn, not marking the actual summit, before backtracking and crossing over the real summit.

The area is a mountainous bowl around which the summits of Striding Edge and Helvellyn sit. Before me is the ridge connecting Striding Edge to Helvellyn: a series of humpbacks with, reportedly, steep drops to either side. I make my way up, pack away my trekking poles, and elect to take the easier path to the right of the ridge. However, curiosity gets the better of me and part way through I get onto the ridge. It is exposed but nothing like what I've experienced in Scotland.

There are two separate couples and a middle-aged lady and her student-aged son also on the ridge. We pass each other, they re-pass as we call encouragement and find a comradeship in the shared objective. The final part, before the steep scramble to the summit, requires the descent of a chimney. I lower myself down and try and give guidance to a couple.

"We've got two dogs with us," they say.

I'd not noticed this before.

"Can I help?" I ask (comradeship feeling rather high).

"Yes, can you take one?"

So I take my pack off and clamber half way up the chimney. I'm then passed Lotte, a small cute wee thing who is lowered towards me with her four paws dangling below her and a look of sheer terror in her small black eyes. I take her close to my chest, offer words of comfort, stroke her as I make my way down to safe ground. She struggles a little – I hush her reassurances and rub her back. On safe ground I make a fuss of her before returning for the second dog. By now the lady of the partnership is able to slip by her man and the other dog is lowered to her, saving me from a repeat experience of things being a 'little hairy' on the ridge.

The next section is a steep scramble to the summit of Helvellyn. A multitude of paths and scree have been created and the group of us work our way up, taking it easy not to dislodge anything. I take it in short bursts, resting often. Lotte takes it gingerly, a couple of times refusing her owner's preferred route and instead making her way across to me.

"She's made a friend," laughs her owners. Lotte looks back with an expression I can only describe as, 'I'm sorted, thank you very much.'

I follow the woman with her son, she complains that all the bending means her bottom is sticking out. Fine by me I can assure you.

Finally we meet the summit ridge, its shelter, memorials, cairn and a cold, chill biting wind. It's noon, my second visit to Helvellyn and I sit in the windbreak shelter and eat my lunch before the easy walk to the plateau of Nethermost Pike then on to Dollywaggon Pike. Here I can't get one of my trekking poles to re-engage, the shaft turns endlessly with nothing to bite against.

It's a considerable drop and a demoralising re-ascent to take in Seat Sandal – my knees complain with just the one pole to support them. With Grisedale Tarn below me, I orientate and study the map hard to ensure that I don't accidentally climb Fairfield. This is a 2000ft peak but is included in another round. The Nuttall's guidebook does allocate the peaks into well-thought-out day walks but it means that, when in the vicinity of other peaks, I have to resist being tempted by them.

I make the drop to just above the tarn before the path that takes a glancing blow up the side of St Sunday Crag. Resting in a hollow, I keep out of the wind and survey what I've done. I manage to get the second trekking pole to bite so I can extend and lock it. Now I make better progress across the series of false summits to the top of St Sunday Crag.

I lose height again before the trek across Birks and a sharp drop, in persistent drizzle, back to Patterdale. At 17:10 I'm sat in my car as the rains close in.

Friday dawns with persistent rain so I bring my walking holiday to an end and make use of the day updating my diaries, washing and taking it easy before the drive back on the Saturday.

November 2011 – English Nuttalls. Over The Hill Club

With the annual Over The Hill Club AGM approaching, the traditional email from Big John Hutchison arrives with details of the club walk for Saturday November 19th. I reach for my Nuttall's guide to the mountains of England; thumb the pages in the proximity of the walk and see what else I can take in.

But this time I can't just go off on a whim: after living alone for thirteen years I have just taken in a receptionist from a gym I attend. She'd lost her job, lost her accommodation and found herself homeless. She then attempted suicide. So I collected her from hospital and gave her my spare bedroom.

Not wishing to leave her alone, I drop her off in Manchester, to stay with friends, while I travel on and seek out the Travelodge at Kendal.

I love the anonymity, no B&B landlord or landlady to make polite conversation with, no problem parking and no fuss about the room. I spread my kit out, load my pack for tomorrow, including one of the three packed lunches I'd prepared for the weekend, lie on the bed, enjoy the memories of egg and chips at an M6 service station and click on the TV.

Having managed without a telly for the last year this feels like a new experience; TV, for me, now has been relegated to *Crimewatch* and Formula 1 on iPlayer. I flick up to the radio channels. It's grim, no Radio 4 and I begin to wonder if I fall into the target market for this establishment. I flick around looking for something that is not pop culture, dodgy or sensationalist news. I finally plump for an ancient repeat of *On The Buses*. Memories of the 1970s come flooding back. Did we really find this funny? Still it was on ITV in its heyday. I recall my mother's shock when, babysitting for a neighbour, at discovering the most dreadful piece of information about them – the ITV button was pressed in on their TV set. Believe me, that kept neighbourhood tittle-tattle going for quite a while; what went on behind the net curtains of 1970's suburbia was nobody's business.

The Friday dawns and I make a slow start. Breakfast is peanuts and rice bread, the drink is my own Rooibos and I again wonder if I fall in the category of the Travelodge target market; they clearly think I do, judging by the succession of emails they send throughout the year offering cheap weekend breaks.

I head for the village of Outhgill to take in the four fells that lie to its east. Navigation proves a problem before I even get out of the car. My cunning plan, of locating the nearest postcode and using my Sat Nag to get me there, is a dismal failure as I end up at some hotel to the north. I use cunning and stealth and drive at five miles per hour, annoying everybody behind me, until I spot Outhgill. In true determined tradition I try to drive as far as I can up the hill I'm about to climb. This peters out after two hundred yards at a narrow dead end and farm gate. Now farm gates don't move, narrow lanes don't get wider and ditches do not suddenly fill themselves in. And steep gradients are not for reversing down. I ponder my stupidity while holding the handbrake with all my might. To my left is a bungalow with a large gravel frontage and a big shiny RAC van. I imagine the conversation (no really, I do imagine this):

"Hello, RAC?"

"I'm stuck."

"Where are you?"

"Erm well."

"Do you have a postcode, sir?"

"Well yes, but well no, well not exactly."

"Do you have a postcode yes or no?"

"No," and I hang up, knock the bungalow's door, explain I am a member, explain my predicament and the RAC man, in true sarcastic tones, agrees that I truly am a member.

Giving up on the idea I gingerly edge the car around with as much anonymity that a noisy power-steering pump will allow.

I roll the car down to the village, park on a little green area, swing the pack through my arms, extend the trekking poles and ascend the track I'd just rolled down.

I cross open ground, follow a stream before the steep terrain through Mallerstang Edge, then boggy ground to the highest summit of the day, High Seat.

It's 11:35 and I survey the view – absolutely bugger all; the mist is down, good and thick.

I close navigate to Archy Styrigg, making use of the GPS to avoid following a path that descends the mountain. It's a windswept plateau which the wind is still busy sweeping. I drop my pack to rest at its summit, munch on some peanuts and yelp as I swing the pack back onto my shoulders; a trapped nerve in my upper left arm is the new ailment of middle age. It recently gave me maximum embarrassment when I had to ask my eldest friend, at the age of seventy-eight, to help me on with my coat.

I follow fences, bogs, bits of cairns across Hugh Seat to Little Fell, arriving at 13:30. I am dry but my feet are soaked so, coupled with not wishing to still be high at dusk, the lofty ideas of retracing my route are abandoned. Taking the quickest route off the mountains I pick up the B road for a lengthy, boring walk back to Outhgill.

At 15:45 I'm driving to Dufton, it should take about an hour but I take considerably longer with a spot of navigation problems. It's a beautiful village with the Youth Hostel bordering the upper slope of the village green and an idyllic pub, with farm buildings behind, adorning the lower slope.

I make my way to the village hall and meet with friends from the club, make my way back, check in and am pleased to be put in a room with just two others. With this new venue, I can start to put Derwentwater Youth Hostel, with its infamous, spacious and snorer-ridden Room 1 behind me.

Supper is served in the Youth Hostel, very tasty and I elect not to attend the annual club slide show and make my way to bed. I drift off and barely hear Sam Hackett and Dave Handley come to bed. Until the snoring starts that is. But, now realising I snore too, I'm more understanding. I switch my radio on and put in the ear pieces. When the snoring outdoes the radio I turn up the volume, if the volume outdoes my ability to sleep I turn it down until the point at which the snoring bothers me.

In the early hours I roll over, the radio comes adrift from the ear piece lead; falls downs the gap between the bed and wall, clobbering Sam in the bunk below. I peer over the edge and an arm hands the radio back.

The morning comes and with it the hostel breakfast. There is confusion after the round of juice, cereal and fruit. Is there a cooked breakfast? Somebody is sent to investigate. All doors are locked and we wonder how long we should remain in the dining area with eyes full of hope.

Watches are inspected, stomachs rumble and eyes gaze to the day outside. The odd non-resident club member can be seen in the car park, nobody wants to miss a cooked breakfast; nobody wants to look a fool. Our patience is rewarded with the clanking wheels of a mobile cafeteria. The smells waft our way, it's a full-English and in true English style nobody wants to be first in the queue. Apart from me whose stomach overrides all social graces.

The food is lovely, so much so I, encouraged by fellow diners, and in true Oliver Twist fashion, shyly ask for some more. My tail drops between my legs as the server thinks not everybody has come down for breakfast yet. I return to the table, plate empty and sit it out. I am rewarded when I'm called across for seconds.

Outside a number of cars are heading round to Kirkland for the walk up Cross Fell. Along with a few others, I pile in Dave Skipp's. When we arrive there's twenty-four of us donning boots, jackets and studying maps. I set off at 10:00 with Big John and Sue Oxley, and manage to keep to their pace for about forty-five minutes before dropping back through the ranks until I'm walking and chatting with those at the rear.

The sky is a rich winter blue and the hills are their greens, greys and russet browns. The path and its crocodile of walkers winds its way into the mist, crossing stone flagged paths and boggy ground. I sink below my right knee in bog and, instinctively, throw my left knee to the ground to protect myself which in turn flicks a large lump of mud into my left eye. I extract myself as the creature from the bog. Immediate concern from my fellow walkers switches quickly to gentle mickey taking.

A boulder field takes us to the summit of Cross Fell, we pause at its windbreak shelter and trig point. I, for some reason that completely baffles me, am entrusted with taking the compass bearing to pick up the Pennine Way track to Little Dun Fell. In the distance Great Dun Fell, with its bizarre arrangement of communications equipment, is literally topped by the most enormous-looking golf ball.

The path is well defined, well made and we make Great Dun Fell in steady time. With our backs to its barbed wire fences, and our eyes from its view, we look into the valley below.

A short excursion onto its newly-metalled access road takes us to the track leading up Knock Fell. By now my legs are tired and I feel chilled in the winter air. The ascent is easy and we gather at the summit for a group photo.

Knock Fell. I'm in the centre with the map case. (John Hutchison)

It's a long walk back to the Youth Hostel, descending amongst streams, rocks and gullies. It's easier to chat without gasping for air as I did during the ascent. Each person's news of the last year is caught up with; plans for 2012 discussed and the evening meal looked forward to.

We cross through a particularly boggy farmyard where we cling to its outer reaches to avoid the preverbal mess that cows make. Our boots and shoes are covered in it and we employ ingenious counter methods in long grass, puddles and shallow streams to rid ourselves of the mess.

We get into Dufton at 16:30, dusk has descended. Villagers walk their dogs for the final stroll of the day; the lights of the pub and hostel beckon us through our final few hundred yards.

I shower and relax in the lounge. I chat to fellow club members as Sam Hackett limps in in a sorry condition. He's strained his knee and ankle on a solo walk in the hills. He starts to slip into some form of shock; an ambulance is called, its blue light flashes ghostly shadows through the glass frontage of the hostel. We watch him taken off amongst the concerned looks of his compatriots.

The evening meal is a grand affair, organised, cooked and prepared by Ann and Alvar Thorn. They sacrificed a day in the hills for us and it is an amazing evening.

Tiredness excuses me from the late revelries and I slip out of the classic village hall into Dufton's night air. A good fire is raging behind the pub. A bit late for bonfire night? But this is up north, clearly they do things differently here. As I approach I start to think that it's a bit ambitious for a Guy Fawkes Night affair. And all the crackling, fizzing and popping? And aren't those flames higher than the pub? I remember the farm buildings behind the pub and the old farmers saying of "Red sky at night, barns on fire."

Indeed it is; a group of villagers and I gather. The fire brigade have been called and we hear their distant sirens as the engines steer their way across the twisting and undulating roads.

Discussions are had about where the farmer might be. Cows bellow in distress as the wind steers the flames in a rotating dance above the roof of the pub.

We stay and watch until the brigade arrives. It's a big job, they empty one tender; another arrives as the first shoots off to the nearest hydrant.

Come morning the fire is still smouldering, the brigade are still in attendance and the talk over breakfast is of nothing else while I slip myself an extra egg and veggie sausage.

On my trip home, via Manchester, I empty my trail shoes of yesterday's mud and take a solo walk up Great Knoutberry Hill through thick fog, following an easy walk from my car. On emerging from the fog, I'm treated to a temperature inversion and fantastic views.

I enjoyed the weekend: company on the journey, a night on my own in a Travelodge, company from The Over The Hill Club then company on the journey back from Manchester. At home I have my lodger's company too while she seeks out the help and appropriate accommodation she needs. It teaches me that perhaps I can share my time and space. That a life of living alone can be challenged.

View from Great Knoutberry Hill

Classification	My Total	Total
Welsh Nuttalls	190	190
English Nuttalls	136	253
Corbetts (Scotland)	20	220
Grahams (Scotland)	6	220
Unique Donalds (Scotland)	0	58
Munros (Scotland)	283	283
Ireland	0	212
Totals (20/11/2011):	635	1436

April 2012 – English Nuttalls

It's Sunday April 1st and I'm laid up in a holiday cottage in Cockermouth with the tail end of a cold. It has dragged on for nearly two weeks with flu-like symptoms, sciatica, a sore throat and a heavily-congested nose.

On the upside the cottage is lovely, full of old world knickknacks, a steep staircase, thick walls and a DVD player – I've come prepared with a stack of DVDs from my "to be watched" pile.

The drive up yesterday flicks into my mind as three distinct phases. I remember setting off, I remember sleeping at a service station for a couple of hours and I remember turning off the M6 at Penrith. But that's about it.

April 2nd and I buck myself up, cold or no cold the fells await. I take the short journey through Lamplugh and pull up at the deserted car park at Ennerdale Water. A check of the guidebook has me backtracking a quarter of a mile. I set off, just before 09:00, in fine drizzle up the steep path which leads to Great Borne. My dubious navigation soon has me going through an amicable divorce with the guidebook as I cut up too soon through a shingle-clad face.

The drizzle clears up; woodpeckers drill into the nearby forest while other birds tweet and call. As I leave the shingle I slip and put my right hand down to steady myself, plumb into a gorse bush. I pull it back, yelp and extract the spines from the side of my nails and watch the blood erupt in minute mole hills. It stings, irritates and I cuss.

I feel tired and rest often as I skirt my way around and look down to the path that I should be on. The slope steepens and I'm down to taking a few paces between rests which, coupled with feelings of being unwell and laziness, makes for a slow ascent onto the broad ridge. Here the mist is clagged in as I make the silent, rough walk to the stone trig point of Great Borne. At two and a half hours in, I shelve my lofty ideas of the peaks beyond Starling Dodd.

Starling Dodd in itself looks a beast but by the time I've dropped and started the ascent it becomes manageable. From its summit I cut east towards Little Dodd but head south too soon and hit Ennerdale Forest. A beck breaks its boundaries and I traverse east to the forest corner then head south to pick up the forestry tracks and the muscle-sapping walk back to my car, arriving at 15:00.

I return to the cottage, accessed through double black doors into an alleyway which is wide enough for a horse and cart. Mr Snowden, the owner, is chopping wood and I stop for a chat. The cottage dates from the 1820s, he shows me how far the river rose in 2009, how close the cottage came to being flooded. There's a mix of buildings towering about the alleyway. It was once a hotel but now divided up.

I wake in the early hours, my right hand throbs and I turn on the light. Counting over fifty punctures from the gorse bush, I resist the temptation to scratch it to oblivion. I pick up the book I'm reading, one from the many that reside in every nook and cranny of the cottage. It's a return to my childhood, *Five Go Adventuring Again*. The antics of Julian, Dick, George, Anne and of course Timmy the dog. I read them all when I was young and this is a welcome return. However, I'm a stickler for continuity and, as a young child, I'd lain out my entire collection then, by taking into account Christmas, Easter and summer holidays, I'd calculated that, by the time of their last adventure, Julian would have been twenty-nine and Timmy would have been stuffed and towed around on wheels.

The book was written in innocent times, their sinister tutor's only claim to such a character flaw appears to be his beard (I must shave soon) and there are lashings of the word "queer" along with "spanking" and the phrase "I'll be bound". I've not yet reached any further references to Uncle Quentin's raving homosexuality (as observed by the Comic Strip's *Five Go Mad In Dorset*) but there's time. Words clearly meant different things back in the 1930s and 1940s and people took them at face value – well Neville Chamberlain certainly did.

I wonder if Enid Blyton felt constrained by her times or whether her mind was simply pure. In the scene where Timmy the dog is hidden under the table, away from the evil tutor, Mr Roland, the pooch gives his presence away by sighing and scratching. Each time the children hide the noise by sighing and scratching themselves. Now my experience of dogs is they give their presence away by means of foul smells, the ones where concern is expressed for the ability of the wallpaper to remain bonded to the walls and people have to leave the room. But old Enid missed that one.

I wake again, rain is ramming against the roof, I don't feel that fit and I elect for a rest day.

Wednesday April 4th brings a cold start. On the short walk, from cottage to car, I notice that many of the passing cars have been de-iced. I feel as if I'm in for a cold day and, knowing I'm far from fit, I have broken one of the suggested routes, from the Nuttall's guidebook, into three. My starting point is the top of the Honister Pass a few miles beyond Buttermere.

As I wind the car down the B roads, I notice the temperature is down to two degrees. I imagine it being sub-zero at the top of the pass and look forward to adding this act of hardship to my write-up. A kilometre short of the top of the pass the weather gods have a surprise in store. On a steep sheltered section, fortunately devoid of an open gully to slide into, my car loses traction, the wheels spin and I have this strange sensation of going backwards. I pull up the handbrake, but it's of no use as my car is hooked on returning from whence it came.

I manage to hold it on the footbrake but this is not a satisfactory state of affairs for any action requires one to remove one's foot. Going forward is not an option and the elements, coupled with gravity, are quite keen on a reverse descent.

I select reverse, for some semblance of control, and ease myself back down to a point where the handbrake will hold. I take another go at it and keep to the right of the road. No joy. I get the owners' manual out and read up on the mysterious ESP button on the dashboard. I can't make sense of it but give it a try and keep to the left; again no joy. There's nowhere to turn and I gingerly reverse for about a quarter of a mile, my neck aching and the car weaving as I fail to find a rhythm.

Another black Golf appears behind me, takes one look at my situation and starts to reverse. Fortunately I see him finding a turning place which I then use.

I catch up with the Golf at a small parking place and its occupants ask me how bad it is. Pointing out the similarities between our vehicles, I describe the ice-encrusted road.

I check my map for alternative walks and choose the four tops to the south-west of Butteremere. I park at Gatesgarth, pay the £3 fee and set off a little after 09:30.

It's cold, I'm slow and, at this level, there's a fair wind. I meet a group descending and ask what the wind is like on top.

"Manageable," she says, "but you'll need to cling on to somebody."

"Unfortunately I'm walking alone," I add.

"There's people behind you," she says.

"Do you think I should introduce myself first," I ask.

The conversation is getting a little weird so I press on.

The path takes me east of High Crag before cutting up to the ridge. I meet the fellow Golf driver, and his companion, heading back down. "Too windy," they say

This puts me in a dilemma. After all they'd taken my advice on the Honister Impassable and now I'm set to ignore theirs: you can tell a man that something is hot but it's not until he's scolded his own fingers will he let the subject rest. Also I'm aware of my middle age. Some men fear losing their hair, some their virility for me I fear losing my tenacity. I'm not one to give up through discomfort so I continue on and meet the main ridge. The wind blasts me and I have to brace myself to drop away from its icy fingers.

On a nice day the pull up to the summit would be rather lovely. Indeed today is blue sky but cold and very windy. A young Swedish woman passes me and we exchange commiserations about the weather as I keep my mind on my tenacity. I ignore the earlier woman's advice of finding somebody to cling on to in the wind. It could get awkward.

The top of High Crag is a flat plateau and my face is pummelled by the wind. I must look like one of those TV presenters that have a go in a wind tunnel – my mouth is forced open and I feel my left cheek vibrating. The wind sucks mucus from my nose and I consider sending the idea to Mr Dyson as a revolutionary new handkerchief. I cling my map to my chest and make for the highpoint of the day, High Stile at 806m. There's a series of cairns and I tag them all.

I drop a little, things ease and I get chatting to a couple with their dog. I ask if he's used to the mountains.

"That's not our dog," says the lady half of the couple, "he's been following us from Buttermere."

Could it be a seventy-five-year-old Timmy the dog having a last sniff around?

I drop and ascend Red Pike where the wind is waiting again and I have trouble making it to the summit as the wind is hell bent on batting me away at each attempt. After making it I retreat and duck down below some rocks for shelter.

I take a compass bearing for the route down. Unfortunately into the wind again, this time so fierce that the neck piece of my jacket is rammed with such strength into my mouth that my head tips back. I try to straighten my neck but there's no go, the mouth piece of my jacket feels like a nightclub bouncer with his hand on my face, pushing me backwards. My neck felt the strain in the long reverse down the Honister Pass, now it's straining to even keep my head tilted back.

I rapidly descend on a rough red eroded path. I keep moving until the wind is manageable and I can get my neck straight. The final summit, Dodd, is a gentle little bump at the end of the ridge spur. I take in the views, the northern flanks of High Stile are well defended and all the peaks look to have been dusted in chalk.

From Dodd there's a good path which takes me to Buttermere where a shoreline path has me passing families out for a gentle stroll. I return to the car at 15:30.

Thursday April 5th brings clear skies and a car to be de-iced. Not wishing to chance the Honister Pass again I elect for the hour-long trip round to Wasdale Head to tackle Kirk Fell, Kirk Fell East Top and Looking Stead. My route is 'off guidebook' as I've previously done Great

Gable and Looking Stead and wish to leave Pillar (plus its infamous rock) to a day in itself.

I start walking a little after 10:05, get some guidance from a farmer to the start of the route and set forth for the steep south-westerly face. I'm very slow but the weather is warm and I walk minus a hat to allow the tan to form on my balding head. This is a recent number two cut to tidy up my balding locks. It's been a decision long in coming, much time having been spent in front of a mirror, tossing my hair around in the hope I can stop the appearance of baldness without looking like I've got a comb-over. On the upside, since the session with the hairdresser's razor I've been getting a few more looks from women. Probably pity.

Kirk Fell

An hour and half into the walk there's a brief levelling of the terrain where I take one of my many rests. The lake, below Wasdale Head, glistens a rich blue, the sky is faultless and the sea shimmers in the distance.

Three hours in I meet a man descending. We stop for a chat;

he'd passed me on the way up, having set out at 11:40. It hits home how slow I am, he'd been up and back in over an hour and a half less than it's taken me so far. To make matters worse he tells me this is the day of his retirement (he's a National Parks employee). At least he did not have a beard; otherwise, in true Enid Blyton fashion, I'd have marked him down as being a trifle sinister.

The going becomes a mixture of scree and boulder fields. I tread carefully as many a rock tips when I put my weight on it. My calf muscles ache and I can walk for no more than a few seconds between rests.

I make the summit at 13:40 at a poor ascent rate of 225m per hour. There are some comforting wind shelters where I eat and take compass bearings to the east top and Looking Stead. Great Gable stands as a proud edifice amongst its neighbours and the blue sky. Ravens sore, catching the thermals they glide majestically with no visible effort.

Great Gable

The east top is an easy stroll before the steep north-westerly descent. I pick my way amongst scree and grass, cross a stream of ice-coated boulders before I start to ascend to Looking Stead. I do a little better, rest not so often and arrive at 15:40. From here I make it back to the car at a little after 17:00.

Arriving back at the cottage my hunger pangs put me off cooking a baked potato. I'd spotted a Chinese takeaway in town so I wander down to have a look at their menu. Mushroom foo yung and chips looks good. It arrives quickly and not bad at £5.80.

Back at the cottage my hopes of a yummy meal are dashed, the mushroom foo yung has no mushrooms and instead various bits of meat. I recognise prawns but am unsure of what the grey and white meat might be. I feel too tired to go back so pick the meat out, but I can't escape the taste of the tainted meal. Retiring to bed, with aching calf muscles, my tummy feels as if it would like to file a massive complaint.

I wake at 06:00, I feel okay but the house stinks of the meat. After drinking some water, I fall back to sleep and wake two hours later with calf muscles that have pulled tight. I hobble to the bathroom then downstairs to breakfast and pack for the day.

The weather is warmer and I give the Honister Pass another try. This time it's really easy and I discover just how close to the summit I was when I had my adventures of the other day.

The car park at the top has a little surprise for me: £5.90 to park for the day. That's more than a dodgy Chinese takeaway. I pay, I grumble, I pack and I walk.

I pass the Honister Mine visitor centre before ascending the mine tracks, passing earth movers and diggers, all silent on this a Good Friday.

Cloud is clagged in and there's drizzle in the air but the track is an excellent gradient and when I leave it the terrain remains manageable for my lungs. Without having to rest I make Honister Crag then Fleetwith Pike in just an hour and a quarter.

My good timing has me surveying the map, checking my location. Previously I'd thought that to do Grey Knotts and Brandreth would require a drop back to the car. Now the obvious strikes me, I can maintain much of the height by cutting across open ground. I worry about my ageing mind not having thought of that sooner.

I cut down, cross rough ground before picking up a path that heads directly south. In mist and drizzle I stop and check my compass bearing, it disagrees with what I think is Brandreth and, assuming there's no iron in the rock I adopt the old adage that the compass never lies. So into the mist I head and reach the flat-topped Brandreth at 12:30 then take a bearing to Grey Knotts where I climb every tor and tag every cairn to ensure I have bagged it.

The rain picks up and I take the, hard-on-my-calf-muscles descent and am glad when the visitor centre comes into view through the mist. I fancy lunch but there's nothing I can eat (not even a dodgy Chinese) so I get back to the car and tuck into my packed lunch.

I'd planned Saturday April 7th as a rest day to allow my taut calf muscles to recover. But with a gloomy weather forecast for Sunday onwards, I decide to walk today. I head towards Buttermere with a plan to do half of the Grasmoor round, splitting the ambitions of the guidebook into two.

At Buttermere I'm faced with parking charges again. I previously paid £3 at Gatesgarth, £5.90 at Honister and today's request is for a whopping £6.20. I'd want mushrooms for that I can tell you. I turn back and park, for free, a shade north of Rannerdale.

It's 09:00 and I set off and survey the steep scree slopes of Grasmoor. It's tough going though I sense I'm quicker than yesterday. I pass across greenery before hauling myself into a cauldron of red heather, rock and scree. From here on my pace is awful. The scree gives way with each step and the heather drags at my heels until I'm pausing every few steps.

At 10:30, having covered 400m of ascent, I take a long rest. I look back, my car is visible as a dot and the scree and boulder field falls away towards it. A couple with a dog, that passed me earlier, are off to my left. Their voices carry and it sounds as if their path is no easier than mine.

Looking down the scree and boulder field on the Grasmoor ascent

At around 11:50, and at 800m altitude, with the couple and their dog well out of sight, the terrain levels out into swirling cloud. The distant views back to Crummock Water and Buttermere highlight how far I've come as I catch my breath, allow my heart to stop racing and my calf muscles to relax.

I make the summit shelter of Grasmoor at 12:10, the cloud is moving around giving a moving window on to the scenery below. Many people are around, some pass, some settle to eat, some say hello, some say goodbye, some say nothing.

I take a compass bearing to Wandope, it's not where I expect it to be. Although I trust the compass I double check it and set off. I soon face Crag Hill, previously bagged and bear right to the easy slopes of Wandope. The morning exertion now feels worthwhile as the terrain on this high-level plateau is straightforward. I have a cut-off point for a level of gradient where my asthma means I can take no more than a few paces between rests. On easier gradients I can walk and breathe without pause.

There's a sheer drop off from Wandope, certainly not a place to wander aimlessly in thick mist. I take another bearing to Whiteless Pike. The guidebook says the meaning of its name is unknown. Unless, of course, the ancients, found it so bland that they decided to name it after an attribute that it did not have. Or perhaps, in this mountainous region, all possible names had been used up and a new scheme was started to use non-relevant names and tack a 'less' on the end. Its subsidiary spur is called Whiteless Breast which gives me a chuckle or two.

I look back to a steep scree face to the south of Grasmoor. Grass dons its summit like a green cloth laid across a head. Its sheer slopes are clad in grey shingle.

The cloud now lifts and, heading for Whiteless Pike, I'm treated to lovely views of Crummock Water and Buttermere. The views hold as I pass over Whiteless Pike, navigate down towards its 'breast' and swing north-west back to my car.

Having taken Easter Sunday off, to give my calf muscles a chance to relax, my next venture is Easter Monday. Amidst rain and a bad forecast I take the short trip to Hopebeck and seek out the minor road to pick up the track that runs to the east of Swinside to Hopegill Head. Passing through two sets of gates, requiring stopping, opening, pulling forwards then shutting, I then fail to find the track. I turn around, with squeaking windscreen wipers and noisy power steering, and pass back through both sets of gates before noticing, on the map, a path between the two gates. So back through the first set of gates I go, I find a place to pull off the road and don my full waterproofs.

The rain pummelling the roof and the warm cab do nothing to urge me out of the car. But around 10:00 I summon the enthusiasm and set out across a splashy field and pick my way round to the path that leads up the stream of Hope Gill. Initially I make good progress but soon the gradient tussles with my asthma and I settle back into the traditional rest per minute as I make slow progress.

Around noon, with gloves ringing and trail shoes feeling the weight of water, I hit an east west path. I check my GPS and work out I'm just north of Hopegill Head. I take a bearing for Ladyside Pike but am unsure that I'm on the right path until, that is, I notice I've marked it 300m too far to the east on my map. With bearing corrected I walk out to it, backtrack and make my way up the ridges of Hopegill Head. Given the cloud-clagged conditions I take a bearing to Sand Hill and head off. I see another walker, also in a red jacket. We stop for a quick chat and discuss nothing but the weather.

The rain is still tapping its fingers on my hood as I reach Sand Hill and retreat to Hopegill Head before the ridge walk, with steep drops to my left, towards Whiteside East Top and Whiteside. At nearly 2Km it feels a long walk across the blustery ridge before I can cut north and traverse around to pick up a path below the southern flank of Dodd. From here I spot my car and make a welcome walk back, arriving at 14:30 where I unburden myself of dripping pack and jacket before a final pass through the gates.

Waking on Tuesday the 10th, I decide it's not a day for the hills. I feel tired, the weather forecast is poor and rain is drumming on the roof of the cottage. I do a few chores during the day, such as shaving off the sinister-looking beard and extracting further gorse thorns from my right hand.

On the 11th I wake at 06:00, take a couple of puffs of my Salamol inhaler and, with a weather forecast of sunshine and showers, lever myself out of bed, breakfast then pack.

I park at Scales, on the A66 east of Keswick, and set off. Within a few seconds I realise I've left my trekking poles in the car and, with keys tucked away in my backpack, decide to do without them for a day. Two minutes later, after a short uphill section, I'm heading back to the car for them.

I get going again at 08:10 and, as per usual, there are more paths than the guidebook, or the map, detail so I navigate carefully. It takes me fifty minutes for what the guidebook claims is a 'good mile'. I peer at the map, trying to measure the distance but, like my hair, my eyesight is starting to go. However, it's considerably longer than a mile.

At Gategill, I pass the kennels where the Blencathra hunting dogs are housed. I strike north up Hall's Fell, leaving the barking dogs behind, and make good pace. After about twenty-five minutes I rest and look back. The A66 rumbles on below, the hills opposite have their heads in the clouds and there's an odd spot of rain in the air.

The upper reaches are a cat's spine of exposed rock which, in drizzle and settled snow, make for some entertaining moments. It becomes a scramble (employing both hands) and one section is across an exposed gully where I have to kick into the snow and take great care while holding my nerve.

The summit has the remains of a trig point. In blustery wind I reckon I've ascended at around 330m per hour – a great improvement on the 225m per hour that I recorded earlier on this trip.

There's a few people to say hello to (or 'How Do' if I adopt the local phrase) as I head, across patchy snow, from Blencathra to Gategill Fell Top.

Gategill Fell Top

It's then a rough stroll out to Atkinson Pike then beyond towards Bowscale Fell. By now I'm feeling hungry, tired and cold but push on to Bowscale Fell where, at 12:30 I settle down, amongst a hail storm blowing in, to munch through a cold jacket potato and a piece of cheese.

The hail gets worse as I work my way back then strike south-east, alongside sheer cliffs, to Bannerdale Crags. I tag the summit then backtrack, with the hail now directly in my face, to pick up the long path back to Scales. I arrive at 14:25, very pleased with my pace.

Having gone to bed with a bad back I wake with a sore throat. Fortunately, for such an event, I have the ingredients for my favourite concoction with me – cyder vinegar and honey. I swear by it – usually when I take the first sip.

I make the drive round to Mosedale then the delightful minor road that runs alongside the River Caldew which glints in the morning sun as its waters tumble over the rocks of the riverbed. Parking where the road peters out at the Cumbria Way, I set off for the round of seven hills to the north of yesterday's walk.

It's tough going, I feel tired and, although I took my inhaler early, I'm slow. I think the long walk in yesterday, before the ascent, is perhaps what opened up my airways. It's something I've noticed before and, perhaps, explains why for other walks my afternoon pace always feels better than my morning's.

After an hour I rest, boiling in my thermal base layer, fleece and jacket. I survey back to the fells of yesterday, their tops dancing with the cloud that steams from their summits. Carrock Fell, the first peak of today, looks a daunting distance but I arrive before 10:00 where I remove my middle layer, the fleece. I check my watch altimeter – 652m, the map says 661m. I check the GPS altimeter and it reckons on the number of the beast: 666m.

There's a fort marked on the map but to my eye I see no evidence. I head west, crossing Milton Hill then, as I meet a ridge, head north-east for High Pike. There's a cairn, a trig point (with a range finder mounted on its surface) and a slate seat in memorial of sixteen-year-old Mick Lewis who lost his life on 8th May 1944.

I sit for ten minutes and take advantage of the tops being out of the cloud and set my compass for each in turn so I can spy them on their horizons. One, Knott, I am unsure of and murmur to myself "That's probably not" before realising my joke.

I head south-west to the third peak, Hare Stones, but cut off the path a bit early and, given its plateau-like top, have to hunt around for the summit. I head west, drop some height, and look back to spy the highest point. As it's only a few stones, I check the time, 11:20, altimeters and GPS to confirm I have truly found it.

I head for Great Lingy Hill. Deviating from the recommended route, I avoid crossing a rather boggy stream and instead keep to a path for as long as I can before striking north-east to find the summit.

I now head for Knott but first rest at the 609m top, which at 1998ft just misses out on the 2000ft summit classification.

Towards Knott I pass a confluence of dramatic gullies which run the water north off the hills before the rather peaty and boggy early slopes of Knott.

I make the summit in beautiful sunshine. The views are superb, birds chirp and the mountains are elegant in the afternoon light and the shadows of the clouds. I look out towards the sea, wind farms dot the view and a large mast sits tall inland.

In under an hour, and feeling drained, I take in the two summit bumps, both marked by rocks, of Little Calva. I check my altimeter, its spot on and has been all day. This implies the weather is settled – over the previous few days it could vary by up to 20m per summit. As soon as I realise this the wind picks up and there's spots of rain in the air.

The second summit bump involves straddling over a fence which then takes me around to the start of the sharp pull up Great Calva. It's tough going; I've hit a wall with my energy reserves. I make the summit, feeling shaky with tiredness.

I head to the end of the fence then take the steep south-east path back to meet the Cumbria Way. As I do so, a RAF propeller trainer plane roars up the valley with its familiar fluttering piston engine.

The Cumbria Way is a welcome reunion and I take its easy footings back to the car.

Friday April 13th dawns bright on my last day of this holiday. I plan to do Wether Hill and Loadpot Hill, two that I missed out on last year.

The sun smacks my eyes as I take the A66, passing the sign for Penruddock (reminding me of the film, *The Thirty-Nine Steps* where Robert Donat tells Madeleine Carroll of his murderous Great Uncle Penruddock) before taking a network of minor roads, and a few hairpins, before parking at The Old Church of St Martin.

It's a fine church, hall shaped with one of those bells that reminds me of a 19th century American school house. There's a cool breeze as the crows call and other birds swoop and rise.

I set off and make slow progress towards some woods. I miss the track that bypasses them and have to make a sharp climb, by a wall, to regain the path. The valley floor below is a mix of lush fields, stone walls and stone buildings.

After an hour I remove my middle layer and, like on the A66, the sun smacks my eyes. As I ascend higher, and admire the westerly views, I notice the distant ridges are capped with such a thin line of continuous snow that it could be mistaken for a seam of quartz. Ullswater glistens and shimmers below.

It's then a final pull onto the plateau which the Roman road of High Street passes along. From here the summit of Wether Hill is easily found and I'm on my way to Loadpot Hill, arriving three hours into the walk. I rest my back against its trig point and eat my lunch.

I now navigate carefully to find the zig-zag path, beyond Brock Crag, that will lead me to Ullswater. It takes a few goes, and a bit of dead reckoning, before I find the path and carefully make my way. I take the chance to sit and admire Ullswater and think through my holiday. Given my health and, at times, poor weather I'm pleased with my efforts – I've done seven of the ten walks I had left in the Lakes to complete in nine days of walking.

From the valley floor I find the path that curves round to Martindale then beyond to The Old Church of St Martin where I arrive (getting to the church on time) at 13:10.

June 2012 – English Nuttalls – Kinder Scout & North Yorkshire

It's June 1st and I'm at Kate Wilson's wonderful wedding reception in a country house a few miles from Sheffield. Kate entered my diaries in 2001 when she accompanied me in a group to the top of my final Munro. In the last few years she's met Paul and had two children. At the wedding, I'm catching up with her family and friends. This includes a fellow Steve who, sat at my table, is making full use of the ample servings of wine. It gets to the point where all of us, on what we note is the 'singles table', get to chatting about what tomorrow will bring. I mention I'll be walking Kinder Scout then heading up to a holiday cottage just south of Kirby Stephen. The conversation then moves on to how each of us knows either Kate or Paul.

"Hill walking, I met her on a walk in Scotland," I say.

"By chance?" asks a table mate.

"No, via Ali and Adrian who I already knew."

"Are you a keen hillwalker then?"

"I do quite a bit," I reply.

"Any Munros?"

"Well," I begin, "it was actually my final Munro that Kate joined me on."

My ratings as a table mate shoot up.

Later Steve (who is now nothing short of out of his head), engages me in conversation. He stands very close, as the inebriated are inclined to do, to the point I feel that I'm propping him up.

"I can't believe you've done all the Munros. That's amazing."

We'd had the same conversation some twenty minutes earlier but I'm happy to go through it again.

"It's something I just set out to do."

"How did you get into it?"

I explain it was a chance conversation with a work colleague some twenty-four years earlier.

"You could like, do Everest."

"Well, I think that'd be beyond me. Quite a few die on their summit bids."

"But you'd know when to turn back."

"There's summit fever, you enter the death zone and it plays tricks with your judgement."

"I'd press on, I know," he replies, "whereas you'd know when to pull out."

"That's very kind," I add, "but I think I'd get summit fever too."

"Nah, you'd know when to stop, whereas I'd go on and die."

"I think," I add, "my caution is not to go there in the first place, that's my judgement because I don't trust myself when I'm there."

"And you're going up Kinder tomorrow."

"Well, I was planning to," I reply, "but it's getting late. I need to be at the cottage between four and six and I need a lie in."

"That's not the spirit of the Munros," he says.

"I know, but I'm a lot older now, I know when to rest."

Twenty minutes later we have the same conversation again.

As it happens, I wake at 09:15 and leisurely boil an egg in the Travelodge room kettle before gathering my things. At gone eleven I'm pulled up at Barber Booth, studying the maps and looking at my watch. I'm minded to blow Kinder Scout out for today; it'll make me against the clock later. Then I remember Steve's words from the night before, I remember my former self, my spirit, my drive, so I set off.

It's tarmac to Upper Booth before following the Crowden Brook. Passing a large group, I say hello and head further. I'm forcing a pace, I don't want to be late and put out the owner of the cottage, who'd written to me with precise instructions to arrive between 16:00 and 18:00.

I criss-cross the stream, motoring fast until the ground rises sharply, my legs turn to jelly and I slump down on a large rock. The large group pass me, slowly and we begin to chat. They are good humoured and are on a "Military Fitness" regime; not actually in the forces.

I walk amongst them as the ground rises. Two ladies start to chat to me (it must be the new haircut). They note my map, compass and GPS and declare me an experienced walker. Again unsolicited praise comes and they ask me about my scariest moments on the hills. There's been many which I tell them of. When we congregate at the head of the brook, just past the steepest section, my antics are relayed to the rest of the group.

From here we part company and I set off, through a corridor of surreal weather-sculpted rocks, to Pym Chair. On route I rest and encounter a couple in radio contact with a larger party. One has sprained his ankle and the couple are attempting to ascertain how bad it is. I listen and get the gist they don't have much first aid. I rustle through my pack, produce a bandage and Ibuprofen and offer it. They radio back that they are on their way with supplies.

I then head off, completely overshoot Pym Chair (where in olden days Pym, a minister, would preach – or was it Chair the minister would drink Pimms – I can't remember which) and find myself hacking through peat hags to the summit cairn. With GPS, map and compass, I head on bearings. Climb down peat gullies, back up, back down until I'm fed up.

A mum, dad and daughter are doing the same, towards me. The girl is young, in tears with the depressing effort of these peat gullies. I understand her upset, you feel cheated, sapped and distraught. Her parents applaud her but it's to no avail, no amount of praise cheers her up.

I find the summit cairn, a depressing pile of rocks on a depressing flat landscape riddled with peat and bogs. I wonder if it's the top, a walker heads towards me and confirms, to his mind, that it is.

"Look it's in a direct line with Pym Chair," he says.

He's a short chap, with balding ginger hair and short trousers. I imagine him bouncing up between the peat hags in true Monty Python fashion. Feeling guilty for my thoughts, I don't have the heart to mention that any two points are in a straight line. He leaves the scene and it allows me to sweep the area for other cairns before I conclude I must have reached the summit – at least my GPS is onside.

I head to Pym Chair, motor down as fast I can and am at my car, in heavy drizzle, at 14:50. I set off, trying to maintain pace without speeding. My car GPS falls off the window, the bracket has broken. I stop and tape it to the screen and it tells me I'll be lucky to do it by 18:00. I stop for diesel and cheese (one thing I could not bring without a fridge). Actually lots of cheese and the assistant comments on my large purchase. "And a cheese sandwich too!" he adds. I wonder if I'm being mocked.

I arrive at 17:40, having played catch-up as best I can. There's a couple of signs at the bottom of the drive informing the best way of tackling the two-pronged entrance. Then there's a sign saying what gear I should be in to negotiate the drive (we're talking gearbox here, not Gore-Tex jackets or anything like that).

I press the door bell (there's a note not to use the knocker) and I think that friendliness is the best approach.

"Tony?" I ask as the door opens.

"Mr Smith," he replies.

I hope I've not transgressed with the over familiarity but he looks friendly enough. He takes me up to the apartment and shows me around (though there are quite a few notes about the place to assist me). When he leaves I use the loo and read the note informing me of all the things that should not be flushed down the loo. Being a single male I conclude I must be the ideal tenant.

The cottage is actually an upstairs flat. Well laid out, I think I'll be happy for the week.

Sunday the 3rd and I struggle to get out of bed. The 'graduates dream' had struck again during the night – that's the one where it's the day of your finals and you've done no revision. Everybody I've mentioned it to has experienced the same thing.

I take the long trip round to the high point of the unclassified road between Thwaite and Hawes. The frost warning pings on my car and, as I emerge into the elements, the wind is there to clip my ear. It's 11:15 and I set my compass for the crossing of the boggy moor to reach Great Shunner Fell.

The gradient is forgiving, I keep apace but am tired, I feel tired to the core but I plod, and plod, over humps, across marshy ground, a deep gulley, cross fences, stiles and walk alongside stone walls. But nothing shifts the tiredness, the will to be back in bed, dreams or no dreams.

I make the summit in over an hour. It's a cross of two short stone walls, one with a terminating trig point, to form a quadrangular shelter, each with two benches. I choose the one that's most out of the wind and eat my lunch – cheese, rice cakes and peanuts. The views sit below the low cloud, good but dull. I look back to where I've come, then up to the next peak, Lovely Seat, that requires a descent to cross the road where I'm parked.

On the way down I recall place markers from the way up. I slump on a rock, drink water and yawn and yawn. I cross the bogs to reach the road and set my compass for Lovely Seat. The gradient is good and I find a pace, resting occasionally. The summit is easily found and as I look back, Great Shunner Fell now has her head in the cloud.

I can see my car and aim roughly for it, arriving just before 14:25. Only three hours. I recall the younger Steve, the Steve of old and those long days of the Munros, those 'bloody' Munros taking eight to twelve hours a walk. Is it age, unfitness or mental determination that I now lack. I just couldn't imagine doing one now, let alone all 284 of them.

The weather forecast promises Monday the 4th as the best day of the week. I wake, feel fitter than when I retired to bed, but not yet up to the biggest round of the week – the Howgills. Instead I elect for the Water Crag and Rogan's seat. The guidebook suggests an extensive route that would pad out a day. I'm more into the easiest route possible and at first decide to park halfway up the minor road between Keld and Tan-Hill then cut east to Rogan's Seat. Further observation of the map shows a slightly longer route, starting from the Tan-Hill Inn, with paths most of the way to the summit.

I find the Tan-Hill Inn but do not find the path. Things start well with a nice-looking track that heads from the inn but whatever I do with the compass it's not the right one. So across heather and peat I set, grumbling and moaning and wondering just how the heck the OS ever spotted a path.

The heather drags at my feet like a terrier, peat bogs have to be circumnavigated and the only rest bites are the moments of mown heather, forming rings around areas that have been burnt off.

I send up grouse and their young, calling out danger as they bat their wings close to the ground. They then lift and glide. One chick brushes my ankle as it gets airborne, literally a touching moment. Yesterday I saw a sign explaining how the moorland habitat is being revived for the grouse, a mile or so on I saw the hides from which gunmen cull them.

I slink into the heather for a rest, the cloud is chopped and the breeze is cool and the views are good if a little dull as no sunlight is there to pick out the distant features.

Passing a deep mineshaft, covered by a metal box grill, I stop and peer into its unknown depths – the moss-covered stones of its lining fall into the abyss where water drips, sending eerie echoes skywards.

After around two hours I make the summit of Water Crag – a brick wall, followed by a trig point and then a stone shelter where I rest. Rogan's Seat is an easy navigation along the line of a fence where I pick up a track for a brief descent before a two-mile slog over heather, peat and a stream gulley.

Again the heather catches my feet, drags my pace. I'm aiming for the track that I could not use from Tan-Hill. As nice as I imagine it'll be, the chance of hitting its head, after crossing miles of moorland, is small. Instead, I aim to its south-west with the plan to turn north and strike it side on. This dumps me in a long peat crevasse which is like wading through chocolate cake.

Back at Tan-Hill the place is a buzz with motorbikes, barking dogs and a noisy generator. It's 14:45 and I fancy a drink. The bar is five deep so I retreat. I look at the outside, the sign advertising it as Britain's highest pub. I admire the wooden sash windows and amuse myself in the thought that Ted Moult's Windows (You only fit double glazing once, fit the best fit Everest) did not last.

Tuesday 5th of June brings another sleep in. Showing my patriotism I'd stayed up and watched the concert from Buckingham Palace and concluded that Paul McCartney wore a very nice jacket.

For the third day running I head north from the cottage and take the B6270 that rises, as a single-track road, over open moorland. I pass gypsy caravans, which have been quite a presence over the last few days. Where Cumbria peters out and North Yorkshire begins I park, survey the ground, then my map and set the compass for Nine Standards Rigg. It's 10:40 and there's a path signed. After yesterday's experiences, I take no notice of it and head directly across country into a squidgy mire that feels like I'm walking on a water bed the size of a football pitch. I learn to detect the texture of the grass that will take my weight and spring like a demented hare between the tussocks.

I begin to ascend, circumnavigating large depressions in the ground, sheep and the quagmire of peat trenches. It's a gentle incline and my pace is reasonable. I check the GPS for a fix and set my compass directly to the summit. I'm surprised when I break onto the ridge, some half a mile south-east of the summit. Setting a new north-west bearing, I conclude I must have misread the GPS when I set the compass before.

I pass a fingerboard, indicating, for those on The Coast-to-Coast (from St Bees in Cumbria to Robin Hood's Bay in North Yorkshire), which route, depending on the time of year, to take. A lot of people are about with heavily-laden packs. I've clearly butted in on something and, as I turn towards the trig point of Nine Standards Rigg, I'm faced with saying hello to a succession of people.

I make the summit at 12:15 and am stopped by an Aussie.

"Is this the way to Keld?" he asks (I think he might have added 'mate' but I'm not sure).

I check my map and confirm that it is.

"Have you got a compass you can set?" I ask.

"No, nor a map. My mate's got them. Say if you see him tell him to phone me. He's wearing a white top."

I assure him I will and press on to take a look at the stone edifices that form the Nine Standards. Some are neatly stacked, like a mathematician did them, others are like a pile of stones in a back yard. I walk amongst them before setting my compass. It points directly to a path which leads me back to the road, picked out from a distance by the tall black, white and red poles that mark it when snowed in. I reach the car in just over an hour, making a note to always at least look for the path before I set off.

I get to bed early and wake early with the idea of doing the Howgills. The weather does not look too good, the forecast does not look too good so instead I choose to do the four peaks to the north-west of Garsdale Head.

Parking near Uldale, I watch as the chasing columns of rain sweep across. I sit tight for a while, wondering whether to abandon the day or wait for it to clear. I think back to what I'd have done in the days of Munro bagging: this weather is 'nothing' so prepare and set off, at 09:00, on the long gentle pull to Wild Boar Fell. The visibility is very poor. I use my GPS and altimeter to fix my location then set a new compass bearing. It reminds me of the Munros where I used no GPS (apart from a brief spell of using a fairly inaccurate one) and no altimeter. Then it was down to close navigation and a fair bit of frustration, especially in mist.

I'm aiming for Sand Tarn but at the 600m contour, set my compass for due east and break onto the wide summit plateau. Here I head north and am relieved to see the OS trig point come into view at the 708m mark. I'm doing well but I decide that the four hills are too much for the day and, if I now take in Swarth Fell, the recommended route is neatly split into two days.

I descend south-west and then south-east until I pick up the boundary wall which I follow. The rain still patters against me, my thin cotton gloves are sodden and my feet squelch as if they've become one with the peat below them.

I navigate by my altimeter, aiming for the 681m mark. At Wild Boar Fell it was over reading by 9m so I ascend hoping for 690m to arrive soon. I'm not sure what the summit looks like, I find a large stone with an 18th century inscription and flip my pack off, rummage for the guidebook and read that I'm looking for a large cairn. The ground rises in front of me and, as I make the ascent, the ghostly image of the cairn comes into view.

It's 11:40 when I tap its top with a trekking pole then head the short distance to the wall. I follow it down, turning left with it until it follows the fall of a stream which I have to cross a few times. Aware it would be easy to slip on the rocks of the streambed, I set off up the gulley in search of an easier route. As I'm about to tread on a large flat stone it crosses my mind that I'm lucky it's not icy. Whether this is a premonition or whether such thoughts are always there, but only remembered when there is occasion to, I don't know. But my foot slips off and I fall downhill landing on my left hand and forearm. The weight of my pack and lower body pivots me on my arm as they fly over my head, taking me off down the slope on my right hip. I slide on my smooth waterproof clothing for around twenty feet until I'm forced onto my back. My pack now becomes a brake.

I stand up, my right hip; lower back, left forearm and left hand all ache. I pick my way back to the stream and follow its safer confines.

As other streams join and the gulley deepens, I ascend the opposite bank, away from the stream and its fearsome slopes. I then edge my way round a forest's perimeter to pick up the track, which becomes the road where my car is parked. It's 13:00, I'm dripping wet and sore.

Thursday the 7th and the weather is looking as doubtful as yesterday. The long round of the Howgill Fells have been beckoning all week. However, a wet day is not the day for them and, with a check of the guidebook against the map, I figure on splitting them into one long day and one modest day. Yorkshire, not being as steep and as high as the Lakes, has the guidebook writer filling a day by connecting walks, with a sharp drop and re-ascent between them, that might be better tackled separately. The walk I cut short yesterday is such an example, so today I choose to do Knoutberry Haw and Baugh Fell to complete it.

I pass the various gypsy encampments on route, with their attendant litter strewn over the open countryside. I pass by the stone barns that are familiar to this district. Something tells me that Wiltshire, my home, has the edge. Wiltshire is only hilly, no mountains, but the chalk downs roll and sweep in their own way.

I park up Uldale and am walking at 09:50. First it's on a steep private road that switches between concrete and tarmac as frequently as it has been repaired. I fork right through the woods and cross the River Rawthey. The sound of it burbling over rocks is accompanied by a deep rhythmic thump of the greater body of water passing through. It reminds me of a distant engine.

The weather is not good as I briefly ascend the riverbank before cutting sharply south. It hits me I'm very slow and it's going to be tiresome day. The rain drills against me and the wind shakes the left sleeve of my jacket in an unknown harmonic.

The visibility is down to fifty feet and, with the ground levelling, I pass a small tarn. There are various cairns and it feels a remote spot as I pass the larger West Baugh Fell Tarn.

I press on, it's very wet underfoot but the rain stops and the weather clears until I can see Knoutberry Haw in the distance. I walk from cairn to cairn until I reach the trig point and the summit at 12:50.

A wall behind it joins with a wall running up from the south-west. I climb over and tuck down on the sheltered corner, eat my lunch and get a text from Kate thanking me for the wedding present.

I now follow the wall, navigating past bog, to Baugh Fell (also known as Tarn Rigg Hill). Here I'd planned to cut down the streambed that feeds the River Rawthey, near to where I started. Recalling the streambed of yesterday, and my slip, I opt to go back the way I came. It feels remote, a long way back but I've had enough of streambeds.

The way back is a gentle decline until I pass West Baugh Fell Tarn. Here I check my compass and head north. Veering into a plateau of bog, I stop to check my GPS. I've wandered too far to the west so set another bearing and hit the river bed, then the track back to my car where I arrive at 15:40 very wet.

By 20:00 I'm asleep and don't wake until just gone 06:00. I pack, breakfast and watch the weather forecast. It's poor and I feel tired, six days on the trot has me continually yawning and I feel achy. The Howgills will have to wait.

Saturday brings my departure; I pack and carry my kit and a bag of rubbish down the flight of steps. At the bins there's the final note of the week – explaining not to overfill the bins. The thing that worries me about all these notes, more than anything else, is that, if I ran the place, I'd do the same.

September 2012 – Scottish 2000ft Mountains

On 6th September 2012 the Scottish Mountaineering club demoted the Munro of Beinn a' Chlaidheimh to Corbett status. I climbed it when it was a Munro so I've added one to my Corbett count and deducted one from my Munro count.

Classification	My Total	Total
Welsh Nuttalls	190	190
English Nuttalls	181	253
Corbetts (Scotland)	21	221
Grahams (Scotland)	6	220
Unique Donalds (Scotland)	0	58
Munros (Scotland)	282	282
Ireland	0	212
Totals (06/09/2012):	680	1436

November 2012 – English Nuttalls. Over The Hill Club

Friday 16th of November sees me setting off for The Over The Hill Club AGM weekend with my new hill-walking accessory – Hugo the camper van. The purchase came after years of inaction, deliberation and procrastination. I've christened him Hugo because of his number plate. He sports heating, a loo, two beds, a table, hob, grill, sink and fridge.

The bean-counting side of my brain has concluded that, over a twenty-year period, I can recoup the entire purchase price on the savings I'll make on my annual spend on holiday cottages. Furthermore I've calculated that I can save on motorway service station meals by cooking in the car park. This latter scheme lasts until I'm hungry, pull off the M6, follow the ever-confusing blue circle signs (which allegedly point you to the car park), pull up and decide I can't be bothered to cook so go in hunt of food.

There's an array of outlets in the service station but only two do hot food. The first has one of those A4 photo frame kind of things on the counter, declaring 'Today's Delicious Vegetarian Meal.' The snag is there is no staff around. I wait, wait and wait a bit more. Somebody mopping the floor glances my way, then carries on mopping. She eventually wrings out the mop, pats her hands on her uniform and comes round behind the counter.

"What can I get you?" she asks.

"I'll have this vegetarian option," I say as I helpfully point to the display.

"I'll just see if we've got any left."

She disappears and, to give her her due, she's less than five minutes. She returns, shaking her head, explaining they've sold out.

"What else would you like then?" she asks, pointing at the variety of meat-riddled meals currently being incinerated under powerful lamps.

I pick up the A4 self-standing photo frame kind of thing (proudly declaring today's 'Today's Delicious Vegetarian Meal') and hand it to her. "Best take this down I guess."

I wander off, annoyed as ever. What did I expect? This is Britain after all – poor service and ignorance all at top prices. When I traded in my VW Golf for the camper van, the offer I got was low but, knowing I'd have to spend some money on it to sell it with a clear conscience, I accepted their offer. A few days after picking the camper up, and saying goodbye to the Golf, the salesman got in touch asking if I'd send them £100 as "They've found that a bearing on the alternator pulley needs replacing". Victor Meldrew was misunderstood I tell you. A fictional character maybe but the fellow deserves a knighthood for all his suffering.

Anyhow I advance to Burger King, buy the preverbal bag of bean burger and chips and pocket as many little tubs of milk that my pockets can muster. Given I hadn't bought a hot drink, technically this is stealing. Somehow I vindicate myself because they'll be useful for the camper van.

I press on with the drive, wondering if such a long trip is worth it for a weekend. I question my membership of the club; it's a long way to go. Should I quietly let my membership lapse?

I pull off the M6 and take the B roads across to Dufton. It's dusk and the headlights pick out the road, snaking through the open moorland. I feel tired and am grateful when I reach the hostel, find a spot to park and make my entrance to the common room.

I'm greeted warmly like an old friend, a comfy chair is offered and I sit in a daze as I'm included in the conversation. Graham Gledhill comes and sits next to me and we discuss our years to date. I tell him about the camper van, he asks about my trips so far.

"South Wales, mainly," I explain.

"Have you been to the Brecons?" he asks.

"Yes," I reply and within moments a map is produced and we are looking at suitable walks for the Club's April meet. Moments later I find I've promised to attend the meet and organise the walk. Thoughts of leaving the club have well and truly ended.

Dave Handley arrives; his opening gambit is, "I'm joining you in having a vegetarian this evening."

"Do we know the young lady?" I reply.

"Not that I'm aware," he adds.

He then announces a prospective new member, David Milton, is in the same dorm as us and that he has been enjoying reading my blog. I bask in the limelight but play it down with a nonchalant rising of my forehead.

"Been away much?" he asks.

"The Lakes, Yorkshire and Devon."

"Where did you go in Devon?"

"Oh," I reply guardedly, "it was a writing course."

"How is the writing going?" he asks.

"How do you mean?" I reply, feeling defensive.

"Well the course, what was it about?"

"Novel writing," I reply hoping to draw this conversation to a rapid close.

"Are you writing a novel then?" he asks.

"Having a dabble," I add.

"What's it about?"

Oh for Christ's sake, my head is screaming and wishing the ground would open up to remove me from my embarrassment. I give a brief plot synopsis, hoping that'll end the conversation.

"You ought to have a word with my wife," he says, "she's been writing a novel for a few years now."

"What's it about?" I ask.

"Haven't got a bloody clue," he replies.

Over dinner, and joined by Ron Reynolds, we get to discussing Waggy (aka Steve Wagstaff). Apparently he's already been spotted in the village hall with his famous beer barrels, one for him and the other for general consumption. The meal is delicious; as are the seconds and the fruit salad tops it off nicely. Dave is ploughing through a bottle of red wine that he generously offers around, including surrounding tables.

"Have you had any further thoughts about my wife?" asks Dave.

The novel writing conversation is a couple of hours behind us now and this sweeping offer takes me somewhat by surprise. And to be honest it puts me a little on edge. Wondering what I might be letting myself in for I reply with a simple, "Erm."

"The writing," he explains, "have you thought about speaking with her to share your writing experiences?"

"Oh," I start (trying to avoid the evident relief in my voice), "well you can pass on my email address."

I wander up to the village hall, two beer barrels fill the entrance lobby along with a sheet complete with names and the number of beers consumed so far. I check Waggy's total – seven and it's only 20:30. He might still be pliable to a conversation.

"Hi, Steve," I start.

"I don't know who in the fuck you are," he replies.

"Steve," I reply, "we speak every year."

He swaggers, shakes my hand (which I fear is a ploy to steady himself) and asks me how I am.

"Good, and you?" I ask, hoping his immediate condition would be overlooked.

"I'm dying," he replies, "I'm in a downward spiral," as he highlights the effect by moving his hands above his head then pressing down on the air either side of his body. "There you are, I could do something about it but I can't."

I must confess to not being able to recall this verbatim. There were words tripped over, pauses, swaggering and alcoholic fumes to contend with.

"Oh," I say, and rather lost for words I add, "Sorry to hear that."

"I could do something about it but I can't," he adds. A true writer does not repeat himself but as Waggy appeared to be emphasising the point I thought I'd continue with the gist of the conversation.

"How are you?" he asks.

Right this moment I'm feeling a bit bloody awkward. I retire to the camper van.

Breakfast is a fine continental 'help yourself' spread. I ensure I consume enough to make only a light lunch necessary.

Big John approaches me and shakes me by the hand. "Well done, lad, for volunteering to organise the walk for April in the Brecon Beacons."

I haven't even filled out the bloody booking form yet.

A few cars make their way to Murton where we disembark amidst an army checkpoint. They do not appear bothered by our presence and nor do we by the youthful young men and their machine guns.

We pull up the track, it's steady going and my recent forays into the Welsh hills pays dividends as I find a good pace. At the path off to Murton Pike I separate from the main group and, with new member David Milton, continue up the track to Murton Fell, a summit of over 2000ft. With grid reference in hand we take a good half hour, amongst peat bogs, surveying the area until we set upon a small stone as the summit. Neither of us is 100% convinced.

We cut across the bog-ridden, mist-clad, terrain until we spy the others approaching the dramatic High Cup Nick. We meet, Big John takes the mick at my deviation, and we swing around this inland gorge, protected by natural stone escarpment walls, which fall away into a wide open valley. It's dramatic and we all stop to admire the view. We climb up Narrowgate Beacon where our orderly line of walkers spreads out to an individual series of zig-zag ascents with chance meetings where one person's zig meets another's zag.

Then it's around Backstone Edge to the trig point which, akin to this area, is built away from the true summit. Again David Milton joins me for the slight deviation – funnily enough everybody else in the group is perfectly content with the fine view from the trig point and not the obscured version on the blip of a rise some 200 metres from the edge.

Myself and Dave Milton on the true summit of Backstone Edge

We then drop past Dufton Pike and I conclude a village is only a village in this part of the world if it has a pike. Here some people deviate for the fine view before Dufton itself is reached in an outing of five and a half hours.

Back in my camper van I study the grid reference for Murton Fell and realise I'd completely messed it up. The true point is some 600 metres to the north-west. I slip off to tell Big John in the hope I'll be excused leading the Brecon Beacons walk.

"Don't worry, lad, don't worry," he says.

It looks like I'm leading the Brecon Beacons walk then.

I alternate between the camper van (where people drop by to admire my purchase) and the hostel until the evening meal. The meal is a fine spread, organised and cooked by Ann and Alvar. I sit next to Ron Reynolds, opposite Bernie and Penny Roberts who sit next to Tim Wood. Tim and Ron are both seventy-seven. Tim, in memory of his wife Kate, has recently walked the El camino de Santiago and Ron, a great grandfather, still runs marathons.

I'm snug and sleep well, waking refreshed I decide to give Murton Fell another go. It's Sunday morning and the day of the club AGM, I breakfast then head back to my camper van and, while arranging kit, there's a knock on the door. Les and Issy Silkowski greet me with a copy of the club's Link magazine. I'd only casually mentioned to another club member that I intend to skip the AGM and word has been passed to the magazine editors to bring me a copy of the magazine before I leave. That's incredible service, I wonder if they could pass on their skills to camper van dealerships and the management of motorway service stations?

The sky is a rich blue and the late autumn light lifts the spirits. I drive to Murton, say hello again to the soldiers of the Black Watch. I climb steadily, using the Land Rover track. Murton Pike hangs on my left shoulder. In under an hour, I break onto mist-clad rough ground and find the same small lake of yesterday. I head north-east, discover an unconvincing cairn, plod on and find the summit cairn described in the guidebook then break off to the real summit. The mist lifts and Murton Pike becomes a navigation beacon back to the Land Rover track. I meet a chap, studying his map. He's heading for Murton Fell and I impart my newfound knowledge of the whereabouts of the summit – I fail to mention my adventures of yesterday.

Classification	My Total	Total
Welsh Nuttalls	190	190
English Nuttalls	183	253
Corbetts (Scotland)	21	221
Grahams (Scotland)	6	220
Unique Donalds (Scotland)	0	58
Munros (Scotland)	282	282
Ireland	0	212
Totals (18/11/2012):	682	1436

April 2013 – Hill and Mountain Walking Club. Brecon Beacons

After my first TGO Challenge crossing in 2004 I joined the Hill and Mountain Walking Club (HMWC). Formed in 1989 by challengers as The Over The Hill Club, I have been regularly attending its November AGM, using it to keep in touch with people.

Never having attended any of its regular club meets I was a bit taken aback when they asked me to lead the main walk on the April 2013 meet in the Brecon Beacons.

Taking my responsibilities seriously I travelled down twice beforehand to work out a route from the accommodation base of The Bunkhouse at the riding stables of Upper Cantref Farm.

It's Saturday April 20th and, after a night slept in my camper van, I breakfast with the others in the bunkhouse and try to ascertain who is coming on the walk.

Stood outside, at the allotted time, the answer to my question becomes apparent, 'Not many'. Just four of us: myself, John Hutchinson, Pete Lee and Graham Brookes.

Undeterred we set off up the minor roads and the long pull, under high cloud, up Cefn Cyff and beyond to the mighty summit of Fan y Big. Here we rest. A small group chat to us and ask where we have walked from.

"The riding centre," explains John.

"And if you see our horses please let us know," I chip in.

I then lead our group to Cribyn with its dramatic impassable northerly escarpment. Thankful the weather is holding we drop towards the bealach with me pointing out the broad shoulder of our next peak, Pen y Fan.

The path is a mix of stone and red earth, a marshy expanse lies at the low point. Also at the low point are, what appears to be, the rest of the attendees from the weekend, led by Dave Skip, doing my route in reverse.

After exchanging our greetings I ask John, "How come Dave just turns up, plans a walk in his head and gets twelve takers and I plan mine in advance, test walk it, prepare maps, have it put on the club website and only end up with four takers?"

John, in his Yorkshire brogue, fills me in. "Well yu see, lad, it's like thiss. Dave looked at yer route and realised pub was at beginning of day. By walking it in reverse pub is at end of t'day."

Being a teetotaller (which I have previously been told is breaking a club rule), I raise my eyebrows and utter, "Good grief."

We make it to the summit of Pen y Fan. Being the highest mountain in South Wales there are extensive views, sweeping around the beacons and north and west to the flatlands beyond.

We then set off down the ridge spur of Cefn Cwm Llwch and a short drop and rise over Allt Ddu.

On descending Allt Ddu we note the path of a family cutting across fields we will soon have to navigate through. As they approach us they stop and ask Pete if this is Pen y Fan.

"Ask Steve," he says, pointing to my map.

"Is this Pen y Van or Cribyn?" asks the denim-trouser-wearing woman.

"That's not Pen y Fan," I reply, turning to look back at the minor bump of Allt Ddu we've just descended.

"Pen y Van," says the woman, correcting my pronunciation.

"That neither, it's Allt Ddu," I reply, playing ignorant.

"I know that's not it!" she barks back at me. "I mean does this lead to Pen y Van or Cribyn?"

"Pen y Van," I reply, now being precise with my pronunciation. I then eye their clothing, shoes and distinct lack of equipment. "Have you enough water?"

"Yes thanks," she says and marches off, family in tow with father carrying the one rucksack between them.

John, ex-mountain rescue, raises his eyebrows.

"I might not be able to pronounce it correctly," I whisper, "but at least I know where the bugger is."

We then follow the paths across the fields and the minor roads back to the hostel.

In all it was 16km, 1000m of ascent and took seven hours.

June 2013 – English Nuttalls

The evening of May 31st sees me setting off from Darlington after two harrowing days of work for a client. They bought a system from the company I work for, agreed the specification and, when on site, it became clear they'd not properly checked the requirement with their working practices. After two days of being questioned, "How do we do this with it?" and my answer, "If only you told us you wanted that" I was fit to explode. In IT the requirements should be defined by what is known as a 'specification', often (quite accurately) abbreviated to a 'speck'. My industry is probably the only engineering discipline where you are asked to rebuild the foundations when the roof is going on. You end up feeling stressed and disrespected as there's usually a blame shift going on for their inability to tell you what they want.

Things came to a head for me whilst training their operators only for their manager to interrupt and ask how they proposed to get their normal day's work done while being distracted by my training.

So, taking deep breaths, I head north for a fortnight's holiday, starting in the Cheviot Hills. With one of my favourite bands, The Zombies, blaring out of my CD player I point my camper van on to the A1 and follow my Sat Nav's instructions until I find myself on minor roads. I don't know if the Sat Nav has an option to avoid fords but if it does I've clearly not set it. In front of me the tarmac drops away and water is pouring over the road. I stop (rather rapidly) and go for an inspection. Whatever the possibilities I decide to reverse, find a place to turn then ignore the Sat Nav's continued advice to make a U-turn.

After making my way through Wooler I find the roads to take me to just short of Langleeford. I park up – it's peaceful with no other people, cars or fords. I turn on the heating, lie down and spend an hour deep in thought about this and that. When I feel like some entertainment I hook up a portable DVD player and watch Hitchcock's *The Thirty-Nine Steps.* The atmospheric Scottish backdrops work well with the mountainous view from the camper van's windows.

I wake, rested, breakfast on porridge and set off at 09:00. The mist is down and there is rain in the air. The weather forecast for Britain today is for a brilliant, sunny day. That is bar the north-east of England where cloud and rain is expected.

It's a long pull up to the minor Scald Hill before the steep ascent to The Cheviot. Arriving at the trig point I check my watch: it's taken over two and a half hours. I scoff peanuts, sup water and chat to a group of three sheltering the other side of the trig point.

The weather improves for the walk out to Cairn Hill. It's a well-laid stone slab path but I'm slow, tiredness is my companion and I'm glad to get to the end of the ridge. I check the bearing. A brand-new signpost tells me I've just walked a section of the Pennine Way – hence the fantastic path.

I take the line of the fence to the top of Harthope Burn before the tiresome pull up Comb Fell through peat bogs. The next objective, Hedgehope Hill, looks steep but, although being slow, I manage it with ample rests. At 15:00 I enjoy its views before the descent back to the camper van after a seven-and-a-half-hour roundtrip.

I'm greeted by a couple that had passed me on the castellated outcrop of Long Crag. We chat for ten minutes about the merits of camping, hostels, B&B, holiday cottages and camper vans. They are impressed by my van, and they are thinking of buying one. The man takes a particular interest, there's clearly some encouragement required regarding his wife.

On inspecting the narrow rear door he says, "Though I'm not sure the door will be wide enough." I detect a twitch from his wife who I could not help but notice was no stranger to the biscuit tin.

"I'm not that big," she says.

"I mean for the kayak," he replies.

Good answer.

The evening is clear skies with a gentle breeze. I sit with the rear door open and, with binoculars, survey the sun-tipped hills. Around 21:00 I doze off and have good sleep.

I wake, June the 2nd, with an achy body and figure the three remaining hills of the Cheviot Mountains will, despite the guidebooks recommendation, have to be split into two days.

I top up the van's water tank from a stream, set the Sat Nav to the nearest place which I figure will tally with the OS map and set off. When I pass the set destination the road dwindles to a single track and I frequently pull up to allow sheep to wander out of my path while the Sat Nav displays 'U-turn Ahead'. Well it amused me.

The View into Scotland from Windy Gyle

I'm walking just before noon, in a warm blue sky day, on well-made farm tracks that, after frequent rests and sips of water, have me at the summit of Windy Gyle in two hours. The hills roll, duck and re-emerge like an amplified version of the southern downs of England. Small patches of forest sit amongst their folds while patchwork hill farms allow my eyes to tread a staircase across the views.

The summit is adorned by a large cairn, trig point and people. A finger board informs me this is another section of the Pennine Way. I step slightly north, into Scotland – my first visit since 2010. I rest awhile, my body catches up and I descend back to the camper van in just over an hour.

I wake at 07:00 on June 3rd, raring to go. After breakfasting and sorting my pack I'm walking at 08:00. Having decided to stay put, and not move to the guidebooks' recommended starting place, the first part of the walk is the same as yesterday.

I pass through the same farms and am soon walking on a gravel graded track on route to the farm at Uswayford. A hare lollops towards me. Not put off by my presence it gets within thirty feet and stops to wash its face with its front paws. I remain still and watch as he comes nearer, to within ten feet. He knows I am there and we survey each other. The pointed face, long back legs and short forearms have me feeling that he's some antipodean cross between a rabbit and a deer. It takes a final wide berth and scurries through the grass to pass me.

I press on, in clear skies and the morning light, to Uswayford where some interesting route finding has me walking amongst the sheep and chickens that grace the farmyard. From here I'm unsure of the path so head east before angling across the energy-sapping, squidgy, heather-clad ground to the first summit of the day, Bloodybush Edge. It's 11:00 and I'm pleased by my pace but Cushat Law looks a great distance off and quite a descent between. A farmer passes on a quad bike as I stretch my legs out on a railway sleeper, abutting the summit trig point.

After a twenty minute rest I set off and am thankful the view is deceptive so, after dropping, following fences and squelching through bog I reach Cushat Law in an hour and ten minutes. From here I look across to The Cheviot and the high ground of the day before last.

I walk back to Bloodybush Edge, followed by the feet bashing tracks back to the camper van.

June the 4th, and the 2000ft mountains of the north-east complete, I head towards the North Pennines. The dead straight Roman road takes me parallel to Hadrian's Wall and the trail of occasional walkers treading its path.

In need of some supplies, I stop at a village shop, pleased to be able to spend money in a privately-run business. I have a mental shopping list which I use to fill the basket. Flapjack eludes me so I ask the middle-aged woman at the till.

"All the cakes are in that aisle," she replies briskly pointing to where I should look. As statements go she was perfectly correct but no flapjack. I wander to a distant alcove and find them amongst the bread.

At the till I debate whether to mention their whereabouts. Having six in my basket might lead her to think her directions were accurate, clear and somehow she could bask in the glory of guiding me so well. "The flapjacks were with the bread," I say. She harrumphs for a fraction of a second before scanning my basket at an impressive rate of knots. So quick in fact that, like the till's display, I have great trouble in keeping up.

"That's twenty pounds and eighty-four pence," she says. No time for a "please" then I think. At that moment the till flicks down the price to £19.84 (she'd outdone the till with the multi-buy discounts).

"It says nineteen pounds and eighty-four pence," I reply.

"Yes, that's what I said, nineteen pounds and eighty-four pence."

I think I'll try a Tesco next.

My next stop is a garage to fill up with diesel. They have a loo, welcome as I try and limit the use of the Chemi-Loo. The camper van is everything I hoped for but I have had to learn about housekeeping. It's easy to use up too much water, easy to fill the loo too quickly. So it's strictly a pee on the grass during the night (which last night gave me a lovely view of Orion and The Plough in the blue-tinged sky) and the use of public facilities wherever possible.

I get to Hallbankgate and find the start of the recommended walk up Cold Fell. However, it's anything but cold – a warm gentle breeze accompanies me up a track, past a small cottage then on towards where a Miner's track is marked as beginning. I follow the OS map and soon find myself ankle deep in tough grass on an open hillside, no sign of the track. It's hard going and I zig-zag my way, legs aching and breathing not doing too well in keeping up.

I keep hoping to find the Miner's track but have no joy so fight my way through the grass and heather until I reach the cairn, and viewpoint, at 547 metres. From here I take a bearing and have another slog across to the summit of Cold Fell, three hours from the start. It's a trig point between two cairns, one an impressive beehive structure. The views are immense, across into Scotland and over to the Lake District. The sky is a rich blue and bird calls surround me.

On the descent it takes me a while to meet with the Miner's track that eluded me on the ascent. It is green and soft and gentle on my feet. I get to its end and wonder if I missed it on the way up because it does not quite match what's on the OS map, or whether I got the angle of the bearing wrong.

I get back to the camper van, four hours from when I set off. With no local water supply to replenish with, I wash with wet wipes and stretch out a clothesline for my things to air.

After a restful sleep I drive around to the Hartside Café viewpoint. It's a fantastic spot with wide open views to the Lakes and Scotland and, at 1903 feet, a good starting point for some 2000ft plus mountains. I'm walking at 08:45 with the aim to take in Black Fell, Tom Smith's Stone Top, Grey Nag then a walk across to the newly-discovered peak of Thack Moor. I harbour lofty ideas of finishing these in no time and taking in the two peaks south of the café.

A pull up to Hartside Height, a fence then a wall leads me to Black Fell's trig point in just under an hour: a timing which indicates I'm looking at a late afternoon finish – my earlier ambitions of taking in the two peaks south of the café are consigned to another day. From the top the views are gorgeous, sat below a light blue sky with the warm wind running around my body.

As I depart, the phone rings. It's buried in my pack and by the time I extract it it's hung up. I recognise the number, a Wiltshire Newspaper. Running a rail user group means the occasional press interview. I enjoy giving the interview from an elevated position. I pack the phone away and set off and immediately it rings again: she probably left a message when I did not answer in time. Familiar with this confounded phone I know it will continue to bug me until I listen to the message. Taking the pack on and off is always a little tiresome but I'm forced into it. When I get to the phone the signal drops so I can't delete the message. Knowing as soon as the signal returns it'll not be satisfied until it's run the battery dry I remove the battery, bury it in the bottom of my pack and look forward to an undisturbed day.

A great starting point for tired legs!

The going gets tougher, there are peat bogs and water-logged ground to contend with. I follow a fence and wall until I arrive at what I believe to be the top, above Tom Smith's Stone. Distant gunfire greets me as does, amongst a rendezvous of walls, an unmarked trig point. After some pondering I realise I'm actually on the third summit, Grey Nag, and have walked over the top above Tom Smith's stone without realising.

Some cloud is now about; the wind temperature has dropped and cools the sweat on my torso. I backtrack to ensure that I have bagged the top before I drop to Tom Smith's stone and take a bearing across to Thack Moor. It looks distant and I have to line up carefully so not to wander onto the fells to its north.

It's nothing short of a route march. Initially I drop then gain height to meet the wide ridge to Watch Hill. Hidden summits tease me as I press on. A descending walker, my only 'companion' of the day remarks how crowded it is. A few stiles and walls later and I'm at the trig point summit of Thack Moor.

As mentioned before this is a newly-discovered peak. Of course it was known about but a recent resurvey, by very accurate GPS, has it no more than an inch or so over 2000ft. On the map it is marked as 609m, 2000ft is 609.6m. I set my GPS on what I reckon, after a climb over a wall, is the highest point. It initially comes in at 608m, then a tantalising 609m before getting carried away with 610m, 611m, 612m and finally 613m. My GPS is the everyman variety and this is probably the best I can hope for.

The walk back looks a staggering distance. I break it down into sections, taking a compass bearing to each. In all it takes me two hours at a route march pace. I'm hoping to get to the café before it closes. I arrive at 16:00, it's open and I ask if they are still serving food.

"I'll have to check with the kitchen, what is it you are wanting?

"Egg and chips," I reply.

She disappears off then comes back informing me how lucky I am that the chef is prepared to cook me egg and chips.

The evening camper van life evolves into snoozing and enjoying the view. This means I'm awake at five and, after a good lie in and a slow breakfast I'm walking at 07:30 to take in the two peaks to the south of the café.

Yesterday's views of the mountainous Lake District are now obscured by cloud and haze. Open heather ground stretches to the nearby summit of Fiend's Fell. A grassy track bends off to the right; I ignore the compass bearing and take it. In twenty minutes it bends neatly back round to the summit. I then set my compass bearing for the minor bump of Little Knapside Hill. There's a faint path that drops me through a peat gully before a pull up, via a couple of stiles. From Little Knapside Hill I head for Knapside Hill, where an impressive cairn arrangement adorns its summit. I press on to Melmerby Fell, the second Nuttall of the day. It's only 08:55, the weather brightens up, birds chirp, sheep wander away and a cool breeze airs my body.

I backtrack across the same ground, arriving back to Hartside Café at 10:25. I take my time sorting out a few things in the van and getting washed. Like last night people pull up for a few minutes and produce cigarettes, mobile phone or camera (for the stunning views). Rarely does anybody just stop to look.

I make my way to the café and order egg and chips again. It's gone up by sixty pence since last night, I negotiate it back down. The food is lovely and I replenish with a chocolate milkshake too.

As I'm walking back to the van a medium-sized Peugeot motor home pulls up. A large, aged male descends. I admire the vehicle and he's pleased to chat about it. I have him down as the archetypal couch potato who's bought himself a camper so he can see the countryside between greasy fry ups at cafés.

"That's a neat vehicle, your Romahome," he says.

"Thanks, I love it," I reply.

"Is it a porta-potty or a proper loo?"

"Porta-potty," I reply while thinking that, like two dogs sniffing one another's privates, that this is a secret code of communication between camper van owners.

"When you get to my age you can't get down to a porta-potty, you need something higher."

"Right," I say decidedly not looking forward to the latter stages of my life. But if I keep myself fit, perhaps I might be spared, unlike Mr Potato here.

"We were cycle tourists in our day," he says. "We used to go all over. The wife used to compete on velodromes as far away as Paris.

I look to his camper and his elderly wife is easing herself down the step on two crutches.

Ashamed of myself, and wishing to move away from the traffic heading to the Appleby Horse Fair, I set off for Alston, buy a few provisions, then on to Nenthead. Here I take the minor road to the 591-metre-point. It's a former mining area and it has that ghostly depressing tinge that I always feel in such areas. I don't know if it's the grassed-over spoil heaps, the simple, grey cottages or the ghost of what has gone by, never to be returned to, but a melancholic unease descends upon me. I get out of the camper and, with just daps on my feet, make my way about a third of a mile across a field to Flinty Fell – by definition a 2000ft mountain. The guidebook writers offer a more interesting approach, but the roads go so near the tops in this area I prefer to save my legs and bag them in the most straightforward way.

The evening sees me parking at Black Hill and, with camper rear door open, I enjoy the views while reading. In the evening a few cyclists pass, a lone middle-aged man stops. He's interested in my camper, a bit too interested for my liking. As he fills the void of the door (and reaches in to check out the quality of the product) he mentions that just eight weeks ago the road was impassable due to snow. If I'd been a rabbit in my cage I'd have given him a good nip.

After he leaves a powerful, skirt-clad, motor-tricycle appears, tucked in behind an open-backed micro car. A cameraman films from the back while the female driver, with L plates, leads the way. As surreal images go this does quite well.

Alone I manage to sleep, waking with the plan to break the guidebook's recommended route, for the peaks from Black Hill, into three separate walks. This starts with 'The Dodd' which sits just over a mile from where I'm parked. I set off, in fair heat, and follow a new fence then wall through peat-soaked bog. At a bench-like stone structure I bear off to find the conical-shaped cairn. It's only half an hour from when I set off as I take in the beautiful views with just a few powder puff clouds.

I make it back down in twenty-five minutes before a short drive round to the highpoint on the road between Coalcleugh and Allenheads. I set off for Killhope Law, at first following a track then tuft-littered ground while I battle heat and tiredness. At the top it feels more like a mountain, compared with the slight rise in the ground for The Dodd. I take in the panoramic views from the high ground. The summit is marked by a tall wooden pole, a trig point, a cairn and an annoying number of flies who feel it's their obligation to bounce off me as regularly as they can.

I'm back at the camper van in a total time of an hour. I drive round to Allenheads where I hope to find a shop, perhaps lunch and some life. Sadly it lacks a little so I look for the signs to the next village, Cowshill. I soon find one but some local wags have used black tape to change the two ells to instead direct me to 'Cowshitt'. Such is local rivalry amongst these villages. On route I take in Middlehope Moor.

Cowshill has a shop but very little I fancy so I drive on to Alston where I lunch and manage to shop and browse around.

I wake on the 8th after a high 'camp' just south of Slate Hill on the A689 between Nenthead and Cowshill. I shiver when I emerge from the van and start my walk, at 07:40, towards Dead Stones via Knoutberry Hill. At first the track is covered in plastic matting, an unusual attempt to control the erosion that walkers like me cause. It soon ends and I'm following wall and fence, through peat bog, grass tufts and heather, reaching the summit in an hour and a quarter. Below me is a stone shelter which I explore. It's unusual as it has a roof and the remnants of a small fireplace. Alas there is no door and barely enough room to sit down.

My next target is Burnhope Seat. Unlike yesterday, where I divided a walk into three to shorten it, today I'm dividing a walk in to two to lengthen it. The rationale being that I feel the walk is too long to do in a single day. Thus today I'm tackling three of the five peaks from the north and the remaining two will be for another day.

Over similar terrain, with the distant golf ball hill-top radar station dipping in and out of view, I reach the trig point of Burnhope Seat in an hour. The guidebook informs me this is the top but two hundred metres west the map shows a spot height one metre higher. I wander over and find a small cairn marking it.

I get to the final peak of the day, Harwood Common, in around forty-minutes before the two and a half hour slog back to the camper van. By now the sun is up and it's a baking day and my approach is rung in by the sounds of motor bikes racing over the pass. After nearly six hours I'm glad for the shade of the confines of the camper van.

I take my time before moving off to Swinhope Head. A number of cars pull up where the occupants lunch or just admire the view. I note a family (man, woman and two young boys) with the woman, map in hand, walking up and down looking out across the open moorland. She approaches the open back door of the camper. "Do you know where the start of the path to Killhope Law is?"

I know the answer to this, there isn't one but also know how she has been fooled. "That's not the path on your map," I reply. "The black dashes and dots denote the county boundaries." She looks a bit embarrassed so I add, "Don't worry we've all slipped up on that one from time to time."

The county boundaries tend to cross the highest points (based on ancient carving up of land) and the markings on the maps do make it look like a very convenient path. Some walls and fences follow the county boundaries but rarely do they form a well-trodden path.

I drive over to Swinhope Head. This is a very quiet spot so I have a lazy evening with two to three hours passing between cars.

I wake at 05:00 on Sunday June 9th to the gentle sound of rain on the van's roof. I roll over and sleep for another four hours. A leisurely breakfast follows while I peep out of the windows to find myself deep in cloud.

When I set off I follow a combination of wall and fence to the summit trig point of Fendrith Hill. The visibility ranges from between ten and forty feet, the ghostly head of the ski tows define the sharp decline into Swinhope Moor. I enjoy the comparative cool day and reach the summit in forty minutes.

The walk out to Chapelfell Top follows a convenient fence. However, the top is more elusive. I read the guidebook and, as I'm doing these in reverse order, I have to unscramble detailed instructions (consisting of 150 yards in one direction and forty in another) until I find the few stones, which mark the summit.

I backtrack and reach the camper van at 12:45, have a quick lunch and set off ten minutes later, reaching the summit of Westernhope Moor (a trig point that is starting to crumble from the top) via fence, bog and rotten wooden paths in an hour. The descent is easy with the cloud beginning to lift.

I rest awhile before driving over Harthope Moor and taking on a resupply of water from Langdon Beck. Struggling to find a suitable place for an overnight stop, I tuck in between two farms on a minor road.

I wake early on the 10th and drive the short distance to a highpoint on the Alston road. Parked with a front wheel partially in a ditch, I'm off at 07:35 along a track that has been recently covered in loose gravel and small stone. This makes the going tough as my feet keep slipping for purchase. I pass two silver camper vans, barely visible in the thick cloud, before a short detour climb to the summit of Great Stony Hill. I then follow the fence back to the track and set a bearing for the pathless walk, across peat-ridden ground, to the summit of Three Pikes.

With no visibility I take another bearing direct back to the van. However, I fall short and walk the last half mile on the road, arriving back after two and a half hours out.

I drive into Alston, use the internet in the library and seek out a hearty portion of egg and chips. I then drive via the lovely village of

Garrigill and on to the single-track road to Tynehead where I set up 'camp'. The weather improves and I dry my socks by hanging them off the windscreen wipers while my trail shoes bask in the sun.

I wake early on the 11th and am walking at 06:30. It's a bigger day ahead with far more ascent than the last few days. I walk a few yards up the track before climbing in a south-westerly direction. I adopt a very slow pace, just positioning one foot in front of the other. This is something I have tried in the past but always had trouble sticking to. The technique is to keep my blood oxygenated. With my asthma-restricted windpipe any kind of uphill pace requires frequent rests as the lactic acid builds up. It works today and I get to the top of Round Hill at 07:50.

The view from the camper van's rear door

From here I climb a stone wall and walk through ankle-deep heather. I come across a regular feature of the last few days – broken grouse eggs where the clutch has hatched. Further on I disturb a grouse mother who scurries off (a technique to lead the predator away from her young) revealing a gorgeous encampment of tiny chicks.

The visibility is good with a brisk breeze. I take a bearing across to a track that leads off to Garrigill. Here there are signs of newly-laid track, silent earth movers and piles of rock. I set another bearing and drop, cross a stream before the pull up Bullman Hills.

I get to Bullman Hills at 09:25 which are a collection of isolated lumps in a windswept moor. The only company are sheep who scuttle off leaving me to cling on to the contents of my pack as I search for my water bottle.

The final peak is Long Man Hill which would normally require backtracking to a track junction then a north-easterly climb. However, I cut due east and cross the stream lower down. Here it is gushing over its bed of rocks, one section of which is about forty foot of solid rock. Layers of compressed sediment have tilted upwards, forming a toast rack of rock lines which the water tumbles over.

I climb through the uneven peat landscape, arriving at Long Man Hill in an hour from Bullman Hills. It's a flat topped with many a tussock contending to be the highest point.

I debate whether to take the track to Garrigill or backtrack via the shorter route, requiring more drop and re-ascent. The latter feels the better option.

I spend the afternoon back in the lovely village of Alston before heading to the parking area at Cow Green Reservoir. I wish to tackle Viewing Hill and Bellbeaver Rigg tomorrow. It is possible to start these from a higher point but this requires a night parked on the uninviting B6277.

It rains during the night so I set off, on the 12th, at 08:05 in full wet-weather gear. I follow a north-westerly track, passing disused mine workings, before taking a bearing to Viewing Hill. Typical of this area I plough through peat and ankle-length tufts of grass which, now wet, drag me down. The summit is flat and my sense of direction poor. The cloud is down and there is rain in the air. I repeatedly take GPS readings, set the compass until I find the summit cairn.

I take a direct bearing to Bellbeaver Rigg but my sense of

direction is lost. What feels like north is actually south and what feels like south is actually north. Therefore walking on a bearing becomes a fight and I have to continually check my location and set the bearing again. After a few false ascents, cut backs and diagonal corrections I find a mist-laden summit cairn. It does not tie with the GPS reading so I set my compass, peer into the mist and see the ghostly image of the correct top.

The route out is tiresome. I make mistake after mistake and make little progress until I feel trapped like the preverbal telephone call where the other end won't let you go. The GPS shows my wearisome progress. I'm aiming for the track I walked in on and it takes an age to appear. I feel drained and head south-east. The reservoir appears but the car park is elusive. When I make it, after being out for five hours, I collapse inside the van and feel glad the day is over.

I wake on Thursday 13th with rain drumming on the roof. I've slept with the light on and the battery is depleted. The tap is showing signs that the water tank is low and, despite being parked right by a reservoir, I'm not feeling the rush to replenish stocks. Something is telling me that I want to cut the trip short by two days. It also occurs to me that the headline, 'Man arrested for stealing water from a reservoir', might be a tad embarrassing.

The rain stops and I drop the blind to look out. It's not too bad and, given I've positioned myself for tackling Meldon Hill, I set out at 08:00.

At first I follow road, track and road again to the dam. I manage to cross the very top of it before the pull up Meldon Hill. I take a slow pace and drop in and out of a series of tiresome fissures carved through the peat. Nearing the summit I find one that heads in my direction of travel, and I welcome no longer having to climb in and out of peat-ridden bog.

I rest near the summit and the day, which has up to now been clear, transcends as cloud blows in, separating me from the view. After making the remains of the trig point around 10:30, without the use of GPS, I check it anyhow and find the grid reference does not quite tally.

The cloud blows through for a moment and I see an alternative top which I make my way over to. It is formed by a series of bevelled out rocks, all holding water, and what looks to be the remains of a shelter.

I head back on the reverse of the bearing I ascended on and drop out of the cloud and, reckoning it will be easier to drop to the north end of the reservoir. I descend, then catch sight of the dam and have a change of heart.

The going is boggy, windy with frequent rain in the air. I'm pleased to make the dam and get back to my camper van around 12:15, whereupon I decide to head home and call in at my friend Jeanette's house in South Normanton. Jeanette has been ill with terminal cancer for some years and has recently moved, with her mother, to live with her sister and brother-in-law. There's no signal on my phone, to warn of my proposed arrival, so I drive to where I'd spied a phone box. Like most BT payphones it no longer takes coins. I get my credit card out and follow the instructions. '1. Lift Receiver. 2. Swipe your credit or debit card in the card reader.' Instruction 2 is where they got me (instruction 1 I managed) – there's no card reader, the coin slot is barred over but the LCD display is working and there is a dial tone. Outfoxed I drive on and pull up at the next phone box. Before opening the door I peer through the side window. The LCD display is active, there's a sign showing no coins accepted and the familiar story of how to swipe one's credit card in the non-existent card reader. Also of note are the knee-high stinging nettles that have grown up inside the phone box. Nobody has been this way for a while. I know BT are apt at stinging you and there's the old phrase 'to grasp the nettle', but this is overdoing it a bit.

Outdone, and with still no signal on my mobile, I drive to Jeanette's to be welcomed by her family and amply fed. I make it home at just before midnight.

July 2013 – Mary Brook

Dread sweeps over me as an email arrives with the subject line 'Mary

Brook'. Experience tells me this is not good news. It isn't. It's from Val Hadden announcing her dear friend, Mary Brook, has been knocked off her bike and killed.

I've walked with Val and Mary a number of times on the TGO Challenge and always loved their company. Mary was fifty-nine. Typing 'was' feels wrong. It should be 'Mary is fifty-nine with many years left to enjoy'.

I last saw Mary in a coffee shop in Hungerford, five miles from where I live. One of those moments where you see a familiar face but five hundred miles from their familiar surroundings it takes a few seconds for it to sink in. She was sat there, smiling knowingly at me, waiting for the penny to drop. She was visiting her brother, who still farms locally where she grew up, and his wife and her two nephews she was very proud of.

Mary had two lives: her home near Drumnadrochit in Scotland and where she grew up in Smannell near Andover. Two funerals have been arranged to reflect this.

On Friday August 16th I join the congregation in the packed Christ's Church, Smannell. Across the sea of heads I spot Val, her partner Merv, her son Graeme and daughter-in-law Marion.

Through the service I learn more of Mary's life. I'd learnt a fair bit while walking with her on the Challenge. After the service I learn more of her death. A neighbour, renowned for his terrible driving, had wiped her out while she cycled along the A831 from her home in Glen Urquhart to Drumnadrochit. Mary had previously said, "He's going to kill somebody one day."

Tragically it was her.

I stand by her grave and whisper, "Oh dear, Mary."

I speak with Merv. Ask him how he is. He tells me he's terminally ill with cancer.

We go back to her brother's farm for the wake. I'm due back at work. But it's all too sad and I stay into the evening. I learn more of her life. How she was badly jilted as a young woman and never really got over it. Instead making a career for herself then running her own smallholding and B&B in Scotland.

I meet her two nephews she was so proud of.

Everybody is floored by what has happened.

I'm one of the last non-family members to leave. I shake her brother's hand and repeat how sorry I am. He gives me a wan smile, shakes his head and says, "I'm a farmer. Farming is all I know. I don't know how to deal with this."

I drive home. Feeling it. Mary wanted people to be happy. She was selfless in that respect.

You've got to enjoy your life. You don't know when it'll end. That's the random hand of fate the universe dishes out. These thoughts spur me on to, after a four-year gap, apply for a place on The Great Outdoors Challenge 2014. I've not taken part for a while because to do the Challenge you can be out of phone contact for days and it's hard to get home at short notice. This hasn't fitted well with a campaign I've been running to maintain the direct train services from my village to London Paddington. In 2009 the Department for Transport announced electrification of the railway as far as Newbury – a non-terminus, with our station three stops further down the line. They gave no indication how our station would continue to be served but, with the only option being a diesel shuttle service to pick up the electric trains in Newbury, the writing was on the wall for our three stations. It's been a massive campaign, drumming up support, leafleting commuters at five in the morning on the affected stations, running petitions, numerous press, TV and radio interviews, fundraising, dealing with correspondence and addressing rail user conferences. Many times I was finishing work at 17:00 and working on it until late in the evening. Only during the last year did the Department for Transport admit we would be on a diesel shuttle service, axing our hourly direct trains to Paddington. Only this tangible proof got the two members of parliament, covering the three stations, to start to lobby for the decision to be reversed. Knowing they were on board has allowed me to relax a bit, but it's been a number of gruelling years. On the upside I got awarded Rail Future's Campaigner of the Year award for 2013.

But Mary's death is a wakeup call. I mustn't put things off.

September 2013 – English Nuttalls

It's the evening of Saturday 28th September and I'm parked up on the streets of Bakewell feeling decidedly grotty. A sore throat has neatly progressed to a cold and a cricked neck is rounding the proceedings off quite neatly. I had been aiming for Kettlewell but, after a visit to my friend Jeanette (poorly with cancer) in South Normanton, I took the shortest route into the Peak District and stopped. I cheer myself with fruit, Uncle Ben's Long Grain Rice, paracetamol, vitamin C and *The Likely Lads* complete box set collection of DVDs to play on my camper van's DVD player.

The BBC euphemistically describes them as 'Surviving Episodes' for which can be read, 'The ones they did not wipe because they needed the video tape for something else'. And they go on to state that due to the archive nature of the material it might not be in the best of nick. For which can be read, 'Episodes that people recorded at home on early video tape machines and have given back to the BBC'.

When I grew up I was led to believe that the BBC was a great, revered, institution not prone to mistakes and ITV was only something that people in what we'll describe as the poorer areas of town watched. Having an interest in 1960s TV I'm finding the stuff shown on ITV has survived in much better condition than the BBC's. The BBC has even lost eleven minutes of the second half of the 1966 World Cup Final. I kid you not – I've had my stopwatch out. Either that or the referee made a horrendous mistake. Of course our German cousins would say that he did make a horrendous mistake in allowing Geoff Hurst's second goal to stand.

I wake on the Sunday morning feeling well enough to drive but not well enough to do the walk I'd planned from Kettlewell. Instead I take a very leisurely drive on to the Lake District, parking up at Greendale with a plan to do the mountains to its north.

I have organised a guide to help me with Pillar and Pillar Rock on Tuesday – requiring a roped ascent. Originally scheduled for Wednesday the guide, on checking the weather forecast brought this forward a day. This leaves me in a quandary – I'm not well but there might only be two days of good weather this week and I have three walks left in the Lake District to complete all its 2000ft mountains.

I wake on the Monday morning, dry mouthed, runny nosed and a bit achy. I get myself going, take paracetamol, a decongestant, vitamin C and top it all off with an orange, an apple and a bowl of porridge. This has me feeling well enough for making a start, at 08:15, up the path to Greendale Tarn. The weather is good, a bit of cloudy but lots of blue sky. I'm sweating out this cold in a thermal top, fleece and waterproof

I soon meet the descending stream and catch a sight I've never seen before. Between a series of rock pools, which the water gushes over, an otter slinks its way. Head, body, tail, head, body, tail as its shiny brown coat, cute face and whiskers slips between the pools. By the time I've extracted my camera it has gone but a wonderful memory nonetheless.

At the tarn I head north-west for the steep incline to Seatallan's back where I take the easier ascent to its summit. I check the guidebook and it suggests if you can see Haycock, head straight for it. This does not appear great advice as that looks a very steep angle. On closer inspection it gives a more detailed route by its eastern flank. I drop to the saddle and start my ascent and begin to feel quite poorly. Popping in more pills, I drink more water and press on. I reach the summit at 12:30, a reasonable timing to take in the final three. I follow the stone wall, in a cool wind, which graces the ridge first taking in Little Gowder Crag then Caw Fell (where I'm on the wrong side of the wall for the summit cairn and have a challenging climb over it). Then it's Iron Crag, stretching out in the distance on a north-westerly spur which involves a steep drop. The pull up is painful; I'm shaking and staggering like a drunk. The wall is my guide then becomes my nemesis as I have to climb it again to tag the summit cairn.

I slip down and rest. The views are wonderful but I feel grotty and am at the farthest point of the day. I'm now bucketing sweat and reduce my torso clothing to just thermal top and waterproof. I follow the wall back to where it turns sharply towards Haycock. Fortunately there is a stile and I'm soon on the other side looking at the descent into Blengdale valley. I take a bearing to what I think will be free from the bog of the valley floor. With compass paraded in front of me its needle swings violently, not directing me to what I can visually see as the route. Realising my mobile phone, in my breast pocket, is disturbing the needle, I lower it to my trouser pocket and head off.

The descent is rugged but easy and I cross the beck and start on the path to take me around to the road then the short walk back to my camper van. However, after about an hour of ascent, with no let up, I start to wonder what's wrong. I check my GPS and find I'm ascending towards Buckbarrow which, although above my camper van, would offer no way to descend. I backtrack, in a sorry state, ill, angry and frustrated with myself to find the path which sweeps me around to the road.

The road is narrow, single tracked and quiet. One car passes me, a Suzuki Jeep. I don't hear it and it whistles by me just centimetres from my left hip. If I'd staggered at that point the driver would probably have been looking at a prison sentence.

I arrive back at the camper van after ten hours and put myself into recovery mode. Having not peed all day, I take on liquids, wash, eat porridge and fruit and have a restless night.

In the morning I move on to Wasdale Head, meeting Iain Gallagher, my paid guide, at 09:00 to climb Pillar Rock. Iain has been recommended to me by Big John Hutchinson (both former members of the Patterdale Mountain Rescue). There are a few forms to fill in before we share out the equipment.

"Do you want to carry the rope or the metalwork?" he asks. I pick up both sets, explain the cold and asthma, and weigh up both sets to find the lightest. He sounds okay about it, but explains if I'd wanted him to carry everything, the day would have needed a rethink.

We set off, I'm blatantly slow. I can't find a pace and need frequent rests as my body complains at what I'm doing to it. The wind is blustery and we both hope that Pillar Rock will be sheltered enough for an ascent. Iain soon realises that I'm struggling and takes the rope off me with no reference to his earlier point about carrying everything. This does help but I still need frequent rests as we take the path to Robinson's Cairn. Here we rest for lunch before the terrain gets more entertaining. The cairn takes an hour then another hour around to Pillar Rock. It looks daunting. A protruded blade with a deep split making the summit look even more exposed. We kit up (or in fact Iain kits me up) and I'm instructed on how to extract the protection, and clip it to my harness, as I follow him up on the rope, leaving our packs behind. The wind whistles through the helmet and I soon take it off, add a headscarf before clipping it back into place.

Iain gives me three instructions – never stand on the rope, always do exactly what he tells me and not to drop any of the metalwork. The latter is easily dealt with as I casually say I'll pay for anything I lose. He gives me a glance, "Thanks, I appreciate that."

So we set off, a simple walk around to the first bit of ascent. Iain goes ahead and ropes up, I climb to meet him. We are then on what is known as 'The Slab'. This is one of the most dangerous parts: a slip here will likely do more damage than a Suzuki Jeep. Then it's another climb, a bit of level, a climb around a ledge before the main vertical ascent to the summit.

I have done rock climbing before and I've always hovered between fear and exhilaration. Well, petrified and demented euphoria might be a better description. But this time I feel very little, I don't once feel fear and the steep drops to the ground far below do not register as anything other than a view. I think the fact Iain talks me through every step, explains what is going on keeps my composure. The hardest part is removing what are called 'nuts' which Iain slots into various cracks to clip the rope to.

Iain shakes my hand at the top and takes a photo. We descend,

Iain remaining above me so I just have to get myself to various platforms and await his descent. It crosses my mind that for £150 a day he's free climbing on my behalf. Somehow it doesn't feel fair; I'm getting the better deal.

I am lowered back to the slab and the harness catches me in a place that any fellow male would appreciate as a little uncomfortable. With my full body weight resting on a testicle I ruefully recall that extracting the nuts on the way up was a darned sight easier.

Ascending Pillar Rock

Back at the packs we stow the equipment, swing them onto our backs and make the way to the summit of Pillar itself. The descent, though long, is the easiest part of the day.

Iain and I get chatting about life, loves and loss. He tells me of a previous partner who, upon buying a house together, refused to allow him to have any of his things about the place. I explain this was the very theme of an episode of *The Likely Lads* I'd watched the night before. We agree that *The Likely Lads* is an accurate depiction of the male condition.

Back at the car park, after an eight-hour round trip, we say our goodbyes and I head off to the nearby inn for a good feed up, two pints of orange juice, and a reflection on all the worry I'd had about Pillar Rock. Now done it feels like a walk in the park, alone I'd have freaked.

I have a rough night's sleep, the weather changes and a storm blows in, rocking the van as the rain batters the roof. I sleep on and off and finally wake at just gone 06:00. Only one other vehicle is in the car park; a Mazda Bongo camper which much have arrived after I'd shut up for the night. It's parked alongside me and with music now blaring I wonder, just wonder in this vast car park why parking alongside me was necessary.

I watch another *Likely Lads* episode then charge my laptop. Not having been able to purchase a twelve-volt charging lead I have bought a small inverter which converts twelve volts from the cigarette lighter up to 240 mains AC. I reflect that somewhere in the Middle East crude oil is extracted from the ground (Mr Bongo has now moved on so I can think), piped to the coast then shipped to Britain where it is refined into diesel and, in a railway tanker, taken to a fuel depot. From here it is taken by road tanker to a filling station where I fill up. I then trundle around with the fuel in my tank, running the engine, driving the alternator which charges the van's battery. This I then convert into 240v AC which feeds the power supply for my laptop, which promptly drops it down to 19v DC and charges the internal battery which I then use to run the laptop. Possibly this is a tad inefficient.

I ponder some more until a school mini bus, failing to spot the vastness of the car park, pulls alongside me and spills out its contents of noisy kids. They surround my van as they don coats and bags and shout and scream while their teachers' voices boom loud above them. Can't a chap get a bit of peace?

I move along to the foot of Yewbarrow and park, hiding the 'No Overnight Parking' sign. My plan is to walk Yewbarrow and the mountains behind tomorrow and thus complete the 2000ft mountains of the Lake District. I wake to rain thumping on the roof, thick low cloud and a recurrence of feeling grotty. Another ten-hour-walk is not very appealing and, having a pass from the military to walk Mickle Fell, in the Pennines, on Saturday, perhaps foolhardy.

I take my time, set the Sat Nav for the general vicinity of the Pennines and set off. I pay scant attention to the bigger picture and follow the narrow roads, discovering that a tall white van has the advantage of being spotted from miles off – drivers are already pulled in to passing places as I go by. This advantage lasts until I find myself parked on a steep-angled bend, gripping the handbrake for dear life while four cars edge by. My camper van, with no traction control, spins its front wheels. I glance down at the Sat Nav which proudly displays the words 'Hardknott Pass' – a notoriously steep section of road.

The camper van is heavy at the back, the weight is off the front wheels and I'm going nowhere. I contemplate bailing out the Chemi-Khazi in an attempt to achieve better weight distribution but in the end I manage a three-point turn and cover old ground

After a stop for lunch in a pub, which mistakes my salad order to include 'no tomatoes' as 'add extra tomatoes' I'm looking, in thick mist, for a place to park on the B6276. This is not only for Mickle Fell on Saturday but also for Bink Moss tomorrow. I drive back and forth, contemplating the best farm gate pull-ins where I can leave room for farm and military vehicles. In all it's five hours since I left Wasdale Head, I'm fed up, full of cold, tired and knowing I have to go back to The Lakes to finish off doesn't help my mood.

I finally find a wide enough gate, batten down the hatches (i.e.

pull down all screens and blinds) and wile away the evening by reading and watching *The Likely Lads* as the rain batters the roof.

I manage to sleep well and come round to my friend, Peter Wanless head of the NSPCC, giving a radio interview. I recall his first, back in 1981 when we were studying for our 'O' Levels, he phoned into a BBC Radio Bristol programme about school revision. He's travelled a long way.

I grew up in his shadow. He got As and Bs in all subjects while I got As and Bs in only half the subjects. He was good at everything and I'm not surprised he has done so well in life. We were in a group of friends who were all in the top set, bar me who was in a mix of the second and third sets. I was living in the shadow of my friends, held back by undiagnosed dyslexia. This lack of achievement drove me on and I'm grateful to have got on to an electronics and computing degree at Brighton Polytechnic where I was able to flourish, equalling Peter's degree grade. My determination in life is partly due to growing up in Peter's shadow.

The radio weather forecast promises that the rain will pass. At just after 11:00 I decide to wait no longer and drive the short distance to the track that leads part way up Bink Moss. The gateway is narrow and I pull in close to the edge so farm vehicles can get through. The front wheels start to spin, no transaction-control. Instead of seeing how stuck I am I decide that this is parked enough and set off at 11:35.

It's a trudge up the track of loose stone. The rain is persistent, I feel damp and absent of enjoyment. The track has been extended so after about an hour I break onto wet, heather-clad ground on a compass bearing in thick mist. There are a number of candidates for the summit and I walk them all, including one marked by a pair of old wellington boots with one slipped over a post. On the final hump I make for the corner of a fence to pick up instructions from the guidebook for the way back down. I follow its instructions of a hundred yards on a bearing, reaching the hump with the wellington boots.

Once off the heather high ground I regain the track and find it an easy walk back to the camper van. I survey how stuck the front wheel is in the rut. To give myself room, to launch myself out, I open the farm gate. With a few spins and glides I get myself free, reverse back, shut the gate then drive to Brough and find a nice café for an omelette. They get the order spot on, no tomato. The place has a religious flavour and advertises a Christian Motorcycling Association. Judging by how some motorcyclists ride on these moorland roads the club could certainly bring one closer to God.

I wake early on Saturday October 5th and phone the guardroom at the local army barracks, explaining I have a permit to walk onto military land to ascend Mickle Fell. The guard room checks my permit number, contact phone numbers, car number and wishes me well. No British inefficiency in this neck of the woods.

Permit No.
3913

MICKLE FELL ACCESS PERMIT
2013

NAME Steve Smith
DATE 5th October 2013

AUTHORISED PERSONNEL

It is a requirement to carry this pass as a means of identification when using the PERMISSVE MICKLE FELL ROUTE
(For further information telephone 017683 43224).

I drive along to the county boundary, between Durham and Cumbria, park up and am walking at around 07:20. The ground is sodden and little trodden. I follow a fence to precise military instructions – which includes not standing on anything that looks like it might explode. Mist soon burns through to reveal Mickle Fell. There are streams to cross and marshy ground to circumnavigate. I pass Little Fell which I failed to get permission to do. It'll have to wait for another day.

After a three hours' trudge I make the final approach to the summit. Mist sweeps in and I stop and take a compass bearing to find the top.

The descent on wet pathless, terrain turns out to be no quicker than the ascent. At one point the fence branches in two. Being me I follow the wrong one and wander off course. Fortunately I sort myself out before being spotted by any military. Back at the camper van I wash, change and drive to get a signal to phone the guardroom and tell them I'm clear before heading home.

Classification	My Total	Total
Welsh Nuttalls	190	190
English Nuttalls	223	254 (i)
Corbetts (Scotland)	21	221
Grahams (Scotland)	6	220
Unique Donalds (Scotland)	0	58
Munros (Scotland)	282	282
Ireland	0	212
Totals (05/10/2013):	722	1437

(i) Thack Mor promoted on 03/04/2013

May 2014 – The Great Outdoors Challenge

It's May 8th, the train is somewhere between Euston and Glasgow and the stops are being called out of turn. A lanky forty-something guy, who boarded at Wigan with the automatic announcer insisting on Warrington Bank Quay, is glaring down at me. "You're in my seat."

"I have it booked," I reply, fumbling for my reservation card.

"No, it's mine," he replies.

We get into pathetic debate whether my reservation is for the aisle or the window seat. An argument I lose and, to be fair to me, I had booked a rear facing, aisle seat close to the buffer car and the railway company has given me a forward-facing window seat as far from the buffer car as possible.

I conclude the negotiation by saying, "I can see you're going to be a pile of fun to sit next to for the next three hours."

Always best to get the last word in, especially when you've lost.

After a further hour, entertaining myself by the train calls mismatching reality, my need for the loo has me plucking up the courage to ask the lanky, officious bastard (for that is how I've come to know him as he appears to have booked the armrest too) to let me out.

He does so without comment and I make my way to the loo and read the instructions. There's a button on the outside to open it (okay I get that) then three buttons on the inside, Close, Open and Lock. I'm never quite sure if I have to press the Lock button after I have closed the door. It's fifty, fifty but I press it and a locked symbol appears and an announcement then begins confirming I have successfully locked the door. It then follows with a list of things not to flush down the loo and I'm certain it includes goldfish. I press the Open button, the curved door swishes back and, while confusing the hell out of a guy waiting in the corridor to use the loo, I press Close and then Lock again and re-listen to the announcement.

Please don't flush Nappies, sanitary towels, paper towels, gum, old phones, unpaid bills, junk mail, your ex's sweater, hopes, dreams or goldfish down this toilet.

I hadn't misheard.

From Glasgow Central I walk towards Queen Street Station, gazing up at the buildings. At lot of years have passed since 1990 when, as a mere twenty-five-year-old, I worked here. I feel the passage of time.

Then it was 'The European City of Culture' and had a good buzz about it. Things feel more serious now. There's lots of people smoking, a badge of honour for the Glaswegians going about their daily tasks.

I buy a ticket for Fort William and start to feel the buzz of the TGO Challenge. I spot a woman, full pack and walking boots already on. Gambling on her being a TGO Challenge participant, I wander into her proximity until the British-ness deserts us both and we strike up a conversation. She's Brenda Manders from Nottingham. We are joined by two others and we exchange notes on starting places and routes and Jim Taylor – a ninety-one-year-old starting at the same place as me – Lochailort. Brenda reckons if I meet him he'll probably not look a day over seventy.

We join the same train but in separate sections as four carriages are for Oban and the other for Mallaig. The carriages are clearly marked on the station but the on-board display has my half for Oban when I need the Mallaig section. The announcement puts our minds at rest and I strike up a brief conversation with fellow challenger Karl Winkler who, with a window seat booked, then promptly drops off to sleep.

He wakes on the crossing of Rannoch Moor and we comment on the station announcements being out of sync with reality. What I had put down as a Scottish brogue now sounds more antipodean. I tease out his life story: originally from Australia he emigrated with his English wife some twenty years ago.

Disembarking at Fort William, I stroll the main street and find the hotel I have booked. I share a memory of the town with the receptionist, Rachel.

"I dunne remember that, I was born in 1993," she replies.

I definitely am feeling the passage of time.

It's Friday May 9th and, having slept well, I make use of the hotel room kettle and cook myself porridge. Once upon a time breakfast was always included in the room rate. These days one has to either part with an extortionate amount of money or make one's own arrangements.

I head for the Fort William bus station and, after a confusing conversation with the bus driver who can't understand my pronunciation of 'Lochailort', climb aboard. Apparently you have to spit as you say it to make yourself understood. Fortunately I'm wearing my waterproofs so it all ended satisfactorily.

After forty-five minutes the bus pulls up at the Lochailort Inn. I make to disembark and, with my eyes fixed on the sea loch where I plan to paddle my feet, step into a large puddle.

With my feet already wet I contemplate missing the walk to the coast but the purist in me wins through and I walk the mile to the coast, take in the sea air, walk back, sign out and note the ninety-one-year-old Jim Taylor has already signed out half an hour before me.

I walk along the road to Arieniskill, glad to be back walking in Scotland again after a four-year hiatus.

As I take the path north-east to the wooded area around Prince Charlie's Cave the preverbal cuckoo keeps me company. One thing I have noticed with Scotland is old Prince Charlie got about a bit – there's caves named after him all over the place.

The path through the trees isn't obvious and, after spotting some distant challengers on a higher path, I start to make my way up towards them. However, my nerves soon start to feel jangled as I find myself in a deep gully with a stream hammering down towards the lower ground. The people above me turn back. Figuring their route is impassable I contemplate descending the gully but, given I may need to backtrack, I scramble my way out the gully and pick my way down to a bridge over the River Meoble. Then follows a welcome track to Meoble where I head east over tough ground.

Pigging peanuts as I go (I have decided to experiment this year with my daytime food restricted to dry roasted peanuts) I find flat ground a kilometre short of my proposed camp. I pitch at 17:30, just in time for the rains which close in at 18:00.

Waking on Saturday May 10th, I find the tent damp and the underside of my sleeping mat soaked. I search for a leak but reckon it's actually condensation. After drying it off with my towel, I pack and, after reviewing the steepness of the proposed route over the Graham of An Stac, I abandon the idea of doing it.

Instead I follow the route until I find a safe crossing over the river before the drop to Loch Morar and the path, through Glen Pean, to Oban Bothy.

I find the uphill sections of the glen painful going. There's headwind and my body isn't getting into the spirit of what I am trying to achieve. I rest often as my legs ache and my breathing is laboured. The ground is boggy and the glen is a deep ravine with boulders the size of houses laying on the floor with the ominous gaps in the overhang marking their departure points.

I make it to a small loch which, on the map, appears trivial. To the right the water meets a sharp rock face, to the left the water laps against a shore-less boundary of an even sharper rock face. There's a path stretching high up which I don't fancy the ascent of. I turn my attention back to the right and figure, with some scrambling and hand/toe traversing, I can get past the 500 metres of loch.

After inhaling a handful of peanuts I set off and have a few hair-raising moments as I envelope my body around land protrusions with the loch awaiting my every slip.

Once safely through I take a deep sigh of relief. It's now downhill and the weather improves and I arrive at Glen Pean Bothy at 17:30, just before the rains set in.

The bothy is a stone building with a wooden internal structure forming a number of rooms. The place is a time warp with only the graffiti, dating from 1966, marking the passage of time.

A party of non-TGO Challenge walkers take the downstairs and I spend a solitary evening in the attic rooms. I note my habit of picking lonely routes with lofty ambitions of Corbetts and Grahams which I invariably abandon due to the weight of my pack.

It's Sunday the 11th and I am off at 06:20 on a tricky route through tree-felling operations. I'm have to backtrack often around boggy ground and felled timber. It saps the strength from my legs until I get onto the decent tracks towards Strathan.

I survey my proposed route on the high ground south of Loch Arkaig and, with the steepness of the contours, promptly elect for the road walk, from Strathan to Spean Bridge, I once swore I'd never do again. I meet fellow TGO Challenge walkers and we share stories. Stories of ninety-one-year-old Jim Taylor are shared: he likes to keep himself to himself, he arrived at Kinbreack Bothy soaked through after falling into a river, he isn't carrying a stove and is mixing porridge with cold water for sustenance.

I find the road walk tiring and boring with my only company being the call of the cuckoo. I munch through handfuls of peanuts and recall how difficult it is to find a place to pitch my tent on this road. After six hours I spot an ideal place to camp – although short of how far I planned to get it gives the advantage of a longer walk into Spean Bridge tomorrow and, perhaps, not a repeat of my last visit when I arrived early and had time to kill before my hotel room was ready.

I put the tent up, it's still sodden from the night before last. I crawl inside and, with the flaps open, it begins to dry out. It starts to rain again, but I have to keep the tent open to keep the downside of over consumption of peanuts at bay. Let's just say striking a match had to be done with some consideration. I manage to tune into an Irish radio station that obligingly covers the English football.

I wake in the early hours of Monday May 12th, but don't get going until 07:20 having spent around seventeen hours tent bound. The weather does its best to be kind through the laborious road walk to Spean Bridge via Achnacarry and Gairlochy.

I stop to watch some tree felling and am impressed and absorbed by the modern machinery. A head of multiple cutters and universal joints sits at the end of a long arm attached to a caterpillar type of vehicle. A tree is grabbed by its base, sawn through and is allowed to drop to the ground with the cutters still gripping it. It is then pulled through the cutters stripping the foliage and bark and chopping the tree into lengths. Each 200ft tree is dealt with in the matter of a minute.

I press on to Spean Bridge via the Commando Memorial and arrive at the Spean Bridge Hotel at 12:55. I ring the bell a number of times and, at 13:10, am greeted with, "Are you waiting?"

"Yes," I reply politely. We then go through the routine of hunting for my booking.

"You are in one of the chalets," she says.

"Not the hotel?" I ask. Chalet to me has the hint of a ninety-seventy's shed.

"No you have asked for a chalet on your booking."

"Did I?"

"Yes, 'a non-dog-friendly chalet' is what you put on your booking form."

I take a look and read back, "A non dog-friendly chalet please as I have allergies."

"That's right," she says.

"No what I meant was I didn't want to be in a dog-friendly chalet as advertised as being available on your website."

"That's right and we are putting you in a non-dog-friendly chalet."

"But I didn't mean chalet," I add.

"But that's what you have asked for."

I give up. I'm a computer person where set theory is important. To me a non dog-friendly chalet is the set of all accommodation minus the dog-friendly chalets which by definition includes the rooms in the hotel.

"No room in the hotel then?" I ask.

"No we have a party of eighteen in."

"Okay, never mind. Does it have en suite?"

"Yes. You are in chalet 2A."

"Okay," I reply while thinking 2A suggests number 2 has been partitioned.

She leads me through the rear car park to a series of ninety-seventy's-looking sheds. At 2A she turns the key and gives the door a deft kick to get it moving. She doesn't go in and instead hands me the key.

At £53 for a room (breakfasts not included) it's lousy. The window frames are caked with mould and set off the pine cladding and woodchip wallpaper a treat. The curtains are pink, threadbare and depressing; the bathroom has equal quantity of mould with a laughable sign explaining the hot water tap, which is barely lukewarm, can scold.

I shower, which floods the floor, and then set about hanging up the tent to dry. I wash out clothes, using hot water from the shower, and switch on the two fan heaters to dry them.

The room is pitiful, I consider going back to reception to complain. But having just littered the room with my wet gear I decide to stay put.

I wander into the hotel for a look around. The commando museum is interesting but I figure the VHS commemorative video at £4 isn't their bestseller. At least it wasn't Betamax. I walk down to the Little Chef, closed for good then back to the coach-trip-orientated café attached to a shop and wool mill. It's as depressing as when I was here in the ninety-nineties. Nothing has changed with tourists presumably underwhelmed by the banality of the food and facilities. Scotland, one of the most beautiful places on the planet, has nothing very exciting for the tourist who doesn't wish to venture out on foot.

I order a baked potato and a peppermint tea. When it arrives I refrain from my tired argument a microwaved potato is a jacket potato, not a baked potato. I've had the discussion too many times, I'm beyond caring, and although I consider I do well on the intellectual side of the debate I never quite feel I get my point across. The tea is a pot of hot water, a cup and an unopened teabag. Getting your teabag supplied in the hot water is like hotel breakfasts included in the room rate and NHS dentistry: both just slipped away with nobody really noticing or complaining.

I spend an hour trying to get a decent picture on the TV in the room. There's a constant buzz on one channel with all the others silent and flicking. I give up, read, do more washing then go in search of an evening meal. At reception I ask, "What time is the dining room open?"

"It's closed this evening, booked out by the party of eighteen. You can eat in the bar."

I venture to the bar, nothing for the vegetarian on the menu but they manage to make me a vegetarian lasagne. I get a text from Ali Ogden, on 'Challenge Control', saying David Albon had a fall and was walked out by Heather Thomas-Smith and picked up by Ali this morning. This has left Heather with a 40km walk with an estimated arrival time of 21:00 in Spean Bridge.

I take a stroll to see if I can find her walking in. There's no sign of her so, at 21:30, I call at her B&B to find she's arrived safely. I text Ali back then hear more of David's accident. He fell around 200 metres, bouncing past Heather and going over a lip. Heather descended to his motionless body fearing the worse. Fortunately David was only badly bruised and had a deep cut to his leg which Heather (according to Doctor Ali) did an excellent job of patching up.

I wake early on the Tuesday May 13th, with the aged thin curtains allowing the sunlight to stream through. I take my time repacking and estimating the amount of peanuts I'll need. My digestion moans at the thought and I manage to give away two packets to the hotel receptionist. Breakfast is served at 07:30, half an hour early, and the hotel further redeems itself by providing an excellent feast which, by all calculations, will delay the need to reach for the peanuts.

Peanuts aren't the only variation I've made for this crossing. Investing in a lightweight pack with a frame is a great improvement on my previous frameless one. It's comfortable whichever way I load it, and there's a large side pocket for the tent which means I can erect and dismantle it while keeping the rest of my kit dry.

Previously I used a pack cover, to fend off the rain, and used a platypus and pipe to sip water from. Concluding these are more hindrance than help I've dispensed with their services. The biggest hardship is now the mere two hundred miles of walking.

I make my way past the railway station and, accompanied by the call of the cuckoo, I take in the minor road to Corriechoille where I branch south-east onto tracks. It's warm and I find the gentle ascent tiresome so miss the planned Corbett of Sgurr Innse and rest for lunch at the bothy.

I am joined by John and Sue Plume, their companion, Jane Aasell and shortly after by John Sanderson. I tuck into my peanuts and, as they pull out readymade sandwiches from the Spar Shop in Spean Bridge, I rue not having done the same. We share humorous incidents from past challenges and hill walking, including stays at Gerry Howkins independent hostel at Achnashellach. We also discuss she-wees at length.

Sue is in the process of describing a group of German lads who are walking through the Glen when they obligingly put in an appearance. On their departure, with reference to Gerry's independent hostel, I take leave to recount the time I was relaxing alone in the common room when I was interrupted by a minor commotion outside terminated by the opening of the common room door.

"Hello, how much is it to stay in the hostel?"

The accent was distinctly German. The figure was a strapping young German man.

"Nine pounds a night," I replied.

"Nine pounds a night. But we have, how you say it, a Youth Hostel discount card."

"This is not a Youth Hostel," I replied in what I hoped was a helpful voice.

"But it says on the map it is a hostel."

These Germans were sticklers.

"Not a Youth Hostel," I explain, "it is a private hostel."

With that the spokesman disappeared. I sensed, heard and saw much movement about the outside. The door then swung open again and there appeared a second appointed spokesman.

"You are Gerry?" he asked.

"No, English," I replied.

Jane, who is Danish, finds this particularly amusing. Though from my perspective I know a comedian is dead when he has to draw on old material to beef up new work.

I mention the impressive tree-felling machine I'd witnessed the other day and John Sanderson explains it is computer controlled with the sawmill's requirements programmed in such that the machine will sense the width of the trunk and cut the logs to length to fulfil the order. For better or for worse the days of two chaps with a saw have long gone.

I press on but take the wrong track and have to cut east, in a bitterly cold breeze, to pick up the route via the Allt na Lairige to the southern shores of Loch Treig. It now warms up, I'm drained and make frequent calculations of the time it'll take to get to Peter's Rock.

The ***Southern Shore of Loch Treig***

At 16:55, eight hours into my day and five days into my walk I catch glimpse of the West Highland Railway line I travelled up on.

At 18:40 and very slow, I reach what Sue Oxley refers to as 'Puke Island', the site of my upset stomach in 2006 where I spent a miserable night, camped alongside Sue, in a massive gale and a stomach requiring me to exit the tent on numerous occasions, all but two of which I made it out of the sleeping bag.

Due to a hydroelectric scheme 'Puke Island' is no more and now sports an impressive bridge.

I study the map and figure I've gone as far as I can for the day and start to pitch the tent. It proves to be a struggle until I discover the inner is twisted such that at one end I'm pegging it upside down.

I cook and remove my walking shoes to discover a new phenomenon – swollen ankles. They are both puffy and I start to prod them in some attempt to explain what is going on.

I doze off early, only aware of the occasional train passing.

It's Wednesday May 14th and it's a real effort to get my aching body out of the sleeping bag and get the tent down and packed away. Half a mile after setting off I smell a cigarette and soon get talking to its owner, an older chap from the north-west with a musical Scottish accent, employed to work on the new roads for the hydro project. He points out Schiehallion and I press on and pass Loch Ossian and, amidst a game of distinguishing between the sounds of trains, plant machinery and rushing water, I take a total of two hours, across boggy ground, to get to Peter's Rock.

My plan is to take in the Corbett of Meall na Meoig but, having started at 07:00 and taken until 12:30 to the branch in the path to start the ascent, I elect to take my foul weather alternative with a view to getting myself on schedule to take in the fellow Corbett of Beinn Mholach tomorrow. However, it soon becomes apparent my pace is so slow my estimate to get to the Struan Inn at Calvine tomorrow is slipping back to a very late arrival.

I survey the map for alternatives and reckon on dropping to the B846 and B847 then road walk it around to the Struan Inn. Not having all of the route on my map is solved by a passing walker with the full OS maps. I'm able to check the route as he points out Schiehallion and gives me an apple and advises the terrain of my original route would have been extremely hard going. I ask if he knows of any places to get food on the road, he shakes his head. It looks like road kill cuckoo for me!

I press on down to where the track meets the road a few miles east of Rannoch Station and begin the long road walk. Schiehallion looks very distant. With a good phone signal I text 'Challenge Control' requesting the grid reference of where the B846 and B847 meet and then text my boss at work asking him to use the AA website to calculate the distance for me.

Both come up trumps and I know the task ahead of me. I pause at the Bridge of Ericht to gather water. The signs of human occupation have me climbing over a fence and lowering myself via the bridge parapet through discarded garden waste to the river below.

With my water bottle filled I press on and am impressed with how the local council have embraced the land reform act by providing bins and helpful signs along the shores of Loch Rannoch. A woman stops her car to check I'm okay and we have a nice chat. At 16:30, and a short distance past the Rannoch Power Station, I camp on the beautiful shores of the loch. The water laps against a sandy beach as birds call and the trees swish in the evening breeze.

I wake early on Thursday May 15th and get going at 07:25 for the twenty-one-mile-road walk to Calvine. It's a long plod without a map to check progress against. Therefore I use my GPS and the grid reference texted by Roger Smith on 'Challenge Control' to plot my progress towards the B847. At last I'm beginning to rein in Schiehallion and, after making use of a café in Kinloch Rannoch for lunch, reach the junction at 13:10.

I slog my way up the B847 and, to mark progress, pick off distant power lines and hamlets until I reach the edge of Calvine. As I take the small road which branches off to the Struan Inn I reflect, after a ten-and-a-half-hour day, I've never been so pleased to see the A9.

"Mr Smith?" asks a man waiting at the gate of the Victorian hotel.

"Yes," I reply.

"Welcome to the Struan Inn."

"Great, thanks."

I'm shown into the bar area where a log burner radiates its welcoming heat, and contemplate whether they'd mind if I dried my undies in front of it.

I complete the registration and my orders for evening meal and breakfast (included in the room rate) are taken. Then I'm shown to my luxurious room and take a shine to the piping hot radiator where I can dry clothes. After factoring in the price of the breakfast it's only six pounds more expensive than the Spean Bridge Hotel. They should pay a visit, especially if they want to watch the telly.

At the evening meal the chair is pulled out for me as I take my table. I couldn't imagine such service at the Spean Bridge Hotel but reflect to be fair, the chairs are bolted to the wall there.

There's distant chat coming from the bar. The baritone of an aged colonial type describes his day's fishing. The food is delicious but I decline pudding and a cup of tea but do suspect if I'd imbibed the teabag would have been taken out of its envelope for me.

I love these 'old-fashioned' places.

I sleep well and head down to breakfast on Friday May 16th.

An elderly lady is shown to the table next to me.

"Is the colonel having a nice time?" asks the waitress.

I surmise she is referring to the colonial type I heard in the bar.

"I think he is," replies the old lady.

The ancient colonel arrives, leg stockings to the knee with tweed breeches above, and announces his presence with his baritone voice. His wife chooses her conversation to test his mood as he complains about the wages he has to pay his gillie.

I get going around 09:20 and cross under the double-decker

bridges formed from the 18th century road bridge and the 19th century rail bridge flying over it. I'm slow along the roads and tracks to Old Blair, but the weather is fine and a gentle breeze rustles the leaves on the trees. A proverbial cuckoo makes its call, seeing me on my way.

Beyond Old Blair I'm on mountain tracks and, as I descend towards Gilberts Bridge, I spy a couple in front of me. They appear to be man and woman and are donned with full packs. Without TGO Challenge company for the last three days I pick up my pace and make better use my trekking poles. Now, with a cooling wind behind me, I'm really motoring and I catch them at Marble Lodge. I then debate whether they are man and woman or woman and woman. It's a close call.

I press on at my newfound pace until I rest beyond Forest Lodge in Glen Tilt. I reflect I was last in this glen in 1998 with my mountain bike aiding my Munro tally.

The glen is stunning, beautiful with a meandering river, rich green grass set off by a deep blue sky. I am caught by fellow challengers Sue Foss and Bill Rettie with Robert and Fionna Ridgwell following on behind. It's good to hear their stories.

"What Challenge is this for you?" I ask.

"The first and the last," replies Fionna.

Only Robert has done a Challenge before, Bill and Sue are enjoying themselves but Fionna is really struggling. We compare maps and discover my campsite is the same as theirs, just beyond the Francis Bedford Memorial Bridge.

I pitch next to Sue on lush green grass in a sheltered nook below the bridge which passed over the tumbling Falls of Tarf. The water from the falls meet below us forming the River Tilt from which the glen takes its name.

Sue and I take in the views and exchange Challenge stories so far. Ninety-one-year-old Jim Taylor is still going well and I catch news of a few other familiar names. She mentions her husband and how a disability prevents him from joining her on the walk. I'm surprised by their closeness – it's rare for me to come across couples who are so close that being apart is a struggle. I've spent my life amongst independent people where time apart is the norm. It's food for thought – perhaps where I'm going wrong. We chat until the cooling air has me snuggled away in my tent and I sleep to the river tumbling on by.

Glen Tilt

I add clothes throughout the cold night and, when dawn comes on Saturday May 17th, wait for the sun to rise to begin to dry the tent.

Fionna discovers a hole in the bottom of her rucksack, a hole in the bag of raisins inside and the bag of raisins now empty. Sue has duct tape to patch up the passage of some pesky mouse.

I finish drying off my tent with my pack towel and we set off together, parting company at 09:00 some half a kilometre north of our campsite. I'm heading across to the ruin of Altanour Lodge where I plan to camp for a foray across the Corbett of Morven tomorrow whereas the others are aiming for Mar Lodge via the Linn of Dee.

The ascent is quick but I'm then very sluggish across the peaty high ground. I descend into Glen Ey and reach the ruin which I recognise from a Munro mountain biking approach in 1998.

I look for a pitch and view tomorrow's proposed route to the Corbett of Morven. It feels beyond me: the Corbetts I have selected for this crossing are straightforward but my mind and body are protesting at the idea. I survey the ascent, descent and re-ascent and, with a sore throat and a tight right calf muscle, elect to head to Mar Lodge, via Inverey, for some company.

Mar Lodge is full so I sit in the annex room and get through two mugs of soup and exchange stories with other challengers. I ask after Jim Taylor and hear he is still going. I mention whether he's the last challenger to cross having fought in the Second World War. He was RAF ground crew – quite possibly he is.

I camp by Victoria Bridge, twisting my body around the lumpy ground and my now punctured sleeping mat.

At just after 07:00, on Sunday May 18th, I'm ready to tackle the road to Braemar, a tedious journey I had vowed never to walk again.

I make Braemar at around 08:30 and attempt to book myself a room at The Fife Arms hotel.

"Yes, we have one room free," says the young Romanian woman.

"How much will that be?"

"Sixty-five pounds."

"Does that include breakfast?" I ask cautiously.

"Yes. Do you want an evening meal?"

"How much extra is that?" I ask.

"For a non-resident it'll be twenty-one pounds."

"Given I'm resident how much will it be?"

"Sixty-five pounds."

"Erm, I think I'll give dinner a miss."

"Okay, let me check again." She types on the computer. "Oh I see it's the same price. Sixty-five pounds is for dinner, bed and breakfast."

"I'll take it. What time can I have the room?"

"Three o'clock."

"Any chance of it sooner?"

We agree on 13:00 and I go in search of today's breakfast. The Old Bakery, a favourite with challengers, does me a fantastic meal and I get chatting to fellow challenger, Martin Angell.

Sat in the lounge of the Fife Arms I get chatting to Alan Sloman, Phil Lambert, Andrew Walker and Mike Akin-Smith. All challengers of old it's good to see the familiar faces. I pop back to the Old Bakery for lunch and am joined by Sue Foss, Bill Rettie and Kate Kowalska. I ask after Fionna and she's still struggling.

On Monday May 19th I breakfast with Mike and Paul Myerscough then, after setting off at 09:00, I walk with Mike for the three hours along the tracks and forest to Gelder Shiel Bothy. Here I settle down for the rest of the day as he heads off to Shielin of Mark.

The skies form a backdrop of tranquillity with the afternoon light contrasting the trees from the land, drawing one's eyes into the distance. The leaves make their whispered hushes as the shadows take over.

I am joined by Stuart Dixon and Darren Fowler, prison officers from Durham. I glance over the bunk-filled room and figure to them this must feel like a busman's holiday. We chat about the state of the nation, the state of crime and the state of the prisons. I ask how drugs manage to get into prisons. There's a variety ways from a dead pigeon thrown over the prison wall, kissing a prisoner goodbye to an offender 'loading up' on the day of sentencing.

Darren declares himself a snorer and duly camps outside. Stuart keeps quiet. That is until about 01:00 whereupon he tests the structure of the bothy with some roof raising snoring. I make do with snatched sleep while listening to the BBC's World Service.

I make a good start at 08:10 on Tuesday May 20th, cutting up from the bothy to the track which, in the cool blue sky of the morning, sweeps around the mountains and drops towards Loch Muick.

My throat feels sore again but the light breeze and blue skies make up for it. I make progress and, with Lochnagar towering on the horizon behind me, I meet a woman ascending. We stop for a chat.

I survey her pack. "Are you camping out?"

"No, I've a wee job collecting water samples."

I contemplate asking her how often she's practised that sentence. A slight mix up could be embarrassing. Instead I ask, "Is that your main job?"

"No I'm an artist, based in Aviemore."

"Watercolour or oils?" I ask, trying to appear knowledgeable.

"Mixed media, I tend to do people and animals."

We enthuse on the beauty of the surroundings. She asks why I don't move up to Scotland. Although the prospect has just got better I relay my time in Glasgow when I got hassle for being English.

"That's a real shame," she adds, smiling.

We then say our goodbyes. I contemplate running after her, but shyness gets the better of me. That's always been the case for me. Too shy. I remember my fresher's week in 1983 at Brighton Polytechnic: partaking in a three-legged pub crawl I was relieved when the shackle was undone. A fellow student came up to me and smiled. "You're Steve?" she asked. We chatted, she was on a bachelor of education course. But my moment of being flattered was soon lost in the crowd of other students. I never saw her again, but I've never forgotten that moment. Life paths twist and turn and if you don't seize a moment it can be lost forever.

From the Loch Muick Visitor Centre I make the streamed gully ascent towards the high ground of the Shielin of Mark. I had planned to stay here but, sat in the bothy at 13:30, with the prospect of a solitary afternoon munching peanuts, I wonder about pressing on. There's an unopened flapjack on the table along with other food left behind.

The flapjack is welcome and I munch my way through. I resurvey the table and a thought strikes me that perhaps this is a walker's supper who is currently out for a hike. With a shaking hand I log my progress in the bothy book and note Sheila Farley is only half an hour ahead of me.

I make a swift exit and reach Muckle Cairn in half an hour and get caught in a brief storm. I check my compass to ensure I make it to Glen Lee where I pass the uninviting Stables of Lee. My throat is still bad and my right calf muscle tight but I am making good ground.

I run into Sheila, resting with sore knee and ankle. We walk to the end of Loch Lee then on to where the path branches off to Tarfside. We say our goodbyes, she's been great company and is very strong with a pack weight nearly twice that of mine.

I cross the fields and tracks to Tarfside where, in the evening sun, I'm chasing down my lengthening shadow.

I run into Bert and Suus from Holland. Other familiar faces appear on the village green and it feels like I've now caught up with the TGO Challenge pack.

I pitch the tent before wandering up to the hostel. This year it's being run by the Hill and Mountain Walking Club. I get made a bowl of soup and made welcome. I drop in at The Mason's Arms and the barman has trouble finding me something non-alcoholic.

Enjoying the company, I ask after Jim Taylor and Fionna. There's no news on Jim but there are many stories of how much Fionna is struggling.

I wake on Wednesday May 21st to rain drumming on the tent and some impressive, canvas impregnating, snoring. I gather my things, make my porridge and set off on the long road to Edzell.

I walk with Barbara Sanders and Peter Kenyon. We catch up with Tina Davis and father and son team of Graham and Peter Lewis. They show me an alternative route via the Rocks of Solitude. Mike Akin-Smith catches us up and we walk out together. The scenery is stunning. With a deep gully to the river below, the path hangs on the edge of the ravine with the light playing through the trees on to the clear, tumbling water below.

In Edzell I eat with Tina, Graham and Peter before the haul, with a painful calf muscle to North Water Bridge.

The evening is sunny with a cloudless sky and people mingle around their tents and the wooden tables. Alas I'm too weary to socialise and retire to my tent.

I wake in the early hours on Thursday May 22nd and, by getting walking at 05:20, dip my feet into the North Sea a bit before 09:00. I can't enjoy the finish as I'm desperate for the loo (the type of desperation where it's impossible to paddle both feet simultaneously) so make a hasty retreat to the Park Hotel.

The receptionist takes a look at me. "You'll be wanting the Kinnaird Room."

"It's been hard enough as it is," I reply.

She doesn't get the joke but tells me the Kinnaird Room is where the TGO Challenge sign out point is.

"I need the loo first." She points me in the direction.

As I wash my hands a sun-bronzed challenger walks in.

"Is that John Hooper?" I ask.

The man stops in his tracks.

"Yes. But I don't know you."

I tell him how we walked together on his first Challenge, about his redundancy package and the death of his mother-in-law.

"You've got an incredible memory," he says.

"Things just stick in my mind," I reply.

"I'm really sorry but I don't remember you at all."

"No problem," I say.

To be fair if some random bloke stopped me in the Gents toilet and told me my life history I'd deny all knowledge.

I walk into the 'Challenge Control' room and am greeted with a hug by Ali Ogden. I never got that service from Roger Smith, but hey ho, times move on.

Ali is in the process of moving her family to Newtonmore, having taken over the hostel there with Sue and Neil Oxley. "We are about to exchange contracts on a house there," she says excitedly.

"Oh great. What's it like?"

"It's a shed with a toilet."

I try and look enthusiastic. To a hillwalker a 'shed with a toilet' is a luxury bothy, but as domestic accommodation I'm having reservations.

"You'll have to come and stay."

"Sounds like it needs a lot of work," I reply.

"It does, it's made of wood, six bedrooms, four fireplaces and up a track. But the toilet is fantastic. Great views."

"What from the toilet?"

"Turret, Steve, turret."

"Oh right," I reply, realising my mistake. "How is Jim Taylor doing?"

"He finished yesterday, amazing and he doesn't look a day over seventy," Ali replies.

I get a handshake from John Manning and some nice comments about my blog from Gayle Faulkner.

I check the train times and head off for the 10:33 direct to Kings Cross.

Challenge number seven complete and the certificate to prove it.

July 2014 – English Nuttalls

July the 4th and I'm laid in the back of my camper van at 473m on the Cumbria, Yorkshire border. I'm attempting to get things dry and reflecting on the last few days. I've just listened to France getting knocked out of the World Cup by the Germany, noted the Wimbledon final will not feature Andy Murray and saddened by the actions of a childhood idol, Rolf Harris, who today has been sentenced to a fairly lenient five years and nine months in prison. A series of negatives shows my frame of mind, I could have said Germany have won through to the semi-finals, Federer has reached his ninth Wimbledon final and justice has been done in that a paedophile, who hid behind his celebratory status, had been brought to justice.

Things started on Wednesday with packing my camper van and discovering my compass, last used on my cross-Scotland walk in May, was nowhere to be found. I felt literally lost without it and after pulling many things apart in search of it, I have brought my well-worn Munro-bagging compass for its first run out in thirteen years. Another sense of loss is a completely shaven head, admittedly this did not take long, but I figure a bald head with a tan may be preferable to the uneven growth that nature has left me with.

Yesterday, Thursday, I set off from home and, with a last minute change of plan, decided to head for the Lake District instead of Yorkshire. With just one Lakeland walk left I'd have spent the week debating when to drive over to do it so instead I decided to get it out of the way. I set off at around 07:00 and by the time I reached the M5 I was fit for not much more than a sleep in a motorway service station. What with fines for staying more than two hours I set an alarm and slept for just over an hour. I took the rest of the trip at a gentle pace. Cumbria was overcast yet pleasant but the number of closed-down filling stations, joining the long list of former pubs, was very notable.

I arrived at Wasdale Head in the late afternoon, parked up and slept for three hours, before moving to park where I'd stopped last year but abandoned the walk due to a heavy cold.

It rained during the night and I set off at 07:20 in a downpour. Visibility was poor and shielded me from the steep view I'd surveyed yesterday. I made Yewbarrow and Yewbarrow North Top in less than two hours before dropping, in howling, wild wet conditions, to the col before Red Pike. My jacket let water and my over trousers were far from doing a good job. I wore a hat and had my hood up, so much for trying to get a tan on the old onion. I clambered through some boulders, slipped and jabbed my left knee hard against a rock. Yelping with pain I staggered to a halt. After a suitable amount of jumping around and cursing, I pressed on, the rain pummelling against my jacket hood as the wind ripped the warmth from me. I stopped to try and put gloves on but my hands were so wet and numb that the lining buckled against them.

I made the desolate tops of Red Pike, Scoat Fell and close navigated, in worsening conditions, to Steeple. Here, with the rain in my face, I backtracked for Black Crag. The visibility was akin to peering down a milk bottle and the rain smacked my eye, stinging like grains of sand being shot blasted against me. The only saving grace was that I felt fit, a cross-Scotland walk in May prepared my body and made my day pack feel light.

I found the descent point into Mosedale via the aptly named Wind Gap. Everything was now wet; I'm soaked through to the skin. Water has got into my map case and penetrated the acetate covering on my map. I watched the ink blur and run and pressed on with the map disappearing as fast as I could cover the ground it portrayed.

Rounding a boulder the wind smacked me so hard I was thrown back. My hands sunk into pools of water as I righted myself and carried on the trudge through the scree, running wild with water.

I got to the Wasdale Head Inn around 15:00 and made use of the hand dryer in their loo to try and dry myself off. Back in the bar I still managed to flood out the area in which I sat. I enjoyed a welcome cauliflower cheese bake and chips before braving the weather once more for the two miles back to the camper van. Half a mile short a transit van pulled up, I protested my sodden condition but I was literally dragged aboard as an Irish family took pity on me. At the camper van I changed into dryer things, arranged essential wet gear in the footwell, turned on the heater full blast and, with the window down an inch, drove over to Yorkshire with a smarting left eye.

So now I'm laid in the back of my camper van at 473m on the Cumbria, Yorkshire border still hoping to finish the 2000ft mountains of England on the trip. A guided walk awaits on the 12th to bag Little Fell, the last on military land, so it's down to me how many of the remainder I can finish by then.

Saturday the 5th has me waking to the sounds of easing rain followed by silence. I lower the blinds and look out on to low cloud. It looks like it might lift so I turn on my radio and listen to a promising forecast and the news that the Tour de France is due to begin in Yorkshire this morning.

I get walking at 08:30, backtracking a few hundred metres before following the handy track towards Blea Gills. I stop short and head east to meet the ridge then the summit of Great Coum. The cloud is lifting and I enjoy good views towards the Howgills. I backtrack and follow the ridge south taking in Green Hill before the boggy crossing to Gragareth where I touch the trig point and the fledgling summit cairn, built on what appears to be slightly higher ground. I take a sharp north-easterly descent back towards the road. It's tough going with an escarpments and gullies to negotiate.

I reach the camper van at 13:50, make myself lunch and do essential housekeeping, such as hanging my sodden underpants, from yesterday's rain, over the door mirror to dry.

I'm back walking again at 14:15, looking for the path which leads to Whernside. It's a little elusive and not as enthusiastic as the cartographer's pen. With use of my GPS I locate it and press on up, passing grazing sheep and stone walls until I reach a cairn where the ground levels out, taking me to the summit trig point. I'm wearing my jacket from yesterday to try and dry it off as I sit in a damp horseshoe open shelter where bits of dried food and rubbish do little for the ambience. Standing up I enjoy the views to Ingleborough and the Ribblehead Viaduct on the railway between Dent and Ribblehead.

Closer at hand is a path which, in hill-walking terms is a motorway connecting the Yorkshire Three Peaks. The descent takes around an hour with my right knee deciding to make some serious protests. Bemused sheep gaze upon me as I roll up my trousers and adjust my strapping.

I wake on Sunday the 6th to a dry day. I'd planned my remaining walks yesterday evening; working out the routes and the roads between to cover the least ground by foot and camper van.

After breakfasting I drive off and, following a stop to take on water from a stream, take the B road to Capel-le-Dale and start walking at 08:45, heading for Ingleborough, the second highest peak in the Yorkshire Dales. I struggle in the heat across the well-laid path – I was quicker in the downpour of the Lake District. A sharp pull onto the summit ridge, then the well-worn summit gives me the sense this is a special place for many. A quadrangle summit shelter, with a plaque celebrating the queen's coronation, adorns the top. Other people are here, enjoying the views. It's one of the few mountains that feels like a pilgrimage.

I rest awhile, take in the views before heading east for the lesser top of Simon Fell which I reach at 11:55 before an easy hour and a quarter walk back to the camper van.

Sat on the bed, still in my full kit, I survey the maps and, with the bit between my teeth, I figure I can take in Drumaldrace and Dodd Fell Hill. A tricky U-turn later and I'm heading towards Hawes, passing signs warning of delays due to the Tour de France which passed through yesterday. In Hawes there's signs for 'TDF Parking'.

A high climb (for the camper van not me) has me parked for the short stroll up Drumaldrace. The view is broken by paragliders and a large chalk bicycle carved into the hills opposite. Wiltshire has its white horses, Dorset the Cerne Giant and now Yorkshire has been updated with a bicycle carved into the hill.

Back at the camper van I drive for a kilometre and park at the gated road to Cam Houses. I could drive on but the road looks very narrow and I worry that there might not be a place to turn. I walk the mile to the second gate and turn north-west across boggy ground for a leg-gruelling pull to the summit of Dodd Fell Hill where the views are extensive, the wind blustery, warm and the clouds sit motionless in the sky.

At the latest I have to be home a week today. In guidebook terms I've just rolled two days into one and I calculate I have a small chance of finishing the English Nuttalls on this trip.

The evening is spent relaxing and watching, rather bemused, a herd of cows taking more interest in the camper van than I feel healthy. When it came to licking the bonnet I banged the wall and they duly departed. Until, that is, around 04:00 when they decide it's a bright idea to lean against the van while brushing along its side. Another bang on the side and they move on. I lay awake as a shower blows in.

I emerge into the morning light, avoid a present one of the cows has deposited by the camper van's rear door, then drive around to Yockenthwaite. The walk up the hill, to Yockenthwaite Moor, looks menacing as the grey skies cast their gloom, and drop their rain, across the hillside. I drive on and take a different approach from the B6160 after first admiring the road based graffiti willing Chris Froome on.

I'm walking at a shade before 09:50 noting that my starts are getting later by the hour by the day. Ground-nesting birds take off and complain at my presence. It's an easy pull up a sun-baked track followed by a cold westerly trudge across ankle-grabbing heather and squelchy ground. I reach the summit cairn and slump with my back to it and admire the views. The return walk is equally as tough, not helped by wandering too far north, requiring me to correct on a compass bearing. In all it takes four hours and I figure that's enough for today. I could push on for another but there's a danger of getting very tired.

I drive to Buckden, admiring further road graffiti and the entrepreneurship of a local farmer attempting to charge £30 per day to park in his field. Bunting is being removed and one has the sense that the passing 'Le Tour' will be remembered for many years to come. I find a pub car park and wander into the adjoining pub.

"Are you still serving food?" I ask.

"We stopped five minutes ago," says the barmaid.

The landlady, spotting that perhaps I'd not spent all my money parking in a farmer's field, interrupts saying they are sure they can do something for me.

"Anything vegetarian?" I ask.

This causes a multitude of confusion. Normally the declaration of vegetarian simplifies things to just one or two menu options. But I sense this has really put a spanner in the works.

The Yorkshire spirit

Support for Chris Froome

"Well, we could do you a cheese and onion sandwich."

"With chips?" I know how to push my luck. A glance between barmaid and landlady confirms that this is within the realms of possibility.

So I eat outside and watch the confines of a small village with its tight parking and too many people in a small space. My friend Rona recently lent me a book on introverts (she has me sussed). I found it very validating – we just like to be alone, pop out only when we feel like it and when things do not go to plan, we find it frustrating

Actually I think Rona had me sussed from my late teenage years as her and our mutual friend Peter Wanless (who I incidentally heard on the radio this morning with his NSPCC hat on), named one of the fish in our local pub's aquarium after me. This fish was a shy sort; whilst all the other fish would be out and about this little chap would hide behind things. Once in a while it would come out, have a quick swim around then go and hide again. So 'Steve the fish' it was christened in honour of the fact they'd not see me in the pub for ages then I'd show up, enjoy the evening then disappear again for weeks on end.

I leave Buckden behind and head south hoping for a nice parking space. On reaching Kettlewell I decide to drive high up on the moor where I find an empty view point, with ample parking, where I can be alone. I blissfully snuggle down to read a book. Well that is until 19:00 when a herd of cows and bulls descend upon me. These buggers have horns and are notably bigger than last night's mob.

One horns the edge of the van, I sound my horn and a few leap back for a moment. One then flattens my passenger door mirror (now devoid of underpants) against the bodywork and sets about giving himself a head massage. Another goes for the flannel drying on my driver's side windscreen wiper while the socks on the other has another fondly extending its tongue towards. I try the washers. This unfortunately activates the wipers so my socks and flannel are wetted and whizzed from side to side.

At the rear door one pokes his head in, held back only by his horns. My walking shoes are sunning themselves by his feet. I grab them and his immediate neighbours sound a low call – presumably to summon some more of the bastards.

I've had enough and clamber into the driver's seat, start the engine and drive off. Cyclists approach from the opposite direction and survey, with some bewilderment, a man driving a white camper van with socks and flannel attached to the windscreen wipers whizzing from side to side. Thank God it wasn't my undies!

Nosey cows

I park about a mile from the incident and continue to read my book. After about an hour and a half I hear the low call of a cow. Up the road one of them is trotting towards me. I suspect the low call is cow-speak for 'Found the bugger' for in no time I am surrounded again. In celebration one decides to lick my tax disc through the windscreen. I set off back to my original parking place and get an hour's rest bite before they gather around me again. They are more determined this time and decide the grass is greener under the van. With horns bashing the underside they begin to munch. I pull forward a hundred yards and clear a cattle grid. They stand and stare with astonished looks of 'Is it something we said?' across their faces.

I wake early on the 8th and set off walking at 07:00 and, in calm refreshing weather, reach the summit trig point of Great Whernside at 08:15. My knees are behaving but a right hernia, which I've been carrying for a number of years, is very painful.

I look back towards the camper van and pick my route beyond to the distant Buckden Pike. I walk back to the van, top up with water then start the ascent to Buckden Pike, first over Tor Mere Top then on past the memorial to five Polish airmen who were killed on this spot on 31/11/1942.

The Polish war memorial

The heavens now open and the walk to the summit is business-like with a quick pat of the trig point and the cairn before heading back. Fortunately the wind is calm so the rain falls on me instead of being blasted at me. A few claps of thunder have me tucked in close to the wall that traces my descent.

By the time I get back to the camper van I am drenched to the skin. Instead of changing I drive to Kettlewell and have a pub lunch in the hope I can dry out. It's still early, the walk so far having taken around five hours. With time on my side I drive round to Litton and, at 14:15 in the dry, take the bridleway onto the high ground of Birks Fell. The trig point at the south-east end of the ridge is slightly lower than the rise at the north-west end. I follow the wall to it, admiring as I do a high-sided open stone structure, presumably giving cover for grouse shooters. A female grouse leads me away from her chicks, I try to say I'm not her predator but alas she is not taking chances. I make the summit in two hours before the easy descent back to Litton.

I drive round to where the Pennine Way crosses the minor road west of Litton. Here I park up, watch lambs master the art of crossing a cattle grid, watch a proud mother grouse out with her brood and listen to Germany thrash Brazil by seven goals to one.

I wake early to a couple of sheep head butting the van. A bang on the window does nothing to deter them and only by opening the rear door and having a quiet word do they move on.

I'm on the go at 07:25 climbing up part of the Pennine Way in a fresh breeze with clouds gliding across the sky. With extensive views I take in Fountains Fell and Fountains Fell South Top. My right hernia becomes very painful and I walk with my right hand tucked into my underpants holding the whole affair at bay. I discover if I hold it in for a few minutes I get about half an hour of relief.

With a weak mobile signal I email a work colleague and ask for the weather forecast for the Horton in Ribblesdale area. (I'm in two minds whether to do another hill or two this afternoon or instead rest up and complete this area tomorrow before taking in the Howgills on Friday and the final peak, Little Fell, on Saturday.) With the email sent I drop height and follow the walls to the trig point summit of Darnbrook Fell at 09:55. With years of erosion the foundations of the trig point are exposed to a depth of about a metre.

I backtrack and, at the junction with the Pennine Way, pick up the reply email, containing a promising weather forecast. I descend back to the camper van but opt to have a lazy afternoon enjoying the sun and reading. Walkers doing the Pennine Way file through within a one hour window, the rest of the day I have the place to myself.

I wake early on the 10th, the temperature has dropped and I switch on the heater as I make slow progress getting ready for the day ahead. Dropping the blinds I find the sky a perfect, cloudless deep rich blue. I drive for about a mile and am walking, on another section of the Pennine Way at 07:05. It's a good track then path across fields before the rocky, sharp ascent of Pen-y-ghent.

Darnbrook Fell

Pen-y-ghent

I make the top in just over an hour and get chatting to three guys walking the Yorkshire Three Peaks. I press on and in half an hour I'm at Plover Hill, fiddling around amongst the walls and stiles trying to locate a small pile of stones which mark the summit. The day is warming up fast and I enjoy the extensive views, including across to Ingleborough and Whernside.

On my way back I meet a multitude of people doing either the Pennine Way or the Three Peaks. The rock begins to throw back the baking heat and I'm pleased for my early start in the cooler weather. I'm back at the camper van at 10:50, wash and set off leaving this beautiful area behind. I find parking on a busy road near the start of the Howgills and miss the solitude of the last few days.

The highlight of the afternoon involves helping the landlady of the nearby Cross Keys rescue a sheep that has strayed onto the road. I enquire about the sign for food and am told, in a manner I take as a hint, that "One needs to book."

I call my parents in the evening. Dad answers.

"Hi Dad, it's Steve."

"Who?"

"Steve, your son."

"I still don't recognise you."

"It's Steve, your son."

"Oh, Steve."

Lord help me.

I wake at 05:00 on the 11th of July with an upset stomach. Undeterred I set off at 06:20 on my penultimate walk of this trip, heading for the seven peaks of the Howgills. I cross the narrow footbridge over the River Rawthey and take the attractive path that sweeps around below the Cautley Spout, a waterfall. It now becomes a steady climb with a branch off to Yarlside, my first peak of the day. It's good progress, 08:05 and the sun is beginning to bake. I'm carrying two litres of water which I begin to eek out as I survey the panoramic views which include the Lake District in the distance.

I pass over Kensgriff before the drop then the very hot ascent to Randygill Top. It's 09:30 and I can see a stream I'll be crossing in the floor of the valley so, as I descend, I drink all my water followed by another litre at the stream before refilling my bottles.

I'm grateful for a long gentle climb, on an excellent path, towards the trig point of The Calf. It's 11:45, I'm probably only half way and I've taken well over five hours. I head out towards Bush Howe and Fell Head at 13:00, it's still warm but some cloud cover has taken the baking element away from the day. The views, in the warm breeze, from here are stunning and best summed up by the dialogue from a video recording I make at the summit:

There's the M6 and I'm stood on the hills that dramatically overshadow it as one drives north. I've travelled that road many times and have admired these hills and now I'm actually on them. Over there is the Lake District in all its glory and where a week ago today I got drenched. It's a beautiful day. There are many regions which make up the English mountains. I've only three mountains left to do. Two today and one tomorrow. This day is so beautiful, a gift in which to have a final look around to see what I've done and what I've achieved. I might well not be back. I want to go on and do all the 2000ft mountains of the British Isles which means there is going to be very little time to revisit any of these hills. So I doubt I'll be back on this spot so it's good to have a look around. Really good.

I retrace to The Calf then head out on its south-easterly spur taking in Bram Rigg Top, by deviating from the path, then Calders at 14:50. From here I follow the fence before the unnervingly-steep descent back towards the stream feeding the River Rawthey. Feeling hot, sticky and tired, I arrive back at the camper van at 16:50 after ten-and-a-half-hours out. I wash then drive over to Hilton for the chance to do Little Fell tomorrow.

As Little Fell is on military land I have booked on a guided walk, organised by Simon Wilson of the North Pennines AONB Partnership. A group of eighteen of us gather, including myself and chap called Ian who is also about to complete his 2000ft English mountains. Given it's military land, there's a safety briefing.

"And," says Simon bringing matters to a close, "as it's a non-firing day there won't be any bangs."

"Unless one treads on something," I add.

It gets a laugh.

This land is seldom trod so the pull up to Little Fell is heavy with vegetation, made harder in the blazing heat. We are a mix of ages so progress is slow, something I appreciate as I feel the effects of the Howgills of yesterday. I'd wound myself up about them, a dauntingly long walk. However, I'm pleased to have pressed on and done them and pleased to have doubled up some days during the week, allowing me this day. A day where I can enjoy companionship and don't have to worry about map and compass.

We make the trig point, two metres short of the summit where we rest for lunch. Then it's compass and GPS, supplied by Simon's colleague Alistair, to find the true summit. We are each asked to collect a rock to build a small cairn to mark it. I watch a line of people each add their rock.

"It's like a Jewish funeral," I quip.

Ian asks me to take a photograph, after much lining up, using his sophisticated camera, I press the button.

"Memory card full," I exclaim.

It gets a good laugh. The rest of us then add our rocks and as I add mine that's it. I've completed all the mountains of England. Or so I thought...

The summit of Little Fell

Classification	My Total	Total
Welsh Nuttalls	190	190
English Nuttalls	254	254
Corbetts (Scotland)	21	221
Grahams (Scotland)	6	220
Unique Donalds (Scotland)	0	58
Munros (Scotland)	282	282
Ireland	0	212
Totals (12/07/2014):	753	1437

May 2015 – Scottish 2000ft Mountains

I've not applied for the TGO Challenge the year, instead opting to make my first trip to Scotland in the camper van for three weeks of walking. I set off on May 1st and make good progress despite feeling the need for frequent stops and the craving for Pringles. The assistant, at one service station, is apologetic at the £3.39 price but when you've got the craving needs must and all that.

I park up north of Moffat on a high pass for the night and settle down to sleep. I wake on May 2nd, and am out walking at 09:00 sporting, of all things, a truss. My right hernia has become so troublesome that a wise investment is paying dividends. Though my family, on my announcing of this purchase of 'my first truss', found this all highly amusing.

A warm wind turns to a bitter chill as I walk a stretch of the Annandale Way with its dips, ascents and spiky grass shimmering while the wind caresses the pale green hills. A tedious wind farm rotates, beyond a plantation of conifers, to my left.

After a couple of hours I reach a tall stile which beckons me across a deer fence to the Donald summit of Whitehope Heights. My first attempt has me slipping off and grabbing at a rail. With a broken thumb nail now catching on the inside of my glove, my second attempt is more cautious. For my efforts there's an attractive cairn surrounded by small outliers poised like a primary school reading group.

I push on, through some high-level snow, and at 12:30 reach the trig point marking the Corbett summit of Hart Fell. With my navigation requiring persistent correction I pass some very impressively horned goats to take in the Donald summit of Swatte Fell and its tops of Nether Coomb Craig and Falcon Craig. It's four hours forty-five minutes into the day and I'm at my furthest point. Snow is blowing in, the undulations are tiring and with frequent stops, pangs of hunger, I make it back to my camper van at 18:20.

As the evening unfolds a storm sweeps in. The exposed position has the van rocking. My Australian friend, Steve Hampton, on first seeing the van informed me that in Australia a sticker stating 'If the vans a rocking don't come a knocking' would be mandatory. Under the circumstances of the storm, a poor soul coming a knocking probably would have been allowed in.

At around 09:00, and with no further chance of sleep, I open the back door which is promptly wrenched out of my hand and swings violently against the body of the van. I fight it shut then try my luck with the driver's door. This also is wrenched out of my hand and unidentified bits of paper, from the door pocket, take off with no chance of catching them.

As I gingerly make my way to Moffat, I reflect on how, in my days of Munro bagging, I used to set off in such conditions. With luck, and wisdom, on my side, I find a parking place by a café.

With a welcome cheese and mushroom omelette consumed I return to the van and take a look at possible routes. Gathersnow Hill is the nearest and lowest but the name gives me the hint to steer clear. I text Ali Ogden for news of weather in Newtonmore: despite dire forecasts she informs me the local Grahams are clear of snow. I get an invite for a visit and supper. I drive up and have great company with her, Adrian and their daughter Ellen. Honouring a pledge I made to myself in 2004, I tell Ellen how, as a baby, I watched her take her first sip of beer from her dad's pint glass.

I sleep in the camper but, with use of Ali and Adrian's loo and washing facilities, I'm in the lap of luxury. Ali, who is building up for the forthcoming TGO Challenge, accompanies me up the Graham of Creag Dhubh. Well to be strictly true I accompany her as my contribution to the route extended no further than lending her my new SMC guide to 'The Grahams & The Donalds.'

My hips give me grief (an old problem steadily getting worse) so I bargain for breaks and, like a child using delaying tactics to avoid going to bed, spark up a new conversation each time she makes to set off.

The summit of Creag Dhubh

A fence crossing, some heather-clad steep climbing, and a final rocky ridge walk leads us to the summit. We take in the view down to

Newtonmore, the snow-clad Cairngorms beyond, scanning the landscape for familiar tops and locations in and around the area. The valley river, with oxbow deviations, tributaries and pools glints in the sun and shimmers in the wind.

We head back down, following the ridge all the way this time. The wind is sharp and I have to rest often as my hips are smarting. We talk about the TGO Challenge, Ali and Sue Oxley are now the event coordinators. It's a mammoth task, sometimes thankless. The final stretch of the walk, through a budding birch wood, sees us to the road.

May the 5th I wake to the ongoing radio election coverage. It's getting interesting with Labour announcing no deals with the SNP which appears to have left the SNP dumbfounded and their plot to hold the balance of power in tatters. I'm parked in Danny Alexander's seat (well not quite as it sounds): he may well lose to the SNP having served the UK, in what I feel is a statesman like way, for the last five years.

Still, never mind, there's hills to be bagged and I'm off at 08:30 heading for the Graham of Creag Liath from the road head of Glen Banchor. Memories flood back of my TGO Challenge and Munro-bagging exploits in this area. My map, dating from 1989, is out of date with forestry plantations so the wisdom of the guidebook is held in check as I walk to Glenballoch. I stop to cover skin worn off my ankle and adjust the truss which experimentally I'm wearing on the outside of my trousers. Though I have slipped my waterproof trousers over the top so I don't appear like somebody a mother would hurry her children past.

I take the rough track on the east bank of Allt Fionndrigh making the bridge at 10:00 in persistent drizzle. To my left the Graham looms above me with an overhanging cornice of snow on the col between the main and minor summits.

From the bridge I climb the slope before starting the ascent for real. Only a minor path tracks through the sodden heather which, in most places, is perpetuated with the imprint of hoofs rather than walker's boots. The col brings some rest before the ravaging wind fights with me to the summit. It's still early so I head west to take in a minor top before the wet descent back to the camper van.

I drive into Newtonmore and order an all-day veggie breakfast at a tearoom as the rain smacks the windows and water drips off me. The café is run by an elderly woman with a gentle peaceful nature that makes one slow down for her and return every smile and every act of kindness.

My next stop is the Co-op to buy cheese and Pringles – fat, protein and carbohydrate, perfect mountain food. I then drive to Garva Bridge with the intention of reading, listening to the radio, cooking supper and having the Pringles and cheese as a late evening treat. Half an hour after parking the Pringles and cheese are gone, half an hour after that I'm fast asleep and don't wake until after 23:00. I stay awake for about an hour and sleep through to 07:00 on the 6th.

My stop at Garva Bridge is twofold, to bag the Corbett of Meall na h-Aisre and to reconnoitre the area as a place to park up next week and offer out hot chocolate to those funnelling through on the TGO Challenge.

I start walking at 08:35 and note a new road carved under the power lines. At my first pee stop I realise I have forgotten the truss but feel none the worse for its absence. I follow the rumbling burn, passing the fresh smell of the pine forests. There's rain in the air but I feel in my stride, home is a distant memory, and I am quite at ease with the 'one a day' nature of the Corbetts and Grahams. It means a lot of days in the hills, but without the option to string many multiples into single walks the days are shorter reducing the need for rest days.

I pass a rotting sheep, where an ill-placed foot would have been most unwelcome, sinking into the water-logged peat. Its hollowed-out eyes and protruding ribs a reminder of the harsh terrain.

I'm casual about crossing a stream and the final rock tilts and my left foot slides for a dunking. I ring out a sock and look ahead, past the trees and, across a snow line to the clouds protecting the summit beyond.

Near the summit is a myriad of channels of melting snow and peat. I cross a snow field, kicking my trail shoes deep and steadying with my trekking poles to avoid a slide. The going now eases and I reach the cloud-clad summit plateau and the rounded trig point pillar of Meall na Arse (as I have just renamed it) at 12:00.

I begin my descent with the rain now a constant drizzle. I find myself in a deep gully, picking my way down towards the stream. It's not a place for a slip and I risk-assess every step, lowering myself slowly on the wet grass and rock. I pass a receding snow field, the grass still flattened on its perimeter. Garva Bridge comes into focus as I squelch my way back.

May the 7th, General Election day with my postal vote already sent off, I head towards Melgarve Bothy to take in the Corbett of Gairbeinn. Pulling up, with snow beating against the windscreen and a view of snow-clad mountain tops, has me turning around and heading towards the bridge east of Glenshero Lodge for an ascent of the Graham, Creag Ruadh.

It's another 08:35 start as I follow beautiful tree-lined gravel tracks with blue sky and white clouds and a blustery chill wind. Birds call, others chirp and there's not a soul in sight. The track hugs the massif of Meall an t-Sithein until I branch off where the forestry fence scoots off up the hill. It forms a virtual handrail and I make good progress through the wet, tussock-ridden ground. There's a rocky outcrop to scramble over, it takes a few minutes and I look back. A wall of snow is belting down the glen and, like a pedestrian about to be soaked by a passing car, I brace myself for its slap. I shudder with its cold, press on and navigate around the water of Loch na Lairige before another pull up onto high ground reveals the summit trig point in front of me.

It's another cylindrical, vertical, concrete affair and I tuck below it, taking in the superb views. To my right is a mountain-surrounded loch with a tree-clad island with waves of water breaking into white ripples. Cloud moves rapidly and the wind chills me.

I make some navigational errors on my descent and make careful use of my map and compass to sort myself out. Another snow storm catches me. I find the deer fence, a useful handrail to navigate by.

The track is as delightful as before, the weather is consistent and varies only with my altitude. I make it back to the camper van at 12:10.

Parking up at the Commando Memorial above Spean Bridge, I look out on the fantastic views of the snow-clad tops of Carn Mor Dearg (my first Munro in May 1990) and Aonach Mor (my last Munro in July 2001) with Ben Nevis poking up behind.

I people watch as various parties stop for photo opportunities of the vista, the Commando Memorial and themselves. Some with arms round one another, others a few feet apart and a few with the new fad of a stick attached to a mobile phone for the modern day 'selfie'.

The election coverage begins at 22:00, I get two hours sleep during the night as I listen to the events unfold. When I open the blinds, on May 8th, the only thing remaining blue in Scotland is the cloudless sky.

I drive past Spean Bridge Station and take the minor road then track to Lairig Leacach at just over 500ft above sea level. The landscape is open with mountains on every backdrop.

I start out on a long track walk towards the foot of the Corbett, Sgurr Innse. It's at least my fourth trip on this track but this Corbett has always evaded me; I climbed its neighbour, Cruach Innse, in 2006.

From the track the ground is wet and I pick my route to keep my feet dry. The earlier ground frost looks to have cleared but my feet slip on semi-icy grass. Sgurr Innse towers as a block of rock sat on a grassy mound. I reach the outer confines and pick my route, taking care not to place my foot on ice. I crack the top of a puddle and press on as the icy air teases my face.

A faint path zig-zags around the hazards until I reach the small summit cairn, three hours into my walk. Cloud is drifting in but the tops remain clear. I backtrack, find what looks like a better path which I then have to abandon at a scree-encrusted chimney. I re-ascend and find the path I followed on my way up. Crossing open peat-ridden ground I pick my way to the track for the lengthy walk back to the camper van.

Saturday May 9th and I start, at 08:10 from the car park below the 15th Century Church, Cille Choirill, in Glen Spean and pass through the well-kept churchyard which sits on either side of a mound. Crossing its corner fence I enter a bracken-clad sloped field. An open gate then takes me onto the open hillside leading to the Graham of Creag Dhubh.

The sky is pure blue, a cuckoo calls and the hills are a mixture of snow, squares of commercial pine forest and red heather. It feels like I'm covering a lot of ground as the forgiving slope covers 2km to reach the summit trig point and cairn.

In all it takes two hours to reach the summit. I sit and take in the views. The road and railway snake through the floor of the glen, a bumble bee takes an interest in my blue pack. I sit for an hour and a half; all thoughts of taking in the Graham on the opposite side of the glen are put to one side as I soak in the peace and shake off my tiredness. I make the hour return to the camper van while the cloud blows in.

Sunday May 10th starts with rain hammering on the roof of my camper van. I get going, from my parking place by the 15th Century Church, at 08:50. The summit of Cnap Cruinn is in cloud as I walk down the church track, crossing the road, rail bridge, river footbridge before walking amongst derelict Land Rovers and ancient Austins converted into sheds. Sheep guard their lambs. The mend and make do nature of the farm is everywhere to be seen.

After some muddy farm tracks, and a few gates climbed over, I make for open ground. The ground squelches pitifully under foot, streams are burst and the ground is awash with running water. I make the lower summit of Beinn Chlianaig and, in thick cloud, navigate the humps, bumps and minor tops across to the Graham of Cnap Cruinn. It's around noon; I'm pretty sodden so I set my compass for a direct descent. It's tough going and I question myself whether I am on the correct side of the mountain. I only settle when the road and a distant speck of the camper van come into view.

Near the river I negotiate a network of fences and gates until I reach its shores. I meet a young lady on the East Highland Way. She's set off from Spean Bridge this morning and, with full pack, now looks bedraggled. We bid one another goodbye and I go in search of the bridge. I overshoot and backtrack through a wood until I glimpse it. It sways as I cross and I am glad to be roadside again.

I drive into Spean Bridge for my regular omelette and chips. My fourth visit and the proprietors are getting the gist of how things pan out. I pop in to the shop and buy two tubes of Pringles (one for tonight and one for tomorrow night) and a block of cheese before heading back to Laggan. I park up on the road to Melgarve Bothy.

I set up my drying rail. This is a length of 22mm copper pipe that I have cut to sit across the shelves which run the length of either side of the interior. Various items of clothing, including the truss, are threaded through the pipe and I have the heater on in an attempt to dry them.

I lay back on the bed – both tubes of Pringles and the block of cheese don't last long.

Waking on May 11th I force myself, at 08:50, out into the wet, along the track, passing Melgarve Bothy, to a ford then a steady pull up the slopes of the Corbett of Gairbeinn. I take in the smaller hump then the higher ground where the weather deteriorates with closed-in cloud and battering rain. There are a few contenders for the summit and only when the ground falls away am I convinced I am at the top. It's two hours in and I, a soggy mass, duck down for shelter, sip some water and turn back on my compass bearing.

The rain smacks me in the face. I draw my hood and collar in so my visibility is a slit through which I have to move my head up and down to survey the ground underfoot and the ground ahead.

I try and keep on my bearing but the weather has me staggering like a drunkard. The minor hump, taken in on the ascent, looms as a mountain in its own right. When I get closer there's a lull, the rains stops and the magnification effect of the water in the air disappears and once more it becomes a minor hump.

I make it back to the track amongst fast-flowing burns – some are raging torrents, as the fallen water makes its way off the mountains.

The weather clears again, the sun appears and I stop and chat to a chap. He's ten days into a hike and has just taken shelter from the storm. I get back to the camper van and use the break in the weather, and the abundance of available water, to fill the water tanks before I shut myself away from the returning storm.

The next two days I spend being, what the Americans call, a 'Trail Angel'. On May 12th I park first at Melgarve then in the afternoon at Garva Bridge handing out hot chocolate to passing TGO challengers. The weather is poor with frequent rainstorms. My standard greeting of "Would you like a hot chocolate?" is not once turned down and at one point I am challenged to reveal whether the Pope is a catholic or not.

I was thinking I'd just be handing out cups from the back of my camper van but soon the welcoming confines of its interior become a small cafeteria. There's no need to actually invite anybody aboard. My query, "Could I interest you in a hot chocolate?" is taken as a welcome to step inside. Some, so eager to please, don't even delay proceedings by taking their packs off.

The only ones to remain outside are a group of Norwegians. On opening the door to them I am presented with a man wearing a tent. It turns out to be a jacket and trousers fashioned from tent material. The chap has made it himself and the stitched seams and poppers are a very professional job.

On May 13th I help out at the Newtonmore Hostel (owned and run by Ali Ogden and Sue Oxley) serving tea, coffee and cake. It's great to be so much part of the TGO Challenge without having to walk in excess of 200 miles. I catch up with a mix of people I saw yesterday and a few new faces.

May 14th, following a large breakfast at a transport café, I am back on the hills for the Corbett of Geal-charn Mor to the west of Aviemore. The track in is what is known as 'The Burma Road': a well-made track which takes me onto high ground. The sky is a perfect blue, there is no wind. I meet a few people passing through on the TGO Challenge. Two hours twenty minutes from the start I make the summit, and its trig point. I sit for an hour and a half and take in the views. The tree-lined glen floor and the Cairngorms to the east and the western Munros are a feast to the eyes.

There is no wind, a distant drone of a piston engine aircraft is broken by three fighter jets thundering through.

I make it back to the camper van and drive into Aviemore and wander between shops. It really strikes me at the space between shops and houses. Down south we are so packed in, up here space is the norm.

I drive in the mellow late afternoon sun to Dorback Lodge to take in the Corbett of Geal Charn tomorrow. The setting sun makes an orange glow as the hills become silhouettes and the air cools and the stars begin to glint in the sky.

During the night I sustain the worst injury so far. I have a dream where I am being attacked. I lash out with my left leg, smash my big toe into the side of the camper van and wake in a mix of relief and agony.

My next stirring is around 06:30 and, given the forecast is sunny first thing with late afternoon rain, I'm off and walking at 07:30. I drop down from the road to an inland beach where oyster catchers protest at my passing and sunlight glistens on the shallow waters of the passing burns.

I miss the main track, rest then pick up its last stretch at the crossing with the Allt nan Gamhuinn. It's a windswept spot with stunted Scots Pine. It's now a long pull up a ridge spur which flattens out and I feel the top is reeling me in. I make the summit, which looks more like a pile of rubble a rogue builder would dump in a farmer's gate.

I make a quick decision, it's early and I need to be in Braemar over the weekend, to catch up with Ali Ogden and Sue Foss on the TGO Challenge. The Corbett of Morrone, which frowns down on the village, is quite straightforward. I set off back: my pace sends a grouse up revealing her clutch of eggs. Finding the track this time, I pass a ruined house then walk through sand dunes to the complaints of oystercatchers.

I park where the transmitter access road branches from the minor Glen Clunie road south of Braemar. There's rain in the air so I set a cracking pace. Departing at 13:25 I make 407m in the first hour, possibly my record. A Dutch couple warn me of icy winds on the top. Slowing off, I reach the summit at 14:50, rest awhile then head straight back to the camper van.

I park up in Braemar and have an interesting evening with Keith Leonard, Graham Gledhill and Charles Karugu on the TGO Challenge. I order a salad which consists of a number of hard-boiled eggs sliced in two and lubricated with mayonnaise. Charles is a native Kenyan and, while placing half a hard-boiled egg in my mouth, he describes, in some detail, his tribal passage of non-anesthetised public circumcision. At the horror I take a sharp intake of breath which propels the said lubricated half a hard-boiled egg into my throat. I can see Charles is touched by my watering eyes as he continues with his tale. I debate whether to cough or swallow, a swallow gets the vote and, with some discomfort, the egg dislodges and makes its passage southwards.

Waking early, I make the short drive to Auchallater where I park and attempt to pay the £2.50 parking fee. The machine rejects all my coins so, with an explanatory note on my windscreen, I set off and take the easy track then branch off onto the lesser track that zig-zags onto the minor peak of Sron Dubh. Forecast rain spreads in but it is light and I make steady progress onto the long ridge towards the Corbett of Creag nan Gabhar. The weather descends into a peppering hailstorm with an accompanying wind that buzzes the hood of my jacket against my face.

With so much water in the air I reach a high point and hope it's the summit. It turns out to be Sron nan Gabhar and, as the rain clears, Creag nan Gabhar looks nearer than I had feared. I make the summit after two hours and spend the next hour and forty minutes battling the wind back to the camper van.

On Sunday the 17th, having moved back to Braemar, I breakfast with Sue Foss, on her second TGO Challenge crossing, at the Braemar Lodge Hotel. Despite her having booked me a breakfast they have no record of it but, with the promise of an extra £10 in the till, they appear to be able to accommodate me.

It's good to catch up with Sue who I met on last year's TGO Challenge in Glen Tilt. She had a mishap in Glen Banchor this time, falling into the river up to her neck. But she appears none the worse for it.

She heads off to church while I read. I get a text, mid-religious service, asking if her walking boots are in my van. I have a quick look around, no luck. A few further texts are exchanged to get a description and I pop back to Braemar Lodge to retrieve them.

We then lunch early which has the net effect that, on top of my cooked breakfast and bowl of grapefruit and my own lunch, I also consume half of Sue's.

We then set off for Lochcallater Lodge, meeting Toby and Vicky Grace on route and, after two hours, arrive at this remote Victorian hunting lodge for the traditional TGO Challenge welcome. Bill and Stan's widow (who now run the place) have laid on a gigantic spread of food and drink. I declare myself as a teetotal vegetarian. A vegetarian option is soon rustled up. Being the only vegetarian there's enough for two portions which, added to my breakfast and lunches, leaves just about enough room for the late-night cheese and nibbles.

There is much singing, reciting of dubious poetry and guitar playing. Andrew McKinnon and Mick Hopkins are the star performers on the guitar. I don't really have any talent to offer, but join in a few songs and chat with old friends Ali Ogden and John Jocys. When the finger is pointed at me I sing a small ditty I learnt in the primary school playground about a young lady from Leeds who swallowed a packet of Sutton's finest only to find some hours later weeds and flowers about her person. It went down well which is in marked contrast to my first recital to my parents during the early 1970s.

I leave at 23:05 and, staggering with tiredness, get back to Braemar and the camper van at 00:50.

I sleep on and off then drive north-east to give the Corbett of Morven a go. Setting off at 09:55, biding 'hi' to a party of three about to do the same, I cross the fields to a ruined farmhouse then start the ascent. My legs are heavy and I feel drained. Too much food and not enough sleep. After a steep ascent I pick up speed as the hill flattens off then gently rises again. Snow blows in and I reach the summit, after a few false subsidiary tops, in two hours. Visibility is down to about fifty feet as the snow falls and settles (mainly about my person).

On the return my feet become soaked in wet heather. I arrive back at the camper van wet, fed up and, with the heaters running, fabricate a diesel-fuelled drying room.

Tuesday May 19th and, after an uncomfortable night of hip pain, I drive over to Cock Bridge. I remember this from a family holiday in 1978 where my parents, spotting the sign a millisecond before their young son in the back of the car, awaited the inevitable guffaws. Thirty-seven years on it still raises a smile.

I start walking at 08:50 for Brown Cow Hill; the easiest of all the Corbetts to pronounce. The guidebook, which gives a phonetic translation of each mountain, declares this to be 'as spelt'. That's as far as I follow the guidebook because the suggested route is a wider circuit and I spot a simpler route that begins on a track then heads across open countryside to an east top before a snow-blasted pull up to the summit proper. The weather has been changeable and the Radio 4 forecast advised, 'Don't be fooled by the bright weather first thing.'

The descent is much the same, the snow turns to rain then sunshine and back to rain. Crossing a small river adds to the fun as a useful rock proves to be clad in slippery moss, resulting in dunking a foot in icy water.

Back at the camper I spy a nearby hotel and enquire about lunch. It transpires the cook is busy ripping out an outhouse so is unable to oblige. I drive up the steep road as a hailstorm sweeps in and, with wipers on full swing, I gingerly reach the summit of the road to find an oasis of a ski centre with an open café. The lady behind the bar is very cheerful, a contrast to the oft dour Scot that is the public face of many a tourist business.

It is too exposed to park up for the night so I spend a sheltered night at the parking spot by The Well of the Lecht. Waking early I return to the ski café area with a view to doing the Corbetts of Carn Ealasaid and Carn Mor. In typical Cameron McNeish guidebook style there's a mistake with one of the grid references extending to seven digits. Grid references can be expressed in different numbers of digits (depending on required accuracy) but one thing for sure is the northings and eastings are never expressed with different levels of accuracy.

I debate whether to do the shorter Carn Ealasaid walk first or the longer Carn Mor. This is settled by figuring if I did Carn Mor first I might feel too tired to do Carn Ealasaid, but not vice versa.

I begin walking at 07:45 via a track amongst the quiet ski slopes. In takes me to open hillside where, across peat bogs, I make the ridge around to Carn Ealasaid. It's blustery with views and I make the summit in an hour. I stay higher on my return and avoid most of the peat. Seagulls circle the hill above the ski centre and I narrowly avoid treading on an egg in a hollowed-out nest. As the seagulls call, swoop and squawk a wind turbine spins with its ghostly hum.

At 09:45 I slump down behind a wooden outbuilding and rest before starting the long route over to Carn Mor. First I cross the road then take the sharp pull up the hill to a spot height of 747m on the Aberdeenshire/Banffshire county boundary. From here it's a very tough walk with deep, soggy-bottomed, peat hags to continually climb down into and out of again. I rely on my hard learnt key to peat hags: (i) Black bottomed is indeterminate, a foot may sink or stand fast (ii) Bright green bottomed is waterborne vegetation guaranteeing a plunge (iii) Stony bottomed is sure underfoot.

A headwind slows my progress and only a newly-installed fence gives any form of comfort. The scattered metal wire of the old one is a persistent trip hazard.

Given there are two tops to cross before the 804m top of Carn Mor, I contemplate turning back. But I press on with the wind continuing to wallop me. The Radio 4 forecast of no rain keeps me going.

The peat hags continue – the bed sores of the mountain tops. One serves as shelter for my lunch. I make Carn Mor at 12:20, a lone trig point on a grassy rise on an ocean of thumb high heather.

The return is aided by the tailwind and I reach the camper van at 14:35 and head to the ski café for lunch. The same lady serves me. She says she spotted me heading for Carn Ealasaid first thing, my return and heading off for Carn Mor followed by my return when I cut across the slopes back to the ski centre. Luckily I was wearing the truss as it was the main thing that prevented me from relieving myself when cutting back through the ski slopes.

She comes from Tomintoul and describes its virtues including a police station, fire station, post office and shop. I go in exploration, the post office is closed (I have a map to post back for Sue Foss) and the shop does not sell Pringles so I'm left having to buy healthy stuff.

May the 21st and I set off at 07:45 for the long track walk to take in the Corbett of Corryhabbie Hill and the neighbouring Graham of Cook's Cairn. A new strategy of prioritising Corbetts, and only doing Grahams where it would be rude not to, comes into play as the walk in is identical for these two mountains.

After a quarter of an hour, and needlessly crossing a bridge and backtracking, I realise I've set off without the truss. I decide to risk it (noting stopping for a pee will now be easier) and press on via a semi-made-up track following the River Livet. This is Highland malt whisky Glen Livet territory.

The walk takes two and a half hours. I feel fatigued and, ideally, need a rest day but as I am so close to my drive home on Saturday I'm determined to keep going.

I pass amongst abandoned houses. By the state of their roofs I'd guess they were vacated in the nineteen seventies. I ponder what characters lived in them and how the glen and isolation shaped them. The homogenisation of education and common media exposure is making unique characters a thing of the past. We talk about diversity these days, but diversity of character is ebbing away.

A fork in the track takes me onto the slopes of Corryhabbie Hill. My hernia aches and there's rain in the air and, as I near the summit the wind picks up which makes the shelter encircling the trig point all the more welcome. A large triangular lump of iron hogs one side so I tuck myself behind the trig point, eat lunch and share texts with Ali Ogden and Sue Foss on their last day of the TGO Challenge.

Cook's Cairn looks a daunting prospect. The lower green slopes are sat on by brown heathery upper slopes. Using my compass I identify a few subsidiary tops before selecting my route. I drop back to the main track, descend to the 450m line then head south-east to pick up the summit track. I reach ankle-snapping heather where animal tracks become welcome as routes through the maze. The climb is steady and I make the top at 13:15.

The descent is into a gruelling headwind. It fills the back of my hood causing the mouth piece to pull hard against my lips. I count off the familiar way marks of my route up and get back at 15:50.

A trip to the post office at Dufftown is as fruitless as yesterdays. Clearly nobody needs to post a letter after 16:00. I console myself with a Chinese takeaway in the back of the camper van.

I wake at 04:30 on the 22nd with a view to bagging Ben Rinnes then drive home. It takes me a while to cook porridge and prepare. Electing to walk without a pack, I drink plenty of water and get going into the early morning light at 05:30. It's cold as I pull my way up the well-made track. I break into cloud and the wind beats a chill. I have my map, compass and GPS buried away in my jacket so, in true Famous Five style, I scratch waymarks into the gravel for my return.

At 07:00 I make the summit with Dartmoor Tor-like rocks to scramble around. The trig point, sporting a direction finder, is fractured but still standing.

As I descend my mind wanders from my trip, back to the routine jobs of home that will need attending. I make it back to the camper van at 08:00 and set off. The drive south takes in much of the ground I've covered over the last week. I find the Braemar post office open and post Sue's map back.

It's a 550-mile journey with plenty of stops. As the south looms, and the roads busy and the buildings move ever nearer together, the peace and purity of the trip morph back to modern living. But enough stays with me and I think I am starting to get the message.

April 2016 – Scottish 2000ft Mountains

April 29th and I'm parked up at the Birdlip viewpoint above the Air Balloon pub in the Cotswolds. Memories of the drag of a drive to Scotland have me putting in an hour before bed so I can be on the M5 first thing.

A fitful sleep and a reasonably early start, coupled with an M5 service station breakfast, a few more stops then the resignation that I need caffeine to keep me safe, has me in Scotland around 14:00. I abandon plans for a first Corbett in the borders and press on, via a complicated set of directions from my Sat Nav around Glasgow, to Arrochar.

On route my mind flits back to the start of my Munro exploits, some quarter of a century ago. I recall no Sat Nav, the frequent search for accommodation, constantly getting lost on route and the hunt for a working payphone to call home. I pat my camper van's steering wheel, glance in the rear view mirror at my bed, check the Sat Nav and glance down to check my mobile is still safely charging. This is good. A quarter of a century has brought many changes. It's a week when the Hillsborough family finally got the justice they deserve and the old boy networks, protecting the likes of Jimmy Savile, and the police are slowly being broken down.

I soon find I'm lost, having set the Sat Nav for the wrong section of road I've overshot my stopping place. A daring three-point turn, on a fast stretch of road, has me heading back. I find an inn to eat at, one of the types where you have to bag a table first and, if on your own, explain to the bar tender that you hope to be on a certain table provided nobody has nicked it in the meantime. At £9.50 for veggie lasagne with £1.85 for a glass of plain soda water, I do wonder if I was hoping too much for table service.

Disgruntled I eat up, head off and park up, listen to the radio and am only disturbed in the early hours by an articulated lorry pulling in for the night.

I start, on May 1st, at 09:30 and trudge, in drizzle, the steep, peat-drenched foothills of Binnein an Fhidhleir (Stob Coire Creagach). The tops are in cloud, I recall the Munro spirit of setting out in all conditions and mental calculations of timings. To the east I note my map has the times scribbled on of three Munros I did with Ady Glover on a bank holiday weekend in 1992: a tortuous day of some eleven hours and three Munros.

I check my GPS once or twice, reset bearings and press on through cauldrons of bog surrounded by deep gullies of despair. I ascend the tiers, my feet wet and icy until a final pull up a deep gulley has me taking the utmost care through minor snow fields and peat which is only too happy to eject copious amounts of water with every step. The wind blows into my mouth and aches every filling before I make the summit ridge. I've hit it too far to the east so have to descend and ascend to the true summit.

There's not much to see as the cloud is down. I descend to the low point on the ridge and then via a soaked gulley that is only too willing to tip my balance with saturated ground and small rocks poised to slide away.

I make it back to my camper van at 13:45, looking forward to seeing if Leicester City can win the premiership title by beating Manchester United. Laid out on the bed I'm relieved that my right hernia operation, last October, has held out with no real discomfort.

I stir around 06:30 on the 2nd and listen to the Radio 4 weather forecast. Rain in Scotland at first (confirmed by the persistent drumming on the camper van's roof) is set to blow through mid-morning. That's good enough for me and I pull the quilt over my head and next wake at 10:30. I make a slow start, emerging, in full kit, an hour later for an ascent of Beinn Luibhean.

Beinn Luibhean

My legs feel heavy but the sun blesses me with a view of the gullies leading to yesterday's Corbett. I make out where I went wrong, schoolboy errors in the mist. I rest often next to the descending burn, crashing from the higher reaches, forming small waterfalls, from which the wind blows spray back up the mountain, and pools of bubble-bath like foam.

The ground is saturated, so are my trail shoes and my feet ache with the cold. I branch west towards the rocky outcrops of the summit. A snowstorm blows in, rattling my hood and peppering my face. Soon I'm leaving deep footprints in the settled snow. The storm breaks as I wind my way to the draughty summit, snack on some food, sip water then, rather casually, head off and am faced with a rather unfamiliar view. I use the GPS to confirm where my lack of natural direction finding has deposited me.

With some close compass work and pauses for reassurance I reclaim the burn of the ascent and drop down to the road. I review my timings – slow. It took me ten minutes short of three hours to reach the summit for a walk lasting a total of five hours.

The evening is spent curled up under the duvet listening to Chelsea putting their rivals, Tottenham Hotspur, out of the premiership title race and giving Leicester City one of the greatest title wins of all times. They started the season at 5000-1 to win the title which, if the bookies and my maths are correct, would mean you could re-run the season 4999 times and they'd not win it again.

Beinn an Lochain

I wake early on the 3rd and aim for the towering, and rather ominous-looking, Beinn an Lochain. I follow the saturated old drovers road to Loch Restil then make a sharp pull up a gully to follow the windswept, and in places precarious, rocky ridge. Mid-morning I get a good view of the summit, a sharp snow-clad protuberance. I make the summit at 11:45 then descend the same way. I endure the odd blast of harrowing wind and the odd slip on grassy and wet ground. Otherwise it's a case of treading carefully down rocky staircases until I reach the road.

It's time to break camp, three days in the same layby has the leisure battery flat and my laptop needing some serious recharging. I consider staying and running the engine but elect to head north to the Tyndrum area. The first thing is to hook up the recently acquired inverter (to charge the laptop) to a two-way extender I've bought for the cigarette lighter – the other outlet is destined for recharging my mobile. It's a first try at this and I note the laptop flickers a light to show the electrons are heading its way and the mobile dutifully follows suit. I start to pull out of the car park and note the light on the laptop flickers and goes out in unison with the mobile phone. I give the wires a wiggle: a technical term that does not improve the situation. Nor does the smoke that starts to bellow out of the two-way extension socket which, given the sudden evidence, isn't really designed for the load. A quick unplug and the inverter plugged directly into the car, has me on my way.

The next chore is to find somewhere to eat. I sail by a number of places which advertise their whereabouts hundreds of yards ahead only to be firmly closed on passing.

The odd hotel looks too posh for a smelly walker so I pull up at a roadside tearoom. It's 15:00 on the first week of the summer season and they have finished serving hot food. I make it to Crianlarich where my need for food has me, shall we say, slightly irritable. I remember the station tearooms and the breakfasts after driving up overnight. Following the signs, gleefully advertising what one could expect, I get to the door to find it closed.

Dejected, I find the local shop and buy a sandwich which I have trouble getting in to. As I finally manage to open its plastic coffin it kind of flops open to reveal a bog-like mire of bread. I take a bite, it's rank. I peel it open and note the mould. Back in the shop I exchange it for something a little more modern and head to Tyndrum.

A café serving hot food, marred by cardboard plates and failing to give me my change, is the best I can find.

I sleep, undisturbed, in the Tourist Information Centre's car park and awake to a dry morning and a short drive to Tyndrum Lower Railway station. Setting off at 09:10 I recognise the track as one I last took in August 1991 – then a mere twenty-six-year-old on route to bag the Munros of Beinn Dubhchraig and Ben Oss. I'd got the train up from Glasgow for the day and walked in sodden rain that quickly penetrated a lightweight coat and suede gloves. I remember being scared, my first solo trip into the mountains with cloud so low that I was forever checking my map and compass.

Today the cloud is higher, the two Munros are shrouded but the timings from twenty-five years ago are still scribbled on my map. I think back to that time, half a lifetime ago, and gently smile at my spirit. With asthma making it against the odds, I was going to do the Munros.

The track passes through pine woods, ascending and (disappointingly) descending to the track that passes Cononish Farm with its lime green corrugated barns. Shortly after I break onto the open hillside of Beinn Chuirn. I'm very tired, I need a day off but I press on with aching legs and an all-in disposition. As I ascend, the summit becomes shrouded by cloud and I meet the hood-drumming wind that rattles everything that can be rattled. I walk away from a sharp edge and press on and reach the summit. Ducking down for some shelter, I graze on food, swig water, draw in every strap and drawstring and brace myself for the descent.

I'm caught by the rain but, for the first time this trip, my feet stay dry. Back at the track I'm glad of its easier pace and glad to be able to reach the pine wood.

I visit the café, once the Little Chef, that I dried myself off in some quarter of a century ago. I recall spending ages hunched over a weak stream of hot air in an attempt to get myself dry as I waited for the train back to Glasgow. Thanks to Dyson the standard of hand dryers has improved.

The café has free wi-fi and I check in emails. There's one from eBay asking 'How do you like the 12v 24v 2 Way Car Cigarette Lighter Multi-Socket Twin Ports Adaptor?' Given it's now burnout and in the bin I delete the email.

In desperate need of a rest I take, what turns out to be, the fine, sunny Thursday off. I read, write and listen to the radio but am generally bored and a little morose. I head to the Bridge Of Orchy Hotel for lunch and am impressed by a series of arrows directing me to its facilities. Only when I read 'Polling Place' do I realise that I'm heading to vote in the Scottish elections.

Once fed I'm off again and tuck the camper van into a pull in on the B8074, warily eyeing what looks to be an abandoned caravan. Sleeping well I'm off at 08:10 for the rare treat of two Corbetts in a day – Beinn Udlaidh and Beinn Bhreac-liath. However, since my map was printed in 1989 somebody has stuck up a forest. Not fancying picking my way through, I change plans to do Beinn Bhreac-liath first; the theory being when I descend I'll be able to see a route ahead.

I'm soon down to my base layer as the sun warms the day. It's a three-hour hard pull onto its long north ridge where I get an unwanted attack of hay fever. At the 2000ft level the air cools and I don an extra layer before the half-hour gentle incline of the ridge walk of small bogs and rocky outcrops. After three and a half hours from the start, I sit at the summit viewing the drop and rise to Beinn Udlaidh. A half-hearted path takes me via a handy gate in a deer fence. I see two other walkers as I ascend to the multi-summited top. I pick the quartz backbone of the mountain to descend and, via the burn, find the access point into the forest and the boggy trail back to the camper van. In all it's been a seven-and-a-quarter hour day of clear views and the background noise of tumbling water.

With a trip via Crianlarich to top up with supplies I get chatting to the shop assistant about yesterday's elections and the general state of the economy and the forthcoming in/out EU referendum.

"What we up here are worried about," she says, "if Scotland votes one way and the rest of the UK the other. We'll have a crisis."

"Yes, and of course England could vote one way and the rest of the UK the other," I reply. The point is lost on her. She's in favour of staying in, saying the local hotels could not run without EU migrants. I'm in favour of staying in too.

"And," she goes on, "the house prices down south are so high."

"Yes," I reply, "a modest terraced house in Brighton now costs four hundred and fifty thousand. Youngsters don't have a hope of getting on to the property ladder."

"Aye," she says, "it's not fair on us up here. We can't afford to sell up and move south."

I give up and take the A85 for a few miles and park up for the night near Auchessan. It's a dry night and the day dawns with high cloud for a 08:50 start. I follow the farm tracks then the new hydro scheme tracks until I'm deposited on open hillside. My right hip starts to nag me so I stop for Ibuprofen and Deep Heat.

Feeling slightly mended I press on: the ground is relatively dry underfoot and I skirt round a succession of boggy terraces. To the north-east are the Munros of Meall Glas and Sgiath Chuil. I avoid accidentally setting my compass for their highlighted points on my map.

I'm slow but not as tired as a few days back, and haul myself to the summit of Beinn nan Imirean in three and a half hours. Descending on a reverse bearing, I catch sight of the hydro road. Abandoning any assistance from my compass I cross the open ground until I'm faced with a six-foot deer fence. Alas it's not the same hydro road I ascended on but does appear to be going in my direction. I make a wobbly climb of the fence and jump down to the building site the other side. A few hundred metres along the track I find it is blocked by another six-foot fence. My climbing skills are required again before the long descent on a modern shingle track.

Near the bottom I find a sign stating, 'You Are Now Leaving the Restricted Work Zone.' Funny as I don't recall entering it. A few hundred metres later and I'm penned in again, another six-foot fence to scale, a river to cross and I'm back on the track I ascended in the morning. Feeling a bit frazzled I get back to the camper van mid-afternoon.

I drive in to Killin for some supplies then follow the Loch Lochay road in the hope to use the Hydro Board mountain road to park up for an ascent of Meall nan Subh. A long and twisty drive terminates with a 'Private Road' sign stating from here on belongs to Kenknock Farm. My 1989 map shows the public road extends further but, to be sure of myself, I set my GPS to adjudicate. It takes ages to settle then comes up with a series of questions involving (i) have I moved hundreds of miles since I last used it and (ii) am I indoors. I take a closer look and note the battery level has dropped back. I change the two AAA cells for the spares I've been diligently carrying in my pack for the last couple of years. These prove to have even less power than the ones I'm replacing. Not wishing to chance it and press on, I return to Killin for new batteries.

I ask at the Co-op's counter, "Can I have a pack of Duracell AAA batteries please?"

"I expect we've run out," replies the assistant.

I point to the shelf behind her and the overwhelming evidence to the contrary that they have not run out. I've noticed this tendency in other shops and especially when asking a hotel if they have a room available. Claims they are full, but they'll just check, result in rooms being available.

I park up for the night on the Bridge of Balgie road and, on waking, drive a mile to the start of the ascent of Meall nam Maigheach. I frustrate myself by losing a number of items around the van so it's 09:30 before I get going. Starting from an elevated point, the cloud is high and the wind is warm, gentle gusts.

I have to rest often, far too often. My body isn't really working for me. The guidebook suggests this Corbett as part of two in a day; I know I'll have to split it. I lay back in the grass and view snow on a nearby mountain that has retreated into the shape of a sea lion. The sun punches its way through then retreats as a warm wind brushes the grass and soothes my face.

I get to a summit in an hour and twenty minutes, it's not the correct one so I arrive for real twenty minutes later. The wind is stronger, I find a foxhole and lean back, rest and enjoy the view.

The descent is straightforward and, with the blinds up in the camper van, I wash and shave. I hear some engine revving outside and am disconcerted as I hear somebody walk around the van. There's a thump from the front so I drop the rear blind to find a car stopped on the single-track road. I then receive a notable level of abuse for having parked in a Passing Place causing this chap to have to reverse. Of course I am in the wrong but the guy (who I guess is around sixty and due a heart attack) has me labelled as having done it deliberately whereas I had just made a mistake and missed the sign. Which to be fair, at some six foot high, which he takes pains to point out is difficult to miss.

"Did you not see me reversing?"

"I had the blinds up," I reply. I think my English accent doesn't help and, given his level of anger, my mind isn't racing towards an apology. When I sense he has finished I say, in a very bemused tone, "Well I hope you have a nice rest of your day."

"I won't be having a nice day thanks to you, pal."

I always know that the use of the word 'pal' is anything but an invitation to friendship. Just like when somebody calls out "Guys, guys" you know they are not really engaged with the rest of the group's way of doing things.

He takes a step towards me then thinks better of it and yells, "Fuck off." I suggest he needs therapy and he returns the suggestion while pointing a finger and reasoning that only a therapist could get me to see the wrong of parking in a Passing Place. I don't quite know whose side his wife is on as she sits impassively throughout the entire proceedings.

He sets off and I see a note on the windscreen (the cause of the thump which caused me to lower the rear blind). His writing is not that good and I can't make out every word but I'm sure two of them are 'cretin' and 'reject'. I turn it over and read his wife's shopping list – I prefer this side.

Moving on, I spend an hour or so mulling it in my mind. I wish I'd been quicker and said, being dyslexic, I'd misread it as 'Parking Place' or claimed to have some form of prostate problem, coupled with dyslexia, and had misread 'Passing Place'.

I enjoy the evening sun, sleep well and start at 09:30 for what I consider to be the easy Beinn nan Oighreag.

After hauling myself up a distant ridge spur of Meall nan Tarmachan I realise I've made a mistake. Below is a drop to a peat plain and then a steep ascent to the Corbett's ridge. I press on, the sky is blue and I'm just wearing a base layer. My right hip decides it's really time to let me know that it's not happy. Every time I put pressure on it a sharp pain spreads around the top of my leg.

I follow the path of a stream. Heavy snow still fills a gulley and a lone patch, on higher ground, looks like a West Country hill figure – yet its shape is more of a flattened hippopotamus than a horse (or some unusual looking fertility symbol).

I make it to a top in just over three hours then realise I'm a bit far south and the real top, of a very similar height, lays half a kilometre to the north-east. I sunbathe awhile, take Ibuprofen and Deep Heat my hip. At the real summit I sunbathe some more before the hobble back on a reverse bearing. I find the re-ascent painful and wonder if I'd have been better doing the walk, and avoiding the descent and re-ascent, from the lower starting point of Glen Lyon.

In a final dip I look up and spy the road via the welcome top of a six foot high 'Passing Place' sign (I've gotten used to spotting them).

I drive round to the Loch Lyon dam, take the Hydro Board road (that I'd failed to get on the other day) from the north side and park on the highpoint where the mountainous views, and tumbling streams, chill me into an early sleep.

The morning of the 10th has Radio Four claiming that the place to be is Scotland as the weather is bright and sunny. I set off at 09:30 for the relatively straightforward Meall nan Subh. Though my body feels a wreck and I find the climb a drag.

There are many humps to navigate over and the footing is often squelchy. A couple of false summits lead me onto a plateau before a final pull to the top. The wind is too blustery to stay for long so I drop down to rest and savour the view of distant hills splattered with snow. The wind whistles through the grass and distant mountains shimmer in the haze.

My right hip gives a twinge as I set off down. With my head full of thoughts I step onto squelchy ground and am dumped onto my rear. I feel the water penetrate my trousers and lower back before gravity has me doing a bizarre twist whereupon I come to a halt, filthy and soggy.

I get back to the camper van just before noon, drive back to the Loch Lyon dam, park up by the side of the road and hang my sodden kit out to dry.

There's activity at the dam, water is being loosed off in a fountain-like spray. A lorry is being loaded and when it sets off it pulls up alongside me and the driver hops out.

"Sorry, am I blocking your way?" I ask while checking for a 'Passing Place' sign.

"No, no I was wondering if you were taking photographs."

"No," I reply in case the Scottish Hydro take a dim view of this.

"Well if you are the best place is from the other side. You can park up and look right long the dam."

I thank him.

"That's okay," he replies, "I'd not want you to miss the best view."

May 11th dawns as another fine day, and I feel more positive for a crack at the two Corbetts of Meall Buidhe and Sron a' Choire Chnapanaich. I start at 07:35 and take the track, past the dam, to the north of Loch Lyon. In just under a mile I reach a dry stone wall heading steeply north. To its left is a wooden post and wire fence. I walk in the metre gap between the two. It's tough going with frequent stops and no opportunity to zig-zag as I'm rather hemmed in. With the ground either side looking rather rough, I figure I'm best off where I am.

The gradient eases at around 2000ft. I spy deer on the high

ground who, upon getting a whiff of me, head off. I haul myself up into a bealach where the remains of an iron fence leads me to a subsidiary top of Meall Buidhe. The wind gusts but the sun is warm as I skirt a snow field and make my way over to the real summit. It's 10:55 and too windy to rest so I drop down and shelter. Another two walkers appear and we exchange distant waves.

View from Sron a' Choire Chnapanaich

I head back to the bealach, take a bearing to Sron a' Choire Chnapanaich and have a distant standoff with a fox. Its coat is a beautiful mottled effect of fox, straw and pepper. I try to pacify it but it elects to bound off to higher ground while making the odd stop to look back and check my progress.

I have to descend, along a tumbling stream, before navigating some corrugated ridges in the gulley. The final climb is a drag, my energy is dropping. I slow my pace, am pleased my hip is behaving, before making the tinder-dry and breezy summit. I rest here and listen to the wind hiss through the grass. The distant mountains all bask in the sun. The descent is straightforward until I hit the road. I feel tired and haul myself back to the camper van mid-afternoon.

After washing and packing up I drive down Glen Lyon and with windows down, music playing, the glen glistening, anything feels possible.

I stop for a few supplies at the post office shop in Bridge of Balgie before the short hop to Innerwick. A picnic area, with ensuite loos, has me stopping for the night.

With another fine day I'm walking at 08:30 via the long rough, hot track to the foot of Cam Chreag. A sharp pull up, crossing some ice-crunching snow, has me on what feels like a Lakeland ridge. The mountains to the west are in all their splendour offering peace and temptation. To the north is the rocky bump of a summit of Cam Chreag. I stagger up its final slopes before laying on the grass and surveying the view.

The return makes for a gentle decline with the blue sky, and warming air, leaving me feeling sticky, having completed this mountain in a shade under five hours.

Friday May 13th dawns with a chill in the air and grey sky. I get going at 08:10 to bag the Graham of Meall a' Mhuic and the Corbett Beinn Dearg. Having diligently copied out the route, around the lower tracks, described in the Grahams guidebook I get it wrong and find myself on the first section of Beinn Dearg. I have three choices, backtrack, press on and do the Corbett first or attempt to correct the error by crossing rough ground.

I elect to backtrack. If I go on for the Corbett I know I'd then abandon the Graham and experience tells me trying to track hop across rough ground is a tiresome affair.

The correct track heads north up Meall a' Mhuic, peters out and deposits me, in chilling breeze, to do the rest unguided. With my hands frozen I reach the clouded summit.

I head north-east to the upper reaches of the track I'd earlier turned back from, set my compass and ascend over rough, heather-clad ground. Picking up the iron uprights of an ancient fence and, with my altimeter counting me down, I reach the summit cairns of Beinn Dearg at 12:30.

I have a choice of descent: either a steep south-west or north-west back to the track. It's one side of a triangle versus two. My knees win the vote and I take the longer route.

About an hour into the return the track irritatingly splits in two. As this is not shown on the map and given they are on such a similar compass bearing, I'm a little stuck. I bargain on the higher one and peer down at its parallel neighbour while the gap between, which would form my way of correcting a mistake, steepens beyond the point of wanting to take it.

I note the lower track is newer whereas the one I'm on looks older and therefore the likely candidate for the one on the map. This proves to be correct, returning to my camper van at 14:25 having defeated Friday the 13th.

The guidebook recommended route for Meall Tairneachan and Farragon Hill is a south-easterly approach. Looking at my recently-purchased Ordnance Survey Sheet 52 the forest to the south of Tummel Bridge has some tracks to tempt an approach from the west. It's one of those very rare areas that overlaps three OS maps and, as one would expect, the tracks through the forest are different on each. Oddly the 1988 version shows more tracks than the 1989 version whereas my 2012 sheet has the most.

So I drive around, confirm the presence of the tracks, sleep over and start out at 08:05 to a weather report that parts of Scotland had dropped to minus five overnight.

The track is steep yet even and I make good time. Leaving the forest in just over an hour I continue uphill. The trig point adorning Meall Tairneachan is a short climb off the icy wind-blasted track. After an hour and a half from the start I pat its summit and take a bearing to check I have Farragon Hill in sight.

I look down on the diminutive Loch Farleyer with its clumps of Scots Pine tugging at its shores. Arable fields are intermixed with areas of brown peat – the runoff from heather-clad mountains which rises to form a snow touched skyline.

The track now twists and drops to opencast mine workings. I see a white pickup that had passed me while I breakfasted. Nobody is around but a strange humming sound penetrates the air and manmade pools with lifebelts dot the ruptured landscape.

After about two miles of descent the, now ropey, track ends and I continue across bog before the final climb up Farragon Hill. The fact it's my fiftieth Corbett escapes me but I'm pleased to have reached it bang on noon. I look back to Meall Tairneachan and the towering form of Schiehallion beyond.

I return via the same way. The open country back to the track is tiresome and I find the ascents wearisome. I spy the white pickup leave then return to the mine workings. At the highpoint I find a BT van and the driver explains that the phone line, to the mine, is faulty. With 6km of buried copper cable, just to reach the road, the job is a tough one. I ask what type of mine it is and he explains it is barite (a barium-based mineral).

"If they strike copper I guess they'll not be able to phone anybody to celebrate," I quip. He gives me a blank look, the joke is lost on him.

I drive on to the B847 which I recall a lengthy walk along while crossing Scotland in 2014. Parking up I'm surprised by a 4G phone signal, the first of this trip.

I start walking at 08:35 on the 15th and have my first battle of the day with a clasped chain holding a six-foot gate shut. The owner has been a bit mean with the number of links requiring it to be tight shut. This is all very well on the roadside but when trying to close it behind me I have a real effort to keep the gate snugly closed and thread the chain and link it from the other side.

That challenge complete, I turn to the hillside for the initial steep ascent followed by a gentler section then a final steep climb through a coire. The cloud is high, the views are distant as I reach the trig point, and nearby massive honeycomb cairn, of Beinn a' Chuallaich.

I pose for a 'selfie', which I post on Facebook, enjoy the views and descend back to the camper van.

I take the scenic route over to the A9 and am surprised that my Sat Nav has heard of my destination, the tiny hamlet of Dalnaspidal. After days of moving around on minor roads the speed of the A9 and volume of the traffic, unnerve me. I keep an eye on things and, having noted the turn-off for Dalnaspidal is just after a stretch of dual carriageway, am glad when the turning appears. With very little room to get my speed down, many a motorist behind not expecting a manoeuvre and me not knowing whether to expect a layby or a road, I'm glad to pull up on a large tarmacked area some thirty foot below the level of the A9.

I'm parked next to some railway cottages and I see a Virgin train heading for Inverness. Close examination shows two redundant platforms. A bit of Wikipedia on my mobile phone informs me that it had a station until 1965.

I sleep rather uncomfortably, the traffic noise is unnerving but I manage to rest up and get walking at 08:15. Noting a typical Cameron McNeish (the author of the guidebook) error of quoting a seven-digit grid reference. By definition a grid reference, having a northing and easting, must be an even number of digits.

Grumbling about the man I set off with a view to taking in The Sow of Atholl and Meall na Leitreach. Crossing the railway, following a track over a bridge I bear off for The Sow. I rest in a grouse-shooting bunker (well made of dry stone) and contemplate my weary body. Everything aches and it screams at me in weakness. I decide to do just the one Corbett, with a round trip of three and a quarter hours.

I snooze during the afternoon which means my night's sleep is shorter. Therefore I'm up and walking at 06:50 on the 17th, accompanied by the Caledonian Sleeper passing through Dalnaspidal.

Passing through the same drained land, with its leats, pools and impressive drainage valves, as yesterday I break off south-east, disturbing a few sheep and geese. I pick up a quad bike track which guides me to the high ground. The surrounding hills hover in the lifting morning mist. I find it tough going, each step tires my legs and, as a quad bike passes me, I wonder if there is room for a passenger.

I haul myself onto the ridge then follow the track south-west, across the plateau-like top, until I reach the summit proper, in cool breeze, at 08:40 before a business-like descent.

A short trip up to Newtonmore has me helping out at Ali and Sue's hostel as TGO Challenge folk pass through on the cross-Scotland walk. It's good to catch up with people and help a few out. The TGO Challenge had appeared in the US press which caused a number of our North American cousins to apply and take part this year. Sadly, many have underestimated and dropped out. Some were disappointed to find out everything marked 'Lodge' is not a place to stay while another, on enquiring if she'd get her boots wet crossing rivers, was told, 'Not if you hang them around your neck.'

On the evening of the 18th I say goodbye to Ali and co, stop for a monster meal in a local curry house before driving up to Glenmore Lodge (above Aviemore) to rest up for the night.

The weather on the 19th starts dry with the threat of rain. I get going at 07:20 for a long walk in to bag Creag Mhor. A well-made forest gets my body off to a good start though my mind (having battled all night with cheese-fuelled dreams) is still far from awake.

The forest gives me a bad bout of hay fever and I'm relieved when I emerge onto open ground. After a series of landmarks (bridges, gullies and cloud-clagged high ground) I'm poised, at some three and a half hours into the walk, for the final climb.

Having been at over 2000 feet for most of the day, it's only another half an hour, in peppering rain, to the rocky summit, of Creag Mhor. As I return I meet ten separate TGO challengers heading south. Conversations are brief – the rain and hay fever (causing a blocked nose and eyes that prick and stream) have me feeling miserable.

Back in the camper van I can barely look at my eyes in the mirror. A couple of puffy, weeping masses peer back. I'm taken back to my summers as a child where, throughout the entire spring and summer seasons, I'd wake each morning with my eyes glued shut. Walking blind to the bathroom I'd feel for the sink, reach for the cotton wool and slowly bathe them open. They'd then prick and weep for the rest of the day. This, asthma and a school where bullying was rife made for a miserable time. One of the reasons I hill walk is to deal with the emotional side of the physical disabilities of asthma – failure at school sports was humiliating and being able to achieve a sport, on my own terms, lifts me. An asthma attack would last four to five days, confining me to bed with what I can only describe as a bag of cement on my chest, my nose taped up and a straw to breathe through my mouth with.

The bullying left me with a distrust of people and hill walking allows me to escape. The asthma makes the ascents tough but all the more rewarding. Hay fever, another of my childhood demons, is an unwelcome addition to the mix. I'm wishing to escape, not be reminded.

I manage to drive into Aviemore and stop at Tesco for some strong relief tablets. There are two options: two packs for £6 or £4.50 a packet. At the till things have gotten worse and I have to keep my head bowed, away from any light. I just make out that they go through the till without the discount. I query it, get it resolved and dwell on whatever my eyes can and cannot do, they still have an eye for a bargain.

Drugged up, I manage to drive round to Braemar, stopping frequently to clear my nose and dab my eyes dry.

Friday the 20th I drive round to the Linn of Dee, pay the £2 to park and set off, on the track to White Bridge for the Corbett of Sgor Mor. This brings back memories of tiresome walks out on the TGO Challenge and long days Munro bagging.

I bump into Val Hadden, on the TGO Challenge. Well into her seventies she's as fit as a fiddle and making good pace for Braemar. We first met on the TGO Challenge in 2004 when she was walking with her friend, Mary Brook. Tragically, as previously mentioned, Mary was killed in a cycling accident some years ago. We both attended her funeral, it's good to catch up again.

I'm wearing sunglasses and, given the fairly dull day, am feeling a bit conspicuous. Needs must and, knowing how disconcerting it can be to talk to somebody whose eyes are covered, I apologise that I can't take them off.

I pass White Bridge and turn onto the rough pass that follows the wide waters of the Chest of Dee. I sit and admire a wide three-tier waterfall and examine the path that overhangs a long drop into the waters below.

Leaving the path I head north over tough, dry heather interspersed by bog. The ground is steep so the view of the summit is only revealed when I make the final pull up, some three and a half hours into my walk, over the windswept rocky lumps that form the highest point. A manmade windbreak is the only concession to humanity. I head south-east and pick up some rain before the path and track. In a warming wind I get back to the Linn of Dee.

A quiet night in the car park is followed by a drive down to the Linn of Quoich and a 08:25 start for the Corbett of Carn Na Drochaide. I'm quickly thwarted by the bridge over the Quoich Water having been swept away. I take the track to a bridge further north to find it has been closed, boarded up and signs saying 'No Unauthorised Access'. It's tempting to climb over it and chance my luck with an angry estate worker. However, knowing my luck the imaginary chap in question will still be getting over a camper van parked in a 'Passing Place'.

I battle on up the track with a plan to cross the Quoich Water by a bridge some four miles to the north-west. About a mile and a half into this detour I'm thwarted for a third time as, with the river changing course, the track has been completely swept away with the river now lapping a sheer escarpment.

It has been steadily raining and realising that all possibilities have been exhausted, I look west to the Graham of Creag Bhalg. It's a very steep climb from the river, through heather and saturated moss. The occasional tree makes for a foothold. Other fallen trees are so rotten that my foot crunches through their remains.

The heather, about shin height, tugs and soaks my boots and legs. I battle this, thumping my trekking poles in hard and pressing down and using them as handholds. After one mile, and seventy-five minutes of this, the incline eases, the rain doesn't, the heather fades and I'm on easier ground. It's 12:05 and a number of cairns and a windbreak adorn the top. The dullness of the day is not helped by my, hay fever deterring, sunglasses.

Heading west, I pick up a track that drops me to Mar Lodge and a road walk back to the camper van.

I spend an afternoon in Braemar catching up with TGO Challenge friends, swapping stories and making some new friends. I take my laptop to a café to write this up. Alistair Pooler sits opposite at the same moment that Facebook tells me it was his wife's birthday yesterday. I interrogate him as to whether he'd performed his husbandly duties! He had.

Another challenger looks across to me, looks at the size of laptop and my suntan. "You've not carried that thing all the way with you have you?" he asks.

The evening gets me an invite to Gordon's Tearooms where a table, for some sixteen of us, has been arranged by Val Hadden. It's a great evening, with stories abound.

I get going at 07:55 on Sunday the 22nd for the drive round to Tarfside to claim Mount Battock. My walking shoes are still sodden from yesterday (in fact they were banished from the van overnight due to their unpleasant odour) so I upturn them on the dashboard and position them for the full flow of hot air from the windscreen vents. I lower the door windows to cope with the heat.

With my Sat Nav taking me on every shortcut known to the A93 I arrive some two hours later at Millden Lodge, slip on my rather toasty walking shoes and set off in the rain. I spend the next five minutes wandering around somebody's front garden. Realising my error, I return to the road and pick up the correct track that leads me into the hills. It soon becomes clear that a great number of new tracks have been cut since my map last saw a printing press. Using my GPS I cross open ground (whereupon my toasty walking shoes return to a sodden mass) and reroute to the tracks via Hill of Saughs.

At just before noon a massive roll of thunder echoes around the hills. It's of such a magnitude that if The Royal Tank Regiment appeared over the hills one could be excused the mistake. I look back to the source of the noise and watch three separate downpours (to the south-west, south and south-east) descend from the sky like strands of dark cotton against a grey backdrop.

I rest awhile, eat and, having ended up on tracks devoid of streams, ration my water. As the storms blow closer I batten down my pack, pull up my hood and press on over the Hill of Saughs.

The track ends and I'm on open boggy ground. I duck my head so I can watch every step. Next time I look up I see nothing. Literally nothing. The cloud has dropped and the visibility is no more than a few yards. At 12:45 I clamber over a ladder stile, touch the trig point and enjoy a brief glimpse of a view.

The sun comes out on the descent, I dry off a little and return to the camper van for a trip round to Tarfside – another TGO Challenge gathering place. After catching up with Challenge friends I drive on to the Park Hotel, Montrose to help out on 'Challenge Control' for four days.

Ali Ogden trains me in answering the phone, as people check in on route, and how to enter this in the paper ledger. I have great fun seeing, and being part of, the Challenge from the organisational point of view. Taking phone calls reporting progress, entering the data into the circa 1981 paper system, collating who has forgotten to phone in and sending texts and making calls until they are located. I look at it from an IT point of view – could this be computerised? In theory yes, but as the system is 'mission critical' it'd need a paper-based backup system. So, in truth, for two weeks a year there isn't much point.

I'm glad to be out of the hills for a few days. My hay fever has been awful this year and, even in a hotel conference room, I have to frequently blow my nose and dab my eyes.

Thursday the 26th is the big day for finishers. The hotel staff give it an hour before they produce air fresheners to combat the arriving hordes of unwashed walkers. I get to shake people by the hand, congratulate them, mark them as completed and ask them to sign out. They then are presented with a new T-shirt (a must), badge and certificate. At times the queue of people waiting to sign out snakes out the door into the hotel corridor.

The comradeship and warmth are unprecedented amongst the modern world in which we now live. People spot one another they saw days, or even a week, ago and fill each other in on their progress since. And to add to the festivities Jenny Wheeler has arranged her wedding, in the hotel, for early evening.

Around lunchtime, with my eyes still streaming from hay fever, I pop out to my camper van to take a Piriton and, at the entrance to the hotel, bump into Jenny. It's the first time I've seen her since we said goodbye on this very spot at the end of the 2009 TGO Challenge. Then, after spending a number of days enjoying one another's company, we planned to meet up in the August. She later cancelled, explaining she was now seeing a chap from her walking club.

"Hello, Steve," she says.

"Oh hi," I reply, feeling slightly awkward.

"I'm getting married this evening," she says.

"Yes, I know. Here in the hotel," I reply. "It's been the talk of the Challenge. Who is the lucky chap?"

"Ian, I met him through my walking club. We've been together for seven years."

"Ah great," I reply.

"Is that your camper van over there?" she asks.

"Yes, I finally bought one."

"That's ours," she replies, pointing to the one parked opposite.

As the afternoon passes things quiet down on the Control Desk. I decide to give the wedding a miss, take my leave and drive to the Brig o' Turk to park overnight before tackling the two Corbetts to its north.

My overnight parking space is midge infested and, however careful I am, hundreds of the little blighters join me for an evening of partying.

I get walking at 08:15, the cloud is low and I first head towards the dam on the Glen Finglas Reservoir. This is the first navigational error of the day, I should have taken the higher track. Realising my mistake, and not wishing to backtrack, I climb the steep wooded slope and pop out on the metalled track.

It's about a kilometre before I branch east, taking another track running parallel, across the glen, to another being bulldozed out of the hillside. I find the going tough so strip back to shirt sleeves whereupon it decides to drizzle so I have to don waterproofs for the long pull, across rough, trackless ground, towards Ben Ledi. My hay fever returns and with my sunglasses and the cloud down, I struggle to see very far ahead. So intent on map and compass I surprise myself with the summit ridge at three hours into the walk. Not sure whether the top is left or right, I'm checking my GPS when another walker has me jumping out of my skin. With the direction sorted I soon make the trig point summit.

With the cloud down I sense it's going to be a tricky navigational exercise over to Benvane. This is not helped by mistakenly following the wrong path – only when the cloud lifts for a few seconds do I see I'm not on the ridge path but instead following a path leading from the low easterly ground. I have to work my way around the steep slopes, and re-ascend, to correct the mistake.

The cloud is still low and my eyes stream behind my sunglasses. I'm now faced with a winding ridge which, given the poor visibility, has me stopping every few minutes to check the GPS and reset my compass. I have to take my sunglasses off to do close map and compass work which, in turn, causes my eyes to sting and prick even more. In my pre-GPS Munro bagging days this would have been an abandonment.

Some reassuring clunks from workmen, building the track, tell me I'm passing the right area. Masses of crane fly dot the ground and circle around. I make the summit of Benvane in a shade under four hours from Ben Ledi. At just over three miles this is painfully slow. A cairn of rocks is littered with crane fly and I appear to have interrupted some form of tipulidae gangbang. A few break off and make some daring attempts to land on my face.

The return is by the long south ridge of Benvane. I reach the camper van at 17:20. I'm fed up and don't fancy a similar day tomorrow. So I set my Sat Nav for home and put in four hours, interrupted only by a series of navigational errors in road works.

Classification	My Total	Total
Welsh Nuttalls	189	189 (i)
English Nuttalls	254	254
Corbetts (Scotland)	59	222 (ii)
Grahams (Scotland)	14	219 (ii)
Unique Donalds (Scotland)	2	58
Munros (Scotland)	282	282
Ireland	0	212
Totals (05/07/2016):	800	1436

(i) Moelwyn Mawr North Ridge Top was demoted on 05/08/2015

(ii) The Graham of Cnoc Coinnich was promoted on 05/07/2016 to Corbett status.

It's the first day back at work after Christmas and I know I've got to do it. My ambition to climb all the mountains of the British Isles is burning too great, work is getting more stressful and, at the age of fifty-one, my technical edge is starting to slip. Mistakes are creeping into my work, I'm managing to catch them and sort them myself but my own standards are dropping.

I ask to go for a coffee with one of the firm's directors. The words come out like I'm asking a girl for a date – I hear myself saying them but it isn't quite me.

"I've decided to retire."

Terry buries his head in his hands and says, "Oh no."

"But I'm giving you three months' notice."

We chat, he's sixty-five and wants out too. He doesn't try and talk me out of it. He can see I'm serious.

Come early April the two directors announce, entirely coincidental to my departure, that they've sold the company. I meet the new owners – corporate types, not like the family feel of the firm I've enjoyed for the last twelve years. My decision was the right one. I wouldn't have been happy.

April the 7th is my leaving do, a meal out at a Chinese restaurant. A card is presented to me. Though Rich's, the salesman, comment leaves me bemused – 'Steve you are a bit odd but I've enjoyed working with you.' Okay I don't have a TV, freezer, dishwasher or a modern car, never raised a family, live alone and am retiring at the age of fifty-one to go and climb all the 2000ft mountains of the British Isles. What's odd about that?

April the 8th I drive to Scotland and park up in brilliant sunshine in the Southern Uplands.

I wake around 06:30 on April the 9th and, being retired, it takes me until 09:00 to emerge from the camper van. Ten minutes later I'm following the well-made path which rises to the north-east of the Tail Burn waterfalls. Though my pace is slow and I abandon my original plan of combining two walks into one.

As I rise on the path my eyes start to prick and my nose starts to run – hay fever caused by heather pollen. Given I felt so miserable with it last year, I've been eating the odd spoonful of Scottish heather honey to try and build up some resistance. However, it's time for more drastic action. I put on my snow goggles and shove the two probes, of a newly purchased red light device, up my nostrils and pray nobody else comes my way. A couple from Selkirk arrive while I'm wiping the last of whatever needs to be wiped off the probes.

My eyes and nose settle straightaway and, relieved, I press on until the path levels off above some waterfalls. I spot a stone wall that is the guide to the summit of the Corbett, White Coomb.

There's a burn to cross which, being out of practice, I manage to submerge my left foot in. Shaking the dripping mass off I press on, slowing now as the slopes are rugged grass tufts. I rest awhile and decide to set my altimeter. In the past it has been in the habit of switching from metres (which match the maps) to feet. With it set to 2017ft I press numerous buttons to try and get it into metres. Only a closer inspection shows I'm actually adjusting the year not the height.

I reach the summit in blustery wind and continue on to the Donalds of Molls Cleuch Dod and Lochcraig Head. Then a navigational error has me striding in the wrong direction until, with the help of my GPS, I navigate back round, then through peat hags, until I meet the path of ascent. The weather clears up and I make it back to the camper van at 16:45.

A couple up from Dumfries are sat in the car next to me. Both middle-aged and smoking. They ask about the falls and I point out an easy walk to a viewing point. They don't look impressed. Only when I suggest they drive 100 metres down the road and look left, to see the falls, do I see any indication of temptation.

Back in the van I attempt to put into practice my regime of better housekeeping. I now have a waste bin and a bedside cabinet in which to store all the things I frequently lose – such as my watch, wallet, keys, compass, pens, notebooks, guidebooks. You name it and I can lose it.

When I say bedside cabinet it's actually something I bought from a charity shop for a tenner. Then realising it was ever so slightly too wide and a bit too tall, I took my electric circular saw to it to, shall we say, trim it down a bit. It now fits a treat but is not worthy of inspection by an expert cabinet maker.

The next change to regime is the elimination of frying eggs. This had three problems: (i) spitting oil around the cooking area (ii) the washing up and (iii) the setting off the smoke alarm. The new regime is pickled eggs, Smash potato and baked beans. To save gas I've worked out I can boil one kettle a day and, with the use of flasks, have porridge for breakfast and lunch, then Smash potato, eggs and beans for supper. Needless to say this new diet does require a degree of solitude and the saving of gas is a moot point.

I wake early on the 10th but again feel lazy so, after a drive around to the foothills of Broad Law, I'm walking at 09:30. Puffing and panting I rest often on my way up the unclassified Cairn Law before heading west towards the Donald of Talla Cleuch Head. I follow a tall deer fence, the wind hums through it like an eerie presence. A distant glen heads south with a wide river, trees and shadows. Only a distant wind farm blots the landscape.

I reach the summit in just over two hours, rest awhile and contemplate the speed at which I live my life. I'm always planning ahead – this morning the remaining mountains have been plotting themselves out in my head. Can I finish in 2018, 2019? And what does it matter, time is now my own? But thirty years of work, following years of education, is going to take some time to detoxify from.

The wind picks up again and sets the fence rattling. I take my leave and head back to Cairn Law then the long pull up Broad Law to its masts, trig point and a very pleasant lady from near Edinburgh. She's walked up the track from Hearthstane and is enthusiastic about the route I've taken. I show her my map, she asks about navigation and I demonstrate how to set the compass and walk on a bearing.

I take the sharp descent and ascent to the Donald of Cramalt Craig. The wind has picked up and the sky now has parallel lines of broken cloud like battleships off to war.

I backtrack, distant hills look like they've been scooped out by a giant ice cream spoon. Light rain patters against my hood as the wind chatters in my ear.

I make it back to the camper van, basking in the early evening light, at 17:15 and set off on a rather twisty two-and-a-half-hour drive to Carsphairn, stopping in Moffat for supplies.

Starting out at 09:15 on the 11th, I take the long track to the foot of the Corbett of Cairnsmore of Carsphairn. I've chosen this one as there are no Donalds in bagging distance. I think I like the purity of one mountain per day.

When the track, as marked on the map, comes to an end I note it continues on the ground, snaking up an outlying ridge. I look at the stone wall ahead and, given the steepness, elect for the longer route up onto the ridge. I drop in to dawdle mode, one foot in front of the other, no big strides. It helps my breathing and, on reaching the ridge, the waiting wind does anything but help my breathing.

I follow a wall and fence for the long, cloud clagged, haul to the summit trig point. An accompanying cairn, wind generator and solar panels, anchored down by 2.3 tonnes of concrete (as advertised) grace the summit. Backtracking, I drop, glad to be out of the wind, to the original track.

I get thinking about my working life. I can't quite believe it's done and dusted and I'll never have to work again. My mind flits between the highs and lows of my education and career. On the high side I recall my achievements. Before I graduated I did a year's industrial placement, designing and constructing electronic circuits for GEC. Late one morning I listened in to a group of senior engineers struggling with a digital circuit they'd designed and built – it wasn't producing the right outputs. I memorised what they were seeing and, when they were off to lunch, I looked over their circuit diagram. I then designed a circuit to match what they were seeing, noting that the only difference between the two circuits was a connection between two pins on one of the silicon chips. When they were back from lunch, I mentioned that they might like to see if there was a short between these two pins. They checked, there was and the room fell rather silent as I was looked at in awe.

Ever since the age of nineteen when I realised, with a big push, I could get a first in my degree I have set myself very challenging goals. I graduated thirty years ago this summer having done a very ambitious undergraduate final year project. I couldn't do something simple, something just enough to make the grade. Instead I designed and built my own bespoke local area network, and not prepared to stop at that I used fibre optics between each access point. And, like there was some angry god looking over my shoulder, I used different types of fibre between each which entailed designing different transmitter and receiver circuitry for each connection. Only when I demonstrated it as a fully working sub-network of the college's own network, and my tutor's jaw actually dropped, did it dawn on me that perhaps I had gone too far.

I always had to be ahead, coursework always in first. Later always hitting deadlines at work. I've pushed myself beyond my limits in education, work, leisure and volunteering.

Looking back I realise coming from a family with a strong work ethic, where even stopping for breath was regarded as being lazy, had rubbed off. I was always trying to prove I was not lazy by being the hardest working and to be seen as the best at whatever I did.

On graduating I set myself a goal of being the technical architect on major public sector IT projects. I got there at twenty-four. First I joined a company where a flaky and slow crime recording system had been developed for Cleveland Constabulary. I took it on myself to fix it, working long hours fixing bugs and improving the performance. I got there. What I didn't really take on board was that I was working above my grade and age, instead my ego liked the adulation. I didn't push on, move on.

There was no mentoring, other than one manager who thought I should, with my first class degree, join the Civil Service. With no hope of programming in that environment it wasn't for me. It didn't strike me then, as it does now with the benefit of thirty more years of life experience, that technical people are not properly rated. If you are good you have to leave what you are good at to get paid properly.

I moved on to developing 999-call-taking systems for various police forces, staying six years in the company. My high moment was with Strathclyde Police – getting a 121 user system to perform on a computer with about 3% of the power of a modern laptop. Having failed a series of performance tests, over a six-month period, we were given one last chance – otherwise the project would be scrapped. I knew I just needed time. Each performance test showed improvement, but not enough. The last set of changes I proposed I felt would get us over the line. However, my company senior bosses decided they wanted to charge the police for them. I knew without them the project would be scrapped, and there was no way the police were going to pay more. It was a crazy position by our management, without the changes they would not get paid a penny of the £1.7m owed for the system. Also, more importantly to me by now, the good people of Strathclyde would not get their new 999-call-taking system. So I started the development in secret and the night before the tests I managed to get the final software changes in and we passed with flying colours. I was hailed a hero, told by the police "You've saved a few careers today, Steve" then dragged to the pub. Two hours later I woke up alone on a pavement in Sauchiehall Street with people stepping over me, tutting. I staggered, very drunk back to the hotel.

My company's senior management never said a word. I didn't get a dressing down for going behind their backs and developing the software, nor did I get a word of praise. My colleagues and immediate superiors were generous in their praise.

I left soon after and got on the property ladder at twenty-seven. When I say property ladder, I went straight in for a four-bed Edwardian semi in Marlborough requiring nearly five years of a gruelling restoration – most of which I did myself. When I look back I feel middle class aspirations ruined my life.

There were many lows to my working life. Not being an alpha male, I found myself plagiarised and bullied by those who were not my betters but felt they were. I've worked for seven firms, three of which I'd now classify my reason for departure as constructive dismissal. Even with the good bosses I felt there was a patronising edge to the praise. That managing people was always going to be held in higher regard and pay.

Also there were colleagues who knew very little about IT but thought they did. They normally got a big voice at the table and I was often left with my head metaphorically in my hands. Some bosses believed in me, but often it took the career progression of the loud-mouths to give me a clear run to do the things that needed to be done. Sometimes I was paid overtime on the quiet – all above board but I was told not to tell others I was getting paid some extra. At the time I felt chuffed, looking back I now realise it was a dysfunctional system where talent wasn't promoted. I wonder about other industries – medicine or law for example. Could you get an upstart trying to blag their way through, trying to appear the expert when they were anything but? The problem with IT is there's no solid professional accreditation. So unqualified people can get in and blag it. Somehow I doubt that's the case with law or medicine.

I press on down the track. Thinking more. My decision to go freelance for eight years mid-career was that I wanted the security of a home from my abilities. I could see staying a permanent employee would likely mean my use to a company would run out before I'd ever have paid the mortgage off. But with being freelance I still worked on police projects, just as hard. I got to design the server transaction management system for the NSPIS (National Strategy for Police Information Systems) 999-call-taking system and rose up to be the architect on the NSPIS HOLMES2 project (for major crime investigations). The latter I was on for six years. The architectural design was non-existent and when I took it on, having done my bit of writing the communications software to link the nation's incident rooms, it was a hotchpot of bits of software that barely talked to one another.

Its performance was awful – a surname search on a fully-loaded database took twenty-six minutes. The requirement was two seconds. I made sure I was well paid, the project was career suicide and, during, the six years I was on it, web technologies had come in and I got left behind.

But with the money I'd learned my lesson. Nobody, customer or supplier, wanted to admit how bad things were. So there was no glory, no awards for fixing it. I held out for the cash, which once invested has now allowed me to retire early. In all I took the technical lead on eight £1m plus public sector IT projects and made a success of them all. I've paid a price mentally, but getting to retire at fifty-one is very welcome. So here I am now having bagged over eight hundred mountains along the way. Perhaps, as Rich the salesman said, I am a bit odd! And now I'm trudging back off this hill, reviewing this whole catalogue of events.

I make it back my camper van at 14:30 and spend part of the afternoon attempting to fix the tap over the sink. It's decided to weep water around the swivel joint which, in turn, is duly making everything it can wet. I fail.

Waking on the 12th I drive round to Forrest Lodge for an attempt on the Corbett of Corserine and its three Donald neighbours. I start at 08:50, an hour and a half later I'm still not out the forest. I check my GPS which decides to paint a black screen and refuse any further communication with the outside world. With the first world problems of a broken sink tap, a broken water softener back at home and now a dead GPS I revert to making some notes in my waterproof notebook with my waterproof pen. The only snag is that I've lost the pen. I'm often quoted as saying, 'It's not the people you've got to watch, it's the inanimate objects' and this is a perfect example.

I'm sure the pen was in my map pocket but alas no luck. Cursing somewhat, I pull my hood tight against the rough wind and pattering rain. As I swing my pack back on I notice the pen on the ground. I don't know who to thank but I say "Thank you" out loud.

I press on and, following some helpful signs about a stile over a deer fence, emerge onto open ground. The signage is welcome but in fact I could have stepped over the deer fence with a simple stride. This is in contrast to the many fences I've come across in the past where I'm climbing over eight foot without a stile in sight.

I recall that my Munros were done with just map and compass. I did have a GPS for a while but it was so inaccurate I barely used it. And it was only during the last one hundred Munros did I carry a mobile phone. Today, with just map and compass, I somehow feel vulnerable, less complete. I reflect I've had the privilege of living through a revolution in technology.

I press on and start to bargain with myself over this entire project. Retirement is supposed to be about fun and enjoyment. I'm having no fun and very little enjoyment. I'm tired, blown about and the rain isn't helping the situation either. As ever I've set myself a tough goal of finishing the Corbetts next year and the Grahams the year after with the plan to pick off the Donalds along the way.

So I re-plan. I'm retired. My body will hopefully last out until I'm sixty so I can slow this down and take the next eight years over it. I can also take tomorrow off, try and get the tap fixed and buy a new GPS. Oh and today I can just do the Corbett and its nearest Donald, leaving the other two, at the far end of a long ridge, for another day. It's a hard bargain I drive, I've got to stop being so driven all of the time.

I follow a faint path onto high ground, pass a cairn then onto the Corbett of Corserine. I then head east, battling wind and rain, until I make the Donald summit of Carlin's Cairn before a return to the Corbett – five hours into a walk that the guidebook advertised, including the two other Donalds, as a five-hour-forty-minute round trip. This is half speed.

I head back down via a fire break in the forest. I then drive to Ayr, in search of a new GPS, park on the windswept promenade and check out caravan and outdoor shops on my phone. My evening meals is a visit to a chip shop. I then locate Blacks and the Mountain Warehouse for early visits in the morning.

I'm rocked to sleep by the wind buffeting the camper van. Knowing I'm just about to spend over £100 on a new GPS I refrain from breakfasting out and instead have porridge in the van.

I walk in to the town centre. Neither Blacks nor the Mountain Warehouse stock GPS receivers. I must have looked incredulous in the Mountain Warehouse for the assistant suggested I could try Argos.

"Where's that?" I ask.

"Here in Ayrton Senna."

"Sorry?"

"In Ayrton Senna."

Hmm, that's what I thought she said. What the late, great Brazilian Formula One star has to do with Argos is anybody's guess. Then it dawns on me. "Oh Ayr town centre," I reply.

"Aye, take a right out the shop then a right again and that's you."

Argos only has ones designed for golf courses so I drive to Glasgow and visit Tiso. They have a good selection and the assistant is very helpful. Sat out in the camper van I try and workout the new purchase. All I want is to be able to switch it on and for it to tell me where I am. But that takes rather a lot of cussing and configuration.

I decide to eat in Tiso's café but soon wish I hadn't. The Scottish food service is up to its usual standards. The veggie option contained slices of beef and they questioned my ordering skills when I queried it.

I drive up the A82 and pull in at Inverarnan with a view to taking in the nearby Corbett tomorrow. However, the volume of Easter traffic sets me ill at ease and instead I head for the tranquillity of the B8074 through Glen Orchy.

Rain sets in as I pull into the newly-laid car park at the foot of the Corbett of Beinn Mhic Mhonaidh. I chat to a lady in a 1972 VW camper van before the weather has us beating a retreat to our separate vehicles.

I read, watch a DVD, sleep then stir to rain drumming on my camper's roof. Emerging at 09:20 the lady in the VW Camper introduces herself as Bridget and walks with me and her husky-looking dog for the first twenty minutes. She's another person that's opted for the simpler life and left the rat race of the south behind her.

I press on alone, along the forestry tracks, for a few minutes before being caught up by John, a sixty-seven-year-old, triple Munroist, retired GP from southern Scotland. He sets a cracking pace and has me through the forest at 10:40. I then confess to my asthma and that if he wants to enjoy his day he'd better go on ahead.

I meet John on his way back down at a point where I still have 150m of vertical ascent, and forty minutes walking, to complete. He says he's just heard, what sounds to me, like 'A couple of plumbers'. I spare my ignorance by thinking this through and, realising he's unlikely to be referring to Eastern Europeans out looking to fix your lavatory, assume he's referring to birds.

"Do you know much about birds?" he asks, confirming my own conclusion.

"Not really," I reply.

I set myself back to dawdle mode, picking my way through the grassy slopes before reaching the summit. There's light snow in the air and I look for somewhere to sit. Having bought new over trousers yesterday, I'm parking myself on grass to avoid scagging the seat on rock. My old ones had gone through on the seat which made sitting on wet grass an unpleasant option.

I take in the views, eat my porridge, send a couple of texts then set off back. Tucked into my driver's window is Bridget's address, phone number and email. I decide not to get in touch. A lovely lady but I felt she wasn't quite right for me.

I drive round to the Cruachan power station and tuck the camper van away in a layby. The leisure battery decides to die a slow death during the night, leaving me without heating. What with the GPS, the tap, and now the leisure battery, the first week of retirement is proving rather expensive.

I set off for the Corbett of Beinn a' Bhuiridh at 08:30 through a narrow, wet steep woodland path of rocks, mud and tree roots. As I approach the skyline the mud thickens until I'm squelching my way through ankle-deep treacle, heading towards a stile over a tall deer fence.

The stile is around five foot high and on a steep left-hand slope. As I mount its first rung the entire structure tilts back towards me. I lean my body in to counterbalance and ascend the slippery steps until I'm perched astride the fence. A massive gust of wind does little to help the situation as I gingerly lower myself down the other side.

I can now see the dam road and the dam above it. I find it tough going on the tarmac, my body aches from yesterday and the distant snow-capped mountains are far from tempting.

At the dam I head north-east across steep, boggy ground. Cloud blows in and out with the icy wind. The summit comes in and out of view and, with the escalating dusting of snow, I'm clearly heading into a storm.

The wind is cruel and blows right through me. At 11:50 I duck down behind some rocks and eat my porridge. Up to now my flask has not been that good but this time, given the contrast with the ambient temperature, the porridge tastes really hot.

I press on into the storm. Snow batters my face and, for once, the snow goggles, to deal with hay fever, do not look out of place.

At times I can barely stand up and my body decides this is the most optimum moment to inform me that it wishes to proceed with a bowel movement. It's never easy at the best of times in the hills but with wind speeds around 60mph and the need to wrestle off the pack, I find somewhere appropriate and do what needs to be done. I am, shall we say, a little frayed around the edges.

Pressing on, I reach the icicle-encrusted summit cairn, four and a half hours into the walk. I hang around for no more than a minute before backtracking. The route isn't obvious so I take a bearing and, after some ten minutes, pick up a line of footprints in the soft snow. I wonder if there's another soul in the vicinity until I press my own sole alongside and compare the result only to confirm that they are my own left from the ascent.

The short grass is ice encrusted, one clump, no more than four inches high, has each blade individually entombed in ice.

I take it steady towards the dam. My knees ache a little and I use my trekking poles to keep myself steady. After negotiating the rickety stile I descend through the steep forest and get back to the camper van, two and a half hours from leaving the summit.

I drive round to Tyndrum and make use of a café and its wi-fi. I manage to order a new leisure battery and a tap for the camper van and have them sent to Ali Ogden in Newtonmore. The first week of retirement has cost me £250 in replacement bits.

I check my maps and elect to head towards Glen Ogle. A National Park car park, with a shut burger van, is my home for the night. My phone has a fair mobile signal and I catch up with friends.

I set off at 09:25 in light drizzle and low cloud, towards the Corbett of Creag Mac Ranaich. I briefly follow a disused railway line before clambering over a low fence and treading carefully across a marsh-ridden plain.

The ascent is a tortuous bog of crags, streams and tussocks. Snow starts to fall vertically (there is no wind) and my eyes focus through it like one of those domed snow shaker scenes that you'd have once found on your granny's mantelpiece.

I press on through the sodden grass with underground streams burbling away. Near the summit I have to map, compass and GPS my way through the crags until I find the summit at 13:00.

I abandon any idea of pressing on towards its neighbour, Meall an t-Seallaidh. In my Munro days, and my youth, I would have done. But the warmth of my camper van beckons and it can wait for another day.

Back at the car park I make full use of the fact the burger van is open and serving vegetarian food.

I sleep well, wake early and, after taking the short drive round to Balquhidder, am setting off, slowly, through the forested Kirkton Glen at 08:35.

My body isn't into it and the pull up the forestry tracks feels like a tortuous slog. However, my spirits are lifted by it being a much nicer day with a warm breeze and many peaks below the cloud line.

After an hour and a half I break out of the forest then head east then south-east for the slopes of the Corbett of Meall an t-Seallaidh. I have to drop and rise a few times as I cross outlying humps. A tiny bit of snow falls but the views from the top, five hours into the walk, are well worth it. A few snow-clad Munros sit in the distance.

I take a direct west route back, barging my way through the forest, via a steep stream bed, to meet a track then, after a bit of backtracking, I follow a shortcut to drop down to the original track up.

Back at the camper van I check maps and, given I'm a bit short of day food, decide to head to Crieff to restock then head to the Loch Turret Reservoir for an attempt tomorrow at the Corbett of Auchnafree Hill.

In the early hours, with a dropping temperature, I realise that I've parked in an exposed spot. I pop out for a call of nature and, with little ambient light, wonder at the sky littered in bright stars.

Back in the van I start the engine to give the dying leisure battery enough juice to run the heating pump, and tuck myself into the quilt and shiver to the bone.

I get going at 08:00 to the myriad of bird sounds coming from the loch. I recognise gulls and ducks but that's about the limit of my ornithological knowledge – I wouldn't recognise a plumber if it was carrying a monkey wrench and a float valve.

The track along the right-hand side of Loch Turret has numerous frozen puddles which glisten in the light permitted by the high cloud. Birds continue to call and sheep scuttle from my path. A line of hills, with their mixed colours of heather and peat, border and guard the south-east shore.

My body is not happy. Yesterday it was bargaining for a day off, today it's demanding one. I'm no longer seeing my body as me. It's a carcass that's getting slower, more painful whereas my mind still holds itself closer to my youth.

The track gently rises and the calls of the birds accompany, until it forks right for a more serious incline. Large black drainage pipes are tunnelled under the track and water splashes out and tumbles down the hillside. Blades of nearby grass have caught and frozen the spray and formed individual fingers like upturned test tubes.

I break off the path at the 700m contour and head, via a burn, for the summit. There are peat fields to cross but the ice gives my feet a firm base on which to tread. I dislodge a couple of hares which bound off, look back then bound off some more.

The summit, which I reach at 11:40, has a cairn but the ground to the right looks higher which I confirm by using my altimeter.

I take in the views and check my phone. Theresa May has called a general election for June (May's election in June) which will probably annihilate the Labour party. With Brexit, the Syrian Crisis and Donald Trump sabre rattling with North Korea, I wonder how much we really need this.

I head back the way I came and, alongside the loch, watch a shepherd whistling and calling his dogs as they round up sheep. He asks me to walk with him so I don't cause sheep, yet to be gathered, to shoot off. I ask about the lambing and he explains the ewes are due in a week and they get them in to give birth. I mention the lambing has already taken place down south and he says "Aye, it's the land of milk and honey down there." The Scots just can't help themselves when they get the chance for a little jibe. I was only being friendly. However, he thanks me for my patience saying that many people wouldn't be so tolerant and hang back for him.

He has four dogs, Jim is sent high up to gather a group of sheep. The shepherd whistles and shouts instructions which echo off the surrounding hills. Jill, a grey with piercing blue eyes, is itching to go and help. But she stays put until some instruction, that doesn't require a second asking, has her shooting up the hill to join her colleague.

After a restful day I get going at 07:50 on the 20th from the minor road, below Kincraigie, and head towards Glen Tilt. The weather is warmer, the cloud higher and my body more fit for purpose.

I'm on a wide grass track with interspersed forestry, fields and pregnant sheep. I look into the glen below for signs of Gilberts Bridge, the only way to cross the river for the long pull up the Corbett of Beinn Mheadhonach. Overshooting, I drop down to the track, double back and find the splendid 18th century bridge.

Across the other side I look for the path that hugs the river bank. It's blocked by a very tall padlocked gate. I then notice, some yards further on, a diamond-shape gate set into the fence. I duck through it and follow the path and track to another bridge crossing an impressive feeder burn into the main river.

Again this is an 18th century bridge which bridges a deep gorge with water pummelling through, thumping like the low drone of a beam engine. The rock has been carved out, leaving menacing deep, dark water where one would certainly not like to find oneself.

I now follow the high path that charts the north-east bank of the burn. It's not a place to have a slip for the slope is an unforgiving slide into the raging waters below.

I make the third, and final, bridge of the day at 10:00. Again it's an attractive stone bridge from the 18th century which leads me on to a two-and-a-half-hour slog up the long slope to the summit. My hay fever starts to play me up and, remembering the misery of last year (where I ended up on steroids), I immediately stop, take a pill, administer eye drops, use the red light therapy on my nostrils and don a hay fever mask. However, the covering over my mouth mists my goggles so I quickly give up on it.

There are three rises on the main ridge, my altimeter tells me the middle one is the higher whereas the cairn size would have you believe the first is the highest.

There is a moderate breeze but there is enough warmth in the air to sit and eat and take in the fine views to the north. The sound of a distant commercial jet is the only interruption to the wind and far off water tumbling through the glens.

I descend into a warming afternoon and, for the first time this year, I'm able to walk without over trousers or jacket.

The route back is much the same as the way up and I get back to the camper van after an eight-hour round trip.

I get a call from Ali Ogden – my leisure battery and new tap have arrived. I drive north and park to take in the Corbett of The Fara tomorrow. The weather forecast is good but it rains throughout the night and I have difficulty motivating myself.

I emerge from the van at 08:55 into a murky-looking day. The rain greets me and in the few minutes it takes me to find the forest track, I'm already dripping and feeling somewhat miserable.

The track is not on my map but, by using compass and GPS, I'm reassured it's taking me in the right direction. It takes just over an hour to reach the top of the forest. There is a tall padlocked metal gate that I need to climb. One foot on it and the entire thing tips towards me. I leap back. On closer inspection I note it's off its hinges so I'm able to prise it open and slip through into the cloud.

The ascent is through sodden, foot-long grass. I keep on a bearing, follow a handy wall and make the summit at 11:30.

I slip off my soaked gloves and have a snack. There's no view and the rain is still peppering me. Putting the gloves back on becomes impossible. The wet lining has rucked and my fingers are too cold to sort it out. I half get them on by fisting by hands and set off back down.

The dam of Loch Ericht comes into view. I recall my long, and tedious, walks towards it in the days of Munro bagging and the TGO Challenge.

Back in the forest I disturb three red deer as they lazily graze in the short strip of open land either side the track. They take a look at me, and possibly have a sniff or two, and lollop into the confines of the conifer trees.

The rain now stops and I arrive, a little bit drier, back at the camper van. I then drive round to Newtonmore, fit the new tap and battery then spend a lovely evening with Ali, Adrian and their daughter, Ellen.

Retreating to my camper van, I have a restless night, not helped by a cockerel crowing from 04:00 onwards. I therefore get going early, drive across to Glen Roy and start up the slopes of Beinn Iaruinn at 09:15.

It's a very steep, heathery slope but the day is dry and the views are fine. At the Corbett's summit I rest, with my back to a good-sized cairn, and take in the views for half an hour. Ben Nevis has her head in the cloud, patches of snow occasionally show through as the wind moves the cloud around.

I continue south-west along the ridge then, faced with an extremely steep south-east descent, continue along a sheep path until the walk off becomes more concave than convex. Even then I follow a steep dried-up stream bed, offering a few more foot holds. I find it very hard to keep my nerve.

The road appears below and it still looks very steep. I drop to my haunches and wobble down a few hundred feet until I find the confidence to stand again.

From around 600 feet up I spot a car draw up alongside my camper van. I imagine it being broken into and only able to watch from afar. After some ten minutes my fears are allayed as three figures emerge and head up the hill.

I make a traverse, along another sheep path, and slip, buckling my left foot in the process. It's painful for a few minutes before settling.

I make it back at mid-afternoon, make use of a nearby burn to fill the camper van's water tanks and bottles, then drive a short distance further up Glen Roy to bag Carn Dearg tomorrow.

Having the new leisure battery, and the heating working, makes for a comfortable night's sleep. I get walking at 08:10, first crossing a footbridge followed by two smaller summits that are reached via grassy slopes, before the final pull up Carn Dearg. There are a few boggy patches to cross before I hit the cloud line, the summit ridge and the summit itself in just over three hours.

The return journey has adjacent similar folds in the hills so I have to get my compass bearings correct to be able aim for the correct route down. The weather is 'draughty' and I get back to the camper van in a five-hour round trip.

Monday the 24th lives up to the expectations of the weather forecast with strong winds and snow. I huddle in the van feeling sorry for myself and ruing the demise of my Windows tablet computer, bought specially for writing up my diaries. Undeterred I continue typing this in on my smartphone.

I drive back to Newtonmore and, as Tuesday 25th dawns bleak and snowy, I note cars in the high street are covered in snow. I am glad I have de-icer with me.

After picking up Ali, we drive south on the A9 to Dalnacardoch for the six-mile walk to bag the Corbetts of An Dun and Creag An Loch.

Looking at the weather I opt for my walking boots. Somehow trail shoes don't feel appropriate.

We cross the A9 and the walk begins as a battle as a strong head wind blows snow into our faces. I have my hood drawn tight, my snow goggles protect my eyes. My gloves have a built-in plastic gadget which I use to clear the goggles.

The boots feel heavy and, with Ali's pace faster than mine, my hips are soon muttering away that they aren't happy.

Conversation is impossible and communication is reduced to the odd turn of the head to check on the other's whereabouts. The two Corbetts are on view but snow clouds are swirling around them and we note the dusting of snow is growing into snow fields. We press on and, surprisingly, cover the six miles in just two hours.

At the end of the track lies the decaying Sronphadruig Lodge, surrounded by a tall deer fence. We push open a slatted gate and are surprised by how heavy it feels against the strong wind. It slams shut behind us.

The lodge's front door is hanging off its hinges. Some of the ceilings are out and the best bit is the hall. We sit on the stairs and eat our lunch – many a decade has gone by since anybody took these stairs up to bed. We debate the weather and decide to press on.

The long walk in to An Dun and Creag An Loch

Letting ourselves out of the deer enclosure, we continue on the track. The two mountains have now disappeared below cloud and the snow is blasting head on: greater than the walk in. Ali and I have a shouted conversation. She asks me what I think. I tell by her voice she is doubting the wisdom of this. "Turn back," I reply. Ali nods. "There's risk of fatality if we ascend," I add.

We have the wind behind us on the walk back. The weather clears but as we take a final look behind us we see the mountains are still in a snow storm. The same snow storm soon chases us down and engulfs us.

I drop Ali back in Newtonmore and feel a bit sad to say goodbye to her and Adrian. Despite being an independent soul, who needs to often be on his own, I have a sense of unwanted solitude as I set off back to Glen Roy.

I get walking on the 26th, at 07:50, from the head of the glen for another Corbett named Carn Dearg. It is the one I accidentally missed on the TGO Challenge in 2010.

There is light snow but I am struck by how still everything is. After yesterday's snow sandblasting, this feels a bit sinister. Like a quiet moment in a film where the director is lulling the audience to only then throw the protagonist into danger.

I pass through the tracks that weave amongst the buildings of Brae Roy Lodge. A diesel generator putters away as the river gurgles its way by.

I follow the tracks until it is time to head north-east to meet the ridge. The horizon is peppered with deer whose silhouettes look like cardboard cut-outs.

The pull up is sharp and my right hip jabs away with pain. At two hours into the walk I reach a snow encrusted plateau. On a warmer day this would be a sodden peat bog, today the ground is solid and I manage to make good progress.

As I rise the snow gets deeper and the best line to the summit is via a knee-deep drift. I drop back to where grass still pokes through the snow and weave a maze like route until I reach the summit cairn at 11:00.

I enjoy some views. A number of glens can be seen forking off from the low ground. I set my compass so I hit the right one and get back to the camper van in two hours.

I drive to Spean Bridge, eat in a café, and then take the short trip around to the base of Beinn Bhan.

After twelve hours of sleep I get going at 09:10 on Thursday the 27th. It's a day to take care as forty years ago today I was in an accident at school where I managed to head butt a Stanley Knife and had eleven stitches around my right eye socket – fortunately this was the last time I ended up in A&E.

I weave my way round a diverted footpath, a tumbling burn, a rickety bridge and a fence. The ground is very uneven, boggy and tiresome. I ache nearly everywhere it's possible to ache. My shoulders, hips, abdomen, knees and legs are all protesting.

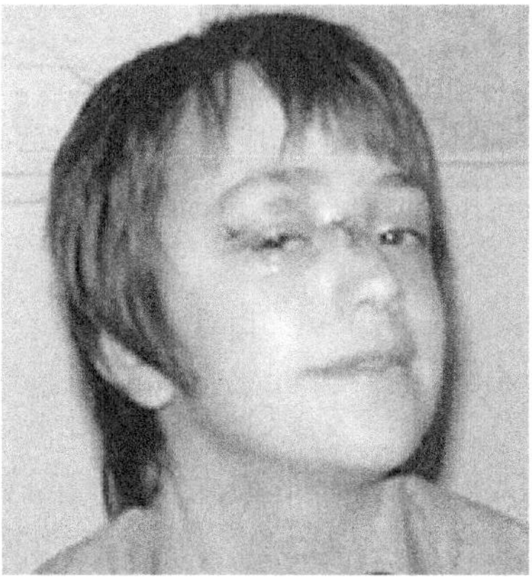

Forty Years ago Today

When I get onto more open ground the wind picks up and light rain, from high cloud, peppers me. I continue on a bearing until the distant outline of a trig point and cairn become visible. Three hours into the walk I reach the top and slump down out of the wind.

I make a navigational error on the way back and find myself on very steep, wet ground. Opposite the hill has a smattering of snow like an artist has flicked white paint against a khaki canvas.

The ground is too steep and too wet. I attempt to traverse but it is unnervingly steep so I head straight back up, at a fear-induced pace, until I reach a ridge which I can descend by. Back at the camper van I take the minor road to Fort William, stock up with supplies, buy a new compass and drive round to Kinlochleven and park up for the night.

I lay in and get started for Glas Bheinn at 09:00. The first thing to navigate is a series of new woodland paths which confuse the hell out of me until I use my compass to cut directly through the trees. I relax when it becomes obvious I am heading up hill, towards the paths and tracks described in the guidebook.

Bagpipes sound in the distance, well at first I think it's somebody murdering a cat until my hearing tunes in properly.

I pick up the track to Loch Eilde Mor then fork onto the path that leads round to the small dam. Within a hundred yards of it I find a sign saying the track across the dam is closed and alternative route should be sought. Like where? A sign like that should be set miles back.

Not only is the track closed, it is in fact entirely absent. Only a wide river channel sits where it once was. I head downstream amongst drainage works and machinery. I find a spot where I am able to make a stepping stone crossing and, with only one foot dunked, I scramble up the civil engineering works that resemble a battlefield.

Checking my time, I note progress is slow for meeting a former work colleague, Mat Skapski, at the Clachaig Inn for the evening. I pick up the pace, following a path until at 550m I branch off north-east for the summit of Glas Bheinn. It is a gentle incline, easier on me and I make the summit cairn at 13:50 in breeze and light rain.

The cloud is high, the views are good. To the north-west are the impressive Munros of the Mamores. They are a series of very individual mountains that each tower above me. I really do wonder how I managed them all in the 1990s.

To the south-west are the equally impressive mountains of Glen Coe. Particularly on show is the Aonach Eagach ridge which Mat and his friends plan for tomorrow.

I head north-west, steeply downwards to take a land bridge across Loch Eilde Mor. From here it's track and path out. The only disruption is a group of people, surrounding a sign, blowing a horn. This appears to attract a group of men carrying a flag who, when passing me, barely say hello. A distinct foreign tongue adds to the mystery.

I take a tumble on the steep wooded descent back to Kinlochleven. One of my trekking poles, stuck in a tree root, is the culprit. I get back to the camper van at 16:50.

Mat (short for Mateus), Gus (short for Angus), Sam (short for Samuel) and Pawel (short for Pawel) arrive at the Clachaig Inn at 19:45.

Having spent the last two hours fending off requests for the table I am holding, my heart sinks when Gus announces they should go and camp before eating. We lay out my map, and line up an array of beers to ward off any further sorties for the table.

They find a pitch quickly and we eat then examine my map – the very one I have used for this area since 1990 – when these guys were either still in primary school, nappies or not even born. Mat is keen for me to join them on the Aonach Eagach ridge tomorrow but, having done it in 1997, nothing will persuade me to go up there again. It is one slip and you are dead land.

I also point out that I am nineteen years older than any of them. A point they, very kindly, say is not a problem. *It certainly feels like a problem to me.*

Mat says he needs his 'manager' up there with him. I point out that, given this is my official last day at Solchar, I ceased to be his manager at 5 p.m. today. A point he concedes.

Gus spots a young lady he knows from a pub in Dorset. He chats her up, she has just moved up and looks keen on him. He gets as far as finding out her name is Emma.

I sleep well and when I step out my camper van I find Mat, Gus, Sam and Pawel emerging from their illicit camp. They sort their kit for the day in the back of Gus's car. Sam is debating whether to take a loo roll. Given my memories of the exposed nature of the ridge I think this is essential equipment.

I get involved in some car logistics so that they have their car at the end of the ridge. With a day off planned, and damp socks that are even offending me, I set off for a village, near Fort William, where Google tells me there is a launderette. I reflect how modern technology makes life so much easier. A smartphone, a car GPS and I find a launderette. Yesterday Mat was able to keep me posted on their long drive up from the south of England. Years ago I'd have been waiting in the Clachaig Inn with no knowledge of their progress. Born in 1965 I'm part of the generation who has lived through the plastic age and now the technological revolution. In the midst of it one might see it as normal progress, looking back the changes are profound.

I pop into the launderette and ask how it works. In fact I am pretty nervous – I've not been in one since 1988. However, the helpful ladies show me how the machines work and I manage to overcome my nerves.

I then pop in to Morrisons in Fort William and stock up with Mini Cheddars, pickled eggs, baked beans and instant potato. Such is the volume, and lack of variety of my purchase, I use the self-service aisle to save inquisitive looks from an assistant. I recall Fort William in the 1980s when it had the one tiny high street Tesco which shut at 17:00 on a Saturday, not to reopen until the Monday morning. Times have changed.

My final popping to places for the day has me going into the town centre where I get chatting to a couple of guys manning an SNP campaign table. We have a constructive chat about future referendums. They want to leave the UK, adopt their own currency and remain in Europe. My view is they would have more chance of independence if they allow the UK to leave the EU first, then go to the people for a mandate to leave the UK, join the EU and adopt the Euro. One of the guys takes the party line but the other nods and agrees with my view.

I drive back to the Clachaig Inn and await the return of Mat, Sam, Pawel and Gus. I doze in my camper and come round to Mat knocking on my door. They've enjoyed the ridge but, being hardened climbers, found it easier than my warnings.

Another evening is spent in the Clachaig Inn where I note the menu of single malts is longer than the food menu. There is a live Gaelic band playing and the place is jumping. Gus spots Emma and hones in on a front row position with her.

There are lively songs involving fiddles, bagpipes and the accordion. The band try and get people dancing and start by asking for a pair to do the gay Gordon's. A woman from LA volunteers and the hunt is on for a man to accompany her. Gus shouts to the band, "Ask Steve." There is a call out for Steve that within a few seconds over a hundred people are chanting. Nobody knows it is me until Gus looks my way and by nature of the fact, and potentially my downfall, I'm the only person not chanting 'Ask Steve', I am pinpointed. Being an introvert this is hell. A chap (not called Steve) steps forward and rescues me by taking the girl from LA as his dancing partner. I return to skulking in the corners.

Mat suggests revenge and I hatch a plan. Gus is clearly keen on Emma and she looks fairly keen too. I suggest we buy a packet of condoms and I go up to him and, in front of Emma, say, "Are these the ones you are after?" But alas there is no machine in the Gents so my plan fails at the first hurdle.

The band play to gone eleven, the place is heaving, the atmosphere electric. It reminds me how the South is so money and career focussed. Nobody has much fun. The pub in our village, that did live music, is now closed with a developer hell bent on turning it into a house.

I sleep in a bit on Sunday the 30th of April before the short journey down the A82 to where the West Highland Way crosses. I alight from the van, fully kitted out, only to notice I have odd walking shoes on. Remembering the 1970's adverts of not mixing radial and cross ply I change one to make a matching pair.

I get walking for proper at 10:10 in a cold wind to take in the Corbett of Beinn a' Chrulaiste. It is a series of steep sections followed by more level ground making me feel like an ant on a giant staircase.

The wind gets brutal and cuts right through me. However, I am feeling fitter and make the circular trig point summit, perched on a sea of red granite on a grey granite mountain, in under two and a half hours.

Back at the camper van I drive down Glen Etive and park for the night with the view to bagging Beinn Mhic Chasgaig, one of four Corbetts in the glen, tomorrow.

It's a windy night and I don't pull back the blinds until gone 09:00. I'm surprised to see a blue sky and my preparation gets a lift.

I get walking at 10:00, crossing a bridge with a very sturdy gate on the far side. Cutting diagonally across, I meet a path following a wide burn. The path rises both in height and away from the burn until it feels like I am peering into a ravine. The drop is very steep and I am glad when it's time to branch away and climb the steep slopes.

I hear my first cuckoo of the year, no doubt enjoying the blue skies and warm winds.

The ascent is very steep. I have another deep drop to a burn on my right. My progress is slow and wary. After three hours I really start to struggle so I sit for a while and appreciate all the mountains that form the skyline. Peaks with specks of snow in the high corries. The green, grey and blues of the grass and rocks – a multitude of hues that glow on a sunny day but brood when the weather closes in.

I press on and, as my altimeter tells me I am approaching the summit, I find a small stream tricking down the mountain. I cup my hands and drink its fine, cool, pure water.

A hundred yards further on and the ground levels into a wide summit plateau: out of sorts with the steep battlements that protect it. It also explains the stream – an impossibility so near to a pointed summit.

I reach the summit at 13:40 – one of the many small rises.

I lay in the grass for forty-five minutes, taking in the grand, pointed peaks that make up this area. They make for sharp climbs but each mountain stands alone and stands out.

I head off down the long ridge that faces Glen Coe. Cars on the A82 are silver dots flashing along the road. I then cut down to Glen Etive through steep ground where I have to take the utmost care.

At the river I am more blasé and hop from stone to stone to get across. It's then a tarmac walk back to the camper van. The river is crystal clear with falls over rocks, twists and turns. There are many people about. Some canoeing, some camping, some just pulling up in their cars to take in the awesome mountains that guard each side of the glen. I get back to the camper van after being out for seven hours.

Driving down the glen, in glorious sunshine playing an old Al Dexter track on the CD player, has me thinking that everything feels just perfect.

I park up for Stob Dubh tomorrow. The mountains, glen and

evening light shimmer in unison. I keep the back door of the van open and drift off to sleep with the blinds down. I come round some hours later to a cool breeze and the mountains as dim shadows against the horizon.

During the night I'm treated to a starlit backdrop between sleeps. I wake around 07:30 but don't get walking for another two hours. Then I set off in the wrong direction along the road. I backtrack to find the track that leads to a bridge which crosses the river.

Turning left I'm faced with the daunting face of Stob Dubh. It looks extremely steep. I pass a cottage, two black dogs belt out and confront me. I take off my goggles to try and calm them. Their owners call them off.

Starting the ascent I feel very tired. There's no let up, it's as steep as it looks – a mixture of rock and grass which I can only climb at a snail's pace. I'm concerned about the descent later in the day. Going up steep ground is much safer than descending it.

Such is the steepness (an average of 1 in 2.3) it's four hours into the walk before the ground levels off enough to be able to slip off my pack and take a drink. I get to the summit at 13:50 in a cold breeze. I take off my over trousers and my map case and stow them away – they are shiny and would slip on the grass should I take a tumble. Then I pack away my compass – it has sharp edges. I then check my telescopic trekking poles are tight at each joint before setting off back.

Keeping three points of contact with each step, I ease myself down the mountainside.

I look for signs of paths, signs where others have trod before me. I follow one and it leads me to a deep gorge, the accompanying hoof prints show me it's nothing more than where the sheep go to drink.

Backtracking I press on, one foot at a time against alarmingly-steep ground. A lizard backs away from one of my trekking poles then climbs onto my shoe for protection. For further protection it scurries up my trouser leg. So there I am standing on one foot, with both trekking poles stuck in the ground, on a perilously-steep slope trying to shake a lizard out of my trousers.

It takes the hint, drops out then scurries away. Spotting better routes down I'm soon on an easier line. I get back to the camper van after being out for seven hours.

May the 3rd is a rest day in which I drive to the end of Glen Etive and spend the day admiring the lochs, mountains and clear blue sky. I even manage to swim and sunbathe. This is such a contrast to eight days ago when Ali and I were snowed off the mountains.

View looking down Glen Etive

Things take a nose dive in the early hours. I first wake at 02:30 feeling nauseous and open a window to get some cool night air. At 04:30 I'm vomiting for England and at 06:30 the other end gets involved.

Feeling very sorry for myself I have to abandon any thoughts of walking today. At 09:30 I pull down the side screen on the camper van and, in this very remote spot miles down a dead-end single-track road, I'm very surprised to see a paramedic, on a call out, stroll past. I get up and ask for advice. This consists of drinking lots of water and getting the contaminated porta-potty emptied as soon as possible.

I laze around, feeling ill but come lunchtime am feeling quite hungry. All the food I have in the van repulses me so I set off, abandoning the last two Corbetts in Glen Etive, to drive to Fort William.

Along the single-track road there are numerous passing places. It's fifty-fifty whether I pull in or an approaching vehicle beats me to it. Until that is I meet a car where there are no passing places between us. It'd be hard for me to reverse but Mr Helpful, in his easy-to-drive car, demands I reverse. I get up onto the bank and get stuck. Forward and reverse both spin the front wheels. Fortunately a few other cars arrive and they push me back onto the road. Mr Helpful then nudges forward as I reverse a few hundred yards.

I get to Fort William and present myself at the till of the café in Morrisons. I order an omelette and a hot drink.

"That's five pounds and fifty-five pence," says the assistant.

"It was only three pounds fifty the other day," I reply.

"That's after 3 p.m.," she explains.

I check my watch, it's 14:57. Given she's already rung it through, and given I feel ill, I pay up. The meal arrives at 15:10 – an interesting point I feel but, again, I can't be bothered.

I eat up, buy some other provisions then attempt to exit the store. People are milling everywhere and it takes me a while to get out the shop, get to the camper van then navigate my way out of the car park and Fort William.

I haven't packed the back of the van very well and, as I drive, bits fly and crash around the back. My temper feels frayed.

I drive past Loch Lochy then cut round, on a single-track road, to the foot of Beinn Tee. There's a handy wide piece of tarmac where I park. Twenty minutes later a farmer appears demanding a fiver. I look at the tarmac, there's no join with the road, so it was laid at the same time. He concedes the road is public but claims the square of tarmac belongs to him. Given he is subsidised by the EU and the Barnett formula I'm reluctant to hand over a fiver from my savings. I opt to leave.

Noting his gate, rather surprisingly, does not display a sign saying 'Beware of the Bull' I drive round to the A87 and park on a nice wide public layby. I get into the back of the camper van. Unaware one of the overhead cupboards has swung open I crack my head on it and completely lose all my sense of humour.

I take Friday the 5th off in an attempt to recover. I'm not over the bug and am suffering bad heart burn so I drive to Loch Loyne, park a bit back from the dam and set up a sickbay. Cars pass, cars pull in. A passing Romahome gives me a toot.

I doze and wake to a woman taking a picture of the front the van. Given my issues with McFiver I open the door and enquire what interest she has. She points to her 55 plate Romahome – she was just getting a photo of them both. I then find out she's a bit of an expert. Perhaps even an anorak. She reels off all the model numbers she's passed, their engine sizes and their MPGs. Her van is a two litre and did sixty mpg on her trip up from Herefordshire.

Saturday the 6th dawns as another faultless day. The views over Loch Loyne, high up from the layby, are stunning.

I push myself to get going to bag Meall Dubh. I feel weak and not myself. However, if I am to complete the Corbetts I need to do at least five a week. So far, I've been here four weeks and done nineteen.

I notice the hill is clad in a wind farm, rendering the guidebook route out of date. I get going at 10:05 and follow an uncharted plod up a very long track. The turbines are numerous and I am in touching distance of many and feel like I am in some HG Wells story.

In bright sun and a low breeze, I branch off the track, cross rough ground and, in a little under three and a half hours, slump down at the impressive summit cairn. I am shot and weak. However, I'm not at all hungry and manage to eat only a very small packet of Mini Cheddars.

I take a more direct route back across rough ground. My legs feel as though they don't belong to me. I cross ground where a digger has cut thousands of square holes. It takes me a while to realise this will soon be a forest and each hole will raise a tree.

I hit the A87 some mile downhill of the camper van. It's a blistering walk up the road in the heat. Back at the camper van I check my watch – it's been an eight-hour walk.

Driving onto Shiel Bridge I park up with a view to taking in Sgurr an Airgid tomorrow.

I get walking at 10:20 and am back at the van forty minutes later – my body just isn't up to it. I hang around the area, eat out twice and enjoy the views over Loch Duich.

Setting off at 09:10 on the 8th I follow the stalkers path up Sgurr an Airgid. Although my pace is okay I'm out of sorts with this entire project. A few weeks back I renegotiated with myself to do sixty-four Corbetts this year and a bunch of the Donalds. Now this feels unbelievably daunting. I'm constantly playing stats through my head. After getting sick I need to do a minimum of five Corbetts this week to catch up. I think through my retirement. The purpose of it is to take the pressure off deadlines and targets. Having started school aged five, I have now had forty-seven years of deadlines and goals. I've retired to make life easier but have just gone and set myself another ultra-ambitious target. I renegotiate with myself again and decide it will be good to finish the Corbetts, Grahams and Donalds in my fifties. That's nine summers in which, from the outset of this year, to complete 429 as yet unclimbed peaks. That equates to forty-eight per year. Okay, that's the new target and, given this is an extended trip, anything else is a bonus.

I press on up the zig-zag path. It's another fine day with clear views and a cooling breeze. I take a call from my local MP's PA. They want to use a picture, in their election leaflet, where I'm standing next to the MP at a rail passenger group meeting. Fine by me.

I reach a ridge, the Corbett is off to my left. I get some rest bite from the gradient before the steep ground returns. Two older chaps pass me on their descent. One has a beard which appears to be full of snot. He snorts out a conversation as bubbles pop from his nose. I make my excuses and get back to my solitude.

The summit area is broader terrain with a number of outcrops. I wind my way through the battlements of the true top, reaching its slain trig point at 12:20.

I eat and take in the views. A haze guards the distant hills and loch.

I'm happier on the descent, now I've cleared my head of tight deadlines I reflect, with the new strategy of forty-nine peaks this year, I am now more than halfway through!

I miss the last bit of path on my final descent and end up on a track that comes out at a graveyard. A short road walk returns me to the camper van.

I drive down the road to a craft shop that also has a few general provisions. It's the kind of shop where there is no hurry. In a trance-like state I spend ages choosing a can of macaroni cheese. My body feels nauseous at the thought of any food I'd had in the run up to the sickness. Even the cover of the DVD I watched on the evening before I was sick has me feeling nauseous. I guess one's body writes anything off that may have been the cause.

I ask if they have peanut butter – I fancy that with jam and bread. Alas the last pot was sold to a family of pine martens at the weekend – actually some humans bought it for the pine martens but it amounts to the same. Further enquiry informs me that they have no idea when the next pot will be in.

I drive on a little further to a garage. I remember, while staying at Ratagan Youth Hostel with a bad cold and throat, it had a restaurant where they did an excellent all-day breakfast. The place ended up being my daily treat as I recovered. Like the Youth Hostel, the restaurant is now permanently closed.

I spend the evening reading Damon Hill's autobiography. In the mid-nineties I was a dedicated fan, travelling to see him race three times. When Munro bagging I would tuck my radio into my hood during his races.

I set off at 09:10 on the 9th on the well-defined track that skirts the south-westerly side of the Corbett of Sgurr Mhic Bharraich. I follow a fast-flowing burn and, to save carrying too much water, pre-load with as much as I can bear to swallow.

The climbing track swings round. I have no more energy than to plod, rest then plod some more.

The day is warm with just a bit of cool breeze. Young trees, with a vibrant green canopy, track a stream joining from the left.

At a lochain I branch on to steep ground and, ever so slowly, take on the final, steep ascent. The grass and heather are tinder dry and crunch below my feet.

I make it to the summit at 12:55. Shiel Bridge is a distant speck below. Its road, with miniature cars, winds round and crosses the head of the loch. Fields beyond are straight edged, flat with each having its own shade of green.

It's cooler, I need my fleece so I start to descend. I meet a couple near to where I started – the only folk I've seen all day.

Back at the camper van, I move along the road and park up for the night in a layby a mile east of the Cluanie Inn. I don't sleep that well so, after a snooze in, get walking at 09:45.

The sky is a blanket of cloud, a real difference from the blue skies of the last few days.

Given there is a Munro beyond the Corbett of Am Bathach there is a well-defined path up its slopes. This Corbett is a ridge back with its navigable width down to thirty feet in places.

I have to wear fleece and inner gloves to keep warm. Resting often, I enjoy the views back towards the Cluanie Inn and the matchbox cars on the road below.

I reach the summit at just gone noon and look across to the Glen Shiel Ridge where, in 1992 in an attempt to do seven Munros in one day, I managed to damage my knees. So much so that to this day I still have to heavily strap them to walk in the mountains. That was a long day and I didn't get off the ridge until late evening and was grateful for a lift, back to my car, from two Italian women.

I start to descend and, given the well-drained profile of the mountain and its narrow undulating ridge, I consider it the best Corbett to date.

Nearly back at the start, I get chatting to a middle-aged chap on his ascent: an ex-paratrooper who, some years back while waiting at a pedestrian crossing, was hit in the head by an overhanging lorry. He shows me the major surgery scar and apologies for his lisp. He's doing well, only twenty-four Munros away from completing.

I drive back round to Loch Loyne and park up for the night. I'm on a slope so I don't sleep well and therefore get going at 08:25 for the long walk to Druim Nan Cnamh.

After a short road walk I find it's not obvious whether one can cross the dam at the head of the loch. I drop down on a track which winds through woodland before bringing me out on the north-west shore.

The east end of the ridge looms above me but first marshy ground has to be covered before I start the sharp ascent through grass, boulders and slabs of rock.

As I pull onto the high ground the ridge, unlike yesterday, is poorly defined. Instead of a neat thirty foot' width there is a mass of hummocks, wet ground and boulders. I'm continually in a dip without a point of reference to follow. I rely on compass and altimeter to find my way.

The ridge has a number of distinct summits. I soon pass the unnamed easterly high point and then head to Beinn Lonnie.

The drop off Beinn Lonnie, and the distant peak of Druim Nan Cnamh are depressing – it's no fun dropping down from ground hard won.

I arrive at the cylindrical trig point of Druim Nan Cnamh, four and a half hours into the day. I'm pleased with my fitness – it's the first day this year I've not had thoughts of throwing the towel in and driving home.

Taking in the views, I am surprised to see the Cluanie Inn and Am Bathach to the north-west; geography was never my strongest subject.

I drop down to the low point before Beinn Lonnie and, instead of covering old ground, take the slightly soggy direct line back to the dam.

After the sickness last week things have been fairly quiet on the need for the loo front. I'm in quite a bit of pain during the night so, first thing, I drive to Morrisons in Fort William and pop the strongest laxative they sell into my shopping basket. With my head down I make my way to the automated pay section. Normally I hate these things – a modern invention which gets me confused and irritated. However, today I am well and truly ticking the 'No Publicity' box. But the modern technology has a twist in store. Apparently I am buying something with an age restriction which requires an assistant to come and type some form of code in. And to add to my embarrassment it's a young female assistant who herself looks too young to be allowed to purchase the said item.

She flashes a card at the machine and it gives a reassuring beep. She doesn't take this as her cue to leave but instead watches over me. The machine beeps again and she utters the words, "Unexpected item in the bagging area." As foreshadowing goes that's spot on.

At 08:00 I'm sat in the station loos at Fort William in excruciating agony. The laxative is not working as advertised. The recommended fifteen minutes rolls into an hour.

I move the camper van to an all-day car park and then present myself at the Belford Hospital A&E department – I spoke too soon about not having been in A&E for forty years.

The nurse's opening gambit is to ask whether I've tried a local GP. I glance around at their empty waiting room. She relents and books me in.

So after a couple of hours of being examined and given a bed by a loo, with some accompanying eye-watering and embarrassing application of an unspecified liquid, the loo, shall we say, is put to full use.

Needless to say, with my dignity in tatters, I take the rest of the day off, make use of a launderette and feel decisively fragile.

In the late afternoon I drive round to Fort Augustus then take the B862 and find a place to park for the night near Glen Doe Lodge.

I sleep well so don't get walking until 10:10 for the Corbett of Carn a' Chuilinn. The track marked on the map has been massively widened as an access road to the Stronelairg Wind Farm.

I pass by a large compound with numerous earth movers, trucks, tractors etc. The track is well signed for the modern ways of site safety. Lots of instructions to drivers, including to be on the lookout for hillwalkers. And the requirement is if a hillwalker is spotted then to radio into control so all other workers can be warned. There's service for you.

In one place the track is three car widths wide with a Passing Place – they must be expecting some seriously larger vehicles than the ones I saw in the compound.

I break off from the track at around the 1000ft mark to the bemusement of a sheep and its lamb. I head across rough and twisty ground, under a gathering black cloud, to reach the lovely pointed summit cairn.

Back at the camper van I start to pick up texts from my old school friend, Peter Wanless. He and his son, Bertie, are big Ebbsfleet United fans and today is there National League South play off final. They are 1-0 down with a player sent off. I then get a text saying it's 1-1 then 2-1 up then a phone call saying they've done it and next year they will be in the National League proper.

Sunday the 14th of May is a rest day so I can be fit for a long day tomorrow, taking in the Corbetts of Geal Charn and Meal Na H-Eilde. I'm due to meet Ali Ogden, crossing Scotland on this year's TGO Challenge, on Geal Charn between 08:00 and 08:30 – outside that window we'd agreed not to wait. She's invested in one of these new-fangled Spot devices which broadcasts your position every ten minutes. I have an App on my smartphone where I can monitor her progress. In conversation with her I refer to it as 'The Ali Stalker App'.

Come 17:30 she's approaching her overnight camp so I drive around to Loch Arkaig to set off early following the Alt Dubh burn.

I get up at 04:30 and set off at 05:40 along a path which had been upgraded to a track. After a few miles it returns to being a rough path which disappears and reappears a number of times.

At its head I branch north-west for the ascent of Geal Charn. About half a mile from the summit the wind picks up and, by the time I reach the trig point, I'm being pummelled by wind and rain.

I only have a base layer and my jacket on. I slump behind the trig point which doesn't really give much shelter. It's 08:12 and there's no sign of Ali and no 4G signal to use the 'Ali Stalker App'. I walk around to get a view into the glen below. The wind fights my every move and I have to brace myself for every step.

I dip down and manage to get enough shelter to get my fleece and inner gloves on. Back at the trig point the wind and rain gets worse. If this were an A road it'd be a severe weather warning.

I wait until 09:24 when, unable to feel my fingers and realising my core temperature is starting to drop, I head towards the col to the north-east.

I slip and the wind bowls me onto my backside. My pack cover becomes a kite and I find I'm stumbling around – a sure sign that I'm borderline hypothermic. I manage to warm my fingers enough to text Ali, giving her the time I'm abandoning. All plans for the second Corbett are now off – I'd not get warm enough to stay on high ground.

I swing south-east, then south to pick up the path and track of my ascent. I get back to the camper van at 11:25, switch on its heater and arrange my trekking poles, and a length of copper pipe, as a clothes dryer.

After sorting myself out, I figure that I should drive back to Spean Bridge for a 4G signal to check the 'Ali Stalker App' in case she has a problem. As I open the driver's door I find a note tucked in the door handle. At first I'm concerned it's a farmer demanding a fiver. A quick read settles my mind as it's from Ali. She'd left it at 10:20 saying she'd abandoned the Corbett, due to the wind, at 08:05 just seventy metres (vertical) from the summit and just seven minutes before I arrived.

I'm now in a dilemma. I really could do with staying put and tackling the abandoned Corbett of Meal Na H-Eilde tomorrow. However, I now have no phone signal and it's possible that if I don't show up in Spean Bridge Ali will be concerned I'm stuck somewhere on the hills. So I drive back and find Ali about an hour's walk away from Spean Bridge. She'd literally got blown off her feet seventy metres from the summit – approximately where I had slipped. In fact on the 'The Ali Stalker App' I can literally see the exact spot she turned back.

We meet later in the Bridge Café, Spean Bridge. She buys me lunch for having waited on the top for over an hour. I then drive back round to tackle the abandoned Corbett tomorrow.

I get walking at 09:00 on the 16th – a far cry from yesterday's 05:40 start – via another well-made track, following a steep-sided glen called Gleann Cia-aig. It's about three miles to a bridge where I branch north-west up the slopes of Meal Na H-Eilde. Here my pace drops to a crawl, the wind picks up and there's drizzle in the air. I just about manage to keep placing one foot in front of the other.

Around the 2000ft mark the wind goes berserk. I find a 'fox hole' in which to shelter. Given yesterday's antics I now get my fleece on, under my waterproof outer. I put on my pack cover, eat as much as I can, redo my shoe laces and tighten my cuffs. I spare a thought for the soldiers of the Great War, exactly a hundred years ago, who left their trenches and faced a hail of bullets. All I have to contend with, when I leave my own private trench, is a raging wind that's about to blast me with rain. Back then, refusal got you an accusation of cowardice, 'lacking in moral fibre' and a volley of bullets in the chest at dawn the following morning.

It's an awful ascent and my mood is dark, almost as black as the sky which lurks beyond the swirling cloud that envelopes me. I have my hood drawn tight and, with my goggles on, I'm peering at the world through a letterbox; my field is narrow. But at least the wind is behind me.

Fifty-five minutes later I make out the cairn of the summit. An old iron fence post sticks out among its rocks. I cling to it as the wind debates what to do with me.

I about turn, the wind and rain now in my face. Water goes through my jacket, fleece and base layer on its way to soaking my stomach.

I feel a strange sensation on my right foot. I look down to discover I've disturbed a frog that has leapt onto it. Who is more surprised I don't know. He leaps off and takes a tumble, rights himself then sits perfectly still.

I'm relieved to get down below the 2000ft level where the weather settles. On the walk back I loosen as much clothing as possible to try and get dry.

I get back, after six and a half hours, in breeze and sunshine. I attach bits of clothing and gear all around the van to dry off in the wind. The evening turns to a blue sky. I reflect on the timing, my freedom from the state, no need to go to war and the letterbox width of time we are all allotted.

I sleep well and drive round to the land of Farmer McFiver for another go at Ben Tee. His hallowed piece of tarmac is taken so I park on the grass and get walking, alongside the burn, at 09:55.

There is heather pollen in the air and I stop to take a pill and use the red light therapy on my nostrils.

The path rises and the drop, into the burn to my left, steepens until I start to become a little freaked. A fine waterfall comes into view: a single long drop of thundering water with a large pool at its foot. The path rises around it then becomes nothing short of a rock climb. Clumps of heather become useful handholds. Normally it is the enemy of the hillwalker, now it is my friend. With rock and heather pressed against my chest I eek out an ascent until a welcome fence denotes easier ground.

At 11:15 I'm glad to be sat on an open moor reflecting the foolhardy nature of the route up. Ben Tee is basking in the sun as I follow the boggy high ground then the windswept climb up its easiest flank.

I rest again around 150ft from the summit and take in the distant views of Loch Ness, forestry plantations, mountains and a wind farm.

I reach the summit, four hours into the walk, in a strong wind. Too cold to hang around I start straight back, picking a route that avoids the waterfall.

Back at the camper van, in case Farmer McFiver should come my way, I beat a hasty retreat. I drive round to Tulloch Station, park up for the night then get myself onto the platform for the first train of the morning to Corrour as my starting point for Leum Uilleim.

A chap, in conversation with another, is waiting for the same train to Corrour. He appears to be rather proud of his poor memory. I've noted that the sayings, 'I'm no good at maths', 'Well I'm not technical' and 'I've a memory like a sieve' are all socially acceptable and often said with pride. This rakes up long battles I've had in the work place. I'm good at maths, am technical with a good memory. Just my luck to have the skills which, if absent in another, are paraded like they are attributes. In my working life I found managers were often devoid of these attributes and, in turn, played down technical people instead of seeing them as allies. There's a lot of ego in the IT world. When did you last hear somebody say, with pride, 'Well I'm no good at English'?

I'm glad to be retired, glad to be out of it.

A woman comes out of the station hostel informing us that Corrour is a request stop with a short platform and we should board the middle coach and tell the guard we need the train to stop at Corrour.

The train arrives, it's two carriages which makes boarding the middle one a bit hard. "Two for Corrour," I say to the guard. He neither replies nor acknowledges me. I ask if he heard me because of it being a request stop. He then answers informing that it is not, and the train will be stopping there regardless.

The trip is beautiful, alongside Loch Treig. At Corrour I say goodbye to my fellow passenger and wish him well for the two Munros he's attempting before, like me, catching the 15:24 back – if he remembers that is.

I take the obligatory photo of Leum Uilleim, framing it as it appears in the film, Trainspotting. I get walking at 08:35, taking the long horseshoe route. It's a sympathetic gradient I'm soon high enough up to be above a Hercules aircraft sweeping its way across Rannoch Mor.

Leum Uilleim

I reach the summit in under three hours and soak in some rain and magnificent views across Loch Ossian. I descend by Leum Uilleim's steep north easterly ridge which becomes a succession of noses by which to descend.

Back at the station I have two hours to spare. I eat at the station house and I'm joined by the chap from the train who's just done his two Munros. He's remembered me and is a lovely chap. I feel a bit guilty for my earlier thoughts about his pride in having a bad memory.

An elderly couple come in with their two small dogs. They were also on the train on the way up and have bagged one Munro today. She's a throwback from the past. Eighty years old, likely public school, and been walking the Scottish hills since her twenties. She tells tales of dodging keepers and staying in abandoned shepherd's cottages long before they became bothies.

Her rucksack dates from the nineteen fifties and sports heavy repairs from when it was washed away in New Zealand.

Her partner has just four teeth remaining, almost protruding at forty-five degrees from the front of his upper jaw. His accent is broad Scots and an ill-fitting bobble hat perches on a head of straggly, long grey hair. They are your preverbal odd couple and questions, such as 'Just how did you two meet?' remain unanswered.

I take the 19th off and first visit Adrian Ogden – Ali, his wife, is now struggling with Achilles tendinitis but is still continuing on this year's TGO Challenge.

We pop down to the hostel which they jointly run with Sue and Neil Oxley. Neil is picking some dandelions for a small, wild rabbit which has, while looking very sorry for itself, parked itself in a flower border. Molly, their female dog, who will see the rabbit as a light snack, is locked indoors. Harvey, the boy dog, is a soppy old thing and takes more of a paternal role by guarding the said bunny from cats.

The rabbit eats some dandelion then perks up and hops onto the lawn for its next course.

Now Maddi, Adrian's step daughter, enters the scene with Pearl, a border terrier. Fortunately Adrian grabs her but, after a quick cuddle, puts her down. We all shout, "No" as Pearl, who by now has clocked the presence of the rabbit, launches herself forward. She gets the rabbit in her mouth, and we all launch ourselves forward to rescue it. Pearl lets go and the rabbit runs off.

I follow the rabbit and find it cowering down the side of the hostel building. Concerned about another attack by Pearl, and cats, I pick it up. It rests in the crook of my elbow. Fortunately there are no puncture wounds but the rabbit is rather wet with dog saliva.

We find it a home in the kindling wood shed and leave it with grass, dandelions and a dish of water.

I do a shop in Aviemore and then set off for Braemar. Just north of the town there appears across the road what looks, from a distance, to be coils of tumble dryer extractor piping.

I slow down and navigate my way through. There's a putrid smell of rotting flesh and it's only then do I realise that the road is covered in the carcasses of sheep that evidently died some while ago.

It's over an hour's drive to Braemar and I can't get rid of the smell. It's an overpowering reek of death. I look for a garage with a hosepipe but, on reaching Braemar, I've had no luck.

Inspecting the underneath and wheel arches I note multiple strands of dripping, rotting flesh.

Ignoring the problem I go for something to eat then drive round to Invercauld Bridge and park up for the night.

I phone Neil for an update on the rabbit. Sadly it died during the afternoon.

I sleep well through a night of heavy rain. I wake and abandon my plans to do the two nearby Corbetts. Instead I plump for the easier Carn Na Drochaide from the Linn of Quoich. Also it's an opportunity to drive through every available puddle to try and wash the underneath of the camper van from the indignity of rotting sheep carcass.

I get walking at 08:25. Last year I had to abandon this one because all three bridges, over the Quoich, had been washed away in December 2015. One has been reinstated by the Cairngorm Club and I am grateful to cross it and follow the track then path, in light rain, around to the minor top of Carn Na Criche before the final pull up Carn Na Drochaide. There are effectively two summits, each with a well-built cairn. The second is the highest. Given it's wet and miserable I take a straight line, through fresh deep heather, back to the bridge. I return to the camper van after being out for just three and a half hours.

I spend the afternoon and evening in Braemar catching up with friends on the TGO Challenge. Alan Sloman kindly posts the following picture of me on Facebook:

I then drive round to Invercauld and park up for the night. I get walking at 07:50 on the 21st, via the estate tracks, for the Corbetts of Culardoch and Carn Liath (Creag an Dail Bheag).

A couple from Dundee – Morag and Dave – soon catch me up. I

pick up my pace, glad of the company. They are then slow over the steeper ground and I get ahead.

There are more tracks than on the map and I have to pause often to take bearings. On high ground, with wind and light rain in the air, I break off the track and reach the summit at 10:35.

Dave arrives within a minute and Morag a few minutes later. Our pace was different over different terrains but over all our times match.

They are great company. She is an accountant and he is the Chief Executive of Mountaineering Scotland. We set off together for Carn Liath. At first we descend the track for about half a mile before taking the rough ground west. There are two summits marked but in fact there are four possibilities. Morag and Dave, not being out and out peak baggers descend, following a fine drystone wall, on the southerly spur from the first spot height. I carry on and, after a few pauses to check GPS and map, find the true summit at 12:40.

Returning to the main track, then to the camper van I drive to Braemar, parking up at the start of the track to Loch Callater. I walk up to the lodge for another legendary TGO Challenge party with singing, musicians and tales of the trail. I don't leave until 01:35, and it's nearly 03:00 before I get back to the van.

Waking around 08:00, I breakfast then promptly fall asleep again. In the afternoon I drive round to Ballater and meet Ali and Sue Foss, on the TGO Challenge, for afternoon tea then later an evening meal.

I then drive, following the A939, to its high point some three miles south of where it meets the A944. In places this A road is single track and there are one or two impressive eighteenth century bridges.

I don't realise how windy it is until I get out the van. The door is yanked from my grip as the rain pummels into me. Back in the living area I switch on the heating and snuggle beneath my quilt. I turn the radio on and, for once, can receive Radio Five Live. Shortly after 22:30 horrendous news starts to edge in of a bombing at a pop concert in the Manchester

Arena. By the early hours it becomes clear that the victims are mainly young and the assailant a suicide bomber.

Needless to say I don't sleep well and, when I set off for the Graham of Mona Gowan at 08:35, I'm particularly slow.

The guidebook warns of adders so I've completely covered myself, including full waterproofs, on what has dawned a clear day. However, the need for a comfort break foxes my plan. I inspect the ground for slippery customers.

I struggle with the climb which, by Scottish standards, is very straightforward. There are a few ups and downs to follow, a fence to use as a virtual handrail and a splattering of cairns to keep me company.

I arrive at the massive summit cairn in an hour and a half then return to the van, feeling hot and sticky.

I drive down to Dalnaspidal on the A9 and park up for the night. Feeling weary I don't get walking until 09:10, on the 24th, for the Corbett of Beinn Mholach.

It takes me two hours to trudge up the track alongside Loch Garry and reach the bridge over the Allt Shallainn. The highlight being disturbing a mouse who runs in a circle and arrives at my right foot. His little eyes look up at me and blink several times. I drag my foot back gently to not alarm him.

From the bridge I make heavy weather of the north-easterly slopes of Beinn Mholach. Beyond the cloud line I'm walking in swirling mist with the blue hue of the sky trying to break through. Without a clear view of the summit, and the numerous humps and bumps of the ridge, I find it hard to find the route up. I eventually reach the beehive summit cairn at 13:25.

The route back is equally hard to navigate until I break through the cloud line around 2250ft. From here I appreciate how the profile of Loch Garry has changed since a 25,100ft pipe was put in during 1937. There's now a mile of flat grassed head land which would have once been below water. After an eight-hour walk I get back to the camper van, hot and tired.

The 25th is sunny and I take the day off. I drive round to near Rannoch Station and chill in this glorious setting.

I get walking, in the hot weather, at 08:50 on the 26th, and follow the track to Corrour Station until I reach the bridge over the Allt Eigheach. Here I drink a litre of water and fill my water bottle with the same amount. Like a camel I don't know when I'll next find an oasis.

I take a bearing and my compass promptly decides to fly to pieces. This is the second compass this year. During my Munros I kept the same compass for ten years. Now they don't last.

There's a welcome cooling breeze up the steep slopes of the Corbett, Meall na Meoig (Beinn Pharlagain) and I'm relieved to be able to walk in just a T-shirt today. I make good progress as I daydream about changes I'd like to make to my house. If I think too much about the terrain, or think negative thoughts on any subject, I struggle more than if I lose myself in planning some project.

The broad summit ridge houses over a mile of significant ups and downs. Fortunately it's a fine day so I can see my way to cut corners. I get to the modest cairn at 12:20, rest, eat, swig back water and take in the panoramic views.

I drop down and pick up the track further north. It's then a route march back to the camper van.

I take the short drive to Bridge of Ericht and park up in a wooded car park alongside the loch. The evening sun glints on the water as it gently laps the sandy shore.

I get to bed early in preparation for a long day to bag Stob an Aonaich Mhoir. The forecast is for afternoon thunder storms so I fancy an early start to try and avoid them.

With lightening forecast I debate whether to take trekking poles: with them their conductive properties could be a liability, without them I'd be slow and increase the risk of running into the storm.

I get started at 07:00, trekking poles in hand, and take the track behind the power station and then follow the massive water pipes that feed its turbines. These date from the 1930s, made of metal with industrial-sized rivets holding them together.

A useful bridge leads me across to the main track I need to follow. However, new forestry tracks fool me and it takes me an hour and a half to do the first mile.

Back on track, after crossing one or two tall deer fences, I rue the lost time and the possibility this could run me into the thunder storm.

It's a long traipse up the track, not leaving it until the 2000ft high point. I navigate through dry peat hags before the ground opens up and I crunch my way across short, tinder-dry heather.

The summit is shy, it appears to forever want more from me. After over five hours I reach it with a sense of relief. However, with the storm in mind, I spend no more than two minutes at the summit admiring the fine view down the steep north-west face to Loch Ericht.

I hurry back, it rains a little. I get back to the camper van, just before the heavy rain starts. However, not a bolt of lightning is to be seen or heard.

I rest until the rain passes then drive round to Kenmore and the picturesque minor road to the south of Loch Tay. Turning up an even more minor road, I park for the night.

I get to sleep early – eighteen miles and nearly nine hours has taken its toll. Between 06:00 and 08:00 I enter one of those half sleeps where you are conscious of your surroundings but still tired enough to have weird dreams.

I ache all over but decide to give the Corbett of Creagan na Beinne a go. I shut the van door at 09:10 and, after testing myself for a few paces, I feel I have enough energy for today, but tomorrow should be a rest day.

It is sunny which prickles the sunburn on my forearms and head.

However, my pace quickens on the track and, as I take to the open hillside, over sheep-grazed grassland, I feel good. So much so that when I hit the broad ridge I'm setting a good pace. A fine view opens up all round: modest mountains, like the rolling hills of the southern down lands, and lush green fields towards the Tay.

A brisk breeze meets me at the summit. I'm two and a half hours into the walk and it takes a further two to return.

I spend the afternoon cleaning out the van, fabricating a watch strap for my altimeter and driving on to Ardeonaig for a look at Creag Uchdag tomorrow.

The warm afternoon air turns to a mid-evening wind, clouds arrive and it rains during the night.

I get walking at 09:00 from the track south-west of Ardeonaig. I want to head south-east but am quickly thwarted by being unable to cross a burn, deep in a wooded ravine.

Instead I walk down the steep track to Ardeonaig. It's a quadruple whammy because I'll effectively have to walk down and back up this piece of track and the equivalent the other side of the burn.

There's a footpath signed from the road but nothing obvious on the ground. So I press on via boggy grassland, scattering ewes and their lambs as I ascend.

At the 2000ft level I pass into cloud. At around 2500ft I come across a murder of crows circling and squawking. I love that collective noun for crows – one crow is a crow, two crows is attempted murder and three or more a murder.

The crows give me no bother and I press on until I meet the remains of a fence. Only the odd iron upright remains with the intermediate tensioner posts still remaining. On one upright I try and spin the tensioner cogs – only one has avoided rusting up.

The posts lead me to the summit trig point, three and a half hours into my walk. I sit in a pocket of warm air – clouds above, below and off to the sides but none immediately around me. I fancy a nearby hump is higher so I walk over to it. Turning to compare it with the trig point I find it has disappeared in the cloud. I use my altimeter to prove to myself that this hump is actually higher.

Initially I backtrack using close compass work to guide me. Then the squawk of the crows confirms my location.

I decide to try and avoid dropping down to Ardeonaig and instead cut across due west to emerge on the track above the ravine. This is a good saving and I return to the camper van at 15:30.

I drive to Killin, stock up at the Co-op and make use of the coin operated launderette, before the drive round to the end of Loch Voil. It's a foreboding, narrow single-track, dark road. Trees and bushes overhang each side and drip with rain. I pull up at the small car park. The evening is muggy and heaving with midges.

I wake to light rain and low cloud and lay in until 11:35. The weather clears, even some blue sky appears. I decide to give the Graham of Stob Breac an afternoon stroll.

To start with the guidebook steers me onto a zig-zag forestry track. However, like all forestry tracks they are open to change and I probably zag more than I zig and find myself on a southerly track. I cut my losses and decide to take a firebreak onto the steep open ground leading to the mountain top.

At this point my compass springs apart and it starts to pour with rain. Fed up I decide to turn back and traipse, getting wet, through the puddle ridden pine needle carpeted track.

I jump as a German voice calls out hello. It takes me a few seconds to spot two German chaps sheltering under the trees. They look like brothers, same shaped bald heads and identical black rimmed glasses.

Like me they were heading to Stob Breac. They make a remark about whether I am skiing. At first I think they mean my trekking poles but then realise they mean my snow goggles. I explain the hay fever. They then question whether I need them in the rain. I insist I do. Then they move on to whether they cause me to sweat. I bid them adieu (German voices coming from trees is getting a little surreal) and plod back to the camper van.

I spend some time drying myself out and building one compass out of two. A strong evening breeze sees off the rain, the mugginess and the midges.

I get walking at 0840 on May 31st for the Corbett of Stob a'

Choin. At first it's an easy walk up a track then, following very helpful signs, through farm buildings before a bridge crossing to the open hillside.

From here things get tough. It's very steep and my first attempt gets me onto unnervingly-steep ground. I backtrack and take its north-east flank. Again this is steep but manageable. The land below me appears to fall away, the track now a mere grey contour through the glen. Munros of old, with dates scrawled on my map from August 1994, guard the northern horizon. A significant burn descends from them with an accompanying roar like distant traffic.

I plod on up the steep slopes. Like the grazing sheep I keep four limbs, via the use of my trekking poles, firmly planted.

The mountain is a myriad of rocky outcrops, each a saw tooth on the horizon. I navigate the steep grass between them and make it to the summit at 12:25. There's two tops with small cairns. My altimeter gives an identical reading for both.

Full of trepidation, for the steep descent, I tread carefully back the way I ascended. The biggest danger turns out to be a field full of bulls. They complain bitterly at my presence. I hurry my way back across a fence and fabricate a longer route back.

I get back in three hours and find the inside of the camper van is cooking in the afternoon heat.

In contrast June 1st dawns a dreary day. I drive round to Ballimore Farm and set off for Ceann na Baintighearna (also known as Stob Fear-tomhais or Beinn Stacach) at 08:05. I follow the Scottish Rights of Way fingerboard for a mile and a half then take to the Corbett's east flank. After nearly eight weeks walking it no longer hurts when I ascend. I still need my rests but the leg pain, due to asthma induced lack of oxygen getting to the muscles, has gone.

It's a long undulating ridge with the wind picking up. The final incline takes me onto a ridge that sits as a T to the easterly ridge.

There's a trig point at the top with a small cairn nearby which, according to my altimeter, is one metre higher. The remains of an ancient fence, heading to the north, sits ghostly in the cloud.

I'm three hours into the walk and it's too cold to hang around. I head back much the same way, passing some earth movers building some unknown works, and get back to the camper van at 13:15.

Back in Killin I lunch then drive to the south side of Loch Earn to tackle Meall na Fearna tomorrow. I find some loch-side parking but it's a miserably wet evening.

I sleep in and don't get walking until 09:25. The weather has lifted, there are high clouds but none threatens rain.

I walk through the park like grounds of Ardvorlich House before following a hill track. In fact I don't follow the track far enough, branching off too early I ascend to ground which then requires me to drop down, cross moorland peat hags before the final pull up to the Corbett's summit.

It's 13:00, sunny and cool as I slump down and take in the views. The Munro of Ben Vorlich is to the west, Loch Earn to the north with a multitude of mountains dotting the horizon.

I cut down and meet the ascent track higher up before the plod back to the camper van.

Feeling a bit tired I drive round to Crianlarich with the aim of taking the Saturday off and make use of the day by catching the train down to Glasgow.

I get to sleep early so end up catching the 06:33 and get into Glasgow before the shops open. I wander around a bit before going in search of bookshops and outdoor shops. Looking for some easy reads, I buy four Peter James detective novels. I then venture to Tiso and, after much deliberation, buy an ultra-lightweight jacket. Hopefully I'll not feel so hot in this one.

As I walk back to Glasgow Queen Street Station I become aware of drums, horns and general shouting. It's an independence march with many shouts of protests against Theresa May, The Tories, Trident, London rule and the fact the BBC are not filming the march.

Making my way through the hoards to the station, I just manage to catch my train and get back to Crianlarich.

I then set off for Glen Etive, with a plan to complete the two Corbetts that I missed due to getting sick. It starts to pour with rain and, just outside Crianlarich, I take pity on a young, Indian-looking female hitchhiker. We put her pack in the back and I clear off the passenger seat for her.

I ask her where she's heading for. In clearly what is not her native tongue she tells me she's going as far as I am.

I try to engage her in conversation but she doesn't respond to any of my further questions. I quickly let the conversation go. To be fair if I was a young female hitchhiker I'd be a bit quiet if I'd hitched a ride off a middle-aged guy who had just bought four detective novels about serial killers.

I switch on the Sat Nav and set it to large scale and turn it towards her. This appears to moderately please her.

Looking at her features I wonder if she's closer to Nepalese than Indian. This is almost confirmed by her complete lack of interest when I point out mountains – presumably to her these are merely foothills with the real peaks lurking behind the clouds.

When we get to Glencoe the rain eases and I pull up in the entrance to Glen Etive to drop her off.

"I thought you were going to a town," she says.

"Sorry no," I explain.

"But I only took a lift from you because I thought you were going to a town."

This isn't quite my memory of it. If I recall correctly she was standing, with her thumb out, in the pouring rain and I was the only person who stopped.

She pulls a face and makes no attempt to get out the van. I begin to think that perhaps, given this outright liberty of accepting a favour then demanding more, she is in fact neither Indian or Nepalese but instead a cat.

"Okay I'll take you to Fort William," I say. I don't fancy getting cross or forcefully evicting her. As a guy I could get myself in a spot of bother.

I drive on and she returns to absolute silence. My previous questions of where she comes from, what's she doing over here remain unanswered. I begin to wonder if her family have sponsored this trip and are busily relocating at this very moment.

I drop her in Fort William town centre. She refers to it as 'the city centre', which confirms my thoughts that she is not long in the country.

As she swings her pack onto her back I notice she has streaks of grey hair. I thought she was younger, either that or the journey has aged her. She thanks me. I drive round to Morrisons and order omelette and chips. In a show of somebody who does not like to be taken advantage of, I argue the toss when I'm overcharged by five pence.

The liberty, of cat-woman, reminds me of an elderly cat I rescued just before Christmas. It was about 17:00 on a freezing evening and I was just popping in to our village post office when a thin, old, threadbare black cat approached me.

"You look like a sucker," she said.

"Are you lost?" I asked.

"Not anymore," she replied.

I bought her some GoCat which she demolished in seconds. Realising she must belong to someone I took her home. After putting her photo on Facebook the local jungle drums pinpointed her as Chloe, who, six weeks before, disappeared from a village five miles away.

However, before this detective work I'd shown her my lounge. She'd had the briefest of glances around and made a beeline for my antique French solid walnut, very comfy chair. The cheaper furniture did not get a look in.

I offered her water, she held out for milk and when her owner arrived, to collect her, she took one look, snuggled into my chest and announced she was now sorted.

I sleep in on Sunday so don't click my radio on until 09:00:

there's shocking news of another terrorist attack – this time in London. It is indeed troubled times. There are many accounts of bravery and kindness. To get people home taxi drivers refuse to take any money. This rather puts my taxi service of yesterday into perspective.

I get walking at 09:35 for the Corbett of Meall a' Phubuill. There's a good track up Gleann Suileag before a steep, rough track branches north just before Glensulaig Bothy.

I get to thinking about the woman I gave a lift to yesterday. Was she suspicious enough to call a terrorist hotline about? She looked scared when I picked her up, she didn't want to be dropped in Glen Coe (and thumb another lift) but instead wanted to go to a town. It then hits me – she's probably running away from something or somebody.

It starts to rain heavily and my pace sinks to that of a snail as I ascend the broad, steep, open ground. The new jacket does its job well.

Eventually the ground levels out and I make the summit just after 13:00. It's too cold and wet to hang around so I descend steeply back to the track. The rain is against my face and makes the goggles appear as if I'm swimming under water.

Back at the camper van I rest awhile then drive a bit further to attempt Streap tomorrow.

Ignoring Cameron McNeish's guidebook, which gives the grid reference of a nearby Corbett for the access point, I park just off the A830 in what can only be described as a midge combat zone.

The van is descended upon by black swarms of the little bastards. When I venture outside, with the door open for no more than a few seconds, thousands of the blighters hop aboard. I have to shut all the blinds and then turn on one light only and wait. Only when they have amassed around the light does the massacre begin.

I am slow getting moving on the 5th and make a mad dash for the track to avoid the midges. After about twenty minutes I do a GPS check – I'm on the wrong track. Its start tied in with points of reference on the road but in the hills I'm about half a mile out.

I descend back to the camper van and from about a hundred

yards survey the scene. Clouds of midges still circle it. I get ready with the keys, take my pack off and carry it in one hand. Within ten yards I press the button to unlock his doors, within three yards they've cottoned on and are swarming around me. I open his driver's door, throw the pack and trekking poles in then dive in myself and slam the door.

Many midges make it through but it could have been worse. I have to climb through to the back to lower the blinds before a quick drive along the road for the correct track.

It's now 10:15 – a late start. I follow the Dubh Lighe river for two miles before realising there is now more forest than on the map. I run out of track so drop to the river. There's a track on the other side but it is impossible to cross.

I follow the bank through trees and swamp. My feet get so wet I may as well have waded across. It's two hours before I'm out of the woods and, just when the river is crossable, I find a bridge.

There's still some wet flat land to cross, with many burns feeding the river, before the very steep southerly slopes of Streap are reached.

It's now 12:45, my typical time to actually be on the top. I feel tired but plod on. At 15:00 I get to a single rock, in a grassy expanse that marks the top of the outlying top of Streap Comhlaidh. It's swarming with crane flies which, give them their due, barely bother me.

From here I am in mist and there's a multitude of spurs. I take the wrong one, it's a bit narrow. Turning back, I can't fathom the way off Streap Comhlaidh. I begin to fear my day might be wasted. Only by using the GPS do I creep along the correct spur.

Again it's narrow. Parts of the mountain's other ridges are described as 'knife edge'; I have the disheartening feeling I might need a guide. However, it still feels manageable, if a little unnerving. I recall trying this mountain, from the west, on a TGO Challenge crossing. It was impossible. Streap guards herself well.

After more ascent I reach the summit at 15:55. Still in mist I lay my trekking poles in the direction I need to return in. This is my 100th Corbett. I take a photo for Facebook. Well, actually I take three before I get one that doesn't show the fear in my eyes.

I descend back the way I came but, on the lowest point before Streap Comhlaidh, I head off down the steep south-westerly slopes. I'm treated to a lovely, warm evening with gurgling burns and waterfalls sliding over rocks.

A bridge then gets me on the right track. In the forest I briefly rest at the well maintained Dubh Lighe Bothy.

The track takes me to the river and another bridge I missed by just a few yards on my way up. If I'd found it I would have been able to miss the earlier swampy walk up the riverbank.

I get back to the camper van at 19:30 feeling pleased I'd persevered through a day of snags.

I take the 6th off to do laundry, recover and to find a hotel for the 8th and 9th to watch the election on a TV. One place I try offers a special discount rate of £122.50 per night. The receptionist looked most put out when I said I'd leave it.

I walk around Fort William, each place I try is full. I resort to the internet and one of those room booking sites. Only one hotel shows as having a vacancy. £188 for two nights. Being the tart that I am I phone the hotel directly and get it for £168 for the two nights. I then check the booking site and make sure it's disappeared.

After eating in Morrisons I drive back along the A830 to climb Streap's neighbour, Braigh nan Uamhachan, tomorrow. I have a moment of confusion locating the access point as Cameron McNeish, in his guidebook, had transposed the eastings and northings.

Being well rested I get going at 06:25. This time I know the way and reach the Gleann Dubh Lighe Bothy in under an hour.

I manage to work out how I got suckered on my way to Streap. An inviting new track had taken me away from the correct route.

I branch off the track and climb the steep south-westerly slopes to get on the long ridge to the Corbett's summit. The ridge is broad with many drops and rises. There's light rain and wind in the air.

On the final pull up a steep, menacing gully lays to my left. After five hours of walking I reach the summit and tag the cairn then note another top, just a few yards away looks higher. I walk over and my altimeter confirms it is superior by one metre.

Despite the wind and light rain there are great views. The Munro of Gulvain is to the north-east and the beautiful Loch Shiel draws out the mountains to the south-west.

I return the same way, resting in the bothy on route.

Evening view from the camper van

After feasting in Morrisons I head south to Ballachulish and the short trip to Callert House – tomorrow's starting place for the Corbett of Mam na Gualainn. I find a layby to park for the night. One other car is there. A boggy track leads into the woods, which border the road, and I wonder if that's the way up.

After about an hour the car owner emerges from the track and confirms the route. He's in his early sixties, has done five rounds of the Munros and now, with over 200 Corbetts bagged, looks set to complete soon.

His fitness makes me realise just how far behind I am from anything close to athleticism. He's done two separate Corbetts today and once did the Munros in seventy-nine walking days.

I wake on the 8th to a weather forecast predicting rain is heading up from England. This is enough to get me out and walking at 07:20. The track through the gap in the woods is easy but the steep slopes to Mam na Gualainn slow me to a snail's pace.

I make it, through long grass, to the blustery summit, depicted by a cylindrical trig point, in under three hours.

There's cloud teasing the tops of the Glen Coe mountains. Loch Leven, far below, looks like a dark piece of roughly-cut sheet metal. There's a bit of rain in the air so I head straight down, getting back before noon.

I eat at Morrisons again then head to the Clan Duff Hotel where I'm staying to watch the election. I'm given the keys to room 10 and I make a quip about having just been handed the keys to 'Number 10'. The receptionist, an eastern European, gives me a blank stare.

A Scottish lady shows me to my room and opens it up for me. I look at the wardrobe and announce it as my new cabinet in number 10. Again this is lost.

Election night is, to say the least, interesting. Theresa May's gamble of a snap election is a political mistake and she's left governing a minority government. She offers no apology, instead announcing that as she has won the most seats she'll remain prime minister.

I've booked two nights in the hotel. The plan is to laze around for the day after the election and catch up on sleep. However, I feel a bit flat and fed up. I'm glad when it's time for bed and sleep.

I wake at 06:30, imagining I'm in the camper van. Only when I notice how far the walls are from the bed do I realise where I am.

I make full use of the inclusive breakfast before packing and venturing out into the pouring rain. A drive round to Loch Arkaig has me on the long single-track road to Strathan.

I start walking at 10:05 for the Corbett of Sgurr Mhurlagain. At first it's a good track but the path following the Dearg Allt burn has been ruined by off road vehicles – it is now miles of bog.

My feet sink into mud more times than I care to count. There's light rain in the air and a troublesome neck muscle lowers my mood. I can't get my pack adjusted to alleviate the discomfort. Instead the pain shoots around my head, giving an ice cream like headache above my right eye and a thumping, migraine like pain at the back. I get some relief with paracetamol and Deep Heat.

Around 1500ft I reach a big barren plateau. From here I branch east, then north-east into the cloud and rain. I feel really tired, fed up and grumpy with the pain as I plod through the sodden grass slopes.

It takes four hours to get to the summit: a cairn on the south end of a narrowing ridge.

I take a couple of aspirin and squelch my way back to the camper van. It's a very lonely, remote spot but it's now parked in a row of four vehicles. One has a note saying the occupants will be back on Tuesday. Another belongs to two women runners who get back a few seconds after me, soaked through. I lay in the back of the van, door open, and exchange a few words with them as they change. The least enthusiastic of the pair, who is being jollied along by her friend gives me a wistful look. I guess in the middle of nowhere a middle-aged bloke in a camper van is more appealing than their plan of walking to A' Chuil Bothy with the intention of doing a Munro tomorrow!

They set off, a minute or so later there's a massive downpour. I have feelings of sorrow for her. I probably got it all wrong but I sensed her outdoor adventure was marking time, that she was tagging along with her friend and instead she'd prefer the domesticity of family life.

Settling down I figure I need to take tomorrow off. I felt lethargic today; the result of staying up for election night is still hanging over me.

I wake around 06:00, the day has started quite brightly. Slipping back into a deep sleep I wake again at 08:35 to a thundering downpour. The two women, who had headed for the bothy, soon return. Clearly they've abandoned the hills. My decision to stay put for the day is ratified.

There are moments during the day when the weather clears enough to consider venturing out. But they are brief, no more than an hour maximum.

A massive storm blows in during the evening. The van rocks on its suspension, rain is hosed against his windows.

I have trouble sleeping but eventually drift off in the early hours. I wake around seven and lower a blind. It's as if I'm submerged in a swimming pool. Visibility is a few yards and distorted by the refraction of light by the water.

I boil water and pour it into my breakfast bowl for porridge. The van rocks in the wind and the boiled water swirls in the bowl. I watch in stunned amazement as it gathers pace, swirling anticlockwise. Seconds later it breaches the rim and cascades over the edge. Only when half the bowl has emptied itself, does the remaining whirlpool stay in the bowl. I pour on porridge to dampen the motion.

Around 10:00 I decide I can't face another day sat in a plastic box being hosed from all angles. I pack a few things away and begin the twenty-one miles of single-track road back to civilisation. To give an idea of how remote this area is it takes sixteen miles before I see another vehicle. I've walked this road twice, while crossing Scotland, and both occasions felt pitifully arduous experiences.

I use the journey to recharge my electric toothbrush via an inverter hooked up to the cigarette lighter – one must have the occasional luxury.

In Spean Bridge I call in at the Bridge Café. There's only one table free: a table for four. The waitress gives me the look of, *I can't turn you away but I'd like to.* Two Americans arrive shortly after, I offer they can join me.

Eric and Neil are interesting guys. Early forties, on holiday, touring around. They immediately apologise for Donald Trump. This is a common occurrence among Americans with passports.

We talk about the state of the USA, Brexit, the UK and Europe with emphasis on the EU. They are surprised by how much I know about American politics. I explain that it's heavily covered in the British media.

We talk for over an hour and we all feel we have gained from sharing our knowledge. When they depart I turn to the weather forecasts.

It looks dire; anywhere near the coast, over the next few days, is to be avoided. I decide to head north to Glen Cannich where it looks a bit more promising.

I'm glad to get walking at 08:35 on June the 13th for the Corbett of Sgorr Na Diollaid. Two days of enforced break have me yearning for the hills. Ten minutes later I'm cursing this hobby as ankle-biting heather, and knee-grabbing ferns slow my progress.

Ahead I hear birds chirping in fear. I look up to see a bushy red fox, complete with a white end to its tail, searching through the undergrowth.

On the map it looks like a straight ascent but in fact it's a long series of rises and dips which are sodden under foot.

Nearer the top, and in drizzly wet cloud, the terrain becomes rockier. The final pull is through a channel of boggy moss between two long walls of rock.

The summit of Sgorr Na Diollaid has two peaks, it's a scramble to the first then a scramble along to the second.

It's 11:45, there's very little to see so I set my compass to the return bearing and begin the descent into the mist.

After about an hour Mullardoch Dam, way off to my right, emerges from the mist. I'm pleased when the bridge, near to where I'm parked comes into view. The weather eases and I get back relatively dry.

I drive back to Cannich and stop to look at The Glen Affric Hotel. I first visited it in 1989 when on a group holiday. Then it was run by a couple from Birmingham who left us feeling ripped off. From charging us for one more mountain bike than we hired, to charging us for more desserts than we ordered, this couple appeared to have no shame. I visited it again a couple of times in the late nineties when, to be frank, it was falling to pieces.

Now it lies abandoned, crumbling back into the earth. The first floor has a mix of boarded up and broken windows. I peer through the downstairs windows: there's white mould covering the fixtures and fittings. Even though the windows are intact I can smell the damp and decay.

The Glen Affric Hotel

I call Andy Glover, who was a co-victim of the rip-offs in 1989, and describe it to him. We share some memories of over a quarter of a century ago.

I drive up the long road to Loch Affric and park up for the night.

Waking on the 14th, I make the short journey to the Loch Affric car park. I put two new one pound coins into the parking meter. It takes my money and issues no ticket. This is not a good start to the day.

I write a note for the windscreen. A couple of women approach the meter. I call out that there's a problem with it. The woman gives me a look like your cat gives you when it's about to correct your diction. I then realise they are French.

At 08:10 I set off along the track on the south side of the loch. There are major earthworks in progress for a new hydro scheme. A temporary sign points me across boggy ground, away from the new road being built. I check my map and conclude it's my best option.

The French couple stop to examine the sign but carry on. They are holding a copy of the Glen Affric tourist map, available free from the car park.

I press on, my feet instantly wet from the sodden path. The path is hard to follow, appearing, disappearing, up and down through the filthiest bog.

I need to cross the river to ascend the minor summit of Na Cnapain on route to Carn a' Choire Ghairbh. There's no crossing point and the abundance of long heather on the hill ahead is off putting.

I eventually pull myself up onto the road being built along the route of the Allt Garbh burn. Whether this is the correct route or not feels of little consequence – I'm just pleased to be out of the squelchy bog and away from the impassable river. The French couple appear. I wave hello, they do not respond.

I plod on and work out where a track, marked on my map, meets the new track, complete with a bridge across the river. The French couple, ahead of me, turn onto the same route. It feels a little odd that they, as tourists, are not sampling the beauty of Loch Affric, but instead are heading into the rugged wilds with a very basic map.

I branch off on the high point of the track and note that the French couple continue on. Good, I've lost them at last.

I start the steep climb towards the main ridge of the Corbett of Carn a' Choire Ghairbh. The cloud is high and I can see all the intricate ridges of the surrounding mountains. So much so the Corbett of Aonach Shasuinn also looks possible.

I look back along the route of my ascent and am rather surprised to see the French couple a hundred yards behind me. I allow them to catch up. The one thing with hill walking is you get a sixth sense when you need to stop and check if somebody else is okay.

"Is this the way to Loch Affric?" asks one of the ladies in broken English. I shake my head and point to where they are on my OS map.

"Non," she replies and points to various geographical features that she has tied up with her map.

I press my case, producing my GPS as proof that I do know where I am. I point to features, point to my map then show her where she is on her own map.

"We go back," she concedes. They don't say thank you, or even merci. I reflect I'm not the first Brit to have got the French out of the poo only never to be thanked. My granddad never did after he landed on the beach at Arromanches in June 1944.

I check my water, I am low. I hear gurgling and make my way across. It's an unreachable underground stream.

I continue uphill and am relieved to get to the broad ridge. There's great views of mountains, the cloud is still high and I make the summit after four and a half hours.

It's now a descent, followed by a sharp re-ascent onto the parallel ridge on the other side of the glen.

I am attracted by the sound of running water. However, it's just one stagnant pool draining into another.

I'm now very hot and sticky. But, having lost two days due to the rain, I'm determined to bag Aonach Shasuinn. I walk the ridge, take in the views before the heart-breaking drop and rise to its summit plateau. A short walk has me at the summit at 16:05. I feel elated – two Corbetts in one day!

I take the shortest descent back to the new track, drink from the river and make the long walk back. It's been an eleven-hour day and I feel tired to the bone.

I drive back into Cannich and listen to the growing horror of the Grenfell Tower block fire last night. I can never understand how buildings can be constructed so tall that they are beyond the reach of a fire engine's hosepipe.

Parking up outside the remains of The Glen Affric Hotel, I sleep the night and visit the local Spar shop. The full horror of the pictures, on the front pages of all the papers, hits me. You can never quite get the impact from radio.

I've never felt comfortable with dumping our poorer people in high-rise. Poorer people form their communities from those around them – never easy in flats when there are no garden fences to chat across. Whereas the middle classes form their communities by the people they've met through their education and work – they don't need the garden fence to chat across.

I drive round to Strathfarrar and get issued with a day pass for the private road. I park at the Culligran Power Station and, at 09:20, begin navigating my way through the myriad of tracks.

It's initially blue sky, interspersed with white clouds shaped like judge's wigs.

I feel tired, yawning often; the eleven hours of yesterday taking their toll. A black cloud swans in and I drag on my waterproofs as it begins to empty itself.

I find the Neaty Burn and a new track running parallel to it. This lifts my spirits. I think back to yesterday, two Corbetts in one day has me metaphorically punching the air. I feel like I've regained part of my youth. It's as if I've just bumped into an old friend and feel on a high because of it.

The track runs out at a new concrete dam. I take to the hillside of Beinn a' Bhathaich Ard, through thick heather, ankle-length grass and am glad to find the occasional animal track to follow.

I get to the summit in a little under four hours, a dome in a sea of short heather with a stone trig point.

An icy wind blows in, I duck down on the sheltered side which, having been in the sun, offers warm rocks to sit on.

I descend into afternoon sun, arriving back at the camper van before driving round to the end of the public road that runs up Strathconon.

The forecast for Saturday is better than Friday so I take Friday the 16th off. In fact it's a nice day and, with bad luck, the 17th dawns dark and wet.

I get walking at 07:15 on the track to the ruined hamlet at Corriefeol. Two decaying stone buildings are all that remain. From here I take to the slopes of the Corbett of Bac an Eich. I feel very weary, each step feels like an effort.

The ground is a steep bog with spectacularly deep gorges down into the burns that run off the mountain.

It takes me four hours to reach the summit. The final hundred yards, of exposed ridge, are in winds so strong I have trouble keeping my footing. The accompanying pummelling rain adds to the misery.

There's just enough room to wedge myself between a stone-built trig point and the wall of the surrounding stone windbreak. This, my 50th Corbett of the year, is celebrated by scoffing down some food, gulping water, tightening my pack and clothing, and then bracing myself to stand up into the violent wind and rain.

I head briskly on a compass bearing; the wind is so strong I even have to battle to keep hold of my trekking poles. I'm relieved to get in the lee of the mountain. From here it's a laborious descent between two deep-gullied burns. The final ground, before the burns converge, is a 'cat's back ridge' which requires careful footing.

From the join in the burns I have to make a sharp climb out of the gully. There are some entertainingly steep slopes to the water below, requiring me to keep my nerve before the ground levels out and I can take the more gentle slopes back to the bridge at Corriefeol. I then follow the easy track back, arriving damp and wet.

I click on my radio, southern England is experiencing the hottest day of the year so far.

The following day, June the 18th, I drive a mile or so back down the glen to take in the Corbetts of Meallan nan Uan and Sgurr a' Mhuilinn.

I get walking at 08:15 at first following the burn then taking to the steep hillside. Finding myself continually yawning and feeling weary I bargain with myself for when I can go home.

I traverse the hillside, gradually gaining height. I reach the ridge at around 2250ft in high wind and spitting rain.

There's a final pull to the summit. It's 11:30 and, despite the cold and light rain, there's a view across to Sgurr a' Mhuilinn which is reached from a sharp descent, almost reaching a small loch sitting between the two Corbetts, then a sharp incline.

After an hour and a half I reach its summit, fantasising about driving into Beauly and getting a pizza. I then descend a ridge, which has more of a Lake District feel about it, before a boggy return and a drive to Beauly for my pizza.

Well-fed I drive to the foot of Little Wyvis with a view to bagging it tomorrow.

I wake on the 19th to rain thudding on the roof, my radio talking of the heatwave down south, and a terrorist attack against Muslims in north London.

I feel a bit ropey: aching limbs and a sore throat. It feels like a mild cold and explains my poor pace over the last few days.

I take the day off and wake, on the 20th, with, what had felt like cold symptoms, manifesting themselves as an upset stomach. Fortunately I'm parked next to a public loo.

I don't fancy another day in the van, and the forecast is that today will be the best weather of the week. This gets me out and walking at 08:55, feeling weak, tired and nauseous.

I cross the road and follow the tracks through trees, passing by a dumped caravan, microwave and television.

I'm very slow, about half my normal pace. Stopping often, I take in the views while feeling rotten and grumpy.

At a junction in the tracks I take the right fork and soon find myself on open ground. This is tough going, the ground is littered with boulders which I continually park myself on to rest.

I hunch over like a crippled old man. Each time I lift my right foot it hovers and wobbles, in mid-air, until I randomly plant it half a yard in the general direction of uphill. I am most definitely 'weak and wobbly' – rather like the Tory government who tried to get elected on the ticket of being 'strong and stable'.

I get to the summit cairn of Little Wyvis at 13:20, pull my pack off and flop down on the grass. Thankful for the warmth, I take in the fine views of mountain tops basking in the sun.

It occurs to me that this is my 111th Corbett – exactly half way through. This cheers my somewhat grumpy mood.

I laze around for about forty minutes before heading back down. This time I work out how I can stay on the tracks. I come across a stag and a goat grazing together. On my way up they were sat side by side, sunning themselves. They are not bothered by my presence. I guess they have found a friendship.

Back at the camper van I make the short drive to Garve. Unable to face any of the food in the van, I hunt for a shop. All I find is a house called 'The Old Shop'. I make do with a burger van that has veggie sausages.

I feel rough all night, sweating, aching but pleased to no longer feel sick.

Through necessity I remain camped by the public loo. My frustrations of not being able to go walking are exacerbated by a few days of fine weather.

It's the evening of the 22nd and I feel well enough to walk tomorrow. Having become discomfortingly familiar with the graffiti on the walls of the Gents loo (company was all but a phone call away) I fancy a change of scene.

I think through my plans. I have done fifty-nine mountains so far this year and, I calculate, if I do just six more I can finish the Scottish 2000ft mountains, by doing forty days walking per year, by the age of sixty. This feels like a more realistic plan. I had high hopes of 100+ this summer but the realities of health, age and weather have scuppered this. Besides I feel a tad homesick and very fatigued – just six more will get me home in early July.

I sleep on and off then take the short drive round to Loch Glascarnoch. On route I pass the Aultguish Inn where, during the foot and mouth year, I was able to stay for £6 per night. The place looks in better condition now and I wouldn't be surprised if the room rate had experienced some inflation.

I park just beyond the loch and, after the rain eases, get walking at 10:45 for the Corbett of Beinn Liath Mhor a' Ghiubhais Li. The wind is very blustery and my pace is awful – I rest every few minutes.

Climbing over a six-foot deer fence, with the wind swaying me on the wire, I shake my head in frustration. Things were going well a few weeks back, now I feel completely trashed.

I plod on through the boggy ground with the wind battering me from the right. Suddenly I am aware of a strange sensation – it feels as if someone is trying to pull down my underpants. I have a quick check around and am rather relieved to find that I am on my own. But there it is again, my underpants are definitely sliding down. I'm aware that they are an older pair. The thing is, with an extended trip away from home, you dig deep in your underwear drawer and pack every pair you can lay your hands on. Even those that should have been thrown out some time ago.

I reach inside my over trousers, then inside my walking trousers and haul them back up. Strangely the elastic is quite tight. Seconds later they are on their way down again. I then note the ventilation zip, on the right leg of my over trousers, is open and the wind is billowing in. It's then blowing through the open pocket of my walking trousers with such velocity it's literally sucking my underpants down. I zip up, pull up and plod on. It takes me a few minutes to realise the irony of wind in one's underpants.

I get to the top at 13:10, my feet soaked. The wind is gusting so strong that I settle down in the summit shelter. The road, a streak of tarmac with the silent dots of vehicles, snakes through the glen below. Beyond is the Munro of Beinn Dearg, basking in sunlight with its three Munro neighbours forming attractive ridges and pathways.

I can see the camper van – it motivates me and I get back in an hour and a half.

I drive to the Aultguish Inn for my supper, opting for a veggie burger and a pint of soda water. It costs me more than the price of two nights' accommodation in 2001.

I park for the night with the view to doing the distant Corbett of

Beinn a' Chaisteil. On waking I look at the weather, the length of the walk and promptly drive south to bag the easy Graham of Carn na h-Easgainn. Easy because it is only a shade over 2000ft, the A9 is high enough to drop me off half way up it, and a wind farm company has built a useful track that leads to the summit.

I get walking at 09:10 minus my trekking poles and my knee supports. With a few inclines, blustery cold conditions, I miss the poles.

I get to the top in under an hour and enjoy the good views across the rolling hills which define this area.

I drive round to Ruthven to take in the Graham of Carn nan Tri-tighearnan tomorrow. It's a nice afternoon and evening and I enjoy chilling out and reading.

I get walking at 09:00 on the 25th with the plan to easily be back in time to listen to the Formula 1 Grand Prix.

There are new wind farm tracks to follow. There are some undulations which I really struggle with. In fact I can't believe how difficult anything uphill has become.

After four miles I branch off onto rough, heather and bog-ridden moorland. Each uphill step feels hard. The tummy bug has left me physically floored. I reach the summit at 12:15 and back to the camper van at 14:40: part way through the Grand Prix. The BBC then lose connection to Azerbaijan So I end up listening to the tennis.

I want to walk on the 26th but feel too tired. I park up in Glen Banchor figuring I'llspend the night here, before going to Ali's and Adrian's tomorrow.

As I settle down to reading Ali calls. She's free this afternoon so I drive round and get involved in a food-tasting session at their hostel. It's for a trail food review for a national walking magazine.

Now trail food comes in pouches to which you add boiling water to allow the contents to rehydrate. The prices vary from £4.50 to £10 per pouch. Around twenty free samples have been sent; being a veggie I'm restricted to ten. This proves to be an outright positive because some of it tastes foul. Even in a tent, in a force eight gale with the prospect of starvation, I'd think twice about some of this stuff.

There's six of us partaking, we score each out of five. We soon have to accept zero as a valid score. Indeed we get the idea of what marks somebody is poised to award by the look on their face after the first mouthful. I further adjust the scoring as follows:

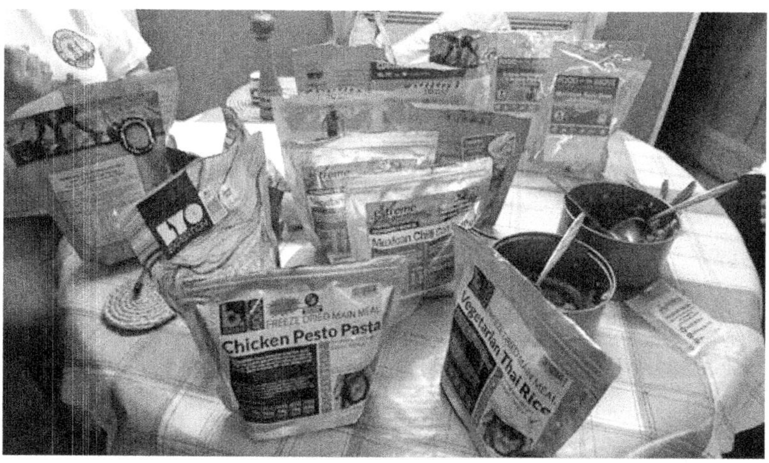

I find two that are very nice and award top marks. A couple more are good but the rest, if forced to finish, would result in an uncomfortable night.

I feel a bit guilty, some of the suppliers are small cottage industries that are just trying to eke out a living. But hey ho, I take my cues from the judges on the cruel world of TV cooking shows.

Ali and Adrian remark on how tired I look compared with my last visit back in May. We reminisce on how we met when, in 2001, I was doing my last hundred Munros. Then I just got fitter and fitter and could have carried on. Now I'm grinding to a halt after fifty-four Corbetts. Ali and Adrian, both retired GPs, say this is normal with the ageing process. It validates my decision to just do three more Corbetts (leaving a neat and manageable forty Scottish mountains per year to bag before I'm sixty) and then go home early.

I stay until the 28th, celebrating my 52nd birthday on the 27th. Despite Ali and Adrian forcing a comfy bed and a bath upon me I still feel beat. Too beat in fact to do any more hills. So, on the 28th I set off home to try and recover.

July 2017 – Scottish 2000ft Mountains

It's the evening of July 24th and I've just driven back to Scotland for three weeks in the Southern Uplands. Well, to be precise, until August 12th when they start shooting things in the hills – that is always a good day to go home.

The three weeks off have been good. In the twelve weeks I spent in the hills I had all sorts of plans of things I could do when I got home. When I got home I kicked most of them into touch on the basis they would involve a certain degree of stress.

Instead I watched Wimbledon, worked in my garden and volunteered to wash artefacts for an archaeological dig going in the village. I also visited the doctor and was diagnosed with a UTI which partly explains why I was struggled so much on my walks.

I get walking at 09:05 on July 25th and, as I record the date in my notebook see that my last walk was on June 25th. It's been a full month.

The gorgeous, cloud-free evening has turned into a cloudy but dry day. The path through farm tracks, farms and forestry is well signposted and, unlike the Corbetts and Grahams in the northern

Highlands, there is a well-made path.

Out of the forest the open ground is clogged up by low cloud, hiding the summit of the Graham, Cairnsmore of Fleet. However, the winding path requires no map and compass work and, in just under two and a half hours, I reach a memorial to the twenty-five airmen killed, in eight separate crashes, including the crew of a Heinkel.

My altimeter reads 707 metres and, with the summit marked at 771 metres on the map, I'm surprised to see the trig point just a few yards ahead. Closer examination of the map shows it at 711 metres – my fifty-two-year-old eyes were confused. I sit for lunch in a shelter, admiring the fine summit cairn.

Heading back down I disturb a herd of mountain goats, bump into a few people on their way up and return to the camper van. I then drive round to Glen Trool with the plan to do the Graham of Lamachan Hill and the Donalds of Larg Hill and Curleywee tomorrow.

It rains during the night and is still peppering the camper's roof when I wake. I listen to the forecast, there's a dry weather window due for around noon to early evening. I look at the length of the walk and figure I need to start in the rain to finish in the dry.

It's hard getting going at 10:15. All my senses tell me to stay put in the dry. But I haven't just driven back to Scotland to laze around in the camper.

I follow a track which goes downhill (again against my senses) and cross a high-sided nineteenth century bridge, straddling a thundering dark river of peat coloured water. It not only flicks up spray but earthy smells too.

I feel hot and sticky in the drizzle. I'm cheered by a fork in the path not marked on the map. No, not a branch in the path but literally a fork (i.e. a piece of cutlery) somebody has dropped. I've been hill walking twenty-seven years and I've just got to do the joke. Shame nobody is with me to share it.

I get to where the guidebook tells me to turn off. It looks harsh. A steep heather, grass and fern-clad slope with two waterfalls smashing their way through the undergrowth.

The Fork in the Path

It's very slow going. The vegetation is waist high in places. The angle is beyond what my lungs are happy with and water is tumbling down the faint path.

I soon penetrate the cloud line and with it the ability to navigate by sight. At this point my compass decides to play up – the liquid-filled bezel has formed a large bubble which causes the needle to drag and stick.

I use my GPS and reach Lamachan Hill at 14:05. It's bleak but calm. I take the spur off to Larg Hill, getting there in forty-five minutes. The cloud clears for a brief moment showing off a fine view out to sea.

I pass back over Lamachan Hill and, with the compass barely of use, get confused with the bearings. I use the GPS to confirm the direction and begin to descend, via rocky protuberances, to the low ground before the sharp rocky pull up Curleywee.

The weather begins to clear with the surroundings blurred, like I'm looking through cataracts. Then slowly the mist clears until there are fine views. The area is not rugged like the Highlands, instead the slopes are gentler, more typical of the Lake District.

I make the summit at 16:50 then head north and begin the sharp drop towards the Southern Upland Way path. Just beyond is the lovely Loch Dee – small but perfectly formed with tiny islands and pier like land masses protruding into it.

From the track it's a route march back, making for a seven-and-a-half-hour day. I pile into the van just before the end of the weather window. Rain thunders on the roof as I wash then eat.

I spend the evening reading, watching a DVD and making a compass out of the remains of three others – the base off one, the bezel from another and the retaining spring from a third.

I then look at my plans to finish the Scottish 2000ft mountains by the time I'm sixty – another eight years. With the effect of retirement slowly permeating my soul, I realise that means quite a few challenging years ahead. I renegotiate with myself (which to be honest is like pushing on an open door these days) and reckon with what I'll do this year I can, if spread over a further ten years, do eight weeks next year then six weeks per year. That'll take me to the age of sixty-two. I reckon I can do Ireland in three lots of eight weeks, taking me to the age of sixty-five. This will be enjoyable, not so challenging and keep me fit for many more years.

I wake on the 27th, drop the camper's blinds and am relieved to see a dry start to the day. From where I'm parked I want to tackle Merrick (a Corbett), Mullwharchar (a Graham), the Donald of Dungeon Hill and finally the Graham of Craignaw. It's a dauntingly big round at twelve miles and nearly 4000ft of ascent. The guide book suggests seven hours forty-five minutes, I know it'll take me around eleven hours.

It's not a walk that can easily be split up so, after yesterday's nine-and-a-half-hour walk, I have to really push myself to get started at

08:40.

I start through a wood, passing a bothy, then more trees until I hit open ground.

The weather is wet then dry, then wet again. A cold wind eats through my jacket as rain peppers me. There's a rough path up and I pass over Benyellary then onto The Merrick.

The weather is too hostile to rest so I descend the steep and slippery ground towards Loch Enoch. A tempting wall, to follow, appears through the mist but, on closer inspection, it's through a bog-riddled plain.

I keep high then pick my way towards the outflow of the loch. It proves difficult to cross, I head north until it briefly forks and I can island hop across.

The pull up Mullwharchar is straightforward. The mist is down but the rain has eased.

I descend south-east where the rain picks up again. At a little over 2000ft I make the summit of Dungeon Hill. It's now dry and I can see across to the final summit if Craignaw. The drop is littered with flowering heather – deep pink clusters on thin stems.

At the low point I feel weak. I eat my last Snickers bar, three packets of Mini Cheddars and wash it down with half a litre of water. This is enough to get me up what feels like the unending rocky battlements of Craignaw: slabs of layered rock with grass and moss as the mortar.

I sit at the top, it's 17:00 and I'm really pleased to have done this round. The weather is now clear, it feels like a fine evening is opening up.

As I descend I stumble across a memorial to the crew of an American military jet that crashed here on 19th December 1979. Bits of the aircraft have been added to the memorial. A bleak place to die and a reminder that, in life, a split-second mistake can mean your time is up.

My energy has now gone. It's a steep descent to Loch Neldricken and I find myself regularly falling over. There are deep pits to lose a leg in and I tumble forwards more times than I care to count. My trail shoes, socks, trousers and over trousers become a dripping mass of mud and water.

The highlight is the golden evening light glowing on the hills above Loch Trool. I get back to the camper van at 20:00 – after nearly eleven and a half hours out.

I take the 28th off and don't get walking again until 08:15 on the 29th from the track near Kirriereoch farm.

Still feeling tired, I find the forestry tracks hard going. I take a wrong path and it's not until I reach a true unexpected fork in the path do I realise my mistake. I backtrack and end up taking a dwindling path, through long, wet grass to the edge of the forest.

The open hillside has equally long grass and it's not until I gain height, on the slopes of Tarfessock, that the grass shortens and my pace quickens. At 2000ft I traverse to avoid the climb to the summit – I plan to do it on the way back from the Corbett of Shalloch on Minnoch.

The wind is blustery but the views are good. I reach the Corbett between 12:10 and 12:15 – the variance in time due to three marked tops which I visit in turn.

I descend south, reach the windswept Donald of Tarfessock before dropping and taking in its minor south top. The rain now sets in and Kirriereoch Hill, another Donald, disappears from view.

Boulders litter the upwards slopes and I have to watch my footing on the wet ground. The top is in thick mist, blowing by at such a rate of knots the wind is ear-shatteringly bad. I walk between all the high points until I come across a significant cairn. One top, which I think is marked by a large quartz rock, turns out to be nothing more than a dead sheep.

I put my full trust in my new compass, bought in Newton Stewart yesterday, and head west until I meet a boundary wall which dwindles into ancient iron fence posts.

The gap back into the forest is long grass, with deep water-filled gullies strategically placed to catch me out and soak me up to knee level.

I'm grateful to reach the track then return to the camper van after another very long day.

I wake on the 30th, drive into Newton Stewart for supplies then via Clatteringshaws Loch to an access point for the Graham of Millfore.

My plans to do it in the afternoon are overtaken by a strong desire to lay in the back of my camper van and go to sleep.

After some twenty hours of rest (reading, watching DVDs and listening to the radio) I step out of the van, into sunshine rain and very dark clouds, at 08:40 on July 31st.

I still feel tired as I trudge up a forestry track – the long days have taken their toll.

In a forestry break I head south-west up the knee-deep grassy slopes of Millfore. My feet sink into hidden pools as I squelch and slurp my way through.

The grass shortens in a stream-filled gully and I make my way onto a cloud-clagged ridge.

A short southerly ascent has me at the summit in two hours. Three cairns and a trig point mark the summit. In this area of the world they appear to be fond of multiple summit markers with the walker left to work out the most prominent. I head back down the same way.

I drive, via minor roads that feel like they head to nowhere, to a parking sign, on my OS map, that doesn't even appear to have a road to it. Fortunately there's a rough track and I park, not surprisingly alone, for the night.

A call of nature, in the early hours, occurs between rainstorms. The sky is briefly clear, the area boasts 'Dark Sky' status and the stars put on a good show above this remote windswept moor.

I get walking at 08:55 on August 1st – probably the first year in which I've bagged hills in five different months.

It starts dry, but the rains soon come in, interspersed with the odd moment of tantalising sun. I aim for the Donald of Meikle Millyea through grass which is long, wet and full of hidden tussocks. I deliberately gain height as soon as I can, finding shorter grass and eventually, after ascending north-west to Meikle Lump, a faint path. The ascent is now south-east and I reach a cairn and trig point in two and a half hours. To some this is the top but the guidebook speaks of a rise to the south: I'm in thick cloud so I set a bearing and use my GPS to hone in on a cairn a full two metres higher than the trig point.

Backtracking I then drop north-west towards the Donald of Milldown. I'm soon out of the cloud so rest, eat, check my mobile (noting Facebook has changed my default settings to Romanian) then head to the summit.

I head back the same way but after Meikle Lump a navigational error has me dropping too far east. This rather inconveniently deposits me in horrible bog-riddled long grass. I can only describe the return to the van, after seven hours, as a wade.

I drive to St John's Town of Dalry to get an evening meal. It turns out to be a rather bland affair and, fifteen quid lighter, I feel my own cooking could have matched it.

I then head north to the minor road running alongside Water of Ken. It becomes difficult to park – a couple of suitable places have unfriendly 'No Parking' signs next to the names of the hamlets, painted on boards shaped in the style of a pair of men's underpants.

I eventually make use of a long Passing Place by reversing onto the grass and just keeping my front wheels on tarmac. This puts the van at an angle and I have to swap beds such that I roll into the offside wall rather than onto the floor. In turn this gives me an uncomfortable night and I wake with hip pain.

I get walking at 08:25, heading for the Donald of Moorbrock Hill. I pass by one of the cottages with the no parking signs. There are one or two other dos and don'ts which, fortunately, do not apply to me. Apart that is from a sign saying that my every movement is being monitored by CCTV.

I navigate up forestry tracks but the effects of a minor cold hold me back. It's been rumbling for a few days but today is the first day that I actually feel unwell.

Two logging lorries descend the hill, I stand aside for each and get a friendly wave. As they pass the smell of freshly-cut pine teases my nostrils.

I check my GPS and find I've missed a junction in the track and unnecessarily ascended. I backtrack and find the correct turn-off, a very overgrown affair that I'm not at all surprised I missed.

Squelching my way to the hamlet of Moorbrock I then take the tracks that fade into grassland shortly before Moorbrock Hill. It's now chilly and I'm glad I chose to wear a warmer base layer today.

I check my GPS again and try and work out where the summit is. There's no ground immediately ahead that's higher, nor is any of the ground behind me. I then look down, between my feet are a couple of rocks – I'm actually stood on the summit!

I line up the route across to the wind farm-encrusted Graham of Windy Standard – with a name like that I'm not surprised the wind farm developers honed in on it.

The cloud level is at the hub height of the highest turbine. Therefore, as it rotates, the top blade disappears from view.

I make its summit at 12:45 after a slow slog up of feeling, rather literally, under the weather.

The turbines swish and drone and, in these robust winds, I get the real sense of power these machines can provide.

I eat and get going into worsening weather. My new jacket, bought in Penrith on the journey up, lets water. I feel miserable as I pop in another couple of paracetamols.

There's a fence to cross – a common occurrence in the hills. But this one, to my cost, is electrified. I get a shock, curse and leap back and grumble at the lack of warning signs. I descend to a large fence post that also acts as a tensioner. By following the cables and insulators I work out which bits are safe to handle. I make it across then descend then rise, in worsening rain, to the Donald of Alhang.

Descending south-east, via a farm, I hit the road at 15:20. I then plod for an hour and ten minutes back. Three cars pass me, none acknowledges my standing to one side. This is an unfriendly glen – The

Glen of Gloom.

I take the 3rd off, shopping in the small town of Dalmellington. I find a small friendly café and have egg, chips, beans and an orange juice for £3.60 – one gets the impression there isn't a lot of money in the Southern Uplands.

I park for the night just north of Carsphairn and get walking at 08:50 to take in the three Donalds that lie to the west.

I walk along a minor road which dwindles into a track to the old 19th century lead mines. There are deep shafts and areas gorged out of the hillside which, I presume, was for opencast mining.

Sheep now meander and graze over this once hub of activity. The industry, like its workers and their families, long forgotten, long dead.

The remains of buildings, not pillaged for their stone or fallen to the weather, poke out of the ground. A solitary chimney stack points like a finger to the past.

I reach the high point of the ruins, pass through a wall and cross bog-riddled long grass and pick up an ATV track.

I briefly manage to do without my jacket and gloves – the first time for days. But as I ascend a biting wind has me wrapping up once more.

I reach the Donald of Coran of Portmark at 11:00. I can see out to sea, a ship reflects the sun like a massive searchlight.

It's too blustery to stop so I press on, via the minor top of Bow, to reach the cloud clogged trig point summit of Meaul.

I'm cold, there's no view so I follow a handy drystone wall to the summit of Cairnsgarroch. There is now a good view of the surrounding hills and the clouds above are zooming every which way.

The descent is initially steep then, after crossing a strong flowing burn, via long wet grass with hidden rivulets to dunk ones foot in.

I pass back through the lead mine, get back to the camper at 15:00 then head to Dalmellington for a repeat £3.60 meal.

I then drive to Glen Afton where I park for the night before tackling the Graham of Blackcraig Hill and the Donald of Blacklorg Hill.

At 08:55 I'm walking, following the track then path via Blackcraig Farm, in a brief interlude between storms.

I'm grateful for the well-cut path, carved through long grass. It begins to rain as I pass over Quintin Knowe. From here I head south-west and make the summit of Blackcraig Hill. The views of the wind farms, some running, some under construction, disappear in the descending mist.

The summit is grass and rock, some made into cairns to tease the walker as to which is the true summit. I visit them all, along with the trig point.

I set a bearing for a tramp over to Blacklorg Hill. This is more rounded and unlike its neighbour is, apart from a stone wall, devoid of rock.

It's now 11:50 and I return the same route. The descent towards the farm brings dry weather and sunshine. Five minutes before getting back a heavy shower has me rather bedraggled as I climb into the camper.

After drying out I drive across to the Lowther Hills. I note a handmade sign saying 'Save the Lowther Hills'. Presumably this is from a wind farm development.

I park at around 1500ft in a steady breeze. I have to run the heating for part of the night, and on one of a number of calls of nature, I note there is a mild ground frost which I do my bit to thaw.

With the heating on I sleep well, waking around 08:00. Radio Four news is reporting that Vince Cable has said, regarding the Brexit referendum, that the elderly have shafted the young. A point I have great sympathy with. At least four people from my village, well into their eighties, voted leave based on a nostalgic view of the past.

I mark up the map and note interesting local place names: Glen Valentine, Cock Hill, Knockconey Dod, Crooked Bank and Meikle Shag.

At 09:05 I get walking – the blue sky of the evening, and very early hours, has given over to cloud.

I follow the tarmac roads that leads into the cloud then onto the radar stations on the Donald of Lowther Hill and the Graham of Green Lowther.

Starving hungry I make use of a brick building, at the summit of Green Lowther, and eat a few packets of Mini Cheddars.

The cloud clears a little and, looking back to Lowther Hill, I note that its radar apparatus looks like a gigantic golf ball set on a tee.

On the way back I break off the tarmac road and take in the Donald of East Mount Lowther. It has a viewpoint mapping out all the places I could see if it were not so cloudy.

It now begins to rain and I return dripping wet. I set up my improvised drying rails, switch on the heater and gently roast.

It's another wet night. It's rained just about every day since I've been back in Scotland. As a hillwalker you accept getting wet but day after day is tiresome.

I drive, with windscreen wipers hinting at the day ahead, through Leadhills to park up and do the two Donalds to the north-east of the Lowther Hills. The guidebook had recommended doing them as part of yesterday's walk but it'd have been a very long day.

I find a parking spot on the B7040 and head down a track to cross the Elvan Water. A group of fisherman, with a nice-smelling campfire breakfast, are camped on the shores.

What should have been a bridge is a deep ford. Too deep in fact. I walk up and down the bank and, passing the fishermen, make my excuses then return to the camper.

I drive three miles to the substantial electrical works that are fed by a multitude of pylons which, in turn, are fed by an even greater multitude of wind farms.

What looks like a bridge on the map is non-existent. I backtrack and park at Shortcleugh where a bridge on a farm track is visible from the road.

So at 09:40 I'm finally off and walking. It starts warm and dry, I take off my jacket. Five minutes later I'm hurriedly putting it back on as the rain blows back in.

It's the usual long grass tromp to the Donald of Lousie Wood Law. I pass by grouse-shooting hides, only five days to go before they are in use. The A74M is in the distance.

I get to the summit, have a bite to eat then, in wind and rain, head south-west towards the Donald of Dun Law. On route there's a really sharp drop of about 300ft that requires careful negotiation.

I make the summit at 12:15 and, given the conditions, and not wishing to renegotiate the sharp drop, head north-west and drop, through deep ankle tugging heather and ferns, to pick up a boggy track back to Shortcleugh, arriving back at the camper van after four hours.

I then drive, with the heater full on to try and dry off, round to the Daer Reservoir and park up for tomorrow's adventure.

The adventure on the 8th begins at 07:40. I have joined two walks together to attempt five Donalds and one Graham in a day, leaving the remote Queensberry for another day and another approach. This will take my total to ninety-five mountains for the year and give me the chance to break the 100 mark before the start of the grouse shooting season.

I trudge up a minor road, passing the hamlets of Crookburn and Kirkhope before taking to the track, alongside the Daer Water burn, to the abandoned hamlet of Daerhead.

Now I'm off the track and, after a tricky crossing of the burn and my first Snickers of the day, I take to the slopes of Earncraig Hill.

I feel hot so take off my jacket. This is normally akin to a rain dance but today looks good.

The actual dance I do make is to try and brush off a pesky midge that has followed me from the burn. However much I flick the air before my eyes it manages to remain in situ. Only when I realise it's inside my goggles do I manage to part company from it.

At 09:30 I make the summit and take in the good views towards Queensberry. I'm half tempted to bag it but it'd make for a very long day as it is out and back, not on the convenient loop of the planned six.

I descend towards the head of Crow Burn before the pull up

Gana Hill. The reservoir pans out to the north with the obligatory wind farm beyond.

I look across to the next peak, Wedder Law. A number of vehicles are parked on a track near its summit. I hear gunfire and realise I'm walking in the stag shooting season. I get there at 11:55 and am pleased nobody is about to order me off the hills.

From here I follow an excellent track for an hour to the summit of Scaw'd Law. It's on the path of a well-built drystone wall so I duck down and eat, sip water and take in the views – the first decent ones for a while.

Feeling tired I make it across to the Graham of Ballencleuch Law. Beyond is the minor top of Rodger Law, it has a trig point so I take it in before the drop towards Comb Law. Here I find a stream to quench my thirst and ascend to the summit – the last of the day. After sitting for a while, taking in the views across to the Lowther Hills with the golf ball-like radar station, I get going for the drop back to the reservoir and the road walk back to the camper van.

I then drive round to Thornhill, have an omelette in a café, before the intricate unclassified roads to the farm at Mitchellslacks. Parking up for the night, I wake on the 9th feeling rather tired for the walk up Queensberry.

I get going at 08:55 but with yesterday's nine-hour yomp I'm aching all over. There's a cooling breeze, I can wear just a base layer as I follow the track, alongside a ravine into a flowing burn, before the haul up the mountainside to the summit at 11:15.

The views are great, I can see the (rather long) route I did yesterday and beyond to the Lowther Hills.

There's a fine cairn to lean against and soak this all in. To the south is yet another wind farm. The turbines turn gracefully in the wind like synchronised swimmers.

Beyond is rolling lowlands which, depending on which way I set my vision, either rise to distant mountains or tumble into the sea.

The return route is the same as the ascent and I reflect this is my ninety-sixth mountain of the year. I reflect further that, given the hanging tiredness of my six in a day on Tuesday, I won't make the hundred before Saturday. However, if I do one a day on Thursday and Friday my total will be ninety-eight for the year.

Therefore I drive up to Fallburn, park up in what has become a lovely sunny afternoon with the plan to walk Tinto tomorrow.

It's a lovely evening only disturbed by one of four dogs, belonging to a woman in an SUV, racing up to me and barking aggressively. I get a lukewarm apology.

As night creeps on, and I contemplate shutting the van's rear door, a serious faced woman appears. "Are you planning to stop here the night?"

I prepare myself for some form of discussion over my right to park up for the night only to then realise it's the woman with the four dogs. Well, to be precise, two dogs as two of them have buggered off. She gives me her mobile number and I promise to text her if they come knocking in the night.

The 10th dawns cloudy, Tinto has disappeared. I lay in then get walking at 09:35 on the excellent path.

As it's popular with walkers, and I'm feeling a little self-conscious, I wear sunglasses instead of goggles. Being slightly darker, they cloud my view of the occasional dog poo, Irn-Bru can and sweet wrapper.

What also clouds my view is the cloud at the top. A fine view-plaque lets me know what I would have seen. It's 11:00, it's chilly and there is a shelter for every wind direction. I find the appropriate one and duck down.

The path back is an easy scar to follow, across the lower slopes, and, with a sore left eye, I get back at midday: I really needed the goggles.

I didn't see the dogs, I text the woman to say as much. She replies saying they'd found them in the early hours.

I drive south and take the minor road to the starting point of Cauldcleuch Head. It's mid-afternoon, the sun is shining and I look forward to this, my final peak for 2017, tomorrow.

The wind picks up during the night, rocking the van and having me turn the heating on. The radio weather forecast is for rain. I peer out at 06:35 to see the hills cloaked in cloud.

All my kit is dry, even my trail shoes. A first for many days. I don't fancy getting wet without a view. I snuggle back into my quilt content with fifty-six new Corbetts, fourteen new Grahams and twenty-seven new Unique Donalds this year. That's enough for 2017.

December 2017 – English & Welsh Nuttalls

Checking the Nuttalls website I note that the Welsh Nuttall of Craig Gwaun Taf (12/11/2016) has been promoted and Carnedd y Ddelw (31/05/2017) demoted. This leaves me with a quandary. The promotion of Craig Gwaun Taf (confirmed by Myrddyn Phillips) is on a walk I've done numerous times. Indeed the Nuttalls website states, "And the good news is that anyone who has done walk 13.1 in Volume 1 of The Mountains of England and Wales has already climbed it – the path goes right over the summit!" However, another website describes the summit as, 'knoll by edge of crag'. I recall the path is a few feet from the edge of the crag. Being the same stickler for accuracy I imagine Myrddyn Phillips to be, I'll have to go and do it.

The same check of the Nuttalls website reveals the English Nuttalls of Long Fell, Tinside Rigg and Calf Top have been promoted and Bram Rigg Top demoted.

Classification	My Total	Total
Welsh Nuttalls	188	189
English Nuttalls	253	256
Corbetts (Scotland)	115	222
Grahams (Scotland)	28	219
Unique Donalds (Scotland)	29	58
Munros (Scotland)	282	282

Ireland	0	212
Totals (10/08/2017):	895	1438

February 2018 – The Milford Track, New Zealand

In May 2017 an email came through from Steve Hampton in Melbourne:

Hi Steve – well, after battling with an overloaded server for a bit more than an hour, I've managed to book us on the Milford Track. Can hardly believe it! Booking details below – starting on 5th Feb which is pretty much the best possible time to do it. I've booked transport from Te Anau to/from the start/end of the walk – can change this if necessary.

All the best from over here. How are the hills going?

Steve.

Sat in my camper van, on my first trip to the wilds of Scotland since retiring, I had read and reread the message with sheer delight. The Milford Track, on New Zealand's South Island, is one of the jewels in the crown of walking and difficult to get on to. Steve had said he was going to try getting us places the moment the 2018 bookings opened. And he'd achieved it.

I've been told New Zealand's South Island is stunning, and the Milford Track the most stunning of all. I figured, with my love life long parked up, solo exploring further afield would be a nice extra to my retirement. As my friend Jeanette (who died of cancer three years ago) remembered me in her will I decided to put the money towards this trip. Jeanette would have approved. She always championed me, wanting me to fulfil my life.

To be free to travel I needed to let go of the daily grind of developing software and take a bit of a break from running a rail passenger group and doing lots of voluntary work in my village

Like anything with a major change in your life plans can change. More on that in a minute!

It's now Friday, February 2nd 2018 and, having flown from Heathrow, via Sydney, and passed through customs, immigration and biological hazard control, Steve is waiting for me at Queenstown Airport, New Zealand.

With my bags liberally filling a rental car we head to an Airbnb for a couple of days of preparation.

We haven't seen one another for a few years and there's some catching up to be done. It starts around his partner, Nadia, and their new daughter, Cara. Steve tells me how cute she is and I look forward to seeing her at the end of this trip.

"Well, Steve," I say, "I have some news too."

"What's that?" he asks, momentarily glancing across at me from the wheel of the car.

"I've met the love of my life?"

"Really!" he replies. Steve is fully aware of my chequered love life and, I sense, is wondering if this is another chapter in doing myself damage.

"Really," I reply with certainty in my voice. I then go on to explain how last July, after a bout of sickness, I retuned early from a Corbett bagging trip to Scotland and met Margaret at an archaeology lecture in our local village hall. Our eyes literally met across a crowded room.

Steve pauses for a moment then adds, "So if you hadn't got sick you wouldn't have met her."

"That's right, and I've lived under a mile from her for the last twenty years."

"Good grief," replies Steve. "All the while she was just up the road from you."

"I know, ironic isn't it. We started with an old-fashioned courtship and we joked we met off-line. Spending Sunday evenings together, ploughing our way through my box set of *Dad's Army* DVDs.

But we didn't get together until January."

Steve nods.

"We've become inseparable," I add, "we get on so well we just spend all the time we can together."

"That's great," he replies, nodding. "How many mountains did you manage last year?" he queries.

"Ninety-seven."

"And how many mountains are there in the British Isles?"

"1438."

"How many have you done now?"

"895."

"Is Margaret happy with you going off to finish them?"

"Yup, she knows how important it is to me."

"I'm glad to see you looking so happy, Steve."

"I know," I reply. "She's done me the world of good. But also I've got to the bottom of some dietary issues which were causing my mood to drop."

"What were they, if you don't mind me asking?"

"You know sugar and alcohol dropped my mood. But also it's certain additives and things like monosodium glutamate. Now I've cut all that out I'm quite cheerful!"

"Amazing!"

"Yeah, I know. I think the western diet is the elephant in the room. I mentioned what I'd found to my doctor and he said, 'Well if it works as a placebo then that's okay'. But I know it's not a placebo because sometimes I've had MSG by mistake, felt low and not realised until I checked back on what I've eaten. I can't be alone in this. There must be tonnes of people out there who feel low, stressed and irritable because of their diet."

It's Sunday February 4th and, with packs packed and food bought, we take Highway 94 to Milford Sound. It rises through the mountains to a Scottish-like drizzle: closed in with clouds to match. The area is one of the wettest in New Zealand. It doesn't bode well. In the previous week the tail end of a cyclone whipped the west coast, causing the relaying of people, through the three huts that adorn the trail, to come to a standstill. This in turn caused others to have their Milford Track bookings cancelled.

We break the journey to walk up to Lake Marian – a twisting path meandering through melancholic moss-covered trees. A suspension bridge leads on to the occasional wooden walkway before the terrain steepens to the Marian Cascades – a river of pure white and blue thundering down the hill.

Onwards we amuse ourselves with making up smutty limericks (the antithesis to Steve's recent PhD in early English Literature) before we reach Lake Marian after a two-hour tramp. The green lake is settled in brooding cloud-clagged mountains. Only the accents of fellow walkers remind me I'm not in Scotland.

We then drive to the Milford Sound Lodge in what can only be described as a vicious downpour. With the windscreen wiper working overtime, we pull up at a mile long tunnel and wait seven minutes for a green light to proceed. This gives us time to survey a series of streams rushing down a bare, grey rock face.

At the lodge, which is at the end of the Milford Track, we are preparing to walk, we get assigned to Room 21. After a rain-soaked dash across the car park, both our hearts sink as we find six other people already ensconced in a tiny sweltering room – only two top bunks are left.

The occupants are all young, all backpackers. To us they look normal, to them we must appear like a couple of old gits – old enough to be their parents. We have to remind ourselves we are no longer young.

We backtrack to the dining area where rain lashes against the windows. It feels like a restaurant at the end of the universe.

In total contrast to our dorm room it is gourmet style, catering for a very different clientele. All I want is some stodge for the walk – egg and chips would be ideal. Instead the waiter insists on describing each dish, how it is prepared, presented and what it contains. We order food I cannot pronounce.

We sit and eat and, recalling all the bad habits we've witnessed over the years in dormitory accommodation, plot how to get the room to ourselves. Options range from choosing the most fart-inducing dessert on the menu, clambering into our bunks with at least one testicle dangling from one's underpants to waiting until 03:00 and yelling out, "Steve, chuck us the wee bottle. No, no the one with the wide top." In the end we settle on relying on Steve's recently diagnosed sleep apnoea.

We go back to the dorm, it's stiflingly hot. We get into our bunks and try and settle for the night. The others play on their smartphones, the light isn't turned off until midnight.

At 04:00 I make my third trip to the bathroom via a very wet tree-lined car park. I get lost on the way back and can't find our dorm. After a few minutes of stumbling through bushes, trees and puddles I find a common room and make a bed on a sofa. I rue these youngsters with their youthful bladders – they don't know what lies ahead of them.

Over breakfast on Monday February 5th Steve informs me Milford Sound is actually a fjord. I have to admit my ignorance, and he explains a sound is a river leading into the sea, whereas a fjord is a glacial scoop out. When the British first arrived there was no English word for fjord and, unwilling to borrow a perfectly good Norwegian one, they declared them all sounds. At least the area is now called Fjordland, even if it is full of sounds. I suppose 'Soundland' might come across as a UK downmarket discount store.

We make the short journey to the bus station, park the car, swing our packs onto our backs and search out the bus to take us south to Te Anau Downs for a boat ride to the start of the Milford Track.

The bus driver, Bruce, fills us in how the road and tunnel was built by unemployed men during the depression of the 1930s. He also explains the Maori myth that the fiords were carved by a giant who, by the 13th, perfected his craft and created Milford Sound.

He drops us off and wishes us well.

Our hearts sink when we get to the jetty for the boat to take us along the Te Anau River. Nothing more than a dredger with a couple of park benches bolted to it.

Bruce had recommended a shepherd's hut to rest in for lunch. With an hour to spare, before the boat departs, we go in search.

We find a display board which tells us it dates from the late nineteenth century and is the oldest building in the area. We open the door to a single room that is nothing short of a slum. Strewn with decaying artefacts, and what appears to be the original horse-hair mattress, we backtrack, find a large rock to park ourselves on and eat our lunch.

A distant throb of an engine lifts our spirits that perhaps the motorised park bench isn't to be our vessel. We wander down and find a handsome boat mooring up. We are first to board, outdoing a coach party on an upmarket version of our walk.

The voyage is in pelting rain and suggestions by the steward one may wish to venture outside to enjoy the views are ignored.

The trip takes about an hour and, with the rain easing off, we follow the start of the Milford Track into trees, with green strands of moss hanging down like an enchanted garden.

A couple of New Zealand robins chirp as we pass and are quite unfazed when we stop to admire them.

We pass the first hut, a posh lodge for the coach party guests, before plodding on, alongside the River Clinton, to the Department of Conservation hut – The Clinton Hut. With the weather clear, our only hazard is a branch which brakes off and crashes to the path in front of us. A near miss – it would have hurt.

With mountains looming steep above the trees we arrive around 15:15, enjoying the short first day.

I wake on Tuesday the 6th at 03:30, sleep done for the night. I contemplate the twelve-mile-walk from the Clinton Hut to the Mintaro Hut. The next three hours are a tedious wait for others to wake up – there's only so many rude limericks one can make up. As I lay awake a number of people get up to use the facilities – the trail attracts an older walker.

The promised rain doesn't materialise, the day dawns bright with mist hanging in the valley.

We get going at 09:05 with the steep-sided mountains towering above the track, kissing the blue sky with the occasional tissue of cloud overseeing the creeks as they fall almost vertically.

These mountains, being newer than Scotland, aren't rounded off. Sheer granite faces picked out by moss and vegetation give a spectrum of hues in the morning light. New Zealand is called 'Scotland on Steroids', and today I can see why.

We come in and out of dense woodland, the trees dripping with moss, with rich orange bark, are home to the most friendly birds imaginable. Some are dark with white breasts, others a khaki green but each unperturbed by our presence – New Zealand once had no land mammals, the birds have evolved to not be wary. Their predators are now rats and the stoat – introduced, against environmental advice, in the nineteenth century to control the rabbit population which was also introduced by the white settlers. It reminds me of the nursery rhyme, 'There Was an Old Lady Who Swallowed a Fly'.

On being released, the stoats, being no fools, took one look at the rabbits munching on the pasture land and, remembering their woodland ancestry, promptly buggered off into the forests and have spent the last one and a half centuries tucking into a ready supply of the eggs of ground-nesting birds and, when not in season, snacking on the birds that do survive – including the flightless ones who gave up flying when they realised their survival didn't depend on it.

Traps, to outwit the stoats and rats, are prevalent on the trail. The odd hedgehog too – in New Zealand they are regarded as pests destroying the bird life.

Out of the trees the views towards the Mackinnon Pass are truly stunning. The ridge lines undulate just enough to draw one's focus, high snow depicts the gullies and the vertical creeks tumble down with their rhythmical pattern that repeats every few seconds. Some blow back and form a swirling mist just below the ridge line.

We rest at a small lake where a flightless Weka bird, a bit like a British fowl, comes to say hello, again confident in our presence.

We scramble across a few river beds, some with running water which requires careful crossing. I help an older lady to find her way, backtracking and taking her hand as she steps from rock to rock.

We rest often, people pass us, it's so beautiful we don't want to hurry. Instead we take our time, taking it all in and savouring each moment, each step and each view. We arrive at the hut around 16:30. We take the advice to tie our boots up as the local Kea parrot population are adept at stealing shoes and boots.

At 19:30 there's a hut talk from the warden, telling us the dos and don'ts plus tips for tomorrow. He's the most laid back young guy I've ever seen, completely at one with his work. I hope middle class aspirations never drag him down.

He labours the point about the Kea, not to feed them and to tie everything down. They nick everything they can, even the lead weights off car wheels are prone to their pesky beaks. He explains how they stole his young son, Tommy and are now raising him as their own. Actually I made that bit up but the warnings made it sound plausible.

On an early morning bathroom visit I note the night sky is awash with stars, the dark sky sharpening the image like modern 4K technology.

Back in the dorm, Steve's sleep apnoea is reaching its rafter-rattling peak. At 05:00, and feeling a tad grumpy, I ferret around for my pen light, click it on and shine it in his face in an attempt to get him to roll over. However, he's outfoxed me by wearing a face mask.

I get some brief sleep but at 06:00 on Wednesday the 7th somebody's alarm wakes the entire hut.

Over breakfast I speak to a lady, "Did you hear that alarm? Really inconsiderate."

"It was me," she replied.

I don't even try digging myself out of the hole.

We get walking at 08:50 for the toughest day of the track, from Mintaro Hut to Dumpling Hut, across the Mackinnon Pass at 1154m high.

The path starts through the familiar trees, draped with moss, which looks like another enchanted garden. We then begin the zig-zag path up to the ridge. It's well made and has a forgiving gradient. But the day is hot, the skies are blue and we are oh so slow.

We are soon passed by the walkers staying at the posh lodges (ours are called huts). We discover they have showers and I'm sure our lack of showers is nasally obvious to them. Other walkers are a mix of New Zealanders, Australians, Chinese and Americans.

There are sheer drops shielded by thick vegetation – a mix of ferns, trees and grasses. At the top the views are stunning, the alpine air is pure and the wafts of mountain freshness skirt past us with each light wind. The steep-sided mountains undulating, some hogging the sky, others dropping to reveal big sky. The odd snow field is still around and waterfalls tumble – the rain of recent days adding to the vista.

At the high point of the day we rest at the Quintin Mackinnon monument. A Scottish New Zealand explorer who, in 1888, founded the route through to Milford Sound. In 1892 he drowned in Lake Te Anau – his body was never found.

The descent is exposed, and therefore very hot. Steve and I swelter in the heat as many people overtake us. We don't care, we want to take our time.

In the distance the Sutherland Falls plummet from the high ground and we reflect how we have had the best of both worlds: perfect weather after heavy rain means the waterfalls, and creeks, are in fine fettle. Rainbows form on their spray with polished silver like reflections as the sun beats on their aqua flows.

Mountains towering above the trail

We drop back to a path that's the spectacle of an enchanted garden. Now wooden walkways help us descend then guide us across boggy ground.

We skip the detour to Sutherland Falls, another uphill section in the blistering heat doesn't tempt us. The path improves and we trudge our way to the hut, arriving 17:00 – two hours later than the estimated time.

I note tonight's hut talk is at 20:00, each night half an hour later. I wonder if this is deliberate, giving everybody an extra half hour a day to catch up as tiredness sets in.

Reading the notice boards I discover Milford Sound is named after Milford Haven following the first European arrival, in 1812, being from Milford Haven. There's more information on the stoat problem – 95% of kiwi chicks end up as snacks for the said mammal. The traps are numerous, the problem momentous.

Thursday the 8th dawns another gorgeous day, we set off at 07:30 – our boat at the end is booked for 15:00 and, given yesterday's pace, we need to crack on.

At first we head through the charmed trails of green twisted trees and mahogany coloured bark that entice us like a fairy tale. We take regular snacks to keep our blood sugars up, yesterday we let them slip which, on the downhill sections, literally caused us to slip.

We walk through a mixture of tree-lined path, suspension

bridges, snatched lake views and towering mountains with their waterfalls.

Steve warns me the end of our walk, Sandfly Point, is one of the most appropriately named places in New Zealand. The sandfly is a bolshie cousin of the Scottish midge and awaits completers of the Milford Track with mouth-watering contempt.

Also Sandfly Point is named more in the Maori tradition of naming places, and wildlife, after some distinguishing feature. Unlike the white settlers who were hell bent on naming things after the discoverer, the discoverer's birthplace or some white man who needed to be appeased – the Maori people are a more humble breed, closer to nature, closer to the earth.

Mitre Peak, Milford Sound

We get to Sandfly Point at 13:50, batting away sandflies as we emerge from the wooded track. With the 14:00 boat about to leave, we take the last two places and, with it powering out into Milford Sound, we look back at the track – our home for the last three days. It's a sad goodbye, au revoir and auf wiedersehen, as the mountains bask in the sun.

Steve and I stay another night in the bunkhouse at Milford Sound. We take a boat trip through the stunning scenery and get a fantastic view of Mitre Peak which thrusts out of the sea in the shape of a bishop's mitre.

The mountains are so steep sided that when the boat pulls up alongside them it's impossible to get a sense of scale.

We drive back to Queenstown and pitch up at a campsite Steve has booked me on to. He is due to fly back to Australia, leaving me to do eighteen days of touring before flying to Melbourne to stay with him, Nadia and the eighteen-month-old Cara.

Steve looks at my dropping face as I survey the rundown shanty town which we pitch his tent amongst. "You'll be okay," he says kindly, "when you get going tomorrow. This is the worst campsite I've ever seen. The others you stay on won't be like this."

I nod. I don't just feel depressed at the thought of staying on this place but with Margaret back in England, and Steve about to fly back to Australia, I'm feeling alone. Eighteen days of solo touring doesn't feel very appealing right now.

After dropping Steve off, and a heart-wrenchingly lonely evening on the campsite, I wake on February 11th, bundle the tent into the back of the hire car which Steve, forever the epitome of kindness, has transferred into my name.

I drive and take in the full glistening beauty of Lake Wanaka from the high point above Lake Diamond. The high clouds glow above the mountains, some dropping down to cover their peaks, others seesawing on the tops. The trees make for dark patches, whereas the lake below glows yellow, orange and red. Silhouetted ridge lines tempt my eyes towards the ones that glow an ochre red. Between the trees and the summits lies a band of floating grey cloud.

It's the evening of February 12th and, having driven up via Lake Hawea and spent part the day admiring the receding Franz Josef glacier, I'm now sat reading in a backpacker's hostel in Franz Josef. My book, *Schindler's List*, is dark amongst the freedom and beauty New Zealand has to offer.

An American chap stops by and, while pointing to my book, announces, "My dad was on that list."

The room stops. Everybody looks on.

We get chatting, his name is Alvin Lewis, son of Victor Lewis. Both he and his later wife were in the concentration camps. Their survival was good will, good survival skills, good timing and good luck.

February 13th I give an American-Italian chap (as he describes himself), Bronco a lift along the coast. He stayed the previous night in the same hostel. Despite very different backgrounds, and he being in his early seventies, we get along well. Chatting away, putting the world to rights.

I note how supple and fit he looks. He puts it down to yoga.

I drop him at a crossroads before turning inland towards Arthurs Pass. Stopping for the night at a small public campsite I get walking on February the 14th to attempt the summit of Avalanche Peak.

I struggle to find the narrow path from which to start the walk. After wasting some time I find it tucked away and begin the ascent from the 1100m of Arthurs Pass to the 1840m summit.

It's a windy walk with a few twists and turns across a rubble-strewn mountain. Some people turn back on the final ridge but, as a veteran of many a Scottish mountain, I brave the gusts and make it to the summit.

While sat down, eating my lunch in mist-obscured views, I feel a tugging on my backpack. On closer examination I find a Kea parrot attempting a break-in and entry. It takes a few goes to see him off.

In the evening I phone Margaret. It's St Valentine's Day and we're struggling being apart. When we hang up I decide I'm too despondent to stay in this clagged-in clouded mountain region so I get the map and guidebook out: Kaikoura, on the east coast, looks sunny with group activities one can book on to and meet people.

Arriving on the 16th I take my first paddle in the Pacific Ocean before going in search of a kayaking trip to enjoy the views and the wildlife.

The woman who takes my booking says, "Awesome" to every part of the transaction. Well New Zealand is awesome. Everybody says so. I notice you only have to hand over a dollar coin for a postcard and the till operator will say, "Awesome." Though sometimes they say "wicked" and I can't help but feel I'm in an episode of Reggie Perrin.

I find a nice campsite with good facilities and a few people to at least nod and say hello to.

On February 17th I wake to a Second World War air raid siren. With nobody looking perturbed, and no Heinkel 111s in sight, I ask around and learn the siren is used to summon local firefighters to attend their station. I can only assume these were shipped over from the UK after the Second World War. Either way it's a chilling sound.

I drive around to the kayaking centre and introduce myself to one of the instructors.

"Awesome, I'm Connor," replies the instructor, a sun-bleached blond, long-haired New Zealander.

Other people arrive and I am relieved, given my age, to be assigned to accompany Connor in his two-person kayak.

That is until a pretty German girl arrives. After one glance from Connor she gets allocated to his kayak and I'm relegated to accompanying an eighty-year-old chap called Alan.

So with Alan and I being the two oldest, with a combined age of 132, we start our paddle.

After about an hour he looks worn out. I take pity on him and tell him to stop paddling. At this point he announces his son and daughter-in-law, in one of the other kayaks, are fitness mad, heading off to the gym each day!

I begin to feel rather 'done'. Why couldn't they have taken him out? They are zipping ahead at great speed, as is Connor and the German girl. And here I am, the second oldest, ferrying their dad, the oldest in the group, and feeing somewhat knackered.

To keep Alan's spirits up I point out the wonderful backdrop of mountains.

"Oh we have plenty of those in Colorado," replies Alan.

I take a deep breath and temper the desire to bash him over the head with the paddle.

There are lots of fur seals and, to my amusement, shags. After two hours of rowing, with our starboard engine stalled, we make it back to the beach. Last.

Just as everybody is set to leave Alan's son thrusts $20 into my hand and says, "Have lunch on me."

I did.

It was awesome.

I get to the evening and book myself on a whale-watching trip. With blue skies the hues off the mountains are awe— no I mean incredibly beautiful. We see a stingray, three sperm whales, a humpback whale, a couple of albatross and, to finish up, a couple of hundred dolphins in one pod.

I wake on February 18th with the plan to climb Mount Fyffe. It's a blisteringly hot day and after walking wooded then open tracks and paths I stop, after 1000m of ascent, to rest at the Mount Fyffe Hut.

With over 500m further to the summit I realise I don't have enough water to carry on so sit and enjoy the views. New Zealand is great in the shade but the sun is far hotter than the UK thanks to an ozone hole.

I gaze down to Kaikoura and the ocean beyond. There are some darker patches where the ocean plunges to 1000m depth, just a bit further out it drops to 2000m. This allows the whales to live close to land as they are a natural deep divers

It's February 19th and, with Cyclone Gita set to hit, I've driven south to Christchurch. I look around the Air Force Museum of New Zealand, the awesome Botanical Gardens and then take a vintage tram ride around the historic regions of the city, much still devastated by the 2011 earthquake.

A lot of work is going on to rebuild the city.

With the news of the cyclone closing in, I drive to the Akaroa, a sheltered costal township. I find a campsite and bang in every tent peg.

During the night I retreat, with my sleeping bag, to the common room. I'm joined by others who have abandoned their tents.

In the morning I survey the tent. Actually I'm surprised it is still there. But it's now flattened. I take it to bits and manage put it through a low heat cycle in the laundry's tumble dryer.

I then retreat back to the common room for the day and night as the cyclone lashes rain against the windows and rattles the roof.

A couple from Worthing provide me with some entertainment. When abroad it's easy to be drawn to those from your own country. Though being from the same country is about where the similarity stops with this couple. For Mr and Mrs Racist are on a world tour which, by all accounts, involves standing in immigration queues at airports waiting to be processed by "Darkies".

"And that's another thing," says Mrs R, oblivious that I've gone a bit quiet, "when we last returned to Gatwick we had the indignity of somebody blacker than the ace of spades checking our passports and deciding if we can re-enter our *own* country."

It's February 22nd and, with a couple of days lost to the cyclone, I drive down to Timaru, find a campsite and book in for two nights. I was attracted to the place for its famous beach. Unfortunately I'd failed to spot it's also a container port. And not just a small affair. Miles of containers line the coast, leaving the beach in their shadow at one end.

Over the thirty-six hours I'm here I manage to eat in every restaurant (there's three of them) and get used to looking out to sea with one hand cupped over the side of my face to hide the containers.

Determined to enjoy my remaining days I get going on February 24th and drive, via the glorious Hooker Lake, around to Mount Cook village.

With high winds forecast for the night I set off walking to the

Hooker Glacier. Through rocks, bridges, moraine humps and wider valley floors, I reach it in around ninety minutes. It's a deep, wide gully with grey meltwater feeding into the river.

Ahead, and to the right is Mount Cook. First climbed by Sir Edmund Hilary its towering 3724m is hard to adjust the eye to. At one level its snow and rock-capped summit appears to be nearby but, when taking in the surroundings, it looks very far away.

I spend most of the night on the phone to Margaret while being bashed by the wind hit tent. I only hang up when I realise I need both hands to keep the thing from being ripped away. It feels like I'm spending the night sharing the tent with and excited Labrador.

At 06:30 the tent collapses and I find myself entangled in a mass of material and poles digging into my legs and ribs.

I extract myself and try to make sense of the remains of the tent. One of the poles is badly bent, I manage to straighten it by hooking it through one of the holes in the steel wheel of the car and bending it straight.

I retreat to the common room. I have paid for two nights but I decide to leave now. After wasted time at Akaroa I don't fancy another day sat in a common room hoping for the weather to improve.

I get chatting to an American chap. He arrived late yesterday and plans to extend his stay by a day.

"Do you want my extra night's camping permit?" I ask.

"Wow!" he replies, his eyes lighting up.

This takes me back a bit. I mean, it's under $20 worth.

Once he has calmed himself down he asks where he can buy gas and matches from. I hand him some spares I have.

"A camping permit, gas and matches," he exclaims.

I leave my 'new best friend' and get chatting to a couple of young women who want to get off this campsite. I give them a lift down to Wanaka where my day improves as I find a room available in a hut on a campsite.

The day improves further by finding a café playing The Kinks and The Beatles.

My final few days are spent on a campsite in Queenstown – better than the 'shanty town' I stayed on last time.

I drive up to Queenstown Hill and, at 907m survey the mountains with their glorious hues towering over sparkling lakes. But I feel a bit lost, missing Margaret. This a new one for me. Missing somebody and them missing me at the same time.

I decide to take a walk up Ben Lomond. With its famous Scottish namesake it'll be great to have both ticked off in my list of walking achievements.

I find the start of the walk, near to a small roadside car park in a suburb of the town. Through wooded tracks, with the sun glistening through the trees, and mountain bikers and zip wire enthusiasts hurtling by, I reach the top of a cable car run.

With the mountain above I'm taken in by a gravity go-kart track. You start from at the bottom, on a cable car, and are whisked up to a hut where, after some basic instruction, you hurtle off down a concrete toboggan-like run.

Well it would have been rude not to. I have two exhilarating goes. The go-karts are very simple – you have a steering wheel which also, by pushing it away from you, acts as the brake.

It's great fun and, after stopping for lunch, I decide to abandon Ben Lomond and take the picturesque walk back to the car.

It's February 28th and I've a long wait at Queenstown Airport. My nerves are jangled, I find airports unnerving places. But the New Zealanders, unlike those running UK airports, are very friendly.

A Tannoy announces the two New Zealand athletes, who have just won medals at the South Korean Winter Olympics, are arriving at one of the gates. So I get to say hello and congratulate Zoi Sadowski-Synnott (snowboarding) and Nico Porteous (freestyle skiing). They are both shy and bemused by the attention and applause.

Later I just make myself out on New Zealand TV.

Steve meets me at the airport in Melbourne. Given his sleep apnoea he's kindly booked me in to a cabin on a holiday park near to his home.

I spend an enjoyable few days here. It's a mix of celebrating his birthday, sightseeing in Melbourne and catching up with old friends, including Chrissy Dorrian – an old friend from my time at Brighton Polytechnic.

Oh and there's Steve's partner, Nadia and their cute little eighteen-month-old daughter, Cara. I love playing with her and, as Cara fetches yet another book for me to read to her, Nadia raises her eyebrows and says, "She's got you around her little finger."

I also note sideways glances between Nadia and Steve as I willingly spoon-feed Cara at the supper table.

"You'll have to have words with Margaret when you get home," says Nadia, pulling my leg.

Steve and I do a final walk on Wilsons Prom, taking in the wonderful Sealers Cove which we visited in February 2006.

Steve drops me at Melbourne Airport for the flight back to England. I'm sad to leave but looking forward to getting home.

I return, enthusing to Margaret about New Zealand and baby Cara.

"She gives me a look of, 'Well'?"

May 2018 – Scottish 2000ft Mountains

It's May the 8th 2018 and I'm saying goodbye to Margaret. Since being together I've spent five weeks away in New Zealand and a week down in Devon. With this pre-planned trip to Scotland, we are both struggling with another parting.

So it's with sadness that I set off to Scotland to continue my quest to climb all the 2000ft mountains of the British Isles. However, the new relationship has got me to rethink my strategy. I'm now going to take until l I'm sixty-five to complete these Scottish mountains with an aim to do twenty-six Corbetts or Grahams this year, twenty-three per year thereafter and add in the remaining Donalds along the way.

The traffic flows freely as I leave the sunny south behind. Passing through Cumbria the rains set in, keeping me company until north of Glasgow where evening sun cheers my mood.

I park up on the minor road in Glen Fruin only to find no mobile signal. I backtrack many miles to find a signal, call Margaret then return to the same spot and notice vehicles glinting as they pass on the ground above me. My OS map shows no road or track so I assume that there's some new wind farm roadway and the vehicles are there for its construction.

I mark up the map for the Grahams of Beinn Chaorach and Beinn a' Mhanaich tomorrow. The guidebook makes reference to a 'new road'. I get out my motoring atlas and note that, what I thought might be an access road for a wind farm, is instead the A817 – built since my OS map was printed in 1989.

It's a chilly night, I sleep on and off until I switch on the heater then wake, very dry mouthed, a little after 07:00.

I set off, in dry weather with cloud hanging over the tops, and follow a track which soon crosses the A817 – it's not fresh tarmac and has obviously been here sometime. Why wasn't I told?

I branch north-east from the track and make steady progress through the short bracken. An annoying drop has me crossing a stream before the grass slopes to the blustery summit cairn and trig point of Beinn Chaorach, two hours into my walk.

I follow a fence as I descend 1000ft to the low ground that marks the ascent of Beinn a' Mhanaich. It looks to be a long pull up and I rue the loss of height. Grahams only need a drop of 500ft in all directions, this one overdid it a bit.

The rain sets in. Fine penetrating stuff that gets into my neck and wets my chest. I make steady progress and, after a check of the GPS, find the summit. The rain gets worse, visibility drops and I have to take a compass bearing to follow the ridge line.

With only a few yards of visibility, and raindrops dripping from my hood to keep me company I traipse the ridge, dropping steadily to meet the A817. I cross a few gates to get myself onto the minor road and the short walk back to my camper van at 14:20.

May 10th dawns clouded over, which is not promising for a long day climbing the Grahams of Mid Hill (Beinn Dubh), Doune Hill, Cruach an t-Sidhein and Beinn Eich. I get walking at 07:20 following the well-signposted route through a field. Realising I've forgotten to pack my fleece, I debate whether to return for it but decide to chance it and press on.

There's light rain in the air followed by patchy blue sky allowing the sun to glisten on the rippling waves of Loch Lomond. Forested islands stand in solitude amongst the lapping waters.

In just under three hours, in hail and snow, I reach Mid Hill. I'm glad to then drop some height. But, with my hands stinging through my thin woollen gloves, I'm not so glad to drop a further 1500ft to the low ground before the very tough ascent of Doune Hill, following a tree-lined gully.

I make the trig point and tiny cairn summit at 13:45. I now briefly drop south-west before dropping to the low ground before Cruach an t-Sidhein. The weather cheers up, I change into dry gloves and I cheer up too.

Cruach an t-Sidhein is a well-behaved Graham with just 500ft ascent to its pap-shaped summit. I slump down and survey the scene from the furthest point of the day. I take in the views of the mountains I did yesterday. The horseshoe of today's hills lay before me. The short grass, in the foreground, cowers against the wind.

I drop back to the low ground and see a rare sight – a fellow walker. Up from Glasgow she's pleased that I share some sultanas and nuts with her. We say goodbye, with her heading up Cruach an t-Sidhein and me off to the final summit of the day, Beinn Eich.

I take a traverse then make the ridge and reach the summit at 17:15. I'm now feeling tired so rest awhile, take a video of my route and post it on Facebook.

View back towards Luss from the summit of Beinn Eich

I start the descent and head towards Luss. It looks depressingly long, the drop to the road then a two-and-a-half-mile tarmac walk back to my camper van. My energy levels are dropping, I've been out over ten hours and it's starting to feel that way.

Diane, the lady up from Glasgow, catches me up and happens to mention she's parked at the top of the road and can, if I like, give me a lift. Do I like? She's my absolute hero. She drops me off at 19:05, she's interested in the camper van. I open the rear door to show her the layout. There's a strange smell, along the lines of a smelly sock crossed with a wet Labrador. She's too polite to make any comment other than praise for my purchase.

I call Margaret in the evening, explaining that after my twelve-hour walk I will have to review my ability to put in a third consecutive day. I wake at 09:25, legs aching with my back complaining about the tumbles, on wet grass, I've taken the previous day. There's no doubt that this will be a day off.

I head into the village of Luss to breakfast. There's a large coach park with an equally large queue for the loos. In the village shop there's a queue for the hot food counter. In front of me are two American men, one sports a pair of tartan trousers to, presumably, acknowledge some distant strand of Scottish DNA. He mentions being part of a former British Colony then corrects himself to 'English Colony' to, I presume, not offend any eavesdropping Scottish person. Personally, if Scottish, I'd have been offended by his trousers! I'm one sixteenth Scottish myself but wouldn't dream of being so presumptuous as to give myself permission to wear a tartan. In fact the only tartan I have is a blanket in my camper van, and that is only because it was a bargain on eBay.

I then drive round to Glen Douglas to position myself to tackle the Grahams of Tullich Hill and Beinn Bhreac tomorrow.

Waking on Saturday the 12th at 05:00, I'm still full of aches and tiredness. I had a bout of the flu about a month ago, I still get phlegm and I think that's holding me back a bit.

I step outside to answer a call of nature. The weather looks promising with light mist, poised to clear, covering the hills. I get walking at 08:10 and the hills are on show, against a blue sky, as I pass the farm buildings and bungalows that make up Invergroin. I take note of the signs requesting privacy when entering and exiting the land for the hills.

Finding the way they want me to head, signposted for convenience, I strike up the hill towards Tullich Hill. I'm very sluggish, back to my old ways of taking a few paces then resting.

After an hour I reach a newly-planted commercial forest. The trees are no more than a foot high, making navigating amongst them very straightforward. It's a forest that'll never make it on to my ageing map.

The disadvantage of the new forest is that it is surrounded by a six-foot deer fence. Still in sight of the farm at Invergroin, and noting that the fence is rather new, I'm reluctant to scale it. Instead I head for the highest point and find a stile.

I make the summit of Tullich Hill in over two and a half hours, very slow and feeling rather hot though, once settled down, a cooling wind airs me. There's the sound of chirping birds as I look out at the rolling grassland falling away to the glen below then rising again with its tucks and creases sheltering the naturally-occurring trees.

I get a good phone signal and, while enjoying the panoramic views, call Margaret. A seaplane, heading towards Loch Lomond flies overhead.

I head east to a couple of lochains before the north-east descent towards the low ground from which I can ascend Beinn Bhreac. I'm soon facing a sheer drop and have to re-ascend before picking up a sheep track that leads me to ground safe enough to descend from.

The ground is marshy and I have to pick my way carefully to the low ground at 1000ft. From here it's a south-easterly ascent keeping, to the side of the hill to avoid an undulation on the ridge line.

My legs complain all the way and I'm tricked by a few false summits before some rocky ground leads me to the trig point.

I set my compass to avoid upsetting anybody at Invergroin. Its boggy going again. I have to cross a few low fences and a stream or two before making it to the road. Passing through Invergroin I get chatting to an old man tending the garden of one of the bungalows. I finally get back to the camper van at 16:30.

Back in Tyndrum I park up for the night and awake to rain pattering on the roof of the camper van. I take my time to get going for the drive around to Glen Coe to tackle the Grahams of Sgorr a' Choise and Meall Mor.

I park by the Co-op in Ballachulish, buy bits for breakfast and mark up the map for the day ahead.

The rain stops so I get walking at 09:30 along Gleann an Fhiodh. I feel slow, drawn and sluggish. I'm trying to do at least two peaks a day so I can finish the twenty-six planned for this year quicker than normal and get home to Margaret. This is making for some long days and today doesn't look like any kind of exception.

There's a good path to follow until I reach a large cairn where I cross a river and pause to drink and take on spare water.

I climb steeply south-east, at a pace befitting a snail, to the summit ridge which, at a shade after midday, I'm grateful to reach.

The weather is now hot and the smell of cut pine, from the forest below, wafts gently in the breeze and enriches my senses. It's a nice ridge, the sun picking out the snow on the north faces of the surrounding Munros. They look menacingly large and I still can't believe that I managed to climb them all. When you are in the midst of a project it doesn't feel as profound as when you look back, years later.

I pass along bare rock interspersed with short grass and make the summit of Sgorr a' Choise, over four hours into the day.

I rest for a while and take in the superb panorama. This is really Munro territory with just the occasional Corbett and Graham squeezed in for good measure. So even though I'm on a summit others tower above me.

I set off south-east to a lower bump then head north-east towards Meall Mor. I'm very slow, painfully slow in fact. My body is protesting at the long days I've given it of late. A few drops of rain have me donning my waterproofs, however it comes to nothing.

I make the summit at 16:40, a cairn on a rocky ridge. I briefly rest then head west to another cairn (just in case it's higher). Ben Nevis graces the distance, the Aonach Eagach ridge, with its menacing pinnacles guards the north side of Glen Coe. Being a Sunday I imagine there are walkers on all the surrounding Munros. However, I'm alone.

I look for a way down. My map is out of date and the forest marked has been felled and another has grown. I head for a phone mast but it's a confusing descent. I eventually end up at the disused quarry near to where I'm parked. From here it's hard to make my way through the wooded paths. I take a few wrong turns but eventually, at 19:10, reach the camper van.

It's been a shade under ten hours, the book time was just over five. It's been a slow day.

The Pap of Glencoe (or Sgorr na Ciche to give it its Gaelic name) is a fascinating mountain. Standing pert and rounded, guarding the entrance to the glen, it is one of the most identifiable mountains of Glen Coe but, at 2435ft, one of the smallest. Of course, being a school boy at heart, I'm minded that 'Pap' means breast and pert and rounded is just what it is.

Anyhow today, May 14th, I decide to give this Graham my complete attention. I get walking at 10:10, following a track that soon dwindles to a rough path through grass, streams, bog and rock. I'm slow going again, finding the need to rest often on this steep mountainside.

There are a few people around today. It's a popular peak so I have some brief chats with French, Dutch, German and Danes.

I struggle to the ridge then take the gravel-ridden paths through the rocky summit region. Here my pace picks up. There's a few twists and turns as the path winds its way around the back before presenting me with the final pull on to the top, three hours into the day. I'm treated to some incredible views: the bridge at Ballachulish spans the throat of Loch Leven and the mountains of yesterday and the Munros of Glen Coe grace the panorama.

I set off back. A man and woman are making their way through the rough rocky path. She is nervous, clinging to the ground. I advise her to look a bit further ahead – she's freaking herself by concentrating on every step.

I get on to the easier ground and pick my way. There's so many paths up that I miss the one I ascended on but, by keeping the starting point in focus, I'm able to wind my way back and, after a slip up on wet ground, reach the camper van.

I then drive round to Garva Bridge where I park up for the night and spend the 15th being a 'Trail Angel' and making coffee and hot chocolate for those crossing Scotland on the TGO Challenge.

I hear news of a guy, Jim Davison, whose stove has broken. Apparently he needs a pair of pliers to have a go at mending it. I get my pair ready and also look out my stove. When he arrives I surprise him by handing him the necessary pair of pliers and, when he fails to fully fix it, my stove and my address to which to post it back. It's a good feeling to be of service!

A group of four Americans call me 'Trail Magic Steve'. My final cup of coffee is made for a woman, not on the TGO Challenge, who parks next to me and goes for a two-hour run. As I hand her the coffee she mentions the two-hour run was up and down the Munro of Geal Charn. Some people are incredibly fit.

I spend the evening with Ali and Adrian Ogden in Newtonmore. They offer me a comfy bed and a leisurely breakfast. I return the favour by going to lend a hand at their hostel. The four Americans arrive and announce, "Hey it's trail magic Steve!"

In the afternoon I drive a short distance down the A9 to take in the Graham of Creag Ruadh. It's a lovely sunny afternoon and I get walking at 13:25 along the hydro track. I overshoot the branch-off point so take a steeper route through the tinder-dry heather. After two hours I settle down, to soak in the views from the summit. A cool wind picks up so I don my jacket. Some of the neighbouring mountains have snow in their high reaches which contrasts with the deep blue sky.

Setting off back I cross rough ground before picking up the hydro track again. I bump into three separate groups of TGO Challenge walkers (five people in all), stopping for a chat with each.

I get back to the camper van at 17:10 before an evening with Sue Foss in Dalwhinnie. We have a nice meal and I hear the stories of her TGO Challenge crossing so far. Other challengers are in the bar and we get chatting to Colin who, on his twentieth crossing, is not far short of what I'm aiming to achieve: all the mountains of the British Isles.

I don't leave until around 22:00 and find myself negotiating the dark, narrow roads around to Glen Roy. An hour later I'm pointing the camper van up the single-track glen road and disturbing sheep and their lambs that have bedded down on the tarmac for the night. They look soulfully into my headlights as they winch themselves to their feet and amble off.

I sleep well at the viewpoint parking area and then take the short drive to a twist in the road where I set off for Leana Mhor (west) at 10:20.

Feeling fitter today I need fewer rests as I take to the hillside, crossing the glen's famous parallel roads (old shores of retreating lakes from the last ice age). I follow a stream under a warm, predominantly blue, sky.

The high ground, in the shade, is damp and the heather flattened – a sure sign that the snow has only recently melted. I press on, the grass becomes tinder dry and crunches satisfactorily below my feet. As I approach the summit cairn the ground softens, my footsteps quieten and I tag the cairn after two hours' walking.

There are great views from the summit. Glen Roy stretches before me, terminating in rising ground. To the south is Ben Nevis with still a reasonable amount of snow.

Resting for a while I then set off back and drive a short distance further up Glen Roy where I park up for what becomes a chilly night by the bridge over the River Roy.

I get walking at 08:20 for the longer ascent, than yesterday, of the also named Leana Mhor.

I head to around 1000ft to pick up one of the parallel roads. Being very visible from afar I thought this would be easy but, in fact, they are hard to distinguish on the ground. So I end up traversing what I think is one of the parallel roads round to a deep-gullied stream. I keep ascending until I can pick my way over the stream then continue my contouring until the slopes of Leana Mhor (east) look sympathetic enough, and dry enough, for my final ascent. Reaching the top after five hours I am, as a reward, presented with a small pile of stones that form the summit cairn.

I sit awhile, admiring the mountains sat below the high cloud. A few spots of rain come down but amount to nothing.

I make my way back and, determined to walk along the 1000ft parallel road, am flummoxed when the battery in my altimeter dies. Arriving back at the camper van, I write up my diary and fill the water tank from the River Roy.

I drive to Spean Bridge, feast at the café then park up for the night at the Commando Memorial with a view to doing Glas Bheinn, above Loch Arkaig, tomorrow. I watch coach parties arrive, I watch the overweight drivers in their kilts, and I watch the passengers take a multitude of photographs of the monument. To me Scotland by coach, or car road trip, doesn't hold enough. If you like the outdoors Scotland has lots to offer, but touring around it feels a little dull.

Saturday the 19th brings the fiddly drive via, Gairlochy, Loch Lochy and the head of Loch Arkaig to seek out the parking spot, at Achnasaul, from which to ascend Glas Bheinn. When I arrive I berate myself for the lack of notice I took to the map – the parking spot is the very same I used last year for the Corbetts of Geal Charn and Meall na h-Eilde. The former of which is where I waited, in a storm, for Ali Ogden. With a bit more careful planning, I could have taken in Glas Bheinn on the same walk.

I get walking at 09:35, missing the royal wedding in Windsor. I follow a well-made track but feel slow and lethargic. My upper legs are complaining as weariness sets in.

Once on open ground I pick up speed and haul myself, through short heather and grass (trying to un-mat itself from the weight of the winter's snow), to the summit.

It's a fair-sized flattened cairn. The distant mountains, misted by high clouds, speckle the horizon with snow-clad corries. The wind is warm but strong enough to have me seeking shelter for lunch – nuts and sultanas have been my staple diet this year.

I make it back to the camper van at 13:20 and set off for Fort William. My first and last Munros, Carn Mor Dearg and Aonach Mor, stand proudly side by side in the glistening afternoon sun. At over 4000ft each they look massive (in fact, compared with the Grahams they are massive). Again I wonder how I managed the Munros. A younger body, sleepless nights in Youth Hostels giving earlier starts, more determination, perhaps?

In Fort William I buy myself a feast from Morrisons, park up and listen to Chelsea v Man United, via a 4G signal, in the FA Cup final. Chelsea win 1-0 and I reflect how, in the past, I'd had to have driven around to find a Radio Five Live reception. Now the phone masts outdo the BBC transmitters. Smartphones have really taken off in the last decade, before that there were simple handsets for phone calls and text only – and I didn't get one of those until 2001.

After the match I drive to Lundavra, on a road out of Fort William that I never knew existed. I park up for the night and get walking, with a festering sore throat, at 08:30 for the Graham of Beinn na Gucaig.

The weather has changed, there's light rain in the air which is driven against me by a jostling wind. I head north-west where the rain and wind picks up and batters me. My pack cover dislodges itself and becomes a sail, flapping wildly in the wind. I look around for shelter and drop below some high ground to sort it out.

I pass a fence which has a sole purpose of carrying a coaxial cable to a TV aerial which services the tiny hamlet of Lundavra. A junction box in the cable has its cover blown off and lying on the ground. I do some maintenance and reattach it.

I press on to the ridge where, paradoxically, the wind drops back a bit and I make better progress, through cloud and rain.

Spying the trig point summit, I am pleased to make the final haul, through some minor craggy ground, and tag it at bang on 11:00. I note what looks like some higher ground to the south-west so go and stand on that before doing the same for a piece to the north-east.

I cut down, in wind and rain, picking up the road nearer to Lundavra. With some relief I get back to the camper van.

The guidebook recommends that Beinn na Gucaig is done with Tom Meadhoin but, to me, it looks like a long walk round. Instead I drive down to Loch Leven to enable Tom Meadhoin to be tackled from the south tomorrow. When I pull up I recognise the car parking place from last year and, like Glas Bheinn from the other day, realise that I could have easily included Tom Meadhoin when taking in the Corbett of Mam na Gualainn. It reminds me that I should mark all the peaks on my maps so when doing a Corbett I can keep an eye out for nearby Graham neighbours and vice versa.

I phone Margaret then my mum and dad while keeping an eye on a Kia hatchback car parked in the layby in front of me – one always worries for other hillwalkers and, as the wet evening sets in, I wonder how the occupant(s) are fairing on the hills.

Around 20:00 two guys, in their sixties, stagger up from the shoreline of Loch Leven. They look dry but are obviously the worse for wear. I feel a bit wary and momentarily check that I'm securely locked in. I wonder what they've been up to. Poaching fish, perhaps?

After they drive off I give it very little thought. They've gone and I'm snug and secure. Around 23:00 their car pulls in front of me again, they get out and swagger around, talking loudly. I switch my DVD player off and lie low. Hoping they'll not bother me. They head back to the shores of the loch. I wonder if they'd baited traps, or fishing lines and are returning to collect their spoils.

I sleep well and, while making a late breakfast, open the curtains. It's raining and their car is still there. It then dawns on me they are camping and had, most likely, spent yesterday drinking before heading off to the pub.

As I pull on my kit, car tyres slash through surface water on the road. The cloud is down to the shore, visibility is very poor.

I get walking at 10:30 into persistent rain. There's no wind so it falls vertically, but it's the kind that soaks through you by finding every chink in the armour of one's hood and collar.

I ascend through forest, then open ground before reaching the corner of an adjoining forest. From here it's a lonely, miserable ascent through bog, streams and squelchy ground.

The lack of wind leaves me hot and sticky, water soaks through my trail shoes, riding up my socks and trousers.

It takes me two and a half hours to reach the summit. I have a walk around to ensure I'm at the top before doing some close map and compass work to get me back to the corner of the forest. Visibility is not much more than a hundred feet.

I meet a couple on their way up. A rare sight on such a murky day and on such a small Graham. I get back to the camper van and take the long route around to Ballachulish, with the heaters on full blast, attempting to dry out.

Tuesday the 22nd dawns with better weather – high cloud and no forecast for rain. I make, what should be, a short trip south on the A82 in search of a layby to tackle the Corbett of Meall Lighiche. I overshoot and feel tempted to keep on driving home. Having only done Grahams so far, I feel daunted by taking in a Corbett.

However, my desire to walk all the 2000ft mountains of the British Isles wins through and, after a bit of backtracking, I find the layby and get walking at 08:55.

The first stretch is on a good track to a farm. A detour path keeps me out of some cottage gardens before a rundown farmyard releases me onto the open hillside.

There's a number of converging burns to cross which has me carefully seeking out a crossing point. My trekking poles aid my balance as I take long strides between wet rocks.

The main joint on my right toe begins to play me up – I noticed it was a little inflamed this morning. Yesterday I had some hip and knee twinges but today it's headed south to my toe, reminding me of the footballing injury that caused it: 1988, exactly thirty years ago. And, to show an example of NHS efficiency, I'm still waiting for the results of the x-ray. I live in hope.

Overshooting the main shoulder of the hill I find myself climbing steeply to reach the ridge path. I make good progress, in fact I begin to feel on fine form. I ponder why some days I do well and others I'm misfiring on all cylinders. It crosses my mind whether it's the amount of pollen in the air.

On the ridge it's a straightforward walk to the summit. It's now just after 12:00 and I take in the views. There's a few glimpses of Loch Leven. Out to sea there are islands dotted like lily pads on a pond. Above me the Munros are in the cloud. To the north-east are the Grahams of

Sgorr a' Choise and Meall Mor that I climbed nine days ago.

The still wind of the ascent is now a cooling light breeze. I turn on my tail and descend by the guidebook route, reaching the camper van in a five-and-a-half-hour round trip – for once, well within the guidebook recommendation of five to seven hours.

I drive to Tyndrum and park up for the night. Waking with nothing aching I drive around to Glen Ogle for an attempt on the Graham of Meall Buidhe. I pull up alongside an impressive modern motorhome parked up in an ample-sized car park servicing a picnicking area.

A man and woman are loitering near an open door leading to the living quarters. By the glance the man gives me he's up for a conversation. I'm not. I rarely am with strangers. Slipping out my driver's door I hurry around to my rear door and let myself in before he's had a chance to clock what I'm doing.

I slip my trousers off and start to slip on my knee supports. Undeterred the man walks around my camper and appears at my long side window on the opposite side to his motorhome. Protecting me is a Perspex window and a fly screen.

"May I ask you a question?" he asks. His accent is German and, if he's not having a laugh, I rather suspect he is a German. I reply in the affirmative while wishing I had some trousers on.

"We are new to this motorhome business. Where do we get water?"

"From streams, rivers, shops or campsites," I reply.

He pauses for a moment. It clearly wasn't the answer he was looking for. I suspect he was hoping for conveniently-placed taps. "Thank you," he replies.

I finish strapping my knees, slip on my walking trousers then feel I could be more helpful. I have four five litre containers that originally came from Morrisons. Each has been refilled from the River Roy. I pick the one that appears the least opaque – river water has a peaty tinge to it which can cause the recipient to question its origin. I knock on their door, hand over my gift and get a few words of gratitude: I'm always more agreeable with my trousers on.

At 09:45 I'm walking, following a very convenient track that zig-zags up the hillside to a transmitter. Some workers have scaled it and appear to be attaching a new piece of apparatus. At ground level another guy is digging a hole and gives me a strange look.

Having ascended 300m in fifty minutes my body is working well. I press on for the summit across bog-ridden undulating land. I climb into the cloud which is eerily still and reach the summit, denoted by three cairns, at 11:20. The distant ghostly noise of a passing motorcycle rises from the glen.

There's some quartz rocks, about the size of toolboxes lying amongst the grass.

I head back, reaching the camper van in just over an hour. The Germans have gone so I relax without interruption and draw up a spreadsheet of all the walks, to complete the Corbetts and Grahams, I've left to do. I give each walk an 'Effort' factor based on height and distance and tabulate it across the years 2018 to 2030. This will allow me to base a year's target on 1/13th of the total effort remaining. Previously I'd worked on number of mountains or number of days walking. But, in an attempt to stop me picking off easy ones first, I'm trying to not be left with the tough ones at the end.

I mentioned the other day that, if I'd only paid more attention, I could combine a Corbett and a Graham on one day. Today, the 24th, I aim to do just that by taking in Beinn Each then the Graham of Sgiath a' Chaise. This will be my penultimate day in Scotland before bagging three newly-promoted English Nuttalls (2000ft+ mountains) and a trip home on Sunday.

I get walking at 08:40, heading in the direction of Glen Ample. The cloud is hanging low as I climb through a pine wood, cross a track and continue up through the forest until it meets a track. I find it tough going, my body does not want to get started. This is the ninth continuous day of walking and I'm starting to feel it.

The track goes through a gate where a sign warns, given the recent harsh winter, that there will be numerous dead deer on the hills. I cross a stream where somebody has piled rocks and stones to form an artistic cairn.

An artistic cairn in a stream

A short distance later a signpost directs me up Beinn Each. There's a path and I begin to find my stride and appreciate the route it leads me on. I'm now walking in cloud and, after a long pull up, I break out into a sunny day. It feels like somebody has turned a light on.

At the summit I look out onto a sea of cloud with distant mountains poking out. I sit for a while, taking in the fine views, the still air and the rich blue sky.

I make my way back down. At the junction with the track is sat a woman. I say hello and she replies with the most gentle and pure of Scottish accents. We exchange a few words about our day before I press on for half a mile up the track then turn off towards the steep ground of Sgiath a' Chaise.

I immediately pass the rotting carcass of a deer and am reminded of the earlier sign explaining they'd be a likely sight.

Above the clouds

The ground varies from bog to the fresh heather shoots of the steeper ground. I feel my hay fever twitching away as I drag my body on.

Near to the summit I meet a chap descending. He's planning a walk for his walking group. I get to the summit at 14:10.

On the return the forest is approached above a deep ravine where very tall straight pine trees compete for the light with those growing further up the hillside. Above, rock and grassy outcrops set the scene like a movie director's dream setting for a western. A cuckoo calls and it echoes off the mountainside.

I drop into the forest where the trees allow no more than slithers of light to illuminate my path. I get back to the camper van then take a long drive down to Hawick to tackle Cauldcleuch Head (a Graham in the Southern Uplands) tomorrow.

After a night camping by the A7 the early traffic wakes me and I drive the final stretch to the start of Cauldcleuch Head. I pull up, the terrain feels familiar and I begin to wonder if I've already done it. A quick check of my diary shows that I had planned it as my last hill of 2017 – although less than a year ago, it'd completely slipped my mind.

While getting ready the wind rocks the camper van and I have a fight with my map. The route crosses an inconvenient fold and I have an embarrassing few minutes trying to get the map under control.

I get walking at 08:00 via the heathery slopes of Stob Fell. The wind picks up and bashes me around, only abating when I've crossed over Pennygant Hill. Cauldcleuch Head looks a long way off. Only a rest, a check of the GPS and some compass confirmation has me realising that I'm looking too far ahead. Cauldcleuch Head is the next 'bump' and a simple walk away.

It's 10:15 and I'm at the summit, presented with nothing more than some old iron fence posts. For such a proud name as Cauldcleuch Head I'd have expected at least a pile of rocks.

I return the same way, the wind waits for me over Stob Fell and gives me a stern reminder that these smaller hills can offer their own challenges.

As I drop back towards the camper van a newly-planted pine forest is in view. There are random spaces between the tress, some are taller than others and it reminds me of a threadbare tapestry.

Shortly before noon I reach the camper van, time enough to set off for England and spend the weekend bagging the newly-promoted Nuttalls of Long Fell, Tinside Rigg and Calf Top. With ten days' walking on the trot already complete, I'm now set to do some more.

May 2018 – English Nuttalls

It's now May the 26th and I'm on my way home from Scotland after a successful three week trip bagging Corbetts, Grahams and Donalds. After ten consecutive days of walking I'm feeling fit, and ready to complete the newly-promoted Nuttalls.

Parking up on the edge of the Warcop military ranges, to the sounds of rifle fire, shells and machine guns, has me double checking that tomorrow is a no firing day. My smartphone confirms this and I settle down for an early night.

I get walking at 06:10 and follow the track, noting the signs to keep to the rights of way. There's also a sign saying that there might be the odd bit of ordnance around that might kill me. I make a note to go careful.

The track starts out well but, due to the lack of access days, soon dwindles to a faint path. The more often trod sheep paths fool me and I find myself rather confused and on land that is technically out of bounds. In fact technically out of bounds is the order of the day because Long Fell and Tinside Rigg are off path and really should not be visited. However, given the early hour there probably won't be many MOD Police about.

It's a very windy day, but there's enough blue sky to make it warm and sunny as I wend my way back onto a track that's marked on my map. This is the final pull towards Long Fell. A fence, with a red and white 'Out of Bounds' sign, sings in the wind.

I reach the summit of Long Fell at 08:50. My GPS is spot on at NY768192 and 2047ft. My carefully set compass directs me to Tinside Rigg, arriving 09:05. There are a few remnants of exploded shells, and a few sheep, to keep me company. Otherwise it's a lonely place.

I make better navigation for the descent, admiring the craggy lines of rock and deep gullies that guide me, via a few tree plantations, back to the busy A66.

It's early enough to think about doing Calf Top today. Starting from the village of Barbon, the route looks to be a long walk on an easy gradient. I drive down, looking for a phone signal (to call Margaret) and a good Radio Five Live signal to listen to this evening's Champions League Final between Liverpool and Real Madrid.

I take the minor road up Barbondale and get reasonable radio reception but no phone signal. From a highpoint on the road, I look at the OS map then look at the terrain. Instead of taking the three-mile walk in from Barbon, on an easy gradient, I can instead do it in a half-mile walk, up a very steep gradient.

Dispensing with the services of my backpack my pockets bulge with the essentials. I eat and drink plenty and set off at 14:30 at a blistering pace, in very windy conditions, following a drystone wall. I ascend 380m in fifty minutes – probably near to my record.

Five minutes along a ridge path has me on the final pull to the trig point. I chat to a man with his dog as we savour some fine views. I don't mention that I've just finished the English 2000ft mountains – today's mountains feel more like a formality than anything to celebrate.

Back at the camper van my Sat Nav tells me home is just a six-hour drive away. A clear journey, while listening to the Champions League final, has me surprising Margaret at 23:00.

June 2018 – Welsh Nuttalls

On the 13th of June I make the three-hour trip to the Brecon Beacons and get walking, from the high ground of the car park on the A470 at around 11:30. Within an hour I'm on the summit of the newly-promoted Craig Gwaun Taf taking in the fine views sitting below a clouded sky.

The grid reference for the summit is SO 00553 20725. I wander about, with GPS in hand, and find the small knoll is within a metre of what my GPS is stating. And technically the summit is just off the path. I'm glad I came back to properly stand on it.

Classification	My Total	Total
Welsh Nuttalls	189	189
English Nuttalls	256	256
Corbetts (Scotland)	117	222
Grahams (Scotland)	48	219
Unique Donalds (Scotland)	29	58
Munros (Scotland)	282	282
Ireland	0	212
Totals (13/06/2018):	921	1438

August 2018 – English Nuttalls

On August 10th the BBC reports Miller Moss has been resurveyed and found to be just over 2000ft. A quick check of the Nuttalls website confirms this.

Classification	My Total	Total
Welsh Nuttalls	189	189
English Nuttalls	256	257
Corbetts (Scotland)	117	222
Grahams (Scotland)	48	219
Unique Donalds (Scotland)	29	58
Munros (Scotland)	282	282
Ireland	0	212
Totals (10/08/2018):	921	1439

September 2018 – Scottish 2000ft Mountains

With Margaret doing a house sit for a week I take the opportunity to pop back to Scotland for four days walking in the Southern Uplands.

Waking early on Sunday the 9th I review that the last couple of days spent lugging tables and chairs around the village, to support the local fete, was, perhaps, not the best preparation for a seven-hour drive. However, the multitude of service stations on the M5 and M6 keeps me safe.

At one I eye up a 55 plate version of my camper. Some three hours later I pull in at another service station and, a few minutes later, it trundles in behind me. I can only assume its occupants have a similar bladder capacity to myself.

With it being out of season I make it to Moffat with no holdups. I park up for the night near Capplegill and get walking at 08:35 for the Donald of Under Saddle Yoke.

It's cool, slightly blustery and my Gore-Tex top is mandatory to keep comfortable. I follow a track to a gate where I branch off up the steep hillside to a grassy ridge where, after a couple of smaller bumps, I reach Under Saddle Yoke. The plan was to just do this summit but, with reasonable weather, time and fitness on my side, I make the rough few miles across to Cape Law.

It starts to rain, I don over trousers and put on the pack cover. The cloud descends and hides some of the surrounding peaks.

A handy fence guides me back but I misjudge and leave its safety too early and find myself crossing boggy ground.

I tire on the pull back towards Under Saddle Yoke and, feeling weary, I'm glad to pass over it again before the long drop back to the track and the camper van at 14:25.

I stop in Moffat and spend ages looking for a food shop. Finding none, I give up and head out of town only to discover a small sign for a Co-op directing me down a minor road.

I stock up on cheese. In truth, rather too much cheese which, after parking up at Tweedsmuir, I consume along with a packet of oat cakes. In turn this fuels a night of complicated dreams where my house has extra rooms that I did not know about, housing every person I've ever had an argument with.

I wake around 07:00 rather out of sorts. I lower the blind on the passenger side which, much to my annoyance, fails to automatically roll up. It's been on the blink for some time but I've always managed to coax it back down. This does not relax me from my night of cheddar dreams and, knowing it'll bug me for the entire day, I locate a Philips screwdriver and set about dismantling it.

A dollop of WD40 and swearing does not retrieve the situation so I dump the larger remains in the passenger footwell and open the top drawer of my small chest to store the smaller screws. The drawer front comes off in my hands precisely one millisecond before I have a sense of humour failure.

Muttering and cursing I get ready for the ascent of Erie Hill and

Garelet Dod. At 09:20 I take the footbridge over the Games Hope Burn then climb the steep, open hillside. I have to stop and rest often, sinking into the grassy slopes before gaining the northerly top then a southerly ascent of Erie Hill.

I take some time, sat in foot-long grass, to enjoy the views. The grass ripples, bends and sways in the wind. The landscape is a mix of green and mauves with dark heather on the distant hills which fold and twist to meet the cloud covered sky.

A deteriorating galvanised fence sports some rust. The remains of a stone wall, down to only its footings, run next to it. I follow the fence south-east and swing round for the pull up Garelet Dod. Although easier I'm tiring and still need frequent rests. I reach its featureless summit at 12:45 and use my GPS to pinpoint what is thought to be the highest bit. In truth a couple of other bits look higher so I visit them.

The cloud lifts, as does my mood. The neighbouring Cape Law looks a long way off. I'm glad I did it yesterday.

I descend, initially back the way I came. With the thought of the re-ascent over Erie Hill as welcome as a broken roller blind, I keep on dropping, over very steep ground, towards the Games Hope Burn. From my high point I try to spy crossing points but the rapidly-flowing white water has me cutting down on a diagonal to cross the footbridge I'd passed over in the morning.

Back at the van I take another look at the roller blind. Some very kind old boy, wearing blue dungarees, on his YouTube channel, shows me how to fix it. After some prejudicial twisting and cursing, I manage to re-tension it, reinstall it and feel a great deal happier with the world.

I spend the evening reading a rather weighty biography on Adolf Hitler and, after calling Margaret, doze off to Radio 4. Waking at 12:30 I hear the sad news that Fenella Fielding has died – "Do you mind if I smoke", was an all-time classic from my childhood interest in the Carry On Films.

I switch on the reading light and it rather spookily illuminates the cover picture of Hitler on the book. With that rather unpleasant image I drift back to sleep rather concerned how the dreams will go tonight. However, Fenella Fielding takes front stage in a rather a nice dream. I wake missing Margaret.

I drive a short distance up the A701 to Kingledores Farm to tackle the Graham of Gathersnow Hill and its accompanying Donald, Hillshaw Head.

Walking up what feels like a private drive, leading onto an active farmyard, has me feeling a bit cautious. However, nobody appears to mind and, as I clank my way through a multitude of gates, I find my way onto the track to Hopehead – a semi-derelict cottage which was once painted white but now is returning to its natural stone colour.

At 09:45, an hour into the walk, I leave the track for the steep open, heather-clad, hillside. I pick my way through the vegetation, rest at a stone shooting hide, and enjoy a few moments in the sun. In fact it is just a few moments as the sun was a false promise and the rain soon sweeps in. I don my over trousers, pull my hood tight and press on to the ridge.

Gathersnow Hill lies ahead and I find it a tiring pull up. I'm pleased to reach my 50th Graham at 11:10 and even more pleased that the highest point is better defined than those of recent days – a few rocks surrounding an old metal fence post. I make the Donald of Hillshaw Head in another half an hour – a few rocks surrounding an old wooden fence post.

The rain has stopped but the wind is blustery, ideal for the surrounding wind farm.

I head back over Gathersnow Hill, taking in fine views of hills undulating their way towards the horizon, before dropping back to the cottage at Hopehead. Now the sky turns blue so I remove my wet-weather gear, pack away my navigation equipment and look forward to the hour-long walk back to Kingledores. Twenty minutes later clouds sweep in faster than a Formula 1 driver making a pit stop.

I get back to the camper van at 14:20, wash, and write up my diary then drive, via Biggar to the minor road south of Coulter. I park on high moorland and, during a star lit night, frequently stir to switch on the heating.

Light rain accompanies me as I get walking at 08:00 on a pull up a track to some trees. My legs ache and I feel weary. The wind bites through me until my pace builds up some body heat whereupon I promptly begin to perspire.

After an hour I reach a gate where, shortly after, an ATV track takes me, via a twisting and turning fence, to a windswept summit of Hudderstone. A small stone marks the top. The views beyond, to the Coulter Reservoir, are tempered by a wind farm with rotating blades dipping in and out of the low cloud. I quick march back to the camper van in under an hour and set off for the Lake District to bag the newly-promoted Nuttall, Miller Moss.

September 2018 – English Nuttalls

It's September 13th and I'm on my back from a brief hill bagging trip to Scotland. Having done Hudderstone earlier in the day I'm figuring on parking up for the night then tackling my final English Nuttall – the newly-promoted Miller Moss.

I check the weather forecast, it looks wet for tomorrow morning. I decide to give it a go today and set my camper van's Sat Nav for the nearest hamlet, Mosedale. The Sat Nav duly shrugs. I try Mungrisdale, again it shrugs. Instead I battle my way through a myriad of tiny lanes until I find the correct road up the valley. It narrows a bit, then some more then promptly runs out. It requires some careful reversing until I can turn around and park up.

I figure on going without equipment to bag it quickly. After a glance at the sky I have a rethink. Instead I make just one concession, I don't bother with my knee supports.

At 14:45 I'm heading up to the derelict mine workings then onwards to the Lingy Hut. There's light rain and I'm glad to rest a few moments at this Mountain Bothies Association bothy. I set map and compass and, given the confines of the hut, it feels as if I'm setting out from Captain Scott's last resting place.

When I reach Great Lingy Hill I realise I set the compass to the wrong peak. I head west and make it to Miller Moss at 16:10 and, for the third time, complete the English 2000ft mountains.

It takes only forty-five minutes to get back to the camper van. I set the Sat Nav for home. It can't shrug at that, it's been there too often before. It duly draws me a map then leads me down an even narrower road until I reach a gate. The gate has a sign, 'Gated Road. Don't follow Sat Nav.'

I turnaround, head home and rest for the night in the Cotswolds.

Classification	My Total	Total
Welsh Nuttalls	189	189
English Nuttalls	257	257
Corbetts (Scotland)	117	222
Grahams (Scotland)	49	219
Unique Donalds (Scotland)	34	58
Munros (Scotland)	282	282
Ireland	0	212
Totals (13/09/2018):	928	1439

Note: When I was later editing this account I realised I had actually done Miller Moss on 12/04/2012. So this was a wasted journey.

September 2018 – A Normal Holiday and another Project

Margaret and I spend a week in late September, holidaying in Boscastle, Cornwall. Margaret, not having had a holiday in a number of years, loves the quaint cottage we take on a farm. After a day or so I realise I've never had what one would normally term a holiday – they've either been spent doing DIY or pushing myself via hill walking.

With my previous ability to make bad relationship choices I'm further amazed at how easy Margaret is to get along with. Every previous holiday with a girlfriend had been marred by my failings being analysed and pointed out on a day-by-day basis.

Margaret even lets me take her hill walking, bagging the highest mountain in Cornwall: Brown Willy.

Towards the end of the year I begin to voluntarily do up the semi-derelict old bowls club pavilion in the village. It's a mammoth job, taking three months, and Margaret comments, "You've got no off button, have you?"

It's always interesting seeing yourself through somebody else's eyes. She's right of course. I've been a workaholic for years. But she's offering me a different life, one where I have somebody to sit and do nothing with. Not always feeling I need to achieve the next thing. I 'blame' education and work. My degree was tough – in 1983 Brighton Polytechnic combined their computing and electronic courses to form a new degree. I felt it ended up being two thirds of each course as the lecturers, between the two departments, felt they needed to impart their entire pet subject matter. Coupled with undiagnosed dyslexia, I struggled until, after being pointed in the right direction with some text books, I began to really master it. Then I couldn't stop. I worked every second I could. Weekends became a non-event, working twelve-hour days, seven days a week. I graduated with a first-class honours degree and took this work ethic into employment, working on multiple public sector IT projects, each lasting for years and always volunteering to write the most technically challenging parts of the systems. I'm now fifty-three and just haven't stopped since I was nineteen.

So I promise Margaret that I'll make the bowls club the last big project. That is until January 2019 when we decide to renovate her house, which she's lived in since she was born, and make that our home. We also agree to try for a baby. Within days I notice a 'Seven Seas' vitamin jar labelled, 'Trying for a baby' appears in the kitchen. It's a long-shot and, with a combined age of one hundred, this is the last chance for both of us. On our side is that Margaret has always looked after herself and some of her cousins got pregnant in their late forties.

So another two projects begin…

October 2018 – Welsh Nuttalls

In October 2018 my adversary, Myrddyn Phillips, was out with his Trimble (a sophisticated GPS) and found that Foel Cedig is higher than Cyrniau Nod. Fortunately I passed over Foel Cedig on my way to Cyrniau Nod so I don't need to go out again.

February 9th 2019

It's a late Saturday afternoon and I'm driving to Devizes with Margaret to meet my mum and dad, at Pizza Express, to celebrate my dad's birthday. Margaret asks, "Is there a Boots the Chemist in Devizes?"

"Yes, what do you need?" I ask, then remember it's never a good idea to ask a lady what she's needs from a chemist.

"I think it's worth getting a pregnancy testing kit."

In other circumstances I might have crashed the car. Instead I give her a curious glance. "Really?" I ask, excited.

"Yes."

We park up in Devizes and make a dash to Boots. We get there as they are closing. In fact there's a young lady on the door not allowing any new customers in.

"Can we just nip in and get something, it's kind of important," I ask.

"Is it a prescription?" she asks.

"No," I reply, feeling a bit awkward. I lower my voice, "We need a pregnancy testing kit."

"Second aisle up, on the left," she announces rather loudly while pointing in the general direction.

We then dash through the shop, with other members of staff guiding us to the rather large choice of test kits. We grab the most expensive, pay up then go and meet my parents. Of course we don't mention what's tucked safely away in Margaret's handbag. But all evening it sits there, on my mind. Am I going to be a father?

February 10th 2019

I'm having a Sunday lie in when Margaret rushes in from the bathroom saying, "You are not going to believe this."

I peer down at the LCD screen of the Clearblue testing device. There is one word: 'Pregnant' and below it '3+'.

I take her in my arms and it then dawns on me: I'm going to be a dad. No, I'M GOING TO BE A DAD. I've never had the chance before, and here I am, holding my partner in the joy of knowing our baby is growing inside her.

I look at the LCD screen again, just to check. "That 3+ isn't the number of babies is it?" I ask.

"No, it's the number of weeks."

"Blimey. Thank God." Margaret's family are famed for their late menopauses and twin births but '3+' would suggest Margaret's run of eggs were having an end of line sale.

February 13th 2019

The following Wednesday we visit the village surgery for a confirmatory pregnancy check. As we sit in the waiting area Margaret reflects that it's not called 'The Old School Surgery' for nothing. It used to be her primary school and there's still the Victorian map of the world, painted on to the wall, which she'd spend her lessons gazing at, longing to be at home.

We get called through and introduced to two female student doctors in their last year of medical school. Personally I thought they were some school kids hanging around from when this place was a school. But after some conversation we discover they must be in their mid-twenties.

"So what brings you here today?" asks the lady sitting at the computer, gesturing for us to sit in the pair of chairs by her desk.

"Well," begins Margaret, speaking our rehearsed words, "I did a pregnancy test on Sunday and it was positive."

"Okay, let's see if we have a test kit," says the other lady sat on the examination couch, swinging her legs. Some rummaging around in drawers then follows and Margaret is handed a sample jar and is shown out of the consultation room to do the walk of shame to the loo. Left alone with the two medical students I explain that neither of us have had children before and we've a combined age of one hundred.

When Margaret returns she hands over the sample jar and, while some device is dipped in it and the wait begins, we chat freely. Both being young they wanted to know how we met.

"In the village hall after an archaeology lecture," I explain.

They smile. I expect most of their generation meet online and meeting a middle-aged couple who met traditionally must come as a bit of a surprise.

"How long have you both lived in the village?" asks the lady sat on the couch.

"All my life," Margaret replies.

"Twenty years for me," I add.

"And you'd never met before?"

"Nope," I reply, shaking my head.

"That's such a romantic story," she says.

Attention is then turned to the test results. "It's positive," the lady operating the computer says.

I take Margaret's hand and say, "Well done you. Well done." Her eyes fill with tears and the medical students both congratulate us.

Doctor Woods, a fully-qualified Scottish doctor, then joins us to see how the medical students are doing. "This is Margaret and Steve," they explain, "they've both lived in the village all their lives, have just got together and Margaret has just take a pregnancy test which is positive."

Doctor Woods, cynical by years in the NHS, looks at us and

says, "You're not cousins are you?"

"No," I reply, stuttering and explain that although Margaret has lived here all her life I've actually only been here twenty years.

"That's a relief," says Doctor Woods, "I was a doctor in inner city Glasgow for many years and you'd be amazed at how many cousins end up having children together. It can cause all sorts of problems."

March 27th 2019

Today's our twelve week scan. Everything goes well, just one baby on board, but we ask not to be told the gender. It's also the day we decide to let my mum and dad in on the news. So, on route to the hospital, we stopped at a farm shop, had tea and bought a card with a duck and her ducklings. We then wrote in it a message to Grandma and Granddad saying there's another little duckling on the way.

After the scan we stop at the Mamas and Papas shop in west Swindon and buy a pair of baby socks, which we pin inside the card, then continue to my parents' house near Devizes.

Mum and Dad are pleased to see us but don't suspect a thing. In their lounge we hand them the envelope, they stand up to open it together. They read the card, it doesn't twig right away. Then all of a sudden it does. Mum does a good impression of a guppy fish at feeding time and Dad takes two paces back and sinks into an armchair while stating, "I didn't see that coming." Mum is then all squeals and hugs for Margaret. After a few minutes they remember me, and Dad gives me a handshake.

May 2019 – Scottish 2000ft Mountains

Becoming a father will, of course, impact upon my hill walking. Previously I'd wanted to do all the mountains of the British Isles but, given my new responsibilities, drop Ireland and adjust this down to finishing off the Corbetts, Grahams and Donalds. This will complete the

2000 foot mountains of Great Britain. Fortunately having not done one of the Irish peaks this was an easy decision – if I had done just one it'd have felt like I was abandoning a project and it would have niggled away at me. I'm not an admirer of Margaret Thatcher but one of her doctrines which struck a chord with me was she valued people that were 'finishers', not those that started a project only to give up when it got tough.

Even with deleting the Irish mountains from the target, my current progress means I'm going to be in my seventies before I finish. So I decide to take a brief break from renovating Margaret's house and, before our baby arrives, make a bias towards the remaining twenty-three Donalds I've yet to climb.

Having just got through our twenty-week scan I drive to Scotland on Saturday May 18th, listening to Man City thumping Watford in the cup final, to take in some hills and also help out on the Control Desk of the annual TGO Challenge (the annual cross-Scotland walk).

At 08:35 on the Sunday morning I begin the road walk from the car park in Glen Artney. As the road peters out I ascend, in a light drizzle, south to the Allt Ollach. Here I'm faced with the preverbal dead sheep in the stream. I say 'preverbal' because to the non-hillwalker the confession that one drinks water from streams is met with, "Ugh, what about dead sheep in the streams." I've never quite known how the non-hillwalker is so knowledgeable about the last resting place of unfortunate sheep but up until now I've always dismissed it with a, "I've never seen one."

Unfortunately this one is blocking the best crossing point and I have to wobble my way across some stones and loosely-attached tree branches to make it to the opposite bank.

I make it to Uamh Bheag and sit, rest, eat and drink. The summit is marked by moss-covered rocks supporting an old iron fence post with a lump of wood stuck on its end.

I continue along the ridge, taking in the trig point and the east top before following the fence, past a wind farm, then across boggy open ground to the minor top of Beinn Odhar before reaching the Donald of Beinn nan Eun at 14:00.

A sharp descent to a hill track has me back at the car park for the drive to Braemar and an evening at Loch Callater Lodge enjoying the company of walkers on the TGO Challenge. I'm greeted like an old friend and my ego is boosted by somebody saying, "You're not *the* Steve Smith, writer of those funny TGO blogs." I have to confess I am and my admirer goes onto say, "I'm only here because your TGO blogs inspired me to come and do it".

The evening progresses with the usual drinking singing, guitar playing and reciting of rude verse and song. As always I love to watch the look on the faces of those that are attending for the first time – varying from utter bewilderment to delight to be included in such an event.

I help out at 'Challenge Control' on the Monday so don't take to the hills again until Tuesday 21st with a plod up the nearby Hill of Wirren.

For the 22nd and the 23rd I'm back helping out on 'Challenge Control' – checking finishers in, dealing with retirements and ailments (of which there so far has been blisters, broken feet, pneumonia and an infected left testicle) answering phone calls from people calling in and generally helping to keep the records straight. Of course I show off pictures of Margaret and scans of our baby. People are delighted and amazed that I have finally settled. It's good to catch up with so many old faces but it's busy and lunch breaks, like when I was at work, are taken at the desk.

On Friday the 24th I excuse myself from Montrose and head to Menstrie to tackle the Donald of Blairdenon Hill and, if time allows, the Graham of Ben Cleuch.

The guidebook says, 'Go up Park Road into Ochil Road where there is parking.' The problem with that is it does not say to turn right or left into Ochil Road. I chance left and quickly find myself at a dead end with limited turning space. A large house has its gates open so I put my front wheels onto its drive to give myself more space. As I reverse, beginning my twenty-point turn, the lady of the house appears and, when I pull forward to make use of her driveway again, she begins to shut the gates.

Not feeling very welcome, with reversing sensors hammering out the theme tune to lord knows what, I complete my turn.

Parked up I get walking at 11:45, passing some cottages before turning onto a Land Rover track, edged with gorse bushes, for the hills.

I make good progress, occasionally looking back to take in the views across the River Forth as it twists and bends through the flatlands below.

I press on then hear a voice behind me – it's the lady who closed the gate on me, accompanied by two dogs. She's deep in conversation on her mobile phone. A white Yorkie dog plods along behind, a blue / grey Pitbull puppy, with testicles the size nectarines, is running around and, with his mistress paying him no attention, decides that I'm his new best friend.

After convincing him that jumping all over me will get him nowhere he decides to leave me alone.

There's a warm wind as I leave the track and follow rough ground to the minor peak of Colsnaur Hill. I make the summit of Blairdenon Hill and stop to take in the distant views of jagged mountains.

I look towards Ben Cleuch and, given I feel fit and it's such a fine day, I press on across boggy ground, reaching its summit two hours later. Here there's a trig point surrounded by a summit shelter. Slightly apart is a viewfinder showing what's before me – folds of mountains rapidly falling away to sea level. I backtrack and, after taking a track to Alva, I road walk back to the camper van, arriving at 19:00.

I wild park on a remote road near Dollar and, on Saturday the May 25th, drive into the village, find parking and, at 08:50, set off along the wooded glen to Castle Campbell.

There's a fine stream and a well-made path to follow through a wooded ravine. People pass with their dogs, I pass others just out for a stroll. A few bridges tempt me but I press on to the castle where I find my bearings and take a path to open hillside.

It's a cooler, cloudier day and the distant River Forth is grey, not sparkling in the sun like yesterday.

I slept awkwardly last night and my neck is stiff, I stop to apply Deep Heat. It starts to rain, I cover my pack and pull up my hood. I pass a memorial to three spitfires which crashed on King's Seat Hill on January 16th 1943. The men were all twenty-one, I wonder if they were in training and somehow managed to get things spectacularly wrong.

I make the summit at 11:15 in miserable drizzle. I take a depressing 500ft descent to a stream where I sit and rest. A chap passes with his two dogs, he stops to chat and the dogs make friends with me.

I get to the summit of Tarmangie Hill in just over an hour – a cairn marks the top, set alongside a broken-down wall. Pressing on I cross rough ground to reach the lowest of all the Donalds, Innerdownie.

I backtrack over one of the flanks of the minor top of Whitewisp Hill. I'm now in thick cloud so double check compass and GPS before following a deer fence, which hums eerily in the breeze, then a sheep fence which takes me onto a forest track back to Dollar.

Just before 16:00 I'm back at the camper van, rather sodden and tired. I dry myself out for a drive down to The Borders to take in Chapelgill Hill and Culter Fell tomorrow.

I start walking the following morning with sheaths of rain lashing their way down the glen. It's blustery and wet, but not too cold. I have to map and compass my way, through sodden grass and heather, to the top of Chapelgill Hill.

I take a bearing to a fence and, using that as a reference, map and compass towards Culter Fell. It gets so windy I'm unable to stop for food or water. A mix up between my left and right feet sends me flying. Regaining my feet, and my dignity, I press on. Only a dip before the final ascent gives me enough cover for a quick snack.

I press on and reach the summit where, due to it being fully exposed, the wind is at its most ferocious. It's such a bleak location that the ground around the trig point has been eroded leaving the concrete overhanging its perch.

With the wind and rain bashing me I spend no longer than two seconds here before I quickly descend and, tucked down in a peat hag, take on some more food and water. My hands are now freezing so I don gloves and, keeping a careful eye on a compass bearing, head into the low ground that bisects today's two mountains.

I eye the weather forecast and, due to predicted rain plus the size of the day required to walk the nearest neighbours to Culter Fell, I drive round to Innerleithen and take the B709. I park up to take in Windlestraw Law and Whitehope Law.

I get walking at 08:50 on May 27th following a grassy track which leads to an easy-to-follow fence and on to the trig point summit of Windlestraw Law in a little over an hour and twenty minutes.

There's a few spots of rain falling from the high grey cloud. The hills around are hues of green and brown, birds chirp as I shiver in the cold breeze.

I make it back to the camper van at a shade after 11:00 where, after a quick lunch, I cross the road and, after being seen off by some rather aggressive sheep, scale a fence, cross a stream and make for the open hillside.

For once there's a consistent gradient so I make steady progress and reach the summit of Whitehope Law in just over an hour and a quarter.

As I eat lunch the rain in the air increases until I see the dark sky of the south-east moving towards me. I batten down my pack, tighten my hood and cuffs and, rather wet, get back to the camper van at 13:35.

I drive round to the Gladhouse Reservoir, in preparation for tomorrow's walk in the Moorfoot Hills, and sleep for the night.

The following morning, as I'm getting ready for the Moorfoot Hills a car pulls alongside me. Its driver, a middle-aged chap sorts out his kit and sets off before me.

I get walking at 08:55 and, after quarter of an hour, feeling tired and achy, I seriously think about turning back. I press on and, while playing with the statistics of how long it'll take me to finish all the Scottish mountains, manage to walk through it.

The first hill, Dundreich, is clouded over. There are a couple of ridges by which it can be reached. I select the most northerly and make good time over the open, boggy ground. As I reach the summit, and cross a fence to the trig point and cairn, the cloud lifts and, in a cool breeze, I'm treated to views of flatlands extending out to more rolling hills.

I follow the fence then cut across open ground, strewn with peat and bog, to reach Bowbeat Wind farm. I bump into the guy who parked next to me – he's doing the same circuit as me but in reverse. He points out the tips of the wind turbine blades are set at a different angle to the main blades.

I notice that some turbines are still, others rotate and others are being switched in and out. The occasional big gust of wind causes the blades to make a sudden swoosh, sounding like somebody jumping into a swimming pool.

I make the summit of Bowbeat Hill then, after lunching near a hare who was barely put out by my presence, press on to the trig point on Blackhope Scar. From here I cut down to a track which leads me back to the reservoir.

It's now a nice afternoon, the hills are in sun with puffs of white cloud against the blue sky. Back at the van I'm invaded by flies – big bastards that fend off fly spray and any attempt to swat them. I phone Margaret and bemoan their presence. She quips that I must really stink to attract so many.

I sleep well but due to physical tiredness I'm tempted to head home. However, May 29th dawns with blue skies and the sun glinting on the reservoir so, even with rain forecast for 14:00, I head round to Peebles to take in the four Donalds which include the Graham of Dun Rig.

I get walking at 07:25 through gentle woodland, following the Cross Borders Drove Road, sprinkled with dog walkers and their pleasant greetings.

I soon feel hot and shed my jacket and take in the pleasant ridge line towards the minor top of Kirkhope Law. Below green fields, with clusters of tress and farm buildings, drift off to rolling hills. Sheep graze and call out to their young.

Just short of Kirkhope Law the cloud descends and it starts to rain. My feet begin to blister through wearing wet socks. I reach Birkscairn Hill and, for my reward, stare at a barren pile of rocks marking its summit.

I press on, map and compassing all the way towards the trig point of Dun Rig. At just after 11:00 it emerges from the mist as a ghostly obelisk.

I'm glad for a bit of descent so that my frozen hands can come back to life. I slip on my gloves, press on and reach Glenrath Heights.

The rain has now stopped but the cloud, scurrying over the ridges, makes visibility poor. I press on using compass bearings and a fence to the minor top of Broom Hill. From here it's a descent and re-ascent to Stob Law. I feel very weary, each step presses on my blisters and my legs feel heavy and tired.

I make it to the top, reverse back to Broom Hill and then take the three-hour walk back to the camper van, reflecting on how close I am to finishing the Donalds. Setting of for home I'm set for the biggest adventure of all – fatherhood.

September 19th 2019

Margaret and I got married on August 1st. Given we've been busy renovating her house, to make it our family home, it was a very small affair. We got the bus in to Marlborough, met up with the two witnesses we'd cajoled the day before, and, in a ceremony which the registrars do their very best to string out, it takes us six minutes to get married. There was no chance of a honeymoon, instead we were straight back to house renovations.

So here I am installing the storage heaters – one of the final jobs. We've now rented my house out – which required me doing some neglected maintenance, including replacing the entire hot water system and fixing the main oven that had been broken for twenty years. As a single man I somehow got away with that.

Our baby is due next week – one week to go and just about a week's worth of work to go. I should be able to get this all finished. It's been a gruelling eight months of renovating her house. Dealing with trades people and working long days on it myself. We rewired, re-plumbed, replaced all the windows, re-plastered and painted throughout, lagged the loft, built me an office, repaired the roof and repaired and repainted its external wooden structure. In this time I fell off a ladder twice, burst a blood vessel in my knee, got a UTI, got diagnosed with an enlarged prostate, tennis elbow, low blood pressure and had two cancer scans to try and find out why I'm passing blood in my urine. On the flipside Margaret's pregnancy has been amazing. She's amazing. No real hiccups, no morning sickness. Just occasional nausea and persistent cramp in her calf muscles to contend with.

So here I am in the hallway, touching in paint and wiring in the final storage heater, waiting for a flooring chap to come and board out and lay floor covering in the kitchen and bathroom. Margaret passes me, eyeing the paintbrush. "Don't get too precious about the paintwork, Steve. You'll soon have a little one whose prime objective is to place sticky finger marks all over the painted surfaces."

"Don't worry, I won't be following him around with a paint brush," I reply.

"Good job," Margaret says, "otherwise he'll think you're Rolf Harris."

She disappears upstairs. Twenty minutes later she calls down, "Steve, you probably don't want to hear this..."

"What's the matter?" I ask, fearing she's spotted a leak in my plumbing.

"My waters have just broken."

I'm not wrong, it is a plumbing leak.

I down tools, go and join her and then phone the hospital. We are told to come in.

I nip to our neighbour, Paul asking him to deal with the flooring man. I show him what needs to be done. In times like this people are only too willing to help. The flooring man arrives, winding down his window as he pulls up.

"This is Paul, my neighbour," I explain. "He'll show you the job, my wife's waters have just broken and I need to take her to hospital."

"I've been stuck on a job all morning," he complains. "I won't be able to get your job done today. But I'll start it, then I'm going home."

This man looked decisively miserable.

"Okay, but I've got to go, my wife's waters have just broken," I repeat, hoping I've out trumped the bugger.

"Won't be able to get it done today," he replies, out trumping me. What did I say about in times like this people are only too willing to help?

I load up Margaret's car with her bag, guide her in and set off.

In the hospital she's put on a monitor and told women often mistakenly believe their waters have broken when they haven't. A midwife examines her in what is optimistically called a 'stretch and sweep' procedure. After a few moments of feeling around, and a strained expression on both her and Margaret's faces, she announces, "Oh, you're not kidding, they've definitely broken."

However, the monitor shows there are no contractions yet. The midwife says she'll go and speak with the consultant but to get ready to go home and come back tomorrow to be induced (to start the contractions). Her parting shot is that a curry and sex are good ways of starting contractions naturally.

Left wondering at this imparted knowledge we watch the monitor. Our baby's heart rate shoots up. Throughout Margaret's pregnancy I've sung "Daisy, daisy given me your answer do", daily to our baby. I sing it now and we look at each other, in slack-jawed amazement, as the heart beat settles back to normal. We both think, Wow!

The midwife returns. "I've spoken to the consultant. Now Margaret, given your age, we are keeping you in. I'll arrange for you to go onto a ward."

We are then left alone. "Bang goes my Indian takeaway and a promise then," I quip.

"Fancy a knee trembler in the toilet then?" Margaret asks jokingly.

"We'd best not, probably against house rules."

Instead we spend the evening walking up and down deserted flights of stairs, to try and get things moving, with me playing Lara's Theme (from Doctor Zhivago) on my mobile phone. Then I leave Margaret in her ward bed, kissing her goodnight. I'd only be able to stay if she'd actually had the baby. Her eyes tell me she doesn't want me to go. I don't want to go either.

September 20th 2019

I wake in the early hours on the Friday morning, cold and uncomfortable while trying to get some kip in Margaret's car, parked up in the hospital car park. My neck is stiff and my prostate is sending messages, via my bladder, that I'm in urgent need of a pee. There's some bushes nearby but also a note, on a lamppost, advertising CCTV.

At 02:30 I wander into the ghostly confines of the hospital, find a loo then the canteen and, by pulling chairs together, make myself an improvised bed.

I sleep on and off, a junior doctor, in full scrubs, joins me at a neighbouring set of chairs. I'm relieved when the canteen finally opens so I can breakfast. At 09:29 I'm waiting outside the maternity ward – it opens at 09:30. I have to pass some reassuring security to get to Margaret. She's slept on and off, being woken every few hours by nurses and doctors checking up. She's also black and blue as they had trouble finding a vein to put a cannula in and take bloods.

We're so pleased to see one another.

The delivery suite is full so we can't yet be induced. Instead Margaret is put on antibiotics to prevent infection (her waters breaking have left her vulnerable). I phone Ali Ogden (now a retired GP) for reassurance that everything is being done properly – it is.

Up until now we assumed that we're having a boy. All the old wives tales pointed us towards this. We'd nicknamed him 'George' but during this long wait we go through names on my phone. We decide on Felix for a boy and, should it be a girl, we choose Nancy.

The day drags on, the delivery suite, according to the staff, is 'rammed'. It's about nine months from Christmas so what do we expect? Margaret tells me she'd have been happier doing it on her own at home. The hospital environment is stressing her.

Late in the evening, as it approaches last orders for expectant fathers, Margaret speaks with the staff. "Please can my husband stay with me?"

We've only been married six weeks so the term 'husband' takes me by surprise – wow, I'm a husband and about to become a daddy!

They go off to ask. I eye the empty bed opposite. "If I stuffed a pillow up my jumper and climb into that bed do you think they'd notice?"

"You'd notice," Margaret says, "when they come and do the stretch and sweep."

Fair point.

The nurse returns and I'm given permission to stay. It's a moot point because soon after a room becomes available in the delivery suite. We get in at midnight and Margaret is induced. It's then a slow process, Margaret's on a monitor – a fascinating piece of IT equipment – which shows her heartbeat, our baby's heartbeat and the level of contractions. I watch the contractions, each time they build I say, "Now," and Margaret takes a whiff of gas.

Margaret is trying to avoid having to go on to pethidine, to manage the pain. She wants things to be natural and is concerned that pethidine, unlike gas, crosses the placenta wall and enters the baby's blood stream. This is all new to me. As a software engineer I was used to the preciseness of bits and bytes – now it is the imprecise science of cells and biology.

At just after 14:00 Margaret's contractions have her 70% of the way to being able to give birth naturally. I'm now pretty hands on and I'm doing things for Margaret that I'd never thought I would be capable of. The midwife does an examination and can feel a hand. This is not good news – it implies the baby isn't positioned correctly. She goes to fetch the registrar.

"He's probably just got his head in his hands over Brexit," I quip.

"Do you think we should ask for a finger count?" Margaret asks. "If it's six then Doctor Woods's might be right and we are in fact cousins."

The registrar appears, does an eye-watering stretch and sweep and pronounces it as an ear.

Phew!

There's not a peep out of Margaret. She doesn't make a murmur throughout all this pain. She's unflappable. The lady in the next room is screaming the place down and the midwife, raising her eyebrows, says, "She's hardly even started."

Come 20:30 Margaret gives in and asks for pethidine. The midwife hooks it up quickly. Margaret feels sick and vomits, I willingly clear it up. What's come over me? I'm normally really squeamish. Things now get easier for her but come 23:30 she's exhausted. We're stood together by the bathroom door, with Margaret hooked up to a mobile drip, and the midwife asks, "What do you want?"

I've never felt this close to anybody, this at one with anybody. As we'd already discussed this I speak for Margaret. "We don't was a C-section."

"Okay, I'll go and chat with the senior midwife."

A few minutes later a no-nonsense woman, in her late fifties, appears, rolling up her sleeves. Two stirrups are flipped up on the bed and Margaret's legs are lifted into each. "Now Margaret, push."

This is where I have to make a decision. Head end or tail end? All the way through the pregnancy I thought I'd be doing the head end. I'd read too many blogs describing how gory things get down below. Other blogs chastised men, saying it was all perfectly natural. I take a look at the tail end and think, 'It might be natural to you, mate, but at this precise moment there's a baby's head starting to appear out of it.'

However, I'm now a tail end guy. Giving words of encouragement to Margaret as she is told to push.

A forehead appears.

This is really happening! We're about to be parents.

An eye appears. Oh my, he's got my long eyelashes.

A cheek appears which twitches. Oh, thank God, he's alive.

His left ear appears. He's got a detached ear lobe, just like mine.

His mouth appears. Not knowing what the customary form of address is I utter, "Hello, mate."

He turns his head towards my voice.

Oh God, this is incredible.

Margaret gives one final big push. His arms and hands appear. He's got very long fingers, just like Margaret's and mine. And he's out, fielded by a midwife who rubs him down, checks him over and passes him up to Margaret. I'm stunned by how much he looks like me.

"That's a beautiful baby," says the midwife. "Looks just like Daddy."

Well, who am I to argue?

It's four minutes to midnight. I check for his boy bits – what self-respecting father wouldn't? Hang on a minute, there aren't any.

It's a girl!

And in that second I realised I wanted a girl all along. A surge of love shoots through me. I join Margaret at her head end. It's just after midnight and the midwife joins us, teaching her how to feed. Nancy latches on and takes her first drink.

"No problems, there," says the midwife.

"Well, she wasn't born yesterday," I quip.

I get a raised eyebrow from the midwife.

I thank Margaret for our beautiful daughter. "Thank you," she whispers back, "I've never seen you so focussed."

"How do you mean?" I query.

"You're normally distracted, away in your own thoughts. But

during my labour you were one hundred percent focussed, you never took your eye off the ball."

I get to cut the cord then, while Margaret is being attended to, I have time with Nancy. Walking around the delivery room with her wrapped up, cradled in my arms. I sing to her, making up rhymes. She sneezes and looks right at me. I poke my tongue out, she pokes hers out back at me.

The midwife attending to Margaret says, "I think we've got a smitten dad there."

Indeed. A proud father and a proud husband too. Margaret was incredible. She didn't make one murmur of pain.

We get home in the evening. The floor layer has left us with no useable kitchen and bathroom. He truly out trumped me in the end.

Classification	My Total	Total
Welsh Nuttalls	189	189
English Nuttalls	257	257
Corbetts (Scotland)	117	222
Grahams (Scotland)	56	219
Unique Donalds (Scotland)	47	58
Munros (Scotland)	282	282
Totals (29/05/2019):	948	1227

Note, having given up on the ambition of including the 2000ft mountains of Ireland, I've removed them from the total aim.

July 2020 – Scottish 2000ft Mountains

Over the winter, between changing nappies and being a really chuffed husband and father, I calculate I have around 215 days of walking left to complete the 2000 foot mountains of Great Britain. I split this down into sixteen years, taking me up until I turn seventy. In turn this works out as about three weeks away a year. But given Nancy will be at school for the greater number of these years I suggest to Margaret that we do six weeks away per year until she goes to school, then two weeks per year after that.

So over the winter we trade my two-berth camper van, for a more spacious Autocruise Alto, allowing Margaret and Nancy, to accompany me on the trips to Scotland. And this is the guy who has just lived and holidayed alone for over twenty years! How times change.

Owning the new camper van does not get off to a good start. It's six metres long and, after only two trips out, I've managed to put two minor dents in it. It takes me a while to get used to its length.

We were planning to travel to Scotland in mid-April for six weeks then the Coronavirus lockdown occurred, relegating us to staying home.

With the lockdown restrictions easing we set off on July the 15th with the aim of me doing my final four walks to complete my twelve remaining Donalds (one of the three categories of mountains – the others being the Grahams and the Corbetts – which make up the 2000 foot mountains of Scotland). To restrict the visits to shops we stuffed the van's lockers full of food and bottled water and plan to buy some fresh veg as we approach the Southern Uplands.

After many miles, and many stops to change, feed and entertain Nancy we pull off the M6, to the welcome sign of an M&S food shop at a service station. I don my mask and set forth only to find the shop closed due to the Covid-19. A helpful sign tells me an identical M&S shop is available on the other side of the M6, across the footbridge. The sign also says #WeAreAllInThisTogether and a helpful arrow points into a broom cupboard. Only after leaving the building, do I find the bridge, tucked away behind the main building amongst some trees. I trot across to find that the sister M&S shop is also closed. So much for keeping us safe, if they'd blacked out the sign on the M6 I wouldn't have had to go wandering where other people were.

We set off again, on the final leg bound for Ettrick. However, Nancy loses her sense of humour and we park for the night just off the M74.

After our first night in the van we drive on towards Ettrick. This takes an age and, on a bumpy road, the cigarette lighter socket, supplying the Sat Nav and the reversing camera (essential in a 6m vehicle) shorts itself out and blows a fuse. By this time I was close to blowing a fuse as with no reversing camera or Sat Nav driving the van, which I was nervous of anyhow, becomes a whole lot more difficult.

We park at the end of the minor road from Ettrick to Potburn and while Margaret and Nancy stay one end of the van, I pack my rucksack and lose find then lose again every possible item I need. Then, for the first time ever, I kiss my wife goodbye as I set off on a walk. Oh and our gorgeous ten-month daughter too.

After a bit of head scratching amongst some tracks I head towards Ettrick Pen. Not that I need the track for long as I soon branch off through long wet grass. Then a bout of hay fever strikes and I have to take eye drops, put on goggles, spray stuff up my nose and take a tablet.

I get to the top, tap the pile of rocks with my trekking pole and survey the cloud clagging in the surrounding summits. I set off and, after a socially-distanced chat with a chap doing this horseshoe ridge of mountains in reverse, cross the Donald top of Hopetoun Craig where the clouds lift for a better view of these rolling hills.

Passing over Wind Fell, which lives up to its name, I get a view of a steep zig-zag path up the shoulder of a mountain to the west. Checking the map I'm daunted to see this is the penultimate mountain of the day, Croft Head.

I make it to Loch Fell at 15:45. Here the clouds become ominous, rain is in the air and my old hip complaint decides it's time for a moan. Crossing the minor top of West Knowe I then make the very steep descent which, even with trekking poles gripped in both hands, is hard on my knees. At the bottom, where the Southern Upland Way passes through the glen I sit next to a circular stone enclosure for sheep. Above me is the zig-zag path I spotted earlier. After a few slugs of water I do battle with the steep ground, glad of the path. Stripping down to just my shirt, I reach the summit of Croft Head after 17:15. I turn to look at the view, across the glen – landslips, a narrow gorge and a waterfall beckon my descent.

Having told Margaret I'll be back by 19:00 I have to miss the last mountain, Capel Fell and instead follow the Southern Upland Way back towards the van.

On my final approach I spot, from a distance, Margaret and Nancy, waiting for me. I get a lovely greeting from them both.

Having missed Capel Fell I set off on the 17th to bag it and Bodesbeck Law on the far end of the actual walk I had planned for the day. This will put me a day behind but will shorten the walk for when I eventually do it.

While getting ready, Margaret points out that I appear quite stressed when I'm organising my kit. I reassure her it's nothing to do with her presence, and that I'm always like this. At 09:40 I start out in pouring rain, which I explain to Margaret as typical Scottish weather, and, after following a gap between two commercial forest plantations, reach Bodesbeck Law, in miserable conditions in an hour and a half

I duck below the summit cairn, glug back water, eat raisins and walnuts before setting off for a 500ft drop following an ancient stone wall. Passing over the minor top of White Shank I then, after hiding out of the wind while shivering and shaking, pass over Graham's Law before reaching Capel Fell around 13:30.

I think about Margaret's words when I set off, that I appeared stressed. This is another gruelling day in the hills. I'm pretty hard on myself. How much do I *really* enjoy this? What *am* I trying to prove?

I get back to the van at 15:05, soaked to the skin. Margaret tells me that after I'd left Nancy pointed to my shoes and said Dada. We both have tears in our eyes as we hug our little daughter.

We then drive onto Peebles where we need to find a public loo to empty the van's toilet. On finding two closed, due to Covid-19, I, in desperation, while Margaret hides her face in embarrassment, lift a manhole cover and pour the contents directly into the sewer.

Back at the van Margaret says, "I don't know whether to be proud of your ingenuity or embarrassed."

I take the Saturday off to spend time with Margaret and Nancy. I also go and try and buy a replacement fuse to resurrect the Sat Nav and reversing camera. I find a hardware shop and, after reading their sign, queue outside, waiting to be called in when the number of customers inside the store drops below three. After a long wait I call in, "How many customers do you have?"

"Two," comes the reply.

"So can I come in?"

"Aye."

I venture in and ask a female assistant, "Do you have car fuses?"

She asks a male who looks at my offered fuse, shakes his head and says, "No."

"Do you know anywhere else?"

"What for?" he asks gruffly.

"A fuse," I reply incredulously.

"No idea," he replies.

I leave, remembering the customary service of small Scottish shops. I try a garage, showing the assistant my broken fuse.

"Sorry, don't sell them individually," he says, turning away.

"How do you sell them then?" I ask. Beggars can't be choosers.

"Only in kits with lightbulbs," he replies, "pointing them out on a shelf."

I take a look. The fuses are the wrong width.

I return to the street and spy, in the distance, a Renault garage. This is fast becoming my walk for the day, but with no mountains to climb (other than trying to buy a fuse).

The Renault garage are apologetic that they can't sell me one until Monday and point me in the direction of a Ford garage. Their service department is open and they willingly sell me a couple.

I cut through the back streets of Peebles, arriving back at the van some hour and a half after saying, "I'm just popping out for a fuse."

We then drive on to Drumelzier, to start tomorrow's walk. However, it's so midge infested we drive back to the Dawyck Botanical

Gardens. Arriving at 16:10 we follow some confusing signs only to be told they shut at five and they don't accept entries after 16:00. I point out it says 18:00 on the road sign. They explain the virus restrictions are the cause of that. I suppose a piece of masking tape and a biro was too much to ask for.

On the morning of the 19th I apply some second skin to my blistered right ankle then drive around to Drumelzier. The parking, up a narrow track, is all taken and, with other cars turning back, I'm thankful for the reversing camera on the van. However, I'm not thankful for the driver impatiently driving towards my bonnet each time I manage to reverse a foot.

So feeling stressed, harassed and bullied we manage to park, angled on a verge, by a bridge over the River Tweed and I set off at 09:25 via a road walk, the full car park then out onto the grass track following the Scrape Burn to a cluster of huts made from green corrugated tin. I peer through the windows of one at a Mary Celeste scene of a long table with the remnants of last night's meal and not a soul in sight.

Pressing on I follow the burn until I break out, wading through knee-high ferns. I rest when I reach the heather and look back to the huts. A tent is pitched next to a stone circular enclosure, a quad bike visits it and there is some conversation.

The hills ahead are a hue of green and purple heather with their flowers budding pink.

I follow the ankle-biting heather until it shortens to a dry crisp crunch, then the summit of Drumelzier Law. There's then a fine ridge to follow which opens out to a plateau on the approach to Middle Hill with a fine cairn marking the way. I get to the top at 12:45 and set my compass to work out which mountain is Dollar Law. It looks possible and, if bagged today, will significantly cut down tomorrow's walk. So I cut west then south-west and take a direct line following a handy fence, reaching Dollar Law.

I now head north, cutting over Long Grain Knowe then the trig point of Pykestone Hill where some rain sets in.

I pass a couple of people, sat socially distanced away, and make my way back to the camper, getting wet for the last five minutes, and arriving back to a warm welcome from Margaret and Nancy.

We then drive, via Peebles and its convenient sewer cover in which to empty the loo, to Megget Reservoir where we park up for the night with the aim of giving Margaret and Nancy a better view, and a place to walk, for tomorrow. However, my attempt to sell the place was scuppered by a bonehead of a young man urinating beside his car, playing his music so loud Nancy began to jig about, emptying the remains of a packet of crisps on the ground, lighting a fag followed by a wheel spin out of the car park.

With the three of us sharing the narrow double bed in the back of the van, I wake in the early hours, squashed between the side and Margaret with an agonising pain in my right hip. I try to move but I'm wedged. I look across, Nancy is the other side of Margaret attached to her twenty-four-seven milk bar. Not wishing to disturb them, and unable to move my leg, I ride out the pain.

With my hip now behaving I get walking at 09:40 on the 20th up the track which follows the glen which divides Greenside Law and Deer Law. Some twenty minutes later I find myself confused where the track crosses the burn, not shown on the map. So I end up branching right instead of crossing it. Only when faced with unfamiliar terrain do I realise my error. I backtrack and pick up the track which crosses the burn then quickly crosses back again, a deviation not shown on the map.

I press on, a hare bounds across the track and dives into the heather. A cairn marks the top of the track and I branch left through rough, wet heather. I plod on and reach the summit of Greenside Law. There's a good view over to the distant Dollar Law – I am glad I did it yesterday. In the foreground there's a steep drop to a green hut between two commercial plantations overshadowed by some rocky inland cliffs.

I take a bearing, across boggy open ground, to pick up the south-west shoulder of Black Law. The gradient on the ascent is sympathetic and there is a fence to follow. I make it to the top in high cloud and a blustery wind.

I pass over Conscleuch Head, Deer Law and then follow an ATV track back to the road. Then it's a steep bit of tarmac to plod up to get back to find Margaret teary – Nancy had just taken a tumble off the bed and clonked her head. Nancy soon recovers, as does Margaret. Nancy means the world to us, she's come late in our lives and we can't bare to see her upset or hurt.

We wake on July 21st, ten months to the day since Nancy was born – a fitting day for me to complete the Donalds.

We drive the short distance to Birkhill, managing to park near the farm. I set off, following the steep stony south-easterly path. There's high cloud, blue sky and a burn, on the opposite side of the road, gurgles and rushes as its sounds echo up towards me.

The path opens up to the traces of an ATV track through the grass. I'm glad to follow this, away from the vegetation pulling at my feet. I reach a fence and, in the warmth, strip down to just my shirt.

It's then over the Graham of Andrewhinney Hill, then onto Bell Craig. It takes me forty minutes to get back to Andrewhinney Hill and I take in the fine views of the hills around, rolling and basking in the sun. I look ahead to the minor tops of Mid Rig and Trowgrain Middle before what will be my final Donald, Herman Law. It then strikes me that this is significant. With only one left I'm about to finish the Donalds!

On the ascent of Trowgrain Middle I spot somebody walking towards me. At first I think it's a lady then realise they're man boobs – quite impressive nonetheless. We stop for a chat. Like me he's fifty-five but has just been made redundant from the closure of the Dunlop factory in Dundee. By the size of him I reckon his severance payment included one or two spare tyres. We chat about our routes, he's parked near me and is out bagging Donalds. I mention Herman Law will be my last. He doesn't take the bait, thinking that I mean the last of the day. We chat on about pensions, wives (mine brilliant, his not so), cars, the dangers of the roads.

"What ones do you have planned next?" he asks.

I know he means which Donalds, so I reply, "Well I've done the Nuttalls and the Munros so after Herman Law it'll be the Corbetts and Grahams."

"Oh, you mean Herman Law is your last Donald Hill!"

"Yes," I reply, basking in the glory of having deliberately steered the conversation around to this.

He congratulates me and I press on, passing over Trowgrain Middle then onto Herman Law (my 89th and last Donald – including the ones that are also Corbetts, Grahams or Nuttalls). With a sense of elation, I take a photo and post it on Facebook along with a note of this achievement. I look around, it's a lovely area but, with the Corbetts and Grahams to finish, I doubt I'll be back to this part of Scotland.

I set off for the forty-minute steep descent to the van. There's a spring in my step tinged with sadness in my heart. It does feel good to have finished the Donalds. When the van comes into view I phone Margaret and we do some mutual waving with Nancy.

Back home I contact the Scottish Mountaineering Club, requesting to go on the register of those having completed the Donalds. I get a query back, asking if I'd included the tops (outliers to the main peaks). I reply no and am told that does not qualify me to go on the list. To complete the Munros, the Corbetts and the Grahams you don't need to complete their tops. Querying the discrepancy I am informed that's the way it is.

I'm disheartened. I'm also finding the camper van a bit daunting. It's very long – I've now put a third dint in it – and its heating, refrigeration and hot water systems are complex and temperamental. On top of that I realise the week away in July was trying for Margaret and her question about my own stress and enjoyment levels are valid.

Nancy wanted to explore everything and the confined spaces of the van weren't the home from home we'd hoped for. On top of that our wild camping was being hampered by the need to empty the loo every other day. I think long and hard. Very long and hard. What am I doing? My life of working nonstop and my obsession to finish all the mountains of Great Britain is playing on my mind. I don't live in the moment, I'm always planning ahead and get very stressed if I don't meet my self-imposed goals. You can sign up for these mindfulness classes but the reality is mindfulness is a way of life. And, when with a child, you can only live in the moment. Anything else and you're in conflict with your and their needs. If I continue down this path I'm going to remain unfulfilled until I'm at least seventy – right through Nancy's childhood. When will I *really* begin to enjoy my life?

On one of our daily walks, in the woods behind our house, I muse this to Margaret and add, "How do you feel if I sell the camper van?"

She pauses for a moment. "It's up to you. But what about your hill walking?"

"How about I just have a couple of weeks away on my own each year and pick off what I can do."

She thinks for a moment. "You mean try and live more in the moment."

"Yes," I reply. "I still want to finish the Corbetts and Grahams, but I'll just take longer over it. Having you and Nancy has changed things for me. I've tried to combine the old and new me and realise they're at odds. What you and Nancy have given me is the much better option. I'm no longer the most important person in my life."

Margaret replies kindly. I think she's amazed by the change in me. But Margaret is the icing on the cake, and Nancy is the icing on the icing on the cake.

We advertise the camper van. Given Covid-19 has made people wary of holidaying we find its value has shot up and sell it to a dealer for just a bit less then we paid a dealer for it only ten months previously. We count ourselves lucky.

After waving the camper van goodbye Margaret, Nancy and I go on our daily walk. Margaret asks, "Are you glad to see the back of it?"

"Given I've put three dents in it," I reply, "I think it's glad to see the back of me. And in truth I'm glad to be starting to see the back of the old me."

Classification	My Total	Total
Welsh Nuttalls	189	189
English Nuttalls	257	257
Corbetts (Scotland)	117	222
Grahams (Scotland)	60	219
Unique Donalds (Scotland)	58	58
Munros (Scotland)	282	282
Totals (21/07/2020):	963	1227

January 2021 – English & Welsh Nuttalls

On 14/01/2021 Black Mountain South Top, Little Calva and Hobcarton End were demoted due to not having enough drop and re-ascent to neighbouring peaks.

On 23/12/2021 the true summit of Green Hill was moved to SD702821. Fortunately I passed over this point on the way to the original location.

Classification	My Total	Total
Welsh Nuttalls	188	188
English Nuttalls	255	255
Corbetts (Scotland)	117	222
Grahams (Scotland)	60	219
Unique Donalds (Scotland)	58	58
Munros (Scotland)	282	282
Totals (14/01/2021):	960	1224

Due to the lockdowns I don't venture into the hills instead I enjoy being a husband and a father, redecorate a rental property, pull together these diaries and self-build a double garage for our cars. I used to joke if I ever moved from my old house it'd be for "A wife, a view or a double garage." Now I've got all three!

February 2022 – A Local Walk

In February 2022 my friend Andy Glover visits for a walk. Andy appears on the first page of my first volume of walking diaries (The Munros: An asthmatic's walking diary) when we were radioing for a helicopter rescue for his brother. He's a long-standing friend and knows my obsession for picking off the peaks. During the pandemic we'd not been able to meet up and do our favourite trip to the Brecon Beacons, overnighting in my camper van after a long walk. Now, without the camper van we drive just a few miles to take in some of the high ground of Wiltshire: Milk Hill and Tan Hill. It's all below 1000ft but spectacular in its own way. I've never done much walking locally. I really do fancy getting to know Wiltshire's high ground.

As ever with Andy we finish in the dark, making an adventure of it. I tell him that last night Nancy had snuggled up next to me on the sofa and said, "I love you, Daddy." He thinks it's brilliant. He's so pleased for me.

June 2022 – Scottish 2000ft Mountains

Over the rest of the winter, with 105 Corbetts left to climb, I play with the maths in my head. Perhaps ten a year for ten years, or five a year for twenty years (taking me in to my late seventies). Then what about the 159 Grahams left to climb? What does become clear is that I need to get back to Scotland to do a week of walking.

Ali Ogden and her husband, Adrian offer to put me up for a week at their home in Newtonmore, with Ali and I doing day trips to bag Corbetts. We plan the five in a day near Tyndrum and the two we missed in 2017 – An Dun and Creag An Loch.

My friend Mike Linnett (who I last walked with when doing the

Munros) and his wife, Rose have just moved to Kingussie. So I plan to meet with them too.

As the holiday approaches I realise I'm really going to miss Margaret and Nancy, so drop the visit to five days (including two travelling on the train). I also realise I've been spending less time planning the final 105 Corbetts and 159 Grahams. The need to keep working out ways to do it has started to ebb away.

Ali contacts me saying she can't walk at the moment due to a hip problem that caused her to retire from the recent TGO Challenge. Ali, forever with the big heart, offers to drive me around so I can still do my Corbetts. As Tyndrum is such a long drive I ask if she'd instead drive me to Strathan so I can tackle Carn Mor and Mike agrees to ferry me down the A9 so we can do An Dun and Creag An Loch together. Three Corbetts in three days sounds good.

I travel by train on June 1st and, late into Paddington, having just ran and missed a tube, I'm stood on the underground platform for the Hammersmith and City line. Anxiously awaiting the next tube, and checking my watch for the connection at Kings Cross, I glance across at the blackened Victorian brickwork. A series of ancient green wooden doors sit, padlocked, behind modern electrical trunking. They can't have been opened for years. I then recall, thirty-five years ago I used to stand on the very same spot, late on Sunday evenings, anxiously awaiting the tube to convey me to where I was staying during my one year student work placement. Such a lot has happened in that time – graduating, working life, a lot of hill walking, marriage and fatherhood. I nod, somehow I feel I've made it through.

I board at Kings Cross, read and look at the photo of Nancy I'm carrying with me. After a mad dash at Edinburgh and Perth I settle into the final leg of the journey, gazing out the train window as the mountains grow around me. Tempting hill tracks wind their way across heather clad moors and up hills. Burbling streams glint in the sun.

Ali greets me at Kingussie and whisks me back to their home. It's great to catch up with Adrian and their eighteen-year-old daughter,

Ellen.

Over supper we discuss my plans, I mention that, now married, I'm trying to curtail my ambitions. "I can be a bit obsessive."

Adrian and Ellen simultaneously, in mock sarcasm, respond "Noooooo."

It's always good to have a mirror held up to you!

They mention how Newtonmore is changing. When I first visited the town in the 1990s it was run down and recessed, suffering from the loss of business the A9 took from it. Since then I've watched it flourish into a smart place but now, post Covid, properties are being snapped up as holiday homes – taking away its life blood. Lack of staff, post Brexit, has led to restaurants, bars and cafés struggling to provide a service.

Ali drives us down to Strathan on the 2nd and walks for just over an hour, along tracks, with me to A' Chuil Bothy. Here we part company as I set off for the Corbett of Carn Mor and Ali returns, resting her hip.

It's a glorious day, blue sky. Apparently the best day so far this year after months of rain and murky low cloud. However, Carn Mor feels daunting – the contour lines are tight on the map and I (having had a bad dose of Covid in February) am far from fit.

It's one slow foot in front of another with frequent rests, wobbles and slumps to the ground. I zig-zag to reduce the gradient. The Munros I climbed sit as elegant giants on the horizon. Their cols, corries, ridges and summits teasing the rich blue sky. I wonder how I managed them all. With my breathing, the rests I needed they were a slog, made by a young man with such determination. Something I realise is ebbing away.

Below, the River Dessarry glistens as it meanders its way through the floor of the glen. It takes me three hours to reach Carn Mor East Top. At 616m, 200m below the true summit, I've climbed at 165m per hour. This is so slow. I don't know if it's age or post-Covid fatigue but I'm hot, tired and low on water. I look up to the Carn Mor itself. It's towering above me, physically and mentally. In the past I'd have pressed on, determined. I now can't do this. I'm done.

The last two years have been a slow transition of going from planning long camper van trips away with Margaret and Nancy to planning two weeks per year down to this. I still want to walk in the Highlands but now, in this moment, I've retired the idea of finishing the remaining 105 Corbetts and 159 Grahams. The two planned with Mike tomorrow are still on. I'll still do the occasional one or two - but just for the enjoyment of walking, not obsessive list ticking to prove myself long after I have proven myself.

I head back, across the minor top of Monadh Gorm, taking in the views down to Loch Arkaig as it shimmers in the wind. Clouds dance their shadows across the hills.

It's then a steep drop into Glen Dessarry. I take a heavy fall and land flat on my front in a soaking peat bog. I extract myself, with a few sucks and pops, then brush the oozing filth from my trousers, arms and torso.

Rather dishevelled, and with a dose of hay fever, I meet Ali back at Strathan. I've been carrying her Garmin tracker so she's been expecting my imminent arrival. It's fitting that this book starts and finishes with Ali. I tell her of my decision, she offers words to keep me going. I shake my head. "I've retired the idea of finishing the Corbetts and Grahams, not retired from hill walking." She gets this. Walking all the 2000ft mountains of Great Britain was once everything to me, now Margaret and Nancy are.

The next day I meet Mike Linnett in Newtonmore. He and his wife Rose are living in a camper van, looking for a property to buy. He confirms Ali and Adrian's view that everything is being snapped up as holiday homes. Having moved here for work it feels unfair.

On the drive down the A9 to the start of the walk, Mike and I pick up where we left off, some ten years ago. Same sense of humour, nothing has changed.

We park at Dalnacardoch and set off up the track to the Corbetts of An Dun and Creag An Loch. They tower in the distance, against a perfect sky. They look daunting. I wonder how to tell Mike that I don't feel up for them. We rest at the abandoned house at Badnambiast, peering in at a swallows nest.

At the head of the track we explore the grounds of the abandoned Sronphadruig Lodge – surrounded by a deer fence where traditional pines are taking hold.

"Mike," I venture, "I don't feel up to the hills."

"It's a great day," he replies, "I've seen a swallow's nest and some great views. I'm happy just to sit here."

Now I get it, you don't need to get to every summit to enjoy life. I've climbed 1343 British mountains and lesser tops – not a bad achievement for a chronic asthmatic. I'll still walk up mountains, but without the pressure of *having* to tick off a list.

In the evening I phone Margaret. We chat then Nancy comes on the line. It's the first time I've ever spoken to her on a phone. She sounds so sweet and tells me about her day. Then she says, "I miss you in Scotland, Daddy. I love you."

If I do need any more convincing, this does it for me. What more does a man need? I've walked it through.

Me with the abandoned house, Badnambiast

Can You Spare Some Time to Give a Review?

Your honest opinion matters. You can rate this book on www.amazon.co.uk (under 'Your Orders' then the 'Write a product review' button) or www.goodreads.com

Many thanks.
Stephen P. Smith

Appendix: All the Mountains and Hills I've Bagged

Classification	My Total
Welsh Nuttalls	188
English Nuttalls	255
Corbetts (Scotland)	117
Grahams (Scotland)	60
Donalds that are not Corbetts or Grahams (Scotland)	58
Donald Tops (Scotland)	19
Munros (Scotland)	282
Munro Tops (Scotland)	85
Corbett Tops that are not Donalds or Donald Tops (Scotland)	42
Graham Tops that are not Donalds or Donald Tops (Scotland)	13
Other Tops	224
Non UK mountains	3
Totals (05/12/2022):	1346

Welsh Nuttalls Bagged (All Completed)

Name	Height	Date
Allt Lwyd	2146ft	24/09/2003
Allt-fawr	2290ft	12/09/2004
Aran Benllyn	2904ft	26/08/2007

Name	Height	Date
Aran Fawddwy	2969ft	26/08/2007
Arenig Fach	2260ft	22/05/2008
Arenig Fawr	2802ft	09/05/2008
Arenig Fawr South Ridge Top	2336ft	09/05/2008
Arenig Fawr South Top	2743ft	09/05/2008
Bache Hill	2001ft	09/02/2002
Bera Bach	2648ft	25/09/2004
Bera Mawr	2605ft	25/09/2004
Black Mixen	2133ft	09/02/2002
Black Mountain	2306ft	13/01/2002
Black Mountain South Top (1)	2090ft	13/01/2002
Bwlch y Ddwyallt	2474ft	24/09/2003
Cadair Berwyn	2713ft	27/08/2005
Cadair Berwyn North Top	2723ft	27/08/2005
Cadair Bronwen	2575ft	27/08/2005
Cadair Bronwen North-east Top (2)	2297ft	27/08/2005
Cadair Idris	2930ft	18/05/2008
Carnedd Dafydd	3425ft	15/09/2004
Carnedd Llechwedd-llyfn	2110ft	22/05/2008
Carnedd Llewelyn	3491ft	15/09/2004
Carnedd y Ddelw (3)	2257ft	21/09/2004
Carnedd Y Filiast	2694ft	26/07/2005
Carnedd y Filiast	2195ft	22/05/2008
Carnedd Y Filiast North Top (4)	2365ft	20/05/2008
Castell y Gwynt (5)	3189ft	16/05/2008
Cefn Gwyntog	2018ft	11/08/2007
Cefn Yr Ystrad	2024ft	24/09/2003
Chwarel y Fan	2228ft	27/01/2002
Cnicht	2260ft	17/09/2004
Cnicht North Top	2251ft	17/09/2004
Corn Du	2864ft	27/03/2004

Name	Height	Date
Craig Cerrig-gleisiad	2064ft	24/11/2001
Craig Cwm Amarch	2595ft	18/05/2008
Craig Cwm Silyn	2408ft	19/07/2007
Craig Eigiau	2411ft	23/09/2004
Craig Gwaun Taf (6)	2711ft	13/06/2018
Craiglwyn	2044ft	21/05/2008
Craig-y-llyn	2041ft	13/05/2008
Craigysgafn	2260ft	17/09/2004
Creigiau Gleision	2224ft	21/05/2008
Creigiau Gleision North Top	2080ft	21/05/2008
Crib Goch	3028ft	15/05/2008
Crib y Ddysgl	3494ft	12/09/2002
Cribin Fawr	2162ft	19/05/2008
Cribyn	2608ft	10/03/1990 & 27/03/2004
Crib-y-rhiw	2198ft	11/05/2008
Cyfrwy	2661ft	18/05/2008
Cyrniau Nod (via Foel Cedig) (7)	2188ft	11/08/2007
Dduallt	2172ft	17/05/2008
Diffwys	2106ft	11/05/2008
Diffwys West Top	2461ft	11/05/2008
Drosgl	2487ft	25/09/2004
Drum	2526ft	21/09/2004
Drygarn Fawr	2103ft	10/06/2005
Elidir Fawr	3031ft	26/07/2005
Erw y Ddafad-ddu	2861ft	26/08/2007
Esgeiriau Gwynion	2201ft	25/08/2007
Fan Brycheiniog	2631ft	28/06/2004
Fan Fawr	2408ft	24/11/2001
Fan Fraith	2192ft	02/12/2001

Name	Height	Date
Fan Frynych	2064ft	24/11/2001
Fan Gyhirych	2379ft	02/12/2001
Fan Hir	2497ft	28/06/2004
Fan Llia	2073ft	24/11/2001
Fan Nedd	2175ft	02/12/2001
Fan y Big	2359ft	27/03/2004
Foel Boeth	2021ft	09/05/2008
Foel Cwm-Sian Llwyd	2126ft	11/08/2007
Foel Goch	2011ft	12/08/2007
Foel Goch	2005ft	08/05/2008
Foel Grach	3202ft	25/09/2004
Foel Gron	2064ft	27/07/2005
Foel Hafod-fynydd	2260ft	25/08/2007
Foel Meirch	2625ft	18/09/2004
Foel Penolau	2014ft	22/03/2008
Foel Rhudd	2162ft	25/08/2007
Foel Wen	2267ft	28/08/2005
Foel Wen South Top	2254ft	28/08/2005
Foel y Geifr	2054ft	12/08/2007
Foel-fras	3091ft	25/09/2004
Foel-goch	2726ft	26/07/2005
Gallt Y Daren	2031ft	09/05/2008
Gallt y Wenallt	2031ft	12/09/2002
Gallt yr Ogof	2503ft	16/05/2008
Garnedd Uchaf	3038ft	25/09/2004
Garnedd-goch	2297ft	19/07/2007
Garreg Las	2083ft	28/06/2004
Garreg Lwyd	2021ft	28/06/2004
Gau Graig	2241ft	18/05/2008
Glasgwm	2599ft	26/08/2007
Glyder Fach	3261ft	25/07/2005

Name	Height	Date
Glyder Fawr	3278ft	25/07/2005
Godor	2228ft	27/08/2005
Godor North Top	2215ft	27/08/2005
Gorllwyn	2011ft	10/06/2005
Great Rhos	2165ft	09/02/2002
Gwaun Lydan	2073ft	27/08/2007
Gwaun y Llwyni	2247ft	26/08/2007
Gyrn Wigau	2110ft	25/09/2004
Llechog	2356ft	27/07/2005
Llechwedd Du	2014ft	25/08/2007
Lliwedd Bach	2684ft	12/09/2002
Llwytmor	2785ft	25/09/2004
Maesglase	2218ft	19/05/2008
Manod Mawr	2169ft	13/09/2004
Manod Mawr North Top	2159ft	11/09/2004
Moel Cynghorion	2211ft	27/07/2005
Moel Druman	2218ft	16/09/2004
Moel Eilio	2382ft	27/07/2005
Moel Fferna	2067ft	28/08/2005
Moel Hebog	2569ft	17/07/2007
Moel Lefn	2093ft	17/07/2007
Moel Llyfnant	2464ft	09/05/2008
Moel Penamnen	2034ft	11/09/2004
Moel Siabod	2861ft	08/05/1999
Moel Sych	2713ft	27/08/2005
Moel y Cerrig Duon	2051ft	25/08/2007
Moel yr Ewig	2280ft	27/08/2005
Moel yr Ogof	2149ft	17/07/2007
Moel Ysgyfarnogod	2044ft	22/03/2008
Moelwyn Bach	2329ft	17/09/2004
Moelwyn Mawr	2526ft	17/09/2004

Name	Height	Date
Moelwyn Mawr North Ridge Top (8)	2119ft	17/09/2004
Moel-yr-hydd	2126ft	17/09/2004
Mynydd Tarw	2234ft	28/08/2005
Mynydd Drws-y-coed	2280ft	19/07/2007
Mynydd Graig Goch (9)	2000ft	14/11/2008
Mynydd Llysiau	2175ft	13/03/2003
Mynydd Mawr	2290ft	23/05/2008
Mynydd Moel	2831ft	18/05/2008
Mynydd Perfedd	2664ft	26/07/2005
Mynydd Tal-y-mignedd	2142ft	19/07/2007
Pen Allt-mawr	2359ft	13/03/2003
Pen Bwlch Llandrillo Top	2037ft	27/08/2005
Pen Cerrig-calch	2300ft	13/03/2003
Pen Llithrig-y-wrach	2621ft	21/05/2008
Pen Pumlumon Llygad-bychan	2385ft	11/06/2005
Pen Twyn Glas	2119ft	13/03/2003
Pen Twyn Mawr	2159ft	13/03/2003
Pen yr Allt Uchaf	2034ft	27/08/2007
Pen y Boncyn Trefeilw	2119ft	11/08/2007
Pen y Bryn-fforchog	2247ft	26/08/2007
Pen y Castell	2044ft	21/09/2004
Pen y Fan	2907ft	10/03/1990 & 27/03/2004
Pen y Gadair Fawr	2625ft	13/03/2003
Pen y Garn	2001ft	11/06/2005
Pen yr Helgi Du	2733ft	15/09/2004
Pen yr ole Wen	3209ft	15/09/2004
Picws Du	2457ft	28/06/2004
Post Gwyn	2182ft	12/01/2002
Pumlumon Arwystli	2431ft	11/06/2005

Name	Height	Date
Pumlumon Fach	2178ft	11/06/2005
Pumlumon Fawr	2467ft	11/06/2005
Rhinog Fach	2336ft	11/05/2008
Rhinog Fawr	2362ft	11/05/2008
Rhobell Fawr	2408ft	17/05/2008
Rhos Dirion	2339ft	27/01/2002
Snowdon	3560ft	12/09/2002 & 1976,1988, 1989, 2017
Stac Rhos	2067ft	11/08/2007
Tal y Fan	2001ft	21/09/2004
Tarren y Gesail	2188ft	14/05/2008
Tarrenhendre	2080ft	14/05/2008
Tomle	2434ft	28/08/2005
Trum y Ddysgl	2326ft	19/07/2007
Trum y Gwragedd	2008ft	12/08/2007
Tryfan	3002ft	16/05/2008
Twmpa	2231ft	13/01/2002
Tyrrau Mawr	2169ft	13/05/2008
Waun Camddwr	2037ft	26/08/2007
Waun Fach	2661ft	13/03/2003
Waun Garnedd-y-Filiast	2133ft	22/05/2008
Waun Lefrith	2221ft	28/06/2004
Waun Rydd	2523ft	24/09/2003
Waun-oer	2198ft	19/05/2008
Y Foel Goch	2641ft	16/05/2008
Y Garn	2244ft	11/06/2005
Y Garn	3107ft	26/07/2005
Y Garn	2077ft	19/07/2007
Y Garn	2064ft	10/05/2008

Name	Height	Date
Y Groes Fagl	2162ft	11/08/2007
Y Gyrn	2031ft	27/03/2004
Y Llethr	2480ft	11/05/2008
Y Lliwedd	2946ft	12/09/2002
Y Lliwedd East Peak	2930ft	12/09/2002
Yr Aran	2451ft	16/07/2007
Yr Elen	3156ft	15/09/2004
Ysgafell Wen	2205ft	16/09/2004
Ysgafell Wen Far North Top	2133ft	16/09/2004
Ysgafell Wen North Top	2195ft	16/09/2004

Notes:

1. Black Mountain South Top was demoted on 14/01/2021.
2. Cadair Bronwen North-east Top was demoted on 19/08/2007 as having an insufficient drop all round.
3. Carnedd y Ddelw was demoted on 31/05/2017 as having an insufficient drop all round.
4. Carnedd Y Filiast North Top was promoted on 02/09/2007.
5. Castell y Gwynt was promoted on 02/09/2007.
6. Craig Gwaun Taf was added on 12/11/2016.
7. Cyrniau Nod was demoted on 21/10/2018 Cyrniau Nod and the nearby Foel Cedig promoted.
8. Moelwyn Mawr North Ridge was demoted on 05/08/2015 as having an insufficient drop all round.
9. Mynydd Graig Goch was promoted on 19/09/2008.

English Nuttalls Bagged (All Completed)

Name	Height	Date
Allen Crags	2575ft	15/11/2008
Archy Styrigg	2280ft	18/11/2011

Name	Height	Date
Atkinson Pike	2772ft	11/04/2012
Backstone Edge	2293ft	17/11/2012
Bannerdale Crags	2241ft	11/04/2012
Base Brown	2119ft	18/11/2006
Baugh Fell	2224ft	07/06/2012
Bellbeaver Rigg	2034ft	12/06/2013
Bink Moss	2031ft	04/10/2013
Birkhouse Moor	2356ft	05/05/2011
Birks	2041ft	05/05/2011
Birks Fell (1)	2001ft	08/07/2014
Black Crag	2717ft	04/07/2014
Black Fell	2178ft	05/06/2013
Black Sails	2444ft	24/04/2011
Bleaklow Head	2077ft	11/04/2004
Blencathra	2848ft	11/04/2012
Bloodybush Edge	2001ft	03/06/2013
Bowfell	2959ft	20/04/2011
Bowfell North Top	2841ft	20/04/2011
Bowscale Fell	2303ft	11/04/2012
Bram Rigg Top (2)	2205ft	11/07/2014
Brandreth	2346ft	06/04/2012
Branstree	2339ft	28/04/2011
Branstree North-east Top	2208ft	28/04/2011
Brim Fell	2612ft	24/04/2011
Broad Crag	3064ft	19/11/2005
Buckden Pike	2303ft	08/07/2014
Bullman Hills	2001ft	11/06/2013
Burnhope Seat	2450ft	08/06/2013
Bush Howe	2044ft	11/07/2014
Calders	2211ft	11/07/2014
The Calf	2218ft	11/07/2014

Name	Height	Date
Calf Top (3)	2000ft	26/05/2018
Carl Side	2447ft	16/11/2007
Carrock Fell	2165ft	12/04/2012
Catstye Cam	2920ft	26/04/2011
Causey Pike	2090ft	20/11/2010
Caw Fell	2264ft	30/09/2013
Chapelfell Top	2306ft	09/06/2013
The Cheviot	2674ft	01/06/2013
Clough Head	2382ft	25/04/2011
Codale Head	2395ft	18/04/2011
Cold Fell	2037ft	04/06/2013
Cold Pike	2300ft	22/04/2011
Cold Pike Far West Top	2198ft	22/04/2011
Cold Pike West Top	2241ft	22/04/2011
Comb Fell	2139ft	01/06/2013
Combe Door Top	2218ft	15/11/2008
Combe Head	2411ft	15/11/2008
Coniston Old Man	2634ft	24/04/2011
Crag Hill	2753ft	20/11/2010
Crinkle Crags	2818ft	22/04/2011
Crinkle Crags South Top	2736ft	22/04/2011
Cross Fell	2930ft	19/11/2011
Cushat Law	2018ft	03/06/2013
Dale Head	2470ft	20/11/2004
Darnbrook Fell	2047ft	09/07/2014
Dead Stones	2329ft	08/06/2013
Dodd (Buttermere)	2103ft	04/04/2012
The Dodd (Nenthead)	2014ft	07/06/2013
Dodd Fell Hill	2192ft	06/07/2014
Dollywaggon Pike	2815ft	05/05/2011
Dove Crag	2598ft	02/03/2002

Name	Height	Date
Dovenest Top	2073ft	15/11/2008
Dow Crag	2552ft	24/04/2011
Drumaldrace	2014ft	06/07/2014
Esk Pike	2904ft	20/04/2011
Fairfield	2864ft	02/03/2002
Fell Head	2100ft	11/07/2014
Fendrith Hill	2283ft	09/06/2013
Fiend's Fell	2080ft	06/06/2013
Fleetwith Pike	2126ft	06/04/2012
Flinty Fell	2014ft	06/06/2013
Fountains Fell	2192ft	09/07/2014
Fountains Fell South Top	2172ft	09/07/2014
Froswick	2362ft	30/04/2011
Gategill Fell Top	2792ft	11/04/2012
Glaramara	2569ft	15/11/2008
Gragareth	2057ft	05/07/2014
Grasmoor	2795ft	07/04/2012
Gray Crag (Hartsop)	2293ft	02/05/2011
Great Borne	2021ft	02/04/2012
Great Calva	2264ft	12/04/2012
Great Carrs	2575ft	24/04/2011
Great Coum	2254ft	05/07/2014
Great Dodd	2812ft	25/04/2011
Great Dun Fell	2782ft	19/11/2011
Great End	2986ft	19/11/2005
Great Gable	2949ft	18/11/2006
Great Knott	2283ft	22/04/2011
Great Knoutberry Hill	2205ft	20/11/2011
Great Lingy Hill	2021ft	12/04/2012
Great Rigg	2513ft	02/03/2002
Great Shunner Fell	2349ft	03/06/2012

Name	Height	Date
Great Stony Hill	2323ft	10/06/2013
Great Whernside	2310ft	08/07/2014
Green Gable	2628ft	18/11/2006
Green Hill (4)	2060ft	05/07/2014
Green Side	2608ft	25/04/2011
Grey Crag (Sleddale)	2093ft	28/04/2011
Grey Friar	2526ft	24/04/2011
Grey Knotts	2287ft	06/04/2012
Grey Nag	2152ft	05/06/2013
Grisedale Pike	2595ft	20/11/2010
Hare Stones	2057ft	12/04/2012
Harrison Stickle	2415ft	18/04/2011
Harrop Pike	2090ft	28/04/2011
Hart Crag	2697ft	02/03/2002
Hart Side	2480ft	25/04/2011
Harter Fell (Duddon)	2142ft	17/04/2011
Harter Fell (Kentmere)	2552ft	04/05/2011
Hartsop Dodd	2028ft	02/05/2011
Harwood Common	2356ft	08/06/2013
Haycock	2615ft	30/09/2013
Hedgehope Hill	2342ft	01/06/2013
Helvellyn	3117ft	26/04/2011
Helvellyn Lower Man	3035ft	26/04/2011
Heron Pike	2008ft	02/03/2002
Heron Pike North Top	2037ft	02/03/2002
High Crag	2441ft	04/04/2012
High House Tarn Top	2244ft	15/11/2008
High Pike	2159ft	12/04/2012
High Raise (High Street)	2631ft	18/04/2011
High Raise (Langdale)	2500ft	03/05/2011
High Seat	2326ft	18/11/2011

Name	Height	Date
High Spy	2142ft	20/11/2004
High Spy North Top	2080ft	18/11/2005
High Stile	2648ft	04/04/2012
High Street	2717ft	02/05/2011
High Willhays	2037ft	02/08/2002
Higher Shelf Stones	2037ft	11/04/2004
Hindscarth	2385ft	20/11/2004
Hobcarton Crag	2425ft	20/11/2010
Hobcarton End (5)	2080ft	20/11/2010
Honister Crag (6)	2067ft	06/04/2012
Hopegill Head	2526ft	09/04/2012
Hugh Seat	2260ft	18/11/2011
Ill Bell	2484ft	30/04/2011
Ill Crag	3068ft	19/11/2005
Ingleborough	2372ft	06/07/2014
Iron Crag	2100ft	30/09/2013
Kentmere Pike	2395ft	04/05/2011
Kidsty Pike	2559ft	03/05/2011
Killhope Law	2208ft	07/06/2013
Kinder Scout	2087ft	02/06/2012
Kirk Fell	2631ft	05/04/2012
Kirk Fell East Top	2582ft	05/04/2012
Knock Fell	2605ft	19/11/2011
Knott	2329ft	12/04/2012
Knoutberry Haw	2218ft	07/06/2012
Ladyside Pike	2306ft	09/04/2012
Lingmell	2625ft	27/04/2011
Little Calva (7)	2106ft	12/04/2012
Little Dun Fell	2762ft	19/11/2011
Little Fell (Mallerstang)	2188ft	18/11/2011
Little Fell (Mickle Fell)	2454ft	12/07/2014

Name	Height	Date
Little Gowder Crag	2405ft	30/09/2013
Little Hart Crag	2090ft	02/03/2002
Little Stand	2428ft	22/04/2011
Loadpot Hill	2201ft	13/04/2012
Loft Crag	2198ft	18/04/2011
Long Fell (8)	2046ft	26/05/2018
Long Man Hill	2159ft	11/06/2013
Long Side	2408ft	16/11/2007
Lonscale Fell	2346ft	16/11/2007
Looking Stead (Pillar)	2057ft	05/04/2012
Looking Steads (Glaramara)	2543ft	15/11/2008
Lovely Seat	2215ft	03/06/2012
Low Saddle	2152ft	16/04/2011
Meldon Hill	2516ft	13/06/2013
Melmerby Fell	2326ft	06/06/2013
Mickle Fell	2585ft	05/10/2013
Middleboot Knotts	2306ft	27/04/2011
Middlehope Moor	2008ft	07/06/2013
Miller Moss (9)	2001ft	13/09/2018
Murton Fell	2215ft	18/11/2012
Nethermost Pike	2923ft	05/05/2011
Nine Standards Rigg	2172ft	05/06/2012
Pavey Ark	2297ft	18/04/2011
Pen-y-ghent	2277ft	10/07/2014
Pike of Blisco	2313ft	22/04/2011
Pike of Stickle	2326ft	18/04/2011
Pillar	2926ft	01/10/2013
Pillar Rock	2559ft	01/10/2013
Place Fell	2155ft	03/05/2011
Plover Hill	2231ft	10/07/2014
Raise	2897ft	26/04/2011

Name	Height	Date
Rampsgill Head	2598ft	03/05/2011
Randygill Top	2051ft	11/07/2014
Red Beck Top	2365ft	15/11/2008
Red Pike (Buttermere)	2477ft	04/04/2012
Red Pike (Wasdale)	2710ft	04/07/2014
Red Screes	2546ft	18/11/2005
Rest Dodd	2283ft	03/05/2011
Robinson	2418ft	20/11/2004
Rogan's Seat	2205ft	04/06/2012
Rossett Pike	2136ft	20/04/2011
Rosthwaite Fell	2008ft	15/11/2008
Rough Crag	2060ft	02/05/2011
Round Hill	2251ft	11/06/2013
Round How	2431ft	27/04/2011
Sail	2536ft	20/11/2010
Sale How	2185ft	16/11/2007
Sand Hill	2480ft	09/04/2012
Scafell	3163ft	27/04/2011
Scafell Pike	3209ft	19/11/2005
Scar Crags	2205ft	20/11/2010
Scoat Fell	2759ft	04/07/2014
Seat Sandal	2415ft	05/05/2011
Seatallan	2274ft	30/09/2013
Seathwaite Fell	2073ft	15/11/2008
Seathwaite Fell South Top	2070ft	15/11/2008
Selside Pike	2149ft	28/04/2011
Sheffield Pike	2215ft	26/04/2011
Shelter Crags	2674ft	22/04/2011
Shelter Crags North Top	2543ft	22/04/2011
Simon Fell	2133ft	06/07/2014
Skiddaw	3054ft	16/11/2007

Name	Height	Date
Skiddaw Little Man	2838ft	16/11/2007
St Sunday Crag	2759ft	05/05/2011
Starling Dodd	2077ft	02/04/2012
Steeple	2687ft	04/07/2014
Stony Cove Pike	2503ft	02/05/2011
Striding Edge	2821ft	05/05/2011
Stybarrow Dodd	2766ft	25/04/2011
Swarth Fell	2234ft	06/06/2012
Swirl How	2631ft	24/04/2011
Symonds Knott	3146ft	27/04/2011
Tarn Crag	2178ft	28/04/2011
Thack Moor (10)	2000ft	05/06/2013
Thornthwaite Crag	2572ft	02/05/2011
Three Pikes	2136ft	10/06/2013
Thunacar Knott	2372ft	18/04/2011
Tinside Rigg (11)	2047ft	26/05/2018
Tom Smith's Stone Top	2090ft	05/06/2013
Ullscarf	2382ft	16/04/2011
Viewing Hill	2129ft	12/06/2013
Walna Scar	2037ft	24/04/2011
Wandope	2533ft	07/04/2012
Water Crag	2192ft	04/06/2012
Westernhope Moor	2215ft	09/06/2013
Wether Hill	2198ft	13/04/2012
Wetherlam	2503ft	24/04/2011
Whernside	2415ft	05/07/2014
White Maiden	2001ft	24/04/2011
White Side (Helvellyn)	2831ft	26/04/2011
Whiteless Pike	2165ft	07/04/2012
Whiteside (Crummock)	2320ft	09/04/2012
Whiteside East Top	2359ft	09/04/2012

Name	Height	Date
Wild Boar Fell	2323ft	06/06/2012
Windy Gyle	2031ft	02/06/2013
Yarlside	2096ft	11/07/2014
Yes Tor	2031ft	02/08/2002
Yewbarrow	2060ft	04/07/2014
Yewbarrow North Top	2021ft	04/07/2014
Yockenthwaite Moor	2110ft	07/07/2014
Yoke	2316ft	30/04/2011

Notes:

1. Honister Crag was promoted on 01/11/2004
2. Birks Fell was promoted on 04/10/2006
3. Thack Moor was promoted on 03/04/2013
4. The true summit of Green Hill was moved to SD702821 on 23/12/2021. Fortunately I passed over this point on the way to the original location
5. Calf Top was promoted on 06/09/2016
6. Bram Rigg Top was demoted on 12/11/2016
7. Tinside Rigg was promoted on 21/11/2016
8. Long Fell was promoted on 21/11/2016
9. Miller Moss was promoted on 06/08/2018
10. Little Calva was demoted on 14/01/2021
11. Hobcarton End was demoted on 14/01/2021

Corbetts Bagged (Partially Completed)

Name	Height	Date	Notes
Am Bathach	2618ft	10/05/2017	
Aonach Shasuinn	2913ft	14/06/2017	
Auchnafree Hill	2589ft	18/04/2017	
Bac an Eich	2785ft	17/06/2017	
Beinn a' Bhathaich Ard	2828ft	15/06/2017	

Name	Height	Date	Notes
Beinn a' Bhuiridh	2948ft	15/04/2017	
Beinn a' Chlaidheimh	2999ft	24/06/2001	Demoted Munro
Beinn a' Chrulaiste	2812ft	30/04/2017	
Beinn a' Chuallaich	2927ft	15/05/2016	
Beinn an Lochain	2958ft	03/05/2016	
Beinn Bhan	2612ft	27/04/2017	
Beinn Bhreac	2994ft	22/05/2010	
Beinn Bhreac-liath	2631ft	06/05/2016	
Beinn Chuirn	2887ft	04/05/2016	
Beinn Dearg	2723ft	13/05/2016	
Beinn Dronaig	2615ft	08/05/2009	
Beinn Each	2667ft	24/05/2018	
Beinn Iaruinn	2641ft	22/04/2017	
Beinn Liath Mhor a' Ghiubhais Li	2513ft	23/06/2017	
Beinn Luibhean	2821ft	02/05/2016	
Beinn Mheadhonach	2956ft	20/04/2017	
Beinn Mhic Chasgaig	2835ft	01/05/2017	
Beinn Mhic Mhonaidh	2612ft	14/04/2017	
Beinn Mholach	2761ft	24/05/2017	
Beinn nan Imirean	2785ft	07/05/2016	
Beinn nan Oighreag	2984ft	09/05/2016	
Beinn Pharlagain – Meall na Meoig	2845ft	26/05/2017	
Beinn Stacach	2532ft	01/06/2017	
Beinn Tharsuinn	2831ft	12/06/2001	
Beinn Udlaidh	2757ft	06/05/2016	
Ben Gulabin	2644ft	17/07/2009	
Ben Ledi	2884ft	27/05/2016	
Ben Rinnes	2759ft	22/05/2015	
Ben Tee	2966ft	17/05/2017	
Ben Tirran	2940ft	17/05/2005	

Name	Height	Date	Notes
Ben Vrackie	2762ft	16/07/2009	
Ben Vuirich	2963ft	14/07/2009	
Benvane	2694ft	27/05/2016	
Bidein a' Chabair	2846ft	15/05/2010	
Braigh nan Uamhachan	2510ft	07/06/2017	
Broad Law	2756ft	10/04/2017	Also a Donald
Brown Cow Hill	2720ft	19/05/2015	
Cairnsmore of Carsphairn	2615ft	11/04/2017	Also a Donald
Cam Chreag	2828ft	12/05/2016	
Carn a' Choire Ghairbh	2838ft	14/06/2017	
Carn a' Chuilinn	2680ft	13/05/2017	
Carn an Fhreiceadain	2881ft	13/05/2009	
Carn Dearg	2520ft	26/04/2017	
Carn Dearg	2680ft	19/05/2010	
Carn Dearg	2736ft	23/04/2017	
Carn Dearg Mor	2812ft	22/05/2010	
Carn Ealasaid	2598ft	20/05/2015	
Carn Mor	2638ft	20/05/2015	
Carn na Drochaide	2684ft	20/05/2017	
Carn na Saobhaidhe	2661ft	12/05/2009	
Conachcraig	2838ft	25/05/2010	
Corryhabbie Hill	2562ft	21/05/2015	
Corserine	2671ft	12/04/2017	Also a Donald
Creag an Dail Bheag	2831ft	21/05/2017	
Creag Mac Ranaich	2653ft	16/04/2017	
Creag Mhor	2936ft	19/05/2016	
Creag nan Gabhar	2736ft	16/05/2015	
Creag Uchdag	2884ft	29/05/2017	
Creagan na Beinne	2913ft	28/05/2017	
Cruach Innse	2812ft	16/05/2006	

Name	Height	Date	Notes
Culardoch	2953ft	21/05/2017	
Druim nan Cnamh	2589ft	11/05/2017	
Farragon Hill	2567ft	14/05/2016	
Gairbeinn	2938ft	11/05/2015	
Geal Charn	2638ft	15/05/2017	
Geal Charn	2694ft	15/05/2015	
Geal-charn Mor	2703ft	14/05/2015	
Glas Bheinn	2598ft	28/04/2017	
Hart Fell	2651ft	02/05/2015	Also a Donald
Leathad an Taobhain	2991ft	22/05/2010	
Leum Uilleim	2974ft	18/05/2017	
Little Wyvis	2503ft	20/06/2017	
Mam na Gualainn	2612ft	08/06/2017	
Meall a' Bhuachaille	2657ft	04/02/2009	
Meall a' Phubuill	2535ft	04/06/2017	
Meall an t-Seallaidh	2798ft	17/04/2017	
Meall Buidhe	2980ft	11/05/2016	
Meall Dubh	2589ft	06/05/2017	
Meall Lighiche	2533ft	22/05/2018	
Meall na Fearna	2654ft	02/06/2017	
Meall na h-Aisre	2828ft	06/05/2015	
Meall na h-Eilde	2747ft	16/05/2017	
Meall na Leitreach	2550ft	17/05/2016	
Meall nam Maigheach	2555ft	08/05/2016	
Meall nan Subh	2644ft	10/05/2016	
Meall Tairneachan	2582ft	14/05/2016	
Meallach Mhor	2523ft	21/05/2010	
Meallan nan Uan	2750ft	18/06/2017	
Merrick	2766ft	27/07/2017	Also a Donald
Monamenach	2648ft	06/07/2009	
Morrone	2820ft	15/02/2015	

Name	Height	Date	Notes
Morven	2861ft	18/05/2015	
Mount Battock	2552ft	22/05/2016	
Sgor Mor	2667ft	20/05/2016	
Sgorr na Diollaid	2684ft	13/06/2017	
Sgurr a' Mhuilinn	2883ft	18/06/2017	
Sgurr an Airgid	2760ft	08/05/2017	
Sgurr an Utha	2612ft	13/05/2006	
Sgurr Innse	2654ft	08/05/2015	
Sgurr Mhic Bharraich	2556ft	09/05/2017	
Sgurr Mhurlagain	2887ft	10/06/2017	
Sgurr nan Ceannaichean	2997ft	08/06/2001	Demoted Munro
Shalloch on Minnoch	2540ft	29/07/2017	Also a Donald
Sron a' Choire Chnapanaich	2740ft	11/05/2016	
Stob a' Choin	2851ft	31/05/2017	
Stob an Aonaich Mhoir	2805ft	27/05/2017	
Stob Coire Creagach	2683ft	01/05/2016	
Stob Dubh	2897ft	02/05/2017	
Streap	2982ft	05/06/2017	
The Fara	2990ft	21/04/2017	
The Sow of Atholl	2621ft	16/05/2016	
White Coomb	2694ft	09/04/2017	Also a Donald

Grahams Bagged (Partially Completed)

Name	Height	Date	Notes
Andrewhinney Hill	2222ft	21/07/2020	Also a Donald
Badandun Hill	2428ft	05/07/2009	
Ballencleuch Law	2260ft	08/08/2017	Also a Donald
Beinn a' Mhanaich	2326ft	09/05/2018	

Name	Height	Date	Notes
Beinn Bhreac	2234ft	12/05/2018	
Beinn Chaorach	2339ft	09/05/2018	
Beinn Eich	2306ft	10/05/2018	
Beinn na Gucaig	2021ft	20/05/2018	
Ben Cleuch	2365ft	24/05/2019	Also a Donald
Blackcraig Hill	2300ft	05/08/2017	Also a Donald
Blackhope Scar	2136ft	28/05/2019	Also a Donald
Blath Bhalg	2101ft	09/07/2009	
Cairnsmore of Fleet	2333ft	25/07/2017	Also a Donald
Capel Fell	2224ft	17/07/2020	Also a Donald
Carn na h-Easgainn	2024ft	24/06/2017	
Carn nan Tri-tighearnan	2018ft	25/06/2017	
Cat Law	2201ft	10/07/2009	
Cauldcleuch Head	2030ft	25/05/2018	Also a Donald
Cnap Cruinn	2434ft	10/05/2015	
Cook's Cairn	2477ft	21/05/2015	
Craignaw	2116ft	27/07/2017	Also a Donald
Creag Bhalg	2192ft	21/05/2016	
Creag Dhubh	2159ft	09/05/2015	
Creag Dhubh	2480ft	04/05/2015	
Creag Liath	2438ft	05/05/2015	
Creag Ruadh	2041ft	07/05/2015	
Creag Ruadh	2159ft	16/05/2018	
Croft Head	2090ft	16/07/2020	Also a Donald
Cruach an t-Sidhein	2244ft	10/05/2018	
Culter Fell	2454ft	26/05/2019	Also a Donald
Doune Hill	2408ft	10/05/2018	
Duchray Hill	2303ft	08/07/2009	
Dun Rig	2441ft	29/05/2019	Also a Donald
Ettrick Pen	2270ft	16/07/2020	Also a Donald
Gathersnow Hill	2257ft	12/09/2018	Also a Donald

Name	Height	Date	Notes
Glas Bheinn	2402ft	19/05/2018	
Glas-charn	2078ft	12/05/2006	
Green Lowther	2402ft	06/08/2017	Also a Donald
Hill of Wirren	2224ft	21/05/2019	
Lamachan Hill	2352ft	26/07/2017	Also a Donald
Leana Mhor	2218ft	18/05/2018	
Leana Mhor	2244ft	17/05/2018	
Meall a' Mhuic	2444ft	13/05/2016	
Meall Buidhe	2359ft	23/05/2018	
Meall Mor	2218ft	13/05/2018	
Mid Hill	2156ft	10/05/2018	
Millfore	2156ft	31/07/2017	Also a Donald
Mona Gowan	2457ft	23/05/2017	
Mount Blair	2441ft	05/07/2009	
Mullwharchar	2270ft	27/07/2017	Also a Donald
Pap of Glencoe	2436ft	14/05/2018	
Queensberry	2287ft	09/08/2017	Also a Donald
Sgiath a' Chaise	2114ft	24/05/2018	
Sgorr a' Choise	2175ft	13/05/2018	
Tinto	2333ft	10/08/2017	Also a Donald
Tom Meadhoin	2037ft	21/05/2018	
Tullich Hill	2073ft	12/05/2018	
Uamh Bheag	2184ft	19/05/2019	Also a Donald
Windlestraw Law	2163ft	27/05/2019	Also a Donald
Windy Standard	2290ft	02/08/2017	Also a Donald

Donalds Bagged (All Completed)

Name	Height	Date	Notes
Alhang	2106ft	02/08/2017	Also a Graham Top
Andrewhinney Hill	2222ft	21/07/2020	Also a Graham
Ballencleuch Law	2260ft	08/08/2017	Also a Graham

Name	Height	Date	Notes
Beinn nan Eun	2070ft	19/05/2019	Also a Graham Top
Bell Craig	2044ft	21/07/2020	Also a Graham Top
Ben Cleuch	2365ft	24/05/2019	Also a Graham
Birkscairn Hill	2169ft	29/05/2019	Also a Graham Top
Black Law	2290ft	20/07/2020	Also a Graham Top
Blackcraig Hill	2300ft	05/08/2017	Also a Graham
Blackhope Scar	2136ft	28/05/2019	Also a Graham
Blacklorg Hill	2234ft	05/08/2017	Also a Graham Top
Blairdenon Hill	2073ft	24/05/2019	Also a Graham Top
Bodesbeck Law	2179ft	17/07/2020	Also a Graham Top
Bowbeat Hill	2054ft	28/05/2019	Also a Graham Top
Broad Law	2756ft	10/04/2017	Also a Corbett
Cairnsgarroch	2162ft	04/08/2017	Also a Graham Top
Cairnsmore of Carsphairn	2615ft	11/04/2017	Also a Corbett
Cairnsmore of Fleet	2333ft	25/07/2017	Also a Graham
Cape Law	2369ft	10/09/2018	Also a Graham Top
Capel Fell	2224ft	17/07/2020	Also a Graham
Carlin's Cairn	2648ft	12/04/2017	Also a Corbett Top
Cauldcleuch Head	2030ft	25/05/2018	Also a Graham
Chapelgill Hill	2283ft	26/05/2019	Also a Graham Top
Comb Law	2116ft	08/08/2017	Also a Graham Top
Coran of Portmark	2044ft	04/08/2017	Also a Graham Top
Corserine	2671ft	12/04/2017	Also a Corbett
Craignaw	2116ft	27/07/2017	Also a Graham
Cramalt Craig	2724ft	10/04/2017	Also a Corbett Top
Croft Head	2090ft	16/07/2020	Also a Graham
Culter Fell	2454ft	26/05/2019	Also a Graham
Curleywee	2211ft	26/07/2017	Also a Graham Top
Dollar Law	2680ft	19/07/2020	Also a Corbett Top
Drumelzier Law	2192ft	19/07/2020	Also a Graham Top

Name	Height	Date	Notes
Dun Law	2221ft	07/08/2017	Also a Graham Top
Dun Rig	2441ft	29/05/2019	Also a Graham
Dundreich	2044ft	28/05/2019	Also a Graham Top
Dungeon Hill	2034ft	27/07/2017	Also a Graham Top
Earncraig Hill	2005ft	08/08/2017	Also a Graham Top
East Mount Lowther	2070ft	06/08/2017	Also a Graham Top
Erie Hill	2264ft	11/09/2018	Also a Graham Top
Ettrick Pen	2270ft	16/07/2020	Also a Graham
Gana Hill	2192ft	08/08/2017	Also a Graham Top
Garelet Dod	2290ft	11/09/2018	Also a Graham Top
Gathersnow Hill	2257ft	12/09/2018	Also a Graham
Glenrath Heights	2402ft	29/05/2019	Also a Graham Top
Green Lowther	2402ft	06/08/2017	Also a Graham
Greenside Law	2110ft	20/07/2020	Also a Graham Top
Hart Fell	2651ft	02/05/2015	Also a Corbett
Herman Law	2016ft	21/07/2020	Also a Graham Top
Hillshaw Head	2139ft	12/09/2018	Also a Graham Top
Hudderstone	2054ft	13/09/2018	Also a Graham Top
Innerdownie	2001ft	25/05/2019	Also a Graham Top
King's Seat Hill	2126ft	25/05/2019	Also a Graham Top
Kirriereoch Hill	2581ft	29/07/2017	Also a Corbett Top
Lamachan Hill	2352ft	26/07/2017	Also a Graham
Larg Hill	2218ft	26/07/2017	Also a Graham Top
Loch Fell	2257ft	16/07/2020	Also a Graham Top
Lochcraig Head	2627ft	09/04/2017	Also a Corbett Top
Lousie Wood Law	2031ft	07/08/2017	Also a Graham Top
Lowther Hill	2379ft	06/08/2017	Also a Graham Top
Meaul	2280ft	04/08/2017	Also a Graham Top
Meikle Millyea	2456ft	01/08/2017	Also a Graham Top
Merrick	2766ft	27/07/2017	Also a Corbett
Middle Hill	2353ft	19/07/2020	Also a Graham Top

Name	Height	Date	Notes
Milldown	2421ft	01/08/2017	Also a Graham Top
Millfore	2156ft	31/07/2017	Also a Graham
Molls Cleuch Dod	2575ft	09/04/2017	Also a Corbett Top
Moorbrock Hill	2137ft	02/08/2017	Also a Graham Top
Mullwharchar	2270ft	27/07/2017	Also a Graham
Pykestone Hill	2418ft	19/07/2020	Also a Graham Top
Queensberry	2287ft	09/08/2017	Also a Graham
Scaw'd Law	2175ft	08/08/2017	Also a Graham Top
Shalloch on Minnoch	2540ft	29/07/2017	Also a Corbett
Stob Law	2218ft	29/05/2019	Also a Graham Top
Swatte Fell	2395ft	02/05/2015	Also a Graham Top
Talla Cleuch Head	2267ft	10/04/2017	Also a Graham Top
Tarfessock	2285ft	29/07/2017	Also a Graham Top
Tarmangie Hill	2116ft	25/05/2019	Also a Graham Top
Tinto	2333ft	10/08/2017	Also a Graham
Uamh Bheag	2184ft	19/05/2019	Also a Graham
Under Saddle Yoke	2444ft	10/09/2018	Also a Graham Top
Wedder Law	2205ft	08/08/2017	Also a Graham Top
White Coomb	2694ft	09/04/2017	Also a Corbett
Whitehope Heights	2090ft	02/05/2015	Also a Graham Top
Whitehope Law	2044ft	27/05/2019	Also a Graham Top
Wind Fell	2182ft	16/07/2020	Also a Graham Top
Windlestraw Law	2163ft	27/05/2019	Also a Graham
Windy Gyle	2031ft	02/06/2013	Also a Nuttall and a Graham Top
Windy Standard	2290ft	02/08/2017	Also a Graham

Corbett Tops Bagged (Partially Completed)

Name	Height	Date	Notes
An Eag	2859ft	10/06/1997	
Aonach Dubh a'	2772ft	06/06/1997	

Name	Height	Date	Notes
Ghlinne			
Aonach Eagach East Peak	2973ft	31/05/1997	
Aonach Eagach West Peak	2968ft	31/05/1997	
Aonach Sgoilte	2785ft	27/06/2001	
Beinn Bhreac	2766ft	13/05/2009	
Beinn Bhreac NW Top	2747ft	22/05/2010	
Beinn Gharbh	2707ft	12/06/1997	
Beinn Liath Mhor East Top	2910ft	09/06/2001	
Beinn Liath Mhor South Top	2523ft	09/06/2001	
Beinn Loinne	2543ft	11/05/2017	
Beinn Tharsuinn North Top	2680ft	12/06/2001	
Beinn Toaig	2736ft	03/06/1997	
Caisteal a' Garbh-Choire	2722ft	23/05/2001	
Carlin's Cairn	2648ft	12/04/2017	Also a Donald
Carn Bhac South Top	2682ft	21/05/1998	
Carn Dearg North Top	2503ft	17/05/2018	
Carn Liath	2598ft	20/05/2015	
Carn Liath	2826ft	21/05/2017	
Cramalt Craig	2724ft	10/04/2017	Also a Donald
Creag an Fheadain	2913ft	14/05/1997	
Creag Feusag	2831ft	14/05/1989	
Doire Tana	2927ft	18/05/1989	
Dollar Law	2680ft	19/07/2020	Also a Donald
Glas Charn	2595ft	19/05/2010	
Glas-leathad Feshie	2818ft	22/05/2010	
Green Hill	2854ft	17/05/2005	
Kirriereoch Hill	2581ft	29/07/2017	Also a Donald
Ladhar Bheinn Far	2815ft	27/06/2001	

Name	Height	Date	Notes
South Top			
Leac an Taobhain	2726ft	22/05/2010	
Lochcraig Head	2627ft	09/04/2017	Also a Donald
Meall a' Bhealaich	2563ft	17/06/2001	
Meall an Tarmachain	2710ft	12/06/1997	
Meall an Uillt Chreagaich	2779ft	22/05/2010	
Meall Garbh	2786ft	24/06/2001	
Meall nan Tri Tighearnan	2926ft	19/05/1997	
Meall Tarsuinn	2877ft	02/06/1997	
Molls Cleuch Dod	2575ft	09/04/2017	Also a Donald
Monadh an t-Sluichd Leith	2625ft	20/05/2015	
Ptarmigan	2552ft	06/05/1991	
Sgurr Beag	2920ft	10/06/1997	
Sgurr Coire na Feinne	2958ft	28/05/1992	
Sgurr Coire nan Eiricheallach	2923ft	16/06/1997	
Sgurr na h-Aide	2821ft	15/05/2010	
Stob Coire a' Chairn South Top	2981ft	03/07/1999	
Stob Coire na Cloiche	2994ft	15/06/2001	
Streap Comhlaidh	2946ft	05/06/2017	
The Cobbler North Peak	2854ft	19/05/2002	

Graham Tops Bagged (Partially Completed)

Name	Height	Date	Notes
A' Ghlas-bheinn South Top	2487ft	17/06/2001	
Alhang	2106ft	02/08/2017	Also a Donald
Beinn Chlianaig	2369ft	10/05/2015	

Name	Height	Date	Notes
Beinn nan Eun	2070ft	19/05/2019	Also a Donald
Beinn Odhar	2054ft	19/05/2019	Also a Donald Top
Bell Craig	2044ft	21/07/2020	Also a Donald
Benyellary	2359ft	27/07/2017	Also a Donald Top
Bioran na Circe	2369ft	27/05/2016	
Birkscairn Hill	2169ft	29/05/2019	Also a Donald
Black Law	2290ft	20/07/2020	Also a Donald
Blacklorg Hill	2234ft	05/08/2017	Also a Donald
Blairdenon Hill	2073ft	24/05/2019	Also a Donald
Bodesbeck Law	2179ft	17/07/2020	Also a Donald
Bow	2011ft	04/08/2017	Also a Donald Top
Bowbeat Hill	2054ft	28/05/2019	Also a Donald
Burnt Hill	2175ft	17/05/2005	
Cairn Caidloch	2126ft	17/05/2005	
Cairnagour Hill	2438ft	23/05/2017	
Cairnsgarroch	2162ft	04/08/2017	Also a Donald
Cape Law	2369ft	10/09/2018	Also a Donald
Carn Mor East Top	2021ft	02/06/2022	
Chapelgill Hill	2283ft	26/05/2019	Also a Donald
Comb Law	2116ft	08/08/2017	Also a Donald
Coran of Portmark	2044ft	04/08/2017	Also a Donald
Curleywee	2211ft	26/07/2017	Also a Donald
Deer Law	2064ft	20/07/2020	Also a Donald Top
Druim a' Ghoirtein	2496ft	09/09/1996	
Druim a' Ghoirtein Far West Top	2031ft	09/09/1996	
Drumelzier Law	2192ft	19/07/2020	Also a Donald
Dun Law	2221ft	07/08/2017	Also a Donald
Dundreich	2044ft	28/05/2019	Also a Donald
Dungeon Hill	2034ft	27/07/2017	Also a Donald
Earncraig Hill	2005ft	08/08/2017	Also a Donald
East Mount Lowther	2070ft	06/08/2017	Also a Donald

Name	Height	Date	Notes
Erie Hill	2264ft	11/09/2018	Also a Donald
Gana Hill	2192ft	08/08/2017	Also a Donald
Garelet Dod	2290ft	11/09/2018	Also a Donald
Glenrath Heights	2402ft	29/05/2019	Also a Donald
Greenside Law	2110ft	20/07/2020	Also a Donald
Herman Law	2016ft	21/07/2020	Also a Donald
Hillshaw Head	2139ft	12/09/2018	Also a Donald
Hopetoun Craig	2077ft	16/07/2020	Also a Donald Top
Hudderstone	2054ft	13/09/2018	Also a Donald
Innerdownie	2001ft	25/05/2019	Also a Donald
King's Seat Hill	2126ft	25/05/2019	Also a Donald
Laird's Cleuch Rig	2244ft	11/09/2018	Also a Donald Top
Larg Hill	2218ft	26/07/2017	Also a Donald
Loch Fell	2257ft	16/07/2020	Also a Donald
Lousie Wood Law	2031ft	07/08/2017	Also a Donald
Lowther Hill	2379ft	06/08/2017	Also a Donald
Meaul	2280ft	04/08/2017	Also a Donald
Meikle Millyea	2456ft	01/08/2017	Also a Donald
Middle Hill	2353ft	19/07/2020	Also a Donald
Milldown	2421ft	01/08/2017	Also a Donald
Moorbrock Hill	2137ft	02/08/2017	Also a Donald
Na h-Uamhachan	2267ft	07/06/2017	
Pykestone Hill	2418ft	19/07/2020	Also a Donald
Rodger Law	2257ft	08/08/2017	Also a Donald Top
Saddle Yoke	2413ft	10/09/2018	Also a Donald Top
Scaw'd Law	2175ft	08/08/2017	Also a Donald
Sgurr Breac	2391ft	15/05/2010	
Sgurr Mor	2010ft	15/05/2010	
Smidhope Hill	2113ft	17/07/2020	Also a Donald Top
Sron Liath	2362ft	07/06/2017	
Stob Law	2218ft	29/05/2019	Also a Donald
Swatte Fell	2395ft	02/05/2015	Also a Donald

Name	Height	Date	Notes
Talla Cleuch Head	2267ft	10/04/2017	Also a Donald
Tarfessock	2285ft	29/07/2017	Also a Donald
Tarmangie Hill	2116ft	25/05/2019	Also a Donald
Under Saddle Yoke	2444ft	10/09/2018	Also a Donald
Wedder Law	2205ft	08/08/2017	Also a Donald
West Knowe	2205ft	16/07/2020	Also a Donald Top
Whitehope Heights	2090ft	02/05/2015	Also a Donald
Whitehope Law	2044ft	27/05/2019	Also a Donald
Wind Fell	2182ft	16/07/2020	Also a Donald
Windy Gyle	2031ft	02/06/2013	Also a Donald and a Nuttall

Donald Tops Bagged (Partially Completed)

Name	Height	Date	Notes
Beinn Odhar	2054ft	19/05/2019	Also a Graham Top
Benyellary	2359ft	27/07/2017	Also a Graham Top
Bow	2011ft	04/08/2017	Also a Graham Top
Conscleuch Head	2047ft	20/07/2020	
Deer Law	2064ft	20/07/2020	Also a Graham Top
Falcon Craig	2374ft	02/05/2015	
Firthhope Rig	2625ft	09/04/2017	
Garelet Hill	2234ft	11/09/2018	
Hopetoun Craig	2077ft	16/07/2020	Also a Graham Top
Laird's Cleuch Rig	2244ft	11/09/2018	Also a Graham Top
Meall Clachach	2031ft	19/05/2019	
Nether Coomb Craig	2376ft	02/05/2015	
Rodger Law	2257ft	08/08/2017	Also a Graham Top
Saddle Yoke	2413ft	10/09/2018	Also a Graham Top
Smidhope Hill	2113ft	17/07/2020	Also a Graham Top
Tarfessock South Top	2034ft	29/07/2017	
Trowgrain Middle	2060ft	21/07/2020	
West Knowe	2205ft	16/07/2020	Also a Graham Top

Name	Height	Date	Notes
White Shank	2039ft	17/07/2020	

Munros Bagged (All Completed)

Name	Height	Date
A' Bhuidheanach Bheag	3071ft	12/09/1996
A' Chailleach	3049ft	13/04/1998
A' Chailleach	3276ft	18/06/2001
A' Chraileag	3675ft	28/05/2001
A' Ghlas-bheinn	3012ft	17/06/2001
A' Mhaighdean	3173ft	24/06/2001
A' Mharconaich	3193ft	18/06/1997
Am Basteir	3064ft	20/05/2001
Am Bodach	3385ft	03/07/1999
Am Faochagach	3127ft	04/06/2001
An Caisteal	3267ft	22/09/1991
An Coileachan	3031ft	04/07/2001
An Gearanach	3220ft	03/07/1999
An Riabhachan	3704ft	10/07/1991
An Sgarsoch	3302ft	20/05/1998
An Socach	3017ft	15/06/2001
An Socach	3097ft	22/05/1998
An Socach	3507ft	10/07/1991
An Stuc	3665ft	30/05/2001
An Teallach - Bidein a' Ghlas Thuill	3486ft	25/06/2001
An Teallach - Sgurr Fiona	3473ft	25/06/2001
Aonach air Chrith	3345ft	28/05/1992
Aonach Beag	3661ft	11/05/2001
Aonach Beag	4049ft	01/07/2001
Aonach Eagach – Meall Dearg	3124ft	31/05/1997
Aonach Eagach – Sgorr nam Fiannaidh	3175ft	31/05/1997

Name	Height	Date
Aonach Meadhoin	3284ft	17/05/2001
Aonach Mor	4004ft	21/07/2001
Beinn a' Bheithir – Sgorr Dhearg	3360ft	25/05/1992
Beinn a' Bheithir – Sgorr Dhonuill	3284ft	25/05/1992
Beinn a' Bhuird	3927ft	28/05/1998
Beinn a' Chaorainn	3442ft	05/07/1999
Beinn a' Chaorainn	3553ft	28/08/1995
Beinn a' Chlachair	3566ft	10/05/2001
Beinn a' Chleibh	3006ft	19/05/1996
Beinn a' Chochuill	3215ft	17/05/1997
Beinn a' Chreachain	3545ft	10/05/1996
Beinn a' Chroin	3089ft	22/09/1991
Beinn a' Ghlo – Braigh Coire Chruinn-bhalgain	3510ft	17/05/1998
Beinn a' Ghlo – Carn Liath	3202ft	17/05/1998
Beinn a' Ghlo – Carn nan Gabhar	3681ft	17/05/1998
Beinn Achaladair	3407ft	10/05/1996
Beinn Alligin – Sgurr Mor	3235ft	05/06/2001
Beinn Alligin – Tom na Gruagaich	3025ft	05/06/2001
Beinn an Dothaidh	3294ft	04/06/1993
Beinn Bheoil	3343ft	07/05/2001
Beinn Bhreac	3054ft	26/05/1998
Beinn Bhrotain	3796ft	01/05/1994
Beinn Bhuidhe	3112ft	09/05/1996
Beinn Chabhair	3058ft	03/05/1996
Beinn Challum	3363ft	04/05/1997
Beinn Dearg	3309ft	14/05/1998
Beinn Dearg	3556ft	25/05/1997
Beinn Dorain	3530ft	04/06/1993
Beinn Dubhchraig	3209ft	10/08/1991
Beinn Eibhinn	3620ft	08/05/2001

Name	Height	Date
Beinn Eighe – Ruadh-stac Mor	3314ft	07/06/2001
Beinn Eighe – Spidean Coire nan Clach	3258ft	07/06/2001
Beinn Eunaich	3245ft	17/05/1997
Beinn Fhada	3385ft	17/06/2001
Beinn Fhionnlaidh	3146ft	07/06/1997
Beinn Fhionnlaidh	3297ft	14/05/1996
Beinn Ghlas	3619ft	09/05/1997
Beinn Ime	3321ft	29/08/1992
Beinn Iutharn Mhor	3428ft	21/05/1998
Beinn Liath Mhor	3038ft	09/06/2001
Beinn Liath Mhor Fannaich	3130ft	19/06/2001
Beinn Mhanach	3127ft	07/05/1996
Beinn Mheadhoin	3881ft	27/08/1995
Beinn na Lap	3068ft	07/07/2000
Beinn nan Aighenan	3150ft	19/05/1997
Beinn Narnain	3041ft	29/08/1992
Beinn Sgritheall	3196ft	29/05/1997
Beinn Sgulaird	3074ft	20/05/1997
Beinn Heasgarnich	3535ft	05/06/1998
Beinn Tarsuinn	3064ft	24/06/2001
Beinn Teallach	3001ft	05/07/1999
Beinn Tulaichean	3103ft	27/08/1994
Beinn Udlamain	3314ft	18/06/1997
Ben Alder	3766ft	07/05/2001
Ben Avon – Leabaidh an Daimh Bhuidhe	3845ft	27/05/1998
Ben Chonzie	3054ft	06/05/1996
Ben Cruachan	3698ft	16/05/1997
Ben Hope	3041ft	09/07/2001
Ben Klibreck – Meall nan Con	3156ft	08/07/2001
Ben Lawers	3983ft	09/05/1997
Ben Lomond	3195ft	06/05/1991

Name	Height	Date
Ben Lui	3712ft	19/05/1996
Ben Macdui	4295ft	26/08/1995
Ben More	3169ft	02/04/1999
Ben More	3852ft	25/08/1991
Ben More Assynt	3274ft	07/07/2001
Ben Nevis	4411ft	30/06/1995
Ben Oss	3376ft	10/08/1991
Ben Starav	3542ft	19/05/1997
Ben Vane	3004ft	29/08/1992
Ben Vorlich	3094ft	28/08/1994
Ben Vorlich	3233ft	04/05/1996
Ben Wyvis – Glas Leathad Mor	3432ft	01/02/1992
Bidean nam Bian	3771ft	22/05/1997
Bidein a' Choire Sheasgaich	3100ft	12/06/2001
Binnein Beag	3094ft	04/05/2001
Binnein Mor	3707ft	29/05/2001
Blabheinn	3048ft	25/05/2001
Braeriach	4252ft	30/05/1998
Broad Cairn	3274ft	25/05/1998
Bruach na Frithe	3146ft	20/05/2001
Buachaille Etive Beag – Stob Coire Raineach	3033ft	03/05/2001
Buachaille Etive Beag – Stob Dubh	3143ft	04/06/1997
Buachaille Etive Mor – Stob Dearg	3351ft	30/05/1997
Buachaille Etive Mor – Stob na Broige	3128ft	06/06/1998
Bynack More	3576ft	28/08/1995
Cairn Bannoch	3320ft	25/05/1998
Cairn Gorm	4084ft	26/08/1995
Cairn of Claise	3491ft	18/05/1998
Cairn Toul	4236ft	30/05/1998

Name	Height	Date
Carn a' Chlamain	3161ft	16/05/1998
Carn a' Choire Bhoidheach	3641ft	25/05/1998
Carn a' Gheoidh	3199ft	03/05/1994
Carn a' Mhaim	3402ft	01/06/1998
Carn an Fhidhleir	3261ft	20/05/1998
Carn an Righ	3376ft	23/05/1998
Carn an t-Sagairt Mor	3435ft	25/05/1998
Carn an Tuirc	3343ft	18/05/1998
Carn Aosda	3003ft	03/05/1994
Carn Bhac	3101ft	21/05/1998
Carn Dearg	3087ft	06/07/2000
Carn Dearg	3103ft	04/06/1998
Carn Dearg	3392ft	08/05/2001
Carn Eighe	3881ft	14/05/1996
Carn Ghluasaid	3140ft	14/05/2001
Carn Gorm	3376ft	13/05/1997
Carn Liath	3301ft	20/06/1997
Carn Mairg	3419ft	13/05/1997
Carn Mor Dearg	4003ft	07/05/1990
Carn na Caim	3087ft	12/09/1996
Carn nan Gobhar	3255ft	12/05/1996
Carn nan Gobhar	3258ft	20/06/2001
Carn Sgulain	3019ft	04/06/1998
Chno Dearg	3432ft	08/06/1997
Ciste Dhubh	3219ft	17/05/2001
Cona' Mheall	3209ft	25/05/1997
Conival	3238ft	07/07/2001
Creag a' Mhaim	3104ft	28/05/1992
Creag Leacach	3242ft	23/04/1998
Creag Meagaidh	3701ft	20/06/1997
Creag Mhor	3434ft	07/05/1997
Creag nan Damh	3009ft	28/05/1992

Name	Height	Date
Creag Pitridh	3031ft	10/05/2001
Creise	3608ft	23/05/1997
Cruach Ardrain	3431ft	27/08/1994
Derry Cairngorm	3789ft	05/05/1994
Driesh	3109ft	09/04/1998
Druim Shionnach	3232ft	28/05/1992
Eididh nan Clach Geala	3041ft	25/05/1997
Fionn Bheinn	3061ft	16/05/1996
Gairich	3015ft	15/06/1997
Garbh Chioch Mhor	3323ft	09/09/1996
Geal Charn	3038ft	19/06/1997
Geal Charn	3442ft	10/05/2001
Geal-charn	3009ft	18/06/1997
Geal-charn	3714ft	11/05/2001
Glas Bheinn Mhor	3273ft	19/05/1997
Glas Maol	3504ft	23/04/1998
Glas Tulaichean	3448ft	23/05/1998
Gleouraich	3396ft	14/06/1997
Gulvain	3238ft	02/07/2000
Ladhar Bheinn	3346ft	27/06/2001
Liathach – Mullach an Rathain	3359ft	06/06/2001
Liathach – Spidean a' Choire Leith	3461ft	06/06/2001
Lochnagar – Cac Carn Beag	3792ft	25/05/1998
Luinne Bheinn	3081ft	28/06/2001
Lurg Mhor	3238ft	12/06/2001
Mam Sodhail	3869ft	14/05/1996
Maoile Lunndaidh	3297ft	11/06/2001
Maol Chean-dearg	3061ft	14/06/2001
Maol Chinn-dearg	3216ft	28/05/1992
Mayar	3047ft	09/04/1998
Meall a' Bhuiridh	3635ft	23/05/1997

Name	Height	Date
Meall a' Choire Leith	3037ft	09/05/1997
Meall a' Chrasgaidh	3064ft	18/06/2001
Meall Buidhe	3058ft	14/05/1997
Meall Buidhe	3104ft	28/06/2001
Meall Chuaich	3120ft	11/09/1996
Meall Corranaich	3507ft	09/05/1997
Meall Garbh	3176ft	13/05/1997
Meall Garbh	3685ft	10/05/1997
Meall Ghaordaidh	3411ft	20/05/1996
Meall Glas	3147ft	05/05/1997
Meall Gorm	3116ft	04/07/2001
Meall Greigh	3284ft	10/05/1997
Meall na Aighean	3219ft	13/05/1997
Meall na Teanga	3008ft	03/07/2000
Meall nan Ceapraichean	3205ft	25/05/1997
Meall nan Eun	3045ft	02/06/1997
Meall nan Tarmachan	3424ft	01/06/1993
Monadh Mor	3652ft	01/05/1994
Moruisg	3045ft	08/06/2001
Mount Keen	3081ft	31/05/1998
Mullach Clach a' Bhlair	3343ft	02/06/1998
Mullach Coire Mhic Fhearchair	3331ft	24/06/2001
Mullach Fraoch-choire	3615ft	28/05/2001
Mullach na Dheiragain	3222ft	15/06/2001
Mullach nan Coirean	3082ft	04/07/1999
Na Gruagaichean	3459ft	29/05/2001
Ruadh Stac Mor	3014ft	24/06/2001
Sail Chaorainn	3278ft	14/05/2001
Saileag	3136ft	13/05/2001
Schiehallion	3553ft	12/05/1997
Seana Bhraigh	3038ft	03/07/2001
Sgairneach Mhor	3251ft	18/06/1997

Name	Height	Date
Sgiath Chuil	3019ft	05/05/1997
Sgor an Lochain Uaine	4127ft	30/05/1998
Sgor Gaibhre	3133ft	06/07/2000
Sgor Gaoith	3668ft	02/06/1998
Sgorr Ruadh	3152ft	09/06/2001
Sgurr a' Bhealaich Dheirg	3399ft	17/05/2001
Sgurr a' Chaorachain	3455ft	11/06/2001
Sgurr a' Choire Ghlais	3553ft	21/06/2001
Sgurr a' Ghreadaidh	3189ft	22/05/2001
Sgurr a' Mhadaidh	3012ft	22/05/2001
Sgurr a' Mhaim	3606ft	03/07/1999
Sgurr a' Mhaoraich	3369ft	16/06/1997
Sgurr Alasdair	3255ft	24/05/2001
Sgurr an Doire Leathain	3314ft	28/05/1992
Sgurr an Lochain	3294ft	28/05/1992
Sgurr Ban	3245ft	24/06/2001
Sgurr Breac	3280ft	18/06/2001
Sgurr Choinnich	3279ft	11/06/2001
Sgurr Choinnich Mor	3589ft	30/06/2001
Sgurr Dearg – Inaccessible Pinnacle	3234ft	21/05/2001
Sgurr Dubh Mor	3097ft	23/05/2001
Sgurr Eilde Mor	3314ft	04/05/2001
Sgurr Fhuaran	3507ft	13/05/2001
Sgurr Fhuar-thuill	3442ft	21/06/2001
Sgurr Mhic Choinnich	3111ft	26/05/2001
Sgurr Mor	3291ft	10/06/1997
Sgurr Mor	3638ft	04/07/2001
Sgurr na Banachdaich	3166ft	22/05/2001
Sgurr na Carnach	3287ft	13/05/2001
Sgurr na Ciche	3413ft	09/09/1996
Sgurr na Ciste Duibhe	3369ft	13/05/2001

Name	Height	Date
Sgurr na h-Ulaidh	3261ft	06/06/1997
Sgurr na Lapaich	3776ft	12/05/1996
Sgurr na Ruaidhe	3258ft	20/06/2001
Sgurr na Sgine	3104ft	27/05/2001
Sgurr nan Ceathramhnan	3776ft	15/06/2001
Sgurr nan Clach Geala	3586ft	18/06/2001
Sgurr nan Coireachan	3129ft	10/06/1997
Sgurr nan Coireachan	3136ft	12/06/1997
Sgurr nan Conbhairean	3638ft	14/05/2001
Sgurr nan Each	3028ft	18/06/2001
Sgurr nan Eag	3039ft	23/05/2001
Sgurr nan Gillean	3170ft	20/05/2001
Sgurr Thuilm	3159ft	12/06/1997
Slioch	3219ft	05/07/2001
Spidean Mialach	3268ft	14/06/1997
Sron a' Choire Ghairbh	3074ft	03/07/2000
Stob a' Choire Mheadhoin	3625ft	04/07/2000
Stob a' Choire Odhair	3100ft	03/06/1997
Stob Ban	3205ft	30/06/2001
Stob Ban	3280ft	04/07/1999
Stob Binnein	3822ft	25/08/1991
Stob Choire Claurigh	3862ft	30/06/2001
Stob Coir' an Albannaich	3425ft	02/06/1997
Stob Coire a' Chairn	3219ft	03/07/1999
Stob Coire an Laoigh	3661ft	30/06/2001
Stob Coire Easain	3658ft	04/07/2000
Stob Coire Sgreamhach	3517ft	02/05/2001
Stob Coire Sgriodain	3212ft	08/06/1997
Stob Daimh	3278ft	16/05/1997
Stob Ghabhar	3576ft	03/06/1997
Stob Poite Coire Ardair	3458ft	20/06/1997
Stuc a' Chroin	3192ft	04/05/1996

Name	Height	Date
Stuc an Lochain	3150ft	14/05/1997
The Cairnwell	3061ft	03/05/1994
The Devil's Point	3303ft	30/05/1998
The Saddle	3319ft	27/05/2001
Toll Creagach	3458ft	24/05/1992
Tolmount	3143ft	18/05/1998
Tom a' Choinich	3648ft	24/05/1992
Tom Buidhe	3140ft	18/05/1998

Munro Tops Bagged (Partially Completed)

Name	Height	Date
An Cabar	3104ft	01/02/1992
An Garbhanach	3198ft	03/07/1999
An Riabhachan SW Top	3563ft	10/07/1991
An Riabhachan West Top	3406ft	10/07/1991
An Sgorr	3031ft	13/05/1997
Beinn a' Chaorainn North Top	3422ft	05/07/1999
Beinn a' Chaorainn South Top	3440ft	05/07/1999
Beinn a' Chuirn	3028ft	07/05/1996
Beinn Achaladair South Top	3293ft	10/05/1996
Beinn Cheathaich	3076ft	05/05/1997
Beinn nan Eachan	3281ft	01/06/1993
Ben Vorlich North Top	3054ft	28/08/1994
Bhasteir Tooth	3009ft	20/05/2001
Binnein Mor South Top	3484ft	29/05/2001
Cairn of Gowal	3251ft	25/05/1998
Caisteal	3629ft	30/06/2001
Carn Ballach	3018ft	04/06/1998
Carn Ban	3092ft	04/06/1998
Carn Ban Mor	3451ft	02/06/1998
Carn Bhac SW Top	3012ft	21/05/1998
Carn Dearg Meadhonach	3868ft	07/05/1990

Name	Height	Date
Carn na Caim South Top	3001ft	12/09/1996
Carn na Con Dhu	3173ft	15/06/2001
Carn na Criche	3155ft	04/07/2001
Carn na Criche	4150ft	30/05/1998
Carn nam Fiaclan	3258ft	11/06/2001
Ceann Garbh	3176ft	25/05/1997
Creag a' Chaorainn	3274ft	14/05/2001
Creag an Fhithich	3435ft	30/05/2001
Creag Coire na Fiar Bhealaich	3301ft	14/06/1997
Creag Ghorm a' Bhealaich	3379ft	21/06/2001
Creag Leacach SW Top	3096ft	23/04/1998
Crow Craigies	3018ft	23/05/2006
Drochaid Ghlas	3361ft	16/05/1997
Druim Shionnach West Top	3069ft	28/05/1992
Gulvain South Top	3153ft	02/07/2000
Luinne Bheinn East Top	3071ft	28/06/2001
Meall a' Bharr	3294ft	13/05/1997
Meall a' Churain	3010ft	05/05/1997
Meall an t-Snaim	3182ft	20/06/1997
Meall Buidhe	3206ft	10/05/1996
Meall Buidhe SE Top	3091ft	28/06/2001
Meall Garbh	3368ft	01/06/1993
Meall Gorm SE Top	3026ft	04/07/2001
Meall nam Peithirean	3197ft	04/07/2001
Meall nan Tarmachan South Top	3024ft	01/06/1993
Meall Odhar	3025ft	23/04/1998
Mullach nan Coirean East Top	3007ft	04/07/1999
Mullach nan Coirean SE Top	3010ft	04/07/1999
Sail Liath	3125ft	25/06/2001
Sgor Choinnich	3048ft	06/07/2000
Sgurr a' Bhuic	3159ft	01/07/2001
Sgurr an Fhuarail	3238ft	17/05/2001

Name	Height	Date
Sgurr an Iubhair	3280ft	03/07/1999
Sgurr an Tuill Bhain	3064ft	05/07/2001
Sgurr Choinnich Beag	3159ft	30/06/2001
Sgurr Dubh an Da Bheinn	3077ft	23/05/2001
Sgurr na Banachdich Central Top	3091ft	22/05/2001
Sgurr na Fearstaig	3330ft	21/06/2001
Sgurr na Sgine NW Top	3091ft	27/05/2001
Sgurr nan Spainteach	3248ft	13/05/2001
Sgurr Thearlaich	3206ft	24/05/2001
Sron Chona Choirein	3041ft	14/05/1997
Sron Coire a' Chriochairein	3258ft	20/06/1997
Sron Coire na h-Iolaire	3136ft	07/05/2001
Stob a' Choire Leith	3625ft	30/06/2001
Stob a' Choire Liath Mhor	3227ft	06/06/2001
Stob a' Choire Odhair	3150ft	27/06/2001
Stob an Fhuarain	3176ft	06/06/1997
Stob Choire a' Mhail	3248ft	03/07/1999
Stob Coire Altruim	3080ft	06/06/1998
Stob Coire an t-Saighdeir	3980ft	30/05/1998
Stob Coire an t-Sneachda	3858ft	26/08/1995
Stob Coire Bhealaich	3612ft	01/07/2001
Stob Coire Cath na Sine	3551ft	30/06/2001
Stob Coire Dheirg	3372ft	19/05/1997
Stob Coire Easain	3543ft	30/06/2001
Stob Coire Leith	3082ft	31/05/1997
Stob Coire Lochan	3008ft	14/05/1996
Stob Coire na Craileig	3307ft	28/05/2001
Stob Coire nam Beith	3632ft	22/05/1997
Stob Coire Sgriodain South Top	3143ft	08/06/1997
Stob Garbh	3221ft	16/05/1997
Toll Creagach West Top	3120ft	24/05/1992
Toman Coinnich	3073ft	18/06/2001

Other Hills & Mountains Bagged

These are hills and mountains outside the above categories.

United Kingdom

Name	Height	Date
A' Bhuidheanach	2891ft	12/09/1996
Am Bathach South Top	2407ft	10/05/2017
Am Beannan	1883ft	19/05/2019
An Cnapach	2889ft	17/05/2001
An Elric	2828ft	14/06/2017
An Socach East Top	3468ft	10/07/1991
An Socach West Top	2761ft	15/06/2001
Aonach Eagach	3281ft	03/06/1997
Barker Bank	1398ft	25/04/1989
Beacon Hill	981ft	05/11/2022
Beinn a' Chlachair East Top	3205ft	10/05/2001
Beinn a' Chlaidheimh South Top	2674ft	24/06/2001
Beinn an Dothaidh West Top	3280ft	04/06/1993
Beinn Bhreac NE Top	2771ft	22/05/2010
Beinn Bhrotain East Top	3635ft	01/05/1994
Beinn Chlianaig East Top	2348ft	10/05/2015
Beinn Dearg North Top	2900ft	25/05/1997
Beinn Gharbh East Top	2575ft	12/06/1997
Beinn Mheadhoin SW Top	3816ft	27/08/1995
Beinn nan Eachan East Top	3121ft	01/06/1993
Beinn Stacach East Top	2253ft	01/06/2017
Beinn Tharsuinn Far North Top	2654ft	12/06/2001
Ben Avon West Top	3732ft	27/05/1998
Ben Lui NW Top	3698ft	19/05/1996
Ben More Assynt West Top	3196ft	07/07/2001
Ben Oss North Top	3088ft	10/08/1991
Bidean nam Bian West Top	3744ft	22/05/1997

Name	Height	Date
Birkett Fell	2379ft	25/04/2011
Black Crag	2628ft	04/07/2014
Black Law SW Top	2283ft	20/07/2020
Black Mountain South Top	2091ft	13/01/2002
Blath Bhalg West Top	2086ft	09/07/2009
Bow Middle Top	2001ft	04/08/2017
Bow SW Top	2008ft	04/08/2017
Bowbeat Rig Head	1919ft	28/05/2019
Bram Rigg Top	2205ft	11/07/2014
Broad End	2730ft	17/11/2007
Brown Cow Hill East Top	2457ft	19/05/2015
Brown Pike	2238ft	24/04/2011
Brown Willy	1378ft	26/09/2018
Bruach nan Iomairean	3182ft	18/06/1997
Buck Pike – Seathwaite Fell	2441ft	24/04/2011
Bullman Hills South Top	2014ft	11/06/2013
Burnhope Seat – Trig Point	2449ft	08/06/2013
Bushie Law	1719ft	17/07/2020
Cac Carn Mor	3777ft	25/05/1998
Cadair Bronwen NE Top	2297ft	27/08/2005
Cairn Hill	2549ft	01/06/2013
Cairn of Gowal South Top	3225ft	25/05/1998
Caisteal na Caillich South Top	2789ft	25/05/2010
Calfhow Pike	2165ft	25/04/2011
Cam Long Down	722ft	15/11/1989
Carn an Fhidhleir South Top	2971ft	20/05/1998
Carn Ballach	3016ft	04/06/1998
Carn Beag Dearg	3314ft	07/05/1990
Carn Dubh	2848ft	14/07/2009
Carn nan Sac	3017ft	03/05/1994
Carn Sasunnaich	3497ft	04/06/1993
Carn Sgulain West Top	2976ft	04/06/1998

Name	Height	Date
Carnedd y Ddelw	2251ft	21/09/2004
Catbells	1480ft	20/11/2004
Cefn Gwyntog Far North Top	2026ft	11/08/2007
Cefn Gwyntog North Top	1970ft	11/08/2007
Cefn Perfedd	1971ft	28/08/2005
Cerrig Coediog	1942ft	28/08/2005
Chalk Rig Edge	1640ft	02/05/2015
Ciste Dhubh South Top	3061ft	17/05/2001
Cleeve Hill	1083ft	12/11/1989
Cnoc a' Bhac Fhalaichte	1273ft	15/05/2010
Coldbarrow Fell – High Saddle	2215ft	16/04/2011
Colsnaur Hill	1814ft	24/05/2019
Cormaud	1663ft	10/07/2009
Corwharn	1998ft	10/07/2009
Cottington's Hill	751ft	14/05/2022
Craig Berwyn	2592ft	27/08/2005
Craig Ffynnon	1931ft	21/05/2008
Craig Lwyd	2264ft	18/05/2008
Craig Portas	1982ft	19/05/2008
Craig Portas East Top	1926ft	19/05/2008
Creag a' Choire Dhirich	2874ft	03/05/1994
Creag Bheag	1598ft	03/11/2022
Creag Dhubh Fannaich	2480ft	19/06/2001
Creag nan Gabhar	2400ft	24/05/2017
Crickley Hill	896ft	13/11/1989
Crinkle Crags – Fourth Crinkle	2730ft	22/04/2011
Crinkle Crags – Gunson Knott	2697ft	22/04/2011
Crinkle Crags – Third Crinkle	2756ft	22/04/2011
Crow Craigies South Top	2860ft	23/05/2006
Cruach Ardrain SW Top	3428ft	27/08/1994
Cruach nam Miseag	2667ft	29/08/1992
Cruach Raineachan	1644ft	12/05/2006

Name	Height	Date
Cyrniau Nod	2186ft	11/08/2007
Ditchling Beacon	814ft	18/06/1989
Druim a' Ghoirtein West Top	2145ft	09/09/1996
Druim Seileach	2756ft	14/06/1997
Drygill Head	2041ft	12/04/2012
East Mealour	1648ft	06/04/1999
Eel Crag	2648ft	20/11/2010
Fan Brycheiniog – Trig Point	2630ft	28/06/2004
Fan Foel	2562ft	28/06/2004
Fiacaill a' Choire Chais	3743ft	06/02/2009
Foel Goch	1983ft	27/07/2005
Foel y Geifr	1690ft	14/05/2008
Foel y Groes	1909ft	25/08/2007
Gale Fell	1699ft	02/04/2012
Gasgale Crags	2307ft	09/04/2012
Glas-charn West Top	2014ft	12/05/2006
Golden Ball Hill	889ft	09/04/2021
Great Hill	1529ft	02/05/2015
Great How	2526ft	24/04/2011
Green Trough	2329ft	06/08/2017
Hackpen Hill	892ft	27/02/2022
Hanging Hill	778ft	18/11/1989
Hay Bluff	2221ft	13/01/2002
Haytor Rocks	1499ft	06/08/2016
High Crag	2899ft	02/05/2011
High Crags	1352ft	20/11/2004
High Pikehow	1883ft	30/09/2013
High Stile	2644ft	04/04/2012
Hobcarton End	2079ft	20/11/2010
Hundleshope Heights	2251ft	29/05/2019
Iwerddon	1913ft	12/09/2004
Jeffries Corse North Top	2011ft	28/05/2019

Name	Height	Date
Jenkin Hill	2411ft	16/11/2007
Kensgriff	1883ft	11/07/2014
Kirkhope Law	1762ft	29/05/2019
Kirriereoch Hill	2566ft	29/07/2017
Knoutberry Hill	2192ft	08/06/2013
Lad Hows	1398ft	07/04/2012
Lad Stones	2021ft	24/04/2011
Ladhar Bheinn South Top	2778ft	27/06/2001
Leckhampton Hill	961ft	13/11/1989
Little Cairngorm	3412ft	05/05/1994
Little Calva	2107ft	12/04/2012
Little Dodd	2575ft	25/04/2011
Little How Crags	2395ft	24/04/2011
Long Grain Knowe	2310ft	19/07/2020
Lose Hill	1562ft	25/04/1989
Maiden Moor	1886ft	20/11/2004
Mam Coire Easain	3510ft	23/05/1997
Mam Tor	1696ft	25/04/1989
Maol Chinn-dearg East Top	2996ft	28/05/1992
Meall a' Bhothain	2985ft	04/06/1998
Meall a' Bhuige	1641ft	13/05/2018
Meall a' Phuill	2891ft	14/05/1997
Meall Buidhe SE Top	3009ft	14/05/1997
Meall Luaidhe	2546ft	08/05/2016
Meall nan Subh South Top	2552ft	10/05/2016
Meall Nathrach Mor	2740ft	06/07/2000
Meallan Odhar	1759ft	19/05/2010
Meikle Millyea – Trig Point	2450ft	01/08/2017
Middle Dodd	2146ft	18/11/2005
Middle Scoat Fell	2733ft	04/07/2014
Milk Hill	966ft	12/02/2022
Miton Hill	1991ft	12/04/2012

Name	Height	Date
Moel Llechwedd	2680ft	09/05/2008
Moel y Slates	1827ft	09/05/2008
Moelwyn Mawr North Ridge Top	2132ft	17/09/2004
Monadh Gorm	1568ft	02/06/2022
Muckle Cairn	2710ft	17/05/2005
Mullach Clach a' Bhlair North Top	3127ft	02/06/1998
Mynydd Gwerngraig	2251ft	18/05/2008
Mynydd Rhyd-galed	1647ft	14/05/2008
Nab Scar	1476ft	02/03/2002
Nags Head	2224ft	08/06/2013
Nitting Haws	1378ft	18/11/2005
Painswick Beacon	928ft	13/11/1989
Pen Pumlumon Llygad-bychan	2375ft	11/06/2005
Pen y Garn Fawr	2001ft	13/01/2002
Pen-y-Garn Fawr	2021ft	13/01/2002
Round Knott	1978ft	12/04/2012
Scars of Milldown	1978ft	26/07/2017
Scraulac	2431ft	23/05/2017
Seathwaite Fell	1972ft	15/11/2008
Sgurr an Fhithich	2215ft	17/05/2018
Sgurr Breac East Top	2338ft	15/05/2010
Sgurr Breac Far East Top	2298ft	15/05/2010
Sgurr Coire nan Eiricheallach North Top	2890ft	16/06/1997
Sgurr Dearg - Cairn	3209ft	21/05/2001
Sgurr Mor West Top	2818ft	05/06/2001
Sgurr nan Ceathreamhnan East Top	3179ft	15/06/2001
Sgurr nan Coireachan South Top	3041ft	10/06/1997
Sgurr Thuilm West Top	2815ft	12/06/1997
Shank of Drumfollow	2765ft	09/04/1998
Silbury Hill	615ft	12/10/2001

Name	Height	Date
Skelgill Bank	1109ft	20/11/2004
Skiddaw - Lesser Man	2674ft	16/11/2007
Skiddaw Middle Top	3047ft	16/11/2007
Skiddaw North Top	3032ft	17/11/2007
Skiddaw South Top	3036ft	16/11/2007
Spidean Mialach West Top	3205ft	14/06/1997
Sron Bealach Beithe	3622ft	07/05/2001
Sron Gharbh	2332ft	22/09/1991
Stake Law	2234ft	29/05/2019
Standing Crag	2005ft	16/04/2011
Stob an Fhir-Bhogha	3376ft	07/05/1997
Stob Coire an Lochain	4052ft	30/05/1998
Stob Coire Dheirg	3504ft	19/05/1997
Stob Coire nan Dearcag	3081ft	15/06/2001
Stob Dubh North Top	2959ft	04/06/1997
Stob Poite Coire Ardair East Top	3445ft	20/06/1997
Stuc a' Chroin North Top	3115ft	04/05/1996
Suidheachan Fhinn	2845ft	24/06/2001
Tan Hill	965ft	12/02/2022
Tarapetmile	1696ft	10/07/2009
The Cairnwell North Top	2858ft	03/05/1994
The Island	282ft	29/09/2018
The Saddle - Trig Point	3318ft	27/05/2001
Thirdgill Head Man	2408ft	07/04/2012
Thornthwaite Crag North Top	2329ft	02/05/2011
Tongue Head	2152ft	20/04/2011
Tor Mere Top	2060ft	08/07/2014
Twistin Hill	2376ft	22/09/1991
Twyn Tal-y-cefn	2303ft	27/01/2002
Uamh Bheag East Top	2177ft	19/05/2019
Ullock Pike	2265ft	16/11/2007
Upper Tarnberry	1811ft	09/04/2017

Name	Height	Date
Urchfont Hill	714ft	08/09/2016
Warren Hill	615ft	10/09/2022
Watson's Dodd	2589ft	25/04/2011
Wether Hill	2201ft	13/04/2012
White Hill	1988ft	26/07/2017
White Pike	1967ft	24/04/2011
Whitehope Knowe	2011ft	02/05/2015

Outside the United Kingdom

Name	Height	Date
Cascade Mountain (USA)	4098ft	18/07/1999
Chli Aubrig (Switzerland)	5387ft	23/04/2005
Avalanche Peak (New Zealand)	6014ft	15/02/2018

Printed in Great Britain
by Amazon

13738412R00417